STATE POLITICS, PARTIES AND POLICY

SARAH McCALLY MOREHOUSE
University of Connecticut at Stamford

HOLT, RINEHART AND WINSTON
NEW YORK   CHICAGO   SAN FRANCISCO   PHILADELPHIA
MONTREAL   TORONTO   LONDON   SYDNEY   TOKYO
MEXICO CITY   RIO DE JANEIRO   MADRID

15955

Library of Congress Cataloging in Publications Data. LCCPD

Morehouse, Sarah McCally.
    State politics, parties, and policy.

    Includes index.
    1.   State governments.   I.   Title.
JK2408.M65   320.973   80–39569
ISBN   0–275–22760–X
CBS COLLEGE PUBLISHING
Holt, Rinehart and Winston
The Dryden Press
Saunders College Publishing

To my father and mother
Ralph and Eugenia Powell

PREFACE

The nature of each state government depends upon the leaders who run it. And that leadership is determined for better or worse, by the political party system. What difference does it make if a state has strong or weak parties? The central theme of this book is that it makes a great difference to the people of the state, especially to the most vulnerable—the children, the poor and the elderly.

This text offers an orthodox coverage of federalism, electoral behavior, pressure groups, formal institutions and policies of state government. While it has faithfully examined these standard structures and procedures its tandem accomplishment has been to affirm the role of the political party as an integral part of the governing process. Within this process it is the party's task to nominate, elect and govern. Thus the party's candidates fill the leadership positions in the government and as leaders they decide whether the needs and demands of the people are met.

No other organization performs as the people's advocate and as the people's decision maker. I could not make the claim that strong parties are able to provide a higher quality of life for the people of a state if my research had not shown this to be true. The fruits of my research are scattered throughout the pages of this book and confirm my belief that cohesive political parties and strong leadership are able to provide a better life for the citizens than self-serving factions built around personalities or issues of the moment. In one-third of our states, political parties are able to fulfill their function of nominating, electing and governing as organizations with a past and a future. These states differ from each other in many social, economic and political aspects, and yet each has party government, or party leaders who can recruit and nominate candidates for public office who are broadly representative of the party's voters and can enact and implement programs which reflect the voters' needs.

By what yardstick do we measure the responsiveness of state political systems? We concentrate on life's most basic needs: food, shelter and health. Without them, life is ridden with hunger and misery; there is no chance for love or contentment. In addition to these basic physical requirements, education is considered fundamental in fulfilling one's life. Education brings personal dignity and accomplishment. In actuality, expenditures for human welfare and education consume nearly 60 percent of state budgets. If the efforts of party leaders make a difference to the way these basic services are provided, then we can say that party government is essential to the quality of life of the people in a state. At the end of this book there is a tentative yardstick in a new area of policy, land use, which measures the role of the party in regulating scarce land resources for important social and environmental goals.

Party government provides the answer to the quest for responsive government. No doubt this position is controversial and must be defended against those who believe that governments cannot be responsive to the people because they answer only to elite demands. The elite theory contends that two groups exist: elites and masses. Governing elites cannot respond to mass demands for a variety of reasons, among them the fact that the masses do not have the education and skills to make their demands known, and in some instances their preferences are frequently not in their own best interests. Elites, according to this theory, control all organizations and have similar backgrounds and values.

The governing elite accommodates the elites in the organized interest groups and together they control society's values and resources. Elitist theory admits that benevolent elites bring the needs of the masses to the decision makers in times of affluence, but claims that this benevolence cannot hold up in times of economic hardship when growth slows down and redistributive policies become even more necessary. At such times, the demands of business and professional associations will be heard over any spoken or unspoken claim of the have nots. This theory offers a gloomy counsel indeed. Consistent with this theory, the political party is no different from any other organization in state government—it is run by elites, who respond to other elites be they the bankers or the businessmen.

Party government advocates do not deny that all organizations have leaders and that the governing elite receives demands from the leaders of organized interest groups and in many cases responds to business and professional associations rather than to the welfare mothers or students or the ghettos. Furthermore, there is no reason to assume that those who have money and education will necessarily espouse the cause of the needy (although they frequently do). How then will the poor be represented in the circles of government? This book argues that the political party may be the only vehicle which can accomplish this. The party is unique in the array of organizations, groups and pressures that make up the political system.

The party is the primary vehicle for connecting the citizen with his or her government. Parties need votes to stay in business and the votes of the poor count as much as the votes of the rich. Political candidates make promises to get votes—promises which must be kept if the votes are to be reaffirmed in the next election. It is vital for the future of the party candidates that they discover the needs of the people and that they act to solve them when they are elected. It is also vital for the party organization that its candidates perform in accordance with the needs of the people if the organization is to be nourished by electoral success. To the degree that the party leaders can deliver promises, the party has a past and a predictable future—it is an organization which is faithful and remembered. No single-interest group can provide this vital function of aggregating the preferences of the mass electorate by nominating candidates for public office and converting these preferences into specific electoral and policy decisions. The Anti-abortionists, the bankers, the industrialists, even the right-wing activists within the Republican Party and the Liberal activists within the Democratic Party are not concerned with aggregating and mediating the preferences of many and converting them into election decisions and policy. Aggregating the preferences of many is not the interest of single-issue groups, and yet aggregating is vital to the existence of the political party.

It takes internal cohesion to accomplish the job of aggregating preferences and converting them into policy and the parties in most of our states are not strong enough to perform these functions. While it is commonly agreed that parties which are split into factions do not represent the needs of the people as well as those which are cohesive in the nominating, electing and governing process, little is being done to strengthen the capabilities of parties. An emphasis on party government is not popular. Party leaders are considered undemocratic because they want to pick candidates at party meetings which are not subject to popular control. Reformers want to facilitate widespread participation in the nomination process, reforms which discourage the efforts of regulars to form coalitions within the party. Yet popular participation in the nominating process has resulted in candidates who are not representative of the party's voters because so few of the party's voters turn out. These candidates, if elected, do not have a broad base of support within the party and cannot represent the needy. Hence the party is weak. What we have done under the guise of democracy is to ruin the possibility of leadership within the party—the only set of leaders who are able to be representative of the people. We have, in effect, destroyed the party organization in most of our states.

Fortunately for the argument of this book, there still exist fifteen or so states in which the parties are cohesive enough to nominate and govern. In these states the leaders can control nominations and work to bring about the policy promises of the candidates. They do not respond to single-interest groups because their support is widespread and they have the cohesion and the need to fulfill broader policy mandates. In these states there is the realization that the business of developing and pushing candidates for governor cannot be settled by the process of self-selection by aspiring office-seekers. At least in these states, candidates who receive the nod of the party leaders have an organization with which to begin the process of winning the election and governing.

Is it true that political party organization affects the quality and distribution of services? By the yardstick which was established; provision for human welfare and education, how responsive is party government? Both education and welfare are redistributive policies—policies which redistribute the benefits of society to provide for more equality across income groups. Because party government involves a continuous leadership over many elections—an organization with a past and a future, it is able to produce redistributive policies. My research proves that this is true. Parties with strong leadership coupled with governors who have extensive formal powers provide for the poor, the children, the elderly and the students more generously than fractured parties and weak governors. A professionalized legislature is also more responsive to the needs of the people. Hence the leadership which is produced by the political party is crucial to the responsiveness of government.

If the political party is able to nominate, elect and govern with a sufficient degree of cohesion, it listens to many needs including the poor and the disadvantaged and incorporates solutions in its policy program. Perhaps it does not heed the demands of the have-nots out of brotherly love, but out of the necessity to represent them in order to be elected. Regardless, in states where there is a party system which is organized enough to listen to the needs of the poor, they are better served.

Responsive government depends upon political parties. That is why this book devotes so much attention to the party as it proceeds to examine the processes and institutions and policies of state political systems. There is nothing sinister about an elite which governs in the interests of the people. Much more dangerous is direct democracy which masks the interests of the few. The task is to hold the elite accountable. This can be done by a strong political party. In this way parties provide an ongoing political vehicle for the mass of people who lack wealth or power.

ACKNOWLEDGMENTS

This book owes a tremendous intellectual debt to the late V. O. Key of Harvard University and to David Truman of the Russell Sage Foundation who introduced Key's thoughts to me in the fall of 1956. I believe I have carried out a task which Key indicated should be done; namely proving that cohesive parties can pass redistributive programs which benefit the needy. I have consistently been encouraged by Fred Greenstein of Princeton University to pursue this challenge. In a time of crisis I also turned to Thad Beyle of the University of North Carolina, Alan Rosenthal of Rutgers University and John Grumm of Wesleyan University who reassured me that I should persist in my emphasis on party government in spite of its current unpopularity.

Without a National Science Foundation Grant in 1973, I could not have performed the research which led me to the discovery of the importance of party leadership for public policy. With the assurance that this was indeed true, I proceeded to write the book on this premise. A University of Connecticut Research Foundation Grant in 1976 aided me in the final stages of preparation.

At least 100 people took the time to help me in my quest for the identification of the governors' program bills. To all the governors and their staffs who answered my queries and particularly to the former governors of the twenty states which formed the basis for my research (Chapter 5), I owe a great debt of thanks. My research depended upon the energy and resourcefulness of governors' assistants, legislative analysts and counsels and the like who often wrote from new occupations in the private sector in response to my pleas. Four students helped me record the roll call votes on the governors' programs. Thanks for poring over legislative journals to accomplish this task go to Rita Micheli and Rose Mary Romano, graduates of Manhattanville College, Mary Ellen Finnerty, graduate of Brown University, and Lorna T. Morehouse, graduate of Tufts University. If it had not been for Diccon Bancroft, Computer Programmer at the Yale Computer Center, judgments with respect to factor analysis, multiple correlation and multiple determination programs could not have been made with such assurance. The manuscript was typed by Rose Mary Noonan, who never flinched at the roughness of the draft she received.

The entire book was read twice by two professional colleagues who gave me advice and criticism. I am indebted to Jeffrey P. Henig of George Washington University and Alvin H. Mushkatel of the University of Denver. Denise Rathbun, formerly of Praeger Publishers, provided the initial impetus, reviewed the first few chapters and has maintained an interest in the book. I thank her for all three functions. Jon Wood, on the staff of *Apartment Life,* managed to make four chapters readable by performing miraculous operations on sentence structure, wordy paragraphs and ponderous statements. Patrick Powers of Holt, Rinehart and Winston has patiently escorted the book into the production process. The fact that the major thesis of this book is controversial, makes me hasten to assume the full responsibility for its genesis, research and presentation. No one mentioned so far is responsible, and while all have been helpful, some have advised me to blunt my enthusiasm for party government. I have not done this and am therefore the prime target for slings and arrows.

My family is in a special category. Various members have provided authoring, editing and encouragement without the slightest worry about responsibility. Former student and now family, Suzan Rolfe, has edited, cajoled, threatened, motivated and inspired to bring my struggles to completion. My lawyer husband endured for a time and then wrote Chapter 7, "The Least Dangerous Branch" to keep it above politics. My older sons Richard and John encouraged their author-mother from job locations away from the nest. My two younger children Catherine and David were 11 and 9 when I started and grew along with the book.

CONTENTS

xi

CHAPTER ONE

STATE POLITICS TODAY

The quality of your life depends in large measure on what your state government is doing for you. The conditions under which you were born or adopted, the manner in which your birth was registered, your childhood education as well as college for many of you, and the conditions under which you will live, work, and strive for fulfillment are all determined by those who run your state government. If you follow a visit to Congress by a visit to your state legislature, you will be struck by the different issues being considered. While Congress discusses war and peace, the state legislators discuss education for prisoners, minimum living needs for the poor, campus disorders, and abortions.

States have been taking a new role in recent years that demands political leadership. When the national government diverted its attention to war and local governments faced persistent opposition to their property taxes, the states increased their share of the financial burden. They gained dominance over the private sector in the field of higher education; individual states have made impressive efforts in public welfare, sometimes in stark contrast to their meager levels of economic resources. While state aid to cities has increased, the local governments' own share of spending for domestic programs has gone down. The states are looking increasingly to the needs of urban residents in higher education, mental health, environmental control, recreation, mass transit, and housing.

There are dramatic differences in the lives of the poor from state to state. If the quality of life among the poor is used as an indicator of a state's sensitivity to the needs of its citizens, the difference in the extent to which they provide for the basic needs of poor families ranges from 22 to 100 percent. While the governor of one state may be describing the starving child gnawing the paint on the wall to fill his stomach, the governor of another may be asking for tax refunds for parents who send their children to private schools to avoid integration. The very fact that there are such differences raises the question: Why is this true? An explanation of the existing political, economic, and social conditions within the states that give rise to such a fundamental problem is the only justification for a book about state politics. We now set ourselves to this task.

QUALITY OF LIFE: THE POLICY YARDSTICK

By what yardstick do we measure the performance of state political systems? Can we tell whether the lives of people in one state are closer to fulfillment than those in another? Do we take state regulation of social mores as a yardstick? For instance, can we say that a teen-ager is better off in a state where the drinking age is lower or higher? Where the penalties for use of marihuana are lenient or more severe? Or where public funds can be used for abortions? State governments make all these decisions. The fashioning of a yardstick is a common problem for all those students of state government and invites help. It is not easy to find a measure of the quality of life. Yet, one must be found if we are to compare.

Perhaps we should concentrate on life's most basic needs: food, shelter, and health. Without them, your life is ridden with hunger and misery: there is no chance for creativity, love, or contentment. In addition to these basic physical requirements, education is considered by most to be basic in fulfilling one's life. An education provides you with the ability to choose your life-style and to select an occupation that best suits your needs. This brings personal dignity and fulfillment. Provision of these basics offers a solid yardstick for measuring the performance of state political systems. Expenditures for human welfare and education do, indeed, take up the largest block in state budgets. Table 1–1 indicates the allocation of money

TABLE 1–1

State Government Expenditures by Function, 1976, All States

FUNCTION	PERCENT
Education	38.8
Public Welfare	19.3
Highways	11.8
Health and Hospitals	7.2
Natural Resources	2.5
Corrections	1.6
Police	1.0
Employment Security Administration	1.0
All other	16.8
Total	100.0

Source: U.S. Bureau of the Census, *State Government Finance in 1976* (Washington, D.C.: Government Printing Office).

by state governments into these major services. The data show that nearly 60 percent of all state money goes to education and welfare. The next largest expenditure is for highways, and the final 30 percent is divided among a host of other functions, including health, natural resource conservation, environmental protection, and prison facilities. Welfare and education can be considered legitimate major components of the states' budgets as well as basic elements in life's fulfillment.

Welfare, Education, and Shelter

Most of the readers of this book have been able to take food and health for granted. In fact, all but 11 percent of our population can do the same. To focus on the provision of basics for the poor may strike you as a narrow measure of the performance of state governments. In this regard, Samuel Johnson once observed, "Decent provision for the poor is the true test of civilization," meaning that provision of basic needs for the poor can be used as an indicator of a government's sensitivity to the needs of all its citizens. Welfare involves taxing the haves in society and giving to the have-nots. Only government can do this—and only a government that concerns itself with its poorest and most disabled. The assumption is that everyone is guaranteed a basic minimum existence. State governments have a controlling say over who will receive this welfare and how much. Some states give generously to the poor and some do not. In our study of welfare policy, we will consider what it is about the characteristics of a state's citizenry and their decision makers that can account for such a variance of dispensation for the poor.

The provision of education also involves redistribution of money from the haves to the have-nots. The prevailing myth is that everyone receives free public education regardless of their ability to pay; education through the twelfth grade is to be provided for all and, to those who qualify, expenses are covered at the university level. However, this has not been the case. Money for education has been distributed to the wealthy suburban community as a direct consequence of state-sponsored disparities in school funding. As with welfare, some states have made an effort to redistribute education on a more equal basis. As a result of recent state court decisions, some states are equalizing the funding for education. It is in those states that educational policy is becoming more redistributive— more money is now going to areas of need and relatively less to the wealthy areas. Again, we ask what characteristics are associated with the states that are working to equalize education for their young people. We would predict that the states that are striving to redistribute their educational funds are those where the needs and demands of the people can find expression through governmental process. Education policy is another yardstick with which to measure the difference in performance of the states.

The regulation of privately owned land for public use is just emerging as a state political issue. While land-use regulation is not a clear example of the conflict between the haves and the have-nots, it does contain this dimension. For the urban poor living in an environment of poverty, rats, carbon monoxide, and noise, the sensible thing would be to pack up and leave; there is a land of promise less than twenty miles away. But to the impoverished family it is no more accessible than a mirage. The suburbs zone their land for single-family use, thus making the price of a house prohibitive. Local zoning also increases the cost of multiple-unit housing and makes low-to-moderate construction impossible. There are many competing claims for each parcel of land. Sometimes they involve mining versus food production, recreation versus preservation, or housing for the poor versus building for business or commerce. In the last ten years, states have come to recognize that some property in private hands must be regulated for the public good. This is an example of redistribution by regulation (as those who have had their property rezoned for a different purpose would be quick to recognize). State governments are better suited than local governments to regulate scarce land resources for important social and environmental goals. As in other areas of policy, social, economic, and political variables may bear on the way critical land areas are regulated in the public interest. If the citizens of a state believe they do not want atomic power plants within their borders, the government can ban them. If the inner-city poor want to move to quarters that are less cramped, the state can buy the land or offer inducements to build or rebuild residential areas.

The Haves versus the Have-nots

A review of the three areas of policy we have been discussing reveals that generally, politics are a conflict between those who have and those who have less. In state politics, crucial issues turn on taxation and expenditure; what level of welfare, what quality of public education shall be maintained? How shall they be financed? Is it the job of government to provide the basic guarantees of existence and some possibility for individual opportunity? Some state governments are better providers than others. Are more people in these states stimulated by basic altruism? Or are the have-nots better served by organizations working on their behalf—organizations that are based on self-interest motives? Groups based on common interests bring the needs and aspirations of people to the governmental market place.

It is the critical theme of this book that it takes political organization to serve the have-nots. The political party is the one organization that can do this. Politicians do not operate out of altruism, they operate largely out of self-interest. But the self-interest of politicians is to represent enough voters to be elected or reelected. This means representing the needs of a sizable block of voters, including the poorest 11 percent. The poor are better served by political party organization than they are with a disorganized politics. In a disorganized politics, the "have-nots" lose because they have no mechanism through which to act and to be represented. Occasionally their demands may be presented by transient leaders who gain their confidence but who do not have the staying power or technical competence to effectuate a program.

While it takes organization to sustain a program on behalf of the needy, it does not take organization to obstruct, and the grand objective of the "haves" is obstruction. A loosely organized political party system gives great advantage to those who can buy candidates to act in their interests. A cohesive political party, on the other hand, can back candidates of its choosing. Because a political party has a past and a future (loose factions do not), it grooms candidates for office who share the collective spirit of party organization. Politicians working under such systems have a regard not only for the present campaign, but for the next. In a state with loose factional politics, there is no continuity or person to hold responsible for policy failures; there is no "outs" group to serve as critics of the "ins." The poor lose in such a system. Parties provide an ongoing vehicle for the mass of people who lack wealth or power. This book will be organized around the theme that men and women who operate under the party label make a critical difference in the quality of life that citizens of a state enjoy.

If we believe that political parties have a central role to play in state politics, we must analyze the states as actors in the federal system. We need to establish the fact that they are viable, decision-making systems with sufficient power of choice. If the states are simply administrative conduits for national policy, then the efforts of politicians make little difference. If the federal government decides who is eligible for welfare payments and appropriates the amount they will receive, then the states become mere administrative units for federal policy. If the federal government decides the curriculum, builds the school houses, and pays the teachers, then the states fade as educational decision makers in the federal system. These are only two examples. In actuality, the federal government funds an average 55 percent of the welfare program and only 8 percent of educational expenses. There is, therefore, great latitude in the funding, quality, and distribution of benefits in these two programs which, jointly, take up the major share of state budgets.

THE STATES IN THE FEDERAL SYSTEM

The answer to the question, "Are states significant actors in the federal system?" involves more than a sharing of funds for programs; it includes the overall place of the states and the division of functions and powers within the federal system. Evolving federalism depends on economic and social events and the reacting philosophy of our political leadership. It can change with changing times or as a new group of leaders assume control in the White House and state houses. In the wake of Watergate, the recession, the energy crisis, and the tax revolt of 1978, candidates for office representing both major parties talk of a "new spirit" in American politics. The nation has moved into a new era of government marked by a massive retreat from the growth in taxes and public services that have been sustained on all levels since World War II. State and local governments have given up many billions of dollars in expendable revenues in the form of tax cuts and spending limits; the federal government, after years of running up large deficits, has committed itself to the concept of a balanced budget and, in a sudden turnaround, has drastically scaled back its plans for a publicly financed new urban policy. Both the president and the nation's governors are critical of "big government" and skeptical of "program politics" and the "liberalism of the 1960s." They are interjecting elements of realism into political debate; resources are not unlimited, government can not solve all of society's problems, spending commitments of today have long-term consequences, and more services and less taxes are incompatible policies. These events, and the reactive philosophy, are hurrying history along and affecting the balance between state and national governments. Certain fundamental issues of federal-centralization versus decentralization of power, the rights and responsibilities of states, and the role of local governments were initially addressed by the founding fathers and are now surfacing again in the evolution of our federal system. We will start our discussion of the states' role in the federal system with the following account of the New York City fiscal crisis because of its ability to capsule many of the elements in the story of evolving federalism.

The New York City Crisis as an Example of Evolving Federalism

In the wee hours of October 17, 1975, as our country was preparing to celebrate its Bicentennial, the governor of New York asked the president of the United States for help. The president was unresponsive. The governor then proceeded to involve himself with the New York City fiscal crisis as the city teetered on the brink of default. Aware that the collapse of New York City would be followed shortly by the default of his state government, the governor worked through the night to arrange a loan for his ailing city. After default was narrowly averted, the governor sent a telegram to the president:

> New York, by exhausting all of its resources, can meet its obligations until December 1. After then the welfare of our citizens rests in the hands of the Federal Government. I seek your cooperation and leadership. We need not a bailout, not a handout, but the recognition by the Federal Government that we are a part of this country, and that we are suffering because of the economic distress in this country.[1]

But the president reaffirmed his position that the federal government would not come to New York's assistance. In fact, Ford's press secretary compared New York to a wayward daughter hooked on heroin. "You don't give her $100 a day to support her habit," he said. "You make her go cold turkey to break the habit."[2] The president's chief economic adviser insisted that the city and state had the means to prevent default. The state should initiate some new taxes so that the city could pay its bills while they worked their way through to a balanced budget. Governor Carey maintained that additional taxing power would be counterproductive, drive industry out of the state, weaken the state's tax base, and victimize the poor and elderly.

The above story vividly illustrates the evolving relationship between the cities, states, and federal government as the Bicentennial approached. New York State had become involved with the city's financial crisis early in 1975—an involvement that surprised many. For the past decade, the federal government had been responding directly to the crises of cities. The state, whose credit was now threatened because it assumed responsibility for the foundering city, claimed that both were now caught up in economic conditions that the national government was responsible for; it was, indeed, appropriate that they receive help from the federal government. The White House claimed that the financial distress of both city and state was brought about by their own irresponsible fiscal management. Therefore, they would have to manage by themselves to put their houses in order.

New York's mayor and the governor both claimed that they had been treated as black sheep by the federal government for some time. They argued that federal grants covered only one half of New York's welfare costs but three-quarters of Mississippi's. (Mississippi could respond that New York's welfare payments are too high). New York City, the governor and mayor argued, has increasingly served as a catchbasin for the nation's home-grown poor instead of a port of entry for opportunity-seeking immigrants. As a matter of fact, federal welfare grant formulas were altered to the city's disadvantage while the poor were crowding in. In the effort to protect states whose poor had migrated to New York City from losses in federal funds, the new formula guaranteed them the same amounts for their reduced numbers while putting a ceiling on the increase in funding that New York City could receive. The federal funds did not keep up with the increasing numbers of New York poor. Albany was $50 million short, while Arkansas saved a 50 percent aid reduction, or $12 million.[3]

If the sight of Cuban refugees arriving in Miami in search of a new life was enough to excite special federal aid programs, New York officials ask, why was there no comparable stir over the great interior drift of similarly motivated, native-born poor to New York? No comparable special consideration was accorded the new urban populations when impoverished blacks were displaced in the final wave of southern farm mechanization. There was the "War on Poverty," but that was reduced to a storefront operation by 1975.

The most exceptional outcome of New York City's plight was when the governor and state government assumed responsibility for the fiscal problems of the city. The state's response was to establish a Municipal Assistance Corporation (MAC) to sell bonds, backed by the state to help finance city expenditures. Governor Carey was called Mayor Carey because of his control (partly by MAC direction) of the city's budget. Although greater than the city's, the state's financial capacity was also limited. In the end, the governor did obtain, from a reluctant president and Congress, crucial short-term help through a series of seasonal loans for 1975–78. The federal government continued to treat New York City as a regrettable but temporary condition resulting from the failure of a single city to "live within its means." As Congress granted federal long-term guarantees for New York City bonds in 1978, both supporters and critics were quick to assert that this would be the last time the federal government would come to the aid of New York City. In addition, they said the program caused an unfortunate federal involvement in local affairs that should not serve as a precedent for other cities.

Except in degree, New York City's plight was fairly typical of the experience of America's older central cities, almost all of which faced growing public demands while losing more and more of their middle-class taxpayers as well as many manufacturing and commercial enterprises. Subsequent events in Detroit, Cincinnati, and other cities suggested that future municipal crises would have to be handled by the state governments. In 1979, when President Carter cut his urban program drastically in response to a wide-spread taxpayers' revolt, the state governments stood as the only port of call. If the financial plight of cities is assumed by the states, many dilemmas will occur. How will the states establish priorities between themselves and their largest cities? Is conflict inevitable? Can the states assume the burden of schooling, welfare, transportation, and environmental protection, which would add greatly to their budgets and bureaucracies? These questions are both political and fiscal. The solutions have the potential of altering the balance of federalism as we have known it in this country over the last 50 years.

Evolving Federalism

Old-style federalism is a legal concept emphasizing constitutional division of authority and functions between a national government and state governments. Both levels received their powers independently from each other by constitutional mandate. New-style federalism is a political and pragmatic concept stressing the actual interdependence and sharing of functions between Washington and the states, while focusing on the mutual leverage that each is able to exert on the other. This modern notion of federalism emphasizes the intergovernmental relationship as one of constant change in response to social and economic forces, as well as changes in the dynamics of political leadership.

A silent revolution took place in the five years prior to the national Bicentennial. The states displayed their independence from Washington by many acts of fiscal rigor and policy resourcefulness. This new American Revolution remains hidden from most Americans even today, in spite of the fact that crises over fuel shortages, school financing, and tax revolts have brought the issue of federal-state-local relations to the front pages of the nation's newspapers. Our federal system is in a state of flux. There is no doubt that the 1970s saw the emergence of states as powerful decision-making entities for major social problems.

After all, it was the states that created the federal system in 1787— the major unique contribution of this country to the art of government. It was an attempt to combine the twin goals of unity and diversity by delegating power to provide central government with the capacity for national leadership and interstate coordination as well as economic and military security from events beyond the seas. However, the new nation was a union of states. The founding fathers intended important roles for the state governments in the federal system. They were to be repositories for most domestic governmental functions and political laboratories in which new ideas could be tested and observed. If successful, they would be adopted by sister states and the nation as a whole. The conception of American federalism has swung like a pendulum from decentralization to centralization and back again.

Prior to the Civil War, the states generally kept with the original concepts of being repositories and political laboratories. The national government had not found it necessary to move much beyond the areas of common defense, promotion of the free flow of interstate commerce—including road and river improvement—and a postal service. But the emergence of the Industrial Revolution during the Reconstruction period, and the economic and social changes that followed, began to put severe strains on state governments. Their political arrangements were not equipped to handle the demands of the urban poor who, in need of work, flocked to the cities. Congress, the president, and the Supreme Court had to step in to provide relief for the beleaguered cities.

The Maligned States

The states may have deserved the criticism that they were untrustworthy, reactionary, wasteful, and obsolete; the record of most states through the 1950s was one of ineptness and seeming disregard for the grave economic and social problems within their borders. They largely ignored deteriorating conditions and presided over widespread abuses of zoning to prevent the movement of the poor to outlying areas. States allowed property taxes, which are the major source of revenue for local government, to lapse into serious disrepair until they could no longer maintain local needs. State legislatures mandated property tax exemptions without replacing the lost revenue. States refused to reapportion their legislatures to allow urban residents their rightful representation, and it took federal court intervention to require this reform.

Despite the fact that most states have undergone the silent revolution that has transformed them into responsive and capable political systems, the criticisms continue. One of the most thoughtful defenders of the states gives us several myths that have been invoked by those who do not want the states to assume a key role in the federal system.[4]

1. *The myth of urban-rural warfare*
    The states are unmindful of local—particularly big city—needs, while the cities distrust the states and refuse to cooperate with them.
2. *The myth of administrative incompetence*
    The states and localities are administratively incapable of properly utilizing any additional powers that might be transferred to them.
3. *The myth of corruption*
    Even if the states and localities now have sufficient administrative skills to handle additional powers, corruption and vested interests will prevent them from utilizing these powers capably.
4. *The myth of shirking obligations*
    The states and localities have failed to assume their proper fiscal obligations, and there is no reason why the federal government should bail them out.

5. *The myth that federal money will be used unwisely*
The states and localities will dissipate federal money given them without any strings attached instead of using the funds where they are most needed.

It is the thesis of this book that states are now vital political systems because they have the economic base, governmental structure, and the political party organization to enable them to assume the grave responsibilities that confront all of us in the 1980s. Not all the states are capable of government that serves the best interests of the people. In some, the poor go hungry and unsheltered and the children are not properly educated. In others, state governments make efforts out of proportion to their resources to provide for their citizens. In the following discussion, we will stress the general potential of the states as we answer the various myths.

The myth of *urban-rural warfare* was not far off base when the rural areas were jealously clinging to their conservative ways in the midst of the change from rural to urban living. Legislators from areas of declining population were reluctant to give up their dominance of state government to the new urbanites, particularly since so many of the former genuinely believed in the moral superiority of rural life and so many of the latter belonged to ethnic or racial groups with decidedly different mores. Because the rural-urban transition took place at different times in different parts of the country, different states have been undergoing its pains since the late nineteenth century. By 1970, few if any states had yet to enter the transitional period. According to Elazar, the transition begins when at least 40 percent of a state's population is urban. It is completed when urban centers account for over 60 percent of the state's population. No state is now below that 40 percent figure, and only 11 (seven of them in the South) are less than 50 percent urban. Before the 40 percent mark is attained, cities find it very difficult to gain consideration in their state capitals because they simply do not have the votes.[5] To be sure, there was a lag in time between the demands for adequate representation and the reapportionment of the legislatures. This lag eventually had to be shortened by Supreme Court action. By 1968, every state had reapportioned one or both houses of its legislature, generally in response to a federal court order. This has brought about a noticeable distribution of state aid in favor of urban areas. There is more spending for education, welfare, health, and hospitals. It is true that new urban-suburban conflicts arise from time to time, and the states have to mediate these disputes. The example of New York City was placed in the forefront of this discussion to point out the fact that states are assuming increasing responsibility for their urban areas. In fact, the states have vastly increased their help to localities, both urban and rural. Most of the new activity involves establishing incentives for economic development such as technical assistance,

public service jobs, tax relief, and funds for building water, sewer, and transportation facilities for industrial parks.[6]

In the last two decades, most states have modernized their legislatures so that they are now more representative and better able to provide needed services. In some states, this modernization was of critical importance. A study of the Mississippi legislature in 1971 suggested upgrading the floor decorum. Visitors were unfavorably impressed by the legislators throwing peanut shells on the floor while the legislature was in session. Not all legislatures started as far behind as Mississippi, nor have all caught up to the demands of the 80s. But most have reformed themselves to become more professional. They have gone to annual legislative sessions, a necessity to meet the demands of today's times. Legislatures now deal with more bills, have longer sessions, enjoy higher salaries, and have streamlined procedures and larger and better paid staffs. Membership is more attractive than it has been in the past and there's a marked increase in the number of state legislators seeking reelection rather than voluntarily retiring after short-term service. These points will be raised again in chapter 6 when we deal with state legislatures.

The myth of *administrative incompetence* had validity at one time. Governors were formally so weak that they could not govern effectively. Professor Michael D. Reagan speaks of giving the states more responsibility as a "cop-out," rather than a panacea, because it gives power to incompetent state governments which have done little to reform their inadequate administrative and fiscal structures.[7] About 15 years ago, a study of state budgeting in Illinois talked about a governor who could not cope with the machinery of state government. This applied to many other governors at that time as well:

> The budget document may be compared to a huge mountain which is constantly being pushed higher and higher by underground geological convulsions. On top of the mountain is a single man, blindfolded, seeking to reduce the height of the mountain by dislodging pebbles with a teaspoon. That man is the Governor.[8]

The chief executive is the single most prominent person in state politics and campaigns for a program that he promises to put into effect after elected. Recognizing the fact that he needs more time in office to put his policies into effect, 46 states now have four terms for governor (compared to only 32 in 1960) and 43 now allow a governor at least a second term (compared to 31 in 1960). Another means for enhancing gubernatorial leadership is executive control of budget making. In all but 19 states, the governor has the sole responsibility for preparing the budget. In 37 states, he has the item veto—a potentially strong instrument for influencing final policy outcomes. During the last 20 years, the executive agencies of state government have been strengthened. State planning agencies are being developed as arms of the governor's office, who uses them to control and coordinate the multifarious activities within the executive branch. None of this is intended to suggest that the armature of state government doesn't creak and wobble. But it does suggest that the myth of administrative incompetence has been effectively challenged as states try to improve their governmental machinery.

The *myth of corruption* argues that, even if the states are well administered, vested interests can buy decision makers. The invisible government seen by proponents of the myth consists of private business and industry representatives. According to the myth, public officials close their eyes to conflicts of interest, lobbyists bribe or use other illegal influences, public officials bend the rules for the rich and powerful, and political parties are fashioned into machines to further the interests of business. A picture of the state treasurer with his hand in the till is left in the citizen's mind as the typical officeholder. Words such as "boodle," "the ring," "juice," "graft," are all leveled against the states and their local governments. Duane Lockard reported that 44 New Hampshire legislators once were employed at the windows of a New Hampshire racetrack.[9] Not long ago, Governor Otto Kerner and some Illinois legislators took the opportunity to turn quick profits on stock in the Arlington racetrack outside Chicago. (They went to prison). Of course, corruption may be found everywhere we find power—the power to allocate contracts and money. But the state and local corruption argument is full of holes. As a group, state and local governments today are far less corrupt than at any time in the last 100 years. It is the federal government that is under a cloud because of the Watergate scandal, although the kind of corruption Watergate represents is far more dangerous than the ordinary old fashioned "boodle." In fact, the crude forms of political payoff are reduced at all levels of government—federal, state, and local. Therefore, the states and their local governments cannot be singled out for corruption over and above the federal government. Payoff laundering and links with organized crime are no more defensible when they involve federal officials than when they involve state bureaucrats.

A second "hole" in the corruption argument is that it ignores the reforms in state legislatures that make them less dependent on outside money and influence. Legislators' salaries are rising, and the office is becoming a full-time career. Legislators with upward ambitions—Congress or the governorship—are becoming more sensitive to possible charges of improper influence.

A third "hole" in the corruption myth may be presented by the fact that corruption does not necessarily affect the delivery of government services. This may be a new idea to the student. Corruption experts say that the older forms of bribery and buying public officials have disappeared. The new forms involve rewarding one's friends with contracts for the delivery of services—this at least supposes that the services will be delivered in one way or another. Consequently, whether corruption exists or not, the services flow.

Corruption, Elazar points out, is a perennial governmental problem and is usually related to norms rooted in the local culture. States like Michigan, Minnesota, Virginia, and Utah are far less corrupt than the federal government. New York, North Carolina, and Pennsylvania are probably similar to Washington in degree of corruption, while Indiana, Louisiana, New Jersey, and Texas are probably more corrupt. Some of these latter states are able to deliver services to their citizens, making the quality of their lives as comfortable and dignified as those in the less corrupt states. Corruption, then, is not a good reason to mistrust the states as providers for their citizens. It exists on all levels of government and does not necessarily affect the delivery of services. Corrupt officials are punished when found, which occurs more frequently in some states than others. This does not mean that we cannot trust the states to provide services for their citizens in this period of evolving federalism.

The last two myths require a lengthy discussion of the states' track records over the last twenty years—a period when issues of war, peace, and dwindling fiscal strength have concerned the federal government. As we will soon see, states have not been shirking their duties to their local governments. They have continued to provide money for over 40 percent of all our nation's domestic services at a time when the local governments' share dropped drastically. To do this, they have had to add income taxes to their revenue base. They are limited in the degree to which they can do this by the heavy federal income tax demands which preempt the field. It is federal policies that cause recessions and continuing inflation. The 1970–71 recession cut back the receipts of state and local governments while it generated increased demands for public services. The welfare rolls increased by 23 percent. Inflation, caused largely by federal fiscal and monetary policies, is perhaps the worst villain in raising costs that state and local governments must absorb. Recall that Governor Carey admonished the President that New York was suffering because of the economic distress of the country.

As for the myth that states will dissipate federal money given them with no strings attached instead of using the funds where they are most needed, there may be an element of truth. But the fault does not lie at the state level. For instance, the formula used for revenue-sharing funds provided by the federal government gives two-thirds of them to the localities. The states must watch while wealthy towns used their funds for town hall extensions and marinas, and the poor cities use theirs for welfare and housing; the states must use their one-third to equalize the burden on hard-pressed cities.

The points just made need to be unraveled gradually. The next few pages will provide a description of the evolving nature of federalism up to the present. It will reveal that the states have assumed their rightful place as keystones of the federal system.

State Renaissance

The importance of states in the federal system can be illustrated by some comparative figures on spending on domestic policy between federal, state, and local governments. Figures, unless scantily clad in bikinis, are not the most popular way of expressing ideas, but these are simplified and tell a powerful story. Figure 1–1 illustrates how much money the three government levels have provided their citizens for such domestic public services as education, health and welfare, hospitals, housing, and highways.

Clearly, local governments carried the major share in the first 30 years of our century. But during the depression (1930s), they began to weaken, and many of them were not able to fund these activities from their real estate tax base. Washington began to help provide for the needs of the poor and jobless. With the Sixteenth Amendment, in 1913, the federal government acquired the ability to tax incomes, which gave it the resources for providing these programs. This tax has proven a relatively efficient, comprehensive method of raising revenues that automatically increase as the economy expands. Extensive federal aid to state and local governments came with the Depression. It grew from $232 million in 1932 to over $2 billion in 1950. It continued growing to nearly $56 billion by 1976. By 1940, however, the state governments assumed a larger proportion of the domestic programs and have continued to maintain it until the present time. States now spend more than either the local or national governments on the "quality-of-life services" consumed or enjoyed by the people. The states took over some of the national government's responsibilities as a larger portion of Washington's budget went to the Defense Department and our allies during World War II and the Korean War. During these two periods, pressure from military and international activities forced the federal government to withdraw its aid for certain programs. During the 1960s, the Johnson administration tried a both guns-and-butter program as it fought the Vietnam War, which can be seen by the increases in federal domestic aid from the 1950s to the 1960s. But at the same time, the federal government developed new programs, like the Model Cities program; it cut back on aid for such things as highways, education, public health, and medical research. The state governments had to try to replace the federal contribution. In spite of all we've heard about revenue sharing, the federal share of

FIGURE 1–1

The States Emerge as Major Providers for
Domestic Services: The Proportion of
Domestic Functions Provided by the Three
Levels of Government, 1922–76

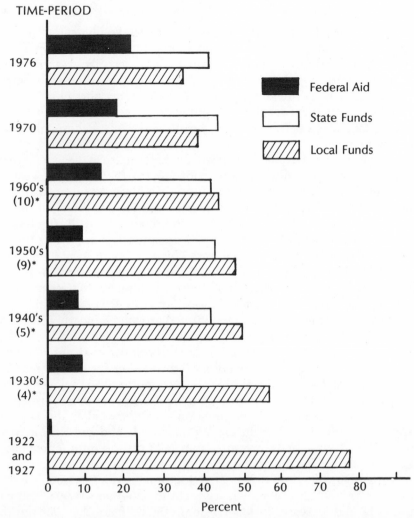

*The number of years for which data are averaged in each decade. Source: This figure is adapted from Table 2 in G. Ross Stephens, "State Centralization and the Erosion of Local Autonomy," *The Journal of Politics* 36 (February 1974): 57. Data for 1970 are from "1974 Appears To Be A Good Time To Be A Governor," *Congressional Quarterly Weekly Report,* 32, no. 33 (17 August 1974): 2218. Data for 1976 are used with permission of The Council of State Governments, from Table 5 in "State and Local Government Finances in 1975–1976," in *The Book of the States, 1978–1979,* Vol. 22, (Lexington, Ky.: Council of State Governments, 1978), p. 296.

the total outlay for domestic services increased by only 2 percent in 1972, the first year of its funding.

Turning now to Figure 1–2, we see that the states give their local governments more help than they receive from the federal government. This has been true since 1940. In 1976, the states received 42 billion dollars from the federal government. They, in turn, gave over 56 billion to their local progeny. Where they got the difference is another part of the picture, but it was not easy. In 1960, only 19 states had both income and sales taxes. Four had neither. By 1976, 41 states collected an individual income tax; 37 had both, and only one–New Hampshire—had neither. In any given year, approximately four-fifths of the states increase taxes to pay for new services or added costs. Between 1969 and 1974, Ohio, Illinois, and Pennsylvania enacted income taxes for the first time, amid bitter conflict involving the governor and the legislature. Connecticut enacted an income tax in 1971 and retracted it the same year. In 1979, Connecticut was still agitating about how to balance its budget. Unfortunately, the great fixed-cost programs such as public welfare, where the fixed costs keep rising, have absorbed a great share of these new funds. The result is that they can't be used for creative programs.

The discussion so far has centered on the increasing responsibility states have taken in all areas of domestic spending over this century. They raise 42 percent of the money for all domestic programs—most of it is for education and welfare—while the local and the federal governments provide the rest. It used to be that the local governments provided nearly 80 percent of the funds for all domestic programs. Their share has dropped by more than half (now approximately 36 percent), leaving the states to make up the difference. At the time local governments were providing nearly all of the funds for education and welfare programs, the states were considered weak and ineffectual. It did not matter a great deal how they ran the small-sized operation, which was state government then. But it matters how the major providers for all our "quality-of-life" expenditures are governed. The record shows that they have not shirked their responsibility.

In 1974, Governor Daniel J. Evans of Washington, chairman of the National Governors' Conference, declared:

> Even a cursory examination of the American past makes it apparent that at intervals of about every 35–40 years significant changes occur which greatly alter the political landscape; the new age of politics ushered in by Andrew Jackson; the Post Civil War years; the Populist/Progressive era; the New Deal all attest to this observation. It is my judgment that when historians write of the fundamental changes that occurred in the federal system during the last one-third of the Twentieth Century, the reaffirmation of the intended role of the states will be the characteristic most commonly noted.[10]

FIGURE 1-2

_The States Pick up the Tab: Proportions of
State Revenues from the Federal
Government and Proportions of Local
Revenues from the State Governments,
1922-76_

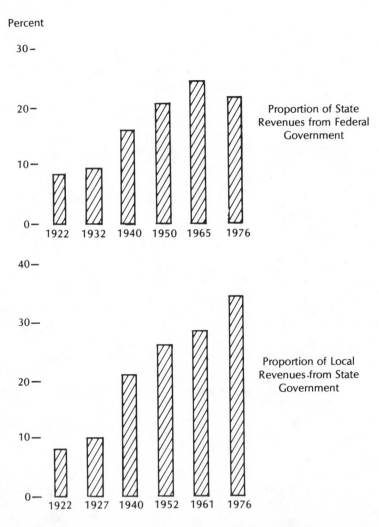

Sources: U.S. Department of Commerce, Bureau of the Census, _Historical Statistics of Governmental Finances and Employment; Census of Governments, 1967_ (Washington, D.C.: Government
Printing Office, 1969); _Historical Statistics on State and Local Government Finances, 1902–1953_
(Washington, D.C. Government Printing Office, 1955); _State Payments to Local Governments_ (vol.
6, no. 3 of the 1972 _Census of Governments);_ data used with permission of The Council of State
Governments, Table 2 in "State and Local Government Finances in 1975–1976," and "State Aid
to Local Governments in 1976," in _The Book of the States, 1978–1979,_ Vol. 22, (Lexington, Ky.:
Council of State Governments), p. 292, p. 602.

The Flow of Power: The Marble Cake

Does power follow the flow of money? In other words, would we expect that, as the funds from the federal government to the states increase, so would the controls? This is a highly complicated question and nobody knows the answer for sure. Whatever the answer is lies at the heart of federalism itself. Many people have ideas, of course. The myth that the states will dissipate federal money if it is given to them without any strings attached (that is, without controls) assumes that control should follow funds. The proponents of the myth would argue that strict controls over the way the money is spent should accompany any funds. State haters are the people who believe that the states are out to deny cities the funds they need for the monumental problems of hunger, housing, and unemployment. They would naturally argue that federal funds to the cities should flow directly to the cities, bypassing the states. Depending on who is the most persuasive in the decision-making circles of state or federal government, the transfer of money to the lower unit carries with it a dependence or independence to correspond with the latest thinking about federalism. (We will consider the relationship between the federal, state, and local governments in the specific fields of welfare, education, and land use in the concluding chapters of this book). In each program, the degree of responsibility for each governmental unit differs. In the discussion below, we will trace the overall trends in the evolving relationships between the national, state, and local governments.

Figure 1–1 illustrates the growth of federal grants. By 1976, the state and local governments received on average 22 percent of all their revenue from the national government compared to 9 percent in the 1950s. The share of this total grant given to the *state* governments has stayed about the same, amounting to just under 25 percent of all state revenues. The *local* government's received share of the total amount has gone up. In other words, federal aid given directly to the local governments has increased more rapidly than that given to state governments. It used to be that 90 percent of all federal funds went to the states directly, much of it to be distributed to the localities. Now the figure stands at 70 percent— a great drop since 1964. And about a third of that amount is to be distributed to the localities—called pass-through money—according to federal formulas. If we expect control to flow from the giving of money, we would expect that the federal government would be maintaining a steady relationship with the states while increasing its control over local governments.

CATEGORICAL GRANTS-IN-AID. This assumption is informed, but we need to know more. Much depends on the conditions under which grants are given. The national government can exercise a great deal of power by establishing the specific purposes for which its grants are to be spent, requiring matching amounts by states or local units or setting rules for administering nationally supported programs. Until recently, the national government spelled out the terms in this way for almost all of its fiscal aid. In 1976, this was the case for 70 percent of the federal-aid package. The method is called "categorical grant-in-aid." The national government maintains over 500 programs of this type spread over 61 federal departments, commissions, independent agencies, and councils.[11] The grants-in-aid support many state and local activities, such as specific agricultural research projects, mental health facilities, vocational training, and highway maintenance. Every cabinet department offers some money to states or communities. Most programs come from the departments of Health, Education, and Welfare; Housing and Urban Development, and Transportation. Not only are they developed and supervised by the departments, they are also under the supervision of the relevant congressional committees. At the state and local level, there are special administrative agencies to carry out the programs. To grab some handle on this whole concept of federal funds delivered as categorical grants-in-aid requires a statement like this: By far the greatest amount of money from the federal government, approximately 70 percent, comes with detailed control over spending, and a portion of this goes directly to the cities and towns. In terms of federal relationships, governors are caught in a dilemma. They need the funds for programs, so they apply for the money. They do exercise some control over its expenditure, but, from their point of view, not enough. What especially grieves the state-level policy makers is seeing their local governments apply for and receive aid directly from the federal government. They have no control over its expenditure. Hence, even if the governor believes he knows what is best for some of the communities in his state, he is not able to control the conditions under which they apply for or administer grants from the federal government. Under the conditions of direct grant-in-aid programs to the cities, the local governments become administrative mechanisms for the implementation of national policies rather than partners in state-wide problem solving. Thus for 70 percent of federal aid that goes to the states, there is no choice over the type of program and only moderate control over how the funds are to be administered.

During the 1960s, the size of domestic problems grew faster than the ability of the federal government to solve them. It became apparent that grants-in-aid were not the total answer to state and local problems. They provided no relief for the increasing costs of basic state and city operations that fell outside the list of aided functions. The states picked up the tab by sharing revenues with their local governments. There was extraordinary growth in state expenditures after 1965, most of which was channeled into the larger urban areas. The governors became sensitive to the needs of their large cities and, as the previous example of New York indicated, provided funds to ease their burdens.

BLOCK GRANTS. The governors object strenuously to direct federal-local relations. They want "pass through" legislation, that is, federal grant programs, that: (1) allow the states to authorize community participation in federal grant programs and (2) allow the states to control the grant money. They also want to receive federal funds as block grants, which is money with broad functional scope, that allows them broad discretion in particular programs such as police, health, or employment. They can then allocate the funds to communities within the state where the need exists. Through lobbying efforts in Washington, state governments have won some battles in their efforts to become federal grant coordinators for community governments. But they have also lost some.

This win-some-lose-some ratio is apparent in the block-grant programs that have been developed on a large scale in the last 15 years. They made up 12 percent of the 1977 federal government grant package. Some of them are "pass-through" programs that allow the states to allocate the money to the most needy communities. Examples of these programs are law enforcement (Omnibus Crime Control and Safe Streets Act), health (Comprehensive Health Planning Act), and manpower (Comprehensive Employment and Training Act), all of which designate the governor as the chief federal and administrative planning officer in the state. The Omnibus Crime Control and Safe Streets Act of 1968, for instance, mandates the states to establish a state planning agency created by the governor.

The governor and his staff are interested in the development of these programs at the state level. They want to ensure that the direction sought in federally funded programs is compatible with the state's overall goals. The villain, with respect to the ability of the states to plan for the health, education, and welfare of its citizens, is the Housing and Community Development Act of 1974. This act incorporates federal funding support for a range of community development activities, housing programs, and planning and management efforts. Eighty percent of the funds are allocated to metropolitan areas and 20 percent to non-metropolitan areas. The act was developed with little input from the states and, as a result, they are largely by-passed. The state role in the federal system is weakened by the manner in which the Community Development Act was written. The states could not allocate Community Development funds to areas of greatest need because the formulas for distributing the money were determined in Washington. An interesting case developed during the early administration of the act. The city of Hartford, Connecticut successfully sued the Department of Housing and Urban Development (HUD) to prevent it from giving $4 million in federal Community Development funds to its suburbs. Hartford's lawsuit argued that the city needed the money for housing its poor and elderly more than the suburbs needed it for roads, sewers, and parks. The city noted that the act creating HUD stated that the agency's purpose was to develop low-cost housing to build economically viable communities. The suburbs around Hartford did not want to undertake low-income housing to provide for the semiskilled workers who work in the suburbs but who must live in Hartford. The Hartford lawsuit argued, in effect, that the federal grant would further enhance the suburbs at the expense of the city.[12]

Block grants have a mixed record as far as the relationships between federal, state, and local governments go. Some of them establish the states as grant coordinators, which is what the governors want. It gives them the ability to allocate funds to areas of greatest need. Other block grants go directly to the cities. No consideration is given to the overall picture of urban-suburban relationships within a state. Each community gets an allotment based on a formula set in Washington. In this case, money goes directly from the federal government to the cities and towns. Ideally, from the states' point of view, money from Washington would be given directly to the states with no strings attached. After all, the federal government has the income tax—and the states are limited in their use of it to what the taxpayers will bear. It would seem logical for federal funds to go to the states for use in areas that they determine are of greatest need, not as the federal government determines it. Another quote from Governor Evans to the National Governors' Conference is in order:

> The need is not so much for additional funds from the federal government, but for funds unfettered by a scope so narrow as to force states into an unproductive lockstep and by restrictions so niggling as to constantly invite the harassment of federal functionaries. Not only does this prevent the best use of funds which are available, but enormous sums are kept from their rightful beneficiaries because of the huge structure of mostly unneeded federal regulations which spawn an army of federal enforcers and require unnecessary state auditors and managers. If Congress would simply follow the model of the 50 states as they share unrestricted revenues with local governments, we would all gain immensely.[13]

GENERAL REVENUE SHARING. The virtually unconditional distribution of general revenue sharing funds to state and local governments for spending as they deem necessary is widely heralded as ushering in a new era of federalism. Statutory formula has entitled state and local units to per capita annual allocations since Congress passed the State and Local Fiscal Assistance Act of 1972. This provided for the distribution of $5.6 billion per year to state and local governments through December 1976, but GRS was extended without major changes in 1976 for almost four more years at a rate of $6.8 billion per year. The change, however, is not a real increase when adjusted for inflation. In fact, the amount has been declining. In 1976, the figure was 12 percent of the federal package and dropped to 9 percent in 1977. While the amounts are still substantial, they are declining in relation to the categorical and block-grant programs.

The major financial argument for revenue sharing, as differentiated from grants-in-aid and block grants, is that the general operation of state and local government needs financial support as much as the specific services embodied in the categories of the existing aid system. In addition to the fact that grants-in-aid do not cover every area of state-local services and are not given to cover the general administration overhead of those governments, the matching-fund requirements of many categorical grant programs place an unbearable strain on the recipient governments. They can't afford to pass up any available federal aid. Yet to meet the matching fund requirements of those programs, they must strip the unaided functions of their share of locally raised revenue. Walter Heller, a strong advocate of revenue sharing, stated:

> It is hard to argue that the benefits of sanitation, green space, recreation, police and fire protection, street maintenance and lighting in one community have large spill-over effects on other communities. Yet, in more or less humdrum services such as these lies much of the difference between a decent environment and a squalid one, between the snug suburb and the grinding ghetto.[14]

General revenue sharing has had a major impact on the evolving federal relationship. Because roughly two-thirds of GRS funds are allocated to local governments, the overall distribution changes between state and local governments. This helps account for the previously noted reduction in the states' share during the 1970s. Both states and localities receive their allotment of the funds based on formulas stressing population, income, and tax effort. While the complex distributional formulas take need and local revenue raising into account, floor and ceiling provisions of the act limit the effects of the formulas. Therefore, while big cities, large urban areas, and poor rural communities have received the largest amounts of aid per capita, substantial redistribution has not been achieved. The problems of the central cities are not ameliorated by general revenue sharing. In the author's views of two detailed studies on the effects of revenue sharing, the provision that all county, municipal, and township governments may receive funds over a certain amount has unfortunate structural effects. No longer do these small jurisdictions need to pay attention to metropolitan problems. The area that receives money without having to prove its need through a competitive grant proposal confirms its autonomy from its own metropolitan area needs.[15] This is a vast departure from the original intent of Walter Heller who proposed that the federal government distribute funds only to states. They, in turn, would have the power to determine which local governments, if any, should receive a portion of the funds and on what basis of allocation. Such an argument can be seen as reflecting the traditional view of American federalism, which defines

local governments as "creatures of the states." States can no longer allocate funds to areas of need because of the distributional formulas of the
revenue-sharing grants. While the impact of revenue sharing is decreasing
due to diminished funding, the formulas represent a recent tendency on
the part of Congress to favor local governments when developing new aid
programs.

Another result of revenue sharing is that very large cities are using
most of their funds to meet operating needs, while in the smaller cities the
money goes into city hall buildings, fire houses, and golf courses.[16] The
contrast could not be sharper. The plight of the largest cities, increased
by the rate of inflation, is such that any additional revenue gets swallowed
up immediately in a desperate attempt to remain solvent without cutting
back on existing services. States, meanwhile, must use their funds to rescue those large cities while building programs of the more affluent suburbs
are financed with money they cannot control.

The situation in central cities is made worse by the fact that the influx
of revenue sharing money was matched by a simultaneous reduction in
funds previously obtained in a categorical grant basis to meet specific city
needs. Revenue sharing was used as an excuse for cutting back on rather
than supplementing, other kinds of aid. Robert C. Wood, former under-
secretary of the federal Department of Housing and Urban Development,
illustrated the plight of Boston. In fiscal 1973, Boston's general revenue
sharing was to be $17 million, but the city was scheduled to lose $100
million in cuts from such programs as Model Cities, The Public Service
Employees Program, and housing. In Wood's view, new federalism
"means the state and local governments of this country will find themselves with responsibility for domestic problems and development without even the present level of resources with which to confront these
problems."[17]

In an effort to ameliorate the large city problems predicted by Mr.
Wood, a large national program called Countercyclical Aid was passed in
1976 (under the rubric of Comprehensive Employment and Training).
The provisions were later extended through fiscal 1978. In line with the
existing GRS formula, the states were limited to one-third of appropriated
funds. The "countercyclical" features of the program make funds available only when national unemployment is above 6 percent, which is now
quite regular. These funds are distributed to state and local governments
in relation to the unemployment levels in their particular jurisdictions.
The purpose of the aid is to help state and local governments maintain
existing employment levels to provide necessary services without having
to raise their taxes during an economic downturn. Countercyclical Aid
resembles general revenue sharing in two ways: It supports already established state and local activities, and it is distributed to state and local

governments according to the one-third/two-thirds ratio. Although it was not renewed in 1978, Countercyclical Aid was considered a vital part of President Carter's urban policy program. The reasons for its failure to pass in Congress may be due to the mood of fiscal conservatism as a result of a taxpayers' revolt earlier in the year. State and local officials, and unions that had benefited from its aid were supporting the extension.

The 38,000 local governments and 50 state governments favoring continuance of both these programs raise an interesting question with regard to federal relationships. Revenue sharing and countercyclical aid have supported a very large number of clients who expect that the aid will continue. These clients like the general funding idea of revenue sharing because it frees them to make spending decisions in line with the desires of their people. State officials would prefer to get all the funds and make allocations based on need. If they insist on this too strongly, however, or try to manipulate the formula to suit their desires, they may lose their one-third share. Therefore, they join with the mayors and county executives in lobbying for the extension of revenue sharing. Despite the differences in support for the formula, states and localities both want the aid and have perfected their lobbying techniques to obtain it. This raises the question of federal control: Can we say that coalitions of state and local officials control the money they obtain? Or do the feds make their regulation a condition? Are the states and localities manipulating federal programs to suit their respective needs? If there are few strings attached, perhaps control has become decentralized, at least in that portion of federal aid given with few or no conditions.

MARBLE CAKE FEDERALISM. Morton Grodzins made an extensive study of the relationship between the three levels of government in terms of a marble cake-theory of federalism. He disputed the layer cake-theory relationship in which each level had separate and distinct functions with its own autonomous sphere of decision making. According to Grodzins' view decisions regarding a particular policy are made at all levels of government, and all levels typically cooperate in funding and implementing common policies.[18] His federalism/marble cake analogy indicates that each policy has its own particular streak in the federal cake, with the width of the streak in each layer corresponding to the power and money contributed to the policy. Overall, we see in the flow of power and money that the states contribute more to all domestic programs than either the local or federal government. We might expect, then, that the states have more to say about how the funds are spent than either of the other governments. This may be true. But the terms under which the money is distributed plays an important part in the amount of power assigned to each layer of government and hence to the marble streak width for each layer. Under revenue sharing, the fact that two-thirds of the federal money goes directly to local governments and only one-third to the states would appear to give the decision-making power to the localities. But, the states have to reallocate their funds to help those living in large cities who do not receive the money needed to ameliorate their problems. Thus, funding itself does not necessarily coincide with responsibility or power.

The last three chapters of this book consider three policy areas in which responsibility and funding are shared between the federal, state, and local governments. The marble cake analogy is used to describe the extent of control exercised by the respective governments over these policy areas. In welfare, the federal government funds just over half of the aid to families with dependent children. But the states may decide who are eligible and how much they will receive. This means the states really determine the conditions under which their poor will live, even though the federal government supplies more of the funding. In the education area, states and localities are the major policy makers because so little of the funds or decisions come from the federal government. In the marble cake division of responsibility for land use, a mere trickle in the federal layer, widens at the state level and is the thickest portion at the local level. Recently, some states have started to change the balance of power by asserting control over some land-use decisions.

In our discussion of the states' role in the federal system, it was intended to show that they are major decision makers and that the quality of life people lead can be shaped, for better or worse, by the policy makers in the state capitols. When the federal government cut services in response to the fiscal conservatism of the late 1970s, the states were left holding the bag. They could cut taxes and spending, but there were still the poor to be helped, the children to be educated, and the environment to be purified. The hard choices had to come with decisions on priorities of expenditures. The states must be responsive to their citizens and act in accordance with their preferences. The thesis of this book is that politicians make a crucial difference in the services people receive. It is the capacity of government to distribute the money and services. The type of government, the type of political party, and the type of leadership underlie who gets what, when, and how.

This notion that the quality of political leadership determines how well the people of a state are served runs into direct conflict with another body of thought which declares that the efforts of politicians have a minor role to play in the output of state governments. In this latter view, economic development shapes both political systems and policy outcomes. This argument is contrary to the one that forms the backbone of this book.

WHY DO THE STATES PROVIDE SO DIFFERENTLY?

States differ in the extent and quality of the services they offer. Presumably, the poor in every state want to be housed and fed. However, some states provide only 22 percent of their needs while others provide 100 percent. Why are the needs of the poor disregarded in one state and given sympathetic consideration in another? Why does one state make valiant attempts to equalize education for all its children while another allows poor children to receive an inferior education? Why do some states try to preserve open spaces for the enjoyment of their citizens while others leave land policy to chance? These differences in public policy outcomes have given rise to different explanations of the underlying reasons.

Economic Development

Rich states, like rich people, spend more for education, welfare, and health. Thomas R. Dye makes a strong argument that a state's social and economic traits explain its public policies. He finds that states with high levels of family income, adult education, urbanism, and industrialization have high levels of government spending for public education, aid to the poor, and hospitals.[19] These states also have higher rates of voter turnout in state elections and strong competition between Republicans and Democrats for state offices. Dye concludes from this that the economy of a given state affects both political activity and the policy outputs of government. In other words, human effort as well as the fruits of human labor are determined by the level of economic development existing in a state. This is a counsel of despair for a political scientist because it reduces all human effort to the impersonal hand of economic determinism. If the economy of a state determines all political activity as well as the outcome of that activity, this makes the efforts of political parties, and their respective candidates for office who work to put election promises into effect, a sham. Before we despair, however, we should examine closely what Professor Dye is saying.

To explore the connections between a state's social and economic conditions and the nature of its politics and public policies, these conditions, politics, and policies have to be measured. It's not very difficult to find how wealthy a state is or how the voters divide between Democrats and Republicans. Nor is it hard to determine the average amount spent on welfare families or school children. However, measuring human effort is a significant task. What makes one political leader successful and another a loser is hard to quantify. This is important because the economic determinism school uses easily measured variables to come to their conclusions. When states score high (or low) on a measure of economic resources as well as a measure of state policy (welfare expenditure per family, for example), the strong association between both measures indicates that the economic factor may have something to do with the policy. Where there are strong associations, it is said that a state's standing on one of the measures "explains" or "accounts for" its standing on the other. While it is true that social, economic, and political conditions in the states stand in the general relationship Professor Dye describes, the associations he finds are not strong. Numerous states either surpass or fail to meet the political activity or policy outputs that go along with their social or economic characteristics. The noneconomic explanations for state politics and public policy are often stronger than Dye's economic explanations. Only one-half of the variation in policy could be explained by all of Dye's economic measures combined, and this occurred in only 35 percent of the cases.

Let us examine the truth about the finding that economic development shapes both political activity and policy. In the underdeveloped states of this nation (those that have a single industry such as mining or farming), a single group is often able to control the politics of a state and govern in its own interests. It is usually a one-party state with few interests to challenge the dominant one—the people are apathetic and do not participate in politics. They see little way of challenging the establishment. Here, as the socioeconomic school rightfully asserts, economics explain the way the system runs as well as the policies it produces. Common sense would lead us to this conclusion. There are about eight states in the nation that still exhibit these characteristics of one party dominance, low voter turnout, and low funding for welfare and education.

However, we would expect that as this southern tier of states experiences an economic boom, they will begin to show the traits of political modernization. Two-party competition will become more prevalent, diverse pressure groups will form, and the people will become more politically active. The services the states provide could therefore increase in quantity and quality. We suspect that there may be a threshold effect at work here. Economic growth may affect policy making most clearly below a minimum "threshold" of development. The poorer the state, the less it can afford to spend on the necessary services for its citizens. The poorer a family, the less it can afford on food or shelter. This makes a great deal of sense. Grinding poverty and starvation go together for people as well as states. However, choices exist for families after a certain income is reached. No longer is life desperate and short. Money can be spent in different ways. It can be spent on education, for example, to improve one's chances in life, or it can be squandered.

So it is with states. Matters other than economic development begin to have an independent effect of their own, so we cannot predict a state's level of services solely on the basis of this measure. Once politics becomes important, economic factors become less so because the conditions themselves can be changed or controlled by the citizens. Economic development cannot explain why political parties in South Dakota, Vermont, and Virginia, for instance, achieve a high degree of cohesion. These states fall below the national average income, but show high political activity. Nor does wealth explain why New York is as far above the educational expenditures expected for its economic base as Ohio is below. Or why Pennsylvania is as far above the expected per capita welfare expenditure as California is below. Wealthy states have the ability to fund generous programs, but ability does not go hand in hand with desire. The efforts by political leaders must convert demands of the people into policy. The quality of political leadership, meaning the ability of leaders to make promises and then build legislative coalitions to put them into effect, is crucial to the well-being of a state's citizens. This is especially true for the most dependent of those citizens, the children and the poor.

If quality of life does depend on political leaders, as this book asserts, what gives rise to leadership in those states that provide generously for their citizens? What kind of political party system can recruit leadership that will be creative and serve the people?

Party Government

The single most important factor in state politics is the political party. It is not possible to understand the differences in the way sovereign states carry out the process of government without understanding the type of party whose representatives are making the decisions that affect the health, education, and welfare of its citizens. Political parties are usually relegated to a "chapter" in the saga of state politics. Yet they permeate every aspect of state government. Republicans or Democrats make the major decisions regarding who pays and who receives in the 50 states. For the last 20 years, with only one recent exception, every governor was either a Democrat or a Republican. Maine elected an Independent in 1974. In 1978, only two state senators were elected as Independents out of 1,920 senators; out of 5,570 state representatives only eight were Independents. The standing committees for each branch of each state legislature are chaired by representatives of the majority party, with only three exceptions: California (Senate), Tennessee (House) and Vermont (House and Senate). Nebraska is omitted from this analysis because its single-chamber legislature is elected on a nonpartisan basis. Clearly, the major decisions are political and are made by the elected representatives of our two major parties.

When we speak of the political party, we speak in terms of coalitions of men and women who operate under a common party label. The major work of the coalition is to recruit, nominate, and elect its candidates for public office. Once in office, they strive to enact programs that will ensure reelection. Any governing coalition has gone through these steps. Popularly elected governors present programs to state legislatures made up of both friends and foes—the number of each indicating the internal structure of the political parties within. It is the governor's political leadership and the coalition he can build within the legislature to support his programs that determine the fate of his political promises. It is curious that so little is known about this relationship between the governor and his legislative party. The ability of elected political party representatives to pass programs to which they have committed themselves at election time is the crux of party government.

PARTY GOVERNMENT AS DOCTRINE.   Proponents of party government say its most ideal form should work in the following manner: Two well-disciplined parties, each with its own conception of what the voters want and a program designed to satisfy those wants, compete for the favor of the electorate. Each party attempts to convince the majority of people that its program is best. In the election, 50 percent or slightly more of the voters choose the party whose policies they favor. The party takes over the executive and legislative power of government and the entire responsibility for what government does. It then proceeds to put its program into effect. The opposition party seeks to control the government at a future time. This goal is reasonably well assured because of the evenness in electoral competition between parties. By voting at the next election, the people decide whether or not they approve of the general direction the party in power has been taking—in short, whether their wants are being satisfied. If the answer is yes, they return that party to power; if the answer is no, they replace it with the opposition. The parties, therefore, are responsible to the electorate because they fear losing the next election. They are cohesive because they know that disunity may mean defeat. This is what is meant by "responsible party government."[20]

According to doctrine, party government performs three indispensable functions in a truly democratic society: First it clarifies the issues and enables the people to express themselves effectively on those issues. Second, it accomplishes the important function of activating public opinion —party government educates the public. Finally, parties establish popular control over government by making the group of rulers in power collectively responsible to the people. Needless to say, the proponents of responsible party government are not pleased with the operation of the American party system.[21]

The controversy over responsible party government has raged recently as the newly enfranchised electorate howled that they were not getting any choice and that both parties were espousing the status quo.

The assumption that parties should perform as vehicles for democratic government is basic to the new generation of discontent. Specifically, the responsible political party must:

1. Evolve and enunciate a reasonably explicit statement of party programs and principles.
2. Nominate candidates loyal to the party program, despite difficulties in controlling the direct primaries.
3. Conduct its electoral campaigns so that voters will grasp the programmatic differences between itself and the opposing party and make their voting decisions substantially on that basis.
4. Guarantee that public officeholders elected under the party label will carry the party program into public policy, thus enabling the party to take responsibility for their actions in office.[22]

PARTY GOVERNMENT AS ACTION. So much for the doctrine. As stated before, political practitioners do not read the doctrine. They go about their work of recruiting, electing, and representing under another set of assumptions—primarily those of *winning*.

An examination of the functions parties perform, as well as the structure that reflects this performance, is in order. The most reasonable explanation for political party activity is that the men and women who make up the party base all their calculations on the desire to be elected or reelected. In contrast to the model of responsible party government, which deduces the type of actions a party should take from some ethical principle about its proper function, this conception of political party is based on the office ambitions of coalitions of men and women. Ambition is not as noble a motive as "responsibility," but it is a more accurate description of the propelling force behind political party organizations in the American states. Positive theory is the school of thought that views political party as a calculating instrument.[23] One of its leading exponents, Anthony Downs, says that democratic political parties plan their policies to maximize votes. Downs defines a party as a group of people seeking to control the governing apparatus by gaining office. Thus, parties formulate policies to win elections instead of winning elections to formulate policy.[24] Self-interest is a more convincing explanation of political action than common good.

If ambition is the dominant motive force in the political party, a party must be reduced to as many factions or groups as will compete for nomination to the vacant elective offices. For each state, county, and local level office, there may be several groups seeking the nomination. Under what conditions do these groups combine for victory? Office-seeking groups under the party label may combine forces to present one candidate for office because they believe cohesion is their only chance of winning. They may also unite to control the nomination for more than one office in the system, or they may see that the nomination or election for one office depends on the nomination or election of another. In this case, the rudiments of a cohesive party structure begin to emerge. If a legislator supports a governor's program because he sees his election chances bound up with those of the governor, the party has a measure of unity. For the governor, legislative leadership is crucial to his policy-making ability. Policies that please the electorate (or at least a majority of it) are crucial to his next election. As a result in some states, a kind of symbiotic relationship develops between office-seeking groups. To the extent that the governors and legislators find it to their advantage to run on the same policy record, we have the makings of party government. This party government has come about because office-seekers must appeal to the electorate and believe that their next election depends on their performance in office. A Republican candidate for governor in a competitive industrial state must offer enough benefits to workers and city dwellers to weaken their normal support for his Democratic opponent. He cannot win the election by appealing only to farmers, industrialists, bankers, and businessmen. These groups are simply not enough votes. Consequently, after he is elected, the program he presents to the legislature will offer advantages to enough groups of voters to ensure his reelection. The legislators will respond if they, in turn, believe that their next election depends on support for the governor's program.

Not every governor runs for reelection, but whatever future position he does have in mind is determined by his record in office. There are only six states that do not allow the governor to succeed himself (Kansas, Mississippi, New Mexico, South Carolina, Tennessee, Virginia). Hence, most governors run for reelection at least once and then look for political advancement on some other level of government, such as a U.S. senatorship or a federal appointment. If they are going to run for the Senate, they'll have to appeal to the same voters that elected them governor. They'll also have to please party or faction leaders on whom they must depend for nomination to another political office. Presumably, these party leaders strive for a good party record to benefit the next gubernatorial compaign as well as the campaign for office to which the governor aspires. A future appointment may very well depend on the good will of party leaders who would require that the governor make a vote-getting record while in office.

A governor represents the totality of interests within his party. No single legislator or faction represents as wide a variety of interests. The governor's legislation is geared to please his state-wide constituency and, depending largely on his degree of control over his party, is passed, modified, or rejected. The governor is head of both his political party and the state government. These two roles are intertwined; the more successful he is as party leader, the more successful he will be as head of state. A governor's ability to capture the loyalty of party chieftains to build winning coalitions within the legislature gives him mastery over the decision-making process. This process allocates the burdens and benefits of the system. The governor's leadership can provide the link between the people and their problems and the extent and direction of resources that state government can allocate to these problems.

Figure 1–3 represents a governing coalition within a policial party. The two elements of political party, the party in office and the party of organized workers, the electoral party, are joined in a governing coalition. The extent to which party government is realized varies. The governor is at the apex of both the electoral and governing parties. It is he who must form winning coalitions both within and outside the government. The gubernatorial electoral coalition may be a permanent one led by a strong state party chairman, such as John Bailey, former Democratic chairman in Connecticut, or Ray Bliss, former Republican chairman in Ohio; or it may be dominated by a powerful leader such as former Governor Rockefeller in New York. Instead of the legislative party being an independent entity, it is subject to the direction and influence of the governor's coalition within the electoral organization. Active and potential factions exist within the party. The governor must compete for the nomination. To do so, he builds a coalition within the party that will be large enough to assure him of an uncontested primary nomination, or at least guarantee an im-

FIGURE 1–3

A Governing Coalition

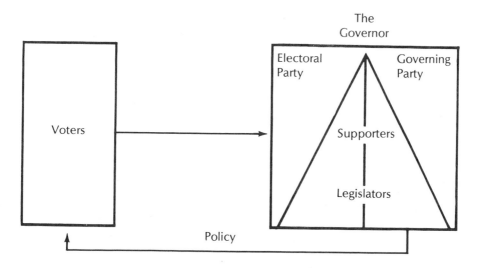

pressive victory in the primary election. This is the leadership faction and includes members of the legislature who come from areas where the governor has electoral organization and support. With his supply of sources, the governor can "pay" other legislators to back him. This model does not separate the legislative party from the electoral, but considers them partners in the forming of a leadership coalition. This is the essence of party government as it exists in a system that has a constitutional separation of powers, as all states have. One would expect that such a governing coalition would be able to present programs to the electorate and be able to put them into effect once in office. The essentials of party government exist if there is a leadership faction with enough power to nominate candidates for public office and to command enough votes in the legislature to pass executive requests.

There are many variations in the degree to which different state political systems give rise to parties that can unite to present programs to the voters and then see these programs enacted after the election. Because the governorship is a powerful position for aspiring politicians, keen competition for the office is natural within both political parties. In all but a handful of southern states, there is the possibility that a well-organized assault on the governorship by either political party will win the rewards of office. However, a potential governor must put together an intraparty coalition before he wins the nomination. Almost no potential governor starts from "scratch." Most of them have been state legislators or public attorneys. They have run for election and have developed a power base from which to operate. With his finite supply of rewards and punishments and his own ability and effort, the candidate forges a coalition to stand by him at election time. The degree of his success is first measured by the primary results and later by the degree of support he musters for his policies in the government.

The play of forces within the major parties is, therefore, the most significant index of a state's politics. In some, a leadership coalition exists that can sift and schedule ambitions among contenders for the nomination. A hard-fought primary is considered a divisive struggle that gives the advantage to the other side. The same is true if the parties are weak, splintered, and ineffectual organizations. The competing factions may be based on personal ambition for leadership or they may represent very real social, economic, or geographic cleavages within the party. The coalitions may be formalized, sub-party organizations with long traditions and different policy outlooks. A strong governor may impose some order on a multifactional situation, as popular governor Dale Bumpers was able to accomplish in Arkansas. In a single state, one party may exhibit a clearly identified and continuous leadership, such as the Massachusetts Republicans, while the Bay State Democratic party is an example of wide factional cleavage and little centralized control over the promotion for the ambitious. It is commonly agreed that parties that are split into factions do not represent the needs of the people as efficiently as those with a more cohesive system of nominating, electing, and governing. The late V. O. Key, Jr., a famous party theorist, believed that multifactionalism within the political party facilitated control over governmental policy by the "haves" in society as opposed to the "have-nots." He said that "A loose factionalism gives great negative power to those with a few dollars to invest in legislative candidates. A party system provides at least a semblance of joint responsibility between governor and legislature. The independence of candidates in an atomized politics makes it possible to elect a fire-eating governor who promises great accomplishments and simultaneously to elect a legislature a majority of whose members are committed to inaction."[25]

We will concentrate on testing Key's proposition that governing parties with sufficient internal cohesion to pass their programs will bring about a wider distribution of state expenditures across income classes.

PARTY GOVERNMENT AND PUBLIC POLICY: A MODEL

Policy-Making Process

The proof of the pudding is in the eating. To what degree does party government affect policies in the American states? While the men and women who compose the party have their own personal motives, the party is not an end, but a means for the society as a whole. We are concerned with the product of the political system and how the political party contributes to that product. If state party government does not affect the quality of services that people receive, then the study of it is not relevant to the needs of the poor, the well-being of the people, the education of youth and the self-respect of the aged. If the capacity of the governor as political leader does not affect his response to the demands of his citizens by proposing programs that will convert these demands into policy, then all our notions of party government are in error.

The policy-making process model we are working with regards policy as the result of the imputs of needs and demands of the people converted by the efforts of politicians acting within certain institutional constraints. While this model is acceptable to most political scientists, there is no general agreement as to the relative influence of the socio-economic, political, and structural variables that contribute to the policy output. Figure 1-4 includes all the influences that may explain policy differences in the states.

FIGURE 1–4

A Model of the Policy-Making Process

Party Organization
Governor's Leadership
Legislative Party Cohesion
Party Program Commitment
P

INPUT
Economic Development
Electoral Competition
Popular Participation
Pressure Groups

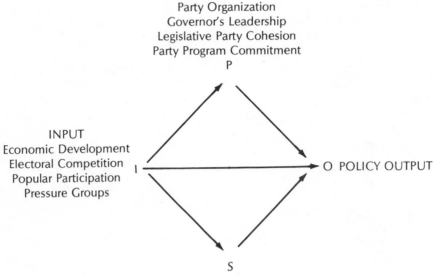

O POLICY OUTPUT

S
Structural Variables
Formal powers of the governor
Legislative party; percent of seats
Legislative professionalism

Inputs

First in the series of influences on the policy-making process are the inputs of needs, demands, and support. These are usually measured by economic development, electoral competition, and the participation of the people in elections and pressure-group activity. Education, roads, jobs, welfare, and health are just a few of the needs of the people. Not all are converted into demands, and it is commonly supposed that only those that are brought to the attention of the decision makers result in policy. Poverty represents needs. Poverty can be ignored by the decision makers if no one espouses the cause of the poor. Most commonly, demands are made by individuals or groups through speeches, demonstrations, visits to public officials, and other forms of pressure. Demands come from the workers and members of political parties, unions, farmers, businesses, banks, and so on. Support, another input in the policy-making process, may be expressed as positive action such as voting or paying taxes, or as negative action such as withdrawal, refusal to pay taxes, demonstrations, or sit-ins.

ECONOMIC DEVELOPMENT. The Thomas Dye School, discussed previously, makes a direct link between the degree of economic development and the major public services adopted by the state. This linkage is represented in figure 1–4 by the arrow that runs straight from state-wide economic development to Policy Output (I—O). Dye concludes that political characteristics have relatively little impact on policy outcomes in the states. Economic development, he claims, shapes both political parties as well as policy output (I—O and I—P). We know, however, that governments in many states either surpass or fail to reach the policy norms that are generally associated with their levels of economic development. This reinforces our hypothesis that party politics, especially political leadership, affects the conversion of need into policy and that this party leadership is not determined by socio-economic forces but by the efforts of leaders (I—P—O).

POPULAR PARTICIPATION. This theory contends that high popular participation brings about generous levels of public service. But, if this is the case, we might conclude that political leaders always listen to voters. But we must check other explanations as well. A high level of economic well-being might influence popular participation. We know that wealthy well-educated people show more than an average interest in politics, and we know that wealth has something to do with the resources needed to support public services. So the economic development in a state may lead to high (or low) levels of political participation, as well as the wealth to back up the demands. What do political leaders need: participation or wealth or both? We will address that question in the following chapters.

ELECTORAL COMPETITION. Another hypothesis assumes that electoral competition between parties is the necessary condition for the electorate to reward or punish the party for its performance in office.[26] This competition-cohesion school believes that close electoral competition results in unified parties acting cohesively in their nominating and governing functions.

Writers in this school of thought differ slightly over the manner in which the electoral division of voters affect this cohesion. V. O. Key, Jr., claimed that competition itself tended to produce party cohesion since each must be united to fight the opposition party, which could take over the government in the next election. Several other writers reject the notion that two-party competition is a producer of party cohesion, and suggest that parties are most likely to be cohesive in states where they are bipolarized along rural-urban lines. Thus, it takes a particular combination of economic and political competition to produce cohesive parties. Unlike many recent researchers, this school never draws a direct link between electoral competition and policy output (I—O). The competition-cohesion school draws two links from the political division of a state's voters to the political party and, hence, to policy output (I—P—O).

Party Organization as Process

Party government theorists assume that the political party brings the needs and demands of the people to the government for "conversion" into policy (I—P—O). It is, of course, those who were elected to public office and their supporters who actually bring the demands and convert them into policy. Party thus provides the link between the people and their government. The ease with which the party can do this is affected to some degree by some constitutional and legal "givens," which differ from state to state and which can be frustrating or hospitable to the performance of party.

Structural Variables as Process

FORMAL POWERS OF THE GOVERNOR. The formal control a governor has over the performance of his administrators affects his ability to bring about policy in line with the needs and demands of the population. Governors must often work with the independent heads of administrative departments to make up their budgets. In some instances, the governor's formal authority allows him to dominate policy making; elsewhere, he has little authority to get what he wants. It is possible to measure variations in the governor's powers, seeking to identify the economic, social, and political influences that are associated with these differences (I—S), and the state-to-state divergence in policy that reflect them (S—O). The formal powers do correlate with the affluent characteristics of a state's population. Wealthy states require a powerful chief executive who, once elected, has the authority to enact needed programs. However, a governor with strong legal authority has no *assurance* that it will yield political power. If he is unable to persuade others of the merits of his position or is unwilling to bargain, he may find himself no better off than the governor with fewer formal powers.

LEGISLATIVE SEATS. The relationship between the percentage of legislative seats held by the governor's party and the degree of control he can exert over his legislators may also affect public policy (S—O). It is an obvious advantage to have a majority in the legislature. The speaker, chairmen, and committee majorities are all from the governor's party. But if the governor's party coalition in the legislature is well *over* a comfortable majority, the surplus may generate rivalries that he cannot control. The percentage of seats held by the governor's party may be a potentially powerful variable that affects his ability to enact legislation. It may intervene between the needs of the people and the governor's ability to meet these needs.

LEGISLATIVE PROFESSIONALISM.   If the legislature has modernized its procedures, it may be more effective at policy-making. John Grumm, an authority on state legislatures, claimed that states with well-paid and staffed legislators are better able to meet their people's needs. He found that industrial states had more professional legislatures and more generous benefits (I—S—O). Grumm discovered that industrialization did not affect welfare benefits directly and concluded that the professionalism of a legislature mediates the needs and demands of the people.[27] Recently, a member of the Connecticut Senate pleaded for office space and secretarial help to better fulfill his duties. Connecticut is low on the list of states with respect to the professional services provided for legislators. However, it is high on the list of states ranked according to per capita welfare benefits. The senator assured his audience that he did not expect life to be as "soft" as that provided for New York legislators—also a state high on the welfare benefit list. One can only conclude from this that some state parties can overcome lack of professional standards and provide the necessary services to their citizens.

Policy Output

Readers who have followed this discussion must be concerned over the number of variables that have been advanced as influencing the ability of politicians to make policy. We considered a policy yardstick in the first section of this chapter. What is needed is a policy measure to compare states according to the quality of services their citizens enjoy. Although education and welfare are the two largest categories of spending, there has been disagreement among researchers as to the measurement of output in these areas. Some researchers use level of expenditures for various programs, but there is a risk in relying exclusively on total per capita expenditures as indicators of public policy. Current disbursements may not be reliable indicators of the services provided to the population. The level of spending does not tell us who is receiving the benefits nor the quality of benefits received.

Equal expenditures in two similar school systems may result in one challenging its pupils to stay until graduation, while in the other, large numbers drop out. Measuring the dropouts is a way of determining the consequences of the services provided by a school system; it is an outcome of the services. Some outcomes are not intended by policy makers. For example, they may decide to spend more on welfare children to help them emerge from poverty and helplessness; but if the money does not reach those most in need, the outcome is contrary to their intentions. Outcomes require different measures from outputs. Whereas state government expenditures for health and hospitals are an output, the proportion of infants surviving their first year of life is an outcome. While expenditures per capita for public education is an output, the percentage of the state's candidates passing the selective service mental examination is an outcome. Outcomes are what concern people most. Citizens formulate demands, pay taxes, and seek to influence the decision makers—all to achieve desired outcomes. No consideration of policy is complete without taking into account the outcomes. The results of public policy have been the least-studied political concept and are often the most difficult to measure—in part because there are relatively few official indicators of outcomes, whereas data about outputs are numerous. In the concluding chapters, we will develop measures of welfare and education that take both spending and outcomes into account.

CONCLUSIONS

This book is based on the assumption that the efforts of politicians are independently consequential and that policy outcomes can be shaped, for better or worse, by the type of party they operate. Policies as important as welfare and education, which consume approximately 60 percent of the general expenditures and government employment of states and their local governments, are proposed to state legislatures by popularly elected governors. The fate of legislation depends on much more than the money available or the political inclinations of the voters. Especially in the present context of American politics and society, governors are caught in a cross fire between growing demands for services and protests against rising taxes, between the demands from cities and resistence to these demands from legislatures that are often dominated by rural and suburban representatives. The urgency of understanding these forces can scarcely be exaggerated. In 1972, Congress enacted the $30 billion general revenue-sharing program. Surveys show that significant amounts of revenue-sharing funds have been used to reduce taxes and make capital improvements, not for new spending on long-term social programs for helping disadvantaged groups. Congressman John Brademas of Indiana said that some of the neediest groups are not those "with the greatest political influence at the local or state level, and it ought not to be surprising that they see so little of the benefits of revenue sharing."[28] In light of the increasing responsibility for all domestic functions that the states have been taking recently, it would appear vital that the policy-making apparatus of the states be examined carefully.

The policy-making process and the central role that political parties play in it, according to the model described above, is of primary importance. We consider the electoral foundations of the party systems found in the various states and the extent to which economics determine the characteristics of state parties. The relationship of interest groups to the party structure will be examined. The factions that develop within both political parties to contest for the nomination for governor will be described because of their intimate relationship to the governing process. The rules of the game that each state imposes on its parties have an effect on the nominating and election functions of the parties.

The political party operates within the government agencies responsible for converting the needs and demands into policy. In every state, the governor presents a program to the legislature indicating the legislation he wants passed. The holding of hearings, the compromises in committee, the debate on the floor, and the final adoption or rejection of the administration's bills are all part of the conversion process. While the courts are generally considered out of "politics," political parties in many states control the nomination and election of judges. In other states, judges are appointed by elected leaders. To what extent are courts involved in the political party process and how does this affect their output?

It is possible to show how policy is affected by the machinery through which it is processed. But to what extent do certain policies depend on political effort? Are some policies less dependent than others on party government? As the demand for new policies arises, what combination of groups align for and against them? How does the political party apparatus mediate among the various groups? These are all questions we will address in the following chapters.

NOTES

1. Steven R. Weisman, "City Avoids Default by Hours as Teachers Relent, Buy Bonds; Financial Markets Disrupted," *New York Times,* 18 October 1975, p. 16.
2. Martin Tolchin, "Ford Again Denies Fiscal Aid to City," *New York Times,* 18 October 1975, p. 1.
3. Francis X. Clines, "New York Says It Is Washington's Black Sheep," *New York Times,* 26 October 1975, Section 4, p. 1.
4. Daniel J. Elazar, "The New Federalism: Can the States Be Trusted?" *The Public Interest,* 35 (Spring 1974): 89–102.

5. Elazar, "The New Federalism," pp. 91–92.
6. John Herbers, "States Step Up Aid To Ailing Localities," *New York Times*, 17 April 1979, p. 1.
7. Michael D. Reagan, *The New Federalism* (New York: Oxford University Press, 1972), pp. 130–31.
8. Thomas J. Anton, *The Politics of State Expenditure in Illinois* (Urbana: University of Illinois Press, 1966), p. 146.
9. W. Duane Lockard, *New England State Politics* (Princeton: Princeton University Press, 1959), pp. 75–77.
10. Daniel J. Evans, "Reaffirmation of the States: Report by the Chairman of the National Governors' Conference," *State Government* 47 (August, 1974): 238.
11. Harold Seidman, *Politics, Position and Power: The Dynamics of Federal Organization*, 2d ed. (New York: Oxford University Press, 1975), p. 170.
12. Lawrence Fellows, "Hartford Battles Suburbs for Federal Aid," *New York Times*, 17 November 1975, pp. 33, 51.
13. Evans, "Reaffirmation of the States," p. 240.
14. Walter W. Heller, "Should the Government Share Its Tax Take?" *Saturday Review* 22 (March 1969): 26–29.
15. Richard P. Nathan, Allen D. Manvel, and Susannah E. Calkins, *Monitoring Revenue Sharing* (Washington, D.C.: Brookings Institution, 1975), p. 308; Richard P. Nathan and Charles F. Adams, Jr., *Revenue Sharing: The Second Round* (Washington, D.C.: Brookings Institution, 1977), pp. 106–107.
16. Advisory Commission on Intergovernmental Relations, "General Revenue Sharing After One Year," *Information Bulletin*, No. 73–79, November, 1973.
17. U.S. Congress, Senate, Committee on Government Operations, Subcommittee on Intergovernmental Relations, *Hearings, A New Federalism*, 93rd Cong., 1st sess., 1973.
18. Morton Grodzins, "The Federal System," in President's Commission on National Goals, *Goals for Americans* (Englewood Cliffs, N.J.: Prentice-Hall, 1960).
19. Thomas R. Dye, *Politics, Economics, and the Public: Policy Outcomes in the American States* (Chicago, Ill.: Rand McNally, 1966). See also Richard E. Dawson and James A. Robinson, "Inter-Party Competition, Economic Variables, and Welfare Policies in the American States," *Journal of Politics* 25 (May 1963): 281–89; Richard I. Hofferbert, "The Relation Between Public Policy and Some Structural and Environmental Variables in the American States," *American Political Science Review* 60 (March 1966): 73–82.
20. This discussion draws heavily on the summary by Austin Ranney, *The Doctrine of Responsible Party Government* (Urbana, University of Illinois Press, 1962), pp. 8–22.
21. American Political Science Association, Committee on Political Parties, *Toward a More Responsible Two-Party System* (New York: Rinehart and Company, 1950), pp. 22–23; Walter Dean Burnham, "Party Systems and the Political Process," in William Nisbet Chambers and Walter Dean Burnham, eds., *The American Party Systems: Stages of Political Development* (New York: Oxford University Press, 1967), pp. 305–306.
22. Frank J. Sorauf, *Party Politics in America*, 3d ed. (Boston: Little, Brown, 1976), p. 389.

23. Joseph A. Schlesinger, "The Primary Goals of Political Parties: A Clarification of Positive Theory," *American Political Science Review* 69 (September 1975): 840.
24. Anthony Downs, *An Economic Theory of Democracy* (New York: Harper & Row, 1957), p. 25.
25. V. O. Key, Jr., *Southern Politics in State and Nation* (New York: Knopf, 1949), p. 308.
26. American Political Science Association, *Toward a More Responsible Two-Party System.*
27. John G. Grumm, "The Effects of Legislative Structure on Legislative Performance," in Richard I. Hofferbert and Ira Sharkansky, eds. *State and Urban Politics* (Boston: Little, Brown, 1971), pp. 308–22.
28. "Revenue-sharing: Some Second Thoughts," *Congressional Quarterly Weekly Report,* 32, no. 27 (6 July 1974): 1758.

CHAPTER TWO

ELECTORAL FOUNDATIONS OF STATE POLITICAL SYSTEMS

In America the people are sovereign. The very existence of political parties and political leaders depends on their votes. The process by which the governor, the head of the state government and his electoral party, is elected reinforces the principle of popular sovereignty. In directly courting the diverse factions among the electorate, political leaders must practice their own form of triage. They must recognize the faithful and reinforce their predilections, ferret out the independents and woo them through promises and actions, and pinpoint the committed opposition as an unnecessary drain on valuable resources. Thus, the elected cannot be far from the people on whom they rely for votes and support.

Just who are these sovereign people? Why are they presently divided so evenly between the two political parties? And what is the exact nature of their sovereignty? Are their needs being met by their elected representatives? These are the issues we will be addressing in this chapter.

In the late sixties, two researchers discovered that, while the people of our country place national affairs first in interest, state affairs come in a strong second in a ranking that ranged from international to local levels.[1] One-half of the citizens asked placed state affairs either first or second. More interesting, geographical location influenced a citizen's orientation to politics. The more urban a person's upbringing, the less likely he was to pay attention to state politics. A similar pattern was discovered in terms of contemporary residence. Residents of urban or metropolitan areas are less interested in state affairs. Although region itself may be a summary variable for many historical, social, economic, and cultural factors, the importance of state affairs varies among the regions of this country. Southerners are most attuned to state matters, westerners next, and midwesterners and northeasterners least. In the case of the southern states, they are bound by the memories, pains, and trauma of the Civil War. For their people, state governments have a unique place in their political spectrum. At the other extreme is the cluster of northeastern and midwestern states, those states generally considered more cosmopolitan in outlook and the original bearers of the political traditions of the nation. Between these two groups are those western states that were settled in large part by immigrants from other states, carved out of former federal territories and left to develop their particular brand of culture and politics. These hybrid states have neither the high cosmopolitanism of the northeastern-midwestern tier nor the bitter memories of the South. They are physically remote from the center of national power and take pride in coping with their own problems. Thus, the people of the different regions of the country provide a divergent reservoir of support for their state governments.

This reservoir of support is based on environmental conditions of birth and residence and weakens as a person becomes more educated and sophisticated. However, the great pulling power of geographical location and native traditions on the loyalties of the citizens indicate that these are powerful factors to be considered in a discussion of the electoral bases of state political systems.

THE TWO-PARTY SYSTEM

A Classification System

Increasingly, the people of the states vote as Democrats and Republicans in equal proportions. All but eight states could be classified as having two-party systems, meaning that both Democrats and Republicans seriously compete for the office of governor. There are now only eight one-party states in the Union—states in which only a major upheaval could move the voters to vote for a Republican governor. This has occurred in four states already, although for limited periods. In 1966 and 1968, Winthrop Rockefeller, brother of Nelson, won in Arkansas, a Democratic bastion state. The fact that he was a well-known leader in the state and the magic of the Rockefeller name helped him win a Republican victory after twelve years of Orval Faubus. But the Arkansas Republican party was not strong enough to win elections on a regular basis, and the following general elections went heavily Democratic. In South Carolina in 1974, a Republican won for the first time since 1876. The Democrats were torn between the traditional conservatives represented by U.S. Representative William Jennings Bryan Dorn, an old-time folksy courthouse politican from a rural district, and a coalition of blacks and young moderate whites, mainly from urban areas, represented by Charles Ravenel, a 36-year-old financier and political newcomer. After a $250,000 media blitz, Ravenel narrowly defeated Dorn for the gubernatorial nomination. But the state supreme court ruled Ravenel ineligible for the governor's race because he had not met the five-year residency requirement. In the end, the disunity in the party ranks set the stage for these elections and allowed Republican James Edwards to win with 52 percent of the vote. A close inspection of the election records for both these solid Democratic states as well as Tennessee and Texas where Republican governors have won recently, reveals that in one or more elections previous to the Republican win, the Democratic vote had dropped into the 50–60 percent range, indicating that the Republicans had been stirring while the Democrats were engaging in intraparty squabbles. Republicans won two gubernatorial elections in Tennessee after close contests, and, in 1978, Texas elected the first Republican governor in 105 years.

The states may be classified according to the degree to which the parties compete in elections. A salient characteristic of the party systems of the states is their dual form. For the last hundred years, power has alternated between two major parties on the national level, and the states have reflected this dualism with varying degrees of competitiveness. For long periods of time, single parties dominated the national scene; yet, even during these eras, the opposition party maintained itself in power in a substantial number of states. Most voters have consistently placed their faith in one of the two major parties; yet, neither party has been able to obliterate the other's following. On the surface it may seem that the parties have remained the same, but, in fact, only the system has remained the same; the parties have changed. They have changed to accommodate the new Americans, the urban masses, the eastern industrialists, and the southern planters. They are in the process of changing from parties that represent geographic areas of our nation to parties that reflect the new urban-suburban-rural division of our people. "New wine has been poured into old bottles and old wine has been transferred from bottle to bottle."[2]

A Belief System

The two-party system has two major aspects: a belief system that at times approaches a religion and a measurement system that varies according to the political jurisdictions, offices, time periods, and inclinations of the researcher. The two-party system as a belief is manifested in the American Political Science Association's assessment of political parties published in 1950 entitled, "Toward A More Responsible Two-Party System." Within this document the claim was made that:

> The two-party system is so strongly rooted in the political traditions of this country and public preference for it is so well established that consideration of other possibilities seems entirely academic. When we speak of the parties without further qualification, we mean throughout our report the two major parties.[3]

Another manifestation of this attitude is found in Schattschneider's work when he claims that we are, for the first time in American history, within striking distance of a competitive two-party system throughout the country. He continues that the extension to all the states of a competitive system will force the party in power to realize that it really can be turned out at the next election. "It is difficult to exaggerate the probable impact of this development on the programs, the organizations, the responsibilities and the reputation and importance of the major parties."[4]

Recall that during our discussion of party government as doctrine, two-party competition was one of the contributing factors. The major assumption of that school was that popular control over government, which is the essence of democracy, can best be established by the popular choice between and control over alternative responsible parties. Only in the competition between such parties can the popular will be translated into governmental action. This theory assumed that electoral competition between parties was the mechanism by which the electorate rewards or punishes the party for its performance in office. It was assumed that, where the condition of two-party competition existed, parties were cohesive and would translate election promises into policy for fear of retribution at the polls.[5] Thus a two-party system is defined as one in which the voters divide their loyalty fairly evenly between the parties, and the parties are able to govern effectively, thus providing a wider distribution of services to the people. It follows from this description of party competition as belief that the states that are governed best would be those that have the most competition. In other words, the degree of party competition is a yardstick with which to measure the quality of the government of the state. This is a tremendously powerful hypothesis.

V. O. Key, Jr., tried to show that the hypothesis did not hold water in the competitive northern states, but his findings were not heeded.[6] Researchers developed measures of party competition on the assumption that they could measure qualitative differences between the American states. Without accepting this belief in the ability of competition to produce responsible government, we can measure the degree of competition that exists in the American states both now and in the past. Some speculation as to why the same two parties have contested elections in all the states since the Civil War might also be in order. Some pondering over the reasons for our states' two-party systems as opposed to multiparty systems is also relevant to our concerns.

A Measurement System

The determination of the degree to which the two parties "seriously compete" for elected government offices is an empirical inquiry. In investigating past returns for various offices, the analyst must choose the offices to study, the time period, and the measure of competition. An examination of the various analyses shows that each scholar tackles the problem in a somewhat different manner, depending on his expectation of the substantive impact of competitiveness.[7] Two researchers examined five widely used measures and found that there was significant correlation between the measures regardless of the time period or offices used. Specifically, the time period ranged from six to over thirty-five years. The offices chosen showed even more variation, with scholars using combinations of the offices of president, United States senator, governor, state legislators, and lesser state officials. Finally, competitiveness was measured by the number of offices held by a party, percent of the vote received by a party, and number of terms in office a party was in power. Since most researchers rank the states according to their own measures of competitiveness, it is possible to compare these values. If the most competitive state on one measure was also the most competitive on the next measure, and this matching continued for all the states in decreasing order, there would be a perfect correlation between the two measures, or a correlation of 1.00. The researchers found correlations of .80 or greater between all the separate measures of competition.[8] Thus, it would seem that each state maintains its own position in the ranking of competitiveness. As the states become more competitive, they maintain the same ranks; in other words, the most competitive state becomes even more competitive, and all others follow in descending order to maintain the original ranks. It was concluded that the degree of competitiveness among the states is relatively stable for the period 1914–63.

More recent measures of state competition have concentrated on state offices alone, omitting those for the presidency and Congress. The governors and state legislators have been chosen because they are the state's most powerful officers. A recent study has combined the following measures of competitiveness: (1) popular vote for the office of governor; (2) percentage of seats for each party in the senate and house; and (3) the percentage of all terms for governor, senate, and house in which one party has control.[9] Built into this measure is the assumption that the percentage of seats the governor's party controls in the legislature is an important measure of the degree of competitiveness in the state. The most extreme example of this may be illustrated by the Arkansas legislature in 1966, the senate of which was 100 percent Democratic and the House 98 percent Democratic under the Republican governor, Winthrop Rockefeller. Obviously, to govern, Rockefeller had to work with the Democratic group of legislators most ideologically attuned to his program, and his program could not overstep the limits of the group's willingness to cooperate.

The objection to combining these two measures of competitiveness for the governor and the legislature is that much of the strategy of the governing process may be obscured. Governors use many devices to gain the cooperation of the legislators from either party. A powerful governor has a collection of resources that may counteract the fact that he has a minority of the legislature. He is the most visible state officer, as head of his party and head of the government. The major point here is that the combination of measures for both governor and legislature may hinder an examination of them as separate entities in the governing process and may disguise the strategy of conflict or cooperation that exists between them. The upshot of this argument is that the degree of competitiveness of a state for our purposes is centered in the office of governor. We will use the division of the voters of a state between the two parties for the office of governor as our measure of the competitiveness of the state.

What can account for the fact that throughout most of our history power has alternated between two major parties on the national level, and that the states have reflected this dual form in different degrees, never deviating long from the same two parties? Given the diversity of interests within the states, one might expect numerous parties to be formed to represent groups with conflicting aims and objectives. Yet, this has not occurred. There are several reasons that push both the national party system and the fifty state party systems toward dualism.

WHY DO THE STATES HAVE THE SAME TWO PARTIES?

The states operate as units of the nation. The "marble cake" notion of the division of responsibility between the states and the national government is that they both share responsibility for the great problems brought about by industrialism and an ever growing urban society. The financial crisis of New York City in 1975 had repercussions among all the states. The poor cross state boundaries and become national problems. In every state, the property tax is failing to support local school systems, and the states need money to provide for educating their students. Increasingly, each state mirrors the national problems. This has not always been the case, as we will see shortly. In the years following the Civil War, the major issues were sectional—the farmers from the farming states vs. the eastern industrialists. At that time, a party that was strong in one group of states was weak in others. It has always been true, however, that national problems are collections of state problems, and national parties are loose coalitions of state parties, whether they represent sectional or class interests.

The Winner Takes All: The Presidency, The Governor, and The Legislature

The first reason for a two-party system on the national level and in the states of the union is an institutional one based on election mechanics. The American presidency and the governorships—the main prizes of American politics—fall only to parties that can win pluralities. Plurality election for a single office means that one candidate is elected and that the winner is the one who receives the largest number of votes. To win this prize, parties make up coalitions of voters that will ensure them a plurality of the vote. The system offers no reward of office to any but the plurality winner, and the weaker minority parties are weeded out by the voters who are loath to support parties that have little chance of winning. Voters cluster around the two parties that have a practical chance of victory, thereby hastening the decline of all other parties. The party strategists do not want to win with less than 50 percent of the vote because they know that a coalition of minorities that exceeds half of the vote might defeat them at the next election. Thus the institutional reason is based on the desire on the part of both voters as well as party strategists to win by a majority in an election in which the winner takes the office and all the benefits of power and the loser gets nothing at all.

Our winner-take-all election system is usually contrasted with that of countries with multimember legislative districts and proportional representation where an executive is elected from the legislature. In this system, a party polling 20 percent of a nation's votes may capture 20 percent of the legislative seats. The main purpose of proportional representation is to guarantee party representation roughly equal to its strength. A governing cabinet in a European nation may be formed by a coalition that includes the representatives of the minority parties. In France under the Third and Fourth Republics, a party winning 10 to 15 percent of the national vote could capture the premiership. In our country with a single national executive and single state executives, the two parties are made up of coalitions that agree in advance of the election to support the candidate.[10] The same reasoning is also used to explain the two-party contest for U.S. senators who run from state constituencies where the winner takes all.

When we look at the congressional districts and the state legislative districts, the institutional winner-take-all reason appears to lose explanatory power. Less than half of the 435 single-member congressional districts or the thousands of state legislative constituencies are even minimally competitive between the parties. But the same two parties compete (weakly in some cases) for the election of the single prize—the legislator who will represent the district. Here we find local minority parties contesting with little hope of victory because they represent minority economic interests. This would seem to be a contradiction to the institutional hypothesis. To be consistent, the winner-take-all hypothesis would predict even two-party contests in all the single-member constituencies of the nation from the local legislative district to the presidency. If the pulling power of a single prize is so great, then two roughly even parties should contest for victory for every contest. This clearly does not occur—only about one-fourth of the congressional and state legislative districts are genuinely competitive. There are many one-party areas of our nation where either the local Republican or local Democratic party does not stand a chance of winning. Why can't the perpetual loser gain enough cohorts to win? If a coalition of interests can get together under a party banner to contest elections, why doesn't a coalition of blacks and young moderate whites get together under a Republican label to defeat the traditional Democratic legislator in South Carolina? Or why doesn't a coalition of farmers and small merchants under a Democratic label try to defeat the local Republican legislator in Idaho? The winner-take-all hypothesis cannot explain the large majority-tiny minority system that exists in many of the legislative constituencies. The explanation must be more complex than the winner-take-all hypothesis of two-party competition.

Systems of Beliefs and Attitudes

From the point of view of the fifty state governors, the tie to the national party is their hope of advancement. The fifty governors, or at least those who are of the president's party, are in line for cabinet appointments and judgeships and other services in the presidential orbit. They are also in line for the presidency itself, either launched from the governorship or from a position in the Senate. Thus, there is an advantage for both the national and state parties to call themselves by the same label.

Attitudes based on Occupation, Religion, and Minority Status

The state parties could be very different in ideological composition from their national counterparts; this occurs in the special case of the southern states. But, in most of the rest of the country, the same beliefs and attitudes divide Republicans and Democrats. These beliefs and attitudes are based primarily on the occupational groupings and life-styles of the voters in all the states. It is fairly accurate to assert that Democratic candidates wherever you find them are supported by union members, Catholics, Jews, and ethnic groups. The skilled workers, the farmers, the clerical and sales personnel and the Protestants divide their vote between the Democrats and their Republican opponents. The Republican candidates are supported by the professionals and managers, Protestants, and a good portion of farmers and clerical and sales personnel. Most voters do not separate state and national politics. Election statistics reveal gross parallels in the voting for state and national offices. When a state or region shifts in party support, both levels of elections tend to shift in the same direction and not infrequently with the same magnitude. Voter preferences in national and state politics tend toward congruent support for candidates of the same party in different levels of office. Party loyalties are fixed by presidential politics which represents the basic economic divisions of voters in all states.

The fundamental loyalty of the voters for one or the other of the two parties suggests the broad proposition that the national parties determine which state parties are able to contest seriously through time for state offices. State parties organized solely to control state government and unaffiliated with either national major party seldom exist or gain power only to dissolve into one or the other major party. Typical of this was the Nonpartisan League (NPL), which was one of the most durable political expressions of western radical agrarianism and played a central role in North Dakota politics. The NPL was active in Wisconsin as the Progressive Party and in Minnesota as the Farmer-Labor party. It arose as a farmer protest against the domination of the state Republican parties by grain and railroad interests. The main tactic employed by the three NPL state groups was to enter the primaries of the existing parties, to nominate candidates pledged to NPL support, and then to back these candidates, regardless of party at the next election. This tactic, in itself, was an admission of the existence of a two-party system on the part of the challengers. Separate third-party activity was seldom indulged in by the NPL and met mostly with election failure. Its only important success was the capture of Minnesota's two senate posts by the Farmer-Labor Party. In all three cases of NPL activity the heavy pressures of the national two-party system forced them to disband and send their loyalists into the two major parties. Because of the farm policy stands of the national parties, the NPL and the Farmer-Labor party merged with the Democrats. The Wisconsin Progressives entered the Republican party as a conservative force. The absorption of the three state parties that arose from the NPL illustrates the capacity of the two major parties to monopolize the two party system, by resisting domination or displacement by third-party forces.

The two major parties rest on the preferences of voters who choose to remain loyal partisans on both the state and national level. Within the national arena, Democratic and Republican parties vie for power on fairly even terms while presenting to the electorate a choice between broadly differing policies. For the past fifty years, the voters of the states have responded to these policy appeals, depending on their work habits and living conditions. As the states become more industrial and more urban in composition, the division between the two parties becomes more competitive *within* each state. No longer does each national party consist of regional blocks of states: rural-farm states within the Republican party and Southern states within the Democratic party. Now only eight southern states are based on the politics of sectionalism. In thirty-four states, the parties are competitive and resemble their national counterparts. This means that many of the same issues that divide Republicans and Democrats nationally divide the voters of these states. Five other states are in transition from the type of southern Democratic dominance based on sectionalism to a more competitive two-party system based on national issues. Three states are leaning Democratic because the composition of the states' voters incline them toward the Democratic party. These states —Connecticut, New Jersey, and Nevada, in which the majority party has averaged between 55 and 60 percent of the vote since 1956, may swing back again into the two-party category if the issues of national politics dislodge a bloc of voters toward the other party.

Anthony Down's Model of Party Competition

Anthony Downs has introduced a spatial model of party competition based on the distribution of voters' preferences. This model summarizes the explanation of a party system based on voter beliefs and attitudes. According to Downs, the political orientation of voters can be placed on a scale running from zero to 100 in the usual left-to-right fashion.[11] The crucial issue being measured is: "How much government intervention in the economy should there be?" Since Democrats have traditionally stood for an expansion of the government's role in the economy and the Republicans have stood for a contraction of that role, the difference between political attitudes of Republicans and Democrats can be measured on this scale. If we assume that the left end of the scale represents full government control and the right end means a completely free market, the parties can be ranked by their supporters on this issue in a way that can be recognized as relating to real-world conditions. Of course, this model is only a representation of reality. We know, of course, that neither party is simon-pure in its notion of government intervention. Republicans have stood for protective tariffs and large government subsidies to industry. The southern Democrats have been states'-rights advocates. Generally speaking, more or less government intervention is a recognized basis for disagreement between the parties over the last fifty years. Downs reasoned that citizens could be placed on a vertical scale according to their preferences on this issue. He also assumed that, because there is widespread consensus within this country on our basic form of government, disagreement is confined to a matter of degree on the expansion or contraction of that government. The continuance of a stable and moderate two-party system depends on a balance between consensus and conflict. For most of its history, the United States has been able to keep that balance. Political conflict based on diverse interests has taken place within a broad agreement on such issues as political democracy, economic enterprise, material progress, and social mobility. Downs assumed that the voters on his scale will be normally distributed according to their preferences on the government's role in society. Since most voters would fall in the middle between full government intervention and complete free market, the parties become moderate to appeal to the crucial middle-of-the-road voters.

Voter Preferences in Three Types of States

The Democratic Party can count on the support of loyal groups of blacks, union members, and the occupants of the central cities in great metropolitan areas, Catholics and non-Protestants. If the Democratic Party appealed to these groups only, it would advocate a great deal more government intervention than it does. To gain enough votes to win an election, the Democrats must appeal as well to the whites, nonunion members, Protestants, and suburban dwellers. The Republicans must also appeal to these same groups while keeping managers and professionals within the party.[12] Since voter loyalty is fairly stable over time between the parties and only about 15 percent of the electorate claims to be truly independent, we can assume that the social and economic composition of the electorate of a two-party state looks like Figure 2–1.

FIGURE 2–1

Hypothetical Distribution of Voters in a Two-Party State

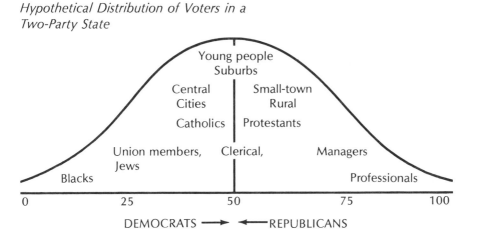

We would expect that states such as Delaware, Michigan, Pennsylvania, Minnesota, Illinois, Indiana, and New York all might look like this. There would be the Democratic coalition of minorities located in the cities, balanced by the managerial classes and the Protestants with the young and the suburban dwellers providing the large group that divides nearly evenly between the parties. On the other hand, a group of states that tends to be Republican would have fewer of the minorities that make up the Democratic coalition, and we would hypothesize that the distribution of its voters' preferences between the parties would look like this: (Figure 2–2).

FIGURE 2–2

Hypothetical Distribution of Voters in a
Republican State

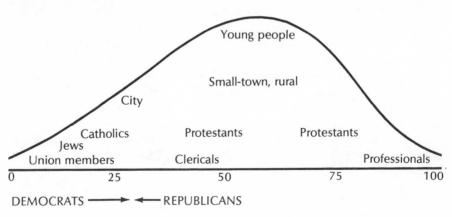

In these states, there are not enough groups that traditionally make up the Democratic party to make up a majority of the electorate. So the Democrats are a minority party in such states. There are not many states in which the Democrats have such a slim chance as this, however. Vermont, Wyoming, South Dakota, Kansas, Colorado, Idaho, and North Dakota look more like this diagram than a two-party state model, but Democrats have captured the governorship in all of these states in the last twenty years. The fact that a Democrat can win the governorship in this group of states may illustrate the pulling power of the office of governor. The "winner-take-all" explanation of a two-party system in combination with a distribution of voters that supports a good-sized minority party can account for a determined Democrat putting together a coalition of minorities and independents that can win the governorship.

The third type of state is the Democratic state of the North.[13] In this hypothetical state, the coalition of minorities and city dwellers and union members outnumber the Republican and independent voters, making a solid Democratic form of politics. Figure 2–3 illustrates the coalitions in this distribution. States that support parties of this kind are Rhode Island, Connecticut, and New Jersey. Republicans have frequently occupied the state houses in these states, but the basic distribution of voters remains favorable to the Democrats.

This discussion began with a question: Why do the states have the same two parties? The answer is complex, as the reader has probably determined—more complex than the two major explanations given. The answer must account for the fact that the two parties that contest for election in all the states call themselves Republicans and Democrats, and the issues on which they appeal to the voters resemble their national counterparts. There are many delightful variations that will emerge in later chapters, but this basic condition is true in all states. Third parties have arisen within the states, but they have not lasted long and have merged into one or the other of the two parties. The contest for the presidency molds the coalitions that underlie both parties over long periods of time, and provides the major explanation for our two-party system. Voters to whom the two national parties appeal prefer to keep their national partisan loyalties when it comes to state politics. Hence, in states where there is only a small contingent of voters who support a party

FIGURE 2–3

---

*Hypothetical Distribution of Voters in a
Democratic State*

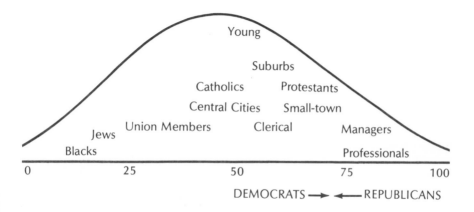

nationally, the party has little chance of gaining the governorship or a majority of the legislature. Thus, the national parties determine which state parties are able to compete seriously for the state offices. This preference on the part of the voters to keep the same partisan affiliation at all three levels of government is reinforced by far-sighted governors who want to proceed to a national office via their party. Hence, there are institutional, social, attitudinal, and strategic reasons for the fact that all the states in the nation have the same two parties that compete with increasingly equal strength.

THE PARTY SYSTEMS ARE BECOMING MORE COMPETITIVE OVER TIME

The social and economic conditions that supported one-partyism are disappearing, and the partisan division of voters is becoming similar to the national two-party division. As Americans migrate about the country, as industry comes to formerly agrarian states, as the partisans of one region move to another, the political composition of the states change. Each state becomes a better sample of the diversity of life and interests that contribute to the competition between the two major parties. Figure 2–4 presents the increase in competitiveness in two groups of states—those ten that were most Democratic in 1946 and those ten that were most Republican compared to a middle group of ten states that have maintained consistent competitiveness. In the Democratic states, the average Democratic vote for governor in 1946 was 88.8 percent. This average has declined steadily over the 30-year period to 61 percent, and six of these states have voted in Republican governors. On the other hand, the rock-ribbed Republican states have shown an impressive increase in competitiveness. The Democrats have moved from a low of 35 percent in gubernatorial races to an even chance for victory if they bestir themselves; as well, the elections of the '60s and '70s brought Democrats into the governors' mansions in all of these ten Republican states. This gradual change in the economic and social complexion of the states that underlies the increase in internal competitiveness is the result of the decline of sectional issues that divided the parties and that produced one-party states based on the economics of farming, cotton, or industry. As the states take on a new form of politics, however, vestiges of the old days remain to give each state the imprint of events long past. The party system of a state is not the creation of a day. The habits of the people are hard to change. Party systems reflect heritage blended with present practices. The electoral groupings of some states bear faint resemblance to our hypothetical curves based on a distribution of voters according to their preferences for more or less govern-

FIGURE 2–4

Average Democratic Percentage of the
Vote for Governor in Three Groups of
States, 1946–78

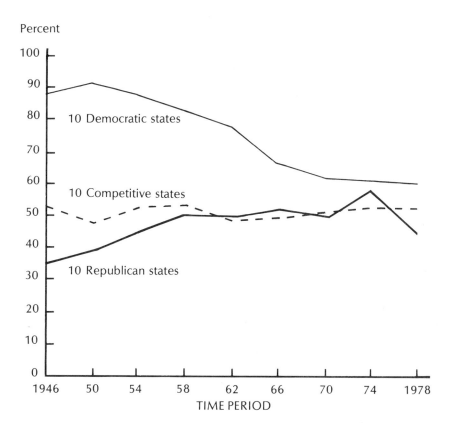

When a gubernatorial election did not fall in one of these years, the election immediately following was used (Through 1976).

The ten Democratic states are: Alabama, Arkansas, Florida, Georgia, Louisiana, Mississippi, North Carolina, South Carolina, Tennessee, and Texas. (Louisiana, Mississippi and North Carolina did not have gubernatorial elections in 1978.) The ten Competitive states are: Colorado, Delaware, Indiana, Kansas, Massachusetts, Montana, New Mexico, Ohio, Utah, and Washington. (Delaware, Indiana, Montana, Utah and Washington did not have gubernatorial elections in 1978.) The ten Republican states are: Idaho, Iowa, Maine, Minnesota, New Hampshire, Nebraska, North Dakota, Oregon, South Dakota and Vermont. (North Dakota did not have a gubernatorial election in 1978. Maine was not included in 1974 because of the size of the Independent vote.)

Source: *World Almanac,* 1947–1954 (N.Y.: Newspaper Enterprise Association, Inc.), Richard Scammon, ed., *America Votes* (Pittsburgh: University of Pittsburgh Press, 1956–1962; and Washington, D.C.: Governmental Affairs Institute, and Congressional Quarterly, Inc. 1964–1974), *Congressional Quarterly Weekly Report* (31 March 1979).

ment intervention in the economy. In the states of the South, it is the Democratic party that is composed of the rural small-town Protestants. "I was born a Democrat just as I was born a Baptist," is a common sentiment. A person of such persuasion is not likely to be "converted" to a Republican. The lively two-party competition of the western states of Montana, Colorado, and New Mexico must be based on some other economic and social base than an industrial economy. This competition may reflect nothing more than the party loyalties of the migrants who settled there after the Civil War and who have found no reason to change their party affiliations since they arrived. It will aid understanding of the variations in political practices and policy decisions in our states if we trace the social and economic foundations of state parties and how these foundations have become merged with the events of this century.

SECTIONALISM, URBANISM, AND PARTY VOTERS

Sectionalism

An explanation for the divergences from the expected party loyalty of a state based on electoral or economic reasons lies in the sectional foundations of our political parties as these developed, matured, and persisted. Sectional interests have constituted important building blocks for the American parties. Each party has had its roots deep in sectional interests, and each has tried to build coalitions on a sectional basis that would give it a majority to govern. Sectionalism is no longer the bedrock for either party, but it lingers today along with the divisions based on new urbanism.

Originally, sectional dualism was associated with the frontier versus the Atlantic seaboard. The states of the Northeast furnished the capital for the development of the western wilderness and created a relationship of creditor and debtor between geographically different groups. Living in hardship and isolation, the western farmer, often in debt for his land, felt hostile toward the more populated and industrialized East. In 1801, Jefferson succeeded in organizing the back-country grain growers from Maine to Georgia into a party to oppose the Federalists composed of the commerical interests of the North Atlantic coast, the tobacco planters of Georgia and the rice planters of South Carolina. This coalition of frontiersmen and grain farmers was also united under Andrew Jackson in 1828 and maintained its force until the War between the States. The "West" was composed of the western parts of the thirteen original states and all the new states being formed: Ohio, Indiana, Michigan, Iowa, and Wisconsin.

Until the restriction of slavery became an issue between the parties, the Democratic party was the party of the frontier—the little farmer arrayed against the commercial party of the Atlantic seaboard.

Of course, migrations of partisans from both parties tended to provide a two-party system based on traditional loyalties within many new states. Most interesting to follow are the deposits of party strength left by the western streams of migrations during this period. Although the new western Republicans became farmers, they remained attached to the party back home. In Indiana, the northern rural counties, peopled by the migrations from Northeast still remain Republican. In the south of Indiana, westward migrations of farmer-Democrats give the Democratic party a stronghold to this day. These two migrations of partisans have contributed to the two-party system of Indiana, a system which has been consistently competitive over the last 30 years, and which exhibits both the two-party complexion of an industrial state overlayed by areas of old-time sectional divisions.[14]

The issue of slavery realigned the old East-West party conflict based on farmers versus the financial East into a North-South conflict. The War Between the States made the Democratic party the party of the South and the Republican party the party of the North. Cotton growing and agriculture dominated the South and created a common economic outlook although, previous to the war, there were decided differences in economic outlook between the slavocracy and the small farmer of the back hill country. The slaveholding segment of the population which had a monopoly of the wealth and leadership managed to "capture" the Democratic Party after the war. Just as remarkable, perhaps, was the fact that the Republican Party of the North was able to consolidate both industrialist and worker into a common bond. This was due to a series of events that alienated the industrial workers from the Democratic Party, the party that would, even then, have been closer allied with their interests. The depression of 1893 occurred during a Democratic administation and produced antipathies among the industrial workers who might otherwise have resisted the Republican-business alliance. Also, under the banner of William Jennings Bryan in 1896, the Democratic-Populist coalition tailored its appeal toward the rural South and West rather than toward the urban proletariat of the Northeast and Middle West. (The resulting realignment of that year lasted more than thirty years until the workers found their home at last in the Democratic party under the Roosevelt coalition.) As a result of the realignment, the Democratic party in large areas of the Northeast and Middle West was wiped out or decimated, while the Republican party consolidated its supremacy in all of the most populous areas of the country. Thus the country was divided into sections: the northern business-Republican party and the southern conservative Democratic counterpart. In the words of Schattschneider:

From the standpoint of national politics the principal function of the Solid South was to make impossible a combination of southern and western agrarian radicals. On the other hand, the establishment of a one-party system in the South simplified tremendously the task of the Republican conservatives because *it isolated the western radical wing of the party.* Thereafter, the western Republican insurgents had no place to go; unable to make any combination able to win a national election, they were reduced to launching a succession of futile minor parties.[15]

Before 1896, the two major parties contested elections on fairly equal terms in many states. According to Schattschneider, in 1892 there were 36 states in which something like a competitive situation existed. By 1904 there were only 6 states in which the parties were evenly matched, while there were 30 states in which the situation could no longer be described as competitive. The decline of party competition was greatest in the South. In 1884, the Republican vote was less than half the Democratic vote in only three southern states—South Carolina, Texas, and Georgia. By 1904 it had shrunk to a tiny fraction.[16] Thus from 1896 to 1932, the voters of the United States lived in one-party areas based on the sectionalism of North versus South. Contests in most states were nearly always so one-sided that the voters had no significant choices.

Rise of Urbanism and the Decline of Sectionalism

THE COALITIONS BASED ON URBANISM. The pull of sectionalism declined steadily within the past several generations. The presidential election of 1932 marked a turning point in American party history. The depression of 1929 brought about the disintegration of the Republican party and propelled the Democratic party into a majority party based on its old foundations in the South and a coalition of minorities, workers', and economically less-favored groups. Under its leadership, the broadest government intervention in economic affairs the country had yet seen occurred, and the difference between the parties turned on this issue of more or less government control over the economy. This basic division between the parties was based on the type of electorate each appealed to. These electorates were no longer divided into sectional areas of the nation based on old war divisions with northern-business versus southern-farming overlays. The diversification of interest intrinsic to the New Deal coalition could be found within most states of the nation and led to the dilution of sectionalism. Outside the South, a barometer of the new coalition could be found in the degree of urbanization of each state. Manufacturing, distribution, finance, and most other non-agricultural pursuits centered in the cities. As well, most of the new ethnic groups also centered in the cities. The process of urbanism created the raw materials for party cleavages more nearly along class lines than the politics of sectionalism. And thus urbanization created new kinds of Republicans and Democrats. Those at the upper end of the income scale became more nearly united in their attachment to the Republican Party as a similar loyalty to the Democratic Party developed in the lower-income brackets. These attachments are not rigid and are crisscrossed by race and religion, but the basic attachments of groups to the two parties has remained since 1932, and the degree to which these groups are found within the states in our country helps to account for the partisan division of the voters in the state.

The fit between the identification of the groups within an electorate and the partisan division of that electorate is only approximate because voters are simultaneously associated with several groups, some with conflicting party loyalties. Also, no group has ever been monolithic in its attachments to a party. The most loyal group within the Democratic party is the blacks who compose almost a fifth of the support the party draws, and in some states are the electoral group that keeps the party competitive.[17] Catholics and Jews are more loyal to the Democrats than the national average and they make up nearly 25 percent of the party support.[18] It has been assumed that the poor as a group have been more loyal to the Democrats, but Axelrod's study shows, rather, that they tend to divide their votes the same way as the nation.[19] Union members, skilled, semiskilled, and unskilled workers have been loyal Democrats, although this loyalty fell off in 1972 and the skilled and semiskilled were considerably less loyal to the Democratic party than the nation as a whole. The inner-city vote has been loyal, but the population living in central cities of the dozen largest metropolitan areas has dropped to less than 10 percent of the nation's population. They now contribute less than 15 percent of the Democratic votes. The national Democratic coalition of minorities is still holding together but at a decreasing rate. If most of the elements of the Democratic coalition—the poor, blacks, union members, Catholics, and central-city dwellers—can be found in a state, the odds are that the state has an active Democratic party, but one that must increasingly make an appeal to the middle-class suburban vote to get elected.

While the Democratic Party is one of a coalition of minorities, the Republican Party is a coalition of overlapping majorities; these groups are the precise complements of the minorities that describe the Democrats. Making up the Republican coalition is a combination of the nonpoor, whites, nonunion families, Protestants and those outside the central cities. Almost everyone is in at least one of these overlapping groups and most people are in four or five. Only the nonunion families and the Protestants have consistently voted more Republican than all voters. The most obvious fact about the coalitions that make up the two parties is that they are very loose. Most groups today do not support their party overwhelmingly.

Except for the blacks who are extremely loyal to the Democratic party, the Democratic coalition is made up of minorities that do not give the party more than 60 percent of their loyalty. In addition, group loyalties are not constant from one election to another, thus indicating a flexibility that can be appealed to by state issues. Each of the groups usually divides its votes no more than 15 percent differently than the nation as a whole. That room for maneuver, however, may be the difference between a popular incumbent Democratic governor maintaining himself in office against a Republican national tide.

THE ECONOMICS OF PARTY SYSTEMS.   If we look at the 50 states according to their competitiveness and certain economic characteristics that the foregoing analysis leads us to expect would account for their competitiveness, we can see certain regularities, but we can also see states which defy expectation. Two measures of the social and economic characteristics of the states are used here. One is a factor called integration derived from an analysis of a collection of many socioeconomic variables found to some degree in each state.[20] A statistical technique called factor analysis clustered the variables around the dimension of integration. The variables associated with integration are listed in Table 2–1. We are in a position to compare the states on the basis of this factor since the technique also provides a score for each state on integration. The variables clustered around this concept are characteristics of modern affluent cultures. In contrast to a measure of the degree of industrialization of an economy, this dimension measures a post-industrial type of economic activity. The variables that are highly associated with integration are wealth and degree of professionalism. States that score high on integration have a disproportion-

---

TABLE 2–1

Socioeconomic Variables in Order of Their Weight on the Integration Factor[a]

Personal income per capita
Percent of the population over 25; college graduates
Percent of employed persons in finance and insurance
Percent of the population urban
Percent of employed persons who are professionals
Percent of the population that is foreign white stock
Retail trade sales per capita
Percent of farms with sales greater than $40,000

---

[a]Only variables with a loading (weight) of at least ± .60 are listed. For the loadings of each variable for both integration and industrialization, see Appendix 1.

ate share of professionals such as doctors or public administrators and are disproportionately middle-class; they are marked by high degrees of education, literacy, and media circulation. Finance and insurance as opposed to heavy industry distinguish this type of socioeconomic development. As with industry, the finance and insurance are concentrated in urban areas. States scoring high on integration are not necessarily the same as those with high scores on industrialization. The two dimensions are measuring different things. It is possible of course to find heavily industrial states with high scores on the integration factor such as New Jersey and Connecticut. Rhode Island, the most industrialized state, does not have the characteristics of a modern affluent culture. Arizona, Colorado, and Nevada have low industrial economies but high scores on the integration dimension. Interestingly, it was not the degree of industrialization but the degree of integration in a state that helped explain its degree of competition.

The second measure of state social and economic characteristics is based on income distribution. High per capita wealth does not indicate that everyone is wealthy. There is a measure of income distribution called the "Gini coefficient." The coefficient ranges between zero and one. A value of zero would mean that there was no inequality of income—that every family had the same income. A value of one would mean perfect inequality—i.e., one family would have all the income. The average figure for the United States and most industrialized countries of the world ranges from .35 to .50.[21] Table 2–2 shows that the mean for all the 50 states is .359. The states of the South have the highest scores on the Gini Index, indicating that income is distributed most unequally there. While it is generally considered that a low score on the Index of Income Distribution, meaning more equality, is associated with a postindustrial economy, this does not appear to be the case with the most competitive group of states in which the margin between the parties is only five percentage points over the 15-year period. These states are low on the integration index but compare favorably with the highly integrated states on equality of income distribution.

Table 2–2 indicates that the first three groups of states which are more competitive than the last two groups are also, on average, wealthier, more professional, and enjoy more equality of income distribution. Within the first three groups of states are all the states with great wealth, middle-class economies and large numbers of minorities such as Massachusetts, New York, California, New Jersey, and Connecticut. High also on this list are Delaware, Illinois, Rhode Island, Washington, Hawaii, Colorado, and Arizona. The second two groupings of states would tend to confirm our notions that states that have a large proportion of minorities, and an urban population, and in which there is great wealth are states that would provide the same bases for two-party competition as those that divide the parties on the national level. Even in this group there are noticeable

TABLE 2-2

The Fifty States According to Competition,
Integration, and Income Distribution

NAMES OF STATES	AVERAGE INDEX OF COMPETITION[a] 1956-70	AVERAGE INDEX OF INTEGRATION[b] 1970	AVERAGE INDEX OF INCOME DISTRIBUTION[c] 1970
Delaware, Illinois, Wisconsin, Idaho, Maine, Minnesota, New Mexico, West Virginia, Montana	5.3 (most)	–.07	.350
Indiana, Kentucky, Michigan, Pennsylvania, Rhode Island, Washington, North Dakota, Alaska, South Dakota, Oregon, Hawaii, Kansas, Massachusetts, New York	8.6	.26	.353
Iowa, Colorado, Nebraska, Arizona, New Hampshire, Wyoming, California, New Jersey, Connecticut, Vermont	11.5	.72 (most)	.345 (most)
Utah, Nevada, North Carolina, Ohio, Missouri, Virginia, Oklahoma, Maryland, Florida	17.5	.002	.361
Arkansas, Texas, Tennessee, Mississippi, Georgia, South Carolina, Alabama, Louisiana	52.7 (least)	–1.28 (least)	.394 (least)
Mean	17.4	.00	.359

[a] The Index of Competition measures the difference between the percent of the vote for governor obtained by each major party averaged over a specified time period. The index is computed for each state in the following manner:

$$\frac{\text{Abs. } (\Sigma \ (\% \ \text{Dem.} - \% \ \text{Repub.}))}{N}$$

Abs. is the absolute value and N is the number of elections. A low value means a competitive state. Several states have changed position within the first three categories since 1970, and Ohio and Missouri are more competitive.
Source: Scammon, *America Votes.*
[b] See footnote 20.
[c] Source: David R. Morgan, *Handbook of State Policy Indicators* 2nd. ed., (Norman, Okla.: Bureau of Government Research, University of Oklahoma, 1974), table 7, p. 26.

exceptions such as Kentucky and North and South Dakota, none of which could be called wealthy or urban. An active two-party competition for the governorship, however, takes place in these states.

In Kentucky, which is a border state, the politics are based on the overlapping flow of migrants from Virginia, Maryland, and the Carolinas which occurred before the Civil War confronted by a postwar influx of Northerners from the Republican states. Outside the cities, the vote was until recently rigidly divided between the Republicans and Democrats who were still waving the bloody shirt. Generally, the cities were strongholds of Republicanism until the New Deal but now deliver a sizable Democratic labor vote. The two-party competition of Kentucky still smacks of the traditional party loyalties of its waves of invaders. Its politics do not yet look like the traditional Democratic-Republican confrontation. The Bourbons, descendants of settlers who brought their slaves and customs from Tidewater Maryland, have traditional control over the Democratic party.

The scales tipped for the North Dakota Democrats when the Nonpartisan League merged with them in 1958. This brought a group of agrarian radicals into the struggling Democratic party and made it a coalition of liberal farmer-labor elements. The struggle in North Dakota has not been waged along national economic lines, and those from an urban state would hardly find the North Dakota Democratic party today an instrument of urban class warfare. The removal of the poorer farmers from the Republican to the Democratic party, however, has divided the state into two equal parties. South Dakota also reflects the origin of early agricultural settlements. Until recently, settlers from northern states as well as German and Scandinavian immigrants made South Dakota a strong Republican state. In the late fifties, the tide began to turn, and the Democrats in South Dakota are today in a strong position, having won the governorship three elections in a row. As in North Dakota, politics is a blend of native issues and national-level articulation. The South Dakota Democrats flourish in spite of the fact that their state is forty-sixth in a ranking of the states by urban concentration and last in terms of population increase from 1960–70. Apparently, the Democrats are able to contrive electoral groupings different from those that exist in the national party. The governorship is a major prize, and the coalitions built to attain it are based on the socioeconomic stuff of South Dakota's flatlands.

Table 2–2 reveals that the most lively competition between the parties exists in the first group of nine states that exhibit different degrees of wealth and population concentrations. Delaware and Illinois are industrialized states that would indicate a two-party split much like that between our national parties. They are also urban wealthy states—another sign of competitiveness. With the exception of these two states, the others are characterized by population diffusion and huge empty spaces. In seven of these states, income is distributed more evenly than in the rest of the country and averages .333 on the Gini index. Apparently, income distribution is even more predictive of the competitive nature of state politics than the integration factor. It would appear that politics in these states is not based on the traditional struggle between the suburban haves and the urban have-nots since these states are not urbanized and widespread equality exists.

The institutional explanation for two-party politics—the winner-take-all explanation—has intuitive merit. In the states of the West (Idaho, New Mexico, Montana), which lack a high degree of industrialization with attendant economic problems and which display agricultural diversity, the state leaders have inherited the partisan division of the migrants since the Civil War. Because they do not have the makings for the typical party coalition, the leaders base political appeals on the outs versus the ins.[22] The state of Maine also illustrates a politics of competition of outs versus ins. It is only 50 percent urban with a traditional Republican party and a Democratic party that is a coalition of Irish, French Canadians, and union workers in the small cities. To the extent that it is made up of minorities, the Democratic party may resemble its national counterpart, but the small-town flavor of its industry makes it a politics heavily infused with Maine localism.

The three midwestern states of Minnesota, Wisconsin, and Michigan became viable two-party systems when the Democratic Party inherited the populist protest groups from the Republican party thus forming parties based on coalitions if not traditional ones. The two parties stand for different economic solutions and John Fenton develops the argument that they are programmatic or issue-oriented parties.[23] The economic issues in Minnesota and Wisconsin, states with low levels of wealth and population concentration, are considerably different from those in Michigan with its highly industrialized economy. In the former two states, the Democratic Party has a sizable rural farm vote. Its politics are based on small-farmer versus large-farmer divisions, indicating that states can develop their own brand of politics, filling their own political bottles with wine different from the national vintage.

The last state to be explained in this enigmatic group that does not have an obvious urban-suburban-rural explanation of politics is West Virginia, a state that has had a fairly even division of the two-party vote for nearly a hundred years. West Virginia, a border state, owes its politics to the streams of migration that left deposits of Republican and Democratic sympathizers across the countryside. The vote of the cities divides between the two parties with the Democrats housing both the new labor vote and the landholding Bourbons and the Republicans making a coalition of the middle-class city dweller and the mountaineers. West Virginia is only 39 percent urban, so the split between the Plateau Democrats and the Mountain Republicans dominates the politics of the state and has not given way to the more recognizeable form of Republican-Democratic division on issues.

Perhaps it is a comforting notion that states develop their own distinctive characteristics based on history and current solutions to differing economic and social problems. In states of the first three groups in Table 2–2, where no struggle between an urban industrial working class confronts a wealthy managerial elite, politics remains based on the political affiliations of ancestors overlaced, perhaps, with such problems as transportation, electricity, water supply, and prices of grain and farm products. In the contest for control of the governorship, the politicians and the electorate separate themselves into two parties—potential winning coalitions for the most important state office.

We turn our attention now to the last two groups of states upon which the heavy hand of tradition has forced a political system that has not been able to respond to current problems by two-party competition. Most of the states in the fourth group are emerging from the searing sectionalism imposed by the War Between the States. (Utah, Nevada, and Maryland, in which oversized Democratic majorities have disturbed a former competition pattern, and Ohio, where large Republican majorities produced the same effect, are temporarily located in this group.) Five states in this group are only slightly less rural, poor, and illiterate than the states in the least competitive category. In North Carolina, Missouri, Virginia, Oklahoma, and Florida, the average index of income distribution is close to the mean for the states of the Solid South. These states border the Solid South, and migrations of both northern Republicans as well as northern industry have cracked the solid wall that separated them from the North and West. In the last ten years, Republicans have been elected to the governorships in all of these Democratic states in which the cultures of North and South meet and are presently mingling. The prediction for this group of states is that they will become increasingly competitive for governor as northern industry moves into them. Florida experienced a 55 percent increase in population in the decade from 1960–70. A change toward more competition will be slow because it does not depend upon "conversion" of individuals from one party to another as much as migrations of voters from state to state. The new generation of carpetbaggers has not settled evenly across the region but has concentrated in industrializing urban areas or in resort settlements along the coast. This uneven distribution has tended to make serious two-party competition a reality in the cities and coastal regions while leaving Democratic bastions in the rural areas.

The Solid South: A Special Case

Table 2–2 documents the effects of history and culture on the eight Democratic one-party states of the South. This region remains the one area in the nation that has resisted the tides of national politics and will remain a Democratic one-party area for some time to come. An average of over 50 percentage points divides the parties in the lopsided contests for governor in this region. The area has not emerged into the mid-twentieth century in terms of middle-class culture. All of the indicators of integration are at the low end of the scale. Poverty, illiteracy, and extremes of wealth are all characteristic of this type of culture. Such extremes of living conditions exist between an aristocracy with firm control over the governing apparatus via the Democratic Party and the exceedingly poor white and black populations. The vast differences in the social and economic conditions in the South as compared with the other states in the union prompted Ira Sharkansky to speak of the United States as a developing country. The contrasts within our postindustrial society are more acute than those of eight other wealthy countries in Europe. He claims that it is more accurate to speak about pockets of postindustrial society within the United States than about a postindustrial United States. He compares the states in the South to the poor countries of Africa, Asia, and Latin America in terms of their dependence on "outside" capital, politics based on traditions instead of policy alternatives, governmental centralization, regressive tax and spending policies, and little support for those programs that have a progressive impact on the distribution of resources.[24] Fortunately for the southern states, there is more opportunity for economic growth because they are situated within a developed country with access to elementary and secondary education, health care, and systems of public assistance and social insurance. An increase in movement of labor and capital in these developing states will provide the major incentive to economic growth and development.

The War Between the States made the Democratic Party the party of the South and the Republican Party the party of the North. That grand sectional division that demonstrated a remarkable persistence rested in part on regional economic differentiation. Cotton growing and agricultural pursuits dominated the South and created a homogeneous culture and outlook. The North had industry, and, so long as the Republican party was able to attract the factory workers, the coalition within the Grand Old Party kept intact. This coalition has fallen apart and the Republicans do not dominate the politics of any state in the North at the present time. There was no way that southern Democratic planters were able to make a coalition with the former slaves as the Republican industrialists had managed to create with the workers. In fact, when it appeared that the newly enfranchised blacks might be able to control election outcomes by providing the swing vote between the discontented farmers and the planters, both groups joined forces against the blacks and took away their vote and hence political power. By designing laws, institutions, and practices to exclude them from the vote, a southern homogeneity was forged.

There was another base on which the sectional division rested, and this was the regional patriotism created by the war. All eight of the one-party states in Table 2–2 were members of the Confederacy. Southern resistence to reconstruction was led by Democrats. Party identification and patriotism were closely intertwined, and, for a long time after the war, the electioneering slogan was: "Vote as you shot!" The sectional explanation of voting patterns in the South remains long after sectionalism as an explanation of voting patterns in the other states has been weakened by the rise of urban, industrial populations. In the heyday of the Solid South from 1880–1916, Democrats controlled the political offices within the states, returned almost purely Democratic delegations to both houses of Congress, and cast electoral votes for the Democratic presidential candidate in election after election. By the late 1920s, the Republicans were able to crack the Solid South around the edges, and, when the Democrats ran a Catholic for president in 1928, the devoutly Protestant South responded by giving the majority of its electoral votes to the Republicans. The South appeared to resolidify as a region as the whole nation swung toward the Democrats in the 1930s and 1940s. Beginning with the Eisenhower Republican trend in the 1950s, the Democratic monopoly on Southern partisan loyalties decayed to the point where the Republicans can now anticipate the Presidential vote of the South. In 1964, Mississippi, Georgia, South Carolina, Alabama, and Louisiana gave their electoral votes to the Republican Party and did not return to the presidential Democrats until 1976 when a native Georgian captured the nomination.[25] The Republicans have hopes of harvesting the governorships in these states and so far have succeeded in electing chief executives in Arkansas, Tennessee, Texas, and South Carolina. It will be a long time, however, before Republican governors can hope to win with any regularity in the subnational politics of the Solid South.

The Democratic South is a historical anomaly in American politics. Outside the South, partisan competition is characterized by rural and small-town Protestant America represented in the conservatism of the Republican party and the liberal coalition of metropolitan minorities and industrial labor supporting the Democrats. In terms of this competition, there is no doubt that the South really belongs to the Republicans in ideological terms, being the most rural, homogeneous, small-town and Protestant section of the country. Partisan politics in the South, however, are the exact mirror of those found elsewhere in the country, and they have shown a remarkable resistance to change. Part of the resistance lies in the organizational advantages in being a Democrat in terms of the flow of benefits, such as patronage and seniority which come from the holding of office. The politicians see no advantage to joining the Republican party simply because it is more ideologically suited to their interests. In addition, the traditional white Democratic voter in the South is "born" into the party. The strength of his partisanship has not changed. The decline in the Democratic percentage of the vote in the Solid South has been due almost entirely to migrations of northern industrialists who are almost as homogeneously Republican as their native social counterparts are Democratic. Philip Converse estimates that about four-fifths of the decline in Democratic partisanship in the South over the 1950s and 1960s sprang directly from rather dramatic changes in the rate and nature of immigration to the region from other parts of the country.[26]. This estimate is based on 15 Southern states that form the Census Bureau's definition of the region. The eight states we are considering are the least likely to be those affected by northern immigrants: All except for Texas and Georgia are below the national average for population increase, 1960–73. The continuing clear Democratic preferences among southern whites on the state level explain why the section is not heading for a two-party system in the near future.

Another phenomenon of note in the politics of the Solid South is the increasing Democratic complexion of the black vote. The black voter sees the National Democratic Party as more enlightened on the racial issue. After 1964, there was a sharp shift in a Democratic direction on the part of blacks throughout the nation. In the South for the first time in history, the black man had developed more solidly Democratic allegiances than his white adversaries. Previous to 1964, the black vote was weakly developed. Converse claims that some 28 percent of blacks in the "Census South" tended on average to be classified as "apolitical" over the course of the 1950s. In less than a decade, the proportion of apoliticals has dropped from 28 percent to about 3 percent.[27] Partisanship among black voters has increased rapidly. The black vote amounts to about one-fourth of the electorate of the South. This vote will undoubtedly affect the appeals and practices within the Democratic Party, but it is not likely to foster immediate two-party competition. Walter Dean Burnham predicts that two-party competition in Alabama will not come in the short run. He forsees, however, that the old regional alignment that formed the basis of party politics in the 1840s and 1890s will probably constitute the foundation of such politics in the future. This would be a "rational" political alignment in which upland whites and enfranchised blacks would join in opposition into Black-Belt Bourbons and urban middle-class conservatives.[28]

WHITHER THE SOUTH?   Most of the former one-party states of the nation are now competitive, and, in most of them, the parties resemble their national counterparts. In many, politicians are agile enough to make state issues relevant to the various electorates so that many local variations exist based on farm issues, irrigation, and historical background. Only the states of the Solid South have resisted the competitive trend, and this may be caused by their poverty, illiteracy, and rural nature as well as by the heavy weight of history. While the historical tradition rests heavily upon the southern states, new generations of voters as well as the steady migrations of northerners to the South may break through this last bastion of one-party sectionalism. All analysts share the view that the South's movement away from the Democratic monopoly will improve its political health and that of the nation's.

A move away from the Democrats expressed in rebellious third-party activity is not the cure envisioned. The Wallace supporters were those most attached to an agrarian set of values, who were willing to sacrifice further economic progress if, in so doing, they could protect their traditional culture.[29] However, most Democrats are not now farmers, and their children will be less protective of their traditionalist values. The cultural impact of the economic changes will reach succeeding generations and traditionalism will be less widespread.

Another caveat is that the new Republican party may not bring about the type of two-party choice typical of most states outside the South. If the Republican party can only offer candidates to the right of the Democrats, the voters do not have an effective range of choices. The Republicans have tended to be right of the Democrats in all Southern states except Virginia, Arkansas, and Tennessee. Unless Democratic politicians and office holders move toward the left, the newly enfranchised blacks plus a sizable portion of the southern electorate will have no party representing them. The South's move toward party competition may not emulate two-party politics as it exists outside the South.

State Politics Versus National Politics

The increase in competition within all the states but a handful has aroused both hopeful and worried speculation among the political analysts. Twenty years ago, E. E. Schattschneider claimed that elections were at least dominated by factors that work on a national rather than regional scale. The development of a competitive two-party system in all parts of the United States increased the importance of the opposition. Hopefully, he declared that: "One of the most significant consequences of the nationalization of politics in the last twenty years, therefore, has been the increased likelihood of a relatively frequent alternation of the parties in power."[30] Schattschneider looked forward to the development of electoral organizations in states that had until recently been dominated by a one-party system. His major concern was with the national party system, however, and he did not consider what effective political organizations opposing each other on the state level might accomplish in terms of the competition for the governorship. The closer the competition between the parties, the more likely each is to capture the governorship. A popular incumbent governor with an effective party organization can be reelected irrespective of the national political contest for the presidency. Thus, the very conditions that have brought about the nationalization of politics and with it the increase of effective state political organization have increased the tendencies of voters to split their tickets between the other party's popular governor and their party's presidential candidate.

Split-Ticket Voting

The substantial increase in split-ticket voting has been revealed in the number of self-styled independents in national surveys.[31] Frank Sorauf notes that split-ticket voting is increasing more rapidly than the growth rate of self-described independents. He wonders if party identifications are losing some of their control over the judgment and decisions of the American voter. He recalls that, in the past, patterns of voting support for the two parties have been remarkably stable. In election after election, individual voters in large numbers voted straight party tickets. The patterns of party support remained stable geographically. A party's pattern of state-to-state support remained steady election after election. He fears that the continued decline in the number and force of party identifications will challenge the stability of our party system.[32] We are on the horns of a dilemma. As we approach the millenium which has been heralded for so long by party theorists—a genuinely competitive party system in nearly every state in the union—we are beset with a new fear that the traditional loyalties may be eroding because of the new possibilities being offered the voters to split their votes between the state and national contests.

Before proceeding further it is important to examine to what extent the states are holding out against the national tides. Figure 2–5 presents graphically the extent to which the states operate independently of presidential politics. During the period 1944–76, there were nine presidential elections with the Democrats and Republicans alternating in power at eight-year intervals. Under each date in the figure is given the number of governors of each party for that election period. Except for 1952, when there were two more Republican governors than Democratic, the Democrats have always had more governors in the state mansions. This has been true in three out of four terms when a Republican president was in the White House.

Over the years the number of states that split their presidential and gubernatorial vote between the parties has increased dramatically. Part of this can be explained by the fact that the state leaders are altering their election timetables to schedule gubernatorial elections in the off-years. In 1944, for instance 33 of the 48 states voted for governor and president simultaneously; in 1976 only 14 states held gubernatorial elections (and Illinois has since gone on an off-year schedule). This does not explain as much of the independence of the states as might be expected, however, because of the 19 states that voted for both president and governor in 1972, twelve elected Democratic governors while sending in Republican landslide votes for president. Evidently the Democratic voters of the

FIGURE 2–5

State Politics are Becoming Independent
from Presidential Politics: Relation
Between Results of Presidential and
Gubernatorial Voting in the States,
1944–76a

Percent of states

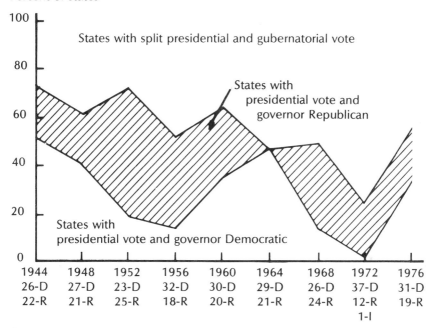

	1944	1948	1952	1956	1960	1964	1968	1972	1976
	26-D	27-D	23-D	32-D	30-D	29-D	26-D	37-D	31-D
	22-R	21-R	25-R	18-R	20-R	21-R	24-R	12-R	19-R
								1-I	

aWhen a gubernatorial election did not fall in one of these presidential election years, the election immediately preceding or following was used.
Source: *World Almanac and Book of Facts,* 1947–1954 (N.Y.: Newspaper Enterprise Association, Inc.); Richard Scammon, ed., *America Votes,* 1956–1974; appropriate issues of *Congressional Quarterly, Weekly Reports* for the 1975–78 election.

individual states feared the liberal McGovern but wanted their own brand of home-grown Democrat. In 1964, another landslide year, this time for the Democrats, the state Republicans feared the conservative Goldwater but wanted their own brand of home-grown Republican, for 10 out of the 29 states voted simultaneously for Republican governor and Democratic president and 11 more states that participated in the Democratic sweep of that year elected Republican governors in 1966. Apparently the voters are reacting to the way their governors are handling the affairs of the state. Governors are a more visible and popular group than they used to be. They are showing remarkable staying power. Incumbent governors have an excellent chance of being reelected. The citizens of the states realize the solutions to many of the problems closest to them are at home and not in Washington. States must solve problems of higher education, mental health, environmental control, recreation, mass transit, and housing. The agony over taxes to pay for these services also falls on the governor's shoulders. The challenge of the states may be attracting a breed of hardy, determined, imaginative types for governor. Genuine responsibility and challenge with room for individual creativity may generate interest among the most talented people in our society. For these and many other reasons, it appears that the people of the sovereign states are judging their governors on different scales than their presidents. No longer does the blue-collar worker pull the Democratic lever in the election booth and register an all-Democratic vote. He may still think of himself as a Democrat, but he votes for his Republican incumbent governor on his record, or because he has not increased taxes, or because he has balanced the budget. For the Republican who supports his president but votes for a Democratic governor in the secrecy of the voting booth, it may be a courageous stand on welfare reform, or health care, or aid to the cities that leads to splitting the vote at the state level. Again, the Republican probably still thinks of himself as a member of that party, but exercises the independence that is becoming so noticeable in the election returns.

The elections of 1974, two years after the Republican presidential landslide, may illustrate the negative rather than the positive influence of the party label. Recall that the landslide itself had not exerted a great influence on the state gubernatorial elections—12 out of 19 states voting simultaneously for governor and president having split their votes. But it appears that the voters in 1974 may have tried to indicate dissatisfaction with the Republican national party which was under the cloud of the Watergate scandal. The president had resigned in August, and in November of 1974, only 5 of the 35 states holding gubernatorial elections chose to reward the Republican Party with the governorship. Three out of six Republican governors managed to hold out against the adverse tide, however, indicating the power of incumbency. It takes no imagination to see what this national party punishment did to the overall picture of Republican politics in the states. Many of the new crop of Democratic governors became familiar and acceptable to their voters, and the powerful effects of incumbency carried them back into office four years later. It may be that state politics holds out against the flood tides of presidential politics, but the ebb tides of scandal and misfortune relegate to oblivion many of the deserving governors of the punished party.

Writing in 1956, V. O. Key noted that in landslide elections there were fewer states that split their presidential and gubernatorial vote, and he surmised that the great swings in the fortunes of the national parties were also associated with alternations in control of the governorships.[33] In the last twenty years, this has changed, as the states became powerful centers of decision makings. The fact that the voters also realize that power has shifted to the state governments accounts for the independence of their voting. Interestingly enough, it is in the states that are most competitive in which the articulation between the national and state voting is closest on the major issues that the greatest possibility for split voting exists. The choice of a few voters can put a partisan of one party in the governorship and electors of the other party in the presidential column. Incumbency and the issues of state politics appear to be the factors that hold the electorate of a state loyal to its governor in spite of national tides.

The End-of-Parties Argument

Returning to the speculation with which we began this discussion of the effects of state competition on the party system, we ask what is the likely impact on the political parties of this willingness of the voters to divide their loyalties between their state and their nation? Must we view this with the alarm of Walter Dean Burnham that the voters are not taking their party loyalties seriously, that they may slip from them into independency. He predicts that the parties may decay and fade away since they no longer perform the functions necessary to bind the voters to them. This is Burham's well-known "end of parties" argument. He believes that if the parties cannot control the economic system for the benefit of the people, cannot integrate the people into the political system, and cannot effectively integrate the voters to the party, we are in for an era without parties as we know them.[34]

A contrasting study by Jennings and Niemi offers some reassurance that voters are not that unattached but continue to think of themselves as partisans of one party or the other. In survey research, party identification has typically been determined by asking the respondent's subjective affiliation with a party. One of the most widely used questions (developed by researchers at the University of Michigan's Survey Research Center) runs as follows: "Generally speaking, do you usually think of yourself as a Republican, a Democrat, an Independent or what?." Jennings and Niemi discovered that the small number of voters (12 percent of their sample) who said that they were "mixed" in their party identifications at the state and national level were overwhelmingly (84 percent) likely to be Independent at one of the two levels. In other words, rarely were they inconsistent enough to say that they were a Republican at one level and a Democrat at the other. These "mixed" voters are highly interested in politics and are more aware of the distinctions between the parties at different levels of the federal system. Eventually they may resolve their conflicting identifications, sometimes reverting to their original identification, but more often changing their basic partisan orientation. Jennings and Niemi do not believe that this leads to the instability of the party system. Conflicting stimulus from different levels of government to some extent results in compensating changes. About half of the mixed identifiers remain Independent at one level of government on a permanent basis, recognizing the difference between the state and national parties. While the mixed identifiers are a large enough group to be important, the writers believe the smallness of the group is the crucial datum for many purposes. There are almost no Democratic-Republican splits, which indicates that a voter thinks of himself as a partisan first and then as a person who can claim independence of voting at another level.[35]

Another "end-of-Parties" argument is the sharp decrease since the mid-1960s in the proportion of strong party identifiers. The decline in *strong* party identification contributes to the overall decline in those who express a party preference. In 1976, 40 percent of the electorate claimed that they were Democrats, 36 percent claimed an Independent identification, and 23 percent identified themselves as Republicans. This indicates a drop in party identifiers since 1960 and an increase in self-styled independents (in 1960 the line-up was: 46-D; 23-I; 27-R). However, of the 36 percent in the Independent category, 22 percent call themselves "leaning" toward one of the two parties.[36] Raymond Wolfinger and associates point out that in every important respect the party leaners behave much more like strong party identifiers than like pure independents. In fact, they are more partisan than weak identifiers in that they are more likely to vote for their party's presidential candidates regularly and less likely to cross back and forth between presidential candidates from one election to another.[37] The increase in independents is undoubtedly related to the more competitive contests for governors all over the country. The states are powerful centers of decison making in their own right. A popular governor can appeal to enough of the "leaning" independents to get himself elected simultaneously with a president of the opposité party.

It would seem inappropriate to hypothesize that we have witnessed an "end of party" in American electoral politics. For one thing, even with a group of self-styled independents, party allegiance remains far and away the strongest determinant of voting behavior in the electorate. The continuing influx of new voters who are not likely to hold strong party preferences can also account for much of the decline of professed partisanship. Young voters make up an increasing proportion of the electorate. Nie, Verba, and Petrocik ascribe the recent decline in partisanship to the "youthing" of the electorate.[38]

We can also look forward to a more educated electorate—one that can and will be interested in discriminating among levels of government. The affairs of state politics will require different political solutions than the affairs of the nation. Given the opportunity to make different decisions at the state and national levels and the increasing sophistication of the electorate, we will have more "leaning Independents"—those who maintain party preference, but exercise the right to reward the governor of the opposite party for program and performance.

THE BENEFITS OF TWO-PARTY COMPETITION

We have already mentioned the supposed benefits of party competition in two previous discussions: the consideration of party government as doctrine in Chapter 1 and the analysis of the two-party system as a belief system in this chapter. What difference does it make if a state has competitive parties? Obviously the campaigns offer the people a choice between two contestants, either of whom is likely to win. Are the citizens more likely to participate in competitive elections? Are the parties more likely to be cohesive in structure?

The Participation of the Citizens

The association between two-party competition and the voting participation of the state's citizens is high and convincing. In fact, the statistical correlation is so high as to be a rarity in social research. Table 2–3 presents the states arranged according to competition as before (Table 2–2) and voting participation. In the first group of highly competitive states, the average voting turnout for governor is 66 percent of those eligible to vote. In the next two groups of states, also competitive, the turnout is also high, although it diminishes with the decrease in competition. In the fourth group of states composed in the main of border states and those of the old Confederacy which lean Democratic and in which a substantial margin of 17 percentage points separates the parties, competition is more depressed. The last group of states, those of the deep South which are non-competitive produce exceedingly low voting participation. The most obvious conclusion to be reached here is that, when parties compete vigorously, they make news and are given much attention by the mass media which generate greater interest in the contest. If the results of the election are in doubt, and citizens believe that their vote is likely to be important, they are more likely to turn out and cast it. Party workers on both sides exert much energy trying to get out the vote because the outcome is in doubt. Angus Campbell classified elections into high-stimulus and low-stimulus elections.[39] In a high-stimulus election, voters generally perceive that the vote will be close and, therefore, that their

TABLE 2–3

The Relationship Between Competition and
Voting Participation in the 50 States

NAMES OF STATES	AVERAGE INDEX OF COMPETITION[a] 1956–70	AVERAGE TURNOUT IN GUBERNATORIAL ELECTIONS[b] 1956–70
Delaware, Illinois, Wisconsin, Idaho, Maine, Minnesota, New Mexico, West Virginia, Montana	5.3 (high)	65.9 (high)
Indiana, Michigan, Kentucky, Pennsylvania, Rhode Island, Washington, North Dakota, Alaska, South Dakota, Oregon, Hawaii, Kansas, Massachusetts, New York	8.6	61.5
Iowa, Colorado, Nebraska, Arizona, New Hampshire, Wyoming, California, New Jersey, Connecticut, Vermont	11.5	59.1
Utah, Nevada, North Carolina, Ohio, Missouri, Virginia, Oklahoma, Maryland, Florida	17.5	50.8
Arkansas, Texas, Tennessee, Mississippi, Georgia, South Carolina, Alabama, Louisiana	52.7 (low)	29.2 (low)

[a] The Index of Competition measures the difference between the percent of the vote for governor obtained by each major party averaged over a specified time period. See Table 2–2 for the formula and source.
[b] Turnout is the vote for governor as a percentage of the civilian population of voting age. If several elections are used, it is the average turnout over the specified time period. Sources: U.S. Department of Commerce, Bureau of the Census, Statistical Abstract of the United States, 1959 and 1969; Current Population Reports, Series P–25, no. 342 (June 1966) and no. 479 (March 1972). Note: The Census Bureau does not give civilian resident population after 1968, so I used an estimation procedure to obtain it for 1970 based on the ratio of civilian resident to total resident population for 1968.

votes will count; they think the office being decided is important; campaign propaganda abounds. People living in a state with high party competition are more likely to experience high-stimulus elections than those living in states dominated by one party.[40]

While competition clearly influences the turnout rate for governor, there are social and economic conditions highly associated with competition that may also influence the participation rates of the voters. Poverty and illiteracy can only serve to alienate people from a system that is founded on the notion of equality. If it is commonly represented that everyone has an equal chance to "make something of himself," how can a poor, uneducated person feel part of such a system? His very failure drives him away. The triangular representation of the relations between the Gini Index of Income Distribution, Competition and Turnout indicates that the three are highly associated.

In a system where the income is distributed fairly evenly—where there are not extremes of wealth and poverty—the citizens feel they have some effect on the system when they exercise their right to vote. Again, we are forced to realize that, on all three of these variables, the eight states of the South rank low. It will be a long time before a large percentage of the citizens of the South participate fully in state elections. There is hope that, as economic conditions become better and as competition increases, the eight states that provide the extreme will deviate less and less from the rest.

QUALIFICATIONS FOR VOTING. Whether election laws have an independent influence on the voting turnout of the state citizens or whether they also respond to the same set of conditions highly associated with turnout is a hard question to answer. Under the United States Constitution, the states rather than the national government are given the power to define legally who is eligible to participate in elections. However, the federal

FIGURE 2–6

Correlations between Income Distribution, Competition, and Voting Participation

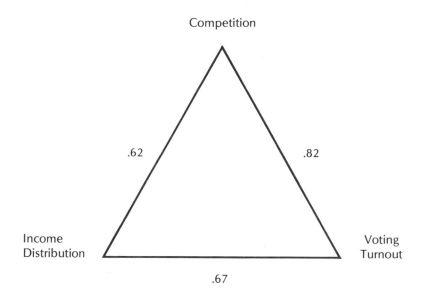

government has limited that power and continues to do so; no one can be denied the right to vote because of race or color, sex, failure to pay a tax, or age (over 18). These four restrictions on the states are embodied in U.S. constitutional amendments. Furthermore, the Fourteenth Amendment's equal protection clause ("No state shall make or enforce any law which shall ... deny to any person within its jurisdiction the equal protection of the laws.") has also been interpreted by the Supreme Court to prevent a state from discriminating against blacks in defining its electorate. In March 1966, the Supreme Court declared the Virginia poll tax (i.e., a head tax of $1.50) as a condition for voting in *state* elections to be in violation of the equal protection clause. The wording was broad enough to include the three remaining states that still required a poll tax. (Although the twenty-fourth Amendment of 1964 had invalidated tax paying as a condition for voting, it applied only to national elections. The other constitutional amendments with regard to race, color, sex, and age apply to both national and state elections.)

Residency requirements have traditionally disenfranchised mobile Americans. Most states used three-layer residence requirements: a period of time in the state, a shorter period of time in the county, and an even shorter period in the voting district. In general, the longest residence requirements were found in the southern states where they tended to disenfranchise migrant and mobile black farm labor. In 1972, 25 states required a minimum of one-year's residence with the rest requiring six months or less. In recent years, the durational residency requirements came under an increasing number of court challenges. On March 21, 1972, in the case of *Dunn v. Blumstein* (405 U.S. 330), the U.S. Supreme Court abolished all such requirements when it struck down Tennessee's one-year state and three-month county residence requirements as unconstitutional under the equal protection clause of the Fourteenth Amendment. For the most part, the court's decision in the Dunn Case was implemented by all states in time for the November 1972 election. It is estimated that 5 to 8 million mobile Americans were enfranchised. In 1973 the court also considered the question of the permissible prior to election registration closing dates in *Marston v. Lewis* (41 U.S.L.W. 3498 [1973]), and *Burns v. Fortson* (41 U.S.L.W. 3499 [1973]), where the issue was the constitutionality of 50-day closing dates in Arizona and Georgia. The court upheld the 50-day closing dates in both states as necessary to promote accurate voter lists. Justice Thurgood Marshall, who wrote the majority opinion in *Dunn,* dissented in both cases and was joined by Justices William O. Douglas and William J. Brennan. Justice Marshall indicated that he thought the states could have considered alternatives such as increasing the registrars' staffs instead of burdening the voters with a 50–day registration closing.

Before the passage of the Voting Rights Act of 1965, 20 states required that the applicant for suffrage demonstrate his literacy. Often the test constituted little more than the test of the ability to write a signature. In other states, literacy involved filling out the application form for registration. In New York, a comprehensive test included questions to test the reader's understanding of brief expository paragraphs. Associated with these literacy tests were alternatives if the applicant could not read or write. He might be asked to explain some aspect of the governmental system or some section of the state constitution. In other states such as Louisiana and Georgia, the local voting registrar could permit an illiterate person to register if he was convinced the person was of "good character." Mississippi, however, required literacy and interpretation as well as "good character." Local voting registrars selected one of the 286 sections of the state constitution for the applicant to read and interpret. The registrar, of course, was the judge of the adequacy of the interpretation.[41] Literacy tests, interpretation, and good-character tests were suspended by the Voting Rights Act of 1965 if less than 50 percent of the voting population of any state or county was registered or voted in November of 1964. Immediately after passage of the act, the attorney general moved to ban the use of the tests in Alabama, Georgia, Louisiana, Mississippi, South Carolina, and parts of North Carolina. Note that these states are at the extreme low end of competition and participation in Table 2.3. The presumption existed that these states used the literacy tests for discriminatory purposes. The Voting Rights Act of 1970 outlawed the use of literacy, understanding, and character tests anywhere as a prerequisite for registration to vote. The Supreme Court upheld the constitutionality of this law.

An objective reading of the qualifications for voting in all 50 states reveals little deviation among them. In only six states do the residency requirements exceed 30 days, and in only one case do they exceed 50. Registration is permanent and covers all state and federal elections in every state except South Carolina which requires the voter to reregister every ten years.[42] There are, then, very few impediments that the laws themselves impose upon the voters at the present time. It is an interesting question whether it was ever the laws themselves that provided the major roadblock to the voting of millions of Americans. Delaware, the state with the biggest turnout had a literacy test well into the sixties. Other states known for the high participation rate of their citizens—Maine, Washington, Oregon, Hawaii, Massachusetts, New York, California, and Connecticut—to name a few, also had literacy tests. Very few states required less than a year's residency in 1970. The conclusion must be drawn that it was not the laws but the general political and social climate in which they were administered that mattered much more to the encouragement or discouragement of the voter.

THE BLACK VOTER.   In the words of Schattschneider, the South was the last
remaining area in the United States in which the struggle against democracy was carried on in terms of legal and extralegal restrictions on the right
to vote.[43] The southern states were able to exclude the black from the
political system only by establishing a political monopoly. Once established, the system was used not only to disfranchise blacks but to depress
political participation generally. In the first four decades of this century
marked by inventive southern legislatures and the disinterest of the Supreme Court, about 5 percent of the blacks in the 11 states of the old
Confederacy succeeded in registering as voters, and most of these were
allowed to vote only in the meaningless general elections. The black population amounted to more than a quarter of the adult citizenry in this
region. The fear of the potential black vote fostered the doctrine of white
supremacy and the patterns of behavior that resulted.

In 1944, the death knell of "lily-white" southern politics was sounded
when the Supreme Court in *Smith v. Allwright* outlawed the "'white
primary," which had been the real election and from which blacks had
been excluded. The decision was greeted almost unanimously by more
than doubling of the size of the registered black electorate in the 11 core
southern states. In 1952, the rate of increase fell off with little more than
a quarter of the blacks registered. The 1960s witnessed further abrupt
change as Congress passed the series of civil rights legislation, the Southern Regional Council conducted a large-scale Voter Education project and
the migrations of northerners into the region brought more moderate
racial views. Philip Converse writes of the increase in registration of black
voters in the 1960s:

> By 1968, the proportion of blacks registered in the old Confederacy was at
> least approaching the rough range that might be expected of a population
> with comparable rates of functional illiteracy under "normal" political cir-
> cumstances. Given the extreme racial polarization in the area, however,
> political circumstances were far from normal, and with proper nurture, there
> was reason to expect that the participation figure might advance significantly
> higher.[44]

Matthews and Prothero detailed the political interest among blacks
in 1961 at the beginning of the new surge in voter registration. Black
motivation to participate politically seemed high. Within groups equated
by education, southern blacks actually expressed higher interest in politics
than their southern white counterparts. For such a depressed minority,
some long-lost political leverage was an attraction. It seemed plausible to
think that, with increased freedom from reprisal and institutional restraint
in the deepest South, levels of participation would increase further. The
authors conclude that the effects of taking part in the process of self-

government on the participant—on his self-esteem and his sense of civic responsibility—must not be ignored. One middle-aged black interviewed was asked why he so deeply wanted to vote. He replied simply: "To be a man."[45]

By 1976, 63 percent of the eligible blacks in the South were registered. This compared to 68 percent of the eligible white population in the eleven southern states. In Arkansas, 94 percent of the black vote was registered, while only 63 percent of the white vote was registered! In Alabama, Louisiana, Mississippi, and North Carolina, there is still a wide discrepancy between the white and black registration rates.[46] Unfortunately, it is still possible for those hostile to the black voter to continue to manipulate the legal regulations to his disadvantage. The redrawing of political boundaries to discourage black candidates from running as well as dilute the black vote is one method of counterattack. Black voting places have been moved without notice on the eve of elections. Voters have been shifted from one precinct to another without notification. District elections have been shifted to at-large elections to weaken the effect of a locally concentrated black vote. It is hard to undo the effects of one hundred years of racial politics. The real undoing will come as a result of the economic and social freeing of the black voter from poverty and discrimination as well as the need for each political party to vie for his vote to win. When his vote really counts, when each party needs him to increase its share of the vote, then he will participate. That this is beginning to occur is visible by examining the voting participation for governor in the 1970s in the eight lowest-participation states. The average turnout has risen to 36.2 from 29.2 in the period covered by Table 2–3.[47]

THE NONVOTER.   Millions of Americans are not participating in the fundamental exercise of the democratic process; enrolling and voting. In 1976, for example, about 68 million eligible Americans did not vote in the presidential election. This nonparticipation exists throughout the country, but it is most prevalent with those segments of the population most disconnected from the rewards and values of the system that has always promised unlimited opportunity. The urban poor, the young, blacks, Mexican-Americans, the American Indian—groups with the largest stake in social change have the least connection with the political process that is the supposed instrument of orderly change. Penn Kimball calls those who do not take part in the political process *the disconnected.* In a study of blacks and Puerto Ricans in the northern cities, Chicanos, Indians, and southern Blacks, he documented their rate of registration and turnout in 1969 and 1970. He discovered the persistent isolation of disadvantaged minorities from the American political process. It was his conclusion that the failure of the American political system to engage millions of voters is a product of the institutional structure by which persons can qualify to vote. The structure discriminates against the poor.[48] He calls for a federal system of voter registration whereby the national government assumes the responsibility and the initiative for seeing to it that every qualified citizen is registered to vote. A careful reading of *The Disconnected* reveals, however, that Kimball believes that those who do not vote are psychologically turned off by the system. "The key difference between voters and nonvoters seem to be their own opinion of themselves, whether or not they felt they possessed the aptitudes for politics, whether or not they felt that the participation of one individual like themselves would make any difference.[49]

The difference between the connected and the disconnected may be the difference between affluence and poverty, between schooling and illiteracy, between a job and no job, between sickness and health. It may be the difference between party responsibility and lack of responsibility. It may be the difference between a system in which every vote counts because the margin is so close and a system in which large blocs of voters make no difference. The statistics in the triangular relationship shown in Figure 2–6 are clear. The distribution of income—not the wealth of the state—competition, and voting turnout are all highly related. Extremes of wealth and poverty do not bring about a political system in which there is a high potential for political participation. The increasing competition within all our states may make more difference to the participation of the previously disconnected than removing the legal barriers to their participation. After all, the poor drop out of school even though it is free. Writing in 1960, Schattschneider said that our political system has nearly reached the limit of tolerance of passive abstention. This was before the increase in competition in all states had been fully realized. Politicians need voters, and any move on the part of an opponent to enlist a large number of the previously disconnected will bring about an equally determined drive on the other side of the political fence. It may be this basic party desire to win in a competitive party system that will bring about the connection of many of our citizens previously alienated from the political process.

The Structure and Operation of the Political Parties

COMPETITION MAKES PARTIES COHESIVE AND RESPONSIBLE. Does the existence of competition really matter to the operation of the political parties? Does it affect the kind of policy that is produced? The thesis with regard to the beneficial effects of two-party competition proclaims that it brings about parties that are cohesive and disciplined to combat the traditional enemy. This cohesion shows itself in the ability of the party to control nominations, to present a united front in the election, and, thereafter, to discipline the legislators to uphold the governor's program to make a good record for the next election. It is generally considered that this type of competition-cohesion situation will benefit the have-nots in the political system. The thought is that the very conspicuousness of competitive party leaderships would have that effect. That is, if the political leaders thought they might lose the next election because they refused to act favorably toward the "have-nots" (who could make the margin of difference in the next election—recall that the poor and the union members are only slightly more likely to vote Democratic), they might, therefore, be more likely to act favorably in their behalf than in a one-party situation where their next election was assured. In the one party situation where the parties are not cohesive electoral units and are divided into one or more factions that do battle within the party, there is little responsibility, because the factions are seldom permanent and are based on personalities or issues of the moment. The late V. O. Key believed that competition forced the parties to be cohesive and responsible. He said in his book, *Southern Politics,* that the absence of competition in the South facilitated the control over governmental policy by the "haves" in the society as opposed to the "have-nots." And that "A loose factionalism gives great negative power to those with a few dollars to invest in legislative candidates. A party system provides at least a semblance of joint responsibility between governor and legislature. The independence of candidacies in an atomized politics makes it possible to elect a fire-eating governor who promises great accomplishments and simultaneously to elect a legislature a majority of whose members are committed to inaction."[50] Key concluded that the factional system provided no institutional mechanism for the expression of lower-bracket viewpoints. We discovered that this situation existed in the states of the South and anticipated that the competitive states of the North would support cohesive disciplined parties that would be able to control nominations, to present a united front in the elections and thereafter to discipline the legislators to uphold the governor's program in order to make a good record for the next election. When Key turned his attention to the Northern states which would provide a contrast to the one-party factional politics of the South he found that the two party system was not consistently producing the disciplined cohesive parties which would be predicted from the model. Key paid particular attention to the primary system of nominations and observed that dissident elements can threaten the party organization by obtaining enough votes in a primary for their candidate. In many states the party organization is so weak that it merely ratifies the candidate who receives the most votes in the primary. Key speculated that parties which were not cohesive in their nominating functions could not produce sustained programs on behalf of the needy. He therefore was forced to modify his stand on the effects of two-party competition on party structure.

Several other writers have rejected state-wide competition itself as a producer of party cohesion and have suggested that parties are most likely to be cohesive in states where they are bipolarized along rural-urban lines. Thus it takes a particular combination of economic and political competition to produce cohesive parties.[51] Duane Lockard discovered that the two-party states in the southern part of New England tended to have programs more liberal toward the poor than did the less competitive three northern states. The politics of Massachusetts, Connecticut, and Rhode Island were based on the rural-urban division, thus lending support to the hypothesis that it is the socioeconomic character of the competition that is important.[52]

COMPETITION DOES NOT AFFECT PARTY STRUCTURE. Another school of thought makes the claim that socioeconomic characteristics of the state's population have more effect on the policy that emerges than the competitiveness of the party system. In fact, these researchers claim that socioeconomic characteristics affect both the party system as well as the policy which emerges from it. Thomas Dye, the major proponent of this hypothesis, concluded that political-system characteristics have relatively little independent effect upon policy outcomes in the states.[53] The fallacy in his argument is that he equates two-party competition with cohesive political parties. After V. O. Key discovered that this hypothesis could not be substantiated in the states of the North, he qualified it to declare that, while *cohesive* parties could function better to produce policy outcomes that would benefit the have-nots, *competition* did not always produce *cohesive* parties. The more refined hypothesis, then, was that competition was related to the social and economic divisions of the electorate and that both competition and socioeconomic conditions affected the type of party that existed in the system. It was the party, however, that had a great effect on the policies of the state. A further discussion of the conflicting claims of the party *cohesion school* versus the *economic determinism* school will take place when we consider the policy-making process more fully.

In summation, the beneficial effects of competition on party structure and function were qualified after research indicated that competition did not consistently produce party cohesion. The socioeconomic school, unsympathetic to the claim from the start, demonstrated that competition has little independent influence on policy, thus further disassociating the connection between competition, party, and policy. The job that remains is to investigate the effects of party structure on policy to test the hypothesis of V. O. Key that governing parties with sufficient internal cohesion to pass programs to which they commit themselves will bring about a wider distribution of the benefits of state expenditure across income classes.

CONCLUSIONS

Two-party systems exist in all but a handful of our 50 states. The centralizing affects of our national parties are such that the same two parties that operate at the national level compete in all but eight states for the office of governor. The states operate as legally separate units of the nation, but, in effect, they are politically inseparable. The national parties are, in effect, coalitions of state parties united for a single purpose—the winning of the presidency and the rewards of national office. The national coalition requires state and local operations of stability and durability, and this requirement is best met by state units that bear the same label as the national parties themselves.

Increasingly, each state mirrors national problems within its boundaries. In most of the country, the same beliefs and attitudes separate Republicans from Democrats. This has not always been the case. In the years following the War Between the States, the major issues were sectional—the southern and western farmers versus the eastern industrialists. The social and economic conditions that supported one-party states are disappearing. As Americans migrate about the country, as industry comes to formerly agrarian states, as the partisans of one region move to another, the political composition of the states change. Each state becomes a better sample of the diversity of life and interests that contribute to the competition between the two national parties.

The only exception to this decline in sectionalism has been the South, which is the historical anomaly in American politics. In terms of partisan competition elsewhere, the South really belongs to the Republicans in ideological terms, being the most rural, homogeneous, small-town, and Protestant section of the country. However, the Democratic party was the party of the Confederacy and remains so to this day in spite of growing Republican inroads in the presidential vote and an occasional state governorship.

The increase in competitiveness within nearly all states has meant that state political contests developed an independence from presidential politics insofar as popular governors can maintain themselves despite national tides in the opposite political direction. Elections for governor have become state contests concerning state matters partially insulated from candidates and issues at the national level. The fact that voters realize that much power has shifted to the state governments may account for the independence of their voting.

Two-party competition is claimed to have great benefits for the citizens of a state. This is the major thesis of the doctrine of party government. The "fall-out" effects of two-party systems in the states of the Union are regarded as tremendously beneficial to three different aspects of state politics:

1. The participation of the citizens;
2. The structure and operation of the political parties; and hence,
3. The type and distribution of policy benefits.

There is unquestionable support for the contention that two-party competition is associated with greater voter participation. It is claimed that two-party competition prompts political involvement, spurs interest in politics and campaigns, and strengthens a person's feeling that his vote counts. It is also believed that the greater the turnout, the more the involvement of ·the poor and hence the more politicians must consider their needs. However, it takes more than competition and participation to bring about a wide distribution of policy benefits.

There is not as much support for the hypothesis that two-party competition is associated with responsible cohesive parties that can control nominations, develop platforms, and discipline their legislative members to uphold the program while in office. There are many two-party jurisdictions where this does not occur. The hypothesis, however, that cohesive parties can engender a willingness on the part of their members to engage in common action to fulfill election promises has not been put to the test in the American states. This type of party exists in many competitive states, but not in all of them. In fact, the most competitive western states do not have strong party organizations. In conclusion, research shows that two-party competition is a healthy sign just as a strong body is a healthy condition, but it does not guarantee that the needs of the people will be met by alternative teams of decision makers who will make good on their promises, any more than a healthy body indicates wisdom, generosity, and fairness.

NOTES

1. M. Kent Jennings and Harmon Zeigler, "The Salience of American State Politics," *American Political Science Review* 64 (June 1970): 523–35.
2. V. O. Key, Jr., *Politics, Parties, and Pressure Groups*, 5th ed. (New York: Crowell, 1964), pp. 228–29.
3. American Political Science Association, *Toward a More Responsible Two-Party System* (New York: Rinehart and Company, 1950) p. 18.
4. E. E. Schattschneider, *The Semi-Sovereign People* (New York: Holt, Rinehart and Winston, 1960), pp. 91–92.
5. Key, *Politics, Parties, and Pressure Groups*, pp. 295–304; W. Duane Lockard, *New England State Politics*, 2d ed. (Princeton: Princeton University Press, 1959), pp. 320–40; *The Politics of State and Local Government* (New York: Macmillan, 1969), p. 179; Malcolm E. Jewell, "Party Voting in American State Legislatures," *American Political Science Review* 49 (September 1955): 773–

91. See also Jewell's discussion of this same finding in his book *The State Legislature: Politics and Practice* 2d ed. (New York: Random House, 1969), pp. 112–17; John H. Fenton *Midwest Politics* (New York: Holt, Rinehart and Winston, 1966). Fenton uses a measure of "effort" to prove that issue-oriented state parties (those bipolarized along rural-urban lines) are more responsible than job-oriented state parties (those not bipolarized along rural-urban lines). "Effort" is measured by the percentage of per capita income collected as per capita state and local tax revenue from own sources. This is based solely on personal income and does not reflect other indices of a state's financial resources (e.g., corporate income and wealth, property valuations), which, if available in addition to personal income data, would be a more accurate measure of a state's financial ability.

6. V. O. Key, Jr., *American State Politics: An Introduction* (New York: Knopf, 1956).

7. The principal measures are described and analyzed in David G. Pfeiffer, "The Measurement of Inter-Party Competition and Systemic Stability," *American Political Science Review,* 61 (June 1967): 457–67.

8. Norman R. Luttbeg and Richard E. Zody, "An Evaluation of Various Measures of State Party Competition," *Western Political Quarterly* 21 (December 1968): 723–24.

9. Austin Ranney, "Parties in State Politics," in Herbert Jacob and Kenneth N. Vines, eds., *Politics in the American States* 3d ed. (Boston: Little, Brown, 1976), pp. 59–61.

10. For a more complete discussion of institutional theory see Maurice Duverger, *Political Parties* (New York: Wiley, 1954); E. E. Schattschneider, *Party Government* (New York: Holt, Reinhart and Winston, 1942); Allan Sindler, *Political Parties in the United States* (New York: St. Martin's, 1966), chapter 3.

11. Anthony Downs, *An Economic Theory of Democracy* (New York: Harper & Row, 1957), chapter 8.

12. For a discussion of the contribution made by various groups to the Republican and Democratic party coalitions, see Robert Axelrod, "Where the Votes Come From: An Analysis of Electoral Coalitions, 1952–1968," *American Political Science Review* 66 (March 1972): 11–20.

13. At the moment, we will not consider the one-party Southern states which do not fit neatly into the analysis just developed (although the southern Democrats have generally favored more rather than less government intervention in the economy). The South has reasons of its own for being Democratic, reasons which we will consider fully later.

14. For much of this discussion, I am indebted to V. O. Key, Jr., *American State Politics,* chapter 8.

15. Schattschneider, *The Semi-Sovereign People,* p. 80.

16. Ibid., pp. 82–84.

17. Norman H. Nie, Sidney Verba, and John R. Petrocik, *The Changing American Voter* (Cambridge, Mass.: Harvard University Press, 1976), p. 240.

18. Ibid.

19. See Axelrod, "Where the Votes Come From" pp. 14–19.

20. For an explanation of the technique of factor analysis and the uses to which it may be put, see Ira Sharkansky and Richard I. Hofferbert, "Dimensions of

State Policy," in Jacob and Vines, eds., *Politics in the American States,* 2d ed. (Boston: Little, Brown, 1971), pp. 326–42. The Factor analysis based on the variables for 1970 may be found in David R. Cameron and Richard I. Hoffer- bert, "Sociopolitical Dynamics and Policy Innovation: The Case of State Edu- cation Finance, 1960–1970," mimeographed (Ann Arbor: University of Michigan).

The technique of factor analysis is based on the assumption that interrela- tions among separate variables indicate the existence of underlying traits— factors—that they share in common. A factor analysis manipulates a collec- tion of variables to discover the various patterns of relationships between them. The groups of variables that relate closely to one another, but only loosely (or not at all) to variables in other groups, are extracted as the princi- pal factors. The individual variables that show the strongest relationships with other members of their factor have the highest loadings. A variable's loading is the coefficient of correlation between that variable and the under- lying factor. The variables with the highest loadings indicate the underlying trait that the factor represents, although it is unlikely that any single variable represents that trait perfectly. It is also possible to construct state-by-state indices for the strength of each factor. Factor scores show how each state compares with all the others on a particular factor.

21. One way to visualize the distribution of income is to draw a Lorenz curve. The chart below shows a Lorenz curve representing the hypothetical distri- bution of income for California families in 1970; it also shows a 45-degree straight line representing an absolute equal distribution, i.e. one in which every family has the same income. The column of figures at the left refers to proportions of total income; the row of figures at the bottom refers to propor-

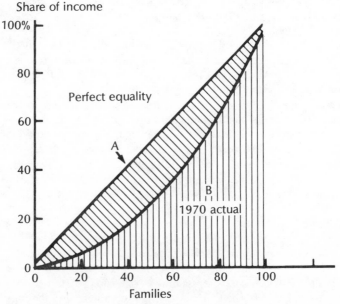

Share of income

Families

Percentiles: lowest to highest

tions of families. The Lorenz curve shows that in 1970 the poorest 20 percent of the families had about 5 percent of the income. Obviously, the greater the inequality in any distribution, the greater will be the area between the straight line and the curve. This fact enabled an Italian economist named Corrado Gini to develop a measure of overall equality. What is now called the "Gini coefficient" is calculated by dividing the area between the straight line and the Lorenz curve (Area A) by the total area under the straight line (Areas A and B). The coefficient ranges between zero and one. A value of zero would mean that the Lorenz curve would become the straight line—that there was no income inequality. A value of one would mean that everything under the straight line could be thought of as Area A. It would mean perfect inequality —i.e., one family would have all the income. For a more complete discussion of the Gini Index and a simple method of calculation, see Oliver Benson, *Political Science Laboratory* (Columbus, Ohio: Merrill, 1969), pp. 8–11.

22. See Frank H. Jonas, ed., *Politics in the American West* (Salt Lake City: University of Utah Press, 1969).
23. Fenton, *Midwest Politics*, pp. 1–113.
24. Ira Sharkansky, *The United States: A Study of a Developing Country* (New York: McKay, 1975).
25. In 1958, all except South Carolina gave their votes to Wallace's American Independent Party.
26. This discussion draws heavily on Philip Converse, "Change in the American Electorate," in Angus Campbell and Philip Converse, eds., *The Human Meaning of Social Change* (New York: Russell Sage, 1972), 303–23.
27. Ibid., p. 306.
28. Walter Dean Burnham, "The Alabama Senatorial Election of 1962: Return of Interparty Competition," *Journal of Politics* 26 (November 1964): 828–29.
29. Harold G. Grasmick, "Rural Culture and the Wallace Movement in the South," *Rural Sociology* 39 (Winter 1974): 454–70.
30. Schattschneider, *The Semi-Sovereign People*, pp. 91–96.
31. Nie, Verba, and Petrocik, *Changing American Voter*, pp. 50–55, 67–68.
32. Sorauf, *Party Politics in America*, pp. 176–79.
33. Key, *American State Politics*, pp. 28–31.
34. Walter Dean Burnham, *Critical Elections and the Mainsprings of American Politics* (New York: Norton, 1970).
35. M. Kent Jennings and Richard G. Neimi, "Party Identification at Multiple Levels of Government," *American Journal of Sociology* 72 (July 1966): 86–101.
36. Austin Ranney, "The Political Parties: Reform and Decline," chapter 6 in Anthony King, ed., *The New Political System* (Washington, D.C.: American Enterprise Institute for Public Policy Research, 1978), p. 220.
37. Raymond E. Wolfinger and Associates, "The Myth of the Independent Voter," paper presented at the APSA annual meeting, Washington, D.C., September 1977, quoted in Austin Ranney, "The Political Parties: Reform and Decline," p. 220.
38. Nie, Verba, and Petrocik, *Changing American Voter*, pp. 64–65.
39. Angus Campbell, "Surge and Decline: A Study of Electoral Change," *Public Opinion Quarterly* 24 (Fall 1960).

40. It is true that states that schedule elections for governor in presidential election years experience high-stimulus elections which tend to increase turnout. However, the correlation between the average presidential turnout and average turnout for governor in nonpresidential years is so high (.88) that we can be confident that our measure is not greatly affected by combining states with different election schedules. Lester W. Milbrath, "Individuals and Government," in Jacob and Vines, *Politics in the American States,* p. 40.
41. Sorauf, *Party Politics in America,* p. 188.
42. "Qualifications for Voting", *The Book of the States, 1974–1975* (Lexington, Ky.: Council of State Governments), p. 38.
43. Schattschneider, *The Semi-Sovereign People,* p. 101.
44. Converse, "Change in the American Electorate," p. 304.
45. Donald R. Matthews and James W. Prothro, *Negroes and the New Southern Politics* (New York: Harcourt Brace & World, 1966), p. 481.
46. U.S. Bureau of Census, *Statistical Abstract of the United States,* 1978 (Washington, D.C.: 1978), Table 834, p. 519.
47. In this case, turnout is based on the total resident population of voting age as reported in the *Statistical Abstract of the United States,* 1974, Table 705, p. 439 and 1978, Table 840, p. 522. Because this includes the armed forces stationed in each state, it may provide an inflated base from which to calculate the turnout.
48. Penn Kimball, *The Disconnected* (New York: Columbia University Press, 1972). Bills authorizing national registration by postcard passed the Senate in 1975 and the House in 1976, but had not become law by the end of 1976.
49. Ibid., p. 295.
50. V. O. Key, Jr., *Southern Politics in State and Nation* (New York: Knopf, 1949), p. 308.
51. See footnote 5 to this chapter.
52. Lockard, *New England State Politics.*
53. Thomas R. Dye, *Politics, Economics and the Public: Policy Outcomes in the American States* (Chicago, Ill.: Rand McNally, 1966).

CHAPTER THREE

PRESSURE GROUPS VERSUS POLTICAL PARTIES

In February 1971, a Pennsylvania state senator rose to his feet and declared:

> Gentlemen of the Senate, let us talk politics. If you receive your support from the high-priced officials of the United States Steel Corporation, and the high-priced officials of Bethlehem Steel, of Westinghouse and of Pittsburgh Plate Glass, then you ought to vote against my amendments because these industries are going to benefit. However, if you are elected, as I am and as many of you are, by the factory worker, the truck driver, the man who works in the coal mines, the school teacher, the small businessman, the blue-collared employee, the farmer, the construction worker, and yes, even the newspaper reporter, and not by big business, then you must vote for my amendments so the corporations can carry their burden.[1]

Those who have been in politics long enough to evaluate strategy under the guise of an emotional appeal will see immediately that the "little people" the senator refers to—factory workers, truck drivers, coal miners, and others—are represented by very powerful unions and organizations. Legislators make laws and adminstrators make decisions every day that affect the lives of these groups. The AFL-CIO, Teamsters, United Mine Workers, teachers' associations, Grange, The Farm Bureau, and "big industries" all speak for the interests in their senator's district and promote them by attempting to influence the decision makers of government. The decisions won between elections constitute the basic stuff of politics. A working conception of the political process must take into account the interactions among groups, parties, and governmental institutions that produce such decisions. The single most important actor in state politics is the political party because it is the only organization that can mediate the demands of organized groups. An inspection of the relationship between parties and pressure groups tells us who is dominating the other. Do certain organized pressures always win? Or can the party leaders decide who wins and who loses in each confrontation?

While the terms "interest group" and "pressure group" are used interchangeably, the latter implies use of influence techniques. Because we are most concerned with the use and results of organized group pressure, we will use the term pressure group. Group interests are the animating forces in the political process; an understanding of state politics requires a knowledge of the chief interests and of their stake in public policy. Those who are elected to public office must reconcile and mediate conflicting group ambitions and restrain group tendencies judged to be socially destructive. An examination of pressure groups and of the interests from which they arise throws light on the demands that politicians must manage and the problems with which they must cope. The political interests of school teachers, for instance, may be advanced through the lobbying and propaganda activities of pressure groups such as the state teachers' associations. While they may call themselves nonpolitical, these organized groups are engaged in politics: a politics of policy. They are concerned with what government does either to help or harm their membership. They do not assume the party's basic function of nominating candidates or of conducting the government. Pressure groups may campaign for party candidates and may even become allied with one or another of the parties, but their main role is to petition the parties and formal instruments of government as spokesmen for the special interests in society.

THE GROUP BASIS OF POLITICS

Earl Latham's Theory of Group Equlibrium

"The chief social values cherished by individuals in modern society are realized through groups."[2] So says a leading spokesman for the group approach to politics. Earl Latham states that organized groups are structures of power because they concentrate human wit, energy, and muscle to achieve their purposes. He claims the state, as an association or group, is not different from other organizations; they all have a common factor of power, the striving for which is a never-ending process extending beyond campaigns and elections. Organized groups may be regarded as systems of private government, while organs of the state represent a system of public government. Latham carries this argument one step further when he says that the legislature referees the group struggle, ratifies victories of the successful coalitions, and records the terms of surrenders, compromises, and conquests—all in the form of statutes. The politics of legislating, for Latham, is primarily a balancing of power among contending groups. Counted in this struggle is the "group" called legislature with its own sense of identity and consciousness that must be considered in the process of policy making. Latham does not give the political party a central role as mediator in the politics of group conflict. He holds that public policy is the temporary equilibrium reached in the group struggle at any given moment.

This theory of the primary role of groups in the process of governing was widely debated two decades ago. Some political scientists agreed with Latham that the most appropriate conceptual unit for the study of politics was the group. Others argued that this was an inadequate view. Much of the literature came to focus on this dispute: whether and to what extent a "group approach" to politics was fruitful. A brief look at this body of theory and some of the implications that flow from it begins with the work of Arthur Bentley. His book, *The Process of Government*, published in 1908,[3] has inspired most political scientists who have followed the "group approach."

Arthur Bentley's Theory of The Totality of Group Activity

Bentley claimed that the analysis of groups, their interests, and their conflicts with one another could explain the totality of the governmental process. Groups had a degree of power or pressure more or less in proportion to their numbers, their intensity, and their techniques. The larger, more nearly general interest would usually tend to defeat the smaller, narrower special interest. Legislatures adjusted group pressures to make policy. Supreme Court decisions were also subject to the group loyalties of the justices.[4] Even political leadership could be explained by group structure: cohesive groups gave rise to strong leaders; fractured groups had weak leaders.

The difficulty with this theory is that the process of policy making in the legislature or the process of judicial decision making or the quality of leadership is more than group phenomena. The legislatures and the courts are more than pressure groups or referees of groups. While legislators are more prone than judges to respond to group pressures, it's an inadequate explanation to say that they respond only to the calculus of pressures. Personal idiosyncrasies, concern for those who have no group representation such as children or migrant workers, attention to numerous, but weak over determined but strong pressures also occur in our decision making process and cannot be explained in terms of group theory.

Even though Bentley concentrated on groups to the exclusion of all other forces, he said very little about why the needs of society would tend to be reflected in politically or economically effective pressure. Nor did he consider what it is that causes groups to organize and act effectively. He

could not account for the fact that groups are more effective in some
political systems than others. More recent advocates of group theory have
modified the extreme positions that Bentley took with his calculus of
pressures.

David Truman's Theory of The Potential Interest Group

David Truman, the major spokesman of group theory among contemporary political scientists, concerns himself with these gaps in Bentley's
work. Truman explains that what drives people to form associations is the
necessity of satisfying their needs. As society becomes more complex and
the division of labor increases, the number of groups increase. An interest
group is a body of people who share common attitudes and make "certain
claims on other groups in the society for the establishment, maintenance,
or enhancement of forms of behavior that are implied by the shared
attitudes."[5] With more specialization and social complexity, more associations will arise. Inevitably, interest groups will turn to government for
resolution of their problems. Both Truman and Bentley conceive of government as an institution or group whose powers are the most inclusive.
Groups will acquire connections with the institutions of government
whenever they deem the relationships important. This is especially evident in the economic sphere. Unemployment, wide fluctuation in prices,
inevitably produced associations among owners, workers, and farmers, to
operate throughout government. These groups will attempt to mitigate
and control the ravages of the system through tariffs, subsidies, wage
guarantees, social insurance, and the like, Both labor and management
historically have resisted the use of governmental power to resolve their
difficulties. But, as one side achieves a governmental decision in its favor,
the other side seeks to reverse that decision or modify it so as to make it
easier to live with.

Truman's amendment to Bentley's theory adds an explanation of why
group needs and interests result in organized political pressure. He
stressed the "potential interest group," a collection of people sharing
certain interests but who have not yet come together to make demands
on society. When these people are pushed far enough, they will mobilize
and demand. Group pressure, however, cannot account for government
actions that serve an unorganized interest group such as the voteless
migratory workers. It is the potential power of these groups, and the
underlying threat of their possible mobilization, that explains why policies
serving their interests are produced.

Truman shared Bentley's belief that group pressures alone determined the final equilibrium position of the social system: group interests,
attitudes, and pressures could account for the outcome of the political

process. Truman believed that this equilibrium was just and desirable because of two major checks on the unmitigated self-seeking of pressure groups. First, most members also belong to other groups in society that have different interests. These "overlapping memberships" would tend to moderate excessive demands. Manufacturers who sought tax advantages, as an example, are also consumers, churchmen, and so on. If the manufacturers' association went too far, thereby threatening the special interests of these other groups, it could lead to conflicting interest battles and perhaps even alienate some of its own members. Second, the potential interest groups considered above would provide another check on the power of existing groups. Truman concludes that the stability of our society rests on the ability of overlapping memberships and potential interest groups to provide us with peaceful change. The group process will proceed as usual.

The Group In Contemporary Theory

Today the belief that all politics can be reduced to group action is not widely shared. Critics claim that the emphasis on the group is a significant advance in our understanding of the political process, but the group does not displace other phenomena of equal significance. Stanley Rothman holds that the comprehension of society requires an examination of its cultural traditions and the structure of the values and beliefs that are held by the individuals who compose it.[6] The last chapter attempted to account for some of the cultural distinctions among the various states in our union. Patterns of migration to the frontier, the tradition of slavery in the South, aristocratic one-party control of some state governments, and the intermingling of ethnic and traditional cultures all account for differences in the way political systems are formed and operate.

In addition, a social system is composed of individuals and groups. Political decisions are a result of both individual and group behavior. A strong governor with a liking for politics will have an effect on the state political system. As Republican governor of New York, Nelson Rockefeller was invincible. His relish for politics made him a master politician. He took his budget to all parts of the state to explain it to the people. He could obtain public support for his program, which the legislative party remembered when the time came to scrutinize and vote on the budget. A legislator who incurred the wrath of a popular governor was not in a secure position. This was Rockefeller's style, and the policy of his adminstration bore its imprint.

On June 29, 1975, the first woman governor of Connecticut was stopped before she could enter the meeting she was to attend by the Huns, a motorcycle clan who wanted to protest the recent helmet requirement. Afterwards she told the audience that she had taken the time to explain the necessity of the requirement to the Huns. She apologized for being late and concluded: "A mother's work is never done." Undoubtedly the personal style of this governor, the first woman to be elected to the governorship on her own record, affects the art of governing in Connecticut.

The group theorists believe government itself is an institutionalized group whose powers are most inclusive. They claim its basic characteristics—interactions among persons—do not differ in kind from those of other groups. This book is based on the notion that the political process is based on the actions of persons. The difference between an interest group based on one specific economic or social interest and a governmental institution formed to represent and moderate many interests is a vast one. The whole purpose of governmental institutions is to advance legitimate group objectives, to reconcile and mediate between conflicting group ambitions, and to restrain socially destructive groups. The very difference in purpose that distinguishes the institutions of government from those interests that bring pressure on it can account for a difference in the way the actions of persons are patterned. Many actors are involved in the legislative process: legislators, pressure groups, governors, parties, party leaders, bureaucrats, and "publics." The legislative rules themselves are bases of power. The adequacy of staffing legislative committees determines the independence of the legislator from information supplied him by a pressure group. Examples can also be drawn from the executive and judicial institutions of government to show that they are not merely neutral registering devices for pressure groups. Nor are they just another "group."

The major premise of this book is that the quality of government in any state depends on the political party system. Party is the most important instrumentality of democratic politics; its major purpose is election and reelection. Votes are the most important commodity with which the politician deals. The politician must appeal to a wide range of groups to be elected and to stay in office; he depends on them for his election. Parties assume responsibility for the conduct of government once an election is won. To do so, they must mediate between pressure groups and the interests from which they arise. This contrasts with the major purpose of pressure groups that have a sharply defined membership, a concrete purpose with which all members are psychologically identified, and the unity essential for concerted action. These organizations promote their interests by attempting to influence goverment rather than by nominating candidates and seeking responsibility for the management of government.

To consider the impact of pressure groups on the governing process does not mean we need subscribe to the notion that policy is the total result of interacting pressure groups. Nor do we have to accept the claim that pressure groups play the major role in expressing and accommodating diverse values of people. Their rather distinctive role in the exercise of power is as a supplement to the party system and formal instruments of government. Pressure groups serve as the spokesmen for special interests within our society.

The remainder of this chapter will be concerned with the relationship between pressure groups, the political party, and the governing apparatus. It will consider the techniques used by pressure groups to attain their ends within the party and the government. The factors related to influence and the points of access to the institutions of government are relevant questions. David Truman provided the guide for considering the relationships between pressure groups and the governmental process on which the following discussion is founded. While Truman's work focused on pressure groups at the national level, most of his framework can be applied to a study of state interest groups.

THE POWER OF PRESSURE GROUPS

Measuring the Power of Pressure Groups

How do you go about measuring the power of pressure groups? Do you ask the lobbyist, the legislators who receive the pressures, a panel of political scientists? Political parties have certain identities whose strength can be measured in terms of votes and legislation. Pressure group candidates do not run for public office under titles such as General Motors or the Teamsters; nor do legislators identify themselves as representing the Farm Bureau or Chamber of Commerce. This lack of identity makes it difficult to measure the amounts and types of pressure interest groups apply. As an illustration of this problem, two teams of political scientists investigated the effects of lobbying activities in chosen states by asking the legislators involved. Tennessee and North Carolina were among the states included. In these states, the legislators believed that lobbyists exerted little influence, despite the fact that previous research had indicated strong pressure systems for both.[7] The only possible explanation for this discrepancy offered by the writers was that both states have traditionalist political cultures marked by a paternalistic and elitist concept of the commonwealth. Consequently, such a culture confines" real political power to a relatively small and self-perpetuating group drawn from an established elite," an elite composed of persons considered to have a "right" to govern.[8] If legislators accept this view, they would admit very little influence from outside, even though it did in fact exist. Also interesting in this regard is that the lobbyists in North Carolina see their influence as far greater than the legislators. Zeigler and Baer found that lobbyists in North

Carolina (whose legislators consider them weak) have almost as high an estimation of the success of their efforts as do the Oregon lobbyists (whose legislators consider them powerful).[9]

At this point, the reader has a right to wonder why the state of the discipline has not advanced further than it has in its analysis of the comparative impact of interest groups. Zeller's study in 1954 remains as the only one that has indicated the relative power of interest groups in all the states. The two more recent studies mentioned above deal with a total of eight states. The methods used to measure the impact of pressures were not the same. Comparisons of regional groupings of states in New England, border states, the South, the West, and Midwest offer data for comparison. With the exception of *New England State Politics* by Duane Lockard, the comparative strength of pressure groups is not a focus of the studies. Different standards for comparison may even be applied among the states of the regional studies themselves. A rewarding and challenging research assignment would be to compare the relative power of the same pressure groups in *two* states, applying rigorous standards for comparison.

That some pressure groups have more power than others is an undisputed fact. Most researchers have an intuitive notion of what power means. If a state has a single industry and if that industry controls the press and the legislators and can keep itself from being taxed, then we can rightfully conclude that the decisions in that state are manipulated for the benefit of that company. If, on the other hand, it is the only industry in the state but does not try to dominate decisions because it fears reprisals, then the task of determining its power becomes much harder. Perhaps the industry has developed such a favorable climate for its existence that the lawmakers don't need to be pressured to act in its behalf. "What's good for the country is good for General Motors, and what's good for General Motors is good for the Country." That famous remark by Charles Wilson, Secretary of Defense in the Eisenhower cabinet, was uttered by the president of a company whose gross income is three times larger than the budget of any state. In fact, with the exception of the United States and the Soviet Union, it's larger than the budget of any country in the world. Such a company might not have to send lobbyists to the state capitol to establish its interests. On the other hand, its very size may generate an opposite force in the form of the powerful United Automobile Workers whose resources are not its gross, but its votes and hence its ability to influence the decison makers. Which of the two pressures has more power?

Robert Dahl's Measurement of Power

The study of power involves resources and the use of resources. It also necessitates specific decisions and action among people: lobbyists, legislators, governors. We could not expect the same pressure group to be interested in or concerned with all the decisions the government makes. Robert Dahl's definition of power as a relationship among people is most useful for the task of comparing the relative degree of power held by the pressure groups in our American states. According to the following simple definition, "A has power over B to the extent that he can get B to do something that B would not otherwise do."[10] According to Dahl, "this power relationship involves at least four major concepts: (1) the base of the pressure group's power: (2) the means used by the pressure group to exert power over the government (or other groups); (3) the range or scope of the group's power over the governmental decision makers, or over other groups; (4) the amount or extent of the group's power.[11]

BASE While this statement can apply to any single actor, group, or institution, we will proceed to make use of it in the study of group power. The *base* of a group's power consists of all the resources—money, status, size, cohesion, and geographical distribution of members—and votes it can control. Clearly, size is an important determinant of the political effectiveness of a group. Since votes are all important to governors and legislators, a large interest group with the potential for delivering large numbers of votes for or against a candidate can command his attention. In terms of sheer numbers, then, farmers, teachers, and union members have more resources than doctors or businessmen. In farm states such as Iowa, Nebraska, and Kansas, the support of groups like the Grange, the Farm Bureau Federation, and the Farmers Union has been important to candidates for public office. The United Auto Workers have been significant in Michigan politics.

A second major resource in the power base is money. Virtually every technique for influencing the political system requires money. An organization composed of wealthy members who contribute as individuals to the campaigns of candidates for public office has a built-in advantage. Labor has a large membership from which to extract money.

David Truman believes that the most basic factor affecting the power of a group is status, the position of its spokesmen in the social structure. Petitions and claims of a high-status group may even in some circumstances appear less as demands and supplications and more as flattery. This is likely to be the case when the legislative representative of a major corporation, the American Bar Association, or the Chamber of Commerce approaches a legislator or junior official. The high-status group is also aided by the fact that the backgrounds of the legislators, administrators, or executives are such that they have similar values.[12] Government officials and pressure groups inevitably overlap in membership. Any of the latter that can claim members in the legislature will thus enjoy a measure of privileged access. The organized bar has had advantages in access to state legislatures by virtue of the number of lawyers elected to those bodies. The Catholic Church in Massachusetts claims many legislators among its membership as does the Morman Church in Utah. The legislator who is a "member" of an active interest group may observe and report on developments within the legislative body and its committees; he may act as the group's spokesman on the floor and he may attempt to persuade key committee members. On the other hand, the legislator may not even be a formal member of the group. He may be unaware that the subtle pressures of a lifetime have given him a point of view which favors a certain group over others. A politician need not be a member of the Chamber of Commerce to listen and respect the testimony of a business leader who is pleading his company's case.

The internal organization of a group is also a part of its resource base. A group that is tightly knit internally will be more effective politically than one with a diverse membership. It will be able to present a strong and convincing show of concern and unanimity. If the group is fragmented internally, it will not be able to display group power, and it may cause decision makers to ignore its goals. Thus organized labor, teachers groups, civil rights interests, and others reduce their political effectiveness if they are unable to articulate a united and coherent set of goals. In the early days of the labor movement, for instance, leaders were able to command allegiance of the union members and present a united front in their fight for better wages, hours, and working conditions. Today, however, the social and economic status of labor has improved tremendously. The individual worker is not as dependent on his union as he once was, making cohesion more difficult to maintain.

MEANS   The means used by a pressure group to exert power over the government or other groups is another concept in the power statement. Unless it makes use of all of its resources, the group cannot control the actions of others. The exception to this is when decision makers anticipate that a group *may* use its potential even though it has not yet done so. An example would be the expectation of a poor people's march if welfare benefits are not adjusted for inflation. The *means* usually involve lobbying, support of candidates in campaigns, demonstrations, propaganda. In this endeavor, the skills and other qualifications of the group's leaders and agents are a crucially important variable. Frequently, interest groups ask former legislators to deal with the government because they have access to the political system and knowledge of the complexities of getting things done in the legislature and the administration. Governor J. Hugo Aronson of Montana, affectionately called the "Galloping Swede" by his constituents, later became a lobbyist after his stint in the governor's office. He announced at one point: "Old governors don't just fade away, they become lobbyists."[13] Consider the effectiveness of access to the Montana administration the ex-governor could attain. His knowledge and connections were invaluable to the group he represented.

SCOPE   The third concept, scope of power, consists of B's responses. The Farm Bureau in Alabama can get the legislature to structure the tax system in such a way as to give the farmers an advantage. This is in spite of the fact that the state could collect many millions more each year if it taxed at the average rate for all the states. In Connecticut, the Farm Bureau *can* get the Republicans to back legislation favorable to its interests, but it cannot get the Democratic leadership to back its proposals. The Farm Bureau must work through the leadership of the Republican party, not lobby the legislators themselves. The legislators of both parties look to their respective leadership for policy guidance and voting cues. Because pressure groups in Connecticut have built-in access to the leaders of only one party, they cannot "get B to do something that he would not otherwise do" if it involves the leadership of the other party. The influence of the pressure group in Connecticut is limited to legislation sponsored by one party—the party in which it has a built-in interest. If that party does not have a majority in both houses, the response to legislation favored by the group is weak or negative. While the Farm Bureau can prevail in the weakly organized party system of Alabama, it cannot get both parties in Connecticut to pass its legislation, and hence its scope is limited.

AMOUNT   The amount of power a pressure group has is measured by its success in achieving policy responses favorable to it. The amount of power is the most important concept and the hardest to measure. A pressure group with vast resources and clever lobbyists may not get its way. The amount of power depends on the decison makers, the legislators, or the amount of power wielded by other groups. If they need the votes, the campaign money, or the information, decision makers will respond favorably. If they do not need these advantages, or cannot be frightened by threats, then the influence will be less. If we can say that the Farm Bureau Federation in Alabama succeeded every time in structuring the property tax classification system so that rural landowners get a special break, and that in Connecticut the same organization cannot succeed in doing this, we have a direct comparison of a pressure group's relative power in two different situations. It is then necessary to explain why the Farm Bureau can exert so much power in Alabama. Does it have enough votes to elect the governor and many legislators? Does it control legislative committee chairmanships? Can it do the same in Connecticut? If not, is it due to a difference in its resources? Its means? Or is it restrained in its activities by a more powerful party system or equally powerful pressure groups?

Comparative Power: An Example

If we were to compare the power of the Farm Bureau in Alabama and Connecticut according to the statement proposed by Robert Dahl, the results might look like the description in Table 3–1. The information in Table 3–1 is oversimplified, of course, but it gives some idea of the relative power of the Farm Bureau in two states. The Table indicates that the relationship between the political party and the pressure group may be a crucial factor in the amount of power a pressure group can wield. In Alabama, the Democratic Party is a "holding company" within which groups contest for power. According to Neal Peirce, the Farm Bureau can elect its candidate for public office. In 1970, Jere Beasley was elected lieutenant governor (and thus presiding officer of the senate) through the efforts of the Bureau.[14] The rural legislators are also given the most powerful committee chairmanships. In Connecticut, as we have seen, the Farm Bureau is closely allied with the Republican Party. The clientele of the Farm Bureau are members of the party, so the Farm Bureau is virtually an appendage. Access to the party leadership is assured. However, this does not mean that the Farm Bureau can dominate decisions. The Democrats, for instance, do not have many farmers in their legislative contingent and ordinarily do not initiate legislation on behalf of the farmer. When the Democrats are in power, it means the farmers cannot count on built-in support. The party plays a crucial role in determining legislative policy in Connecticut. According to Duane Lockard, parties make use of pressure groups to accomplish their legislative ends; party leaders may

TABLE 3–1

Comparative Power of the Farm Bureau in
Alabama and Connecticut

STATE	BASE	MEANS	SCOPE	AMOUNT
Connecticut	Votes Money	Built-in Republican Party Lobby Former legislators as lobbyists	Agricultural policy only (can influence decisions of Department of Agriculture)	Weak
Alabama	Votes Money	Nomination and election of candidates for executive and legislature. Controlling votes of legislators Legislative committee chairmanships	Agricultural policy Tax policy	Strong

consult the pressure groups to develop their position on legislation.[15] Often the party leadership will ask for pressure to be applied on particular bills, sensing a political gain by their enactment but needing help to popularize the idea. The parties are so powerful they will occasionally discipline an unruly pressure group. Lockard describes how the Democratic Party cracked down on two groups that had opposed it in previous campaigns. The dentists had proposed a bill to prohibit dental laboratories from providing false teeth directly to patients, claiming that the patients should have a dentist's prescription. Governor Bowles vetoed the bill and the dentists worked to defeat him in the next election. When the dentists reappeared the next legislative session to push for the same bill, the Democratic leaders announced that they were going to kill it. One Democratic leader said that "the dentists were going to be taught a thing or two about politics since they appeared so anxious to get into the game."[16] While the Connecticut political parties may not be as strong as they were 25 years ago when this incident took place, they are still strong vis-a-vis the pressure groups; the party leaders still exert control over legislative policy. That means pressure groups must do business with the party leaders who "clear" legislation.

In Connecticut and Alabama, it appears that party strength underlies the differences in Farm Bureau strength. If we discover that the utilities, highway interests, and Associated Industries of Alabama (a local version of the National Association of Manufacturers) can all exert clout in Montgomery, whereas the same groups cannot prevail over policy in Hartford, then we can talk of states in which pressures have power and states in which they are weak. All of this measuring, however, is crude at the present time. Very few studies have made use of rigorous methods of measuring power to determine the relative strengths of pressure groups in different states. The tools exist, but they have not been used.

THE ECONOMIC AND POLITICAL BACKGROUND

Strong, Moderate, and Weak Pressure Group Systems

Table 3–2 is a listing of the "significant" pressure groups by state, indicating which states have strong, moderate, or weak pressure-group systems. Strength is an estimate derived from reading the recent state literature. It was not measured according to the power statement discussed above because the evidence is not available to make comparisons. As evidence

TABLE 3-2

Listing of the Significant Pressure Groups
by State

STATES IN WHICH PRESSURE GROUPS ARE STRONG (22)

Alabama	Farm Bureau Federation, utilities, highway interests, Associated Industries of Alabama
Alaska	Oil, salmon, mining, contracting, labor unions, Chamber of Commerce
Arkansas	Transport, agriculture, utilities, natural resources (oil, timber, bauxite), insurance, local government (County Judges Association, Arkansas Municipal League), labor, Chamber of Commerce, Arkansas Free Enterprise Association
Florida	Associated Industries, utilities (Florida Power Corp., Florida Power and Light) Farm Bureau, bankers, liquor interests, chain stores, race tracks, Phosphate Council
Georgia	Atlanta business group, Citizens and Southern Bank, Coca-Cola, Fuqua Industries, Delta Airlines, Trust Company of Georgia, Woodruff Foundation, Education lobby, Georgia Municipal Association
Hawaii	Big Five Companies: C. Brewer and Co., Ltd. (sugar, molasses, insurance, ranching); Thro. H. Davies & Co. (sugar, merchandising, foreign investment), Amfac, Inc. (sugar and merchandising); Castle and Coke, Inc. (sugar, pineapple, bananas, seafoods, coffee, macademia nuts, discount stores, steamship agent in Hawaii, land development, and property management); Alexander and Baldwin, Inc. (docks and warehouses, sugar, pineapples, merchandising); Dillingham Corporation (construction)
Iowa	Farm Bureau Federation, Truckers
Kentucky	Coal companies, Jockey Club, liquor interests, tobacco interests, Kentucky Education Association, rural electric cooperatives
Louisiana	Oil Companies (Exxon, Chevron, Texaco, Gulf, Shell, Mobile, Mid-Continental Oil and Gas Association); gas pipeline interests, Louisiana Chemical Association, forest industry, rice industry, Louisiana Manufacturers Association, Farm Bureau, AFL-CIO
Mississippi	Mississippi Economic Council, Farm Bureau, manufacturers association, medical association, public school teachers, associations of local officials (county supervisors, mayors, sheriffs, etc.), segregationist groups (Citizens' Council, John Birch Society, Association for Preservation of the White Race, Women for Constitutional Government)
Montana	Anaconda Copper Company, Montana Power Company, State Chamber of Commerce, Northern Pacific Railroad, Great Northern Railroad

TABLE 3–2

Continued

STATES IN WHICH PRESSURE GROUPS ARE STRONG (22) (continued)

Nebraska	Farm Bureau, Omaha National Bank, Northern Natural Gas Company, Union Pacific Railroad, Northwest Bell Telephone, education lobby
New Hampshire	Public utilities, paper manufacturing, lumber, race-track lobby
New Mexico	Oil and gas, school teachers, liquor dealers, banks, truckers, cattlemen, business groups
North Carolina	Textile, tobacco, furniture, utilities, banks, teachers
Oklahoma	Phillips Petroleum, Kerr-McGee, other oil companies (Texaco, Mobile, Humble, Atlantic-Sinclair, Sun-Sunray, DX Division, Hess Oil), transportation companies, power companies, local public officials
Oregon	Utilities (Pacific Power and Light, Portland General Electric), lumber companies, public school teachers (Oregon Education Association), railroads and truckers, organized labor (AFL-CIO, Teamsters, Longshoremen), Farm Bureau, Agricultural Association, insurance lobby
South Carolina	Planters, textiles (DuPont, Stevens, Deering-Milliken, Fiberglass, Textron, Chemstrand, Lowenstein, Burlington, Bowaters) Electric and Gas Company, banks
Tennessee	Manufacturers association, County Services Association, Farm Bureau, Municipal League, Education Association, liquor lobby
Texas	Chemical Council, Mid-Continent Oil and Gas Association, Independent Producers and Royalty Owners, State Teachers' Association, Manufacturers' Association, medical association, Motor Transport Association, insurance organizations
Washington	Boeing Aircraft, Teamsters, government employees, school teachers, AFL-CIO, highway interests (oil, asphalt, contractors, car builders), timber, banking, commercial fishing, pinballs, public and private power, gravel, wine and beer, Grange
West Virginia	Union Carbide, Bethlehem Steel, Occidental Petroleum, Georgia Pacific, Baltimore and Ohio Railroad, Norfolk and Western Railway Company, Chesapeake and Ohio Railway Company, United Mine Workers

STATES IN WHICH PRESSURE GROUPS ARE MODERATELY STRONG (18)

Arizona	Copper companies (Phelps Dodge), oil companies, farm groups, Arizona Power Company, "school lobby," liquor lobby
California	Pacific Gas and Electric, Standard Oil of California, Bank of America, California Teachers Association, Lockheed Air-

TABLE 3–2

Continued

STATES IN WHICH PRESSURE GROUPS ARE MODERATELY STRONG (18) (continued)

California (continued)	craft, Transamerica, Kern County Land Company, Bankers Association of America, California Real Estate Association, California Growers Association, University of California, AFL-CIO
Delaware	DuPont Chemical Company, insurance lobby
Idaho	Idaho Power Company, Idaho Farm Bureau, stockmen, mining and forest industries, railroads, county courthouses, Morman church, Idaho Education Association, AFL-CIO
Illinois	Illinois Manufacturers Association, Illinois Chamber of Commerce, coal operators, insurance companies (State Farm and Allstate), Illinois Education Association, Illinois Medical Society, AFL-CIO unions (Steelworkers), retail merchants, race tracks, Farm Bureau, *Chicago Tribune*
Indiana	AFL-CIO, Farm Bureau, Indiana State Teachers' Association, Chamber of Commerce
Kansas	Banks, power companies, pipeline companies, railroads, Farm Bureau
Maine	Big three: electric power, timber, textile and shoe manufacturing; Farm Bureau; Grange; liquor and beer lobby; horse-racing lobby; conservation groups
Maryland	Bankers, industrialists, AFL-CIO, liquor lobby
Missouri	Missouri Farmers Association, AFL-CIO, Missouri Bus and Truck Association, Teamsters, Missouri State Teachers Association, brewers
Nevada	Gambling, utilities, banks, mining, livestock, insurance, railroads
Ohio	Insurance, banking, utilities, savings and loan associations, Chamber of Commerce
Pennsylvania	Steel companies (U.S. Steel, Republic, Jones and Laughlin, Bethlehem); oil firms (Standard, Gulf, Sun, Atlantic); public utilities; service industries; Pennsylvania State Teachers Association; Welfare Rights Organization; AFL-CIO
South Dakota	Farmers Union, rural co-ops and rural electrification interests, Farm Bureau, Chamber of Commerce, banks, South Dakota Wheat Growers Association, South Dakota Stockgrowers Association, Northern States Power, Homestake Mine, liquor lobby
Utah	Utah Mining Association, Utah Manufacturers Association, Utah Industrial Council, Utah Farm Bureau Federation, Salt Lake City Chamber of Commerce, Utah Education Association, AFL-CIO, Farmers Union

TABLE 3–2

Continued

STATES IN WHICH PRESSURE GROUPS ARE MODERATELY STRONG (18) (continued)

Vermont	Farm Bureau, Associated Industries of Vermont
Virginia	Virginia Electric Power, Virginia Manufacturers Association, Chamber of Commerce, railroads
Wyoming	Wyoming Stock Growers Association, Rocky Mountain Oil and Gas Association, Farm Bureau Federation, Wyoming Education Association, Wyoming Association of Municipalities, Union Pacific Railroad, Truckers

STATES IN WHICH PRESSURE GROUPS ARE WEAK (10)

Colorado	Colorado Cattlemen's Association, Denver financial interests, oilmen, Chamber of Commerce, billboard interests, Colorado Education Association, Colorado Municipal League, AFL-CIO, Colorado Farmers Union, League of Women Voters
Connecticut	Connecticut Manufacturers Association, Insurance Lobby, Farm Bureau Federation, Grange, AFL-CIO
Massachusetts	Labor, Catholic Church, Public-utility interests, Real Estate Lobby, Associated Industries of Massachusetts, Chamber of Commerce, Insurance Companies, Massachusetts Federation of Taxpayer's Associations, race-track interests, state employees, liquor interests
Michigan	General Motors, Ford, Chrysler, American Motors, United Automobile Workers, AFL-CIO
Minnesota	Railroads Association, 3M, Dayton Hudson Corporation, Northern States Power Company, Honeywell, Northwestern Bell Telephone, banking, beer, iron mining, liquor, Minnesota Education Association, Teamsters, Minnesota Association of Commerce and Industry, AFL-CIO, Farm Bureau, Farm Union, League of Women Voters
New Jersey	Johnson and Johnson, Warner-Lambert Pharmaceuticals, Prudential Insurance, Campbell's Soup, Becton Dickinson, First National State Bank in Newark, New Jersey Manufacturers Association, Hess Oil, Garden State Race Track, New Jersey Farm Bureau, New Jersey Education Association, Chamber of Commerce, AFL-CIO
New York	Education Lobby: Board of Regents, N.Y. State Teachers' Association, N.Y. Federation of Teachers, Associated Industries of New York, Empire State Chamber of Commerce, Bankers Association, AFL-CIO, Teamsters, state medical association, Roman Catholic Church, New York City Lobby
North Dakota	Education lobby: North Dakota Education Association, PTA, School Boards, Department of Public Instruction;

TABLE 3–2
_____

Continued
_____

STATES IN WHICH PRESSURE GROUPS ARE WEAK (10) (continued)

North Dakota (continued)	Farmers Union; Farm Bureau; North Dakota Stockmen's Association; Association of Rural Cooperatives
Rhode Island	AFL-CIO, Associated Industries of Rhode Island, insurance companies, public utilities, banks, race-track associations
Wisconsin	AFL-CIO, United Auto Workers, business interests, Farmers' Union, liquor lobby, local public officials

_____

Table 3–2 is based on judicious consideration of the available evidence. It is offered with some hesitation because tabular presentation tends to "harden" the data. There are undoubtedly sins of omission and comission in this table, and the author will appreciate any correspondence on the subject. The following sources were helpful: the highly perceptive, although journalistic volumes of Neal R. Peirce still in the process of publication and to date: *The Megastates of America* (1972), *The Pacific States of America* (1972), *The Mountain States of America* (1972), *The Great Plains States of America* (1973), *The Deep South States of America* (1974), *The Border South States of America*, (1975) all published by W. W. Norton and Company, New York; John H. Fenton's two books: *Midwest Politics* (New York: Holt, Rinehart and Winston, 1966) and *Politics in the Border States* (New Orleans: The Hauser Press, 1957); Duane Lockard, *New England State Politics* (Princeton: Princeton University Press, 1959); William C. Havard, *The Changing Politics of the South* (Baton Rouge: Louisiana State University Press, 1972); Wahlke, et al., *The Legislative System*; Frank H. Jonas, *Politics in the American West* (Salt Lake City: University of Utah Press, 1969); V. O. Key, *Southern Politics in State and Nation* (New York: Knopf, 1949); and last, in an effort to find out about Delaware, Lewis A. Dexter, "Where The Elephant Fears to Dance Among the Chickens," *Human Organization* (Spring 1960–61), pp. 188–94.

is gathered on the four components of power—base, means, scope, and amount—this list will be altered. A casual inspection of Table 3–2 reveals that states with strong pressure groups are also states that do not have modern integrated cultures. In most of them, a single major economic enterprise dominates the economy: farming in Alabama and Iowa: oil in Alaska, Louisiana, Oklahoma, and Texas: coal in Kentucky and West Virginia: copper in Montana; power in New Hampshire and Oregon. The elements of a postindustrial type of economic activity are missing. Income is distributed unequally. Wealth, professionalism and urban-suburban life, —the signs of modern diversified economy—are lacking. Diversity brings a strong and active group life in which the power of one group can curtail another. The states that exhibit weak pressure groups are disproportionately middle class. They are marked by high degrees of education, literacy, and media circulation. The Gini Index (see Chapter 2, Table 2–2) indicates that states with weak pressure groups are also those in which the income is distributed most equally. Table 3–3 illustrates this discussion.

Inspection of Table 3–3 shows that in rural, sparsely populated states, a single large company, corporation, or interest group may wield great amounts of power in that state's political system. On the other hand, interest groups appear to have somewhat less impact on public officials in

TABLE 3–3

Interest Group Strength by Economic
Background

ECONOMIC STRENGTH	State Pressure-Group Strength		
	WEAK (10)	MODERATE (18)	STRONG (22)
Average Index of Integration[a]	.78 (high)	.20	−.52 (low)
Average Gini Index of Income Distribution[b]	.34 (high)	.35	.37 (low)

[a]See Table 2–1 for an explanation of this variable.
[b]See Table 2–2 and discussion in text for an explanation of this variable.

systems containing a diversified economy and large numbers of groups and organizations. As the number of competing groups increases, so do the opportunities for government officials to play the demands of one group off against those of another. In such a situation, no single group is likely to predominate.

West Virginia: A Strong Pressure-Group State

West Virginia is an example of a state run by a single industry—coal. The inability of West Virginians to better their lot is grounded in the fact that they control such a small portion of their state's wealth. The overriding interest of the outside corporations is to maximize profits from their West Virginia operations. Through inordinate influence by the coal industry and other major corporate interests on the state legislature, the tax system has beeen kept so regressive that government services are doomed to remain inadequate. Paul J. Kaufman, a former state senator, pointed out that the entire coal industry paid less in taxes to the state of West Virginia than the state collected in cigarette taxes.[17] Long overdue corporate and severence taxes have been imposed in the last few years, but their yield is a fraction of what is collected from the regressive sales tax.

The example of West Virginia demonstrates the grip a single industry can have in a "one-horse" economy. Coal is the economic lifeblood of West Virginia, but the state does not reap the benefits of its wealth. Because the economy is not diversified, no interests have arisen to compete with the giant corporations. The only hope for a challenge to the coal industry appears to lie with the United Mine Workers. The new leadership could play a leading role in elections and in changing the policies of state government. The companies have controlled the political structure from the county level on up. Under the leadership of Arnold Miller, a Coal Miners

Political Action Committee was formed in 1973. Its purpose is to lobby for specific legislation and to help candidates friendly to the union's views win office.

A single industry, corporation, or establishment can dominate the affairs of a state when, as a result of insufficient economic diversity, labor, political parties, or other interests fail to produce counter-activity. The West Virginia story could be repeated by the moneyed establishment in Texas, copper interests in Montana, oil in Louisiana, or the power companies in Oregon.

California: A Moderate Pressure-Group State

Pressure groups exercise a moderately strong, but not controlling influence in other states where (1) the former power of one interest group is challenged by other groups or an increasingly active party system, or (2) where all interests exert power on the decision makers within their areas of scope with no one interest dominating. Arizona, California, and Maine are examples of transitional states in the moderate category.

Increases in the power of both political parties accounts for the change. The following example of pressure politics in California illustrates the point. During the forties and fifties, the lobbies held sway in California. Both parties were exceedingly weak. The manufacturer's association, the oil lobby, the utilities, and the retailers were able to successfully oppose Governor Warren's budget. These were the years of *"Artie Samish,"* about whom there is more information than any other state-level lobbyist. Samish was able to keep the legislators from approving liquor and beer taxes proposed by the governor. By 1953, California had the lowest liquor tax rate among the states for which data were available. Taxes had not been raised from the original level set when prohibition was repealed 20 years before. William Buchanan estimates that the liquor industry's investment in Samish brought back several millions of dollars in tax savings.[18] Three governors also proposed tobacco taxes. But among Samish's clients was the Philip Morris Company. No tobacco tax existed in California by 1953. Samish also represented buses and race tracks. The successful pattern for them was much the same.

Strong and well-organized parties did not exist in California until recently, and thus there was no party responsibility for candidate selection or policy making. Auxiliary or volunteer party groups existed for the purpose of making endorsements. Candidates refused to identify themselves publicly with any party. Since 1960, a two-party system has been growing by leaps and bounds in California and, with it, more party responsibility for grooming and presenting candidates and policy. The new leadership of both parties has succeeded in curtailing the power of the lobbies. But the lobbyists are not in a hopeless position. The new Democratic party will need money. Since the savings and loan and insurance companies are an important fund source for them, a strong antibusiness tone to new legislation is unlikely. However, direct bribes and skulduggery on the part of lobbyists have diminished. The new lobbyists have governmental expertise that makes them more acceptable to the issue-oriented legislators. Thus, while the "third house" of lobbyists still flourishes in Sacramento, their power is checked by the growth of the parties.

Michigan, Minnesota, and Wisconsin: Pressure Groups Within Parties

All but one of the ten states in which pressure groups are weak have well-developed and strong two-party systems. The economic structures of the states are diversified, and income is distributed more evenly. This political and economic setting gives rise to another type of pressure-group activity. There are many competing groups but no "ruling elite," because none of them is large enough to dominate the others. Nor are the groups actively interested in more than a few issues among all those under consideration at any given time. In states with weak pressure-group and strong political party activity, the pressure groups are likely to align themselves with one of the parties. Connecticut, previously discussed, is an example of this form of operation. In both Massachusetts and Michigan, labor aligns itself with the Democratic party and industry with the Republicans. The parties are "built-in pressure groups." Their clientele is so aligned with, and their interests so dominantly represented by the general position of one or the other party, that they have become working partners. The close relationships between the party and its respective pressure groups pay dividends when the party controls the governorship and legislature. When the opposition takes over, this built-in relationship has difficulties.

In Michigan, the Democratic party was formed in 1947–48 by a coalition of liberal labor leaders and intellectuals. On the labor side, Walter Reuther of the U A W and August Scholle of the Committee for Industrial Organization (CIO) were the chief figures. A group of respectable liberals also cast their lot with the Democrats. The diametric opposite of the Democrats who wanted to reallocate the power, goods, and opportunities of society were the Michigan Republicans. With twin pillars of support in the automotive business and the rural hinterland, they favored low taxes, minimal government services, and the protection of private property. These circumstances promote the conflict between union and management that has been a consistent theme in Michigan politics. Major issues of public policy such as taxation, social legislation, or labor legislation are decided in consultation with automotive, labor, and management leaders within their respective parties. The United Automobile Workers contribute to the Democratic election coffers. They do so to maintain a strong bargaining position, but even then, the party maintains the machinery for contesting elections. To return to Robert Dahl's definition, the pressure groups in Michigan cannot "get B to do something he would not otherwise do." They are strong only within their respective parties.

Minnesota and Wisconsin are similar to Michigan insofar as the groups that affiliate with the Democratic and Republican parties are distinctly different. The Farmer-Laborites and Progressives of the two states cast their lot with the Democratic party which brought together farmers, laborers, immigrants, and liberals. These groups demanded positive governmental action to redress their grievances, mainly in the form of more egalitarian distribution of goods and opportunities. The Republicans were left with most of the people who felt relatively comfortable with the given distribution and who felt threatened by the demands of the urban and rural disinherited. John Fenton has proposed a provocative theory regarding the relationship between pressure groups and the type of "issue-oriented" parties described above: Parties based on clear economic differences tend to attract the pressure groups whose interests form a natural alliance. The parties aggregate and synthesize the separate goals of the interest groups into programs they hope will attract a majority of voters in an election. If a party wins an election, it then has a mandate to translate its programs into policy. In Fenton's view, if interest groups become actively involved in political parties, it facilitates the development of a closer consensual bond in society. If, on the other hand, interest groups have no political alliance, they feel free to make extreme and self-seeking demands on the parties and the government. As Fenton explains:

> ... when interest group leaders are members of political parties, they must actively participate in the aggregative and synthesizing functions of the parties. This invariably affects the policies of the interest groups and reduces the policy differences between the interest groups and the parties.[19]

Pressure Group Strength versus Party Strength

The rough outlines of a strong political party weak pressure-group theory have been painted with a broad brush. Table 3–4, which arranges the pressure groups by party strength, illustrates the broad outlines just portrayed. Party strength is measured by the strength of the governor's electoral coalition within his party. It anticipates that this electoral coalition will carry over into the governing process, thus indicating the governor's ability to convince members of his party in the legislature to formulate

TABLE 3–4

Pressure-Group Strength by Party Strength

PRESSURE-GROUP STRENGTH[b]	Party Strength[a]		
	STRONG	MODERATE	WEAK
Weak (10)	Connecticut New York Minnesota North Dakota Rhode Island Wisconsin Massachusetts Michigan Colorado	New Jersey	
Moderate (18)	Delaware South Dakota Arizona Vermont Virginia	Missouri Maine Nevada Utah California Idaho Maryland Kansas Wyoming Pennsylvania Ohio Indiana Illinois	
Strong (22)	Iowa	South Carolina Hawaii Washington Montana Nebraska West Virginia New Hampshire	Oregon Arkansas New Mexico Alaska Kentucky North Carolina Georgia Florida Texas Oklahoma Alabama Louisiana Mississippi Tennessee

[a]Party strength is measured by averaging the governors' vote percentages in the gubernatorial primaries of 1956–78. In a state with strong parties, the average primary vote received by governors-to-be was 80 to 100 percent. In states with moderately strong parties, the average primary vote received was 64 to 79 percent. In weak-party states, the governors-to-be received 35 to 63 percent of the primary vote. The reasons for using this measure of party strength will be explained more fully in the next chapter.

[b]Pressure-group strengths are estimates derived from reading the most recent state literature. This classification agrees with an earlier one by Belle Zeller in 34 out of 45 states. Political conditions in 6 out of the 11 states in which we differ (Minnesota, Wisconsin, Michigan, Arizona, Maine, and California) have changed drastically in the 25 years since her study. See Belle Zeller, ed., *American State Legislatures*, pp. 190–91.

policies that implement his program. Strong parties can control the entry of pressures into the government. With the exception of Iowa, strong state parties are able to prevail over the policy-making process. In states where the parties are moderately strong, pressure groups share the making of policy with them. In California and Maine, for instance, the parties may be gaining strength while the pressure groups are declining in influence. Interest groups in Ohio, Illinois, and Indiana have traditionally supplemented party activity. According to Fenton, party strength in these last three states is based on jobs rather than issues. The result is election battles between the "ins" and the "outs." Interest groups operate outside the parties because their concern is with issues.[20]

Interest groups are the major supplement to party activity in those states where the party machinery is inefficient in channeling their demands and translating them into policy. Typical of the weak party states are parties that are nothing but holding companies for the diverse groups that contest under the party label. Politics in those states tend to be a politics of personalities, not issues. The party as an issue-oriented organization does not exist; party labels are meaningless. Most of these states are the traditional one-party systems of the South. The Democratic Party has held its umbrella over the most diverse assortment of cliques, factions, and groups. In this situation, it is the pressure groups that govern. The major organized groups in the state control the policy because there is no party to synthesize their demands. In states with nondiversified economies, unequal distribution of income and weak political parties, the dominant pressures can control the policy output of the system. The strength of pressure groups, then, is related to both the economy of the state and the condition of the political parties. When the economy is diversified, parties are likely to be stronger than the pressure groups and control their entry into the decision-making process.[21] The relationship of activities between pressure groups and parties justifies the assertion that where parties are strong, pressures are weak or moderate; where parties are weak, pressure groups are strong enough to dominate the policy-making process.

FUNCTIONAL RELATIONSHIPS WITH POLITICAL PARTIES

Our original definition of a political party distinguished the functions of a party from those of a pressure group. Political parties are coalitions of men and women operating under a common political label to recruit, nominate, and elect candidates for public office. When in office, these parties work to enact programs that will ensure reelection. The major function of a pressure group is to attempt to influence the decisions and actions of those in public office. They do not nominate their own candidates or seek responsibility for the mangement of government. Their interest is the politics of policy. Pressure groups are concerned with what the government does either to help or harm their membership.

We have seen that the type of party system defines the activities of the pressure groups within it. At one extreme, the organized group pursues its objectives in dealing with those elected to public office unencumbered by the political party structure, which is too weak to challenge its efforts. At the other extreme, organized groups tend to operate in the closest collaboration with one or the other party. Between these two extremes are groups approaching one or the other poles on the scale. No single pressure or combination of pressure groups has replaced the party in mobilizing votes. Pressure groups spend time and money trying to influence the nomination and election of candidates for public office, but they do not run people under their own banner. Generally, parties make commitments on broad questions of public policy. Pressure groups have the task of formulating and supporting recommendations in specific areas of government action. These may include the concerns of a limited number of persons, technical matters, or the details of government policy and action as they affect particular interests. Some of these matters are so minute that the parties cannot be expected to take a stand on them. For instance, V. O. Key reports the example of the American Beekeeping Federation opposing the "discriminatory part of the proposed prune juice order that prevents honey from being used as an added ingredient."[22] No one would fault either the Democrats or Republicans for not taking a stand on such a matter.

There are many points where pressure groups try to influence the activity of a political party as it goes about its work of nominating, electing, and governing. What follows are descriptions of the methods used to "win" political parties or, more explicitly, the men and women who seek office and govern in the name of the party. This recognizes, of course, that a group's success or failure to influence will depend on the type of party system and the assets of the group.

The Party Platform

The party platform is hardly an accurate indication of future performance. A governor can make few promises if he doesn't have the votes in the legislature to put them into effect. The degree to which he can carry out his promises depends on the strength of his political party. After extensive correspondence with governors, I am convinced that they do indeed view the platform as a serious declaration of policy and present bills to the legislature to implement it. But the party platform is more than a significant declaration of policy; it serves as a means of forging a coalition of leaders, factions and groups that can elect a governor. From the standpoint of pressure groups, the significance of preparing a platform lies in their ability to determine whether they will have access to the elected party. Interest groups will seek to insert planks that are as explicit as possible. They realize that settlement of the issues they are concerned with will take place in the governing process, but they want the assurance of having a foot in the door.

Integration of pressure groups into the political system is a function of the parties. Where parties are weak, pressure groups strive to walk a line between them. Weak parties are not responsible for a program, so the pressures must begin again once either is elected to office. In the case of one-party states (typical of weak party systems), the pressure groups wait until the primaries are over and a candidate has been selected. Then they will apply their influence on him to draft a favorable platform. Since the candidate represents the dominant faction and is certain to be elected, the primacy of the pressure group's demands is assured.

In the moderate-to-strong party systems, the policy orientations of each party divide the major pressure groups into two clusters. In Massachusetts, for example:

> Closely allied with the Republican Party are the public-utility interests, the real estate lobby, the Associated Industries of Massachusetts (the local version of the NAM), the Chamber of Commerce, the insurance companies, and the Massachusetts Federation of Taxpayer's Associations. All these groups have easy access to the leaders of the Republican Party. Through shared opinions, campaign contributions, and at times common business connections, the lobbyists for these groups know they can present their arguments to attentive ears within "their" party, even as labor has similar access to the Democrats.[23]

The claim is not that either party commits itself unreservedly to its camp followers among the pressure groups. Given the drift of policy in either party in moderate or strong party systems, party platforms will attract some groups and repel others. Occasionally, partisan or ideological differences may develop between groups with similar economic concerns. For example, the policy differences between the Farmer's Union and the Farm Bureau Federation are wider than the economic circumstances of their membership. The Farm Bureau has a long-standing conservative and Republican orientation. In the one-party states, it is a powerful pressure group; in two-party states, it aligns itself with the Republican Party and is less powerful. The Farmers' Union attracts a membership tinged with an old populist verve. Its liberal views align most naturally with the Democratic party. A pressure group's association with a particular party's ideological platform does not necessarily mean party adoption of that group's program; the platform may be altered or merged to suit the broader objectives of the party.

Nominations

Pressure groups inevitably have a stake in who will occupy the offices to which they want access. Elective positions determine policy and fill important appointive offices. Nominations, whether by primary or convention, occur under the umbrella of the political party. Pressure groups may actually promote a candidate for nomination, or they may induce their members to vote in the primaries for those whose records, backgrounds, or promises best meet the claims of the group.

In the first case, a group may promote the fortunes of an aspirant through the party machinery, be it a primary, caucus, or convention—to secure organizational support or, where that is nonexistent, to gain the advantages of the party label. Where two well-organized parties exist, groups maneuver among rival factions or negotiate with the dominant faction of each. A legislator from a suburban Republican district who consistently supports labor measures has no right to be astonished if he faces primary opposition financed by business interests. Where party ties are not persistent, but loose and temporary, the interest group itself may provide the organization and financial effort. The Farm Bureau, for example, succeeded in nominating and electing its candidate to the lieutenant governorship of Alabama in 1970. In many legislative districts, the interest groups may serve as party for a candidate. John Kingdon investigated the supporting coalitions of candidates for the state legislature in Wisconsin. He found that Democratic candidates tend to obtain compaign funds directly from an interest group (organized labor), whereas Republican contributors were more likely to channel their funds (business and professional) through the party organization.[24]

In the second case, a group may promote the fortunes of those who are most acceptable in the primary. This effort may be open where specific endorsements are made, or it may be more concealed. The latter usually involves listing the qualifications and records of candidates and then relying on its members to vote in accordance with the group's policies. Specific endorsements are not made. The group may also try to increase voter registration or primary voting among its supporters. Whether a group's support of a candidate is given openly or in a disguised fashion will depend on its acceptability to the public. If a group's prestige is not high, open campaigning may harm its candidate. Race track or gambling interests are deeply concerned with nominations in many states, but their efforts are largely behind the scenes. Campaign contributions and speakers' bureaus are also methods used to help the favored nominees. This can account for the influence of organized labor in the nomination process.

In some jurisdictions, a prestigious interest group may establish the notion that certain elective positions are its proper concern. Thus, in many states or localities having an elected judiciary, the bar association is widely regarded as entitled to a say in the nomination of judicial candidates. The special relationship between bench and bar may give the latter an advantage in the nomination of judges.

Our knowledge of the nomination process is too limited to permit more than speculation at this point. From the interest groups' perspective, entering the nomination process provides another point of access to the decision makers. Whether or not they can enter the nomination process depends primarily on the type of party operation. If it is strong, the group may have built-in access to the leadership coalition. If the party system is weak, groups may substitute for party functions and run candidates for the nomination in an effort to capture the party label. The matter of most importance to the group is access. This may come through the party leadership or by individual efforts on behalf of a nominee who, it is hoped, will win the next election.

Elections

The importance of a nominee lies in his ability to get elected. An interest group does not desire access to a person but to a position that commands ultimate decision-making power. More interest groups participate in the election stage than in the nomination stage because the danger of antagonizing another faction within the party is minimized; the fight for the nomination is over and the field is limited to two contestants for the office. Groups vary in their orientation to political campaigns. We discussed the tendency for certain major interests representing labor, management, and farming to cluster about each party. These groups participate in the campaigns of the party congenial to them. They do, however, try to avoid complete identification with any one political faction. Duane Lockard reported that the state CIO president in Rhode Island, a state where labor support counts in elections, said organized labor should not be too tightly bound to any party. Mr. Policastro granted that labor's ties with the Democrats had been strong, but this was so "because the labor movement generally has been helped much by the Democrats." Labor would be "happy" to endorse any "truly liberal" Republican who ran, he said. But Christopher Del Sesto, the Republican gubernatorial nominee, "was not acceptable to the CIO because Mr. Del Sesto had made some 'nasty cracks' about organized labor during the years he served as state OPA Director."[25] The reasons behind Mr. Policastro's remarks lay in the legislative session just past. He had tried to win the support of three or four Republican Senators for a minimum-wage bill by promising them CIO support in November. [26] If the marginal votes of the opposite party are crucial, it pays a pressure group to maintain cordial relations, if not wholehearted support.

There are many groups, however, that cannot engage in campaigns becase they might offend their own members or their public image. Widespread attitudes toward the medical profession, for instance, probably would not permit that body to engage in open electoral activity on an extreme scale: Doctors aren't expected to get up on soap boxes. Nonprofit or educational groups that enjoy tax exemptions are usually reluctant to jeoparidize that privileged status by engaging in political activities.

In spite of internal restrictions on the partisan activity of groups, it is clear that a very large number do participate in election campaigns. This support may come in the form of campaign contributions, volunteer workers to disperse materials and get voters to the polls, public endorsements, and other forms of aid. Pressure groups make such forms of support available to candidates who are clearly in sympathy with their goals. They may also direct their efforts toward the defeat of a candidate they find particularly objectionable.

PUBLICITY The simplest and most common form of group participation in elections is publicizing the political records of incumbent candidates for their members and sympathizers. If the candidate is a legislator, this means a tabulation of his recorded votes on measures considered important by the group leaders. This is standard procedure by the AFL-CIO, the National Association of Manufacturers, and the League of Women Voters. Candidates may be asked to commit themselves on governmental policies in which the group is interested. Such requests put the candidate on the spot when the results are made public.

Another contribution a group may make to the campaign of a favored candidate is the provision of their highly valuable membership and mailing lists. These may be used to solicit money and votes. Groups may permit their meetings to become opportunities for candidates to appear and become known both to those present and to the newspaper reader. They might offer their meeting halls with little or no charge. These tactics reveal that money is not the only way groups can contribute to the election campaign of a friendly candidate.

MONEY Campaign contributions, gifts, or loans from group members to a candidate are welcomed by those who are rarely able to finance campaigns out of their own pockets. Although some states have moved toward public financing through various tax incentives in recent years, candidates still have to procure most of their campaign funds. Campaigns are expensive, and limitations on expenditures are not permitted by virtue of the Supreme Court decision in January, 1976. To what extent and in what amounts organized interest groups provide money to aid candidates' campaigns has only recently been made available through a series of disclosure laws. These were passed by state legislatures feeling the reverberations of the Watergate scandal. By December 1976, campaign finance disclosure statutes were law in all 50 states. The trend was to tighten up the disclosure requirements a great deal. and to mandate lower disclosure ceilings.[27]

It is still early to analyze the results of new legislation. Partisan differences are revealed by the traditional sources of money for each party. Republicans frequently receive large gifts from individuals through the party structure. It can be assumed, however, that many of the contributions nominally coming from individuals actually represent groups with which they are affiliated. This is especially true of corporations. Democrats rely on political committee activities to raise most of their money. Because of their different sources of funding, Democratic and Republican reformers have different views regarding setting limits on campaign contributions. Republicans want to limit the activity of political committees, such as the AFL–CIO's Committee on Political Education (COPE), by requiring low disclosure floors. Democrats, on the other hand, favor lower individual-donation ceilings and higher limits on donations from union and other political fund-raising committees. They argue that permitting small givers to aggregate their money encourages some contributors who otherwise would not have donated. Opponents of pooling donations contend that committees are political interest groups that should be allowed to function but not contribute funds. In Michigan, for example, it was estimated that 64 percent of all money donated to the Democratic State Central Committee and directly to statewide candidates in 1948 came from United Auto Workers and other CIO-union funds.[28]

Three states moved to limit the activities of political committees in 1974: California, Connecticut, and Wyoming. In Connecticut and Wyoming, the laws were passed by Republican legislatures. In the case of Connecticut, the limitation was repealed by the new Democratic majority in 1975. In Wyoming, the law required political committees to use only those funds collected from members living in the candidate's district. Both the Wyoming Education Association and the AFL-CIO brought suit, but the law was upheld by a Cheyenne court. In the case of U. S. Representative Teno Roncalio (D), the law was affecting his re-election campaign "harshly and adversely." He estimated that by late July he had returned between $5,000 and $6,000 in contributions from labor and education groups, thus "crippling" his fund-raising efforts. His opponent, State Senator Tom Strook, was a Casper oil leasing executive with supporters from Wyoming's oil industry who donated as individuals.[29]

What these accounts reveal is that candidates in states where a two-party system exists depend on contributions from groups who are attuned to the policy orientations of the party. It appears to be a system of mutual benefit: financial support for access to governmental decision making. Since the two political parties are generally supported by very different coalitions, whichever party gains control of the governmental machinery becomes important.

If we count both individuals and committees, monetary support comes from a very small proportion of the electorate in any constituency. The rank-and-file voters do not contribute significantly. It is important to inquire into the meaning these donations have for the relationship between candidates and the few who supply money. The easiest assumption is that the campaign contribution is a "bribe" to obtain legislative or administrative policy advantage. Very simply, it's a way for those with means to protect their interests.

In the Kingdon study of Wisconsin candidates for office, it was clear the rivals of both political parties perceived their supporting coalitions very differently. Democrats have support from labor but not from business and professional groups; Republicans tend to have the reverse. Distinctly different groups of people will have the share of influence on governmental policy depending on which party wins the election. Influence can only be successful when a decision maker is willing to listen. A man will probably listen more readily to those who helped put him into office than those who opposed him. This does not necessarily mean that either party is the "pawn" of the groups that back the party's candidate, but simply that the politician is more likely to be available to those who actively support him. Kingdon discovered that most politicians prefer to believe they are relatively free of their coalition of supporters and able to exercise their independent judgment in making public policy. Their supporters expect something of them in a general sense, but the parameters of their decision-making alternatives remain relatively open. Their coalition probably helps set the boundaries within which they must make their decision, and helps prescribe the general path which they must follow.[30] Several respondents in the study indicated that Democrats would choose the same policy direction, organized labor or not. Indeed, labor was not seen by candidates to "expect" anything in return for support more than any other group, perhaps because, as one politician put it, "They never had to ask."[31] Henry Teune confirmed the fact that policy orientations of a political party draw ideologically supportive groups. Teune found that legislative candidates in Indiana, who have the backing of a strong party organization and substantial support in the public's voting habits, are also favorably inclined toward interest groups. There is a strong relationship between commitment to the political party and favorable attitudes toward interest groups.[32] The legislator is receptive to interest groups as an integral part of his or her political world. It represents a fusion of interest groups with party organization.

MOBILIZING THE VOTE   The third type of group participation in election campaigns—getting out the vote—cannot be clearly distinguished from the other two. Contributions of time to get out the vote can be equated to contributions of money. While all groups want to maximize the vote for a favored candidate, not all will attempt the task of ringing doorbells and getting voters to the polls. Truman hypothesized that the size and distribution of a group's membership determines how active a role the group will play in getting people to vote. As an example, the National Association of Manufacturers has a scattered membership. Its organizational pattern during elections is to contribute money to party committees and satellite groups, and not for its members to pound the pavements. This latter type of activity is uncharacteristic of local N.A.M. members. In contrast, the AFL-CIO can count on its large, geographically clustered membership to be of maximum advantage to candidates. Local canvassing committees conduct registration campaigns, ring doorbells, provide transportation to the polls, and supply many other monotonous but important services.

A variety of groups have worked to get voters to the polls for state offices. The American Legion has done so especially when issues dear to the heart of veterans have been at stake. Farm Bureaus have also provided this service when farm issues have been in question. Artie Samish, the famous California lobbyist of the 1940's, used his liquor lobby as a political machine in the weak party system which existed in California at the time. The Lobby had a corps of workers throughout the state on the staffs of retail liquor dealers. Since there was a need for anonymity, tavern owners and package dealers could not engage in visible campaigning. In this respect, Samish's organization resembled a machine, not a party.[33]

The effect of interest-group activity on the outcome of elections is not easily determined. As long as the candidate feels beholden to a group that has supported him with time and money, the group's major objective has been met. When a group has access to the decision-making circles of government, the campaign effort has been successful. Research linking political candidates and their elective coalitions indicates that successful candidates whose elections are not in doubt are especially receptive to groups, make use of their efforts, and grant them access to the governing process. The nature of a political party conditions the kind of election activity engaged in by the pressure group. In the California party system of the 1940s, powerful liquor interests gained access by supporting candidates who would vote for their limited range of legislation. In a two-party system where each party has strong policy commitments, candidates seek out groups with similar policy orientations. When an alliance with labor or business can provide the needs of their campaign effort, candidates do not have to depend on the hidden support of disapproved lobbies.

ACCESS TO THE INSTITUTIONS OF GOVERNMENT

Both political parties and pressure groups provide the link between citizens and their government. In states where parties are weak, segments of people are represented by narrow pressure groups. In about one-third of the states where parties are strong, no such power is conferred on lesser forms of organization; the groups align themselves with the party whose interests are of mutual advantage. It is apparent that in nearly two-thirds of the United States, state politics does not provide the coherence of policy strong party systems can provide. In these states, politics minimizes the voices of significant elements of the population. Many issues are settled without the controversy a strong party system could produce. In the moderate to weak party systems where pressures are strong, the government's structure helps determine the strategies employed by interest groups. Decision-making authority is widely dispersed. This results in many points of access for groups to influence decisions. The separation of powers, bicameralism, the plural executive, and the existence of a plethora of boards and commissions all shape the political system in such a way that power is dispersed. Groups find it advantageous to try to affect legislative decisions, gubernatorial appointments, agency policy, the operation of boards and commissions, and court decisions. In the following sections, the access and influence of pressure groups will be considered in the context of the institutions of state government.

The State Legislature

Access to the legislature is important to most groups because the chance to promote or block legislation is vital to their interests. Depending on their resources and the skill with which they use them, groups gain access with different degrees of success. However, there are many other factors which also affect access. We will turn attention to these first.

The formal structural arrangements within government benefit or burden access to the decision-making process. The separation of powers, especially between the legislative and executive branches with their accompanying system of checks and balances, ensures that effective access to one does not guarantee effective access to the other. The constituencies of the governor and the legislator are different. The governor represents the whole state and must consider this in planning his next move. The legislator represents a small portion of the state and must please it to be reelected. The only unifying influence here is that of the political party. If a party is able to elect the governor and a majority of the legislature in a moderately competitive system, access to the government is gained through the leaders of that party. Discipline provides the power to govern because it controls access to the decision-making points of government. In a situation where the party is an umbrella for factions in both branches, there is no stability; different groups achieve power over different points of decision making. When Duane Lockard spoke of New Hampshire's legislature (the General Court) and the influence of outside interests, he said this body of 400 people is not organized to function as a policy-making group. They are the medium through which decisions are made but rarely are they the decision-makers.[34] The strongest pressures in New Hampshire come from race tracks, public utilities, and lumber/paper manufacturing interests. The party organization is weak and cannot discipline its members.

LEGISLATIVE LEADERS Every legislature has a system for setting the order of business and ensuring that debate takes place according to established procedures. The speaker of the house and the president of the senate are the most powerful positions within their respective chambers. If a pressure group can ensure that these leaders are friendly to its interests, it has gained much. The Alabama Farm Bureau succeeded in electing the lieutenant governor who became presiding officer of the senate. As a result, they obtained the most powerful committee chairmanships.[35] In the states where there is a strong party leadership, the party leaders determine who will be appointed committee chairmen. In Arizona, where parties are fairly strong, faction membership is the principal criterion used for making committee assignments. When "liberal" Democrats are in a majority, the "minority" or "conservative" faction in the party is discriminated against, at times receiving no assignments to major committees.[36] Conservative Democrats in Arizona are to the right of Republicans on many issues. The complicated and technical rules have an important effect on access. If a speaker is friendly, he or she may be able to use the procedures to see that legislation is advanced or sent back to committees. If the pressure group has hired a clever lobbyist, he may know how to manipulate the procedures to serve his ends.

LEGISLATIVE COMMITTEES A thorough discussion of legislative committees will be given in chapter 5. However, it is necessary at this point to mention how important they are to the success or failure of legislation. In all but a handful of states (those with joint committees), each legislative chamber has a number of standing committees. These committees consider legislation and report it out of committee for the consideration of the legislative body. Refusal to report a bill out of committee usually dooms the proposal. Both houses generally follow the recommendations of their committees for two reasons: (1) the members do not have the time to consider the legislation as thoroughly as the committee, and (2) if the bill is an important piece of legislation, the party may have demanded their support or opposition. In some states, committees are managed by chairmen who owe their allegiance to the legislative leaders and the governor. In this case, pressure groups must deal with the party leaders. In weak party states, committees are more like their congressional counterparts, and exert great power over the content and form of the legislation. Access to the committee chairmen becomes vital to a pressure group. Until recently (1965), Florida's conservative leadership within the Democratic Party (The Pork-Choppers) stacked the committees with special-interest legislators. Senator Fred Karl recalls that a majority of the banking committee, including its chairman, were bankers; the pari-mutual committee was made up of racing enthusiasts. The insurance, real estate, and citrus committees had similar makeups. In fact, before announcing committee assignments, the leadership often submitted a list to the major lobbyists for approval. Any real regulation of the banks, insurance companies, or liquor industry, state tax on corporate income or real estate, severance tax on oil or mining companies, or effective conservation or consumer-protection measures became literally impossible.[37]

The formal structure of a legislature thus affects the points of access which pressure groups must have if they are to achieve power. In some, the formal structure is integrated by the party's leadership and access to the rules and committees is through the party structure. Most likely, however, in a majority of legislatures the formal structure will be indicative of the existing power structure. Thus pressure groups will exert their influence on the committees of both chambers where the effective decision-making occurs. The formal structure, therefore, affords advantages to some groups and handicaps to others.

INFORMATION NEEDS   There are other aspects of the legislative process which create the advantage of access to pressure groups. These relate to the information needs of the legislators themselves. They may want to know the advantages and costs of environmental legislation, for instance. If a bill to prevent non-returnable bottles will mean the loss of jobs in a legislator's district, he may want to compare the effects of this result with the costs of converting to the heavier duty, returnable kind.

Both labor and the environmentalists can provide him with this technical information. He must evaluate it, make a choice and then explain his action to his constituents. The more reliable and accurate the information is, the more access a pressure group will have. If it provides the legislator with credible information, future access is guaranteed. This adds confirmation to the finding that secure and long-term legislators tend to favor the acitivites of pressure groups more than those who are new at the game.

Another type of information pressure groups can supply is more strategic; it has to do with coalitions which favor or oppose particular legislation. This takes skill, and only an experienced legislator can judge the credibility of a group wich presents this information to him. If, over time, the group can accurately judge the line-up on issues of such importance, the legislator will accept and depend on its advice. In situations where legislation is controlled by neither the party nor the governor, the legislator is free to decide on his own. Occasionally, the party takes a "hands off" policy on sensitive social issues such as abortion legislation. Similarly, the legislator will need substantive information and a realistic assessment of the sensitivities of his district in order to make his decision.

The Techniques of Lobbyists

A "lobby" is an interchangeable term for a pressure group because the legislature has traditionally been its major focus of attention. To lobby is to communicate views or policy matters to government officials. Power involves both resources and the means of using these resources. Lobbying is a method of utilizing the resources of a group to achieve its ends. Not all organizations are of equal size or possess equal resources. Hence, they do not use the same techniques in the lobbying process.

Some smaller organizations wage their campaigns at a distance— through calls, telegrams, and the mails. Powerful interest groups include a professional lobbyist (or legislative agent) to represent their views personally to government officials. Lobbying is a profession, and a lobbyist is considered indispensable if a group is to have its point of view represented effectively. If a group has resources as well as access, a skillful lobbyist can employ these to his advantage. The value of a lobbyist increases year after year as he becomes known and trusted.

REGULATION OF LOBBYING   Lobbying is the most regulated area of interest group activity. Table 3-5 summarizes the regulation requirements in the states. By 1976, all states required regulation of lobbyists by statute and made information on registration available to the public. All but seven make lobbyists report their expenditures. It would appear from Table 3-5 that states with stricter requrements have weaker pressure groups. They require pressure groups to report more frequently and impose stronger penalties for failure to do so.

The lobbying regulations are loose and do not define the extent of lobbying that takes place; nor are the laws applied uniformly. In 1973–74, California passed a law prohibiting registered lobbyists from making political contributions. But the officers of corporations are not lobbyists, even though they make phone calls to members of the house and senate on crucial issues. To summarize, the state lobbying laws do not accurately reflect the extent of lobbying. Even an accurate set of facts with respect to the activities and expenditures of lobbyists, however, would not reveal

TABLE 3–5

Percent of States with Specific Lobbying
Regulations by Pressure-Group Strength

PRESSURE-GROUP STRENGTH[a]	FREQUENT REPORTING (QUARTERLY OR MORE OFTEN)	EXPENDITURES REPORTED	STRONG PENALTIES FOR NONCOMPLIANCE
Weak (10)	50%	90%	30%
Moderate (18)	33	89	22
Strong (22)	36	82	18

[a] The states in each pressure-group strength category are the same as those identified in Table 3–4.
Source: Data used with permission of The Council of State Governments, *The Book of the States, 1978–1979*, Vol. 22, (Lexington, Ky.: Council of State Governments, 1978), pp. 76–77.

their real power. Access, so vitally important to a lobbyist, cannot be captured by statistics. Money spent or salaries paid do not indicate successful lobbying efforts. An organization of consumers, for instance, spends little money but swings considerable weight. Probably the major advantage to be gained from lobby registration is disclosure and, hence, public confidence. Lobbying would continue much as before, but the public could, if it chose, find out the extent of the effort.

THE NEW LEGISLATORS A recent article in the *Harvard Business Review* warned corporate government that real power now rests in state government; business must engage in energetic, better-organized and better-planned lobbying, or legislation adverse to their interests will become prevalent. "A lot has changed since the days when smoke-filled cars rattled toward state capitals, their occupants clutching cash-filled black bags to 'do a little business' with the legislature. Gone are the days when lobbyists set up card tables in the rear of the house chamber in Wyoming, for example, to pay for votes as they were cast. In the 1890's, when the states were the focus of business concern, a state lawmaker was worth as much as $20 in gold per vote."[38] The article continues with a description of the new legislator:

> The new legislators tend to be activists, independent thinkers, and strong individuals. They are consumer-and-ecology minded. While not necessarily antibusiness, they are certainly not business-oriented. They share neither the perspective nor the value judgments that come from knowing how to read a P & L statement and examine a balance sheet. Most have never been called on to weigh the costs and benefits of economic activities in terms of the community's livlihood, and they have only hazy notions about alternatives to many business practices which they comprehend little and appreciate even less. They are prone to view with disfavor proposals from old-style lobbyists representing business.[39]

The authors say even the "old guard" legislators are changing; they will no longer respond to the old-style means of communicating characterized by logrolling and exchanging favors.[40] This undermines the traditional propriety of voting with friends and against established enemies. Old-style lobbying is obsolete. The new legislators welcome lunches, banquets, small favors, and year-round remembrances as tokens of civility, but not as techniques of influence. According to Haley and Kiss, this makes the job of lobbying more difficult than ever before. They see the new lobbying efforts centered in sound research and professional expertise. State legislators lack well-staffed committees and good research services. The lobbyist can be a critical resource for them. His effectiveness depends on his degree of specialization and his ability to impart precise information, even on technical matters. The legislator must be able to see the relationship between his issue and the needs and demands of society.

This advice "from the horse's mouth" illustrates the new techinques of lobbyists as they adjust to the changed coalitions of the seventies. It does not apply to all states—especially those in which political parties are weak and the logrolling mentioned above may be the only organized effort which permits legislation to be passed. However, the tone in the *Harvard Business Review* article presents lobbying in a far different light form the rough dictum on lobbyists attributed to Jesse Unruh. As Speaker of the California Assembly, Unruh achieved renown for his efforts to professionalize the legislative process: "If you can't take their money, drink their booze, screw their women, and look them in the eye and vote against them, you don't belong here."[41]

NEW TECHNIQUES   The practical advice offered by both of the above sources is confirmed by Harmon Zeigler and Michael Baer in their careful study of lobbying in four states. Considering lobbying as interaction between legislators and lobbyists, the writers research this reciprocal relationship in an attempt to discover its nature and effect. Direct communications involving personal presentation of arguments, research results, and testimony at committee hearings were perceived by legislators and lobbyists to be the most effective forms of influence. Least effective according to both groups were such means as entertaining legislators, giving a party, giving or withholding campaign contributions, and bribery.[42] Of the four states studied, only Massachusetts had a strong party system. Zeigler and Baer discovered that lobbyists tend to concentrate their efforts on the leadership in that state, although there was no indication that the leaders were unduly influenced by this effort. In the strong lobby-weak party state of Oregon, the average legislator turned to the lobbyist more frequently than the leaders for information.[43]

No matter what the lobbying effect is, and this is difficult to measure, a substantial portion of the interchange between legislators and lobbyists takes place at committee hearings. A committee hearing is the most important source of information for legislators. Lobbyists flock to committee rooms, the focal point of their contact with legislators. However, if they rely solely on testimony as a means of communicating, they may not find the results as satisfying. The object of supplementary communication is to make formal testimony credible. Lobbyists believe their testimony will be better received if the committee members know them and have been given some personal summary of their statements. Informal group meetings—coffee breaks, breakfasts, corridor chats—are the most effective way lobbyists have of making themselves known before the committee hearings. One lobbyist expressed himself this way:

> If you walk into a committee hearing and nobody knows who you are, your testimony is not likely to make much difference. If you have to spend a lot of time explaining who you are, who you represent, why you are here, and so forth, everybody gets bored. If they are not familiar with the organization you represent, they are likely to consider you as some kind of interloper. So what you have to do is to cultivate their friendship long in advance of the actual hearing. As soon as I know who will be on the committee, even before the first meeting is held, I make certain that they have at least met me. Since you frequently have to deal with freshmen who have never seen you or heard of you, this can be a pretty difficult job.[44]

ALLIANCES AND LOGROLLING In states with weak political parties, mutual assistance of pressure groups provides a means of forging a leadership structure. Two principal forms of mutual assistance among pressure groups are alliances and logrolling, although at times they are not separate. The alliance involves development of a common strategy among several groups in pursuit of a policy that is substantively related to the interests of each. An act of a legislature may, in reality, be only the ratification of an agreement negotiated by group representatives interested in the policy. In Washington, where parties are moderately weak and there is no discipline in party caucuses, interest groups are enormously important. Peirce reports an article that appeared in the *Seattle Post-Intelligencer* that claimed Washington's state legislators pay less heed to the poor and minority groups than to the unions and industry. "Highway interests—oil, asphalt, contractors, car builders—have the run of the place. Urban mass transit interests barely have a foot in the door."[45] We don't know how often lawmaking occurs by negotiated alliance, but it's much more likely when political mechanisms don't exist for forming coalitions of like-minded legislators. Zeigler and Baer reported an example of logrolling in the 1965 legislative session in Oregon. An amendment to the constitution prohibiting public employees from serving in the legislature was being considered. Labor, believing that public employees were generally more sympathetic to its cause than were legislators with business or professional backgrounds, opposed the amendment. When they discovered that a crucial number of the members of the Constitutional Revision Committee were prepared to support it, the labor lobbyists asked the private power, trucking, and insurance lobbies for their help in defeating the amendment. None of these businesses had any position on the amendment and agreed to help. Zeigler claims that the business lobby helped labor without anticipating any specific exchange of favors because their interests are so different.[46] This account illustrates at least one-half of the concept of logrolling—supporting a proposal is not related to the group's interests. Perhaps the business lobby anticipated that on some future day it could cash in its credit.

PUBLIC OPINION   Pressure groups try to influence the content of public opinion and therefore try to exert indirect pressure on legislators. Since his district's votes are most important to the legislator because it ensures his continuance in office, he must pay attention to such efforts. Public utilities use the mass media to convince voters of their critical role in providing valuable services. Farmers, insurance companies, Chambers of Commerce, teachers, and laborers try to create a climate of public opinion that is favorable. Andrew Hacker's account of the struggle between the railroads and truckers in Pennsylvania illustrates the power of an organization that has money to spend on public relations (railroads) versus the power of an organization which has votes (truckers). The railroads, organized under the Eastern Railroads Conference, hired a public relations firm to create favorable public opinion. They believed that activating as many strong and agressive groups as possible to block the truckers would make the most effective campaign. The plan was to enlist the support of motorists who were outraged by all the road hazards, taxpayers' associations who do not want to pick up the tab for damaged roads, and other similar groups. The campaign was essentially negative: anti-truck. While eliciting the support of the Grange and the Pennsylvania State Association of Township supervisors, the railroads remained shrouded in the background. Mass media were used to reach unaffiliated members of the community. For many years, public relations firms have been doing political work; their services are particularly suited to business firms, which are usually unable to directly influence public opinion on legislation.[47]

Several conclusions can be drawn from this discussion of the lobbying effect on the legislative process. Where parties are strong, the effects of lobbying are contained by the party leadership. In this case, representatives from interest groups deal directly with the leaders and may be able to influence their actions. But lobbyists are just as likely to be used by the leaders as they are to use them. In weak party states, alliances and logrolling take the place of party-inspired coalitions: Lobbyists can be effective. In either case, the power of a lobby is achieved primarily by its resources, whether economic power or votes. The work of skillful lobbyists will maximize this power to the group's advantage by lubricating the flow of communication. The skills of lobbyists are without value unless the group has resources. Even with resources, the group's power is curtailed and limited by the strength of the political party.

The Executive Branch

REGULATORY AND CLIENT-ORIENTED AGENCIES   The passage of favorable legislation may be an important focus of pressure group activity, but equally important are the continuing relationships with the administrative agencies of government. After legislation is passed, the execution of the act falls to the hands of an administrative agency. A group may threaten, encourage, or aid an agency in its attempt to get favorable treatment. With the growing complexity of government, legislative bodies have had to delegate authority to administrative agencies to make rules and regulations. An example would be the creation of a licensing board to regulate insurance operations or public utilities. This procedure involves the creation of a new set of rules for the protection of society. Licensing boards concerned with hairdressers or real estate salesmen are intended (or at least proclaimed) to protect the public by demanding high standards. These boards are often taken over by the very profession they are suppposed to regulate; the regulations may become meaningless or the licensing standards impossible for outsiders to meet. An independent public utilities commission may overlook the public welfare in its favoritism toward the utilities it in fact represents.

When the legislature places a policy-determining agency outside the control of the governor or its own body, if often throws control into the hands of the special interests, which are its clients. The Farm Bureau wants a state's extension service under its control, not subject to the general control of the governor or legislature. Teachers, as another example, may feel that the education department should be sacrosanct and untouchable by "political" hands altogether. Clientele groups not only want their agencies separate; they also want their money separate. It has taken massive efforts to pry gasoline tax revenues away from traditional highway usage and divert a portion of them to mass transportation. This is because highway interests are more organized than the users of public transportation. Each group identifies itself with the public interest. They believe they can best ensure proper consideration of the public's affairs by keeping the agency and the funds "independent"—meaning independent of everyone but the particular interest invloved.

A typical pattern of state administration is the multiplicity of elective offices. Although there is considerable variety among the states, most of their ballots have long lists of offices to be filled by direct choice of the electorate. At last count, Oklahoma, North Carolina, Mississippi, and North Dakota led the list with 10 agencies headed by elective officials. They are closely followed by Louisana (9) and Georgia (9).[48] In fact, most of the states have at least five elected officers: governor, lieutenant governor, secretary of state, attorney general, and treasurer. Others may include the auditors and the directors of education, agriculture and labor. The multiplicity of elected offices stems from the notion that people should have the greatest possible degree of participation in their own government. The move toward reform has met with resistance from pressure groups who have established preferential positions for themselves in state government. The prosepect of appointment and removal powers in the hands of the governor is a serious threat. The multiplicity of executive offices is a guarantee of the governor's inability to require conformity with his policy. It is unlikely that all the different offices will be of the governor's party or faction. The obscurity of many offices allows interest groups with large constituencies to elect their own candidate as administrator.

Before the Florida legislature reorganized the executive branch in 1969 and gave the governor power over several major departments, the elective cabinet had extraordinary power. Its members were not only elected directly, but had a right of succession (which the governor lacked until 1969). Cabinet officials also sat ex-officio on many boards and commissions. Some called it the "seven governor" system because the six other elected officers—secretary of state, attorney general, comptroller, state treasurer, superintendent of public instruction, and commissioner of agriculture—could and did build their own independent political bases. They served an average of 12 years and knew the bureaucracy and legislature better than the average governor. The system was tailor-made for entrenchment of special interests. The comptroller was often supported by the banks in election campaigns and was thus indebted to those he was supposed to control. The same was true of the state treasurer with respect to the insurance industry, the attorney general with the bar, and the agriculture commissioner with respect to big farming interests. The reorganization did not abolish the cabinet but it succeeded in giving the governor more power to control it.[49]

ADVISORY BOARDS   Grant McConnell, author of *Private Power and American Democracy,* is concerned about the extensive use of boards and other devices to make or advise on policy for administrative agencies. Despite their diversity, they have one common feature: They limit the responsiveness of policy to the large constituency represented by the governor. A common pattern is for a board to be chosen from members of a trade or industry—sometimes even by recognized units of the trade or industry.

These individuals will advise or make policy for the state department or agency charged with that responsibility for the area involved. Often the board is able to impose its policies on the line administrators. McConnell claims, "In the long run only a strong governor can protect the strong-willed and independent line administrators, and strong governors are not common in the American system.".[50]

The power of pressure groups to influence policy is made easier by the multiple access points in the administration of state governments. However, this group power can be hemmed in by an equally powerful or determined governor backed by legislators who are responsive to his policy requests. Funds for the agency can be cut if it does not cooperate with the governor, or its powers may be thwarted by a reorganization plan. If the governor wields political power, the agency may see that its best interests lie in cooperation.

The Judiciary

Pressure groups have discovered that courts make policy by deciding what is constitutional or unconstitutional; by the interpretation of statutes, administrative rules, and regulations: the decisions of lower courts; and so on. They have often turned to them in recent years. Relations between pressure groups and the judiciary are not identical with those between groups and the legislature or the executive. The difference is one of degree. Pressure groups are as concerned with the courts as they are with operations of the legislative and executive branches of government. Still, judicial decisions may benefit one group's aspirations and impede those of others.

Data on interest group activity in litigation are not yet complete. What indications there are tend to affirm the observation of David Truman; groups that are trying to defend the status quo have an advantage over those who are trying to change the established order of things. Truman claims that the defense advantage stems first from the strength of established relationships in society and second from the opportunities for delay and obstruction offered by existing procedures. More than any other governmental institution, the courts are looked upon as guardians of the "rules of the game." Privileged access by groups representing the status quo may be seen in zoning decisions that generally strengthen the power of local boards to decide the character of their communities. Zoning boards themselves represent the middle-class status quo in the communities and not the lower-income groups. The role of interest groups in the Connecticut case of *Senior v. New Canaan Zoning Commission* reveals that there is little question that zoning cases are rife with organized interests.

In the area of public education, however, an activist judiciary has been applying new tests to state and local practices. Public education is an important issue in the states, and many organizations have drawn the judiciary into the consideration of various aspects of local school affairs. Racial segregation was outlawed in cases sponsored by the National Association for the Advancement of Colored People Legal Defense and Education Fund. We are now in a period of follow-up litigation and conflict over implementation of the decision which has spread to northern cities. In addition to integration, state and local officials have been faced with serious problems of finance. Much of the problem has been traced to local property taxes. In the early 1970's, several lower courts were asked to decide the validity of property tax as a method of financing education on the grounds that it resulted in great disparities in the amount of money supporting the education of students. In California, for example, the court invalidated a property tax system because the school district of Baldwin Park in Los Angeles spent $563 educating each pupil while a school district in Beverly Hills spent $1,232. That's more than twice as much on each pupil.[51] There can be no doubt that court decisions are having important ramifications in the educational policy making of the states. Where decisions are made, so also will organized pressures be found.

An appeal to the courts may achieve other ends than a policy decision. In the case of the truckers versus the railroads in Pennsylvania, the truckers sued the railroads under the Sherman and Clayton antitrust laws for conspiring to put them out of long-haul freight business with dishonest publicity. Part of the purpose of the suit was to utilize the courts to reinforce the truckers position in the eyes of the public. The announcement of a $250 million suit for damages made the front pages of newspapers. The case lasted almost four months and eventually reached the Supreme Court, which overturned the verdicts of two lower courts and decided in favor of the railroads. Justice Hugo Black, speaking for the court, said that the Sherman Antitrust Act could not be applied to the political arena. Were the antitrust laws to be extended to this sphere, the very workings of democracy itself would be impaired. He then commented on the activities of pressure groups as vehicles of representation. The fact that the railroads intended to keep legislation on the books that would help them and harm the truckers is no ground for a lawsuit, he ruled. There is no requirement that lobbying or public relations compaigns must have altruistic motives or be in the general interest. People seek action on laws in the hope that they may bring about an advantage to themselves and a disadvantage to their competitors. Such a hope for personal advancement provides much of the information upon which governments must act.[52]

CONCLUSIONS

Justice Black's words provide an appropriate summary of the role of pressure groups in our democracy. Pressure groups are the vehicles by which political needs are made known to the government. The more diverse a society, the more each segment of the social order is represented by an organized group. A working conception of the political process must take into account the relationships among groups, parties, and governmental institutions that make the decisions. In the main, activities of pressure groups are directed at policy. They are concerned with what government does either to help or to harm their membership. They do not assume the party's basic function of nominating and electing candidates to public office or of conducting the government. Their main role is to petition the parties and formal instruments of government to act as spokesmen for the special interests in society.

The relationship between a pressure group and a political party is a crucial one for the democratic process. Where parties are strong internally and can elect governors and legislators committed to a common program, pressure groups do not have power over the decision-making process. Their demands must be channeled through the party and usually through only one party. The party mediates among the pressure groups attracted to it. However, there are strong party systems in only about one-third of the American states. In the others, power of the organized pressure groups is greater. In weak-party states, the pressures assume the entire task of representing people to their government. Only organized groups are represented. Their lobbyists do not run for election, nor are they held accountable to more than a small fragment of the society. If they have resources that can effectively be brought to bear on the government, their power can only be checked by another pressure—and often there is no opposition.

States with strong pressure groups are often states that do not have modern integrated cultures. A single major enterprise dominates the economy. There are vast differences between the rich and the poor. The political system is characterized by a single weak party which operates as a name for the factional winner. If the public officials cannot be held accountable because they have no opposition, there is no effective representation of the consumer or the poor who exert power by vote in other states. It is in these states—nearly one third of the total—that certain pressures may dominate the policy-making process. There is no aggregating or synthesizing of interests.

The fight goes on between the many thousands of competing groups that comprise the political scene. We assume, as did Justice Black, that free speech implies the right to petition the government and make desires known. The case of truckers versus the railroads raises the question of disclosure. Can one group work through another, even if the membership of the second is not aware? Can the public discern the effects of a public relations campaign? Can we continue to count on group pressures canceling each other out, or do conflicting groups even combine to gain cumulated demands against the interests of the rest of the public? This situation may not be uncommon in one-third of our American states.

NOTES

1. Commonwealth of Pennsylvania, *Legislative Journal—Senate, 1971*, p. 146.
2. Earl Latham, "The Group Basis of Politics: Notes For a Theory," *The American Political Science Review* 46 (June 1952): 376–97.
3. Arthur F. Bentley, *The Process of Government* (Chicago: University of Chicago Press, 1908).
4. Ibid., p. 205.
5. David Truman, *The Governmental Process* (New York: Knopf, 1951), p. 33.
6. Stanley Rothman, "Systematic Political Theory: Observations on the Group Approach," *American Political Science Review* 54 (March 1960): 15–33.
7. The studies that asked the legislators were: John C. Wahlke, Heinz Eulau, William Buchanan, and Leroy C. Ferguson, *The Legislative System* (New York: Wiley, 1962), p. 322; Harmon Zeigler and Michael A. Baer, *Lobbying: Interaction and Influence in American State Legislatures* (Belmont, Calif.: Wadsworth, 1969), Chapter 7. The study that ranks the states according to strength of pressure groups is: Belle Zeller, ed. *American State Legislatures* (New York: Crowell, 1954), pp. 190–91.
8. Daniel Elazar, *American Federalism: A View From the States*, 2d ed. (New York: Crowell, 1972), p. 99.
9. Zeigler and Baer, *Lobbying*, p. 156.
10. Robert A. Dahl, "The Concept of Power," *Behavioral Science*, 2 (July 1957): 202–203.
11. Ibid., p. 203. The order of (3) and (4) are changed.
12. Truman, *Governmental Process* pp. 265–68.
13. Neal R. Peirce, *The Mountain States of America* (New York: Norton, 1972), pp. 115–16.
14. Neal R. Peirce, *The Deep South States of America* (New York: Norton, 1974), p. 295.
15. W. Duane Lockard, *New England State Politics*, 2d ed. (Princeton: Princeton University Press), pp. 285–91.
16. Ibid., pp. 289–90.
17. Neal Peirce, *The Border South States* (New York: Norton, 1975), p. 154.

18. William Buchanan, *Legislative Partisanship, The Deviant Case of California* (Berkeley: University of California Press, 1963), p. 40.
19. John H. Fenton, *People and Parties in Politics* (Glenview, Ill.: Scott, Foresman, 1966), p. 64.
20. John H. Fenton, *Midwest Politics* (New York: Holt, Rinehart and Winston, 1966), p. 115.
21. The statistical correlation between party strength and the economic variables of Integration and Income Distribution (Gini Index) are + .39 and –.40. The latter correlation is a minus quantity because, as inequality increases, party strength decreases. These correlations indicate that there is a relationship between party strength and economic conditions. There is probably a stronger relationshp between pressure group activity and economic conditions, although this cannot be subject to rigorous statistical manipulation. The strongest relationship appears to be between pressure groups and political parties. Again, this correlation cannot be measured exactly because the activities of pressure groups have not been quantified.
22. V. O. Key, Jr., *Politics, Parties and Pressure Groups,* 5th ed. (New York: Crowell, 1964), p. 155–56.
23. Lockard, *New England State Politics,* p. 165.
24. John W. Kingdon, *Candidates For Office: Beliefs and Strategies* (New York: Random House, 1966), p. 145.
25. Lockard, *New England State Politics,* p. 224.
26. Ibid., p. 223.
27. "Campaign Finance Laws: Filing Requirements," in Council of State Governments, *The Book of The States:* 1978–1979, pp. 250–53.
28. Harry M. Scoble, "Organized Labor in Electoral Politics: Some Questions for the Discipline," in Robert H. Salisbury, ed., *Interest Group Politics in America* (New York: Harper & Row, 1970), p. 317.
29. C. Q. Political Report, "Campaign Finance: The States Push for Reform," *Congressional Quarterly Weekly Report,* 32 (31 August 1974), p. 2361.
30. Kingdon, *"Candidates For Office,"* pp. 78–81.
31. Ibid., p. 145.
32. Henry Teune, "Legislative Attitudes toward Interest Groups," *Midwest Journal of Political Science* 11 (November 1967): 489–504.
33. Buchanan, *Legislative Partisanship,* p. 47.
34. Lockard, *New England State Politics,* pp. 69–70.
35. Peirce, *The Deep South States of America,* p. 295.
36. Dean E. Mann, "The Legislative Committee System in Arizona," *Western Political Quarterly,* 14 (December 1961); 931–33.
37. James Nathan Miller, "How Florida Threw Out the Pork Chop Gang," *National Civic Review* 60 (July 1971): 367.
38. Martin Ryan Haley and James M. Kiss, "Larger Stakes in Statehouse Lobbying," *Harvard Business Review,* 52 (January-February 1974): 126.
39. Ibid., p. 129.
40. Logrolling involves a group's giving support to a proposal that may bear no relation or only the most remote relation to its own objectives in return for similar support from the group it has assisted.

41. Neal R. Peirce, *The Pacific States of America* (New York: Norton, 1972), p. 35.
42. Zeigler and Baer, *Lobbying,* pp. 173–83.
43. Ibid., pp. 166–67.
44. Zeigler and Baer, *Lobbying,* p. 172.
45. Neal R. Peirce, *The Pacific States of America,* p. 242.
46. Zeigler and Baer, *Lobbying,* p. 186.
47. Andrew Hacker, "Pressure Politics in Pennsylvania: The Truckers vs. the Railroads," chapter 7 in Alan F. Westin, ed., *The Uses of Power* (New York: Harcourt, Brace & World, 1962), 323–76.
48. Council of State Governments, *Book of the States,* 1978–1979, pp. 135–137.
49. Neal R. Peirce, *The Megastates of America,* pp. 469–70.
50. Grant McConnell, *Private Power and American Democracy* (New York: Knopf, 1967), pp. 185.
51. David L. Kirp, "Judicial Policy-Making: Inequitable Public School Financing and the Serrano Case," chapter 3 in Allan P. Sindler, ed., *Policy and Politics in America* (Boston: Little, Brown, 1973), p. 89.
52. Hacker, "Pressure Politics in Pennsylvania," pp. 365–66.

CHAPTER FOUR

THE PARTY OUTSIDE THE GOVERNMENT: THE ELECTORAL PARTY

If this book serves no other purpose than convincing you, the reader, that the operations of our two political parties are central to the form of government under which you live and move and have your being, then it will have accomplished its goal. Our political party process must be seen as the primary vehicle for connecting the citizen with his or her government. For better or worse, the party provides the decision makers who make policies that affect the lives of us all.

It is the fundamental job of the party outside of government, the electoral party, to recruit, nominate, and elect candidates for public office. Parties are electoral machines. Their primary purpose is to size up the electorate, provide candidates who appeal to a majority of the voters, and then raise the money and manpower to see that those candidates are elected. A good example of this process is the skill and organizational ability that characterized the Democratic party in Michigan during the Staebler era. This effort was coordinated at the state level and permeated all local organizations with an ideological as well as practical unity. Most state parties do not reflect such programmatic or political fusion. State parties present an array of personalities, as well as factions, ranging from the unity of Michigan Democrats to the disunity of the same party in Mississippi. This chapter will consider the diverse groups of people who make up the two major political parties in our 50 states. The political party represents more than a conglomerate of office-seeking groups to the extent that the groups combine their efforts to capture more than one office under a common political banner.

PARTY DOCTRINE

We must first clear away some dogma with respect to the proper functions of the electoral party before we can discuss the realities of the situation.

In chapter 1, we made a distinction between the type of political party the proponents of responsible party government advocate as doctrine and the type of political coalition called party that forms around office-seeking groups. Recall that the normative description of the party calls for party program and principles, candidates loyal to the program, education of the electorate in the understanding of the program and, finally, translation of the program into policy by the elected office holders. This school has also been referred to as the party democracy school because it advocates rank-and-file participation in defining policy. Electoral success is viewed not as an end in itself but as a means of implementing policy ends. We distinguished this model from a more action-oriented model in which a party is viewed as a coalition of men and women whose principal goal is office seeking. Realizing that no program can be made into policy unless the proponents are elected, we based this model on the ambitions of groups clustered about the offices to be filled. It is furthest from the minds of the party men and women to "structure societal conflict." Their efforts are directed toward getting their candidate elected and enjoying the rewards of money, jobs, favors, and legislation that flow from his obtaining office. Political conflict arises when the "outs" and the "ins" debate the most fundamental issues of the moment. But they don't do it to perform a social function: their motives are solely practical and directed toward winning elections. To the extent that one group sees advantages in uniting with another, such as candidates for the state legislature identifying with the program of the governor, a more structured, hierarchical organization exists.

The 100 state party organizations with which we deal are not pure types. Some are more ideologically oriented than others: Some are more office oriented. The Michigan Democrats in the 1950s would have satisfied both the party democracy school and the office-ambition model of party organization. State chairman Neil Staebler summarized the attitudes of Michigan Democratic leaders in a speech given in 1955:

> If I may oversimplify just a little, I'd describe the mainsprings of politics as patronage, money, program, and morale. Without minimizing the importance of money and patronage, I would say that the other two, program and morale which are closely related, are more important.... When the merit system was introduced it gave our parties a great setback.... But it has led to the growth of a new species of Party worker, the volunteer, who works from sheer belief in Party principles and is motivated by this thing I call morale....[1]

Staebler encouraged mass participation in party activity to gain the cooperation of party workers. He believed that party workers should participate in developing the liberal platform which they were being called upon to produce. The era of the party boss is passing, Staebler claimed. Party leaders will begin to work harder by common consent and less by maneuver. This Camelot of new politics, based on responsible party leadership and a scheme of organization rooted in an issue-oriented approach to politics, began to crack in 1959. The remarkable unity achieved in the decade of the fifties was now being threatened by internal dissension. The Michigan Democrats were not able to win the governorship for 20 years after that. The principal causes of discord were of a programmatic nature. Moderates in the party became restive under the New Deal-Fair Deal program that the liberal-labor leadership promoted for a decade. The restoration of party unity will lie with programmatic adjustments that are consistent with the trend toward "moderation." Michigan Democrats illustrate the point that both ideological and office-seeking motivations can be present in the same party, but it is an unlikely occurrence. Proponents of the responsible party government school and those who see the party primarily as a coalition of office seekers could both find confirmation of their respective theories of party organization in the Michigan Democrats. This book will investigate as many party organizations as possible to find the existing combination of motives and incentives that successfully unites a group of people for whom office holding is a primary objective. The conditions under which these different types of organizations are found are also important to the study of party structure.

TWO-PARTY COMPETITION AND PARTY STRENGTH

According to traditional theory, two-party competition is one of the major conditions of party government. Only in the alternation of office by two responsible parties can the popular will be translated into governmental action. If genuine competition between the parties exists, the electorate can "throw the rascals" out of office and install the competitors. This notion of the efficacy of party competition is found in both the normative theory of party and the more action-oriented view. In the former, two well-disciplined parties present programmatic choices to the electorate based on their analysis of its needs and wants. It is the parties themselves who educate and divide the electorate. They are internally disciplined because they're composed of groups of people who are loyal to the program and want to put it into effect.

The office-seeking theory of the political party includes competition between two relatively matched coalitions. Competition is the best guarantee that the parties will be internally cohesive and, as a result, better able to perform the job of electing and governing. In this view, the function of the party is to recruit and elect candidates to public office who will translate election promises into policy, not so much from conscience as from fear of retribution at the polls. One of the major propositions of this theory is that close electoral competition between the parties results in unified parties. Each must be united to fight the opposing party which threatens to take over the government in the next election. United parties will be able to control the type of men and women who are nominated for public office. Because winning is the primary goal, candidates who represent majority opinion will be selected by the party leaders. Factions within the party will be appeased by the promise of policy, patronage, prestige, and the like. A slight modification of this basic theme was offered by Duane Lockard and John Fenton. They claimed that parties will most likely be cohesive in states that are polarized along rural-urban lines.[2] Thus, it takes a *particular kind* of economic and political competition to produce cohesive parties.

A Measure of Party Strength

It's possible to test this hypothesis and draw some conclusions about its validity. We measured party strength in the last chapter with the promise that a fuller explanation would follow in this one. Because the highest stakes in the opportunity structure of state government are winning the governorship, the greatest amount of energy is expended on the nomination for this office. The primary vote indicates the strength of the coalition that the party leaders or the nominee himself have been able to build to win the nomination. If possible, the coalition will be large enough to assure the candidate an overwhelming majority. The governor will need as large an organization as possible to compete for the office in the general election. Accordingly, the more competitive the state, the more united the party should be. The competition-cohesion theory, when followed to its logical conclusion, predicts that the majority party would be composed of many factions in states where there is little or no competition because internal politics provides controlling decisions with respect to the personnel who will man the governor's office. Primary votes register the strength of factions competing in the nominating process in both parties for states that have all degrees of competition. In this way, we can test the hypothesis that parties are more unified in competitive states.

A Test of the Competition-Cohesion Theory

Table 4-1 shows the strength of political parties arranged by the degree of competition in the state. A glance at the table shows there is only a tendency for strongly competitive states to have strong parties and for

TABLE 4-1

Two-Party Competition and Party Strength,
1956–1978

PARTY STRENGTH[b]	Competition[a]		
	STRONG	MODERATE	LOW
Strong	Delaware Wisconsin North Dakota Michigan Minnesota South Dakota Colorado Arizona New York	Massachusetts Iowa Rhode Island Vermont Connecticut Virginia	
Moderate	Illinois Maine Pennsylvania Washington Hawaii Indiana Kansas Montana Wyoming New Hampshire	California Idaho New Jersey Nebraska Missouri Ohio	Maryland Nevada South Carolina Utah
Weak	Oregon New Mexico Alaska	Kentucky North Carolina West Virginia	Oklahoma Florida Texas Tennessee Arkansas Georgia Mississippi Louisiana Alabama

[a] This is the Average Index of Competition which measures the difference between the percent of the vote for governor obtained by each major party averaged over a specific time period, in this case 1956–1978 (inclusive). See Table 2–2 for the formula. In this table there are three categories instead of five which means a merging of the five categories in Table 2–2. Note that the 12 least competitive states are the same in both time periods. The average percentage difference between the parties in the strong category is 8.5, in the moderate category 13.3, and in the low category 36.6.

[b] Party strength is measured by averaging the governors' percent of the primary vote in gubernatorial primaries 1956–78 (inclusive). In a state with strong parties the average primary vote received by governors-to-be was 80 to 100 percent. In states with moderately strong parties the average primary vote received by governors-to-be was 64 to 79 percent. In states with weak parties, the average primary vote received by governors-to-be was 35 to 63 percent. In four states, Delaware, New York, Connecticut and Indiana—which nominated by party convention, the vote for the gubernatorial nominee in the convention was tabulated. This may impose a hardship on Indiana parties, which appear to relish intraparty squabbles within the convention but which may patch things up sufficiently to contest the ensuing election.

those where competition is low to have weak parties. In fact, competitive states are as likely to have moderately strong as strong parties. The correlation between competition and cohesion is not high (.40). In the group of 22 states where competition is strong, only nine show unity in the nominating process for both parties over the past 22 years. In ten others, nominations are contested vigorously, although the gubernatorial nominee receives over 64 percent of the primary vote. In three strongly competitive states, the party organizations do not even have the unity to nominate a gubernatorial candidate by 64 percent of the primary vote. Surely we can lay to rest the proposition that competitive states produce united parties. The other end of the continuum appears to be true, however, in that low-competition states have weak parties. The nine states listed in the low-competition-weak party cell are the familiar southern Democratic states. The main competition for the governorship takes place within the Democratic primary where opposing factions represent a conflict of personalities or amorphous issues. There is no need to develop large electoral coalitions because a candidate can win by a small percentage of the total electorate—that portion that supports him in the Democratic primary. At times, party factions arise that resemble the coherence and continuity of parties in the strong party states. Table 4-1 tells us little about the substance of the factions existing in all the states. A few illustrations drawn from the literature of political parties are in order. The wealth of case studies and area books gives us glimpses into the internal struggles that develop within the parties over the gubernatorial nomination.

Connecticut Democrats: Competitive and Cohesive

In Connecticut, both the Democratic and Republican parties were dominated by unusually strong leadership until the 1970s. The leadership of the Democratic party, in the form of the state chairman, John Bailey, was able to maintain a majority control of delegates at the state nominating conventions where major statewide nominees for public office are selected (see Table 4-1, note b). John Bailey became Connecticut state chairman in 1946 and within two years had united the Democrats who had been split into factions for many years. He recognized the party's need for ethnic votes and recruited candidates with ethnic ties who supported legislative programs to the liking of ethnic groups. Bailey made the state chairman's position a full-time one. He divided the state into six regions and met with one regional group each week. He worked well with the big-city bosses whom he consulted on a regular basis. Through Baileys' working with the city organizations, the potential for factionalism within the state was sharply reduced. They gave him legislative support, but he gave them patronage and places on the state ticket. Bailey supported potentially strong candidates such as Abe Ribicoff, the first Jewish governor, and Ella Grasso, the first woman governor, regardless of ethnic ties. By 1970, however, the party organization became weaker. The convention's choice was challenged in a primary in 1970 and the challenger won. The party has appeared to drift since Bailey's death in 1975. Governor Grasso could not control the choice of a new state chairman. What was behind the success of this acknowledged political boss? Bailey had all the earmarks of a boss for 30 years, at a time when bosses were fast fading from the scene. He apparently had the perception to see new sources of power and the new style by which the game must be played in the second half of the twentieth century. Lieberman describes Bailey as "the power broker" who was able to attract the influential Democratic elements in Connecticut and to convince them to form an association which he—Bailey—promised would pay them handsomely. "His simple pitch was that disparate elements had more to gain if they united around him."[3] People learned they could trust him. He was able to immerse himself in politics for the best part of his lifetime and build a political party around his personal capacities, the wise use of patronage, and his ability to attract good candidates and win over 70 percent of the time. It takes time for such a power broker to develop. Whether Connecticut Democrats are spawning another is not yet known; if they are, he or she has not emerged as yet.

While the above description is meant to indicate one type of party organization without fully describing the causes for such a phenomenon, there were several features of Connecticut's politics that gave rise to a strong party system. During the first part of John Bailey's regime, all major state-wide nominees for public office were selected in a nominating convention in Hartford, and the choice was not subject to challenge. In 1955, Connecticut adopted a challenge primary that weakened the hand of "the power broker." Bailey told me he could no longer make the type of compromise necessary to ensure a well-balanced ticket. Disgruntled factions could now call for a primary to choose the party's nominees. This, he openly admitted, was a challenge to his power. Until 1970, however, Bailey was able to hold the party together by sheer ability. The Connecticut example indicates that parties are affected by the "rules of the game"; their ability to function is aided or stunted by the laws governing their actions. It also indicates that the rules need not determine their behavior and that the efforts of men and women can circumvent the rules. The interplay between rules that attempt to structure the operations of the political party and the actual actions of the people within it is central to any analysis of the party as an electoral and governing instrument.

Illinois Parties: Competitive and Fighting

Connecticut was a highly competitive state during most of John Bailey's term (although it has recently "leaned" Democratic) and exhibited the type of party structure that standard party theory would predict. There are, as Table 4–1 reveals, many other state party systems that are highly competitive and moderately strong. Illinois has a state party system in which considerable clout is expended. In both political parties, regular battles are fought between the "ins" and the "outs" with sufficient consolidation behind one candidate to permit him to win by a significant percentage. The legendary Chicago Democratic political machine under the late Mayor Daley could usually produce one-sided pluralities for its candidate in the gubernatorial primary. In 1972, however, the machine was beaten by Daniel Walker, former chairman of the Chicago Crime Commission and author of the controversial "Walker Report" that condemned police activities at the 1968 Democratic National Convention. The Chicago machine reasserted itself in 1976 by beating Walker, the incumbent governor, in the primary, thus reestablishing the machine as the major force in the party. This fight between the "reform" Democrats and the "regulars" was crucial to the continued operation of Illinois politics as played by either party. Nothing could be worse to the Chicago machine than to have the most dreaded monster—a Democratic governor making decisions on state and national political matters *independently* of City Hall. There is bipartisan support for the use of patronage and contracts to build strong political organizations. The poorer counties in both parties can use jobs to reward the faithful for their votes. These faithful vote for the "organization" man out of gratitude. John Fenton concluded that the Illinois job-oriented, two-party competition produced politicians who were not crusaders. They were not issue conscious. For them, issues were a means of getting government jobs. "The result was a government which tried to do something for everyone but did not try too hard."[4] The government spends a relatively modest amount of money in relation to the wealth of the state.

Since 1968, it would appear that two crusaders have emerged only to be beaten down by the regulars. Governor Richard Ogilvie distinguished himself in office by reforming the budget-making system, increasing state support for local schools, creating a department of law enforcement, and, finally, forcing through the first income tax in Illinois history. This gained the wrath of downstate Republicans. Ogilvie had to fight hard to win the ensuing primary within his party. Governor Walker, another reformer who followed Ogilvie, was beaten in the primary by the Daley machine in 1976. Illinois still has not emerged from the grip of Cook County's patronage system and the Republican county courthouses. Here, there is no benevolent despot in the form of a John Bailey, although candidates receive sufficient backing in the primary. State-wide issues are not as important as patronage for the dominant electoral machinery within either party. And the leaders of geographically located machines are not anxious to share patronage on a statewide basis. Hence, competing factions struggle to obtain sufficient political power for their candidate. Modest pluralities are better strategy within each party because there are fewer people to reward with the spoils of success.

Southern Democrats: One Party and Fractured

A variety of political structures exist within low-competition one-party states, from the traditional bifactional structure of Louisiana Democrats to the loose factionalism of competing personalities that mark the politics of Georgia, Mississippi, and Alabama. In these states, general elections usually do not determine the leadership of state government. The predominance of the Democratic party pushes into the direct primary of that party the controlling decisions of the state. In most of those states, there are no well-organized, stable, and continuing factions within the Democratic party. Leadership cliques are poorly defined and are not viewed by the electorate as differentiated groups. At widely separated moments of tension, cleavages may outlive candidates, and the voters may show some stability in their voting habits, but these clusters of voters soon dissolve and are replaced by other groupings around the candidates of the day. In this type of party structure, it can hardly be said that the voters have any policy choice. A choice of personalities exists within a dominant party umbrella —personalities who do not represent continuing policy committments but only colorful promises for a limited term in office, promises that have no guarantee of fulfillment because they are not backed by more than the utterer—and a few loyal followers.

Louisiana: One Party and Bi-Factional

The factional systems of some one-party states seem to be party systems within the dominant party. Two groups develop each with a recognizable policy orientation and a continuing hierarchy of leaders who fight it out in the direct primary in much the same fashion that candidates from a two-party system compete in the general election. In a few cases, this bifactional structure has maintained itself over a long period. A system of bifactional competition within the Democratic party characterized Louisiana's politics from the time of Huey Long's election in 1928 through the election of his brother Earl in 1956. The factional alignment included the

Longs and their supporters on one side and the reformers, or anti-Longs, on the other. In eight consecutive elections spanning a period of 28 years, the run-off primary in the Democratic party involved a contest between a Long and an anti-Long candidate. This pattern of political conflict ended in 1960 when the Long faction failed to place a candidate in the second primary. Supporters of the Long and anti-Long candidates were from geographically distinct sections of Louisiana. Huey Long made an effective appeal to the less-favored classes and rewarded their support with programs of concrete action. His successors continued the appeal of increasing social welfare spending, while the conservative interests of the state rallied around whoever happened to be the anti-Long leader of the moment. The political cleavage resembled that between Republicans and Democrats in two-party states. Alan Sindler claims that the Kingfish's (Huey Long) domain developed "A politics of class protest which *in turn developed* a structured politics of deep meaning. . . ."[5] The voters of Louisana had a choice not only between conflicting personalities but also among competing programs. Such was seldom the case in other one-party states of the South. In fact, recent trends in Louisiana indicate that politics is no longer bifactional but based on a multifactionalism led by personalities and ad hoc coalitions that shift from election to election.

Virginia: One Party Oligarchy

Until recently, Virginia represented another form of one-party system. V. O. Key maintains that a majority faction within the Democratic party dominated Virginia's politics.[6] This faction, led by the Byrds, was oligarchical in nature. It was organized, persistent, and provided policy continuity in the form of business conservatism. It was dedicated to maintaining a low level of public services and succeeded in keeping welfare expenditures minimal despite the fact that it had greater wealth than its sister states. In Virginia, the "have-nots" were represented by no one. The old order has changed rapidly in recent years, and Virginia politics have become competitive between the parties. A Republican governor won in 1969, and 1973 saw a former Democratic governor, Mills E. Godwin, run and win as a Republican. Governor Godwin has the distinction of winning both the Democratic primary in 1965 and the Republican convention in 1973 without opposition. Whether this means that each party will now continue in an "oligarchic" mold or the opportunity for power will generate factions within each party remains to be seen. Virginia provides another variant in the rich descriptive list of party systems.

These illustrations do not add up to a comprehensive theory of party structure. They are intended to show that the degree of competition that exists within a state does not indicate the type of structure existing within the state parties themselves. Competitive states appear to encompass a variety of party structures based on a rivalry between the "ins" and the "outs," as in Illinois; more programmatic differences between the middle-of-the roaders and the wings; and rivalries between upstate and downstate or between suburbs and farms. In some competitive states, there is an attempt on the party of leaders, such as the late John Bailey of Connecticut and Michigan's Neil Staebler in the '50s to try to suppress internal strife so as to present a united front in the election. In other competitive states, no such attempt is made; the factions slug it out in the primary, and the leaders acknowledge the results and back the nominee with whatever effort they can muster. In the states with low competition, reduced now to the Democratic states of the Solid South, the intraparty squabbles appear to develop around personalities and less around issues or geographical areas. Because anyone who can get a good-sized plurality among the Democratic voters can aspire to the governorship, there is no need to join in a coalition for a large block of votes until the run-off primary. This encourages factions and the grouping and regrouping of allies at the last moment—hardly a politics of coherence. This pattern predominates, but we have noted the bifactional rivalry of Louisiana as well as the one-party oligarchy of Virginia in the pre-1960 period. Generalization is hazardous but we turn now to a theory of the structure of political parties which may be of help to the analysis.

PARTY STRUCTURE: THEORY, LEGAL, AND REAL

Party Structure: Theory

At this point we have destroyed more ideas than we have contributed. We have, I hope, successfully questioned the doctrine that commits the party activist to "educating" the public to the issues of the day. We have knocked down the notion that competition brings about cohesive parties and suppresses factionalism in the interest of party unity. Perhaps a discussion will be useful of the type of party structure we might expect to find if we assume that political parties are composed of coalitions of office-seeking groups.

A NUCLEUS: THE BASIC UNIT   For Joseph Schlesinger, political parties are dominated by their office drives. He claims that, if a party is to remain viable over the long run, it must choose its alternatives in terms that will appeal to the voters. The basic unit of party organization is "collective effort devoted to the capture of a single public office."[7] Schlesinger calls such an effort a nucleus. A nucleus may be a very simple electoral effort, such as the candidate for state legislature and his supporters, or it may constitute multiple activities involved in a gubernatorial campaign. Complex party organizations emerge out of the relationships among nuclear organizations. Schlesinger holds that these nuclear organizations are the building blocks of the party. In some states, there is no cooperation between them. Certainly in most states of the Solid South, the political primary shows several nuclear organizations competing for the prize of office. The party itself is nothing but an umbrella over the struggle. Occasionally the candidate organizations merge after a first primary for the purpose of winning the run-off. This merger indicates the attempt on the part of two nuclear organizations to strive for a common victory.

Another form of cooperation is that between nuclei with different office ambitions, such as candidate organizations for the legislature and the governor. In Connecticut, state party leaders could punish an unruly local legislator by denying him the opportunity of running again. Control over patronage, contracts, and promotions can force unity between two electoral organizations; the local nucleus cooperates because it can be punished if it doesn't. Usually, however, the cooperation works the other way. The more inclusive gubernatorial nucleus coaxes the local organization by exchanging votes for favors. Schlesinger points out that nucleus A cooperates with nucleus B only to the extent that A finds cooperation useful in achieving its own goals. It had traditionally been assumed that competition between the parties would force this kind of cooperation. It would appear that this is not necessarily the case, although there is a tendency for the most unified parties to appear in competitive states. The shape a political party organization takes in a state can depend on many factors. It might be the sheer ability of a leader such as a John Bailey or a Neil Staebler to put together an electoral organization that attracts the cooperation of various nuclear organizations. It may be that clever use of patronage can control a party—or majority portion of a party—as in Illinois. A strong belief in the party's program may foster cooperation among nuclei. Not enough is known about what generates cooperation between various units of a party. But it appears to be a workable hypothesis that there will be no cooperation unless there is a mutual advantage to do so. This advantage is cast in office-seeking and office-keeping terms, for the parties are by definition coalitions to capture public office.

To return to the concept of nucleus, the central focus is to capture a single public office. A nucleus is not the same as a precinct or voting district within the formal party hierarchy. Unless the precinct elects an office within its boundaries, it is not a nucleus by Schlesinger's definition. For a true nucleus to exist, there must be the expectation that the activities of the men and women within it will be devoted to the capture of a public office. When a governor is in office, he is constantly calculating his chances for future election. His supporters, both within the electoral party and the governing party, work with him in this effort (see chapter 1, Figure 1–3: A Governing Coalition). He weighs his policy decisions, legislative program, and political appointments according to their contribution to his future. Examples come to mind of governors who have been defeated for reelection because they have approved and brought about a state income tax. No governor wants to be in office when an income tax is enacted but this burden falls on the best of them. The agonizing choice is to back the legislation with the hope that he or she can educate the electorate to see the state income tax as the only alternative. To summarize so far, every party nucleus must be devoted to the capture of public office by appealing to the voters in a constituency; it must have a candidate and the support of a coalition.

CONTRIBUTIONS TO THE NUCLEUS   Schlesinger describes the party nucleus in terms of various functions he calls "contributions." These are: (a) leadership; (b) recruitment and nomination; (c) issue formulation; (d) memory, intelligence, and communications; (e) technical services; and (f) money. The most important of these is leadership. Party leaders may be either public leaders (candidates for public office, including incumbents) or associational leaders (those whose office is limited to the party organization). The relationship between these two leadership positions has never been the subject of analysis. New York's Governor Rockefeller was the "real" leader while he held office. In Michigan, Neil Staebler shared leadership with Governor Williams (Staebler ran for Governor after Williams left office). John Bailey of Conneticut never ran for public office after he assumed leadership of the state party. The extent to which associational leaders or public office holders exercise actual power within a nucleus probably depends on the tenure of the public office. There are only 23 states (including the four two-year-term states) that do not limit the term of office of the governor. Hence, the continuity of a state party organization may depend on the ability of the associational leadership to recruit, nominate, and provide an orderly succession to public office every four to eight years. In many state legislatures, there is heavy turnover of candidates, thus increasing the potential power of the associational leadership. Very little systematic research has been done on this point.

Of the other chores, or functions, of the party organization, more will be said later. Of course the discovering and promoting of candidates for public office, as well as the discouragement of those who are unsuitable, is the major task of the leadership. In most constituencies, the direct primary forces the top contestants to battle for the nomination. It is up to the leadership to try to keep these contests from becoming fratracidal and to guarantee that the winner will be supported by the others who lost in the primary. The most effective control the party has is the defeated candidate's own hope for preferment. Schlesinger takes the view that parties formulate issues to ensure election victory rather than the other way around. To succeed, a party must devise a program or platform. To a great extent, selection of candidates determines policies for which the party will stand. Closely related to issue formulation is the need for memory, intelligence, and communications. To formulate issues, the party needs to gain accurate information about voters' reactions and to disseminate information favorable to the party via the mass media. The party needs and uses the services provided by polling organizations and campaign specialists. Money is essential to this entire operation and has been carefully limited by recent legislation at the state level. The devices used to garner money and the candidates' dependence on the sources were major considerations of the 1970s.

OFFICE SEEKERS AND BENEFIT SEEKERS In a later work Schlesinger describes the goals of those who work for the party.[8] There are two kinds of people who participate in a political party: (a) the office seekers and (b) the benefit-seekers—the receivers of political power and patronage.[9] These two groups need each other to win but their goals are different and sometimes conflict. Office seekers may want to advance to a higher rung on the political ladder. The current office is but one step in that direction. Governors, for instance, can't count on more than eight years in office if they are successful in winning a second term. They think of Washington as their prospective next move. State legislators may want to advance to be U.S. representatives or governors. If advancement is not their aim, control of a particular office over a long period is important to some. Elected offices at the state level, such as secretary of state, commissioner of motor vehicles, or attorney general, may become permanently attached to a personality who can win election after election with immunity from the fortunes of his or her party. This type of motivation is also held by many state legislators. These office seekers have static ambitions—they want to be elected and reelected to the same office. Another category of office seeker is that of candidates who look on public office as a way of gaining recognition on a "one-shot" basis. They take time from their law firms or insurance businesses to spend a term at the capitol to gain contacts and business. All these goals are related to the holding of office. It is the inherent value of office—the benefits it can bring to the office-holder—that is important to the office seeker.

Benefit seekers want all the nonoffice goals that people bring to politics. Benefit seekers are persons who hope to affect government activity in terms of policies ranging from control of pollution to jobs, contracts, or individual favors. They work within a party nucleus because they want to influence the office holder after the job is won. On the other hand, they may simply want the status that comes from helping a favorite person gain office, being members of the team, and being able to go home after the hard fight and rest on their laurels and reminiscences. It's important to emphasize that winning is the best strategy for both office seeker and benefit seeker. They need each other. If office seekers were not concerned with benefits, no one would have any reason to work for them. Both office seekers and benefit seekers must win elections to see their goals realized.[10]

Samuel J. Eldersveld conducted an extensive study of party organization in the Detroit metropolitan area that confirms many of Schlesinger's assumptions.[11] Both writers view parties primarily as office-seeking organizations with emphasis on the party's electoral function. Eldersveld adds to Schlesinger's analysis by considering the motivational and career pluralism existing in the party organization. He discovered that different goals within the party make organizational satisfaction of a diversity of motives and aspirations difficult. The office holder would prefer to be left alone to develop his own policies while in office but he must pay those who helped get him elected to guarantee their support when he needs them next. The tension between material and purposive motivations of party activists has been the subject to much research. Some studies find that within the group of benefit seekers is a difference in performance: those whose incentives are purposive (amateurs) and those whose incentives are material or social (professionals). Amateurs are active in campaigns, and they are supportive of programmatic functions. But they are less likely to be effective in developing party and electoral coalitions. Professionals are oriented toward conciliating and aggregating party interests, understanding that the achievement of material incentives depends on electoral success. Because the solidary and material incentives are more enduring than the purposive motivations, professionals are also likely to be more experienced political leaders.[12]

The previous discussion under the heading of *structure* can be confusing unless we realize that, by structure, we mean the pattern of activities of people within the political party. We have seen that there is no need for those seeking office within one nucleus to cooperate with those seeking office in another unless it is to their mutual benefit. If the value of cooperation is seen as mutually helpful, the rudiments of a party hierarchy emerge; however, it is usually the nucleus with the smaller number of voters rather than the larger electoral nucleus that can set the terms of cooperation. Party workers have differing motivations and goals that can create tensions within the organization. We now turn our discussion to party structure in the framework of legal formalities that have been set by the different states.

Party Structure: Legal

Two hundred years ago the founding fathers warned about the dangers of faction but did not try to control the budding political parties through constitutional prescription. While the United States Constitution makes no mention of parties, the constitutions and statutes of the 50 states contain detailed definitions of party organizations and the duties they are to perform. The degree to which statutes specify the entire party structure varies from state to state. State constitutions or statutes generally ordain the county and state committees; some then mandate the other levels while others leave the full articulation of the organizational hierarchy to the parties themselves. The paper organization is rarely identical with the real or working organization; the man with the title "boss" may not be the state or county chairman, making the formal structure an empty shell. Nevertheless, even in states where the real structure of party power does not coincide with the written structure as in Wisconsin, both parties operate through duplicating, but separate voluntary organizations that parallel the statutory organizational structure. The voluntary organizations, bolstered by some 20,000 dues-paying members, retain and exercise the substance of party power.[13] Hence, there is justification in setting out the formal structure because the real structure is often intertwined with it. The reason is that both formal and informal structures are built around electoral divisions of the state. Figure 4–1 diagrams the legal structure we are considering.

The precinct, composed of several hundred voters, is generally the smallest formal unit in the state party structure. A precinct captain usually administers party matters. In larger cities, the next higher level of party organization is formed about the ward, or district, composed of several precincts and presided over by the ward leader. These jurisdictions generally elect councilmen or legislators. More commonly, the next higher level of party organization above the precinct is the county committee, consisting of precinct executives or persons chosen by them. The county is an electoral unit for a variety of purposes—the choice of county officials or election of state legislators, for example, and it may coincide with the boundaries of a congressional district. Each party has a state committee and a state chairman, generally an important political figure. It is important to keep in mind the difference between the "real" and the "legal." Schlesinger and Eldersveld have offered a theory of party structure based on the ambitions and motivations of human beings. Figure 4–1 diagrams a party structure that is commonly assumed to represent the flow of authority from top to bottom. It is indeed rare that both forms coincide— that the legal structure represents the real power hierarchy. We took note of the fact that Michigan and Connecticut Democrats may have given us the best illustration of the convergence of form and power. Some candidates are able to "capture" the party structure to their advantage. Others must build up their own electoral nucleus which does not coincide with the formalities. The precinct may or may not be composed of an energetic group of party workers. If not, the candidate will have to develop his own basic organization.

FIGURE 4–1

Diagram of the Typical Formal State Party
Organization

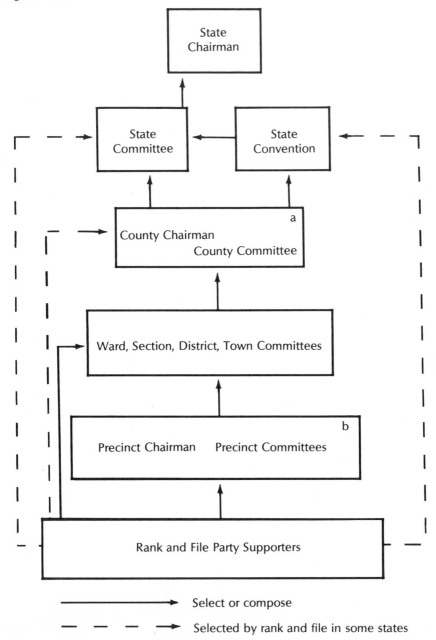

State
Chairman

State
Committee

State
Convention

a

County Chairman
County Committee

Ward, Section, District, Town Committees

b

Precinct Chairman   Precinct Committees

Rank and File Party Supporters

Select or compose

Selected by rank and file in some states

[a]3,000 in each party in the United States
[b]100,000 in each party in the United States

Party Structure: Real

What follows is intended to describe briefly the operations of a party organization's legal units. This description is a mixture of the real and legal aspects of party structure. Many gaps exist in the knowledge of both the legal and the actual operation. In 1966, the National Municipal League discovered that neither of the national committee offices in Washington had a collection of the rules of their constituent state parties. The compendium published by the National Municipal League in 1967, in my opinion, is the most thorough public collection extant of state laws and party rules governing the organization and procedures of political parties in each of the states.[14]

THE PRECINCT ORGANIZATION   Because the precinct is the basic building block of the legal party organization, and because power in the party is based on the active support of these strategic units of party, our discussion will begin with a look at the precinct organization. V. O. Key claimed that while levels of party organization are intimately interrelated, the linkage is from the bottom up rather than from the top down. Members of party committees at any level have a power base in an organizational level lower than the level represented by the one in which they sit. Hence, a county committeeman is likely to have influence in a precinct or ward. A member of a state committee is likely to be a power in his county. As Key points out, "Advancement in the political organization tends to be an expansion of influence from a geographical base rather than an ascent up a ladder."[15]

The selection of a precinct captain or committeeman may go through the formalities of a primary in which any voter may place his or her name in nomination with a few signatures. The handful of local partisans who show up duly elect their leader. It often happens that no one volunteers for the honor, and the precinct committeeman may be elected (occasionally to his surprise) by a write-in vote. On the other hand, the self-designated party loyalists may converge at a caucus and elect their next captain by a show of hands. That person is quite likely to be the incumbent, if he is willing. Party organizational fiction has it that this precinct committeeman can capture the "friends and neighbors" vote. He is the connecting link between the people and the organization—the one with the direct link to the voters. (I found out who my committeeman was when I changed party affiliation, and he asked me how I could perform this disloyal act "under his very nose.")

To build a following, the precinct captain begins with his family, relatives, and friends. He recruits others with promises of election-day duties, such as manning the polls (a 16-hour day), for which he can pay about $25.00. In the suburbs these chores are performed by hungry students or public-spirited housewives. It is in the cities that the precinct captain may fulfill a real need for his small group of voters through social work. This consists mainly in introducing them to the correct government agency to process their forms for aid of various sorts. He may go with them, "glad hand" the administrator, and see that they feel at home. He may recommend his people for employment. Or he may see the judge and beg for mercy for a misused partisan. In all these ways, the precinct captain can collect a hundred or so votes for his faction's candidate in the primary or for his party's candidate in the general election. If the precinct leader is active, as described above, he can perform a vital role for the party organization. This type of personalized leadership, however, is not universal. In some localities, the precinct organization is active; in others it is most attenuated. If there are 100,000 precincts in the United States, we would expect a fully manned two-party system to produce 200,000 precinct leaders. In truth, many of these local positions are either vacant or only nominally occupied.

Organization at the precinct level is highly important for party success. A precinct captain and workers who are active and in contact with the families in the area perform a vital function in the winning of electoral office. One would think that precinct organizations would be active and vigorous, but this is not the case. It is hard to find people who want to perform the personalized canvassing and convincing at this level without some sort of monetary reward. The vitality of the party at higher levels is an inducement to work with the hope of reward. But, if the party is in bad shape, county or statewide, it is hard to convince a local partisan to perform a thankless activity with little hope of reward. In areas where the party organization is alive and vigorous, the precinct captains are also motivated; in areas where the party does not stand a chance of winning or where it is listless and unproductive, the precinct organizations are also weak. There is another reason for lack of interest in electoral activity at the precinct level. Occasionally, precinct chairmen are "pawns" in a power game played out at the ward or county level. They are recruited solely for the purpose of loyalty to a factional leader who wants to be elected or appointed to the ward or county post. When this is their only reason for being, they are paid off by the higher candidate. They often lose interest in the precinct and retire as soon as his election is determined. Thus, the precinct becomes a link in the intraorganizational power structure of the party and not an active electoral unit that can deliver the vote to candidates for public office. The upshot of this discussion is that the precinct is an important electoral unit for any candidate seeking a "nucleus," but it often fails to perform this function.

In larger urban areas, there are levels of party organization between the precinct and county. Wards are composed of several precincts, and ward leaders perform most of the same duties as the precinct chairmen, but on a grander scale. They may preside over a group of precinct workers whom they supervise in shepherding the local electorate. In many cities, the ward serves as the electoral district for members of the municipal assembly and is, hence, a "nucleus" as well as a structural entity. In some states, other intermediate levels between the precinct and the county have importance in the party structure. The assembly district in New York is the smallest political unit from which a public official is elected; the district leaders are important personages in the party structure. In New England, counties are divided into towns and townships which are the significant links in the state organization. County government does not play as important a role in New England as elsewhere in the country; the county party committee is not a basic link in the state structure. Nor are there powerful county chairmen. The state committees are built on the town organizations. Very often the precinct committeemen collectively make up the ward, district, city, or town committees, or elect the committeemen who do. Occasionally the ward committeemen are elected by the party members voting in primaries or caucuses (see Figure 4–1). The leaders of these intermediate electoral level organizations operate much as the precinct leaders. They are fearless of any discipline that might come from the state organization because it has so little leverage over them. They can be rewarded and are open to suggestion but they maintain a high degree of autonomy from the state organization. It is carrots, not sticks, that can elicit their cooperation.

THE MACHINE   To be sure, there are a few local organizations in the country that still resemble the prototype "city machine." The heyday of the urban machine was at the turn of the century. Tammany Hall in New York City, The Hague Machine in Jersey City, The Prendergast Machine in Kansas City, and the "Robin Hood" of Boston (Mayor Curley, who ran for office from prison), epitomized city organizations that could "do" for their people—jobs, favors, Thanksgiving baskets—and receive votes in return.[16] Today, with the decline of available jobs and the state and federal assumption of the welfare function, political machines cannot hold workers by monetary and social rewards. Their decline has been rapid: reform organizations have been elected in cities, and old organizations have dwindled due to lack of nourishment, leaving few "machines" left today. The late Mayor Daley of Chicago may have represented the last thriving machine. Neal Peirce says of this juggernaut:

> Under this authoritarian, hierarchical organization, some 500 patronage jobs are allotted to each ward. Virtually every precinct committeeman has a city job; the public, in effect, subsidizes the system by salaries paid to patronage workers. Many ward committeemen own insurance agencies and do a land-office business with retailers and real estate owners who see an obvious way to get access to City Hall. But the ward and precinct committeemen, in turn,

are under tremendous pressures to contribute and work on election day, or they can expect to be thrown out on the street. The machine knows what they are doing, and it brooks no election day inefficiency—or dissent. . . .[17]

Loyalty to the typical machine is by no means entirely dependent on monetary ties. Strong and lasting friendships develop in crisis situations. The comradeship of exhaustion after a successful fight does not wither after each primary or election. The belief that the "machine" has helped people in a hostile world is enough to engage volunteer workers in the great game of politics. Material or financial gain is not the only reward. The ties of party loyalty, individual bonds, the control of patronage, and the upward ambitions of men and women may create a manageable coalition of party workers. Where these occur, as exemplified by the Daley organization in Chicago, the Jersey City machine, or the boss-run organization in Brooklyn, it is almost futile to challenge the machine in the primaries. With control over the primaries comes major or controlling leverage in the party organization at the county or statewide level. The Daley machine was typical of old-fashioned organizations because it could determine the party's nominations, not only city wide, but all over the state. It could deliver Cook County votes by substantial margins in the state elections. Daley's was the classic machine with a hierarchical form —a boss at the head of an electoral organization that became the government. Those elected to office owed their success to the machine's efforts; major decisions were made to please the organization. With the death of Mayor Daley in 1976, the future of old-fashioned political structure is in doubt. Big-city machines are not typical of party organization today, which is composed of self-designated candidates who pull together an electoral nucleus that may or may not include viable wards and precincts. Nor is it typical for a candidate to be reviewed for acceptability by a city boss who can deliver the vote in a primary or election. This is contrary to the style of politics in our states. We return, then, to the more typical party organization.

THE COUNTY COMMITTEE The county committee is usually the most important unit below the state level for a number of reasons: it coincides with the electoral units that elect a considerable number of public officials at the county level; the county courthouse is still an important source of patronage; and the county is also a basis for defining other constituencies —congressional, state legislative, and judicial districts. County organization is an important electoral nucleus as well as composing the nucleii of many other electoral offices. The county committee is commonly an assembly of the party's ward or precinct chairmen, township chairmen, or functionaries from other subdivisions of the county. Occasionally, the county committee is elected by party members. Its size and functions vary greatly. In small, rural counties, the committee may have only 10 or 12 members while in the large urban counties its membership may number several hundred. In Bronx, New York, the Democratic county committee is composed of 3,750 local committeemen who are elected by the state assembly district leadership. The county chairman, selected by the committee, is usually a powerful leader in local politics. In most counties, the perquisites attached to this position are substantial in terms of jobs, contracts, services, and legal fees. The county chairman is the contact man between the state party organization and the local leaders and constituents.

Occasionally the county organization is "captured" by the "courthouse gang." They use it to further the material purposes of a small clique of leaders, politicians, suppliers, contractors, and so on who have no higher ambition than to exist off the comforts that can be derived from minimal efforts. If the county is in the hands of one party—and many counties in the United States are one-party districts—very little effort is required to maintain the status quo and reap the rewards. Little attempt is made to develop electoral participation because the favors would have to be spread thinner. This, of course, is not the sort of activity wanted by state leaders who need as many votes as possible for their state and national candidates. Occasionally the entrenched county group must be bypassed by upwardly mobile candidates who have to develop their own parallel electoral organizations. These county courthouse cliques may not be of the same faction in power at the state or national level. Their natural instinct is to "sit on their hands" and let their county lose the election that may bring unsympathetic occupants into the state house. The result of such laggard behavior is severely detrimental to any party organization that must operate on a statewide basis. The state can't discipline the unruly county because it has its own separate existence and is not dependent on the state or national organization for its livelihood.

Noticeable differences arise in the interest of the voters if the county organizations are active. In an attempt to build up their party in North Carolina, the Republicans had difficulty recruiting dedicated and resourceful party workers at the grass-roots level. Moreover, they were unable to find candidates to run in local races. Douglas Gatlin discovered that there were 21 North Carolina counties where no Republican candidates ran for sheriff, county commissioner, or as members of the lower house in the state legislature.[18] He found that, in those counties where Republicans were able to build an active organization with candidates for these offices, party competition increased. An organization that generates interest for its candidates and campaigns for them gets out the voters. In inactive counties, local Republicans settled for small favors that came from the Democrats to keep them happily inactive.

In 1972, for the first time in living memory a Republican became governor of the state. Governor Holshouser faced an overwhelmingly Democratic legislature (In 1975, the senate had 49 Democrats and one Republican; the house had 111 Democrats and 9 Republicans). A state with a Republican governor and only a corporal's guard of Republican legislators who made it to the capitol reveals lack of effort at the local level. The county party organization does make a large difference to the overall activity of a state party effort. Gatlin concludes that the local party activists are exceedingly important for the party system:

> Where one, or even both, of the party organizations is only a paper organization, where its candidates are unknown, unattractive, or even nonexistent, its potential voting support cannot be realized in any races. Socioeconomic conflicts cannot be effectively aggregated through the party system if party cadres do not carry out their partisan activities. Perhaps some inefficiency in interest aggregation by parties promotes the stability of a democratic political system in an environment of conflicting factions. On the other hand, there is some point at which empirical inefficiencies of party cadres become a matter of concern to the democratic order.[19]

THE STATE CHAIRMAN   The next higher level of party organization is the state convention, the state committee, and the state chairman. Although not all states have conventions, in those that do the convention shares a policy-making function with the state committee. It is made up of delegates selected from the counties or, in some cases, by the rank and file. The major functions of the state convention are drafting the party platform and electing some of the state and national party officers (state chairman, national committeemen and committeewomen, presidential electors, and delegates to the national conventions). In 16 states the convention is used as a means for nominating state officers or it's used in conjunction with primary elections. The votes on issues or candidates may often be an indication of the strength of various factions in the party.

General direction at the state level is provided by the state committee. Variety characterizes their composition, method of selection, duties, and even nomenclature. Sizes range from 14 in Iowa to mass-meeting size (750 for each party in California). In most cases, the state committee is composed of members elected in county delegations of variable size according to party strength; by convention, by county delegations to state conventions, by county committees, or by primaries. In some cases, there are ex-officio bigwigs such as county chairmen, state office holders, congressmen, and senators. The role of the committee varies but in many states they play some part in the preparation and adoption of general party policies and platforms, promotion of party harmony, coordination of organizational policy, and fund raising for the party. The chief function of the state committee is conducting campaigns. However, since the nominating function is now usurped by the direct primary in all but a few states, the state party structure has been reduced in importance. Candidates who have waged a struggle for the nomination on their own may not consider the state organization worth bothering with at election time. They have built up an electoral nucleus of their own that they can use to win the election. Lack of control over nomination of candidates for public office has gradually brought about the decline of many state party organizations. We will consider this point later in the discussion of the direct-primary form of nomination.

At the head of the state party committee is the state chairman who is usually an important figure in party circles. The social and career characteristics of state chairmen do not differ markedly from other groups of political leaders. They are generally white, moderately young, successful, and well educated. Some work full time and some part time. There is nothing dramatically different about the ways in which they became politically active, although, at this stage in their careers, they have opted for "administrative" political office as opposed to "policy-oriented" elective office. A significant portion go on to elective office once their service as chairman is completed.[20]

Numerous chairmen serve as true leaders of their respective parties, the chief executive officers of the state organization. As such, they are in charge of state party headquarters and are responsible for the day-to-day operation of the party. If their party controls the governorship, they usually operate as the right hand men of the governor helping him with the distribution of patronage, contacts with local party leaders, legislative liaison, and political advice. Neil Staebler and Douglas Ross make the following statement about the job of a state party chairman:

> The closest we can come to a general theory of state party management is to say that a party leader's every action and pronouncement, be his motivation program or patronage, must be measured in the light of his natural desire to preserve his position of leadership. His concern may be simply to hold on to his prestigious title. In most cases, however, a party leader, like anyone else, takes pride in his work. Whatever plus or minus values society may put upon his programs and procedures, he has an investment of time and talent to protect. If he is primarily patronage oriented, the careers of others are often dependent on his maintenance of power; if he is issue oriented, he sees loss of power as a setback to his programs.[21]

Staebler, joint author of this statement, served his entire term as state chairman under a popular Democratic governor with whom he operated on a most friendly basis. He was a trusted advisor and maintained a close relationship based on many years of loyalty, faith, and trust. State party chairmen who operate as Staebler did are the political agents of the governors, but the relationship is a two-way one. They believe that the governor's success guarantees the party's success and serve as the governor's political arm by organizing, campaigning, mediating, handling public relations, dispensing patronage, and maintaining legislative liaison. Occasionally, state chairmen are members of the state legislature, permitting them to "arm twist" from close range.

It is equally possible that a state chairman may be a power of his own fashioning—elected without the approval of the governor—or by occupying a place of party power in his own right. He occasionally has a fixed term that antedates the governor's. Some chairmen have been in power for a long time and have seen several governors elected during their tenure. These chairmen are found in all types of party systems and in all geographical areas. John Bailey of Connecticut was the typical independent chairman. He played a major role in the election of four governors. The independent chairman is also exemplified by several southern Democratic chairmen who preside over a faction different from that of their governor's. An example is Robert Vance, Democratic chairman of Alabama. Vance defeated the Dixicrat elements of the party in both 1970 and 1974 to serve as an independent chairman during the administration of Governor George Wallace. Vance considered himself the leader of the "Democratic Party" in Alabama while Wallace was the leader of a separate party faction. The independent chairman may be the John Bailey type of leader who can groom, elect, and work with governors he believes are best for the party or the type exemplified by Vance who must preside over a party of warring factions.

Another situation is presented by the out-party chairmen. Some preside over hopelessly weak minority parties, and as the recognized leaders, must build up the party to win the first state office, such as the Republican chairmen do in the South. The temporarily out-of-power party chairmen who need to groom a good candidate to get back in the running also typify the out-party chairmen. The state committee is generally of considerably more importance to out-party chairmen because it elects them and serves as their source of strength. Ray Bliss, former Ohio Republican state chairman, is most often cited as an effective out-party chairman. He appeared to have established goals for the party, exerted his native ability and experience to accomplish them, and worked doggedly to succeed. He was rewarded by election as national chairman. Hence, the state chairman may be strong or weak, agent of the governor or independent, out-party or in-party. The strongest appear to be those who see the governor as the success of the party and work in close association with him when in office, or they will work to recruit and groom a successor if they are out of power. Nevertheless, even those who possess the requisite leadership traits are often unable to make their mark on the state party. Many of those elected to office do not remain in power long enough to make an impact. The loss of continuity in state parties, which change chairmen on the average of once every two and one-half years is one of the principal problems facing state party organizations.[22]

Later, under our discussion of the governor and legislatures, we will see that a governor who is elected by a party that has had a strong and continuing leadership coalition is better able to get his legislation enacted into law. Evidently a leadership group that has consistently recruited, groomed, and provided support for gubernatorial candidates can gather around the governor when he needs support for his policies. The support comes from those men and women in his electoral and governing coalition who have helped him obtain and are prepared to provide him with the support he needs in the governing process.

The fact that there are strong leadership parties that can groom and support governors is all the more impressive when we consider that the party organization is a system of party committees growing up from the grass roots. The result is to build into the state party structure a strong localism and distaste for statewide direction. Because the state party is not a disciplined hierarchy but a system of relatively independent layers, power may reside in those who do not hold the formal positions of leadership. The state treasurer, the purchasing agent of a public works commission, or the appointments assistant to the governor may wield more power than anyone in the formal power structure. It is generally true that, even in states where the chairman is not the holder of considerable political power, he normally does the bidding of those who do hold power. He may represent a geographical or occupational faction within the party. Whether strong in his own right or doing the bidding of others, he must obtain the collaboration of the lower layers of organization. Each has its own local following and each is comparatively independent of external control. The manner in which they join forces to carry on the business of the party—selection of candidates and the conduct of campaigns—varies greatly from place to place and from time to time within the same state or locality. The extent to which the formal party organization, prescribed by rule or statute, is the real organization differs from place to place. While there is a moderate tendency for political leadership to be more cohesive in competitive states, this is only a tendency. What actually affects the ability of some state parties to provide a determined and continuous leadership is as yet unknown. We do know that this leadership is a vital part of the ability of the governor and his administration to provide better education and welfare services for the people of his state. Hence, the unknown becomes a matter of crucial importance to those who study party leadership.

The Rewards for Party Work

What reward is there for those who spend countless hours of their time pounding the pavements; licking and sticking; meeting commuter trains in the wee, small hours to hand out campaign literature; encouraging and recruiting candidates—in short all the chores connected with the political party as an electoral organization? We have seen that Schlesinger has identified two major types of people who work for the party: office seekers and benefit seekers. Office seekers want the status and power that come from elective office but they cannot achieve this goal alone. They're dependent on the labor of those who attach themselves to the party for one reason or another, and they must reward these faithful workers.

There is an occasional conflict between the goals of the office seekers and those who work for their election. The latter seek benefits from party work that can usually be provided by the successful office seeker. Clark and Wilson describe the three major incentives that motivate people to work for the party—or any organization, for that matter. They are material, solidary, and purposive.[23] Material incentives are paid in tangible rewards; that is, rewards that have a monetary value or can be easily translated into those that have. These include jobs, contracts for public works, purchase of real estate for public improvements, and judicial spoils such as appointments by the courts of receivers, trustees, and other judicial functionaries. Solidary incentives concern rewards that are basically intangible. These inducements derive from the act of associating and include such rewards as community recognition, socializing, being around important people, and fun and conviviality. These are independent of obtaining political office—the main function of party organization. The workers enjoy party activity separately from the major ends of association. The third incentive is purposive and is paid off in policy—the elimination of corruption, enactment of a charter or amendment, beautification of the community. Unlike solidary incentives, purposive incentives are inseparable from the ends being sought. The members seek some change in the status quo, not simply activity to enjoy each others' company. A political party must appeal to many motives that occasionally are in conflict. We turn our attention now to an illustration of the way the parties satisfy these varying motives of the workers and how the differences between them create tensions for the party organization.

MATERIAL   Not long ago, material rewards and political payoffs in the form of patronage were regarded as evil. Reformers reacted violently by placing most state jobs under a merit system. Many local governments also sought to reduce political influence in "nonpartisan" governments by instituting merit appointments. It was thought that the lack of patronage as payoffs would limit party activity to those virtuous types who sought solidary, or better still, purposive rewards. According to one's perspective, this was considered either a disaster or a triumph. It is now conceded that the role of patronage in holding a party organization together was overdrawn by both friends and foes. Studies have shown there is no simple correlation between patronage positions available to a state government and the strength of the parties in the state. Neither Connecticut nor New York has a high percentage of state administrative positions available to the political leadership for dispensing to the party faithful; yet both party systems are considered strong.[24] Party strength would seem to depend on many factors. A generation or so ago, patronage flourished among the uprooted, illiterate, and unassimilated groups in the urban centers of America. Without wealth or political tradition and involvement in the issues of the day, these groups could be wooed by the boss to produce for the party.

Today, labor unions and well-organized interest groups provide the parties with alternate sources of political workers. Patronage has declined but the parties are still around. In fact, Frank Sorauf suggests that patronage may be self-destructive for the party. In the hands of a faction or city machine leader, it may be used to destroy party leadership or as a weapon in intraparty squabbles.[25] Certainly the 35,000 jobs the late Mayor Daley of Chicago controlled were not used to help candidates for state office who opposed his politics. Patronage is a mixed blessing. If used skillfully by a state party leader, it may build up intraparty cohesion or vitality. It is still an important commodity in which many state chairmen trade. The positions involved are generally of two types: paid government positions involving the public's business and unpaid honorary memberships in various party councils and committees. The former are the most important since they reward the party worker for his services. Jobs represent the currency of politics. Honorary memberships are of less importance in terms of monetary reward but carry with them honor and prestige. A knowledgeable state chairman or governor can use patronage appointments as a means of maintaining control over party affairs.

Some states still maintain large numbers of patronage positions. A former state chairman of Pennsylvania said that the governor of that state has 65,000 patronage positions to reward, while in Indiana about 8,000 of the state's 22,000 public employees are patronage appointees. In West Virginia, a Democratic party official reported that the party controlled all state offices except the governorship and could distribute 300 state jobs. He noted, however, that if his party had elected the governor there would be 15,000 jobs to distribute.[26] These are exceptional cases. Even those who distribute patronage express ambivalent attitudes toward patronage policies. Most of them, both party chairmen and governors, still view prospective jobs as an important incentive to party workers. Between 1955 and 1959, Governor Harriman used patronage to assert control over the state wide party. By the judicious clearing of appointments through a chosen leader rather than his rival, the men in Albany were able to influence the choice of local candidates for elective office. Patronage appointments were important as much for their symbolic as for their practical value. A bypassed leader not only loses control over the income of a particular person but also loses legitimacy in the eyes of his followers.[27]

SOLIDARY AND PURPOSIVE   If jobs and contracts can be used to control the party organization because they provide material rewards, how can we explain the mass of party workers who labor without the expectation of pay, contracts, or even appointments to boards and commissions? The other two types of benefit seekers are those seeking solidary rewards and those seeking purposive rewards. Recently, studies have shown that political parties are more "ideological" or purposive than had been supposed. A study of state party chairmen reveals that they were motivated primarily by what might be termed idealistic, philosophical, or impersonal motives. Motives such as influencing governmental policies, fulfilling a sense of community obligation, attachment to party, and political work as a way of life were regarded as more important than business contacts and material reward. In fact, nearly 50 percent said they saw campaign work as a way of influencing the policies of government.[28] A study of Detroit precinct committeemen found that they began their party activity with impersonal or purposive motivations of moral, philosophical, or ideological satisfaction (74 percent of the Democrats and 85 percent of the Republicans).[29] If it is true that party work is increasingly "fed" by policy motives, doesn't that give rise to a problem for the party leaders with respect to satisfying policy demands? When jobs are used to pay workers, they may walk away satisfied. But policy cannot please all the workers—it may be too little for the militants or too much for the moderates. As V. O. Key said, "The top party leadership must try to restrain the extremist within the party ranks. . . . Lower-level leaders may flourish by the fanning of extremist and particularist emotions, but the top echelon must seek to hold together divergent and often conflicting elements."[30] In doing so, the top leadership may be persuaded that the state must fund public schools more equitably, provide for the needs of the poor more generously, provide job training, and so forth when these issues may not be the ones dividing the party rank and file. It is the radicalism of those drawn to the party by ideological motives that affects the policies of the top leaders and makes them less representative of people who vote for them.[31] Hence, those who are drawn to the party for ideological reasons may be the hardest to please insofar as they disagree with the more moderate attitudes of the top leadership. It may be important for leadership to try to instill a "solidary" reward through various means to moderate those activists it cannot please in the ranks immediately below. Some evidence exists to indicate that, the longer a party worker stays with the organization, the more his rewards become solidary and are derived from social contacts.[32] This may be the saving of party organization. Those who seek solidary rewards find them in party work among old friends. If a sufficient number of the ideological activists move toward this reward as their motive, the leadership can keep the party together.

PARTY FUNCTIONS

The basic functions of the electoral party are the recruiting, nominating, and electing of candidates for public office. Under these headings come other important jobs, all related to strengthening the party's prospects for victory at the polls. It is necessary to recruit candidates as well as secondary leadership to work for them and carry out the thousand and one tasks that are part of a successful election bid. Nomination procedures are complicated by the direct primary which takes away the assurance that party leaders can control the nominations. The firm attachment of a party label to a candidate in a primary is a feat that can be performed by a cohesive party, but it is far from a common occurrence. Under the heading of election management comes the formulation of issues, publicity, and fund raising. We will consider these functions in a sequence from recruitment to nomination to election.

Recruitment: Candidates and Leadership

The recruitment of able people to run for office is necessarily bound up with the recruitment of party leadership as well. The type of person who chooses to remain within the party structure and the one who decides to make a bid for election are both found within the pool of party regulars. Hence, any discussion of recruitment takes in both groups. Neil Staebler discusses the importance of recruitment to party control: "This explains why party leaders usually prefer candidates who are of, by, and for the party, and why a state chairman often will battle bitterly to secure the nomination of those who are friendly to the regular organization. Only when winning appears essential to the survival of the party, and thus to the chairman's position and power, can he be expected openly to encourage an attractive candidate with whom he has little or no political leverage."[33] Huckshorn found that, among chairmen of both parties, 74 percent engaged in some form of candidate recruitment. Considering the number of states where self-starting has become the common method of entry into candidacy, these figures represent surprisingly high levels of recruitment. Most state chairmen concentrate on ticket filling at the county level or in state legislative races. At times, recruitment demands months of work. A state chairman may spot a likely candidate in a county organization and begin trying to persuade him or her to consider running. A Democratic chairman from a competitive state comments:

> When we see a young man or woman that we think would be a good candidate for the legislature, particularly the House, we begin to groom him. I see that the individual is appointed to party committees in order to increase exposure and establish some limited name-identification. We send him out on the trail to speak at dinners and other events. If he stands the test we then approach him about running for office. I don't think that some of them ever realize that we consciously groomed them for office.[34]

Recruitment is not a process without dangers to the power of the state chairman. If the party is fractionalized between two ideological or geographical wings, the chairman may have to assume a neutral position on recruitment and let the candidates "emerge" or recruit themselves. Any approach to a prospective candidate may appear to be favoritism, and the chairman cannot then remain a mediator and conciliator, which he may regard as crucial if his party is going to win the election.

Recruitment activities for city and county offices traditionally have been left to local party organizations, and most of them have been unwilling to call on the state chairman to persuade local candidates to run. They do accept other forms of assistance such as patronage, research, fundraising assistance, and get-out-the-vote drives, but most have viable local organizations that traditionally prefer to handle recruitment responsibilities on their own. Because it is vital to a local organization to have its leaders and candidates friendly, they find the people to fill the ticket and provide the leadership. Of course a high percentage of the county, township, city, or precinct organizations have defunct operations. In this case, the state party chairman tries to find a few capable people to get the ball rolling. He may obtain the names of potential leaders from other party people in the area. Often a civic leader, lawyer, businessman, teacher, or journalist may make a good prospect. Any individual who enters politics briefly to aid a particular candidate may be persuaded to accept a continuing commitment. In the case of a new sprouting local organization nurtured by the state leadership, recruitment of local candidates for public office is performed jointly with the state organization. The state leader has extracted commitments of loyalty from them in advance.

CHARACTERISTICS OF RECRUITS   Since the leadership of the state party organization, both organizational and elective, arises out of the local-level parties, their ability to recruit active and vigorous leaders is vitally important to the organization. It is from this pool that the leadership "fishes" for state organizational or elective office, appealing to the prospect on purposive or monetary grounds, whichever seems to be more appropriate. The chairman must see that his recruit is trained in the fundamentals of party organization and that he survives the political break-in period to become a dependable addition to the party. Obviously the characteristics of the environment affect the type of people who will be tapped for leadership positions. In a university town or "silk-stocking" district, an ideologue would be a preferred candidate. In a working-class district, a person who can identify with the problems of the blue-collar worker is preferable. This person does not necessarily have to be a blue collar himself but he must be able to speak the language of the working man. Republicans from the industrial Northeast are very different from their fellow partisans in Kansas. The Democrat who stems from the liberal university district is a different creature from the candidate who represents the peanut-growing section of Georgia. Neither could be elected to statewide political office in the other's state. It is, then, a delicate matter to choose the candidates who will be representative of their respective jurisdictions. It is a process that requires political risk on the part of the candidates themselves. How they assess their election chances affects their willingness to work or run for the party.

THE PARTY ACTIVIST   What kind of person is a party activist? How does he differ from the voters in terms of social, attitudinal, and personality characteristics? Research indicates that the individual who is likely to be a party activist, and thus eligible to run for party office, is most likely to be a middle-aged, married, business or professional man with a comfortable income and some standing in his community based on long residence and organizational contacts there. Political leaders and activists tend to be of higher socioeconomic status than party members or voters. Furthermore, the higher the leadership level, the higher the socioeconomic status of its occupants. The Republican Party tends to draw its activists and officials from higher status groups than the Democrats. This generalization breaks down, however, when the officials and activists of the Southern Democratic Party are investigated. In these states, for instance, Democratic county chairmen represented the "establishment" party and drew upon higher-status groups in the community. Some writers have found that upwardly mobile people—those who want to better their occupational position—will rise to prominence within a party.

Certain occupations may produce a larger share of party activists than others because of the type of "brokerage" skills that they encourage. Many lawyers, for example, are found in party organizations and elected offices. Herbert Jacob believes that elected officials have characteristic personality traits, the core of which consists of a greater need than the general population for prestige, power, helping others, and being in the public eye. They enter professions that encourage this brokerage role. Hence, elected officials will come principally from occupations that stress this personality type.[35]

Also of interest is the political socialization typical of party activists: the type of family background and the development of interest in politics. Leaders and activists tend to have been raised in "politicized families" or have grown up in homes where at least one parent was politically interested and active, giving the family a major role to play in stimulating interest and entry into the field of politics. This interest tends to develop at an earlier age than in ordinary people. Political leaders and activists are those individuals who feel sufficiently competent and able to create changes in line with their interests; they are generally more ideologically sensitive and consistent than voters.

The model of political recruitment considered above suggests that party leaders recruit from the community people they see to be potentially available and encourage such persons to seek nomination to party or elective office. They encourage the beginner to believe that political office is important both to himself and to the party. This selection is an important part of the recruitment process because it develops a pool from which candidates will rise to fill higher positions in the party and government. Recruitment is perhaps the most important function that party leadership needs to perform for the political system. To the extent that they can attract able, interested people from the political community to participate in politics, the system can continue. It is immensely important to our democracy that this recruitment process select those who are representative of the voters. It is vital to the parties themselves that their leadership continues to identify, groom, and promote candidates for statewide office.

Primary Nominations: Legal Procedures

The uniquely American direct primary form of nomination exists in all states, although it takes on different shapes.[36] A direct primary requires that nominations be made by the voters, usually party members, rather than representatives in a convention. Ushered into the American states in the period 1896 to 1915, the direct primary form of nomination replaced the delegate convention as a means of selecting candidates to run for governor and other statewide offices. Convention nominations had been indirect, with the voting delegates chosen by mass meetings, caucuses, and conventions in counties or other local areas. The adoption of the direct primary, under the guise of making the internal control of the party more democratic, struck down the intermediate links between the party rank and file and would-be candidates, allowing the voter to express his preferences for the nomination.

The primary system first came into use in the southern states—those most stubbornly attached to a single party. It permitted a measure of popular government within the dominant party. Because nomination was tantamount to election, the voters were given a choice within the confines of the party. Outside of the South, statewide direct primaries first took hold in the West and then spread to the Eastern Seaboard. The fact that there remained a semblance of an opposition party in these states may explain in part why they embraced the primary procedures later than the southern states. Introduction of the direct primary into most states substituted an intraparty politics for an interparty politics. Prior to the primary form of nomination, cliques of leaders operating within their respective party conventions bargained and fought over the nominees their party would present to the voters in the general election. Now they must convince the primary voters that their candidate must win the party label to contest for the election. Primary voters are a very different lot from the general electorate and hence may pick a candidate in the primary who is not necessarily representative of the party.

Primaries in the 50 states are usually divided into three categories, differing chiefly in the way they define the party membership that can vote in them.[37]

THE CLOSED PRIMARY   Found in 39 states, the closed primary requires that the voter declare his party affiliation so he can vote only in his respective primary. In most of these states, the voter declares his affiliation when he registers. Then at the primary election he is given his party's ballot so he may choose among his fellow partisans seeking the nomination. In other closed-primary states, the voter simply declares his party membership or preference when he goes to the polling place and is then given the primary ballot of his party.

THE OPEN AND BLANKET PRIMARIES   In the eight states of the open primary —Idaho, Michigan, Minnesota, Montana, North Dakota, Utah, Vermont, and Wisconsin—the voter appears at the polls, receives the ballots of all parties, and makes his selection privately. He may not, however, participate in the primary of more than one party. The blanket primary, found in Alaska, Louisiana, and Washington, has been called the "free-love" primary because it does not restrict a voter to one party; he need not disclose his affiliation and may vote in more than one primary. That is, the voter may choose among Democrats seeking the nomination for one office and among Republicans seeking the nomination for another. Louisiana has a single primary for both Democratic and Republican candidates.[38]

Party leadership clearly prefers closed primaries. At least they know, within limits who their constituency is and can therefore groom candidates to appeal to that segment of party voters who are most typical of the larger voting public. The lottery of the direct primary form of nomination was a serious setback for the party leadership, which was the intention of the reformers. They mistrusted the party and fancied it to be a tool for all sorts of hidden interests. In effect, they made it very difficult for leaders to recruit candidates for public office by using the assurance that they would win the primary. Too often, a last-minute challenger would enter the scene, declare his candidacy for the nomination, and then sweep the primary. It's debatable whether he is more qualified than the party-sponsored candidate carefully chosen by the leadership. In sixteen states, the party still has a place in the nomination of state candidates, although it's usually in combination with a primary.[39] In four others, the party officials can choose whether or not to have a convention or primary. The norm in these predominantly one-party states is for party officials to choose the direct primary because they can't control the nomination and so prefer to be neutral. This is typical of the pattern in Alabama, Georgia, South Carolina, and Virginia.

Participation in Primaries

The party organization's most important function is nominating candidates for public office. Outside of the South, where voter turnout in primary and general elections is about equal, primary turnouts have averaged 27.5 percent. In general elections, the average is 22 to 29 points higher.[40] If primary voters reflected the preferences of a party's rank and file, there would be no problem with this meager turnout. But are those people who vote representative of the whole? Down south, voters in the Democratic primaries make the final choice of candidates. In other states, about 30 percent of a party's rank and file determines which candidate will win the nomination; aspirants for office need only command the loyalty of a few friends and neighbors to win a place on the party ticket. This fact has undoubtedly affected the overall health of the political party in the United States. Candidates appealing to small groups of voters can make it difficult for politicians to present popular slates. These blocs of voters may be rooted in an ethnic group, a religious group, a newspaper, or a neighborhood—any biased group that is organized enough during the primary to create headaches for the party leaders. In some cases, statewide parties have disintegrated under the influence of a direct primary. In others, the leaders try to get out the party faithful to support their hand-picked man.

While studying party leadership in the states, Robert Huckshorn asked the chairmen of all the state parties if they would become involved in a primary fight between two or more candidates for the same nomination. In both parties combined, 57.5 percent indicated that they would intervene, at least provisionally. Many (28.7 percent) said they would involve themselves if it was necessary to protect the caliber of the ticket. Others felt that intervention would be desirable only if the candidate had been officially endorsed. Only 28.8 percent said they would not intervene under any circumstances.[41]

Huckshorn quoted the following lament from a leader who had tried to keep his party organization together by controlling the nominations:

> ... I worked long and hard to put together a list of candidates who might give us a chance at some legislative seats in one key county. But in two of the three districts we got an outsider who had never been in party affairs. ... The primary was held about three weeks ago and we got a Bircher nominated in one, a housewife with no experience in another, and we got our own guy nominated in the third. How in hell are we going to go to the people with that? To make matters worse, the Bircher is probably going to win and will be around to embarrass us for the next two years, if not forever.[42]

The Politics of Gubernatorial Nominations

This section is concerned with the politics of winning gubernatorial nominations. The importance of understanding the intraparty coalitions a potential governor must put together before he wins the nomination can hardly be underestimated; they are what he works with in the policy-making process. If the gubernatorial candidate puts together a successful primary coalition—one that will work to get him the nomination—he can count on its support in the governing process. A candidate who receives a bare majority of the primary vote can count on a powerful alliance against him in the legislature. His closest rival usually has allies within the legislature who are more eager to bolster their candidate for the next round than to help the incumbent achieve success.

Almost no potential governor starts from "scratch." Most have been state legislators or public attorneys, have run for election, and have developed a power base from which to operate. With his finite supply of rewards and punishments and his own ability and effort, the gubernatorial candidate forges a coalition to stand by him at election time. His degree of success is measured first by the primary results and later by the degree of support he musters for his policies in the government.

THE CHANCES OF WINNING THE GOVERNORSHIP CONTROL THE PRIMARY CONTESTS A pioneer study of the intraparty politics of the nominating process has been made by the late V. O. Key.[43] Key's hypothesis is that the operations of a direct primary occur within the framework fixed by the two-party division of the electorate. The nature and function of party primaries will vary roughly with the degree to which the formal party system diverges from the pattern of two-party competition. In states where one party is dominant, internal politics provides the controlling decisions in respect to personnel to man the governmental machine. Key's studies of the 11 southern states support his hypothesis that lack of competition results in multiple-faction parties. The party machinery is impartial toward personalities and factions competing in the primaries. Key points out that no external pressure from a minority party exists to drive the majority party toward internal unity and discipline. Key noted in the 1950s that North Carolina, Tennessee, and Virginia had the makings of an organized faction within the majority Democratic Party. He explained that this was created by the presence of a small Republican opposition party, thus supporting the claim that even minimal competition can bring about a degree of cohesion.[44] Since that time, these three states as well as Florida have elected Republican governors and have moved out of the solid Democratic ranks.

When Key turned his attention to the Northern states, which would provide a contrast to the faction-torn one-party South, he found that the two-party system was not consistently producing the disciplined cohesive parties he had predicted. He concluded that the primary system has affected the structure of the northern parties. Gradually, party organizations were weakened by dissident elements that won in the primaries until many state organizations merely ratified the successful primary candidate. In the most competitive states, rivalry for the nomination is keen as different groups try to control the process. In a few, party organizations make some attempt to control the nominating process through preprimary conventions or informal party assemblies.

Conditions have changed since Key's analysis, which ended with 1952. There are now only seven one-party states in the Union-states in which nothing short of major upheaval could move the electorate to vote for a Republican governor.[45] The remaining 43 states fall into different classifications, depending on the measures and time periods used. We are interested in a measure that will indicate the chance a potential governor has for winning an election and will use the popular vote for governor for a 22-year time period to measure competition.

Ten states "lean" Democratic—where Democrats averaged 55 percent or more of the two-party vote from 1956 to 1978. Most of these states are in the process of transition from solidly Democratic to a more competitive standing, except for Connecticut, Nevada, and Utah, which have been leaning Democratic in recent years. In all ten states, a Republican has been elected governor at least once in that time period. This indicates that Republicans have a chance if they bestir themselves.

The remaining 33 states offer either party a good chance to capture the governorship. This group includes those traditionally true-blue Republican states of New Hampshire, Vermont, Kansas, and North and South Dakota. In all 33 states, the voters swing back and forth in their preference between parties. There are no longer any solid Republican states, or even "leaning" Republican states, if the yardstick is composed of "chances for winning the governorship."

Given the chances for election just outlined, we would expect that aspiring politicians would aim for the governorship in state parties where their election chances were best. The 33 competitive states offer this opportunity for both parties; the ten "leaning Democratic" states give the Democrats an edge, while the solid Democratic states ensure that a Democrat will be elected. Table 4–2 presents evidence of the struggles Democratic contenders had for the nomination in the 50 states, grouped according to the candidate's election chances.

TABLE 4–2

Proportion of the Vote Polled by Democratic Nominees in Gubernatorial Primaries, 1956–78[a]:

STATE INTERPARTY COMPETITION	Percentage of Primaries, According to Proportion of Vote to Nominee in Primary					TOTAL NUMBER OF PRIMARIES
	UNDER 50	50–59	60–79	80–100	TOTAL	
One-party Democratic[b] (7)	71	17	3	9	100	35
Leaning Democratic[c] (10)	51	27	7	15	100	45
Two-party (33)	26	25	19	30	100	184

[a] Involving no incumbents.

[b] The seven one-party Democratic states are those that average over 65 percent Democratic of the general election vote for governor: Alabama, Arkansas, Georgia, Louisiana, Mississippi, South Carolina, and Texas.

[c] The ten leaning Democratic states are those that average 55–60 percent Democratic of the general election vote for governor: Connecticut, Florida, Maryland, Missouri, Nevada, North Carolina, Oklahoma, Tennessee, Utah, and Kentucky.

Note: There is substantial overlap between the states listed as Democratic and Leaning Democratic in this Table and the states in the least competitive categories in Table 2.2. The measure of competition and the time periods differ, so there is not perfect correspondence.

Source: Richard Scammon, ed., *America Votes* (Pittsburgh: University of Pittsburgh Press, 1956–62); and (Washington, D.C.: Governmental Affairs Institute, and Congressional Quarterly, Inc. 1964–76). Appropriate issues of *Congressional Quarterly Weekly Reports*, 1977–78 (Congressional Quarterly Inc.).

The One-Party Democratic States

When these struggles for the nomination are put into the context of chances for election victory, an interesting pattern emerges. Seventy-one percent of the primaries in one-party Democratic states are won by less than 50 percent of the primary vote, which indicates a fierce competition for the nomination. Once the primary is won, the candidate is virtually assured of the election. It is no wonder, then, that the real struggle takes place *within* the dominant party. Competing factions may be based on personal ambition for leadership, or they may represent very real social, economic, or geographic cleavages within the party. The 1974 Dorn-Ravenel primary in South Carolina indicated an economic and social struggle between two factions of the Democratic party. This will undoubtedly re-emerge in the future. It is commonly believed that factions are more likely to have social and economic bases in the seven one-party states where the real contest is in the dominant party's primary. So, in effect the party is no more than an umbrella covering major factional strife.

The Leaning Democratic States

Another pattern emerges in the ten leaning Democratic states. Only 51 percent of the primaries are fought so bitterly as to give the victor less than 50 percent of the primary vote. Because a Republican could win, the party label is coveted as a meaningful vote-winning mechanism for the election. Battles are more interparty than intraparty. Capturing the party nomination means that bargaining among potential contenders may take place in advance of the primary to ensure a nominee of a respectable showing and hence some party support in the election. Bargaining might consist of agreements for appointments within the administration if the leading contender is elected. Or a possible timetable of ambition might be worked out among aspirants in which each could run without major competition in a future primary. Whenever such bargaining takes place, the stakes are high in capturing the nomination.

The Competitive States

Either party can win in the 33 competitive states, making the party organization much more than a holding company. Here, a powerful group of state chairmen and others, with some semblance of leadership, can sift and schedule ambitions among contenders for the nomination. A hard-fought primary is considered to be a divisive struggle that gives the advantage to the other side. Airing one's "dirty linen" in public gives the opposition a campaign platform on which to operate. The primary voting trends shown in Table 4–2 tend to confirm that Democratic state parties are more cohesive in two-party states. The nomination is won by a larger proportion of the primary vote (80 to 100 percent) than in any other contests, which indicates at least some cohesive effort by the party leadership. But, even if this hypothesis appears to be confirmed in a general way, the fact remains that 50 percent of the primaries involving nonincumbents in competitive states are won by less than 60 percent of the primary vote. The coalitions that the governor and party leaders build to get nominated and elected are the same ones used to pass programs in the legislature. Thus, in the 33 competitive states, as many Democratic candidates are nominated through fierce intraparty struggles as by grand coalitions that agree in advance to work for a candidate bearing the party's banner into battle. It would follow, then, that the struggle for nomination carries over into the government by limiting the governor's ability to build the coalitions he needs to govern.

The Republicans: Contests for Nominations

Party analysts like to ridicule the Democrats for being in a permanent state of disorder—the party tends to exaggerate its internal disagreements in the most visible arena. Republicans, on the other hand, tend to minimize their internal disagreements. Politics is a business to the Republicans, while with Democrats, it's a pleasure. Bearing this in mind, we should expect Republicans to exhibit different tendencies from their joyously squabbling competitors. A first look at Table 4–3 would appear to confirm this notion of the Republican party. Many more primaries are won by candidates receiving 80 to 100 percent of the primary vote. However, as V. O. Key pointed out, minority-party primaries are not contested when an election appears hopeless. No serious aspirant for governor would make a major effort to gain the Republican nomination in Alabama, for instance. The table indicates that few Republican nominations were closely contested in strong Democratic states. In fact, Alabama Republicans did not even run a candidate for the governorship until 1974 when Elvin McCary was unopposed for the nomination. He went on to receive 15 percent of the vote in the November election. In most of these strong Democratic states, the Republican nomination goes to a person who is willing to make the run just to keep the Republican name before the voters. In Alabama, Georgia, and South Carolina, Republicans usually nominate their candidate in convention while the Democrats nominate in the primary. In view of the general power situation between the parties of those states, this makes political sense.

In leaning Democratic states, more frequent contests occur within

TABLE 4-3

Proportion of the Vote Polled by Republican
Nominees in Gubernatorial Primaries, 1956–78[a]:

STATE INTERPARTY COMPETITION	Percentage of Primaries, According to Proportion of Vote to Nominee in Primary					TOTAL NUMBER OF PRIMARIES
	UNDER 50	50–59	60–79	80–100	TOTAL	
One-party Democratic[b] (7)	6	11	11	72	100	36
Leaning Democratic[c] (10)	11	27	22	40	100	55
Two-party (33)	20	21	22	37	100	178

[a] Involving no incumbents.
[b,c] Same states as in Table 4–2.
Source: Same as for Table 4–2.

the Republican party. There is a decent chance that voters may become disgruntled with the way majority Democrats are "running the ship" and turn to the Republican candidate. The Republican nomination has much more than honorific value. Obviously candidates recognize this, and nominations are contested almost as much as in the two-party states. In these states, the decorum hypothesis of Republican management can be fairly tested. Table 4–3 does not indicate a peaceful nomination process within the Republican ranks. While they may not compete as openly as the Democrats, 40 percent of their nominations are hotly contested. Apparently the race for the state's most important political post does not impede slugging matches within the businesslike GOP. Party leaders are no more able to keep the fight out of the public arena than their Democratic counterparts. Thus, a Republican governor arriving on the steps of the capitol has no better chance of coalition support than a Democrat. Over 40 percent of the time, a governor faces opposition left over from his primary match.

Incumbents Usually Renominated

There is one unwritten rule followed faithfully by both parties under competitive conditions: Incumbents are usually renominated unopposed, which again makes good political sense. A governor has a reservoir of publicity he accumulated during his four years in office. He has also been able to distribute political favors to the faithful (and deserving) and hence build up a pool of supporters. This gives him a great advantage in the primary because he has created a supply of rewards and punishments that can be used to further encourage supporters. Promise of appointments within his next administration appears a likely possibility. Gubernatorial careers are longer now. An incumbent governor running for reelection in a competitive state has a better than 70 percent chance of winning the general election. Helping him are those who have aspirations of one kind or another. He has the power to reward support. Table 4–4 illustrates these points. Note that within the Democratic party in the seven southern states nomination, even for incumbents, is still hotly contested. No group of decision makers within those southern Democratic parties agrees to let the incumbent have the nomination. More likely than not, a shiny new contender believes he has as much chance as the incumbent.

Although there are not enough primaries to make ironclad generalizations about the southern states, the data show that most of the time the incumbent governor faces a stiff contest. The leaning Democratic and two-party states reveal a different trend. Here, the incumbent will most likely win the next electoral contest and put his party into office—with all the flow of rewards that fact can bring. The incumbent is the best bet for the nomination, and, well over 90 percent of the time, he gets it. Many willing members of his party bestir themselves on his behalf. Figures show that the Republican party is just as prone to give the nomination to an incumbent. With too few cases (four) where an incumbent Republican has

TABLE 4–4

Proportion of the Vote Polled by Democratic
and Republican Incumbents in Gubernatorial
Primaries, 1956–78

STATE INTERPARTY COMPETITION	Percentage of Primaries, According to Proportion of Vote to Nominee in Primary					TOTAL NUMBER OF PRIMARIES
	UNDER 50	50–59	60–79	80–100	TOTAL	
Democratic Party						
One-party						
Democratic[a] (7)	0	29	59	12	100	17
Leaning						
Democratic[a] (10)	13	7	27	53	100	15
Two-party (33)	4	10	19	67	100	75
Republican Party						
Two-party (33)	6	16	16	62	100	82

[a] These are the same states as those given in Table 4–2.
Source: Same as for Table 4–2.

run again in the one-party Democratic or leaning Democratic states, we cannot test any theories in those categories. Winthrop Rockefeller received over 95 percent of the primary vote in Arkansas in all his bids for governor; but it must have been obvious that he was the only candidate who had any hope of winning Arkansas for the party.

To summarize, it appears that few governors can count on the support of a party organization to help them in their attempts to capture the governorship. In a sense, they must "capture" the party to make a bid for the nomination and election. They have serious competition for this prize —the party label. The average number of candidates who compete for the nomination varies with the competitive conditions in the states, as Table 4–5 shows. In strong Democratic states, a Democratic gubernatorial candidate must beat out an average of three contenders for the nomination. As a general rule, in the leaning Democratic states, he contends with two others. In a competitive state, the Democratic candidate can concentrate on one opponent. This shows the internal structure of the party in relation to its power position in the state. Presumably there is some concentration of effort to support a winner in the competitive states. The Republican pattern shows a different trend but one that can be explained from its relative power position. In states where election is more or less hopeless, a "sacrificial" candidate is drafted or runs unopposed in the primary. In states where there is hope, Republicans exhibit the same disposition as Democrats to unite behind an uncontested winner in the primary—or at least a strong candidate who will encounter little opposition. They are a little more successful at this, which may buttress the general notion that Republicans minimize their internal differences while Democrats exaggerate theirs.

These statistics give broad generalizations. What needs to be refined is the nature of party factions, which appear as votes in the primaries. No single concept can describe the varieties of political structure appearing in the states. Factions may be amorphous and transient, relatively durable, economically based, or, on occasion, ideologically oriented. The primary

TABLE 4–5

Average Number of Gubernatorial Candidates
Polling 5 Percent or More of the Total Primary
Vote, 1956–78

	DEMOCRATS	REPUBLICANS
Strong Democratic	3.7	1.7
Leaning Democratic	3.0	2.2
Two-party	2.2	2.0

provides a picture of these factions at one moment in time, indicating the strengths and weaknesses of the contenders in terms of votes.

Nominating Conventions: A Sign of Party Cohesion

In five states we can glimpse the nomination stage of both parties from another perspective. Colorado, Connecticut, Delaware, New York, and Utah are among the 16 states which use party organs to nominate candidates for governor. All have viable party organizations ready to back candidates for nomination. Colorado and Utah have preprimary conventions within the parties to endorse gubernatorial candidates. A convention winner in Colorado is listed first on the gubernatorial ballot. While anyone who receives over 20 percent of the convention vote also goes on the ballot, the candidate preferred by the convention majority usually wins. In Utah, if a candidate receives 70 percent of the delegate vote, he is the certified candidate and is not required to run in the primary.

In Connecticut, Delaware, and New York, primaries are not mandatory and are used infrequently. These states have a history of two closely matched political parties that take their partisanship very seriously. Potential governors make a try for the nomination within the party circles. A primary can be held if this intraparty decision is contested by a candidate receiving a specified minimum percentage of the convention vote (Connecticut, 20 percent; Delaware, 35 percent; New York 25 percent).

All five states exhibit several varieties of factional contests and agreement. Both party conventions in Colorado were able to keep factional strife from erupting into a public settlement in the primary until 1974 when close contests occurred in each party. Both contests were fought between liberals and conservatives and both were won by liberals. In Utah, on the other hand, lively primary contests between the two leading contenders in both parties characterized four out of the last six primaries. In Connecticut, New York, and Delaware, the factions usually join together within the framework of the convention.

New York Democrats are the exception to this rule, three times in the past 20 years carrying their contests to the party's voters. In 1974, Hugh Carey won a sweeping victory over the party-endorsed candidate in the primary. Within a few days, he had drawn support from virtually every segment of the party. Democratic party regulars who had given his opponent their official backing thus implied that Carey was as much to their liking as their former champion. In 1978, party-backed Carey won a decisive primary victory over his lieutenant governor who challenged him for the nomination.

Until 1976, Indiana used conventions to nominate statewide candidates. Apparently, factions within the parties could not be contained within their respective conventions, and the contest was shifted to the primary arena. Indiana party factions have a traditional tug-of-war over nominations. One student of Indiana's nominating conventions says that control over outcomes was widely dispersed. Even the top leaders holding massive party and patronage powers were unable to control the results at the top of the ticket. They followed the ever-changing coalition of delegates who responded to the qualities of aspirants for the nomination.[46] On the other hand, another student of Indiana politics claims that the governor held extensive control over the convention. A large number of delegates were state employees. They, of course, voted the way party leaders told them to. The county chairmen usually received some form of state patronage and in return were expected to deliver their delegates' votes. This description fitted the party in control of the governorship from which flowed the patronage that held factions together. More open conventions occurred when the party was out of power.[47]

The advantages of a working party cohesion appear in Iowa and South Dakota. In both states, if no candidate receives more than 35 percent of the primary vote, a postprimary convention is held to select a candidate. While this would appear to be putting the cart before the horse in terms of moderating factional strife, the threat of a potential postprimary convention has resulted in its total absence of use in either state.

The eight states mentioned in this discussion have recognizably little in common. Indications are that party organizations in the three northeastern states and Indiana may have withstood the onslaught of the party reformers in the early part of the century and maintained a semblance of party cohesion. In the other four states, there may be signs of party revival. Perhaps the parties in those states recognize that a primary, unlike the convention system, fails to provide opportunity for consultation, consideration of alternatives, or compromise in resolving intraparty disputes and differences. This distorts one of the vital elements in the process of party government.

In a number of other states, no official endorsement by a state convention or party committee is authorized by law. Support of a particular candidate by at least a considerable segment of the organized party leadership may be the decisive factor in a primary contest. In California and Wisconsin, voluntary associations within the parties have influenced the outcome of primary contests by giving their endorsement to favored candidates. Perhaps there is a growing realization that the business of developing and pushing candidates for governor cannot be settled by the process of self-selection by aspiring office holders. At least candidates who receive the nod of party leaders in these states have an organization with which to begin the process of winning the election and governing.

ELECTIONS: DO FACTIONS COMBINE
FOR VICTORY?

The Factions Continue in the
Governing Party

If the gubernatorial candidate who won a handsome percentage of his
party primary invariably won over the candidate whose party was weak
and divided, the political process would accord with the party theorists.
A united party would implement its election promises, motivated by the
need to face the electorate in the next election. Unfortunately, this pleas-
ant myth dissolves when the results are examined. Figure 4–2 shows the

FIGURE 4–2 Primary Record of Winning Gubernatorial Candidates,
1956–78[a]

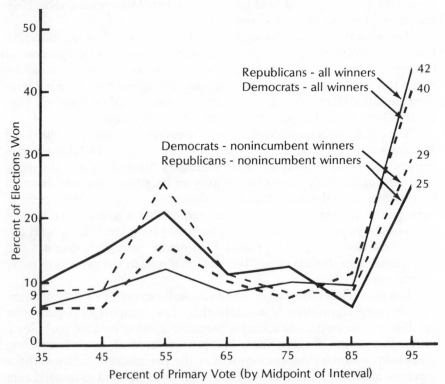

[a]Distribution of 257 gubernatorial elections in 33 competitive states won by Republican and Demo-
cratic candidates according to their percentage of the primary vote.
Source: Richard Scammon, ed., America Votes (Pittsburgh: University of Pittsburgh Press, 1956–62;
and Washington, D. C.: Governmental Affairs Institute, and Congressional Quarterly, Inc. 1964–76).
Appropriate issues of Congressional Quarterly Weekly Reports, 1977–78 (Congressional Quarterly
Inc.).

distribution of all gubernatorial elections won by incumbents and nonincumbents from both parties according to their primary percentage for the period 1956–75. All four curves indicate the same fact. Elections are won many times over by gubernatorial candidates who have *not* taken their party by storm. For all winners in both parties, barely 50 percent of the elections put a governor into office who had a working majority of his party behind him (80 to 100 percent of the primary vote).

The notion that a divisive primary hurts the candidate in the general election can't be proved by examining the nonincumbent gubernatorial candidate's electoral record. In the 68 contests where a nonincumbent Democrat was running, only 38 percent were won by candidates who had a consolidated party backing them (over 80 percent of the primary vote); for the 57 nonincumbent Republicans, it was only 30 percent. Both parties usually send green governors into the state house with less than 70 percent of their party's backing. The new governor faces a legislature in which sit bitter remnants of the factions that opposed him in the primary contest as well as the recognized opposition of the other party. With this start he must put together a coalition to back his policies.

The State Chairman

What role do these faceless men who sit astride the 100 state parties play in the campaign for governor? Apparently they believe that their major role is to build up the party organization, raise funds, and provide campaign strategy.[48] Most candidates employ a manager to assume overall direction of their campaigns, but the state chairmen tend to see themselves as managers of the state party's total ticket with the responsibility of getting as many persons elected as possible. In states where there is a cohesive organization at the top, the chairman works to unite the party. Our figures show, however, that this happens less than 50 percent of the time. The success or failure of a party's candidates reflects on the evaluation of the state chairman. A high rate of resignation or defeat of incumbent chairmen occurs after each election. This is particularly true in very competitive states where expectations run high as to the party's possibilities. The state chairmen are caught in a bind. If they involve themselves in campaigns, they run the risk of losing or being deposed. On the other hand, they cannot actively attract campaign workers and volunteers when they remain isolated from the conflict. A party has to be nourished by new recruits. This dilemma has been fostered by the weakening ability of the party to make nominations for office and hence to push for party-approved candidates in the campaign. The state chairman's role is increasing in importance with the growth of more competitive parties, the increase in types of campaign techniques, and the improvement in party operations.

As this occurs perhaps the job of state chairman will become a highly skilled task that is isolated from the fate of individual candidates.

Platforms

To an unusually high degree, the party platform is a serious document in our state parties. All 24 governors who were asked stated that they took the platform seriously and tried to put its provisions into effect after they were elected. After the gubernatorial primaries, platforms are usually adopted by the state conventions or state committees. The nominee or incumbent governor is consulted with respect to the platform, and his wishes are generally incorporated. The state chairmen are almost always involved in platform drafting. The state central committe in Michigan through its resolutions subcommittee plays an important part in the preconvention platform drafting process. In 1956, the Democratic party instituted an issues day to which local party organizations were invited to send representatives. Special groups were also encouraged to participate in the drafting process. The preconvention drafting committee consulted with such groups as farmers, veterans, and business and professional organizations. This work culminated in a preliminary draft of the platform which was then approved by the resolutions committee of the convention and subsequently by the whole convention.[49] Some states in the South do not hold state conventions because there is no way of uniting a party rent by factions. Platforms are presumably the work of the individual candidates for governor in a system of this sort.

According to Neil Staebler and Douglas Ross, issues are susceptible to exploitation by party interests in various ways: to attract specific groups needed to win the election, to improve the party's cohesion by refreshing its sense of direction, to resolve an intraparty struggle, to stimulate the enthusiasm of party workers, to attract the attention in the mass media, and to promote realistic solutions to pressing public problems. In each party, issues create a constant psychological appeal. Graham Wallace noted, issues are "something that can be loved and trusted, and which can be recognized at successive elections as being the same thing that was loved before."[50]

Techniques of the New Politics

The spread of two-party systems in 33 of our states and the stakes in running for office, coupled with the rise of computer science, have ushered in the new profession of political public relations and campaign management. This development has made the expert commonplace in political campaigns and has raised fears that the relationship between a candidate and his party is becoming severed. Professional media consultants, national opinion polling firms, public relations and campaign management firms, and commercial advertising companies are standard for gubernatorial candidates in competitive states.

In the 1960s the idea of private campaign management firms spread from California to her sister states. Whitaker and Baxter, Spencer-Robert, and Baus and Ross, are three of the best-known firms centered in California. Fees may run as high as $100,000 for a campaign. These firms provide a variety of services—depending on the candidate, a firm may serve in a consulting role or it may direct all aspects of a campaign—from the use of media and scheduling public appearances to polling the voters on the issues of the day. A public relations firm probably cannot increase a candidate's chance by more than 5 percent of the total vote. Hence, such firms do not like to take on high-risk candidates. Since the late sixties, firms have suffered losses and their aura has dimmed. They are no longer looked upon as a guarantee of election in a competitive race.

Buying public opinion polls is another device that may bring the candidate back into the party fold. The importance of computer politics has long been recognized but its cost has prevented it from being widely used by impoverished state parties. By 1972, 65 percent of the state parties were engaged in some form of polling activity.[51] Party officials use the polls in several ways. The most common is to aid general campaign strategy. Issues concerning the voters can be determined by polling. The party can then concentrate on those issues to its advantage. The ability to determine a party's image can also be accomplished through polling. If the Republican Party discovers that voters think it is run by big business, the party can try to change that image by carefully pointing out that it is also supported by blue-collar workers, unions, farmers—or whatever happens to be nearest the truth. Occasionally, candidates and managers leak the results of favorable polls to the press. This is risky, however because such leaks may produce overconfidence on the part of the workers. The leaders hope for a bandwagon effect. The successful use of polling by state political parties may bring candidates back into the fold as campaigning costs skyrocket and contributions to candidates are limited by legislation. Most party officials do not believe that campaign consultants, polls, or data processing will replace handshaking on street corners or the "good old-fashioned seat-of-the-pants" campaigns. State parties will have to make use of the new technocracy or be displaced by private campaign consultants.

Political Money

Political parties must have money if they are to perform their functions of nominating and electing candidates. In 1966, a political consultant, Joseph Napolitan, ran Milton Shapp's campaign for governor in Pennsylvania, reportedly spent $2.5 million, and lost! (Shapp became governor in 1970 and again in 1974). Prior to the 1974 regulations on campaign financing in California, it took $3 million to wage an effective campaign for governor. In the 1972 primaries, candidates for the legislature spent an average of $65,000 with some divided races costing as much as $100,000.[52] Campaigns for primary elections increase the total costs by one-third or more. Because winning is the most important motivation for candidates and their parties, campaigns are the largest consumers of political funds. The cost of maintaining the party organization between elections, is minimal compared to the massive effort expended on the campaigns.

If party leaders want to have control over the candidates, they must have control over campaign financing. To the extent that parties raise and dispense campaign funds, party organizations are better able to control nominations and be a significant influence on the office holder elected under the party's banner. Potential candidates may be discouraged from seeking the nomination if they know that available money generally flows through the party treasury and is disbursed to the candidates receiving the party's endorsement. Moreover, a party platform is likely to be taken more seriously by candidates and office holders if the party provides a significant portion of the campaign funds and organization.

Where does the money come from? In patronage states such as Indiana and Pennsylvania, percentage assessments on the salaries of all those who owe their jobs to the party are an effective way of filling the party coffers. Wisconsin's Republican party has a group of wealthy patrons upon whom they have been able to draw.[53] Many states depend on large donations by a few donors. In two-party states, the Republicans are financed mainly by businessmen and the Democrats by labor unions. But parties like to ask for small donations from small contributors as well. This is usually done by solicitation, house-to-house canvassing, or a street-corner project like a tag sale. The middle group of contributors respond to cocktail parties or a call by an influential party member. Large donors are the subjects of very careful planning. They may be invited to an exclusive dinner visited by a high-ranking public official or offered membership in a president's club at the rate of $1,000 a year. The task of a party state chairman is to try to raise funds, reconcile competing demands for funds from the national committees and state legislative campaigns, and meet the needs of all state and local candidates. In most states, the contribution process is a welter of competitive contests with popular incumbents doing better than the newcomers. Neil Staebler, Michigan party chairman, points out that contributors have a natural inclination to give to a candidate rather than to an impersonal party organization, placing the state committee in some danger of being starved. One of the main roles of the state finance chairman is to make sure this does not occur.[54]

Because of the tremendous expense connected with recent state campaigns and the post-Watergate fear that political money has to be controlled in some way, all the states have now enacted laws to govern the expenditure and reporting of funds for campaigns. Details vary from state to state, but the principal forms of regulation are these: prohibitions against contributions by unions (8 states), prohibitions against contributions by corporations (26 states), and individual donation limits (24 states). All states except North Dakota require that a candidate disclose his contributions and expenditures.[55] Reports are filed with either the secretary of state or a separate elections commission. Those commissions with enforcement power can issue subpoenas, investigate violations, and hold hearings but prosecution usually is handled by the state attorney general.

To take these regulations in order and comment on them opens a Pandora's box of regulations, evasions, and, most recently, the effect of the Supreme Court decision of January 30, 1976, on the whole idea of spending limits. In late 1976, 24 states limited spending by or on behalf of a candidate. Some states limited certain kinds of expenditures, either to curb total spending by restricting certain high-cost activities or to ban campaign techniques regarded as immoral or improper. At the simplest level, some states ban the bribery of voters. Some states *prescribe* the purposes for which money can be spent. Such legitimate expenditures include headquarters and hall rental, postage and mailing expenses, campaign literature, posters and banners, advertising, wages, expenses, and whatever else was familiar to the legislators who wrote the bills. Whether any form of limitation on spending, aside from that on bribing voters, is constitutional has been opened up by the recent Supreme Court decision. In Buckley vs. Valeo 1976, the Court found limitations on overall campaign expenditures contained in the federal campaign finance laws to be infringements on the First Amendment's right to freedom of speech. This decision affected state limits on expenditures and several acted to bring their laws in conformity with the Supreme Court decision. In Connecticut, the General Assembly removed all limitations, thus allowing expenditures by individuals independent of any candidate or committee. In conforming with the Supreme Court decision, individuals may spend as much of their own money as they wish to support a candidate so long as they do not clear or coordinate the expenditure with him or his campaign organization. An individual may give $2,500 to a gubernatorial candidate, for example, and then spend $100,000 for his own newspaper, television advertising, or billboards on behalf of that candidate. This freedom to spend also applies to state political parties as well as political action committees set up by unions, corporations, groups of individuals, and trade associations. If the political party does not coordinate its activities with a candidate's campaign, the party may spend on campaign items such as media time, polling, or research.

Not only did the Supreme Court lift the ban on expenditures, it also removed the limits on the amount a candidate or his family may spend. Campaigns may now generate a great deal more money than before. It would appear that the effect of the Supreme Court decision would benefit wealthy candidates who can foot the bill for their campaigns. In 1966, Nelson Rockefeller reported expenditures of $5.2 million; his Democratic opponent, $576,000. In 1970, Rockefeller had 370 employees in his campaign organization, while his opponent, Democrat Arthur Goldberg, had 35. Rockefeller's effort included the use of three family-owned airplanes, while Goldberg flew chartered commercial airlines. Rockefeller's media expenditures surpassed the cost of Arthur Goldberg's total campaign by almost $1 million. A large percentage of Rockefeller's expenditures were derived from family sources.[56] On the other hand, there is no limit to the money a party committee may spend to benefit a candidate. Parties are beginning to use polls and other mass communication techniques. They can use television on behalf of a candidate with no limit to their expenditures; they can swing to computer storage of information, which will benefit all candidates in an election and which can be brought to bear on any campaign; parties can send out mailings on behalf of their candidates. As a result, private funds of wealthy individuals may soon be matched by those of a party.

The Supreme Court did not strike down the limits on how much individuals and political committees may *contribute* to candidates directly. State laws prohibiting contributions by unions, corporations, or individual donors are still constitutional. However, they have long been evaded through "private" contributions by corporate executives or members of their families and the formation of labor union political action committees, which collect worker contributions for their activities on behalf of candidates. Most states hold gubernatorial campaign donations to under $5,000. New Jersey's $600 is the lowest limit, but it is matchable under the state's public financing plan. A cursory inspection of the state laws reveals that contributions to political parties are not restricted. Hence, the parties themselves may go after big donors and then spend money independently on behalf of the candidate by registering voters, building the party organization, and preparing research materials.

In an attempt to control contributions and minimize the undue influence, extortion, and corruption accompanying private fund raising, some states have turned to public financing akin to the national provisions for presidential candidates. In August 1973, *U. S. News and World Report* polled all 100 state chairmen regarding their attitudes toward tax support of political campaigns. Fifty-four chairmen responded. The survey revealed a strikingly partisan division on the issue. Twenty-five of the Democrats and one Republican answered affirmatively on the question: "Does the United States need a new system of financing political parties?" Twenty Republicans and five Democrats answered negatively. Among the respondents, Democratic critics of private finance argued that politics has become a rich man's game and that the little man is outweighed by special interests.[57]

Watergate provided an incentive for several states (17) to enact public financing plans. While they do not follow the federal pattern, these laws embody a rich diversity of fund-raising methods, eligibility requirements, and distribution formulas. In Maine and Maryland Massachusetts and Montana "public financing" schemes are in fact income tax surcharges where the taxpayer adds one or two dollars to his tax liability. Most states have a checkoff system similar to the federal income tax provision. Three states (Alaska, Minnesota, and Oregon) provide a direct tax credit, and another 11 allow a state income tax deduction for small campaign contributions. Taxpayers' response to the checkoff plan has been good (17 percent in Rhode Island and 14 percent in Iowa, which compares favorably with the 15 percent citizen support for the presidential fund). With respect to the surcharge, fewer than 5 percent in affected states chose to increase their personal tax liability by even one dollar. Most interesting is that eight states allocate public funds to parties, not candidates. These states allow the taxpayer to designate the political party that is to receive the funds. This would tend to alter the relationship between the candidate and his party and provide the party with more leverage over candidate selection. Three states have funded primaries as well as general elections (Michigan, Massachusetts, and Hawaii). Minnesota provides public funds in races for both legislative houses as well as for five executive offices. States have shown remarkable willingness to enact public financing of campaigns, which is a first essential step to providing enough money for politics and curbing the abuses that now accompany fund raising. When public funds are given to the political parties, it's possible that control over nominations and elections will be increased, because the money can be used to control the entry and support of candidates.

Many people have predicted that party organization will end as candidates hire their own consultants, dig into their own pockets, and smile at political committees and individuals working in their behalf. On the other hand, new campaign laws may operate to enhance state party organizations. The parties are not affected by finance limitations so long as the funds are used for party activities and not for candidate support. These activities may include sophisticated computer information systems, which are getting out of reach of all but the very wealthy candidate. The computer is a storage facility for much basic information about individuals all over the state. When it is linked to high-speed mailing systems, the computer system can reach every voter and replicate most of the functions performed by the old political machine. Use of these electronic gadgets requires substantial funds to initiate and they are available only to those who have the start-up money. Political parties have begun to utilize the computer for its ability to store, process, and analyze political intelligence. It's possible that the political party may be able to collect unlimited funds for such activities. Wealthy persons may contribute without limit, providing services for their candidate as well as the entire ticket. The many small donations made possible by a computerized mailing system may also enhance the party's coffers. But only relatively well-financed organizations can afford this new technology. Computers are most efficient when used over the long run, providing a continuing and up-to-date source of information. The combination of money and technology will enable state committees to exert considerable influence over party nominations, perhaps leading to a shift in power from local organization to state party. Money talks. Potential candidates may have to conform to the policy criteria of party leaders if they wish to obtain help for their campaigns. This degree of control has enormous implications for party government.

CONCLUSIONS

While the pollsters and prophets are predicting the decline of the party system in the United States, small groups of men and women are busily engaged in party activities: collecting petitions, convincing local notables to run for election, raising funds, trudging from door to door to get out the vote, meeting trains, walking through factories, standing a required distance from the polls and handing out last-minute literature, and, finally, gathering near the radio to hear the results. All across the country, elections are won and lost in this fashion. The party belongs to these people, not to the voters. The voters do not contribute their time and money, but merely express a preference at election time, much as a customer might buy a particular brand of toothpaste. The toothpaste manufacturer does not expect a customer to help him make his product, although he does pay close attention to consumer preferences in producing a product that will sell. In the same sense, a politician is none too eager to embrace a direct primary and let the voters select the person who will run for office under the party label. It takes skill to pick a winning brand and the voters can't be counted on to have that necessary skill. All states, however, allow voters to help in the nomination process, so party activists must cope as best they can with the method of selection.

Pollsters say that traditional party loyalties are breaking down, which spells the demise of the party. It is to be expected that a highly mobile and educated electorate would increasingly wish to reserve judgment as to their choice between two candidates. Traditional party ties fostered by family or region are no longer relevant. While they certainly were convenient to the politician because he could count on blocs of votes, he must now appeal to a larger group of undecided voters. His beliefs, his personality, his stand on issues are all crucial to bringing him an election-winning number of votes. Does the volatility of voters spell an end to the party itself? Probably not. Candidates are as eager as ever to capture the party label in running for public office. So long as status, fame, power, and money attract men and women to run for public office, there will be coalitions of aspirants to capture, groom, nominate, and elect. Party loyalty of the electorate has never been a major prerequisite for operating the party system of this country. The work of recruiting, nominating, and electing candidates for public office has never been performed by the electorate. Coalitions of men and women have always carried out this function for various rewards such as money, sociability, or ideology.

This chapter has been concerned with the activities of men and women who operate within the structures or our two major parties. The primary job of the party outside of government is to provide the candidates for public office—the decision makers who make the policies that affect the lives of us all. The more unified and cohesive a party, the better it can perform this function. A party rent by factions cannot unite behind candidates for election, nor can it govern if its candidates are elected. We have discovered that parties in competitive states are more likely to be unified in the nominating process. But, even here, factions develop. If there is no state leadership to control access to the nominations, they are fought over bitterly. The end result is to weaken the party's ability to contest the election or fulfill its major function of governing in the name of the people. In one-party states, factions are usually based on personalities or amorphous issues. There is no state leadership to channel ambition or provide an orderly ladder of succession to higher political office.

The fact that there are party leaders who can groom and support governors is all the more impressive when we consider that the party organization is a system of committees growing up from the grass roots. The result is that a strong localism and distaste for statewide direction are built into the state party structure. What actually affects the ability of some parties to provide a determined and continuous leadership is as yet unknown. We do know that this leadership is crucial if a governor and his administration are to provide better education and welfare services for the people of his state.

The direct-primary form of nomination is hard on the party leadership's ability to groom and present well-qualified candidates. As head of his party ticket, the governor must put together a coalition to win in the primary. This coalition is the one he works with in the policy-making process. If the gubernatorial candidate puts together a successful primary coalition, he can count on its support in the governing process. A candidate who receives a bare majority of the primary vote can often count on a powerful alliance being formed against him in the legislature. His closest rival in the primary will usually have allies in the legislature who are more eager to bolster their candidate for the next election than they are to help the incumbent achieve success. A number of states are starting to realize that endorsement of a candidate by the party leadership may be a decisive factor in a primary contest. There may be signs of party revival in the recognition that the business of developing and pushing candidates for governor cannot be settled by the self-selection process of aspiring office holders. In these states, candidates who receive the party nod have an organization with which to begin the process of winning and governing.

The new campaign laws may operate to enhance the organizational power of state parties. With no limits on the money a committee may spend, parties can use the most modern techniques of mass communication. Use of computer storage for information benefits all candidates in the state and can be used to hold various segments of the party together. Parties can send out mailings to help all candidates; the efforts are paid for, in part, by the donations received through mass mailings. New campaign laws and new technology may work to enhance the influence that state political parties can exert over party nominations. These factors [trends, developments,] have significant implications for the role of the party in the future.

NOTES

1. Robert Lee Sawyer, Jr., *The Democratic State Central Committee in Michigan, 1949–1959: The Rise of the New Politics and the New Political Leadership* (Ann Arbor: Institute of Public Administration, University of Michigan, 1960), p. 78.
2. See chapter 2, footnote 5.
3. Joseph I. Lieberman, *The Power Broker* (Boston: Houghton Mifflin, 1966), p. 340.
4. John H. Fenton, *Midwest Politics* (New York: Holt, Rinehart and Winston, 1966), p. 217.
5. Allan Sindler, *Huey Long's Louisiana; State Politics, 1920–1952* (Baltimore: Johns Hopkins Press, 1956), p. 248.
6. V. O. Key, Jr., *Southern Politics in State and Nation* (New York: Knopf, 1949), pp. 19–35.
7. Joseph Schlesinger, "Political Party Organization," in *Handbook of Organizations.*, edited by James G. March, (Chicago, Ill.: Rand McNally, 1965), pp. 764–801.
8. Joseph A. Schlesinger, "The Primary Goals of Political Parties: A Clarification of Positive Theory," *American Political Science Review* 69 (September 1975), pp. 840–49.
9. Ibid., p. 843.

10. Schlesinger developed the point that both size of the vote and margin of victory are subject to different strategies depending upon whether one is an office seeker or a benefit seeker.

11. Samuel J. Eldersveld, *Political Parties: A Behavioral Analysis* (Skokie, Ill.: Rand McNally, 1964).

12. See James Q. Wilson, *The Amateur Democrat* (Chicago: University of Chicago Press, 1963).

13. Leon D. Epstein, *Politics in Wisconsin* (Madison: University of Wisconsin Press, 1958).

14. National Municipal League, *State Party Structures and Procedures: A State by State Compendium* (New York: National Municipal League, 1967).

15. V. O. Key, Jr., *Politics, Parties and Pressure Groups,* 5th ed. (New York: Crowell, 1964), p. 328.

16. Mayor Curley has been romanticized in the novel (and movie) *The Last Hurrah* by Edwin O'Connor (Boston: Little, Brown, 1956). See also Justin N. Feldman, "How Tammany Holds Power," *National Civic Review* 39 (1950); pp. 330–34; James Reichley, *The Art of Government: Reform and Organization Politics in Phildelphia* (New York: Fund for the Republic, 1959).

17. Neal Peirce, *The Megastates of America* p. 347. Also see the recent work immortalizing the mayor by Milton L. Rakove, *Don't Make No Waves—Don't Back No Losers: An Insider's Analysis of the Daley Machine* (Bloomington, Ind.: Indiana University Press, 1975).

18. Douglass Gatlin, "Toward a Functionalist Theory of Political Parties; Inter-Party Competition in North Carolina," chapter 6 in William Crotty, ed. *Approaches to the Study of Party Organization* (Boston: Allyn and Bacon, 1968), p. 241.

19. Ibid., p. 243.

20. Robert J. Huckshorn, *Party Leadership in the States* (Amherst: University of Massachusetts Press, 1976), pp. 21–43.

21. Neil Staebler and Douglas Ross, "The Management of State Political Parties" chapter 3 in Cornelius P. Cotter, *Practical Politics in the United States* (Boston: Allyn and Bacon, 1969), p. 49.

22. Robert J. Huckshorn, *Party Leadership in the States,* pp. 45–67.

23. Peter B. Clark and James Q. Wilson, "Incentive Systems: A Theory of Organization," *Administrative Science Quarterly* 6 (September 1961): 129–66.

24. Daryl R. Fair, "Party Strength and Political Patronage," *Southwestern Social Science Quarterly* 45 (December 1964): 264–71

25. Frank J. Sorauf, "Patronage and Party," *Midwest Journal of Political Science* 3 (May 1959): 115–26.

26. Huckshorn, *Party Leadership in the States,* pp. 111–12.

27. Daniel Patrick Moynihan and James Q. Wilson, "Patronage in New York State, 1955–1959," *American Political Science Review* 58 (June 1964): 286–301.

28. Charles W. Wiggins and William L. Turk, "State Party Chairmen: A Profile," *The Western Political Quarterly* 23 (June 1970): 330–31.

29. Samuel J. Eldersveld, *Political Parties: A Behavioral Analysis,* pp. 277–92.

30. V. O. Key, Jr., *Politics, Parties and Pressure Groups,* 4th ed. (New York: Crowell, 1958), p. 241.

31. This problem is considered by Herbert McClosky et al., "Issue Conflict and Consensus among Party Leaders and Followers," *American Political Science Review* 54 (June 1960): 406–27; Edmund Costantini, "Intraparty Attitude Conflict: Democratic Party Leadership in California," *Western Political Quarterly* 16 (December 1963): 956–72.

32. Eldersveld, *Political Parties: A Behavioral Analysis,* pp. 277–92; M. Margaret Conway and Frank B. Feigert, "Motivation, Incentive Systems and Political Party Organization," *American Political Science Review* 62 (December 1968): 1159–73.

33. Staebler and Ross, "The Management of State Political Parties," p. 57.

34. Huckshorn, *Party Leadership in the States,* pp. 103–104.

35. Herbert Jacob, "Initial Recruitment of Elected Officials in the United States," *Journal of Politics* 25 (November 1962): 703–16.

36. Portions of this chapter appeared in slightly different form in "The Governor as Political Leader" by Sarah Morehouse in Herbert Jacob and Kenneth N. Vines, eds., *Politics in The American States: A Comparative Analysis,* Third Edition, copyright © 1976 by Little Brown and Company Inc. and are reprinted by permission.

37. "Constitutions and Legislation," Primary Elections for State Officers, *The Book of the States, 1978-1979,* 22 (Lexington, Ky.: The Council of State Governments, 1978), p. 241.

38. For the 1975 Primary, the Louisiana legislature abolished the partisan primary for governor and some other offices. Instead there was established a single primary for both Democratic and Republican candidates—with a runoff between the top two—replacing the general election. Consequently, the Republican Party cannot hold its own primary and cannot have a candidate in the runoff unless its candidate runs first or second in the first primary.

39. Malcolm E. Jewell and David M. Olson, *American State Political Parties and Elections* (Homewood, Ill.: The Dorsey Press, 1978), pp. 93–104.

40. Austin Ranney, "Parties in State Politics," chapter 2 in Jacob and Vines, *Politics in the American States,* pp. 71–72.

41. Huckshorn, *Party Leadership in the States,* pp. 106–107.

42. Huckshorn Ibid

43. V. O. Key, *Southern Politics In State and Nation* and *American State Politics: An Introduction*

44. See James R. Spence, *The Moore-Preyer-Lake Primaries of 1964: The Making of a Governor* (Winston-Salem, N.C.: John F. Blair, 1968). This is an account of three men and the campaigns they waged for the Democratic nomination for Governor of North Carolina in 1964. Two major continuing factions were represented by candidates: The Old Guard Conservatives and The Sanford Forces. The Old Guard won with Judge Moore.

45. In Table 2.2, I used an Average Index of Competition that placed Tennessee among the one-party states, making a total of eight. In this chapter, Tennessee becomes a "leaning Democratic" state based on percent of the vote Democratic for governor over a longer time period. This measure is more appropriate for the present discussion of party competition and primary voting.

46. David Calhoun Leege, "Control in the Party Convention Nominating System: The Case of Indiana," chapter 11 in James B. Kessler, ed., *Empirical Studies of Indiana Politics* (Bloomington: Indiana University Press, 1970), pp. 200–226.

47. Robert J. McNeill, *Democratic Campaign Financing in Indiana,* 1964 (Bloomington: Indiana University Institute of Public Administration; and Princeton, N.J.,: Citizens' Research Foundation, 1966), pp. 31–32.
48. Huckshorn, *Party Leadership in the States,* p. 100.
49. Sawyer, *The Democratic State Central Committee in Michigan,* pp. 167–71.
50. Staebler and Ross, "The Management of State Political Parties," pp. 60–61.
51. Huckshorn, *Party Leadership in the States,* p. 132.
52. Bernard L. Hyink et al., *Politics and Government in California,* 9th ed. (New York: Crowell, 1975), p. 102.
53. See McNeill, *Democratic Campaign Financing in Indiana, 1964;* and David Adamany, *Financing Politics: Recent Wisconsin Elections* (Madison, Wis.: University of Wisconsin Press, 1969).
54. Staebler and Ross, "The Management of State Political Parties," p. 68.
55. "Constitutions and Legislation," Campaign Finance Laws: Filing Requirements: Expenditures: Contributions, *The Book of the States, 1978-1979,* pp. 250–58.
56. Joyce Gelb and Marian Lief Palley, *Tradition and Change in American Party Politics* (New York: Crowell, 1975), 221–22.
57. This survey was reported in Huckshorn, *Party Leadership in the States,* pp. 151–52.

CHAPTER FIVE

THE GOVERNOR AS PARTY LEADER AND POLICY MAKER

The governor is at the apex of the power structure of the state. The job is sought because of the recognition it brings to the holder. It is the highest office in subnational politics and usually leads to federal office. To obtain the governorship, a candidate must campaign for both the party nomination and the electorate's approval. A governor is at once the head of the party and head of the government. His success as a party leader is vital to his success as a governor who can convince legislators and administrators to follow his bidding.* Because of the importance of the governor and his policies to the health and welfare of the people of each state, the office is eagerly sought. In only a handful of states does the weaker party draft a sure loser and the stronger party nominate a sure winner. In all but seven states, competition for the office is keen. The governor must deliver his promises to the people or he has little chance for future election and, with it, the chance for political advancement.

To deliver on his promises, the governor must deal in the politics of personalities and issues. He must put together a coalition large enough to ensure him the nomination by his own party. His coalition must convince the legislators of his party that he is the strongest candidate and that their future lies in supporting him. They, after all, also have ambition for reelection or advancement. Blessed is the governor who has a party leadership corps that will back him and finance his efforts and provide him with doorbell ringers and help him control his party's legislators after he takes over the state capitol. Chapter 4 documented the tasks of the electoral party as it recruited, nominated, and elected governors. We saw that there is a tendency for parties in competitive states to be more unified in the nominating process: Perhaps a leadership elite schedules the ambitions of the future contenders for the governor's office. Perhaps this is done by more informal processes among the aspirants themselves. At any rate, competitive parties try to minimize conflict for the purpose of entering

*The terms "he, his, him," and so forth refer to both men and women. Now that Connecticut has elected Ella Grasso and Washington has elected Dixy Lee Ray—the first women to be elected on their own records—it is assumed that gubernatorial politics is no longer a male occupation.

the election with a strong electoral organization ready to do battle against the opposition. Even with these intentions, however, factional strife breaks out in the most competitive parties, and a newcomer for the nomination must often battle fiercely to seize the party banner. This struggle for the nomination carries over into the governing process and affects the governor's ability to govern effectively. Those who suffer are those who usually suffer—the sick, the poor, the prisoners, the jobless. It takes coalitions to pass programs. Without coalitions, groups with money and influence—and these are not the groups mentioned above—can block legislation intended to ease the burden on those who suffer from economic and social dislocation.

This chapter will consider first the political atmosphere within which the governor prepares himself for leadership. What is his structure of opportunities and how does he groom himself for the apex of the political system in his state? How long can he expect to be governor in such troubled times? Where does he want to go next? Can we assume that all his political actions are taken with the idea of making an impressive record to help him win a federal elective or appointive office?

Second, with respect to his role as head of the governing party in his state, what resources does he command to help him move men to his point of view? What are the institutional and political restrictions on his ability to see his program through the state legislature?

Third, what relationship is there between the coalitions he formed during the election process and the coalitions that support him in his role as governor? What are the political and formal powers of strong and weak governors? The central theme that dominates this discussion is that governors who head political parties with sufficient internal cohesion to pass programs to which they have committed themselves will bring about a wider distribution of the benefits of state expenditures across income classes.

THE GOVERNOR AND POLITICAL AMBITION*

Tenure in Office

The turnover in the office of governor has traditionally been high. This is a product of two factors: the constitutional limits on the term of office and the high risks of leadership in a constituency where there are inadequate

*Portions of this chapter appeared in slightly different form in "The Governor as Political Leader," by Sarah Morehouse in Herbert Jacob and Kenneth N. Vines, eds., *Politics in The American States: A Comparative Analysis,* Third Edition copyright © 1976 by Little Brown and Company Inc., and are reprinted by permission.

TABLE 5–1

Changes in Governors' Tenure Potential,
1960–78

FOUR-YEAR TERM	1960	1978
No restraint on reelection	12	19
One consecutive reelection permitted[a]	7	21
No consecutive reelection permitted	15	6
Total	34	46

TWO-YEAR TERM	1960	1978
No restraint on reelection	14	4
One reelection permitted	2	0
Total	16	4

[a] Includes three states with absolute two-term limitation (Delaware, Missouri, and North Carolina).
Source: Data used with permission of The Council of State Governments, *The Book of the States, 1960–1961*, Vol. 13 and *1978–1979*, Vol. 22, (Lexington, Ky.: Council of State Governments), p. 122 and p. 116.

revenues to meet the demands of the people. Recently, governors have been spending more time in office. This is primarily due to the increase in the number of states adopting four-year terms. Forty-six states now have four-year terms for governor compared with 34 in 1960. Only Arkansas, New Hampshire, Rhode Island, and Vermont now consider it necessary to submit the governor to public approval every two years. The increase in the gubernatorial term means that in 46 states a governor can now count on a respectable time to prove himself. If he decides to increase taxation to pay for burgeoning education and welfare services, he can do so in the first two years of his term and hope that the results will appear before he comes up for reelection. His record can also attract attention on the national scene where he hopes to advance to elective or appointive office. Statistics on the actual time spent in the governor's chair show an increase in tenure. Joseph Schlesinger demonstrated that the number of years spent in the office of governor in the 1950s begins to approach the experience of the typical governor in the first decade of the nineteenth century. In both periods, approximately 69 percent of the governors spent four or fewer years in the governorship while 30 percent could count on five to ten years. By contrast, in no period between 1830 and 1940, according to Schlesinger, could more than 16 percent of the governors count on five to ten years in office.[1] The figures for 1970–79 are shown in Table 5–2.

The trend toward longer tenure is again confirmed by data from the 1970s. Thirty-seven percent of the governors spend five years or more in the statehouses. The office would appear to be gaining in popularity and

TABLE 5-2

Tenure in Office of Governors (figure is percentage of all governors who served during
the decade)

NUMBER OF YEARS SPENT IN OFFICE OF GOVERNOR	1970–79
10 plus	8.0
5–9	29.0
3–4	61.0
1–2	2.0
N	119

respect in the eyes of the electorate. After years of declining influence and
financial hardship, state government is losing its image as the "sick man"
of the federal system. In a time of discontent about politics, governors are
among the least unpopular politicians. In 1974, the trend toward increased optimism in the nation's statehouses was related to the national
Watergate scandal (which discredited politics generally, but Washington
particularly) as well as the improved financial position of the states. Governor Rockefeller predicted, however, that the costs of government would
catch up and that the temporary popularity of the incumbent governors
would sink again. The figures in Table 5-2 seem to deny the fact that the
governorship is a yo-yo with gyrations depending on the temporary pock-
etbook status of the state's electorate, since governors are lasting longer
on the job than ever before.

A study by J. Stephen Turett of 19 states from 1900 to 1969 confirms
the fact that incumbent governors, historically viewed, have not become
more vulnerable.[2] There has been, especially in the past three decades, no
detrimental change in the status of governors seeking reelection. In fact
they are running farther ahead of their party's congressional nominees
than ever before. In spite of the increasing ability of governors to maintain
themselves in office, it is commonly supposed that governors running in
presidential years are more subject to the tides of national politics. In line
with this supposition, a series of state constitutional amendments has
shielded gubernatorial elections from presidential contests by scheduling
them on off years. There are now only ten states with four-year terms for
governor that schedule elections in presidential years. Turett's study of
voting trends in those states that held elections in presidential years from
1944 to 1968 reveals a gradual disassociation of presidential and gubernatorial voting.[3] From 1970 to 1976, Democrats won statehouses in ever-
increasing numbers while Republicans presided over the White House. If

TABLE 5-3

Vulnerability of Incumbent Governors Seeking
Reelection by Year

YEAR	NUMBER OF ELECTIONS HELD	NUMBER OF INCUMBENTS PERMITTED	PERCENT INCUMBENTS RUNNING	NUMBER OF INCUMBENT DEMOCRATS		NUMBER OF INCUMBENT REPUBLICANS	
				WON	LOST	WON	LOST
1970–71	37	30	73.3	5	0	9	8
1972–73	21	16	56.0	4	0	3	2
1974–75	38	30	73.3	14	2	3	3
1976–77	16	13	61.5	4	1	2	1
1978–79	39	24	70.8	8	1	6	2

there was ever a time when Republican incumbents might have been fearful, it was the 1974 off-election when their party was under the cloud of Watergate.[4] Table 5–3 reveals, however, that they won as many as they lost. Three Republican incumbents were able to convince their respective voters that state politics were more important than national scandals. A second look at Table 5–3 shows that the incumbent Republicans have won many more than they lost in the last three elections. Turett found that the impact of presidential elections on governors' races depends on the type of presidential election going on. He found that only in landslide years did the incumbents of the party winning the White House do better than incumbents of the defeated presidential party, a finding that was not verified in 1972 when Nixon's coattails were too slippery for most of his fellow Republicans. In other presidential years, the success of the governor's presidential party was not a controlling factor.[5]

For many, the governorship is not an end in itself. Once elected, a governor can generally count on four years to cope with the problems of education, welfare, decreasing resources, inflation, and integration before he runs for reelection. He has better than a 74 percent chance of being reelected to repeat the performance. But, even with luck, most governors do not spend more than eight years in the statehouse. Just what motivates them at all? What ambitions do they have for advancement?

The Lure of National Leadership

It is not unnatural to assume that all governors want to make a good record, even though many will return to their law firms or businesses following a stint in the statehouse. The truth is that the lure of national leadership overcomes the raw fact that not all can succeed. About 60 percent of the governors have returned to private life after retiring or being retired. It is an honor to have been elected to the state's highest office, and the rewards for service are measured by plaques in prominent places, highways personalized by name, renown, proud memories, and the probability of good contacts with prominent members of the "establishment," including other governors in the peer group—to say nothing of recognition in the form of a lucrative law practice or a top position in an insurance agency.

We now turn to those who have gone on to national office and who provide an incentive for the others. The governorship is a stepping stone to what Joseph Schlesinger calls "the presidential office complex."[6] This includes not only the presidency itself but also those offices that the presidents influence or appoint. The vice-presidency, the Supreme Court, and the cabinet all draw persons from major offices in the Congress and the states. From 1900 to 1958, two-thirds of the men who held posts in the presidential office complex had held some kind of state office. Schlesinger discovered that the states vary in their relative contributions to the national structure. Twelve states had no representatives among the presidential office group, while the states of Massachusetts and New York had more than twice the number of representatives warranted by their populations.[7] Governors in states with strong prospects for national office, whether elective or appointive, have leverage over others. The lure of following a national leader to Washington can bring action out of legislators and administrators. Governors also covet a Senate seat. The Senate is called the "Ex-Governors' Club" because one-fourth of its members have been governors. These career lines boil down to an opportunity structure that potential governors keep in mind as they assess their chances. While only about 40 percent actually go on to Washington to become administrators or senators, Potomic fever—the prospect of operating on the national scene—motivates many whose hopes are eventually disappointed. Although governors realize that many are called but few are chosen, they hope that their record may prove them to be worthy of the leadership group.

The 156 occupants of the 50 statehouses during the 1950s were, as we have already seen, much more successful in gaining reelection to one or more terms than their predecessors. Sixty-seven governors had one or more reelections to their credit. Thirteen governors found their way to the U.S. Senate. One governor, Robert T. Stafford of Vermont (1959–61), was the state's congressman from 1960 to 1972. Vermont has only one congressman and the office carries considerable prestige, making it a natural gubernatorial aspiration. Some three dozen governors received presidential appointments to cabinet, subcabinet, ambassadorial, judicial, or special mission posts during the 1960s.[8] They included three cabinet members and as many appellate judges. The facts of political life are that governors of the president's party are generally chosen for appointed office or special assignment. The only exception to this is the case of Republican presidents trying to woo the South by appointing its favorite sons to federal offices. An ex-governor with the administrative and political experience acquired on the job does not "fade away" but can expect to be sought for new federal assignments—*if* he is of the right party .

The election of 1976 brought Governor Jimmy Carter of Georgia into the White House, the first governor to be elected president since 1944. This provided a collective ego boost to the governors who had long described their role in terms of its excellent preparation for the office of chief executive. The fact remains that both the Senate and the governorship have been the two main president- and vice-president-producing conduits over the years. With the recent exception, the odds seem to favor senators as opposed to governors. Of the 15 men who obtained a major party nomination for president or vice-president from 1960 to 1976, 11 were senators or former senators, and only two (Spiro Agnew of Maryland and Jimmy Carter of Georgia) were governors. The three preceding elections had produced two governors as presidential candidates, Dewey and Stevenson, and one for the vice-presidency, Warren, out of a total of nine men. Schlesinger suggests that governors of states lying in areas of sectional strength have the greatest chance of becoming the party's (particularly the out party's) standard bearer.[9] Since the presidency has become a "swing" office and most of the governorships are also competitive, there are no longer solid areas of sectional strength for either party to fall back on to select a sure sectional vote getter. President Carter may have provided the final test of this theory as he brought the traditional Democratic South into the Democratic party fold once more. But the vote in half the southern states was close, predicting the continued erosion of the South as an area of traditional Democratic strength. Hence, governors will have to count on national prominence rather than sectional strength if they are to continue to capture the presidential nomination.

At the National Governor's Conference in June 1974 in Seattle, governors were speculating about their chances for the White House. They believed they had a chance to assert themselves in national politics now that the attention of the nation was turned toward inflation, unemployment, and the complexities of life. A governor striving to accomplish solutions to these problems may attract a sympathetic national electorate. Governor Rockefeller of New York was hopeful that the era of the governor may be returning. Most governors agreed with Rockefeller that their jobs are excellent training for the White House. They believe, however, that he underestimated the problems they face in getting national attention. Governor Gilligan of Ohio described the problem this way: "The Senators have 30 to 50 people around whose whole purpose is to make them look good. I have 55,000 employees, any one of whom could get me into trouble tomorrow. Ohio has a budget of about \$5 billion, a population of 11 million people. It keeps you busy."[10] With Governor Carter in the White House in 1976, the odds shifted back to the governorship as a direct route to the presidency, and a current crop of governors are eyeing that office with ambition.

The discussion to date has emphasized the fact that the governorship enjoys prestige in itself, but that it is also a good stepping-stone to higher office. My assumption is that governors have progressive ambitions. They want to make good names for themselves to advance to higher office or positions of importance in private life. Even with an ever-increasing opportunity to serve two terms or more in the statehouse, the governorship is a transitional office. Of all major political offices in the system of American politics up to the presidency, it is the least secure. Its occupant has a mandate to prove himself in short order. He has the very human problems of educating the state's children, providing food and hope to its needy families, making sure that the sick and the elderly are properly cared for, protecting the air and streams from pollution, keeping the population from becoming buried in its own refuse—thus entering the daily lives of all its citizens. His success in coping with these problems on his own will predict his chances for advancement.

The Gubernatorial Career

The actions of Connecticut's woman governor are watched with curiosity by the nation. Inside the system, however, Ella Grasso is well known. In 26 years of politics she has held three statewide offices. For twelve years she was secretary of state (1959–71) before taking the 6th District congressional seat for two terms. Her career is not unlike that of the typical governor. In recent years there has been an upsurge in the number of incumbent congressmen running for governor. There are two reasons for this. The first is the increased attractiveness of the office. The second is the increasing functional relationship between the offices of governor and U.S. representative. Because the national government is an important source of funding for state programs, the congressman is likely to be aware of the intricacies of federal procedures and may perceive himself to be a well-qualified candidate for governor.[11]

The largest percentage of governors hold a statewide elective office just prior to their election as governor. (This category includes all the offices elected by the state at large—attorney general, lieutenant governor, secretary of state). The state legislature ranks second as a direct feeder into the governorship. Other offices held by governors shortly before making the race include state administrative and local elective offices. Schlesinger discovered that the offices that are the key positions for advancement have a clearly defined relationship with the goal office.[12] For some states, there is an orderly succession to the governorship running through the state legislature to statewide elective office to governor. The state legislature provides the base office for most of the state leadership. Most state politicians cut their teeth there. Other first stepping-stones are the various public or government attorneys. The two categories of state legislator and public attorney account for about half the first offices in the opportunity structure that revolves around the governorship.

Given the structure of opportunities for governor, what type of person is tempted to make the race?[13] Two-thirds of the governors from 1960 to 1970 held law degrees. One hundred twenty-four of the 156 governors were attorneys or businessmen (attorney—92; businessman—32). The median age at inauguration was 47, leaving plenty of time for advancement to federal office. Governors are family men, providing TV with ample human-interest coverage (children sliding down the statehouse banisters). Of the crop of governors who held office from 1960 to 1970, some 65 percent had served in the armed forces. So much for the all-American credentials. The path that leads to the governorship takes more than an attractive personal profile. In most cases that path is deeply involved in politics. The success with which a potential governor handles the politics of getting the gubernatorial nomination is a powerful predictor of his success in office.

THE GOVERNOR AS ELECTORAL PARTY LEADER

A great deal was said in the previous chapter about the politics of the nominating process. A governor who has been able to convince his party that he has power and prospects and has received the backing of the majority of the party leaders and, along with this, the support of the voters is in good shape to make policy. We have seen how rare this phenomenon is, even in competitive states where one would suppose that parties would unite to battle each other. We hypothesized that the factionalism within parties in competitive states might resemble a conflict of leadership elites, which appeal to changing nonrecurring segments of the party's voters. In states in which there is little competition between the parties, the factions in the majority party are more likely to be durable groups of voters led by an elite with similar interests. These competitive elites are likely to be represented in the legislature and can represent a very real stumbling block to a governor who needs the votes to pass his programs. To illustrate the point, gubernatorial faction making from competitive, moderately competitive and one-party states will follow.

The Governor as Factional Leader in
the South: The Carter Campaign for
Governor, 1969–70

The coalition Jimmy Carter put together to win the gubernatorial primary in Georgia in 1970 was composed of rural whites and urban blue-collar whites. To defeat former governor Sanders, who was also a contender in the primary and had the support of most black leaders, he had to put together the Wallace-Maddox coalition of agrarians as well as make an appeal to the blue-collar workingman in Atlanta and other urban areas.[14] Because Carter had moderate racial views, he appealed to the Wallace-Maddox rural whites, not on the race issue, but as a populist—a man who understood their problems, was of them. Populism, he calculated, was a large enough umbrella for blacks to come under, should they want to after the primary when they had to choose between him and a Republican. Groups to whom Carter did not appeal for primary support were the blacks, urban professionals, and white-collar classes. Beginning in the fall of 1969, Carter began roaming about central and south Georgia where the agrarians lived. He strolled down main street, visited the country stores and gas stations meeting the folks. In Atlanta, he spent his time at factory gates during shift changes and in the heart of working-class districts. Carter counted on keeping a serious segregationist out of the race. Unquestionably, a segregationist would draw support away from Carter rather than from his opponent. In other words, a segregationist would have taken away many votes from the rural and small-town whites whom Carter was courting on a populist plank.

The other groups in the Democratic party—the urban professionals, the white-collar classes, and blacks who supported former Governor Sanders—were declared to be a part of the wealthy liberal establishment of Atlanta and Washington. In the last three weeks of the gubernatorial primary campaign, the following 20-second commercial appeared to link Sanders with the upper-middle-class big-money boys.

> This is the door to an exclusive Country Club where the big-money boys play cards, drink cocktails, and raise money for their candidate: Carl Sanders. (Country club door opens; close-up of man writing check.) "People like us aren't invited. We're busy working for a living." (Footage of Carter talking with an "average man.") "That's why our votes are going for Jimmy Carter. Vote Jimmy Carter. *Our* kind of man. *Our* kind of governor.[15]

Carter won the first primary by a 48 to 38 percent lead. Because he did not have an absolute majority, a run-off primary was held two weeks later which he won by a 60 over 40 percent victory. The results of that primary indicated serious splits within the Democratic party in Georgia with which

Governor Carter would have to contend after he presented his program to the legislature. In an effort to bring the business community of Atlanta around before the election and to defeat his rival, he proclaimed that "The last time the Republicans had power in Georgia they burned Atlanta."[16]

In his inaugural address, the new governor said, "I say to you quite frankly that the time for racial discrimination is over. Our people have already made this major and difficult decision. No poor, rural, weak, or black person should ever have to bear the additional burden of being deprived of the opportunity for an education, a job, or simple justice."[17] In spite of this commitment, the major program of the Carter administration was a reorganization scheme, which was completed in less than a year. Carter was able to get the legislature to give him the authority to reorganize the state government subject only to legislative veto. Lieutenant Governor Lester Maddox, president of the state senate and a segregationist, was bitterly opposed to this plan. Thus, after the honeymoon, the party in the legislature returned to its factional wars. Despite Georgia's economic advances, its programs for local schools, higher education, highways, and welfare have continued to lag well behind the national average. These programs take legislative approval, and the party is too divided for much concerted action. In a state in which the 1971 Democratic legislators outnumbered the Republicans in the house by 173 to 22 and in the senate by 50 to 6, policy making is done within the Democratic party. A combination of blacks, segregationists, businessmen, rural whites, and blue-collar workers cannot handily create a major social program. Too much power lies with veto groups within the party.

The Conservatives versus the Liberals in Texas

The liberal-conservative alignment takes place within the Democratic party in Texas instead of providing the basis for two-party conflict as it does in many states of the north. From the mid-1870s until 1952, the Texas Democratic party dominated the political life of the state. The Republican party, associated with Reconstruction and Yankee dominance was distasteful to most Texans. While the Republican party has won federal offices and Texas has gone Republican for president four times, the party just succeeded in electing the first governor since 1869 but claims only a handful of legislators in the Texas house and senate. Hence, the conservative-liberal split within the Democratic party is the real key to the way Texas politics is played. The effect of the New Deal is still felt within the party. The New Deal strengthened the hand of labor and weakened the favored position of business. The loose confederation of farmers and ranchers, oilmen, manufacturers, professionals, blue- and

white-collar workers, and housewives realigned themselves into a liberal
conservative alignment. In 1956, the liberals formed their own organization and called it the Democrats of Texas (DOT). They were rendered
powerless in 1960 when Lyndon Johnson, whom they considered an arch-
conservative, joined the liberal cause as John F. Kennedy's vice-presiden-
tial running mate. The liberals are beginning to challenge the leadership
of the Democratic party, but, for the past quarter of a century, the governorship has continued in the hands of conservative to moderate Democrats.[18]

Traditionally, the September convention of the Democratic party
which meets in even-numbered years has been dubbed the "governors'
convention," as it has provided a ready-made opportunity for the gover-
nor-nominate to secure control over the party machinery and to incorporate his campaign promises into the state platform. In 1956, Governor
Price Daniel, a moderate, was able to gain control over the state executive
committee by a narrow margin over the liberal forces of Ralph Yar-
borough. When asked about the importance of the position of governor as
political leader, he replied:

> Of course the leadership of the governor as titular head of his party is not as
> important as it is in a two-party state. On the other hand, here in our state
> with our division that we have within our Democratic Party, it is very impor-
> tant that the governor exercise his power as titular head of the Democratic
> party and that he have that power through the conventions because there are
> many influences through our state Democratic Executive Committee and our
> precinct conventions that are important in the life and government of our
> state. And if the governor is not the titular head of his party, of course, he does
> not have the power of persuasion to get over his program that he would have
> if he had the party leadership.[19]

In the state convention of 1974, the battle for the leadership of the
party emerged again. In the ballot for state chairman, the governor's
choice, Calvin Guest, won over the liberal candidate, Leonel Castillo, by
3,125 to 2,183 votes. Guest claimed support from both rural and urban
conservatives, Wallacites, moderates, and, surprisingly, the leadership of
organized labor. Although labor was usually aligned with the liberals, the
leadership wanted more to unite the party than to contribute to a liberal-
conservative split. Castillo claimed support from a coalition of blacks,
Mexican-Americans, traditional liberals, rank-and-file labor, the young,
the disaffected Wallacites, the party progressives, the "open party caucus"
interested in procedural changes, and the Texas Woman's Political Caucus
seeking more power for women.[20]

The factional alignment in Texas favors the conservatives. For the
sake of party unity, even the labor leaders support the winning faction and

can trade the certainty that their candidate will win for repeal of the right-to-work or anti-picketing laws or the establishment of agency shop provisions. Given the conservative three to two edge, pro-labor legislation stands little chance of passing. The liberals have no organized spokesmen —only the knowledge that they can claim the allegience of about two-fifths of the majority party. The low voter interest in the inner cities may account for the fact that the liberal wing does not win votes for its candidates. The liberals are incapable of raising funds anywhere comparable to what the business–oil establishment can and does make available to more conservative opponents. With scarcely a major newspaper or major television station friendly to their cause, the liberals have great difficulty getting their point across. There is little point in voting if the cause of your candidate is hopeless. The conservative wing can keep control if it can please the oil-insurance-banking-construction businesses and rancher interests. Keeping the coalition together means conservative government. In the words of Governor Briscoe who was speaking of his role in the 1974 Constitutional Convention: "If I had taken an active part, it would have resulted in more chaos, and we had enough of that."[21]

Texas fails to place well in any of the tests one might impose to measure the output of state government in terms of serving its children, the poor, the old, and the sick. Its tax structure is unfair, benefiting the wealthy at the expense of the low and middle classes. In 1972, Texas stood forty-seventh in terms of tax effort—a measure of actual tax collections as compared with tax capacity. Texas ranked fortieth in expenditures for public elementary and secondary school education; thirty-ninth in average monthly payments for aid to families with dependent children; forty-eighth in average monthly payments to the elderly.[22] What can account for the fact that Texas does not offer its poor and middle classes breadth of services, innovative programming, or a fair tax structure? In a state where three-fifths of the majority party can control with the aid of big-business money, the press, and labor leaders—the people who need these services suffer. It will take more organization and initiative of the type displayed in the state convention of 1974 to organize the needy in Texas to fight for services they have been denied.

The Governor as Moderator
of Factions: Factions and Parties
in California

Since 1959, California's political parties have joined the other two-party states in providing a semblance of order and predictability in the nomination of candidates for public office, dividing on issues, keeping the voters informed, staffing the offices of government, and providing leadership for the legislative branch. With the inauguration of Edmund G. Brown in 1959 as the second Democratic governor in the twentieth century and the first to have his party in control of both houses of the legislature, the modern era of California politics began. The recent migrants to California recognized partisan politics as the type they left back home, and the native Californians were mystified by the change from nonpartisanship.

> An era was drawing to a close—the era of EPIC, of Ham 'n Eggs, "Goodie" Knight, of nonpartisanship and cross-filing—the era, above all, of Earl Warren. During the quarter-century from 1934 to 1959, the influence of parties in California politics varied substantially. It increased sharply in the mid-1930s, waned in the 1940s, then grew steadily stronger throughout the 1950s.[23]

Throughout the 1940s, the party system had deteriorated to the extent that three-fourths of the members of the legislature were elected by cross-filing in the primary (winning in the primary of each party simultaneously). The Warren era was the nadir of party influence in California. In winning office for himself and other Republicans under the nonpartisan banner, Warren weakened the already disorganized Democrats. His adoption of a liberal program deprived them of a reason for their existence. The Democrats could not fall back on local party organizations because there were none. They were divided into regional (north/south) and urban-rural factions. Because the Democrats constituted a majority of the registered voters, they began to try to organize their party into a cohesive whole after Warren departed for Washington. One of the first steps was to abolish the cross-filing system. Pat Brown was elected governor in 1958 on a platform that included a promise to eliminate the practice, and his legislature under strong Democratic control changed the primary law to prohibit cross-filing. The practice had weakened party responsibility and cohesiveness. It would be ridiculous for a Democratic state convention to meet after the primary, adopt a platform and pledge all Democratic nominees to support it when most of the winners of the Democratic primary were Republicans who had successfully cross-filed.

California politics has become a politics of issues—which make sense to the electorate. Each party tries to appeal to the moderate middle-of-the-road California voter who is still prone to nonpartisanship. Each party has a more ideological wing—conservative for the Republicans and liberal for the Democrats. The California parties mirror the national parties, but they are not cohesive electoral units. There is a lack of a strong state party organization. The gubernatorial primaries in each party have been contested by six to ten personalities. In the Democratic primary in 1974,

Governor Edmund G. Brown, Jr., won by 38.1 percent of the vote in a contest involving eighteen candidates. The winner of the gubernatorial primary for each party must try to appease enough of the enemies who ran against him in the primary to mount a united campaign. Brown, son of the governor who ushered in the birth of two-party politics in California in 1959, was considered a liberal and was supported by the minorities who comprise about one-fourth of the Democratic voters as well as by young voters. His major opponents, state assembly speaker Bob Moretti and Mayor Alioto of San Francisco, had the support of liberals and conservatives, labor unions, teachers, and lobbies. Brown got the support of the unions after he won the primary, but the more conservative Democratic fund raisers helped his Republican opponent, Houston Flournoy—an event that would not likely happen in a state where the political parties were more united. Flournoy himself had to try to make peace with conservative Republican leaders in exchange for their support after their candidate, Lieutenant Governor Ed Reinecke, was indicted for perjury. Both gubernatorial candidates must scurry around to gain enough support from their respective party groups to win in the general election.

Each candidate must also deal with extra-party organizations. Within the Republican umbrella, the California Republican Assembly—a conservative organization with local units in all of the state's 58 counties—provides financial and other campaign support to those candidates it believes best represent the standards of true Republicanism. The organization was instrumental in making Earl Warren, Goodwin Knight, and Richard Nixon major political figures. On both sides of this assembly are two others that represent the Goldwater Republicans (United Republicans of California) and the moderate Republicans (The California Republican League). The Democratic candidates must contend with the California Democratic Council, the statewide organization of the once-powerful liberal Democratic club movement born in 1953, to bring some order into the Democratic party and organize it on a local basis. The CDC's primary purpose is to endorse candidates in the primaries and recommend action on important issues. Its power is not what it used to be, and it has been ignored by the successful Democratic regulars who do not need its efforts.

Politics in California, a two-party state, does not resemble the virulent factionalism of the internal politics of the Democratic party in Georgia and Texas where the divisions are based on firm economic and geographical groupings. In California, the governor deals with intra-party opponents who are supported by a more-fluid party electorate, an electorate that can be appealed to on the issues of the day. His opponents, however, may give him trouble when he becomes governor. They may reemerge in the legislature to harass him. He must constantly be assembling and reassembling his coalition to win support for his programs. No strong party organization does this for him.

Factions and Parties in Pennsylvania

Pennsylvania political parties are ideologically similar to their national counterparts, and the electorate responds to policy issues as does the national electorate. Within each party there is an old guard, which is conservative, and a liberal-to-moderate wing. Leaders emerge from each wing and try to "capture" the party organization for their candidate. Invariably, a primary fight ensues for the governorship based on the old guard (or professionals) versus the liberal challengers. The challengers have been successful within each party recently, but their terms as governor entail working with or placating the built in old guard within the party. The regulars are based in the party strongholds, and their power is derived from long and faithful service as party chieftains. For the Republicans, the strongholds are in the prosperous southeastern part of the commonwealth as well as in the rural counties along the northern tier. The Democratic base, outside of Philadelphia and Pittsburgh, has been in the depressed northeastern coal counties as well as virtually all of western Pennsylvania, territory that includes all the tired steel and coal counties around Pittsburgh.

The Republican party might have slipped into permanent minority status if it had not been for a succession of moderate liberals who took on the old-guard faction allied with the Pennsylvania Manufacturers' Association. The first of these, Governor Duff, was elected in 1946. He put through amazingly progressive reforms that included a tough clean-streams law, which cleaned up the Schuylkill River, and a tax law, which gave the hard-pressed local governments new sources of taxation. He called the regulars the "high-buttoned shoes reactionaries."[24] The old guard have not succeeded in electing a governor since. They were persuaded to run William Scranton, a liberal young congressman, in place of their first preference—a professional party politician—in 1962. This was a winning maneuver and Governor Scranton gained national recognition for his ability as a progressive governor of a large industrial state. The Republican party is now a more moderate coalition than before, and its gubernatorial nominees have succeeded in obtaining unified support in the primary and have won without significant opposition in the last three. There is still a liberal-old-guard split, however, which any candidate must forge into a working whole to unite the party.

The Democrats are also composed of similar factions, although the electoral groupings are made up of the unions and minorities and big cities. On the one side there are the regular organization politicians who rose to the top through the precincts and wards. David Lawrence, elected governor in 1954 at the age of 73, was the state's first Roman Catholic governor and a member of this faction. Lawrence was a man able to combine a strong party organization with a progressive administration.

The other camp consisting of insurgent reformers began with the two men who upset the traditional Republican machine in Philadelphia 25 years ago, Richardson Dilworth and Joseph S. Clark. Their modern successor is Governor Shapp. The regulars were clever enough to keep things patched together until the early 1960s, giving the statewide nominations to the insurgents from time to time. (Dilworth was nominated for governor in 1950 and 1962 but lost both times. Clark ran for the Senate in 1956, 1962, and 1968, winning the first two times.)

In 1966 and 1970, the regulars put up Robert P. Casey against Milton Shapp in the primary, and each time Milton Shapp won. In 1974, Shapp had convinced the regulars that he was a successful incumbent and should have the nomination without opposition. It was the first time a governor could run again, and Shapp had apparently consolidated the party behind him, indicating that a term limitation is a handicap to a governor attempting to unite a party. Shapp, a self-made millionaire businessman, immersed himself in the study of state government believing that it is a place where an executive can make a contribution. He spent $4 million in the primary and general election campaigns of 1966. After he had succeeded in becoming a familar figure, he ran his own campaigns in 1970 and 1974. Shapp has had trouble with the regulars who accuse him of ignoring their choices for state jobs. But he was able to get his party majority behind him to pass an income tax after many years of argument and stalemate. In the meantime, the old-guard Democrats have passed from the scene, as the Pittsburgh and Philadelphia machines have fallen into disrepair. With the end of old-style machine politics may come a decline in the ability to slate-make. There may not be politicians who can deliver the vote. The former old-guard versus the reformers factions may give way to a more fluid contest for control of the party. Perhaps the Shapp organization will become the regulars who may be challenged by a new generation of reformers. Perhaps the moderates in both parties may sense the value of unity and schedule the major rivals, depending on their ambitions and abilities, into a unified politics. In summary, the governors who contest for control over either party in Pennsylvania can usually count on unifying the party, even though it may be a struggle. The value of winning is great enough to promote unity.

The Governor as United Party Leader in Minnesota and Wisconsin

The political parties in Minnesota and Wisconsin are based on the ideological, economic, and ethnic lines that divide the voters in those two states. The parties are cohesive, and the statewide organizations are able to recruit and groom candidates for governor and provide them with money and modern campaigning techniques. Governors are likely to have proved themselves to their respective parties by previous service in the legislature. In 1974, both gubernatorial candidates in Minnesota had served in the state legislature. In Wisconsin, Governor Lucey, a former legislator, was opposed by William Dyke, a former mayor of Madison. In both states, the state party organizations have meaning as electoral and financial units geared to electing the candidates of their choice.

In Wisconsin, the polarization between the two parties rests on liberal-conservative lines. The conservative and relatively prosperous Catholics and Yankee Protestants tend to congregate in the Republican party. On the other hand, the relatively liberal, lower-income Scandinavian farmers, the Milwaukee and Madison working class, and the former LaFollette Progressives are encompassed within the Democratic party. Both parties established extra-legal governing organizations to circumvent stringent state laws, and both are able to recruit a mass membership for their parties. Many citizens are card-carrying Democrats and Republicans.

The Republican endorsement procedure for governor is an excellent example of what party-theorists would call a positive role in leadership. Two or three thousand activist delegates gather in May or June of a gubernatorial election year and endorse a single candidate in the September primary for governor. This enables the full force of party finance and activity to affect the primary campaign. The endorsed candidates win in the primaries and are not seriously opposed. The Democratic party organization does not always endorse candidates in the primary. Labor, however, frequently participates in the primaries by endorsing and contributing to candidates; furthermore, the party leadership frequently prefers one contestant and attempts to influence the primary outcome by directing volunteer efforts and individual contributions to the candidate.[25]

Party control over finances is another aspect of party responsibility. To the extent that parties raise and dispense campaign funds, party organizations are better able to control nominations and be a significant influence on the office holder elected under the party's banner. Potential candidates may be discouraged from attempting to challenge the favored one if they know that available money flows out of the party treasury and is disbursed to candidates receiving the party's endorsement. The party platform is likely to be taken seriously by the candidates if the party provides both money and campaign effort. The centralized fund-raising system employed by the Wisconsin Republicans has meant that the party organization collected and controlled the money available from major conservative financial sources. The Republican financial picture has been dominated by the party organization. The major portion of the spending for the gubernatorial campaigns is handled directly by the Republican state organization. Adamany states that, since a major share of their volunteer effort as well as most of their money comes from the ideologically conservative Republican Party, it is not surprising that many Republican candidates have tended to be conservatives, or at least to be attentive to conservative opinion.[26]

While the Republicans have collected and controlled the money available from major conservative financial sources, the Democrats cannot have as centralized a fund-raising effort because they have no natural base of wealthy individuals upon whom to draw as a party. Labor usually gives directly to the candidates selected through the endorsement process because it is these candidates to whom they wish access after they are elected. A party endorsement, however, means that these labor funds will be released, and thus it is a tremendous advantage to the designated candidate. The party also raises some money from fund-raising events and dues, and, in 1964, this—along with some labor money—amounted to 37 percent of the gubernatorial candidate's (John Reynold's) total.[27] The liberal activists who control the Democratic party machinery have been able to groom, recruit, and endorse candidates whose programs and principles are acceptable. Thus, the financing pattern in both Republican and Democratic parties has tended to be compatible with the strong party government model. Gubernatorial candidates must convince the ideologically active party machinery that they deserve the nomination before funds and support will be forthcoming. The Wisconsin parties have been strong and programmatic. A governor has a built-in base of support when he reaches the government. He looks toward the same organization for support for his legislation and the administration of his programs. Wisconsin governors "deliver" for the voters when they are elected.

Minnesota is another state with "programmatic" parties that are able to impose a form of discipline over the candidates who run under their respective banners. When the Farmer-Labor and the weaker Democratic party joined forces in 1944, the merger meant the joining of urban Irish and Polish Catholics and rural Scandinavian Lutherans. It also brought together some extreme left-wing elements from the Farmer-Labor party with relatively conservative middle-class Democrats. Hubert Humphrey (a man to achieve fame as senator, vice-president and Democratic presidential candidate in 1968) and his entourage fancied themselves to be a middle ground between the top elements of the Democratic-Farmer-Labor Party. After 1954, the consolidation of the party had been achieved with the moderate Humphrey wing in control. The state's farmers shifted in massive fashion to the new party. The party also enjoyed political gains in the cities, but the gains were small in proportion to the rural-farm increase.

The Republican party meanwhile was also trying to get its liberal and conservative wings under control. The conservatives longed for a Republican party in the image of Robert Taft of Ohio. The liberals wanted a candidate in the image of Harold Stassen, former liberal governor who controlled the party until 1954. By 1960, the Republican party was a relatively moderate, middle-of-the road party, and in most elections the choice was not between a reactionary Republican and a liberal but between a middle-of-the road Republican and a liberal. In Minnesota, the political divisions are not along urban-rural lines. They tend to follow ethnic, occupational, and income lines. The Scandinavian low-income grain farmer is most likely to vote Democratic, whereas the Yankee or German high-income dairy or livestock farmer votes Republican. There is no significant relationship between percentage urban and percentage rural-farm and the Democratic or Republican vote. This means that a person in the city is just as likely to vote Republican as Democratic. The Republican party has an opportunity to make inroads into the Democratic-Farmer-Labor strength in the cities. Apparently, the increase in home ownership in the cities brings a concern with taxes, an issue on which liberal Democrats are vulnerable to Republican charges of extravagance with public funds.[28] Hence, the urban vote is not as decisive as in most states that are divided into two evenly competing parties. The major industry is food growing and processing, and Minnesota is a rurally oriented state.

In Minnesota as in Wisconsin, the state parties play a central role in recruiting, nominating, and electing. When speaking of the parties of these states, one speaks of party platforms, party conventions, and party state central committees. Party conventions make preprimary nominations in both states, and the party-endorsed candidate has a great advantage because of the resources coming his way. The experience of the Democratic-Farmer-Labor party in Minnesota demonstrates that parties at the state level can play a central role in modern campaigning by assuming the leadership in making the new technology available to party candidates.[29] The Minnesota Republicans have been experimenting with statewide campaigns in terms of opinion polling, automatic computer processing of voter data, and other forms of election analysis.

What difference does it make if the governor has professional party machinery able to support him in his efforts for winning the governorship as well as getting his program passed after he becomes governor? In both states, the governors "deliver" on policy promises. The voters expect their leaders to respond. When they became unhappy over the excesses of big business, they protested with their votes and were rewarded with legislation that regulated the railroads, the insurance companies, and the lumber interests. Voters' protests against corruption brought them strong civil service laws. When the laborers protested their insecurity, they received unemployment compensation and workmen's compensation laws. Both states must tax heavily to provide the services expected by their citizens. In 1972, Wisconsin and Minnesota were seventh and second, respectively, in relative tax effort. They ranked in the upper fifth in average monthly payments to families with dependent children and in the upper fourth in expenditure per pupil for public education. In both states, by way of summary, the governors and legislators know that they will be held responsible for delivering on promises. If they do not, the other party will unseat them. Both parties are cohesive and run unified campaigns. A continuing leadership group exists in each. The nominee for governor must be at home with the party ideology and platform. Unlike the other states mentioned previously, the party leadership can help or hinder the ambitions of future governors. It is the party that governors must persuade if they are to be successful.

Table 5–4, which ranks each of the six states discussed on the variables of party strength, tax effort, education, and welfare policy, illustrates the thesis that it is the parties that are unified that are better able to provide their citizens with services of benefit to all. Whether the party is Democratic or Republican, generous education and welfare benefits are provided the people if the party is united behind the governor. The states with the strongest parties are at the top of the welfare and education services rankings; those states at the bottom of the party-strength category do not provide their people with adequate education and welfare policies.

It has been a major hypothesis of this book that the factions that contend during the process of nominating the governor are represented in the governing process. To the extent that a governor has captured the machinery of his party he can count on its help in governing. His faction, if it is large enough, can be counted on to produce the votes he needs when he proposes measures to the legislature for passage. A governor

TABLE 5–4

Party Strength and Public Policy[a]

STATE	PARTY STRENGTH RANK[b]	TAX EFFORT RANK[c]	EDUCATION POLICY RANK[d]	WELFARE POLICY RANK[e]
Minnesota	4	7	8	10
Wisconsin	8	2	12	3
California	20	9	20	16
Pennsylvania	29	12	9	6
Georgia	43	37	37	45
Texas	45	47	40	39

[a] Each of the six states are given ranks on a 50-state basis.
[b] Party strength is measured according to the description in Table 4–1. The years are 1956–1976.
[c] Actual tax collections as a percentage of personal income adjusted for tax capacity, 1971.
[d] Expenditure per pupil for public elementary and secondary day schools, 1973.
[e] Average monthly payments for aid to families with dependent children (per family), 1972.
Source: David R. Morgan, *Handbook of State Policy Indicators*, 2d ed. (Norman, Okla.: University of Oklahoma, Bureau of Government Research, 1974), pp. 33, 43, 62.

hamstrung by factions cannot hope to govern effectively. Governing parties with sufficient internal cohesion to pass programs to which they commit themselves will bring about a wider distribution of state expenditures across income classes. The test of this claim can only be made by an inspection of the efforts of governors as chief executives and leaders of the governing parties.

THE GOVERNOR AS CHIEF EXECUTIVE

Governors are faced with problems such as growth of crime, poverty, and environmental pollution. Most of these problems have an important urban aspect at a time when more persons live in suburbs than in central cities or rural areas. At the same time the residents of the states are expecting the governor to solve the urban problems, they also expect improved health, educational, recreational, and other services. Yet there is ample evidence of an increasing public resistence to increased taxes necessary to take care of these problems.

The Governor as Federal Systems Officer

The governor plays an important innovative role in the federal system. Although he has been given the title "federal systems officer," he has little choice but to be a political activist. He is chosen by the people of the state to lead and is the undisputed policy innovator. He lobbies for funds in Washington and then strives to ensure that federal dollars entering his state are spent in accord with his goals and conceptions of how the state should develop. He must complement lobbying for funds from Washington with pressures on his own legislature for the authority and money needed to support his programs. He must mediate between the cities and towns and coordinate their actions.

Since 1966, the 50 governors have seen the advantage in maintaining a Washington office to represent their interests before the Congress and the administration. This office was organized by the National Governor's Conference, an organization that has been in existence for some time but has not been energetic enough in representing the interests of the governors vis-a-vis the federal government. Its annual meetings had been ineffective in influencing federal policy. By establishing the Washington Office, the Conference embraced new organizational purposes aimed at directly influencing federal-state relations. It created a full-time governors' lobby in Washington. In response to weekly analyses and special research reports, the office receives constant feedback from governors and their staffs on the anticipated effect on state government of pending legislation. To bring the Conference and its members in closer contact with federal policy makers, an annual midwinter meeting of governors is now held under the aegis of the Washington office. The meetings are attended by nearly all the governors who put partisan considerations aside for the purpose of acting collectively for state interests. These meetings inform the governors of the major legislative proposals expected to be taken up by Congress during that particular session and alert them to the probable consequences of the action for their state programs and policies. By their fourth annual midwinter conference in 1970, the governors expected their conference to be attended by the president, cabinet officers, and Capitol Hill leaders. They make their collective presence felt by demonstrating their concern with the course of domestic policy.

The demands of the new federalism have also moved at least 27 states to establish their own Washington offices to obtain more federal funds and keep track of them.[30] Since national aid contributes an average 24 percent of a state's budget, the amount and character of such aid is crucial to the states with large urban centers. In these offices, staffs lobby on behalf of the individual states. These lobbyists are attuned to the recent developments with respect to much legislation affecting their states. They keep close check on their congressional delegation, testify before congressional committees, contact government officials, and provide an office where the state officials can convene when in Washington.

When the governors turn their attention to the impact of the federal programs on the cities, towns, and counties in their own states, they are caught in a web of intergovernmental program and policy relationships. These include the assistance state agencies under the governor's policy direction give to local governments and the coordination of federally funded programs at the state and local levels. There has been a trend in federal legislation—for example, the Omnibus Crime Control and Safe Streets Act, the Comprehensive Health Planning Act, the Land and Water Conservation Act, and various regional development programs—to designate the governor as the chief federal planning and administrative officer in the state. For example, the Omnibus Crime Control and Safe Streets Act of 1968 mandates the states to establish a state planning agency created by the governor. The governor and his staff are interested in the development of these programs at the state level. They want to ensure that the direction sought in federally funded programs is compatible with the state's overall goals. The governor desires to use his office to influence the procedural and policy guidelines that accompany the federal programs and to see that they conform to state objectives.

While governors want to oversee the programs that are funded with federal money within their borders, they must often see some localities spending funds for golf courses and marinas while others cannot meet decent standards of housing and welfare. This problem with respect to revenue sharing, under which the states receive one-third of the funds and their localities receive two-thirds, was discussed in chapter 1. The governors must watch as the cities use their funds to continue operating programs for the poor and elderly while the suburbs use the funds for parks and firehouses. Because the funds are allotted automatically without the governor's option of saying which local governments should receive a portion of such funds and on what basis, the governor loses control over coordinating policy within his own state. For instance, if FHA insurance were to be jeopardized in any state where exclusionary zoning is a problem, the governors would likely do something about it. If local governments can receive federal insurance without such restrictions, the governors have a difficult time initiating such action. Lacking incentives, such action is usually politically impossible.

Until recently, fear, distrust, and disdain characterized the relationship between the states and their localities. This was well deserved in the past. The states tended to let the localities manage with a dwindling tax base. This has been changing as cities see that the states are contributing more money to solve their problems. The state governor may be a better friend than the federal government administrators. In the past two decades, the federal government has developed a host of programs to deal with local problems. Some of these fostered good state-local relationships, and some were detrimental to these relationships. Several programs in the package of federal largesse served to provide the governor and his administration with the few real incentives they had to strengthen state-local relationships. Among these were funding for state assistance to Model Cities and HUD's (Housing and Urban Development) 701 Planning Assistance Program. When this program was initiated, few states except for New York had a community affairs agency through which to establish this relationship. At present there are between 35 and 42 state community affairs agencies.[31] In general, the federal programs that best served the states in the sense that they could control the policies and programs within their borders were those that were channeled through the state.

The "new federalism" concept is supposed to restructure federal aid around block grants or revenue sharing. Supposedly the concept was developed to afford the state and local governments the opportunity to sort out their own priorities and make their own spending decisions. Over the past several years, the states and localities have seen the emergence of block-grant programs in such functional areas as law enforcement (Safe Streets Act), manpower (Comprehensive Employment and Training Act), and community development (Housing and Community Development Act of 1974). The first two programs do provide the governors with a way of planning and assisting the cities in the use of funds. Under the Safe

Streets Act, all planning and action grants are made to the state governments, which, in turn, must make 40 percent of the planning monies and 75 percent of the action grant funds available to local governments. While the Safe Streets Act may not have accomplished its end of reforming the criminal justice system, it did lay the groundwork for the cooperation needed between state and local governments. Under the Comprehensive Employment and Training Act, funds are awarded to states, cities, and localities to plan and operate manpower-related programs. Much of the money, however, is channeled directly to large cities and metropolitan areas. It is not as desirable a program from the governor's viewpoint as the Safe Streets Act and does not promote the "new federalism" concept.

The villain with respect to the ability of the states to plan for the health, education, and welfare of their citizens is the Housing and Urban Development Act of 1974. The act incorporates federal funding support for a range of community development activities, housing programs, and planning and management efforts. Eighty percent of the funds is allocated to metropolitan areas and 20 percent is earmarked for nonmetropolitan areas. The act itself was developed with little input from the states, and, as a result, the states are largely bypassed.[32] States are not entitled automatically to any funding under Title I of the act, and they have not been assigned specific responsibilities relative to the administration of the Community Development Block Grant Program. The state role in the federal system is weakened as a result of the manner in which the act was written. The previous three cases have served to illustrate the proposition that the federal grants, which provide approximately 20 percent of all state and local funding, have not in all cases provided the proper milieu for allowing the states and localities to cooperate in solving joint problems. From the state point of view, say the authors of an article on the impact of federalism on state-local relations, the theme of new federalism was to "cut the states out of the action." No funding was provided to the states to provide the technical assistance that localities needed to develop and perform their new tasks. The major struggle governors have is trying to convince the Congress that they need to be consulted in the planning and execution of federal programs and in convincing the mayors and local officials that they are willing to assume responsibility with respect to urban problems.

Formal Powers

APPOINTIVE POWER   The vestigial survival of Jacksonian democracy is evident in the number of elected administrative officers in the American states. The selection by popular vote of such officers as lieutenant governor, attorney general, comptroller, treasurer, auditor, and secretary of state represents the Jacksonian formula aimed at preventing abuse associated with legislative choice of these officials. (The former position of the legislature as an electoral body gave it powerful leverage in the extraction of patronage from executive officers.) This system of popular election, however, has its own system of side effects. It has created a multiheaded leadership of state government consisting of independently elected officials who do not owe policy loyalty to the governor, unless, by happy accident, they think the same as he does. In addition to sharing responsibilities with officials who are independently elected, many governors share appointive power with the legislature which can veto their choice of administrators. Thad Beyle discovered that governors mentioned the importance of the appointive power more times than any other formal power. Sixty-seven percent of the governors who replied (39) stressed the lack of the appointive power as the most crucial weakness in their performance as chief executive.[33] Table 5–5 ranks the states according to a formula developed by Joseph A. Schlesinger.

If the governor has complete control over appointments, his state's rank is 100. If he needs the approval of one house of the legislature for all his appointments, his state would receive a score of 80. If both houses of the legislature must approve his appointments, the score would be 60. The least control of all is the case where the official is elected by popular vote. Table 5–5 shows how far the states deviate from theoretical full control over appointments. Virginia's score of 84 is highest. The secretary of state, attorney general, treasurer and auditor are still elected in a majority of the states. Now that most of the states are internally competitive between parties, either party could capture some of the offices. In these situations, the governor shares fiscal power and judicial power with his opponents— a doubtful privilege. Some consolation is afforded a governor if an official with whom he cannot work can be removed. But even the gubernatorial appointing power does not necessarily include a general power to remove. The governor may not remove elective or judicial officers, many of whom are subject to impeachment. When Governor Brendan Byrne of New Jersey tried to remove his secretary of state plus a member of an independent commission, both men having come under clouds of suspicion, they resisted and clung to their jobs![34]

Is it possible to live with the oddity of state governmental situations that permit control of the governorship and minor offices to be divided between the parties? Are most of the minor administrative offices entrusted with minor responsibilities and so permit the states to get along well enough despite the eccentric manner in which they operate? We know that the governors do not think so. Thomas Dye, however, found that there is little evidence to support the notion that executive fragmentation in itself affects the content of public policy in the states.[35] While he found that states that remain content with the long ballot pursue some-

TABLE 5-5

The Appointive Powers of the Governor, 1975

State Rankings

STRONG	MODERATE	WEAK
84 Virginia	49 Connecticut	30 Oklahoma
70 New Jersey	49 South Dakota	30 New Mexico
70 Tennessee	48 California	24 Texas
69 Hawaii	48 Idaho	23 Arizona
68 Massachusetts	46 Delaware	23 South Carolina
66 Wyoming	46 Georgia	21 Florida
64 Indiana	44 Rhode Island	19 Mississippi
63 Kentucky	44 Michigan	
59 Pennsylvania	44 Washington	
59 New York	43 West Virginia	
59 Montana	43 Kansas	
56 Illinois	41 North Carolina	
55 Nebraska	41 Maryland	
51 Ohio	40 Louisana	
51 Alabama	39 Missouri	
50 Minnesota	39 Iowa	
50 Colorado	39 North Dakota	
	38 Wisconsin	
	38 Vermont	
	36 Utah	
	36 Alaska	
	35 New Hampshire	
	35 Nevada	
	33 Arkansas	
	33 Maine	
	33 Oregon	

Note: The figure for each state is based on the governor's powers of appointment in 16 major functions and offices. It indicates the degree to which the governor can be assumed to have appointive power over the sixteen functions or offices. The functions are: administration and finance, agriculture, attorney general, auditor, budget officer, conservation, controller, education, health, highways, insurance, labor, secretary of state, tax commissioner, treasurer, and welfare. See the formula in Schlesinger's chapter in Jacob and Vines, eds, *Politics in the American States*, 2d ed., p. 227.

what different policies than states with streamlined executive branches, most of these policy differences are attributable to the impact of economic development rather than the structure of state executive functions. There is a tendency for states with many agency heads to spend less money per pupil for education, to pay lower teacher's salaries, to provide lower welfare benefits, and to have fewer unemployment recipients. Dye found that these relationships appear to be a product of economic development rather than fragmentation of the executive. Dye's policy variables are levels of spending for various policies that would naturally be related to the wealth and economic development of the state. He may not be providing us with the test we are looking for to examine whether a governor with appointive power can affect the distribution of money and services from the haves to the have-nots. As a matter of fact, the strongest correlations between governor's power and public policy lie in the fields of taxation and welfare. Even after controlling for economic development, weak executive power is related to the sales tax, a regressive tax to the extent that it falls on the wealthy and poor alike. It is my contention that it takes organization to put forward and pass a sustained program in behalf of the needy. Disorganization can obstruct such a program. A fragmented executive may be a holding operation—a bastion of the status quo. A governor who can appoint those who share his views can develop programs to present to the legislature and can use the resources that are available to him to build a coalition to pass the proposals.

JOINT ELECTION OF GOVERNOR AND LIEUTENANT GOVERNOR   If the lieutenant governor is elected separately from the governor, he might be from the opposite party as well, compelling the governor to share legislative power with his opponents. Under the extremely narrow majority the governor may have in the state senate, any arrangement that would throw control over to the other side is a thorn in his own. This very condition occurred in Illinois in 1971. Republican Governor Ogilvie had a Republican majority in the house, but an even split in the senate. Lieutenant Governor Simon, a Democrat, tipped the scales in favor of the opposition party in the senate. A quick check of the 31 states outside the solid south that elect lieutenant governors reveals that, in 1979, seven states had a divided team; the governor and lieutenant governors were from different parties. There are eleven northern states in which this situation could occur because separate elections are held for the two offices. Since a lieutenant governorship is an attractive base from which to launch a campaign for the governorship, consider the irritant influence on the governor—his second-in-command watching and waiting to make political capital out of his mistakes. Consider how an opposition lieutenant governor could throw road blocks in the way of the legislative program of the governor from the former's position of power in the senate. Is it possible to say that the voters, in their infinite wisdom, have elected the best men for the job, regardless of party? Is this the proper exercise of judgment, or should electoral arrangements deny this opportunity to the voter? In my judgment, voters who live in internally competitive states have the opportunity to overthrow the government at frequent intervals. They should *not* have the opportunity to hamstring the governor—whom they elect—and prevent him from gaining internal unity sufficient to propose and enact a program that reflects the opinions of the majority of those who supported him.

GOVERNOR'S STAFF   Fortunately for the governor, he can surround himself with loyal staff members who are chosen to be an extension of his personality and interests and who owe him allegience by virtue of their appointments. Professional policy advisors and legal assistants who serve the governor are the key to his successfully handling the policy load he inherits as governor. In the smaller states, the governor's office may consist of no more than an administrative assistant and several secretaries. In larger states, the governor will have administrative and legal assistants as well as policy experts in a broad range of state functions and processes. Recent studies reveal that the staff members selected by governors are political animals who tie their political fortunes to the governor's. They tend to be long-term acquaintances of the governor who have helped him with his primary and election campaigns.[36] Thus, the picture emerges of a governor with a loyal corps of supporters trying to get control over an unwieldy and balking administrative apparatus. Undoubtedly some of the major pieces of legislation the governor and his staff see passed become bogged in the administration. This accounts for the plea for reorganization powers the governors have been making recently.

BUDGETARY POWER   There are two more weapons in the arsenal of the governor's formal powers that are widely recognized as powerful ammunition, depending on the skill of the governor in using them. The first is the power of the purse, which the governor shares with the legislature, of course, but, over the years, the responsibility of preparing the budget has been given to him. In 35 states, the governor has the sole responsibility for preparing the budget, meaning that he appoints his budget director who answers to him. In 15 states, he shares this responsibility with a civil service appointee, an appointee of someone other than himself, or a legislative committee. Beyle discovered that only 8 percent of governors he observed mentioned the lack of budgetary power as a problem in their performance as chief executive.[37] Apparently in most states, the budget is seen as a major expression of gubernatorial policy and as an important means of administrative control. For this reason the governor is able to control the official who prepares the budget. The budget office must be able to prepare a budget that is an accurate expression of the governor's proposed program. In most states, the governor *does* appoint the budget director, in some cases with one or both houses approving. In Virginia, for example, the governor not only appoints the budget director but can remove him at his pleasure. Next, from the point of view of gubernatorial control over the budget, might come a state like Kansas where the governor appoints the head of the department of administration with the advice of the legislature, and he in turn appoints the budget officer from the civil service. In this case, the governor cannot dismiss the budget officer because he is protected by the merit system. In South Carolina, from the point of view of gubernatorial control, an even weaker system exists. Here the budget is prepared by a board on which sit executive and legislative representatives headed by the governor. Weakest of all, in Mississippi, a commission of budget and accounting located primarily within the legislature is responsible for the budget preparation. This is the weakest form from the point of view of a governor who wishes to be responsible for financial control over policy making.[38] In the second and third states on the list, however, the governor may assume control over the budget by persuasion, if not by formal power.

VETO POWER   On the other end of the budgetary process is the power to veto items in appropriation bills. This is a potentially powerful weapon. It is a means by which the governor can prevent administrators from going over his head and getting support from the legislature. By vetoing particular items in the bill, the governor can keep the budget within the spending confines he chooses. In 35 states, the governor has the item veto combined with a two-thirds to three-quarters majority of the legislature (elected or present) needed to pass the item over his veto. Practically speaking, this means that the governor need persuade only a small percentage of his party members to support him if the question of repassing the item over his veto arises. Because most legislators know that it is almost impossible to overturn a veto unless the governor's party is hostile and divided or unless his party commands less than one-third of the legislature (such as the case of the Republican governor of South Carolina), the threat of a veto is effective. In nine states, the governor has the item veto with a majority or three-fifths of the legislature needed to override his decision. In spite of this veto power, the governor uses it sparingly, more as a threat than as actuality, so that when a veto *does* come before a legislature, the most intense party activity attends it.

This discussion is concerned with the item veto as a weapon in the arsenal of the governor to affect appropriation bills as a vital part of his policy program. In all states but North Carolina, the governor has veto power over all legislation, and in only five can his veto be overturned by a simple majority. As with the item veto, it usually takes a large-sized majority to override the governor's veto. One might question why a governor who had considerable influence with his legislative party would ever let unapproved legislation slip through. In this regard, it must be remembered that the governor recommends for passage only a small amount of the total legislative product. If offensive legislation is called to his attention, he may threaten to veto it if passed and must do so to give credibility to his threats. Cases have arisen where the governor vetoed a bill in his program because it was altered substantially in the legislative process. Occasionally, when the governor's party is a hopeless minority, he vetoes offensive legislation passed by the opposition party. On the other hand, when he has a swollen majority he cannot control, he may veto offensive legislation passed by legislators bearing the same party label. Generally, the veto calls for a vote of confidence in the governor, and his party leaders exert maximum influence to ensure that the veto is sustained.

Joseph Schlesinger has compiled an index of the formal powers of the governors of all 50 states.[39] This index is composed of the previously discussed components: governor's tenure provisions, appointive powers, responsibilities for budget preparation, and the power to veto bills passed by the legislature. The index (for 1971) ranges from a low of 8 in South Carolina to a high of 20 in New York, Illinois and Hawaii. (See Appendix 2 for complete rankings). This means only that the governors of these latter three states have more *formal* power with which to influence and persuade. The governors of South Carolina, Mississippi and Texas lack these formal powers. They may not need them to accomplish the same ends—for example, influence policy, since they may have informal powers such as the use of patronage, jobs, and contracts to win necessary support from the members of their party. Schlesinger did discover that the more competitive urban states tended to give their governors more formal power. I suspect that strong political leaders would propose and support measures to strengthen their hands. Dye, on the other hand, did not find that the governor's formal powers significantly affected policy outcomes in the states.[40] He found that economic development is more important than the governor's powers in determining public policy; he observes that the governors with strong formal power come from states that are wealthy, urban, and industrial while the governors with weak formal powers tend to come from states that are poor, rural, and agricultural.

"CHIEF EXECUTIVE" Typically a state constitution declares that the governor shall be invested with the "chief" executive authority rather than "the" executive authority of the state, thereby implying that other independently chosen executive officers share the executive power with him and hence affect the manner in which his policies are carried out. Does the arrangement of state agencies and personnel have anything to do with the fate of the governor's program so carefully nurtured into law through the legislative process? Obviously so, because as shown in the study by

Beyle mentioned earlier, the governors see problems of control within the executive branch itself as the most important constraints on their ability to perform as heads of government.[41] The lack of reorganization power was mentioned by 46.2 percent of the governors, ranking second to lack of appointive power on their list of frustrations. These two powers are closely related in their substance and indicate that the bureaucracy and its personnel can hamstring the political goals of the popularly elected governor.

American state governments consist of a variety of agencies whose powers are so ill-defined that administrators are uncertain of their jurisdictions or so well-defined that they can act independently of each other. States have failed to develop well-ordered administrative hierarchies because, in part, state governments are not created at once but are the products of the gradual accretion of new functions and the related agencies. The simplest administrative solution to a new problem is to create a new agency to assure the citizens that the state is "doing something" about the problem. In the process of creation, the new agency is put under the control of the governor or of the legislature or established as an independent commission to take administration "out of politics." Hence, agencies and departments that ought to be grouped into functionally related units have developed "minds of their own" since their creation and refuse to merge or cooperate. The sources for independence are many and varied, but one recurrent and pervasive concern is that interest groups and professional organizations have developed symbiotic relationships with state agencies that manifest themselves in resistence to change.

A recent study of the attitudes of top state administrators toward reorganization indicates that only 42 percent preferred to be under the primary control of the governor. Those agencies actually under the control of the governor, however, indicated overwhelmingly (77 percent) their preference to stay there. At present there are more agencies under the direct control of the legislature than that of the governor, and only about half (47 percent) of those under legislative control prefer to stay there; 22 percent indicate a desired shift to gubernatorial control, while an even larger percentage (31) desired a shift to independent commission control.[42] These data disclose a clear preference for a shift *away* from state legislative control. While preference for the governor's primary control is expressed by a majority of all who are currently under his control or who find him sympathetic to their agency goals, one-fourth of all state agency heads favor independence. This indicates clearly the extent to which there are strong pressures fractionalizing the control of the governor over his administrative establishment.

On the other hand, a recent study of the views governors hold toward top administrators confirms the fact that they believe administration is a political process. Administrators, according to the governors, should support them publicly even though the administrator disagrees with the governor. On occasion, the administrator should implement the governor's plan even when he does not agree with it. Sixty-five percent of the governors believe that the administrators should help the governor carry out vote-getting programs. They should be political spokesmen for the governor as well as becoming involved in gubernatorial campaigns.[43]

While executive centralization and authority are regarded as important for management purposes, no governor will make the assumption, characteristic of the reformers, that management is the entire answer to the weighty problems facing state government today. The reformers believe that there exist eternally valid goals of efficiency or sound business practice that should dictate organizational forms. In the view of Martha Weinberg, governors can never exercise rational, calculated control over their administrators. Because they depend on the public for election, they must always maintain sufficient support to be reelected and must react to the public's demands. In this way they rely on "crisis management" or the response to the public's concerns at any given time. These demands are often unpredictable or uncontrollable.

> Governors do not *manage* in the customary sense of the word, that is, they do not direct or oversee the affairs of agencies over some sustained period of time. Instead, management for elected chief executives usually involves sporadic intervention in the agencies' business, often only for a short period of time. This intervention is most often initiated because of a crisis.[44]

Administration is deeply immersed in the policy process. A given administrative agency invariably favors some of the participants at the expense of others. Rearranging the structure may increase the power of some groups over others; it may make it possible for a governor to appoint those favorable to his program to head the departments in his administration. This he needs to do because he cannot exercise continuous supervision over them. He needs those who agree with his policies to head the departments in his government. Decisions on governmental structure, then, are not neutral, but rather are decisions on policy. And no governmental structure, however favorable it may be to the strong governor, can make the value decisions concerning the inequalities between the inner city and the suburb, between black and white citizens, between corporate power and the public interest. These decisions the governor alone must make.

The power to reorganize the executive branch is becoming an important executive power. In the years between 1965–78, 21 states went through the throes of executive branch restructuring. More than thirty states conducted studies of executive branch organization. In many instances, the governors have initiated the studies and have frequently drafted the reorganization bills. To take one example, on December 20,

1976, the Committee on the Structure of State Government presented its final report to Governor Grasso of Connecticut. The committee believed that major restructuring of the state government should take place with primary emphasis on improving the staff support available to the governor and on reducing the number of separate departments and agencies reporting to the governor.[45] By the committee's count, its mandate included 210 units of government in the executive branch. To better organize these units, the committee recommended that 15 major departments be established together with an office of policy and management and an executive office of the governor. This report was similar to many in the last ten years. The purpose of most executive reorganizations is: (1) to reduce the number of agencies reporting to the governor; (2) to make the governor responsible for administrative departments by giving him or her power to appoint their directors and making their terms of office coterminous; (3) to eliminate duplicate and obsolete functions; (4) to achieve better coordination and more logical assignment of related functions; and (5) to give principal department heads the power to make decisions for which they are held accountable. One development during the decade was the adoption of constitutional amendments restricting the number of executive departments. At least twelve states now have such limitations, the most common limit being 20.

The Connecticut Committee on the Structure of State Government recognized the fact that some groups strongly support the status quo. It offered to assist the governor to get the reorganization plan approved by the General Assembly, recognizing that the consideration of the plan would be lengthy and difficult because of the large number of groups who would feel that their ox was being gored. The final result was the formation of 22 major departments, not 15 as recommended. There is no question that executive reorganization is a very political process. The governor must have legislative support to accomplish it. Even in states that have given their governor the authority to reorganize by executive order—subject to veto by one or both legislative houses—the authority has been little used, the governor preferring to get full legislative approval for such drastic proposals. In Massachusetts, for instance, "reorg" as it is inelegantly called is a major political issue and modification of the executive structure has been slow and modest. In every instance, the governor has presented reorganization plans to the legislature as routine statutory proposals rather than through taking advantage of his initiative powers.[46] This may have been because a Republican governor faced a Democratic legislature during the period of reorganization. The political climate dictated the need for legislative approval—if not, a legislative veto was a certainty.

The fact that the reorganization process is heavily involved in politics means that there need be no fear that governors will become so strong that tyranny will develop. The countervailing forces will continue to ensure that the governor will not go on a rampage. The difficulties of building legislative coalitions, the power of pressure groups, the eagerness of journalists to expose "political scandals" will still continue to hold the governor in check. The first years of this century saw a wave of reform to reduce corruption and keep stealing on the part of government officials to a minimum. Reformers were prepared to accept a paralysis in policy making to keep the governor and his administrators honest. State government is now being called on to provide a high level of human services for its people, and governors need to integrate, innovate, and execute if they are not to lose the capability of providing these services and hence to lose the confidence of their people.

Matthew E. Welsh, governor of Indiana from 1961 to 1965, states that state governments are charged with an awesome responsibility today which makes it necessary that the governor lead and lead actively in adapting the apparatus of state government to do a more effective job. He believes that major changes in state constitutions will be necessary. Claiming that it is not possible or desirable for the federal government to operate the state schools or universities; or administer the state's water and air pollution programs; or operate state and local health programs and hospitals; or build state and local road and highway systems; or administer city, county, and state courts; or see to it that racial minorities are given equal opportunities on an everyday basis, Governor Welsh called for basic structural changes to grant broad authority to the governor because our federal system can only be preserved by the presence of high-quality government at the state level.[47]

Goodbye to Good-Time Charlie, a book by Larry Sabato, claims that governors are now in a position to exert leadership, the kind that inspires the confidence of men. He believes that governors of greater capacity and training have been elected in the last decade more than ever before. They have the foundations of persuasive power, but that is not enough for success. "The brightest, ablest governors could be stopped dead in their tracks by the multitude of institutional obstacles placed in their way."[48] Since most of the institutional barriers have been removed by reorganization and increasing appointive and budgetary powers, the new governors are in position to use their competence and personality to serve the people.

The major question to be asked is: "What powers, or combination of powers, have the strongest impact upon the quality of life which the citizens enjoy in the states? Is a governor with considerable political and formal power able to promote and get his legislators to pass programs that will distribute the benefits of the state to those who most need them? Is it true, as V. O. Key has often stated, that political organization affects the quality and distribution of services? We can proceed with this type of analysis after we have considered several other resources which are directly related to the ability of the governor to get things done.

THE GOVERNOR AS POLICY LEADER

On January 17, 1977, John D. Rockefeller, IV, finally became the governor of West Virginia, ending the mountaineer suspicion that denied him the first election bid four years earlier. The noonday temperature was so bitter for the inauguration that many stayed indoors to watch it on television. In his address, Rockefeller, the third member of his family to serve as governor of a state, declared that West Virginia's "time has come." He called on the people to leave behind the stigma of Appalachian poverty that has characterized West Virginia as a poor and almost helpless state and to reach out for their fair share of the American dream. He added that coal would pay the bills that would bring West Virginia out of the past and into a more comfortable and healthier world. In his losing 1972 bid, Rockefeller took a strong environmental position against strip mining, pledging to abolish it in the state if he were elected. The southern coal counties saw that as a threat to their jobs and he was not given the necessary votes from this region. For his 1976 race for governor, Rockefeller supported strip mining and the coal industry backed him. "We are blessed with 17,000 square miles of coal and a growing coal industry at a time when suddenly coal is again critical to the energy of the nation," he said. Not until the end of his 15-minute speech did Rockefeller remark that "we must be certain not to sacrifice the rugged beauty which surrounds us, 'this gift from God,'" which was the main theme of his campaign in 1972.[49]

Rockefeller was speaking as head of his faction of the Democratic party, as chief executive and as legislative leader. He as the chief policy maker in the state put together policy based on his roles in partisan politics, administration, and legislation. These three roles in policy making are very difficult to separate, and I have done so in this chapter mainly for the purposes of discussion. This section on the governor as policy leader shows the relationship between the governor as leader of the electoral party, the governing party, and the legislative party. I will trace his development of policy as a candidate for election, his development of this policy into an administrative program, and his guidance of this program through the legislature as chief legislative leader. In Governor Rockefeller's case, he put together his pledge of a large building program for secondary roads, removal of the state sales tax on food, and a modified policy on strip mining versus environmental concerns. He presented this program in the form of program bills to the legislature, which is overwhelmingly Democratic. As leader of the majority faction, he tried to convince enough of his party to back his legislation. His overwhelming primary victory meant that he had good backing to lead his party. He planned to run again in 1980 and held out rewards to those who backed him in 1977, as well as to those who will back him again. The fact that he consolidated the party (as well as can be done in West Virginia) meant his promises had meaning. He pledged a harmonious relationship between his office and the legislature. A Democratic governor in West Virginia, however, has at least two major factions to contend with. The party is divided between the traditional Bourbon Democrats—conservatives with their roots in southern, rural, former slaveholding counties—and miners and workers from the coal counties and industrialized areas controlled by the United Mine Workers and the AFL-CIO. The liberal-conservative split is crisscrossed by personalities and county courthouse cliques. The Democratic governor in West Virginia inherits a party that is divided and has no continuing state leadership to help him get support for his program.

As party spokesman, the governor has the responsibility of defining the issues and making the commitments that form the basis of his legislative program. How do these issues proceed from a gleam in the governor's eye to a set of administration bills introduced by party leaders in the legislature? The political circumstances dictate the conditions under which the governor operates to fashion the gleam into reality. For example, in the one-party states, the governor has a very free hand in the formation of his platform, which he tries to convert into legislative policy. In a one-party state, the party has no platform except those platforms of the individual members of the party who are running for office. In the primary contest, the platforms of the candidates for the governorship— in fact, all other administrative and elected offices—represent the views of the candidates and need not, and usually do not, contain uniform provisions. As a result, when the primary is over, the platform of the winning gubernatorial candidate, the other elective candidates, and those of the legislative members are not necessarily related. The party itself has no platform in the primary, of course, because it cannot impose one on such a diverse assortment of hopefuls, and, since the general election is a formality, it develops no platform in that contest. Hence, the party's platform is that of the winning gubernatorial candidate.

In the election year of 1970 in Arkansas, an obscure candidate, Dale Bumpers, ran as one of eight hopefuls in the gubernatorial primary. In the primary he placed second to the well-known segregationist governor Orvil Faubus. In the run-off primary, Bumpers received 59 percent of the vote and proceeded to win overwhelmingly in the general election. He had ambition for national office and immediately proceeded to go about his duties as governor in an aggressive manner. According to a loyal staff member, he presented his program to the General Assembly on the first day of its regular session and attached 26 bills to implement it. This was an unprecedented effort on the part of a new governor and "set the stage for an atmosphere of cooperation between the governor and the legislature which in the end was essential to the success of the legislative session."[50] Well might the new governor need cooperation. In his first primary he had received 20 percent of the vote, hardly an impressive backing to start building a united party. In the General Assembly of 135 members (including both senate and house), sat 132 Democrats. The governor had to deal with the members of his own party. In the legislature there were at least three members who were waiting and watching for the chance to become gubernatorial challengers. When we see him faced with this lineup, it is impressive that the governor was able to get an average of 59 percent of his party behind him on his program. He failed to get a kindergarten bill passed as well as a merit-system bill. Extensive bail reform and campaign advertising limitations also failed to pass. In Arkansas a governor cannot count on a party united behind him. He must calculate his odds in winning approval of a program of his own making. He may not try ambitious, but sure-to-be-defeated programs because defeat is not a mark of a successful politician, and the governor wants to make a good record. This record he must make on his own. There is no party organization, no party support for his efforts.

In the modified one-party Democratic states, the governor is in much the same position since he is actually elected in the primary, and the platform on which he is elected is one of his own choosing. If the weaker party has shown signs of strength, the candidate may alter his platform to conform to collective party wisdom. This collective judgment may come from the state chairman, the state senators, the party committee. At any rate, if the party feels challenged in any way, the individual candidate in the modified Democratic state may have to yield slightly in the interest of winning. Governor Robert Scott of North Carolina, however, who received about 48 percent of his party's vote in the primary of 1968 and won a fairly close election, did not indicate that he was interested in making a record for himself or his party in terms of program. In Governor Scott's words:

> I do not know of any way that an accurate listing of bills supported by my administration could be obtained. A very few I supported strongly, many more, passively, some I didn't like, but did not oppose for various reasons, and some I opposed strongly.
> Some bills were given a great amount of vocal support, but very little, if any actual support. It all depended on a great many factors: some political, some economic, and some were simply strategic moves.[51]

In a two-party state, the potential governor heads the state ticket, and the others who run on it such as the state legislators and other candidates

campaign on the same platform. The governor may have to accept altera-
tions in the name of the party. Since all of the ticket must back the
platform, it must be one on which they can all campaign. For the party
in power, platforms originate in draft form in the incumbent governor's
office. Once adopted by the state convention, the platform for either party
provides the party leaders and candidates with a convenient source for
political positions on the issues, and it also offers a reasonably effective
means for the leaders and candidates to dodge taking personal positions,
since they can refer questioners to the platform.

In 1971, in his state-of-the-state message, Governor Reagan of California quoted the speaker of the assembly as saying that the time for talk had
passed and that "what will be necessary is we have the courage to take
effective action." The governor then proceeded to outline five goals for
action in the areas of education, environment, public safety, taxation and
fiscal policies, and public assistance—both welfare and Medi-Cal.[52] The
governor faced an assembly, both houses of which contained slight majorities of the opposition party. His was the problem of obtaining loyal support
from his own party as well as convincing portions of the Democratic
opposition to support his program. Both parties, however, recognize the
fact that a platform is to be taken seriously by the whole of the ticket. In
cases where the parties are divided between the legislature and executive,
a certain amount of cooperation is necessary to act on the budget and the
various issues facing the government. Because either party has a chance
of winning the next election, neither wants to be regarded as an obstruction to the popular mandate—so closely divided between them.

The governors of all states, therefore, go into office with a platform
that is dictated by the gubernatorial candidate and his advisers, be they
personal or political. This platform reflects enough of the governor's major
policies so that it can be used as a basis for his legislative program. When
a newly elected governor takes office, especially when this represents a
change of parties, he is generally forced by lack of time and possible
suspicion of those already in office to have most of his program prepared
by the members of his own staff, who may be outside the government. A
member of Connecticut Governor Meskill's staff said that all commissioners in Connecticut serve until March 1. This is so that the newly appointed
commissioners can become experienced in their jobs. It also means that
a full-fledged program cannot be developed by a new governor of a different party for two years. (In Connecticut, even-year sessions are devoted
exclusively to budget and "left-over" business of the previous session.) The
staff member said that Governor Meskill's real program came in 1973, two
years after he was sworn in.[53] When the governor has been in office for
awhile, many of his administrative measures are the products of the departments under his supervision. The preparation of legislation is also
influenced by pressure-group activity, and many administration bills are
prepared by the legislative representatives of these groups. (The legisla-

tive activities of pressure groups were discussed in chapter 3.) Out of this mixture of the governor's desires, the party platform, the work of the governor's staff, the pressure of various groups, and legislation prepared by the governor's department heads come the major pieces of the governor's program.

Each year the governor presents a state-of-the-state address to a joint gathering of both legislative houses (in 1977, only one state did not hold a regular or special session). In this, the governor outlines the substance of the program he wants passed for the session. This is translated into administration bills that are introduced in most states by the governor's party leaders in the house or senate or by legislators whom the governor may specify. All 50 governors were asked to submit lists of 1971 program bills and 24 were able to produce such lists. This was largely a function of their occupancy of the governor's chair at the time. Of those governors still in office, only the Pennsylvania and Wyoming governors were unable to conjure up the lists, and their staffs made every effort to help by submitting newspaper clippings, speeches, and recollections. Former governors, as well as their legislative assistants scattered about in various occupations, were able to piece together the bills that had been included in the governor's program. The average program included 50 bills including the appropriations bill and any revenue proposals. New York's list was 133 items long, and that of Illinois was over 200.

Of the 20 states for which the program bills were eventually determined, the following issues predominated: (In each case, the number of governors who presented these issues is indicated in parentheses.)

Environment   (18)
Traffic safety   (17)
Welfare   (15)
Education   (14)
Health   (13)
Prison reform   (12)
Drugs-alcohol   (10)
Election reform   (10)
Consumer protection   (9)
Reorganization   (9)
Tax reform   (8)
Housing   (7)
Ethics-financial disclosure   (6)
Reapportionment   (5)
Economic development   (4)
Reform-civil service   (4)
Reform-judiciary   (4)

In 1971, Governor Ogilvie of Illinois exhorted the legislators to consider the legislation he was about to present:

> During the coming months, you will receive many recommendations and requests for legislative action. You will receive messages from me relating to my concerns and ideas for better serving the citizens of this state. But only you in this assembly can make those specific legislative decisions which will shape our destiny. That prerogative is yours alone—and responsibility for the results is yours as well.
>
> Your goal must be nothing less than to enhance the quality of our lives. The people are demanding—and they deserve—a state that is safer, healthier, cleaner, and more responsive to their needs.[54]

Through his power of policy initiation alone, the governor's influence over the legislature is substantial. He sets the agenda for public decision making, and he largely determines what the business of the legislature will be in any one session. Few major state undertakings get off the ground without his initiation. He frames the issues, determines their content, and decides their timing.

Resources at the Disposal of the Governor

The success of the governor in getting his program passed will depend on his ability as party leader. All governors have resources at their disposal, but their skill in using them marks the difference between a successful and unsuccessful governor. A governor who has built up a good-sized coalition within his party can expect to have a nucleus of support. He already has a group who have worked for him and have shared the fruits of winning. Friendships, loyalty, psychological rewards—all have a part to play in the legislative coalition he must fashion to pass his policies. Here are some of the resources at the disposal of the governor:

1. *Patronage.* The amount of patronage at his disposal differs from state to state. Jobs, contracts, and other favors are not put at the governor's disposal the way they used to be, but he can still use skill in dealing out his store of treasures at times of maximum advantage to himself. The latter may take the form of the appointment of a friend of a given legislator to a government position, or the promise of a future appointment to the bench or to some other position for the legislator himself. The patronage also takes the form of awarding contracts to a firm in which the legislator is interested or paving highways in the legislator's district. Occasionally, the governor will use his pardoning power as a lever in influencing legislation and pardon one of the legislator's constituents in exchange for that legislator's support.

In the past half century, many states have adopted legislation placing most state jobs under the merit system. However, Huckshorn reports that the governor of Pennsylvania has 65,000 patronage positions to award, while in Indiana about 8,000 of the state's 22,000 public employees are patronage appointees. In West Virginia, a Democratic party official reported that the governor distributed 15,000 jobs.[55] These are exceptional cases but illustrate the importance of patronage as a political system.

In the one-party states of the South, various types of patronage seem to be more important tools for the governor than is true in the more competitive states because the governor must forge a coalition devoid of help from party leadership. It is standard practice for the governor to make a careful tabulation of legislative votes on gubernatorial programs and to tell dissenting legislators that, if attitudes and votes are not changed, they will get no more jobs for constituents, no more state aid for rural roads in their districts, no more of the favors that are the lifeblood of state legislators.[56] The idea that a governor may use patronage to build a block of votes in the legislature is obnoxious to the reformers. It seems to be one of the realities of political life, however, that must be accepted. The governor, after all, has been elected by the voters on a statewide basis and represents a larger conception of the public interest than those who are elected by district. In those circumstances, there may be considerable justification for the governor's using such methods.

2. *Publicity.* The governor has guaranteed access to newspapers, radio, and television that the legislator cannot command. The governor has repeated opportunities to speak, to capture the headlines, and to appeal to public sentiment as a way of bringing attention to his legislative program. Many governors use weekly or biweekly radio or television programs in which they explain to the people the major issues before the legislature and their own position. Added to these means of direct access to the citizen are the daily press conferences held by most governors. No single legislator or group of legislators can hope to command the audience held by the governor largely and simply because of his position. There is great variety in the skill and imagination with which governors use these techniques and opportunities. Governor Rockefeller of New York, for instance, was an expert at getting the public behind him. Armed with a chalkboard, he went about the state explaining his budget. His personality made him adept at winning crowds to his point of view. On the other hand, an observer points to Foster Furcolo, the Massachusetts governor, who relied on public opinion to gain support for his sales tax. He held weekly press conferences, spoke widely across the state, and made use of all the radio and television time available. This would not make up for the fact that he was not a party organizer, was ill at ease with the legislators and could not bring himself to bargain effectively with his own party members. In the end, he did not get the new tax and was defeated soundly in the primary following his first term.[57]

3. *Promise or threat of campaign support or opposition.* The support of the governor in a primary or election campaign can be a powerful stimulus to a legislator, particularly one from a constituency where his own nomination or election is in doubt. In Connecticut during the term of John Bailey as state chairman, the state leadership could persuade the local party to deny renomination to a recalcitrant legislator (the primary is seldom used to challenge the endorsements of local caucuses). In New York, also, there is a similar pattern of cooperation between state and local party organizations. In Michigan, the Legislative Liaison Committee of the State Central Committee agreed to a resolution which stated that candidates running on the Democratic party ticket would be expected to abide by the platform adopted in party convention.[58] In the absence of a strong party organization, the governor may lack allies at the local level who can be counted on to carry out a campaign for his endorsee. Purging legislators is risky business, unless it works. Otherwise, an angry opponent may face him in the next session. In states where the governor can expect to find a majority of the opposite party in the legislature, his major objective is to help build up his legislative contingent so that he can count on a basis of support from which he can bargain with the opposition. Generally, legislators hope their gubernatorial candidate will give them a plank upon which to campaign. The legislator in the governor's party has a personal stake in the governor's success.

4. *Promise of advancement within the governor's party or faction within the legislature.* Committee assignments, majority party leadership, and the speakership are attractive resources. The tenure of legislative leaders is shorter in state legislatures than in Congress, giving the governor frequent opportunity to influence the choice of leaders. The governor is vitally concerned with this process because the fate of his program will depend on the treatment it receives in the legislature, and this treatment depends primarily on the actions of those individuals who hold those important positions. If the governor is adept at politics, he will have his nominees for those posts selected and their election guaranteed before the legislative session starts. The speaker and the president pro tem of the senate are formally elected in their respective legislative bodies. This need not present an obstacle to the alert governor who should be able to select the members of his choice to those posts. In most state legislatures, the committee chairmen and committee members are appointed by the speaker of the house and the lieutenant governor or president pro tem of the senate. If these officers are supporters of the governor, they will make sure that individuals friendly to the administration are selected for important committee posts. This will ensure prompt and friendly consideration of important administration measures in committee.

In states where the governor must resign himself to a minority party status in the legislature, his choice of minority leadership and also friendly committee members of his own party may also be crucial. He must have leadership who can deal with the majority party leaders in the kind of compromise legislative process that occurs in that type of situation.

It is quite common in many one-party states for the governor to select one or more legislators to serve as his floor leaders. These may be regarded as the governor's spokesmen, and, in several one-party states, it has been traditional for the legislators to accept the governor's choice as the speaker of the house and the president pro tem in the senate. This spokesman is supposed to represent the governor's views on measures before his house. The legislators who make up the governor's faction look to the floor leader for guidance in much the same way as members of the majority party look to the majority floor leader in a two-party situation.

5. *Calling of special sessions.* The governor who has this device at his disposal can use it skillfully to call attention to particular aspects of his legislative program. The power given to the governor to call a special session of the legislature is based on the belief that certain emergencies might arise which would make it necessary for the legislature to meet at some time other than a regularly scheduled session. The governor can use a special session as a threat to the legislature to complete its work before the constitutional adjournment date. He can also call the special session to get the people of the state to become aware of the immediacy of a financial crisis and his program to cope with it. The legislators are then in the position of going along with the proposals of the governor or taking the consequences, which can be serious if the electorate is really alarmed. In December 1971, Governor Rockefeller called the New York legislature back into special session to deal with a 1.5 billion budget gap that made the state short at least one-third of the cash it needed to make its payments and pay its bills through the end of the fiscal year. The governor, in asking for additional sources of revenue, said that to close the gap entirely with cuts would shift the situation from a fiscal crisis to a "human disaster."[59]

Most of these resources depend on the skill of the governor. A governor at odds with his legislative leaders will find that many of these resources will fade. A governor faced with a strong rival candidate sitting in the legislature may discover that his influence cannot go far because the rival may be building a power base for himself, using the very resources the governor has in his arsenal.

The Governor as Chief Legislator

To what degree does gubernatorial leadership affect policies in the American states? The political system is not an end but a means. We are concerned with the product of a state political system and how the governor contributes to that product. Party politics—especially state political leadership—affects conversion of need into policy. As head of his political party, the governor is the recognized legislative leader. There is evidence that the influence of the governor over his legislative party is based on his political leadership within the electoral party, the party outside the legislature. If the governor has been successful in building a coalition to support him in the primary and election, he is also successful in building a coalition within the legislature to pass his legislation.[60] The governor's formal powers of appointment, budget control, and item veto may also affect his ability to see his program through the legislature. Certainly the possession of a majority is an asset to any governor. Common sense suggests that, if a governor's party controls the legislature, success in obtaining the passage of his program would be increased. This gives the governor, through the speaker, a control over legislation he does not have with a minority, in which the leadership positions are in the hands of the opposite party. The degree to which the legislature has professionalized its operations may be relevant to its ability to be responsive to the needs and demands of its constituents, presumably the same as the governor's. More will be said about the professionalism of the legislature in the next chapter. We mention it now because it enters into the following analysis of the factors that affect the ability of the governor to get his program bills passed.

A minor test boring into the factors that affect the ability of the governor to see that his program legislation is passed would proceed by measuring several concepts we have previously considered. The first—and this is the dependent variable or the variable that needs to be explained—is the support of the legislators of the governor's party on the bills he presents to them as administration bills. Almost all the votes on these program bills are recorded (roll-call votes) and it is a simple matter to determine the percentage of the party members who supported the governor for each vote. This is called the index of administration support. I found the average index of administration support for the governor's party in state legislatures in 1971.[61] The states represented different degrees of interparty competition, equal numbers of Republican and Democratic governors, and a geographical cross section of the country. Table 5-6 lists the states selected to test the ability of the governor to get his program passed.

Now that we have the dependent variable, the index of administration support for the 20 states, we need measures of the governor's influence. We will use the familiar measure we used before of the governor's electoral party influence, namely, his primary voting strength.[62] A measure of the governor's formal powers has been developed by Joseph Schlesinger and combines tenure potential, veto powers, budget control, and appointive power in one index.[63] We suspect that a governor who has party influence will be able to make maximum use of his formal powers. If he operates without the advantage of generous formal powers, he may be constrained in his ability to put his program across. Governors must

TABLE 5–6

Twenty Selected States Classified According to
Index of Competition, 1956–70[a]

ONE-PARTY DEMOCRATIC	MODIFIED ONE-PARTY DEMOCRATIC	TWO-PARTY	MODIFIED ONE-PARTY REPUBLICAN
Arkansas–D	North Carolina–D	Kentucky–D	**Ohio–D
Mississippi–D	*Nevada–D	*Wisconsin–D	Wyoming–R
**Tennessee–R		Rhode Island–D	New Hampshire–R
		**California–R	
		**West Virginia–R	
		*Washington–R	
		*Montana–D	
		Pennsylvania–D	
		Colorado–R	
		Illinois–R	
		**Massachusetts–R	
		New York–R	

Key: D/R. For each state, the party affiliation of the governor for 1971 is given.
*/** Divided control: One (*) or both (**) houses in the hands of the opposite party, 1971.
[a] This is the index of competition described in Table 2–2. It measures the difference between the percent of vote for governor obtained by each major party, averaged over the time period.

often work with the heads of administrative departments whose positions do not depend on them, and they make up the budget with the help of bureaucrats who are independent of them. In some instances, the governor's formal power allows him to dominate policy making; elsewhere, he has little authority to get what he wants. One should be cautious, however, with an index of formal powers. A governor with strong legal authority has no *assurance* that it will yield political power. If he is unable to persuade others of the merits of his position or is unwilling to bargain, he may find himself no better off than a governor with fewer formal powers.

What we are attempting to do in this test of the governor's influence is to see if governors with both formal and informal powers can get legislative support. If we correlated the measures of governor's strength with the loyalty of legislators on administration bills and found that they could indeed explain the loyalty, we would be pleased that our test succeeded so well. But, certainly at least one of the readers of this book would be bound to say that there might be other things that could exert an influence on the legislator's support. We have already mentioned several in the previous chapters. We know that economic factors such as integration and industrialization affect the character of politics in a state. We know that persons who are more likely to participate in politics can exert an independent influence on the legislators. We suspect that a legislature can develop an independence of its own, vis-a-vis the governor, which could explain its reaction to his program. Unless we can control or include all these variables to see how they interact with each other, the results will be cast in doubt. Appendix 3 gives all the variables mentioned so far and how they are measured. If we can account for all these and still be able to say that the governor exerts an independent influence, we can be reasonably sure of ourselves and of the reliability of our analysis.

Fortunately for the human brain, computers can cope with many variables at once and distinguish between those that are important and those that are not. Human intelligence can instruct a computer to perform an analysis on many variables, note the relationship between them, compute their individual effects on the phenomenon to be explained, and tell how much of their joint effects can explain the phenomenon. The reader can discern that we are now at that point in the analysis of the influence of the governor on public policy. The simplest measure of association between two variables takes considerable time, even with the help of a pocket calculator. We have indicated an interest in the simple relationships between at least nine variables—amounting to nearly 100 such calculations. We have also indicated an interest in the joint effects of variables, which takes a more sophisticated technique called multiple-regression analysis. Multiple regression allows one to study the relationships among a set of independent variables—in our case economic, leadership, and structural variables—and one or more dependent variables—such as support for the governor's program bills—while taking into account the interrelationships among the independent variables. We know for instance that researchers have found that economic development influences the interest and participation of the citizens of a state. Citizens in wealthy states participate more. Multiple regression analysis can take this relationship into account and indicate the independent effects of both voter participation and economic development on support for the governor's program. The results of a multiple regression analysis give us the effect of each variable on the governor's support, while taking all the others into consideration (the regression coefficient). The strength of the total relationship between support and all the economic, leadership, and structural variables is given by a multiple correlation coefficient (multiple R). This multiple correlation coefficient ranges from 0 to 1 and is interpreted in the same way as the simple correlation coefficient. The square of this multiple correlation coefficient (R-square) indicates how much of the policy can be explained by all of the variables we are considering. Needless to say, researchers hope that this R-square will be high. It is reassuring, for instance, to learn that one has been able to account for 70 percent or more of the governor's legislative support.

We now have all the elements of a complicated analysis in order. We have indicated the economic, leadership, and structural influences that we believe have a direct effect on legislative support for the governor's program in the American states. We have indicated ways to measure these various influences, recognizing, of course, that any measure of human activity suffers from error. We have a multiple regression analysis that can instruct a computer to do the work. We are now in a position to examine the relationships that exist between the economic variables, the leadership variables, and legislative support.

Figure 5–1 confirms the hypothesis that the governor's political leadership and his ability to use his resources can explain more of his legislative support than any other variable. His power as a legislative leader depends on his control over his electoral party as well as the formal powers that are part of the administrative apparatus with which he works. The economic variable, industrialization, appears to be weakly and negatively associated

FIGURE 5–1

---

*Relationships Among the Economy, The
Governor's Party Leadership, and
Legislative Support*

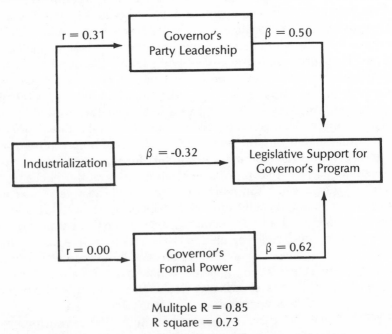

Mulitple R = 0.85
R square = 0.73

Note: The beta weights shown in the figure indicate the relative contribution of each independent variable to accounting for variation in the dependent variable (legislative support). The figure shows governor's formal power to be the most important explanatory variable in the 20 house sessions analyzed. See Appendix 3 for measures of these variables.

with legislative support for the governor's program. Economic development has been found to shape political systems, and it is not surprising to find this factor exerting some influence over both the political system and the policy produced by it. An industrial economy lacks the wealth, professionalism, education, or literacy of the postindustrial states. This may explain why an industrial economy exerts a negative influence on the support some legislators give the governor. Legislators can't support services they believe they can't afford. This analysis does not support the contentions of the economy-policy school, which state that the economy is the major explanatory variable in both the political process and the policy produced by it. Industrialization is the weakest of the three variables influencing the support of the legislators. Its association with the governor's formal powers and political leadership is not impressive. It has no association with the governor's formal powers, and it has a moderate correlation with his political leadership. There is no support for the contention that the political leadership variables do not exert a powerful influence over the distribution of the services in a state.

The analysis in Figure 5-1 shows that the influence of the governor over his legislative party is partially explained by his formal power of budget making, veto capability, appointment control, and tenure potential. A governor who may run again or who can at least present running again as a possibility has a greater supply of rewards and punishments than a lame duck has. A governor who can threaten an item veto can exert a great deal of control over the budget. A governor who has the power of appointment of those sympathetic to his views can count on a loyal administration—one that cannot be subjected to legislative interference. All these formal powers depend on the skill of the governor.

The influence of the governor over his legislative party is also influenced by his skills as a political leader within the electoral party, the party outside the legislature. If the governor has been successful in building a coalition to support him in the primary and election, he is also successful in building a coalition within the legislature to pass his legislation. In terms of measurement, the governor's party leadership measured as the governor's primary percentage *after* the legislative session has a high correlation with the degree of loyalty obtained from his party's legislators *during* the session. The high correlation between outside party cohesion and legislative loyalty would seem to support the theory that the governor's outside party organization generates discipline within the legislative party. The direction of this influence needs to be explained, since the legislative discipline predates the governor's party cohesion. One possibility is that the progression of events would start with the efforts of the governor to build support within his party—both electoral and legislative —to help him win the next primary and election. With his supply of rewards and punishments and his own ability and effort, he forges a coalition to stand by him at primary time. The degree of his success is measured both within the legislature and by the primary results. His influence grows as the time for the election approaches. His strategy is oriented toward the next election and the strength of the coalition he builds is measured both in legislative and primary support. Based on my findings, a model of gubernatorial influence would give the most weight to the ability of the governor to form winning coalitions both within and outside the legislature. There may not be a time lag here. The two processes probably occur simultaneously. Instead of the legislative party being an independent entity, it is subject to the direction and influence of the governor's coalition within the electoral organization. While it is an advantage to a governor to have a majority in the legislature, this is not an automatic guarantee that his legislation will pass. The impact of the popularity of a governor must be given a much higher value in explaining the success of program legislation.

CONCLUSIONS

The governor is the chief policy maker in the American states, and his ability to provide political leadership affects the quality and distribution of public policy. The governor is undoubtedly the most important participant in the subnational politics of the federal system. As the states become more active in urban problems and in the designing and implementation of domestic programs at the state and local levels, the governor is assuming a more important intergovernmental role.

This discussion has examined the governor's influence over his political party, both within and outside the legislature. The major theme of this chapter is that the coalitions formed by the governor to get him the party nomination affect his ability to influence his party's legislators. Other formal powers of the governor also affect his ability to see his program through the legislature. The overriding consideration is the skill with which the governor makes use of these resources. A strong governor with an electoral coalition behind him can get support for his policies.

The principal task of the governor in the decade of the eighties is to lead and lead *actively* in adapting the apparatus of the state government to do a more effective job. The total capacity of state governments to deal with urban problems demands attention. The relationships between state and local government must be critically reviewed, and the metropolitan areas must be given assistance. The nature of federal-state and state-urban relationships demands that the states have more capacity. The ability of the governor as the key political figure to provide the leadership for these extensive commitments is the key to the continuation of our federal system.

NOTES

1. Joseph A. Schlesinger, "The Politics of the Executive," in Herbert Jacob and Kenneth N. Vines, eds., *Politics in the American States,* 2d ed. (Boston: Little, Brown, 1971), p. 225.
2. J. Stephen Turett, "The Vulnerability of American Governors, 1900–1969," in Thad Beyle and J. Oliver Williams, eds., *The American Governor in Behavioral Perspective* (New York: Harper & Row, 1972), pp. 17–30.
3. Ibid., p. 25.
4. One would suppose that it would be a good time for Republican governors to retire. Three governors who had been in office for six to eight years decided not to make the race. Only Meskill of Connecticut would appear to have been discouraged by the predicted Democratic wave.
5. Turett, "Vulnerability," pp. 25–30.
6. Joseph A. Schlesinger, *Ambition and Politics: Political Careers in the United States* (Chicago, Ill.: Rand McNally, 1966), pp. 22–36.
7. Ibid., p. 195.
8. This discussion of the careers of ex-governors draws heavily on the article: Samuel R. Solomon, "Governors: 1960–1970," *National Civic Review* 60 (March 1971): pp. 138–42.
9. Joseph A. Schlesinger, "The Governor's Place in American Politics," in Beyle and Williams, *The American Governor in Behavioral Perspective,* pp. 13–17.
10. "1974 Appears to be a Good Time to Be a Governor," *Congressional Quarterly Weekly Report,"* p. 2220.
11. Paul L. Hain and Ferry B. Smith, "Congress: New Training Ground for Governors?" *State Government* (Spring 1975): pp. 114–15.
12. Schlesinger, *Ambition and Politics,* pp. 89–118.
13. The following paragraph draws upon Solomon, "Governors: 1960–1970," pp. 128–31.
14. James Clotfelter and William R. Hamilton, "Electing a Governor in the Seventies," in Beyle and Williams, *The American Governor in Behavioral Perspective,* pp. 32–39.
15. Ibid., p. 34.
16. Ibid., p. 38.
17. Neal R. Peirce, *The Deep South States of America* (New York: Norton, 1974), p. 328.
18. The previous discussion draws heavily on Eugene W. Jones et al., *Practicing Texas Politics,* 3d ed. (Boston: Houghton Mifflin, 1977), pp. 114–17, 122.
19. This interview was reported in Fred Gantt, Jr., *The Chief Executive in Texas* (Austin: University of Texas Press, 1964), p. 322.
20. Walter Noelke, "Democratic Convention: Texas Style," *Practicing Texas Politics,* p. 128.
21. Jon Ford, "Analysis of the Briscoe Campaign," in Jones, *Practicing Texas Politics,* p. 374.
22. These statistics can be obtained by consulting the following: U.S. Bureau of the Census publications: *Governmental Finances in 1971–1972,* p. 45; *Statistical Abstract 1973,* pp. 128, 311, 101.
23. William Buchanan, *Legislative Partisanship, The Deviant Case of California* (Berkeley: University of California Press, 1963), p. 1.

24. I am indebted to Neal Peirce, *Megastates* (New York: W. W. Norton, 1972), pp. 245–53 for much of this section.
25. David Adamany, *Financing Politics: Recent Wisconsin Elections,* p. 228.
26. Ibid., pp. 225–26.
27. Ibid., p. 227.
28. See John H. Fenton, *Midwest Politics* (New York: Holt, Rinehart and Winston, 1966), p. 111.
29. Robert Agranoff, "The Role of Political Parties in the New Campaigns," *The New Style in Election Campaigns* (Boston: Holbrook Press, 1972), pp. 96–116.
30. Donald H. Haider, *When Governments Come to Washington* (New York: Free Press, 1974), p. 299.
31. Jay Gilmer, James W. Guest, and Charles Kirchner, "The Impact of Federal Programs and Policies on State-Local Relations," *Public Administration Review* 35 (December 1975): 776.
32. Ibid., p. 777.
33. Thad L. Beyle, "The Governor's Formal Powers: A View from the Governor's Chair," *Public Administration Review* 28 (November/December 1968): 540–45.
34. Duane Lockard, ed., "A Mini-Symposium, The Strong Governorship: Status and Problems," *Public Administration Review* 36 (January/February, 1976): 95.
35. Thomas Dye, "Executive Power and Public Policy in the States," *Western Political Quarterly* 27 (December 1969): 926–39.
36. Sprengel, Donald R. "Governor's Staffs—Background and Recruitment Patterns," in Beyle and Williams, *The American Governor in Behavioral Perspective,* pp. 106–18; Wyner, Alan J. "Staffing the Governor's Office," ibid., pp. 118–24.
37. Beyle, "The Governor's Formal Powers," p. 544.
38. *The Book of the States, 1978–1979,* pp. 146–50.
39. Schlesinger, "The Politics of the Executive," pp. 220–34.
40. Dye, "Executive Power and Public Policy," pp. 934–39.
41. Beyle, "The Governor's Formal Powers," p. 543.
42. Deil S. Wright, "Executive Leadership in State Administration," *Midwest Journal of Political Science* 11 (February 1967): pp. 1–26.
43. E. Nelson Swinerton, "Administrative-Political Role Consensus Among American State Executives," *Social Science Quarterly* 50 (September 1969): 267.
44. Martha Wagner Weinberg, *Managing The State* (Cambridge, Mass.: The MIT Press, 1977), p. 209.
45. Committee on the Structure of State Government, *Better Organization For Better Government* (Hartford, Conn., 1976).
46. Victoria Schuck, "Massachusetts," in Lockard "A Mini-Symposium," pp. 91–92.
47. Welsh, Matthew E. "The Role of the Governor in the 1971's," *Public Administration Review* 30 (January/February 1970): 24–26.
48. Larry Sabato, *Goodbye to Good-Time Charlie* (Lexington, Mass.: Heath, 1978), p. 91.
49. Ben A. Franklin, "Jay Rockefeller is sworn in West Virginia," *New York Times,* 18 January 1977, p. 1.

50. From material provided by the Governor's Office, 1971.
51. Letter from Robert W. Scott, 26 October 1973. Mr. Scott was associated with the North Carolina Agribusiness Council, Inc., at that time.
52. *California Assembly Journal,* 1971, pp. 137–38.
53. Phone Conversation with John Doyle in November, 1973. Mr. Doyle was Governor Meskill's legislative liaison from 1971 to 1973.
54. Illinois, *Journal of the House of Representatives,* 1971, p. 19.
55. Robert J. Huçkshorn, *Party Leadership in the States,* (Amherst: University of Massachusetts Press, 1976), pp. 111–12.
56. Robert B. Highsaw, "The Southern Governor-Challenge to the Strong Executive Theme," *Public Administration Review* 19 (January/February 1959): 9.
57. John P. Mallen and George Blackwood, "The Tax That Beat a Governor: The Ordeal of Massachusetts," chapter 6 in Alan F. Weston, *The Uses of Power,* pp. 285–322.
58. Robert Lee Sawyer, *The Democratic State Central Committee in Michigan, 1949–1959: The Rise of the New Politics and the New Political Leadership* (Ann Arbor: Institute of Public Administration, University of Michigan, 1960), p. 265.
59. New York State, *Senate Journal,* 1971. Second Extraordinary Session, Monday, 27 December 1971, p. 4.
60. Sarah McCally (Morehouse), "The Governor and His Legislative Party," *American Political Science Review* 60 (December 1966): 933–41.
61. Every bill in each governor's program was followed through the 1971 House Journals. Every roll call on which there was over 10 percent disagreement with the majority position was recorded. The index used for measuring the degree to which the party supported the governor was the Index of Administration Support. This index indicates the percentage of party members who supported the governor. For a single roll call, the index is obtained by dividing the number of votes cast by party members who voted in favor of the governor's bill by the total number of party members who voted. An average index for all roll calls is the arithmetic mean of the indices derived for the roll calls in the session.
62. The strength of the governor as electoral party leader is measured by the governor's percent of the primary vote. This can be averaged over a time period e.g., 1956–1970, using the primary votes obtained by the party's successful gubernatorial candidates.
63. See Appendix 2 for the Index of the Formal Powers of the Governor, 1971.

CHAPTER SIX

THE LEGISLATURE AS PARTNER OR RIVAL

In March 1971, Speaker Fineman of the Pennsylvania House of Representatives rose to his feet and declared, "The Chair would like to make a statement that concerns this House." He then proceeded to review an evaluation study of the decision-making capabilities of the 50 state legislatures.[1] Pennsylvania's state legislature placed twenty-first in that study. In light of that rating, it was important that the legislature understand the intent and thrust of the evaluation. Fireman's words ring as a monument to the pride with which a dedicated legislator views his job. Here is a portion of what he said:

> The Citizen's Conference chose to measure the forms, the organizational structure, and the procedures of the legislatures because they believed these features to be overridingly essential to the quality of legislative performance. I must question this assumption. This is very much like evaluating a football team by the quality of the stadium it plays in, the kind of coach it has, the kind of locker room facilities that are provided, the equipment that is provided, the quality of the training and the table food and the uniforms that are furnished to each player. The best-equipped team is not always the best performer. An accurate evaluation of a football team so far as its performance is concerned requires much more than a consideration of these factors, just as an accurate evaluation of a legislature's performance requires more than an appraisal of its facilities and its procedures.

> ... For, what better measure of democracy at work is there than a legislative body that is representative of the population it seeks to serve and which does the kind of job and produces the kind of legislation which the people desire and need, no matter what the circumstances under which that legislative body operates?[2]

LEGISLATIVE RESPONSIBILITY VERSUS LEGISLATIVE INDEPENDENCE

Speaker Fineman believed that a legislature must be judged on its ability to provide for the quality of life for the people it represents. He argued that this yardstick should be the test of a legislature's worth. They cannot be measured by the degree to which they have modernized their procedures any more than a football team can be judged by its locker room. When professional legislatures are more truly representative of the people they serve, it is a measure of performance, not desk space, salaries, and procedures.

In their zeal to make state legislatures more representative and professional, reformers lost sight of the major purpose of their reforms. Legislatures were judged on district representation and the degree to which they were professionalized, not on the way they solved the life-and-death issues that confronted them. To be sure, legislatures deserved the criticism that they were unrepresentative and inept—their records through the 1950s were futile, characterized by seeming disregard for the grave economic and social problems within their borders. It took federal court intervention to require states to reapportion their legislatures so urban residents would gain their rightful representation. This reapportionment was followed by a reform revolution that claimed as much impact on the legislative decision-making capability as the previous set of revolutionaries. In some states, this modernization was of critical importance. One Illinois legislator complained that members of the house did not have offices, secretaries or personal staff to research the enormous number of bills that came before them. He believed that the public suffers in such a situation:

> Quite often the private interests prevail over the public interest, as groups with particular ends to further fill the vacuum created by the absence of adequate facilities and staff. Knowledgeable lobbyists armed with selected statistics are extremely persuasive with overly busy, understaffed legislators.[3]

The reformers accomplished many of their aims. In the last two decades, state legislatures have become more representative and better able to provide needed services, have reformed their fiscal processes, have instituted annual sessions, have received adequate compensation, and have reorganized and staffed their committees. Membership is more attractive than it has been in the past and there is a marked increase in the number of state legislators seeking reelection rather than voluntarily retiring after short-term service.

Speaker Fineman did not dispute the need for better staff, better facilities, higher salaries, or more professionalization; he disputed the ultimate purpose of many reformers, which is a denial of the political process. The object of a more-professionalized legislature was to be independent from the executive branch. This philosophy prompted the Citizens Conference on State Legislatures to make one of its major tests: How independent was the legislature from "domination" by the executive branch of government? Legislative independence from the governor is a denial of the whole idea of party government. In the independence model, legislators would not operate as members of political parties; they would not owe allegiance to a party program nor feel any need to support it. When elected, they would use their own judgment and rely on their own perceptions of their constituents' desires. Under party government, in contrast, the governor and his legislative party members constitute a team. His program is the result of agreement among party leaders, and, when he presents it to the legislature, he expects team support. A party government is better able to represent the citizens of a state than is an independent legislature, which represents only itself.

Policy is the Yardstick

In chapter 1, we considered a model of the policy making process that viewed policy as the political result of input constituting the needs and demands of the people (Figure 1–4). The degree of party organization in a state—in terms of gubernatorial leadership, legislative party cohesion, and party program commitment—was measured by the efforts of politicians. Structural variables included the formal powers of the governor, legislative party majority status, and legislative professionalism. Using this model in the last chapter, we found that the governor's political leadership as well as his formal powers could explain a large part of his ability to get programs passed in the legislature. To continue along this line, we will consider the new variables that apply to the legislature by asking what the relationships are between party strength, gubernatorial leadership, and professionalized legislatures and how these factors will affect the legislature's ability to make quality-of-life decisions for its citizens.

THE LEGISLATURE AS PARTNER IN THE POLICY-MAKING PROCESS

Party Government

The success of a governor as chief policy-maker in the American states is linked to his degree of party leadership both within the legislature and in his electoral party. This theory does not minimize the role of the legislature but makes it a potential partner in the policy-making process. The degree to which it is a partner is deeply involved with the type of political party that operates in the state, both inside as well as outside the legislature. By common agreement, the definition of a political party as a governing instrument would include its ability to control nominations for the legislature and the governorship, to present a united front during the election, and to uphold the governor's programs for the purpose of making a good record for the next election. In this way, the people know what the policies are of their elected representatives and can hold them accountable. This model is seldom matched in practice, but the states can be measured according to the strength of their political parties in the nominating, electing, and governing functions. Legislative policy making, then, is divided between the governor and (with due respect to Nebraska) the two legislative houses, with the former usually taking the lead. A governor represents the totality of interests in his party, with no single legislator or faction representing as wide a variety of interests. His proposals are geared to please his state-wide constituency and, depending on party support, are passed, modified, or rejected.

Functions

Those on the party government side as well as those on the legislative independence side of the fence would agree that there are certain functions a legislature performs for better or worse, depending on the perspective:

1. *Lawmaking.* In legal constitutional terms, lawmaking is mainly, if not purely, a legislative task. The burden of settling conflict and making authoritative decisions for society has always been lodged essentially within the legislative jurisdiction. Of course the legislature shares this function with the governor, interest groups, its constituents, the party, and others. But the moment of truth comes when the vote is taken from those people who have been properly elected to the legislature.

2. *Representation.* Remembering our basic diagram of the policy-making process, we hold that the legislator represents the needs and demands of his constituency. But he is also a member of a political party that makes demands on him concerning the state-wide interests as seen by the party leaders. There may come a time when the legislator believes he should be a free agent, responsible only to his estimate of the public good. This concept of representation permeates all aspects of a legislator's job. Every vote, every decision, every service is performed with the thought of representation in mind. To be reelected—and remember we have set this up as the prime consideration of all politicians—means to represent the needs and demands of enough constituents to garner an electoral victory. Since he needs both electoral and party support for his next election, the legislator must consider the demands of his constituency as well as those of his party.

3. *Oversight of administration.* Recent surveys have shown that this is the job legislators believe they are least able to perform. Many of the procedural improvements in the legislatures, such as staff, research assistance, or creation of fiscal strength, are calculated to improve the capacity of state legislatures to oversee the work of the executive agencies in performing the tasks they have funded. The legislature's self-interest demands that it knows whether agencies are complying with the legislative intent. This does not necessarily imply independence from the executive. The governor may not be able to control the elected agency heads and welcomes legislative surveillance. Any oversight of the proper administering of their program should thus be shared by both the governor and legislature.

4. *Legitimation.* This function is more elusive than the others and involves the respect that members of the public display toward the legislature as a legitimate branch of government. Statements of the legislators, their decorum, reports of debates, and their passage of legislation may or may not represent to the public an aura of legitimacy. Several recent studies of the level of diffuse support for the legislature have been made. Diffuse support is a reservoir of goodwill that the legislature can engender and that is not dependent on any particular output. Such research has found that public support for the legislature is quite high, with attentive constituents vastly more supportive than the general public. It is based on how the citizens view the legislator, how they perceive their relationship to the legislature, and how they interpret the legislature's performance.[4] It may well be that the main impact of the reapportionment revolution, for example, is improved public respect for the legislature. If the redrawing of legislative districts on a "one-man one vote" basis made no major substantive differences in the output of legislation, the result may confer an aura of legitimacy on the state legislatures themselves.

The Reapportionment Revolution

The design of the revolutionaries was to make state legislatures more representative of the people they served. If the legislature was more representative, then policy reflecting the needs and demands of people would result. This group of revolutionaries did not concern themselves with independence: representation was their major purpose. They believed that the only way a legislature could be representative was to require that each legislator represent the same number of people. This could be brought about by apportionment—the drawing of legislative district boundary lines and assigning legislative seats to these districts—so that each legislator represented the same number of constituents.

Their concern was based on the fact that most state legislatures had been seriously malapportioned for many years before 1962. Since the turn of the century, when many of the states were last apportioned, the United States changed from a nation three-fifths rural to three-fourths urban and suburban. But the state legislatures did not reflect this shift, and, as migration from rural to urban and suburban areas continued, population inequities in the districts of most state legislatures became very large. In 1961, citizens of the five largest cities in Connecticut (with one-fourth of the state's population) elected only 10 out of 294 members of the lower house. The six million citizens of Los Angeles County (almost 40 percent of California's population) had only one of 40 seats in the state senate. This type of malapportionment was not as severe everywhere, but there were 14 states in which a majority of the members in one or both houses could be elected by as low as 20 percent of the population from the most rural areas. There were very few legislatures in which egregious malapportionment could not be found.[5]

The reformers reasoned that malapportioned state legislatures were unfair to the underrepresented urban populations. They claimed malapportionment resulted in the development of state governments designed to serve the needs of rural rather than urban residents. State legislatures dominated by representatives of rural areas tended to be conservative and very slow to respond to changing social problems. Taxing and spending decisions favored rural interests both in direct program funding and in formulas for state aid to local governments. This conventional wisdom about malapportionment was especially pertinent in the South, where a Democratic body of small-town or rural white men represented a minority of the white population. But, outside the South, the popular impression about the effects of malapportionment encountered difficulties. New York, California, and Connecticut were widely honored for keeping government current with developing needs, economic growth, and technological change. Yet, all three states were malapportioned prior to the reapportionment decisions. There is reason to believe, therefore, that factors such as party responsibility and other forms of representation also influenced the ability of a state to provide for its urban problems.

The reapportionment revolutionaries carried their cause to the doors of the U.S. Supreme Court. Tennessee's legislature, subject of the Supreme Court's scrutiny in the case of Baker v. Carr, was a prime example of an unequal apportionment system. In the 60 years since its last apportionment, the state's uneven growth of population led to major inequalities not only between metropolitan and rural counties but among rural counties as well. In the Baker v. Carr decision, the Supreme Court declared that lower courts had responsibility for determining whether, in specific cases, the rights of citizens to equal, legal protection under the Fourteenth Amendment were being abridged by malapportionment. The

Court did not establish standards of population equality or explain what factors might justify deviations from such equality. Various state and federal court judges were sharply divided on mathematical standards of equality and even on the question of whether population principles should be applied to one or both houses. Two years later, the Supreme Court held in Reynolds v. Sims that the equal protection clause requires both houses of a state legislature to be apportioned on a population basis. Speaking for the Court, Chief Justice Earl Warren declared, "Legislators represent people, not trees or acres. Legislators are elected by voters, not farms or cities or economic interests." The apportionment rule is that of "one man one vote." What this means is that, barring persuasive exceptions, state legislative districts must be equal in population according to the most recent federal census. In some cases, the courts have allowed districts to deviate from exact population equality if the boundary lines coincided with the boundaries of cities or counties. Thus, the reapportionment revolution was promulgated, and, by 1968, all significant malapportionment in state legislatures had disappeared. Almost all districts in the states are within 10 percent above or below the mean population per district. Continuing problems remain, however. In 35 out of 99 legislatures, some state legislators are elected from multimember districts. For the state legislatures faced with reapportionment, the appeal of multi-member districts was in their simplicity—It was much easier to allocate an additional seat to a county than to divide the county into districts. Three main objections arise as to the use of multimember districts. In some, the voters vote for as many as ten legislators, making it difficult for them to exercise an intelligent choice. The second objection is that the majority party often wins all or virtually all the seats in such districts, preventing the minority party from winning seats in proportion to its strength in the area. Third, there is some evidence that these multimember districts in some states have made it difficult, if not impossible, for black citizens to elect black legislators because their votes are swallowed up in the white community.

The gerrymander, or art of drawing legislative districts for maximum partisan advantage, continues in spite of the equalization of district size. It is possible to disperse the party's faithful into majorities in several districts rather than concentrate them in smaller numbers where their support would be wasted. The practical aim of the party in control of the state legislature where apportionment is made is to increase its security. Gerrymandering achieves this end. Occasionally, racial gerrymandering is used by a legislative majority to reduce the political effectiveness of a racial minority.

The Supreme Court has never ruled directly on the question of partisan gerrymandering or the use of multimember districts for partisan advantage, but the federal court system has been more sensitive to the discriminatory effects on racial minorities. The courts are likely to reject the gerrymander or multimember district if the courts are convinced that their use is part of a pattern of deliberately trying to minimize the voting strength of racial minorities.

Results of the Revolution

Reapportionment was often cited as the way urban Democrats would wrest power from rural Republicans—at least in the northeastern states. The reasoning was that the Republicans were overrepresented in the rural areas of these states. As those areas lost power, so would the Republican party. This expectation proved to be exaggerated. The Democrats, however, did gain seats in the Northeast where reapportionment tended to restore the party composition of state legislatures to a more equitable representation of election results. In some instances, but certainly not all, the Democratic party was the beneficiary. Erikson found that out of his sample of 38 northern state legislatures, the average partisan impact of reapportionment was an increase in the Democratic legislative strength of about 2.9 percent of the legislative seats.[6] The states, however, where reapportionment has produced the greatest apparent gains for the Democratic party appear to be the most densely populated and industrialized. In both Connecticut and New York, reapportionment meant an end to Republican domination of the lower house. In New York the critical margin of five additional seats meant that Democrats could control the Assembly.

What difference in policy did the reapportionment revolution make? After all, policy *is* the major focus of our interest in the legislatures. Recent studies show that reapportionment of state legislatures has changed the distribution of state aid in favor of urban areas. There is more spending for education, welfare, health, and hospitals. Of major interest to those who predicted a spending spree by the newly elected urban contingent is that the total budget size did not increase. While spending increased in social welfare areas, cutbacks in other functions limited overall budget growth. Those who predicted that reapportionment would make a difference in the way state funds were allocated were correct.[7]

A thoughtful summary concerning the impact of reapportionment on New York State indicates that in addition to evening the balance between the Democratic and Republican parties, reapportionment moved Republican districts into areas where interparty competition and intraparty tensions were more acute. In the Republican party, a new crop of suburban legislators may be less willing to appeal to New York City for votes on a statewide ticket than legislators who knew that their party could not win with a rural appeal. Less secure in their districts, they are not about to do favors for New York City in return for future support in a statewide race for governor. As the population and representation of the suburbs increases, a Republican governor will be less inclined to support the interests of New York City in the face of opposition from the remainder of his party.

The impact of reapportionment for the Democrats was the loss of some New York City legislators. But the party still remained basically a city party. Unlike Republican leaders, who find it difficult to defend New York City's interests within their party, the Democratic leaders from the city pay little heed to their suburban or upstate colleagues. Top Democratic leaders today come from New York City as they did during the 1950s and 1960s and try to funnel state aid to the city. Democratic Governor Carey has solved the problem of doing city business with an unfriendly Republican senate and a Democratic house that thinks in city terms by focusing more on state provision of services. This avoids the problem of distribution of state aid to the city. The state takeover of the City University is a good example. In spite of the reapportionment revolution, however, the agenda of New York's legislature is dominated by the proposals of the governor who continues to take the lead in legislative policy-making.

THE LEGISLATOR AND POLITICAL AMBITION

When the dust settled following the reapportionment upheavals, the traditional problems of legislative policy making remained. This process is divided between the governor and the legislature, with the governor taking the lead. To repeat a point made earlier, his program is geared to please the totality of interests within his party and, depending on the support of his legislators, is passed, modified, or rejected.

The governor's agility to garner support from his legislators depends on the rewards the party can offer them for their loyalty. The conditions under which a legislator supports his party versus his constituency is related to the political ambition of the legislator and the way in which his political party can further that ambition. Thus, strong state parties can be of great aid to legislators seeking reelection.

Whether the political party can help the legislator advance is related to the character of the district he represents. We noted that, in many cases, reapportionment tended to shift districts from both rural and urban areas to the more competitive suburban areas. Either shift has meant that the districts are more competitive than they used to be, with legislators increasingly having to fight for their seats. What this means in terms of party loyalty is that, if given a choice, new legislators from competitive districts will tend to represent their districts first before the interests of their state party. They must please their districts if they want to be reelected to the same or higher office, which is the ambition of virtually every politician. On the other hand, legislators from solidly one-party districts may not need the support of a state party for election. If they want, however, to advance within the legislative party hierarchy, they must please their leaders, who control committee assignments and political positions. Several hypotheses emerge from this discussion.

1. Legislators have ambitions for advancement that are related to the political opportunity structure in their districts as well as in the state.
2. If the legislator sees his chance for reelection bound up with the record of his party, he will support the governor's program.
3. If the legislator is from an atypical district and from a faction opposing his governor, he will support his district's needs over those of the state party.

The legislator is seen as a political animal who needs to be recruited, nominated, and elected for political office. Two unavoidable questions are: Where does he come from? and What does he think his chances are for advancement?

Recruitment

Because the state legislative office is the most common starting point in the political career of elected officials, it is important to know just what motivates candidates to run for this first steppingstone. For many political aspirants, campaigning for this office is their first experience in electoral politics. They must compete against a party candidate in the primary as well as run a campaign against the other party's candidate in the general election. With incumbents very difficult to unseat, the neophite legislator can expect defeat. So what prompts him to run again, as do many defeated legislators?

When the legislator calculates his chances for advancement, he probably takes into account the following conditions: Is he fairly representative of his district's social characteristics? If he's not too far out of line with the general racial, ethnic, and religious backgrounds of his potential constituents, he may conclude that he would make an acceptable candidate. The potential candidate must establish relationships with many groups and interests to win widespread approval. But he must also determine whether his district is representative of those in the majority of his party, which may establish him in one or another of his party's factions.

The degree of competition existing between the parties in a legislative district may also influence the decision on who is chosen for the legislature. In our study of gubernatorial nominations, we noted that competition between state level political parties does not necessarily mean that disciplined party organizations exist that can control the recruitment and election of gubernatorial candidates (Table 4–1). However, some researchers believe the degree of competition in a district does affect the control parties can exert over the recruitment process. A recent study in Oregon offers generalizations which illustrate that this is true in most states. The writers claim that social and economic conditions determine the degree of competition within and between parties and that there are four types of districts that shape the character of the recruitment process for any legislative candidate: (1) The urban two-party, (2) the urban one-party, (3) the rural one-party, and (4) the rural two-party. These combined factors determine who the principal actors in the recruitment process will be, whether the political party will be important, and where in the process the real decision is made.[9] The Oregon study shows that heavy competition prevails in both primary and general elections in urban districts where social cleavages cross-cut the parties. Political activists and the politically ambitious find strong incentives to become candidates because an urban constituency is a springboard to higher office. Party leaders and interest groups seek standard bearers from prominent persons who have a good chance of victory at the polls. The eventual winners come from backgrounds that make them personify the various political, social, and economic characteristics of those districts.

A second recruitment pattern is found in urban districts where social cleavages divide the electorate into two unequal parties, where one clearly predominates. The majority party's primary is competitive between candidates who represent different interest groups but, within the minority party, another process takes place. Party officials must solicit candidates to fill slots on the ticket. Only one candidate enters the race and he must be persuaded. This is in sharp contrast to the recruitment processes in rural one-party districts. Here, candidates usually run unopposed or face only token opposition. A small circle of farmers, businessmen, and local professionals control the recruitment, with only a few individuals responding to the meager incentives to run for office. Successful candidates for the state legislature cannot aspire to higher office because their thinly populated rural constituency does not serve as a springboard. At most, a candidate from a rural one-party district may reach the state senate. The primary and election are mere ceremonies because the legislator is chosen in the recruitment process.

The last type of district is also rural but one where competition is based on local issues. Elections are not ideological contests between competing persuasions or parties, and the political inducements to run are no greater than in rural one-party districts. However, candidacy means becoming a champion of one faction, win or lose. Victory brings prestige not only because the winner becomes a state legislator, but also because he becomes a leading spokesman for his faction. The major difference between the Seligman study and that of V. O. Key lies in the character of the political party in the competitive district. Whereas Key would predict that the party leaders exert some control over primaries in competitive legislative districts, Seligman and his associates found that the greatest competition for nomination took place in competitive districts. Groups, factions, party officials, and the self-recruited all vied for the nomination, repudiating the thesis that parties would exercise more centralized recruitment in such situations.[10]

Key hypothesized that the statewide strength of the political party would exert an important influence over the nominations within legislative districts. Using Indiana and Connecticut as illustrations, he argued that strong state parties foster more centralized recruitment in legislative districts. This is also the case in Pennsylvania. Sorauf found that, in all sections of the state, legislative candidates were usually induced to seek the office by a party representative. Even in the safe districts of large cities as well as in small towns and rural districts, party leaders select which candidates will run for the legislature.[11] Both Key and Sorauf contend that the statewide pattern of party strength influences the legislative recruitment process as much as the individual prospects for success in each district.

The Direct Primary

State nominating systems differ from each other in significant ways, as was indicated in chapter 4. When the nominating system restricts the numbers of participants, the type of office holders differ from those selected under a nominating system open to all. Restrictive systems, such as Connecticut's party convention or Pennsylvania's closed primary, limit public participation, strengthen a party's control over nominations, and increase the power of politicians. Both a closed primary and a party convention ensure that the legislative nominee is a partisan regular, since party leaders control the nominating process. The candidate is likely to have made an early commitment to politics and have lengthy political experience. The use of preprimary endorsements and organizational help usually means that a united party can see to it that its preferred nominees are selected. If the nominating system is open, such as Washington's blanket primary or Minnesota's nonpartisan primary (prior to 1974), the electoral conflict is broadened and expands the range of participating groups. Hence, the party leaders' control over recruitment is reduced. Influence is more widespread and the outcome's predictability decreases. The responsibility for nominating candidates is wrested from the parties and legally given to the electorate at large. Thus many opportunities arise for mavericks, nonpartisans, and political novices to run for office without the prerequisite party experience or loyalty as necessary requirements to gain a legislative nomination.[12] Nominations go to individuals who have managed to build a personal following or have captured a coalition of interest groups. In sum, the structure of the nominating system affects the party's ability to determine the outcome by endorsing and sponsoring candidates for the state legislature.

A bewildering array of party structures exists behind the facade of a direct primary. In the northern states, there is very little correlation between party competition in a legislator's district and the primary support he receives.[13] All 1,300 legislators tested in a recent study won the general election in their districts, but their primary vote did not indicate the struggle among factions in one-party districts or the confident margin of being the party's candidate in competitive districts. A study of Democratic legislative primaries in eight southern states reveals that a high proportion are contested, which indicates that the primary is the real point of decision in southern one-party districts.[14] What this all boils down to is that it takes a high degree of sophistication to study the efforts of men and women as they go about the business of politics.

Starting from the assumption that winning is the most important occupation for a politician, the study of winning coalitions under many different circumstances requires imagination and understanding of human nature. The circumstances under which strong party leadership exerts itself to groom and nominate candidates for public office are diverse. The type of state primary in existence, the character of a state's party leadership, the social and economic conditions in a district, and the way these are reflected in party strength all affect party effort. The primary is a facade behind which the real struggles for leadership take place. One generalization can be made, however. Primaries are often not contested. The evidence, although not complete, suggests that only about 40 to 50 percent are contested in the northern states. Two types of primaries are not contested at all. The first is a district primary that is hopeless for one party or the other. V. O. Key demonstrates with Ohio's legislative districts that, when a party's chances are poorest, the contested primaries are lowest. His material also shows that incumbents are able to run unopposed much more frequently than nonincumbents.[15] Key gives us two reasons that partially explain why the primary form of nomination is not put to use. We have one additional explanation for the lack of contests in primaries. Party-endorsed candidates are less likely to be challenged than nonendorsed candidates. A study of one period from 1966 to 1970 reveals that

80 to 90 percent of all nonendorsed candidates faced opponents in the party's primary or district convention, while only 40 to 55 percent of endorsed candidates faced opponents.[16]

The major purpose underlying the study of recruitment and nomination for legislative office is to discover the type of people, and their organizational loyalties, who will soon participate in the policy-making process. If we believe, as do most political theorists, that a party should adopt a platform and recruit, nominate, and elect those who will be faithful to the party once in office, the conditions under which legislators are nominated and elected is of vital importance. If a governor cannot control his legislative contingent, we can hardly expect him to see his programs passed.

Party Competition in Legislative Districts

The extent of two-party competition for legislative seats varies widely among the states. In a few, such as New York, Michigan, Connecticut, and Rhode Island, all or very nearly all of the seats are contested. In southern states, with some exceptions (Kentucky and Tennessee), the search for two-party competition becomes a search for Republican candidates. Generally, two-party competition in all legislative districts is more likely to be found in states having a closely competitive two-party system. But in districts where one party is clearly dominant, contested elections may not occur.

Competition for legislative seats is more likely to be found in metropolitan areas because both party organizations are stronger. More money and personnel are available to contest elections on all levels. Also, the distribution of suburban voters heightens the competition between parties. This is especially noticeable in the more heavily urbanized counties of southern states where Republican candidates are becoming more numerous and are achieving electoral success more rapidly. If Republican presidential and gubernatorial candidates run well in the southern metropolitan counties, their coattails will benefit legislative candidates in those districts.[17]

We started this section with the hypothesis that the pattern of competition in a legislator's district would affect his relationship with his state party. If he believes he needs its help to win, he will support its leaders and program. If his election campaign was aided by a particular interest group, by a group of friends, or a rival faction within the party, he will not support his state leadership. If the socioeconomic character of his district resembles that of the majority of districts in his state party, we would expect the legislator to be loyal because he must campaign on the state program and presumably needs the help from state headquarters to win.

If the legislator comes from a one-party district, he or she may be independent of the state organization for electoral help, and another set of calculations may influence loyalty. On the other hand, a legislator from a noncompetitive district may face primary competition and need the support of the party. The rewards for hard work and loyalty within the legislature are the committee chairmanships and other leadership positions. Naturally, these will go to those who have been around the longest and have shown the most consistent support.

Turnover in State Legislatures

Observers of American state legislatures have lamented the fact that there are so many newcomers in each election because this fact reduces the effectiveness of the legislators. Committee chairmen and experienced legislators need to be knowledgeable enough and to exercise enough independent judgment to guide the committees through the legislative process.

There is disagreement about whether turnover of the state legislators is caused by voluntary retirement or by defeat of the incumbent at the polls. A recent study in eight state legislatures of the turnover phenomenon and the reasons for it reveals that there has been a gradual but very substantial decline in the number of legislators who voluntarily retire. For example, 70 percent of Wisconsin assemblymen did not seek reelection in 1897, while only 14 percent chose not to do so in 1967. In all the states, the percentage of legislators who have sought reelection and won has increased over the years. Of those who did not return, more have been defeated in elections than have voluntarily retired.[18] There was a temporary setback when the states reapportioned and made many legislators fight for reelection in districts new to them. But this flurry is now over and the legislatures are becoming more tenured all the time. The average percentage of new members in 1971 was 24.6 in state senates and 32.3 percent in the legislative houses, a noticeable decrease since 1963. Turnover may be expected to decline in the future because the rewards for legislative service are becoming more attractive, compensation is greater, and there is more confidence in state government.[19]

THE ROLES OF A STATE LEGISLATOR

Recruitment patterns and the process of nomination and election make up the socialization process that influences how a legislator views his job and delineates those on whom he or she is dependent. A district's needs and demands are filtered through its legislators. Figure 6–1 presents the

FIGURE 6–1

*Linkages between the Legislator's
Constituency and his Voting Behavior*

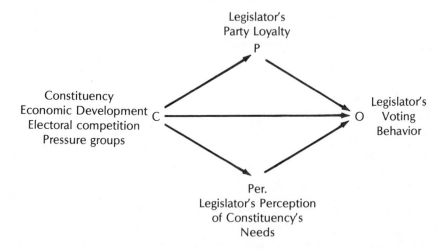

Legislator's
Party Loyalty
P

Constituency
Economic Development C
Electoral competition
Pressure groups

Legislator's
O   Voting
Behavior

Per.
Legislator's Perception
of Constituency's
Needs

hypothesized linkages between a legislator's constituency and his voting behavior. Whether the legislator represents the desires of his district depends on his loyalty to his party, his perception of his district's needs, and his views of his job as legislator. Early studies of legislative behavior assumed that the representative automatically voted according to the socio-economic development of his district. In this case, the path runs directly from the constituency to policy output (C-O). These assumptions were soon modified when it was seen that legislators from similar constituencies did not vote together as a bloc, but were more likely to follow the leadership of their party. The connection, therefore, between a constituency's interests and the legislator's output is modified by the intervening variable of party loyalty (C-P-O).

Another body of research we are about to examine is concerned with the role styles of the legislators. The term *role* refers to a coherent set of behavior "norms" that guide legislative actions. Each role reflects a particular orientation to legislative duties, the legislature, and to the way in which a legislator gives expression to the values and interests of his or her constituency (C-Per.-O). Many studies have been made of the roles of state legislators. Usually they are descriptive, informing the reader that there are various types of people in the state legislature, but not helping us to predict what the future decisions of a legislature will be based on this knowledge. If the major reason for political science as a discipline is the ability to predict the future, then it has failed. The whole subject of role description so far has not helped us predict the policy output of state legislatures. We only know that legislators view their jobs differently, and some state legislatures have more of some type than others.

This author believes that the way a legislator views his or her duties is related to his political socialization—the way he is recruited by his party faction or interest group. In addition, his role conception as legislator affects the perception of his constituency's needs and, hence, his voting behavior. While the evidence is shaky, what follows are the major role types that have been used to describe state legislators and the probable connection between these role types and the action a legislator takes when faced with a decision. This is based on the hypothesis that most legislators are upwardly mobile (that is, they want to use the legislature as a steppingstone to higher office) and that the way they view their role is related to their plans for advancement. There are, of course, some legislators who have been identified as having very little ambition. They are probably not too important to the total legislative output.

The major breakthrough in the research on role behavior was that of Wahlke, Eulau, Buchanan, and Ferguson, who published *The Legislative System* in 1962.[20] Their study of the self-perceptions of legislators from California, New Jersey, Ohio, and Tennessee has been commonly accepted as usable and helpful in the study of role concepts. While the researchers identified several self-perceptions a legislator may entertain, we will concern ourselves here with the legislator's notions of himself as a representative in a system based on representation, as all state legislatures are. It is through the system of representation that legislatures are enpowered to act for the whole body politic; their actions are regarded as legitimate and authoritative. Representation involves two concepts: focus and style. The first involves a legislator's perceptions in respect to the importance of his electoral district compared to that of the whole state as being a focus of his actions. Is the legislator concerned with his district and does he seek to discover its interests? If so, the writers of *The Legislative System* call him district oriented where he conceives of his job explicitly as that of sponsoring and supporting legislation to the benefit of his constituency. If, on the other hand, the state is the salient focus of his orientation, he is labeled state oriented. A third group of legislators mentioned both district and state as equally relevant to their legislative or service activities. They were given the intermediate title of "district-state oriented." The writers discovered, as we might well hypothesize, that those legislators who placed the needs and demands of their district first were those from competitive districts. In other words, the sanction of removal if they did not perform in accordance with the interests of their district focused their attention on district rather than state as the crucial point of reference. Legislators from competitive areas are, therefore, more likely to be district oriented than legislators from one-party areas. The writers also discovered that competition was more important than a district's socioeconomic character in determining the focus of a legislator. In both metropolitan and suburban areas, legislators from competitive districts focused on their constituency more than the state or a combination of the two. Still, 40 percent or more of all legislators deviated from this finding. There is no way of telling from the research whether those legislators whose districts were adequately represented by their party's program would tend to be state or district oriented. After all, a political party's program must satisfy its state-wide constituency, which would tend to favor district majorities regardless of whether they were competitive.

The representational style first introduced by Wahlke and his associates received the most notice by researchers who succeeded them. The latter writers take great pains to separate these self-perceived representational styles from the above discussion of self-perceived focus. Even a legislator who realized he must consider his district first, for political reasons, could also feel free to make up his own mind as to its needs and not be bound by its demands unless he chose to do so. What follows, then, is the description of the three major representational roles that has greatly influenced the literature on role concepts. The role description was derived from the legislators' responses to questions. The role orientation of *trustee* is that of a free agent. As a premise of his decision-making behavior, the trustee claims to follow what he considers right or just, his convictions and principles, the dictates of his conscience. If he finds himself in conflict with those he represents, he should not submit but rather try to persuade them to his convictions. He believes that he was elected to follow his own judgement. The second major style of representational role orientation is that of *delegate*. The delegate believes that he should not use his independent judgment or principled convictions as decision-making premises. He should determine the wishes and desires of his constituents and act accordingly. The third and final category is that of the *politico*. He represents an overlap of the other two. Depending on the circumstances, a representative may hold the role orientation of trustee at one time and that of delegate at another. Within this range called politico, the trustee and delegate roles may be taken simultaneously, possibly creating a role conflict, or they may be taken one after another as legislative situations dictate.

Wahlke and associates discovered that there were more self-styled trustees in their four state legislatures than any other type. In California, New Jersey, and Ohio, they comprised 55 to 61 percent of the legislatures and 81 percent in Tennessee.[21] Since 1962, when the book by Wahlke and associates was published, researchers have asked the same question in other legislatures and have come up with different proportions of legislators taking the three role styles. In Wisconsin's assembly, two-thirds of the legislators were delegates, and a preponderance of Pennsylvania and

North Carolina representatives were delegates.[22] It is interesting to hypothesize about the policy difference that would result if a legislature were composed of 20 percent delegates compared to one made of 70 percent. From what we know about Wisconsin, that state has a very active party system that endeavors to make promises at election time and to fulfill them when elected. Yet, only 21 percent of Wisconsin's legislators claim to be trustees. In Tennessee politics, the Democratic factions prevent any overall party program, and the gubernatorial candidate's promises constitute what the electorate may expect to be enacted. It would seem more logical for a Tennessee legislator to consider himself a delegate with a district focus if his party has no program. Hence, it is hard to discover just what causes a legislator to assume one role over another. And it is equally hard to predict what his voting behavior may be if we *know* how he looks at his representational role. But we suspect that the delegate style and district-oriented focus are highly related. While the writers of *The Legislative System* do not correlate the two roles directly, they draw several conclusions with respect to the way a district-oriented legislator performs service functions as opposed to a state-oriented legislator. A district legislator stresses communications and errand-boy functions more than a state-oriented legislator, who tends to persuade or educate constituents.

To summarize, we do not know what the knowledge of role orientations means to the problem of legislative behavior. Will a delegate support his party if it makes demands upon him? Will a trustee vote for his district if its interests conflict with those of his state wide party? There probably is a connection between the way a legislator looks at his job and the perception he has of his constituency's needs. We can be reasonably sure that the attitudes and perceptions of legislators affect the way they respond to demands. But the question remains whether we can get accurate enough information about roles to contribute to the study of voting behavior.

Despite the interest shown by legislative scholars in both roles and roll calls, there have been few attempts to demonstrate that particular role orientations are related to the voting behavior of legislators. Sorauf found that legislators in Pennsylvania who voted most consistently with the party were more likely to be trustees than those with a less-loyal voting record, but the differences were not large.[23] In a more recent study, Hedlund and Friesma examined whether differences in representational role orientations were related to the ability of Iowa legislators to predict accurately the opinions of their constituencies on four referenda issues subsequently voted on. Contrary to what the literature would suggest, they found that trustees—not delegates—were better able to accurately predict constituency opinion on the issues.[24] In similar fashion, Erikson et al. measured the capacity of Florida legislators to predict constituency opinion on three straw referenda issues. Trustees were again found to be more accurate predictors of constituency opinion than either delegates or politicos, leading the writers to note the ironical fact that "legislators who claim to pay the greatest attention to constituency preferences appear to be least able to determine what their constituents want."[25]

At this point it is hard to see the relationship between the use of representational roles and the actual behavior of the legislators. The legislator probably does not know precisely what it is that his constituents want except on highly important issues such as taxation, birth control, abortion, and bussing. In general, he knows the tendencies of his district and uses this information to guide his specific acts. If he is a delegate, he is probably more representative of his district than the trustee. We would also expect that a delegate would be more sensitive to his district's demands if the district was a competitive one. Hence, representative role orientations have some value in our attempt to explain and predict legislative behavior. For the party leaders, the proportion of self-styled delegates may be of crucial importance if the party program deviates extensively from many of the districts. The legislator may see his political survival dependent on voting against the party position, especially if the district is competitive. But we have not answered the most important question of all: What makes a trustee take the position he does? He is just as likely to come from a competitive constituency as the delegate. In spite of this, however, he does not feel bound by its demands even if he is better able to predict them. Perhaps the trustee throws his lot in with that of his party. He wants to progress through the ranks and run for higher office. One study of Michigan legislators discovered that the trustees were more likely to have future ambitions.[26] In summary, the study of legislative roles may be of importance if we can actually predict the behavior of legislators from their self-perceptions. As we shall see later, the major explanation for legislative voting patterns is that of the political party. The governor's program places heavy demands on the legislators to muster the necessary loyalty and vote yes. The governor is more visible and the constituents are more likely to know who he is than to know their legislator. Some deviations are allowed by party leaders, even on votes for the governor's program, if the constituency is particularly opposed and the necessary support exists. But regardless of whether he's a delegate, trustee, or politico, when the chips are down his party leaders expect support.

POLITICAL ORGANIZATION OF THE LEGISLATURE

New members of the Ohio General Assembly, as their legislature is called, find guidebooks on their desks describing the legislative process. The hope is expressed in the preface that "it will suffice as a useful document until the legislator gains the knowledge that can come only from direct experience."[27] While Ohio's legislators may not compare themselves with the other 7,400 or so state legislators assembling in January in their respective capitols, the Ohio legislature and the conditions under which the legislators work are not unusual. The Ohio Senate has 33 seats, which is close to the average size of 38 or 39. [The largest Senates are Minnesota's (67) and New York's (60); the smallest are Alaska and Nevada (20).] The Ohio House has 99 members, which is nudging the median of 100. [The largest lower houses are in New Hampshire (400) and Massachusetts (240); the smallest are in Alaska and Nevada (40).] Their terms of four years for senators and two years for members of the house are also typical of their sister states. (Four states have four-year terms for the house, and twelve have a two-year senate term.) The Ohio General Assembly meets in annual sessions, which is typical of the recent trend in the state legislatures around the country. In the early 1940s, only four legislatures met in annual sessions; by 1976, 42 were doing so. This has greatly increased the amount of time spent in actual session—regular and special. Being a state legislator means acquiring an important position and one that is increasing in stature as the burdens on states increase. All the trends point to the increasing professionalism, capability, and representativeness of our states' legislatures.

The Legislative Process

The Guidebook for Ohio Legislators describes the process by which an idea becomes a law. This legislative process is reproduced in Figure 6–2. Pretending for the moment that we are new members of the Ohio General Assembly, we eye the chart in dismay. It would appear that our favorite legislation may not make it through the interstices of the legislative process. We note that there are eight asterisks which indicate that the bill may be lost at a particular stage. Actually, we can add two additional asterisks to indicate the risk of losing the bill in the second house. Of these ten points where a bill may be lost, only four involve voting on the assembly floor. All the other stages where a bill may fail are in committees or in the hands of the party leadership. We note that the House Reference Committee routes all bills to standing committees. In the Senate, however, the process remains mysterious and we are told that this function is performed by the president pro tem, the elected leader of the senate. We also note that the committee that considers the bill in either house may postpone or "kill" it. Even if the bill emerges from the standing committee, it must pass the rules committee, which can also dispose of it. If it is passed in different form by the two houses, then it can languish in a conference committee. Clearly, the selection of all committee members that can decide the fate of legislation is of paramount importance to any

FIGURE 6–2

The Legislative Process

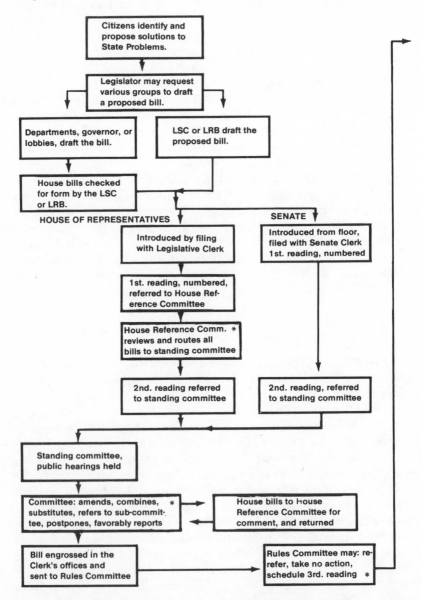

Note: After the bill is introduced, it is given a series of "readings" (usually three) as it proceeds to committee and is returned to the full house for deliberation. This custom derives from the British Parliament, where, before literacy was common, a clerk read a bill three separate times so that it would be understood. Even now, it is customary to discuss process in terms of "readings," although the reading usually consists of having a legislative clerk read the number and title.
Source: Ohio Legislative Service Commission, *A Guidebook for Ohio Legislators,* pp. 62–63. Reprinted by permission of the Ohio Legislative Service Commission.

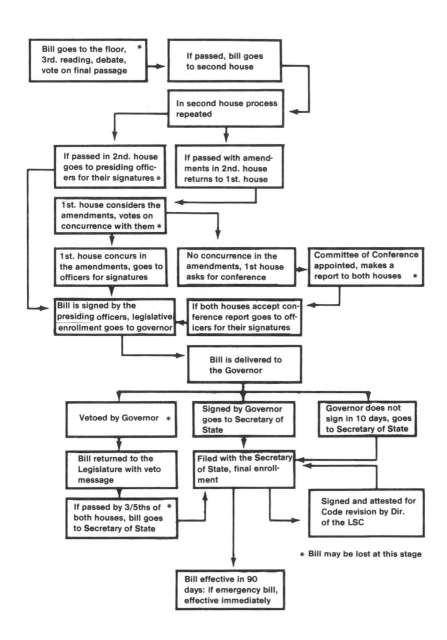

Bill goes to the floor, * 3rd. reading, debate, vote on final passage

If passed, bill goes to second house

In second house process repeated

If passed in 2nd. house goes to presiding officers for their signatures *

If passed with amendments in 2nd. house returns to 1st. house

1st. house considers the amendments, votes on concurrence with them *

1st. house concurs in the amendments, goes to officers for signatures

No concurrence in the amendments, 1st house asks for conference

Committee of Conference appointed, makes a report to both houses *

Bill is signed by the presiding officers, legislative enrollment goes to governor

If both houses accept conference report goes to officers for their signatures

Bill is delivered to the Governor

Vetoed by Governor *

Signed by Governor goes to Secretary of State

Governor does not sign in 10 days, goes to Secretary of State

Bill returned to the Legislature with veto message

Filed with the Secretary of State, final enrollment

If passed by 3/5ths of * both houses, bill goes to Secretary of State

Signed and attested for Code revision by Dir. of the LSC

* Bill may be lost at this stage

Bill effective in 90 days: if emergency bill, effective immediately legislator, group, or governor wanting something passed. In formal terms, bills may be introduced only by legislators or special legislative bodies such as the Legislative Service Commission (LSC) or the Legislative Reference Bureau (LRB). It is even common to refer to the legislator who introduces a bill as the "author," but actually very few proposals emanate from the legislators themselves. The initiative for most proposals comes from executive departments, the governor, or special interest groups. A governor's legislation is usually "authored" by his floor leaders who give it to their clerks. Since it is the political power structure that really has control over the fate of legislation, we now turn to a consideration of the party leadership in the legislative process.

The Party Leadership

The majority-party leadership in each legislature makes the crucial decisions about party membership on committees, the party ratio, appointment of chairmen, the rules, and settling the chamber down to its job. There's a considerable amount of prodding by the governor throughout. The decisions that count have usually been taken before the session is convened. It is by no means uncommon, however, for intraparty conflict over the choice of speaker, president pro tem, or the majority and minority floor leaders to be settled after the session has begun. This indicates that the leadership has not consolidated its support among the members of its legislative party.

The speaker of the lower house is clearly the most powerful figure in that branch; he is elected by the membership and represents whatever party or faction has a majority. Traditionally, the lieutenant governor, elected state wide, presides over the senate. However, as state parties became more competitive and the possibility increased of having a minority party lieutenant governor chairing the senate, the legislative powers of the lieutenant governor were considerably curtailed. Indeed, many of them are no longer allowed to preside. All state senates now elect a president pro tem who is the real political leader, both in his majority party and in the senate. In all but a handful of states, the one-term limitation on legislative leadership has been abolished. Legislatures are now willing to recognize the advantages of partisan leadership and have been gearing up to take more of a political role in the decision-making process.

In two-party states, the speaker of the house and the senate's president pro tem are in fact chosen by the majority party caucus as its first order of business at the start of the session. Though the minority party nominates its own candidates for these posts, this is a time where party lines remain firm and the majority party candidate wins. In moderate to strong party states, such as Rhode Island, Pennsylvania, Wisconsin, New

York, and Connecticut, there is a regular advancement pattern from party whip to floor leader to speaker for one or both parties. In other states, such as Illinois, Iowa and Montana, the speaker and floor leaders have been chosen more often from among committee chairmen or members of the judiciary or appropriations committees. These chairmanships are held only by members of the majority party. Needless to say, the governor tries to influence selection of the majority leader and president of the senate. The fate of his program depends on friendly leadership. If his party does not control the house or senate, he has a more complicated set of interests. He wants a party leader from his minority party who will work well with the opposition and who will try to get his program through a legislature with the least amount of loss or mangling.

In one-party states, the house and senate leaders are invariably from the governor's party. But they are not necessarily of the governor's faction. In Texas the lieutenant governor has almost total power over the management of the senate. If he is from a different faction than the governor, he can create difficulties for legislation the executive wants passed. The speaker of the Texas house is so important to the legislative power process that his selection requires a great deal of political activity. Lobbyists representing special-interest groups make every effort to secure the selection of a sympathetic speaker. Aspirants to the position begin lining up support from legislators and legislative candidates several months or even years before the beginning of a speaker's race. This campaign is unique because it takes place entirely within the legislative domain. Those who supported the winning candidate can obtain important committee assignments and chairmanships; and they will form the speaker's coalition that controls most house activities.[28] Only if the contest is very close does the governor of Texas have any opportunity to influence the outcome. And even then he usually operates behind the scenes to change a few minds in his favor. In this situation, even though the speaker is of the governor's party, the governor may not have his cooperation in the passage of legislation he wants. Recall that often in a situation like this the governor does not have much of a program.

The choice of leaders is important because most of them exercise great control over the organization and functioning of the legislature— particularly the appointment of committees. The speaker and senate president have the authority to choose members of the standing committees and usually their chairmen. A strong presiding officer who represents the interests of the governor will place dependably loyal men on certain key committees. It is here that the greatest contrast with Congress is noticeable. When a new session begins, the presiding officer can and sometimes does remove a legislator from a choice committee to discipline him for a disloyal voting record. Where factions are important in the dominant party, factional loyalty is likely to be a prerequisite for choice committee

assignments. The importance of leadership control over committee assignments is magnified by the fact that the speaker of the house and president
of the senate can assign bills to committee. In Ohio, the House Reference
Committee is also involved in assigning bills to committees, but the
speaker appoints that committee and is an ex-officio member of it. Hence
he can control its decisions on matters that are important to him.

In addition to assigning legislators and bills to committees, the house
speaker and president of the senate exercise considerable power in presiding over their chambers. Their party or faction often has complete dominance. One-third of the members are new and ignorant of the rules, which
may explain why these presiding officers can choose whom to recognize,
when to prolong or cut off debate, when to pretend not to hear demands
for a roll call, and so on. Electronic voting, which has been installed in all
but a handful of lower houses, does not seem to curtail the skill of the
speaker. He may determine when the machine is to be closed and the
votes counted or whether to leave the machine open while votes are
changed and absentees rounded up. Speaker Anthony Travia of New York
asserted his leadership as evidenced in the following scene:

> Occasionally Travia displays his power in a shout. In the rush for adjournment
> after a six-month session last year, he wanted Assemblyman Joseph St. Law-
> rence to recommit a bill to committee instead of opening a floor debate.
> Assemblyman St. Lawrence stood and began to speak about his bill. Travia
> interrupted him with a shout: "I only want to hear one word from you!"
> "Recommit," St. Lawrence said. "That's the word," Travia said, banging his
> gavel lustily.[29]

In addition to the speaker and president of the senate, there are floor
leaders for the parties or factions. They are often chosen along with the
candidate for speaker or president at the party caucus which takes place
before the session. In some states such as New York, the speaker picks the
majority leader. The minority party leader is also chosen at his party's
presession caucus, and may, of course, manage his governor's program if
they are of the same party. The majority leader often assists the presiding
officer in planning committee assignments and developing legislative
strategy, and, on the floor, he manages the administration bills for his
governor. A floor leader is often found in a legislature dominated by a
single party. He is not likely to be elected but rather designated formally
or informally by the governor. The Louisiana governor, in consultation
with his floor leaders, plays a major role in the appointment of committees
and especially the choice of chairmen. In making appointments, the
speaker and senate president usually approve the choices worked out in
advance by the governor and his legislative leaders.[30] The factional floor

leader in a one-party state plays much the same role as a majority leader in a two-party state. There is usually no opposition leader unless a well-organized anti-administration faction exists.

The Party Caucus

The caucus is the most common form of party organization. We have already referred to it as the meeting of a party's membership within a legislative house. The order of business is to tend first to such matters as the selection of leaders. In some legislatures, the caucus meets frequently to discuss legislative strategy, to count the members who will be loyal on the vote and to give others permission to vote "their conscience," or, more likely, "the interests of their districts." In Connecticut, party caucuses meet frequently to discuss the bills on the calendar. In Iowa, a veteran floor leader discusses one of his most important tasks:

> One of the main jobs of a floor leader is to preside at his party's caucuses. As caucus leader, he attempts to unite the party and prevent splits. Naturally, the issues that we make decisions on are sometimes divisive. They tend to create antagonisms, and it is the duty of the leader to see that the wounds are healed and that the party leaders operate as a group and get back to implementing the party program. It's his prerogative and duty to call caucuses for the purpose of maintaining *esprit de corps.* [31]

There has not been a recent survey of the use of party caucuses. The increasing two-party competition within states and their legislatures, however, would probably make the party caucus a regular phenomenon. In some states, caucuses meet every week; in others, they meet when important issues arise. The majority party usually holds caucuses in states with moderate to strong party organizations. New Jersey, Connecticut, Pennsylvania, Massachusetts, Rhode Island, and Washington are examples of states where the caucuses meet regularly to consider the important measures before reaching the floor.

The Leadership Committees

The asterisks in Figure 6–2 indicate trouble at two points in the legislative process, which are both controlled by the party leadership. The House Reference Committee and the senate and house rules committees in the Ohio General Assembly are the so-called leadership committees; they play an important part in directing the business of the legislature. They are chaired by the house speaker and senate president in their respective chambers and consist of leaders from both parties. They are, however,

under the firm control of the majority-party leaders. The Ohio House
Reference Committee, authorized to eliminate frivolous or duplicate bills,
is one of the most powerful in the country.

Most legislative bodies have rules committees, although most of them
do not have the function of assigning bills to committees. Again, this is
usually done by the presiding officer of either house. The rules committees
usually make recommendations on changes of rules, a power that occasionally assumes importance because it can give the majority leader priority recognition on the floor of the house. (In most states, it is the floor
leadership that determines the priorities for floor consideration of legislation once it has been reported by a standing committee.) In some states,
the rules committee has the power to determine priorities and select those
bills that will reach the floor of the legislature during the closing days or
weeks of the session, that is, when the most important bills are passed.
Malcolm Jewell reports that, in states where the rules committee controls
which bills reach the floor late in the session, it is often a powerful committee and the primary tool of majority control. Alabama provides a good
example of powerful rules committees in both houses that use special
orders to advance bills to prompt floor action. In the closing days of the
session, the committees meet daily to consider requests for special orders.
The legislative calendar is so crowded by that time that bills are most
unlikely to pass without such prior treatment. The rules committee is
utilized by the dominant legislative group to ensure that it can get orderly
control over the process in the closing days. In Alabama, the governor's
faction is the dominant group.[32]

Legislatures often have a committee on committees (at least 16 senates and a handful of lower houses). Their function is to make appointments to all the standing committees when it is not customary for the
presiding officer to do so. They are usually bipartisan and are generally
under the control of the majority leadership.

The steering or policy committee, on the other hand, represents the
leadership of a single party and usually meets with the governor to plan
party strategy. If the parties are strong, they can be a determining factor
in the successful passage of legislation.

The Standing Committees

Standing committees, at least in Ohio, obviously have a major impact on
legislation. The governor, pressure groups or constituents doing the proposing have a vital interest in who will take their bills and perform the
given rites of passage, particularly when the committee's functions include holding public hearings, amending, combining, substituting, referring to subcommittees, postponing or favorably reporting. The average

number of committees for lower houses is 17 and 13 for senates. Membership varies but averages 15 for the house and 12 for the senate. Ohio's standing committees in 1971 and the number on each were as follows:[33]

HOUSE		SENATE	
Agriculture, Commerce, and		Agriculture Insurance and	
Labor	(18)	Financial Institutions	(8)
Environment and Natural		Education and Health	(8)
Resources	(19)	Commerce and Labor	(9)
Finance-Appropriations	(22)	Elections and Retirement	(9)
Health, Education, and		Environmental Affairs	(8)
Welfare	(22)	Finance	(9)
Highways and Transportation	(19)	Judiciary	(8)
Insurance, Utilities, and		Rules	(9)
Financial Institutions	(21)	Urban and Highway Affairs	(8)
Interstate Cooperation	(7)	Ways and Means	(9)
Judiciary	(19)		
Local Government and			
Urban Affairs	(19)		
Reference	(11)		
Rules	(13)		
State Government	(22)		
Ways and Means	(18)		

The two most important functions of legislative committees are making decisions with regard to legislation and the authorization and oversight of administrative actions. Conflicts develop, however, in the exercise of these two functions. One is between the executive and the legislature; the governor is elected by all the people of a state while each legislator has only a small constituency. They do not always represent the same interests, especially if the governor is of a party different from the legislative majority. A second source of conflict is between the political party and the committee leadership. Where party leadership is strong, the committee leadership is part of a majority coalition. Where party leadership is weak, committees may be strong and independent. Any study of the power of legislative committees, therefore, begins with an examination of the political party structure and how committee members and chairmen are appointed.

When a legislative body is under tight control by party or factional leaders, they will choose the members of key committees and even replace them if they do not go along with the party program. Each house member gets on two to three committees and each senate member serves on at least three. These numbers translate into rewards and punishments for the party leadership to dispense. Each legislator has a set of ambitions that relate to his future plans for advancement. He may see his plans closely tied in with the leadership and will, therefore, be a loyal party member. If the leaders can structure things their way, the legislator will be rewarded with choice committee posts. On the other hand, a legislator's best interests may be served by declaring his lot with one or another faction in a divided party. He may lose out in his choice of committees if that faction does not control the legislature. And there is still another possibility. In a legislature where parties are weak, the committees themselves may be strong. A continuing set of leaders may have developed, determined by seniority or time spent in the legislature or on the committee. In this case, the same legislators hold chairmanships for long periods of time, and a small group of senior members hold the power. This situation is likely to occur in a one-party state where the power of senior members does not change after an election. Seniority was recently approved in Texas as a device for selecting and retaining committee members. In 1979 the party lineup of Democrats to Republicans in the senate was 27 to 4 and 127 to 23 in the house, meaning, of course, that there is no party competition to upset the senior members. Arkansas is another state where party leadership is weak. Committee chairmen in the house are chosen by seniority. In 1979 Arkansas' ratio of Democrats to Republicans was 35 to 0 in the senate and 94 to 6 in the lower house.

In legislatures with two effective parties, the majority party normally has all committee chairmanships, and the ratio of Republicans to Democrats on each committee usually approximates that in the legislature. This is becoming the norm as two-party competition increases within the states and minority parties increase their legislative contingents. Seniority is by no means ruled out as a reason for committee chairmanships, even in these situations. Common sense dictates that members who have served for a long time on their respective committees will have developed a valuable expertise. It is likely that the chairmen will be those who have served longest on their committees. There is, however, more opportunity for the leadership to replace them if they are not loyal to the party because there is no entrenched seniority system.

The notion that committees must be weak where parties are strong is prevalent in today's reform literature. But this lacks comprehension of the role that political parties are supposed to play in bringing the needs and wants of the people to their government's points of decision. A governor and legislators committed to the same party program have the obligation to produce legislation when in office. This process is aided when subject matter committees are chaired by those sympathetic to this legislative intent. Committees are not necessarily weak under these conditions; they are part of the leadership coalition. The real question, which has not been answered adequately by the research to date, is how a minority governor gets his legislation passed when all the committee chairmen are his formal political enemies. We know that this situation exists in many legislatures today. This becomes, then, one of the more fascinating inquiries and one that is still veiled in mystery. Exactly what happens when the governor's program hits an opposition legislature? One thing is certain: Many governors are facing this problem right now, but the answer lies in the future. Committees are a vital link in the policy-making process; the extent to which they are equipped to research and deliberate, regardless of party affiliation, is directly related to how well the people of a state are served.

TOWARD MORE PROFESSIONAL LEGISLATURES

This chapter began with a quote from Speaker Fineman of the Pennsylvania House of Representatives. He spoke eloquently about the true functions of legislatures as being representative and "producing the kind of legislation that the people desire and need." Fineman believed those to be more important than reform of organizational structure and procedures. The reapportionment revolution was followed by a reform movement that claimed as much impact on the legislative product as the previous set of revolutionaries. The same forces and pressures that brought about the Supreme Court decisions were responsible for the reform efforts. Rapid transformation of American society from rural to urban living and the need to tackle the most pressing human problems on the state level made the press and various private organizations question the ability of state governments to handle the job that faced them in the seventies. In Mississippi, for instance, legislative operations were hardly adequate to cope with the demands facing the state. Even their floor decorum was frequently criticized. One legislator described the reaction of his constituents:

> "Whenever I talk to any of my people who have been to Jackson and seen the legislature, it seems the first thing they question is how disgusting it was to watch members breaking peanut shells and throwing them on the floor or reading newspapers or jabbering with lobbyists while the House is in session and conducting business. . . ."[34]

The need for floor decorum was obvious in Mississippi, but most state legislatures started somewhat ahead of this condition.

A relatively small number of legislators and certain organizations such as the Citizens Conference on State Legislatures (the one to which Speaker Fineman was referring), The Eagleton Institute of Politics at Rutgers University, and Common Cause have tried to generate interest in reform. The goals set forth in all the studies and publications can be summarized under a few headings.[35]

1. Legislative-executive relations need improvement in such areas as appropriation of public funds and the post-audit of public expenditures, review of administrative rules and decisions, and retaining some control in the legislature over the powers it delegates to administrative agencies.
2. Legislative sessions should be free of undue restriction in length of session, frequency of meetings, and subject matter to be discussed. (It was noted earlier that all but eight legislatures now meet in annual session, so the states have nearly met this requirement.)
3. Legislative compensation should be fixed by statute rather than by constitution and should reflect the responsibilities vested in a legislator (as compared to the practice in the executive branch). Legislative compensation should also be high enough to attract qualified persons from all walks of life. Recently, legislative salaries have been raised in many states. Only nine fix basic pay levels in the State constitution while most now allow their legislatures to set the salaries. By 1978, the mean compensation figure for a two-year period was $23,000. California's lawmakers were the highest paid with $51,110. New Hampshire paid its legislators $200 for a one-year session.
4. Legislative staff should be selected on the basis of merit and competence. The information needs of a state legislature are as crucial as those of the administrative branch. The legislature should provide itself with sufficient (and full-time) staff so that it can meet its information needs on a continuing basis.
5. Legislative standing committees should be assigned broad functional areas of responsibility. This will make it possible for their members to develop expertise in the area of committee responsibility. The number of committees should be reduced in most legislative houses. Citizens interested in legislation should be able to attend public hearings, and notices of such hearings should be published sufficiently early to enable interested parties to attend.

This list could be extended but these are the major suggestions for reform. They are a matter of common sense. Legislators who are trying to solve the most agonizing human problems should be given adequate sources of information, secretarial services, space, and so on. Legislatures are truly becoming more professional. With the heavy weight of responsibility they carry, legislators are due these necessary tools. A state that gives its legislators the staff and help they need may also give them an awareness of their importance in the political process. A feeling of self-respect is another kind of aid that will help in meeting the demands of the eighties.

Many proponents of legislative reform, however, claim too much for the reforms they advocate. The major emphasis seems to be independence from the executive branch of government as an end in itself. This is typified by the studies and recommendations of the Eagleton Institute of Politics, which stress independence from the governor as a major goal of their studies of seven state legislatures. In 1975, the director of research and service for the Institute concluded that enhancement of the committee capacity does not necessarily make for "independence of the legislature." He admitted that in New Jersey the governor still dominated:

> In 1970–1971, for instance, despite greater committee capacity and better committee performance, what the governor wanted the governor generally received. Of the 112 administration bills submitted, as many as 104 passed the Assembly and were enacted by the legislature without being changed very much in the process. . . .
>
> As long as a legislature is dependent, it will not have much incentive to strengthen its standing committees so that they can perform better in formulating state policies and programs. This would challenge the executive. As long as a legislature is dependent, it will have less incentive to strengthen its standing committees so that they can perform better in controlling state policies and programs. This would surely challenge the executive.[36]

Clearly this position leads inevitably to the assertion that both a strong governor and strong parties are an impediment to legislative effectiveness. This view is diametrically opposed to the one asserted here.

In the first place, any kind of reform is not neutral. It is a highly political process. Someone is bound to lose; someone wins. For instance, political appointees who had been doing secretarial work for the legislative committees are now replaced by professional staff people. In several states, these professional staffers are hired by the party leadership. New York, Connecticut, and California recognized that there was a need for professional staff, but one that would propose legislation to serve a partisan point of view. There are both majority and minority staff members in these legislative committees. When party balance changes in the legislature, so does the ratio of majority to minority staff members. But, according to New York's minority staff director, there is great demand for the previous majority staff to serve under the new partisan label.[37] Jess Unruh, speaker of the California legislature, tells of the collaboration between both minority and majority staff personnel on a study of the chronically unemployed. The result was a bipartisan package of legislation that received the full support of the governor because most of the potential objections had been overcome by the staff. Here is an example of a situation in which bipartisan effort produced major legislation. This could never have been produced by a "neutral" staff, which researches but does not recommend.

The upshot of this discussion is that partisan politics is good. There is no reason to believe that an elected governor should not formulate a program that represents the promises he makes to the electorate. There is no reason the legislature cannot have the staff to research thoroughly these proposals, to react to them, and to modify them. There is no basis for believing that, because a legislature passes this legislation, it is dominated by the governor. They are part of the same team. Partisan politics is better able to represent the citizens of a state than is an independent legislature which represents only itself.

The ability of a professionalized legislature to be more representative of the needs and concerns of its citizens is the focus of two recent studies. Rather than assuming legislative independence as the goal of a professional legislature, the studies took welfare policies as the measure of a professionalized legislature being more responsive to the needs of lower-income people. John Grumm measured the degree of professionalism by including the compensation of legislators; expenditures for legislative staff, services, operations, and printing; number of bills introduced in a session; length of the sessions; and a measure of legislative services. He assigned each state a score based on a factor analysis of the variables[38] and found that in states where legislators are well paid and staffed, their ability to perform is enhanced and they are better able to represent their constituents. These states have more liberal welfare benefits.

The second study, by Carmines, used Grumm's index and discovered that the relationship between a political party and the welfare needs of the people is made even stronger in states with professional legislatures.[39] Because a legislature is the principal political institution for converting party conflict into public policy, and because the conversion process should be effective to the degree that the legislature is organizationally capable, it is reasonable to conclude that the linkage between the party and welfare expenditures would be stronger within states with strong effective legislative systems than within those with weak legislative systems. The research indicates that responsiveness rather than independence may be the end result of a professional legislature. This is in accord with those theorists who place a high value on party government and the ability of a party to bring the needs of the people to the decision-making arenas of government.

THE LEGISLATIVE PARTY

A responsible party nominates gubernatorial and legislative candidates who represent a common program commitment. The governor as head of the party proposes legislation to fulfill that program and works to obtain enough voting support for his bills to ensure passage. It is possible to measure the extent to which this happens in various states. A legislator's party-voting loyalty can be determined by analyzing roll-call votes, which are an essential part of reaching decisions on bills. They become public record and are a means of judging party loyalty by those making demands on the legislator.

The party is regarded as the legitimate organizing force in a legislature, whether it is found to be present or absent. Another factor, however, is an individual legislator's reaction to the conflicting demands of party, constituency, or pressure group. Under what circumstances does the legislator heed these respective demands? This section considers both the ability of a legislative party to provide the major voting cues for a legislator and the conditions under which the legislators act according to alternative loyalties.

Party Issues

Policy is our major concern as we examine the behavior of legislators. It is the end point in our diagram of the policy-making process. We have assumed throughout this book that the bills in a governor's program represent the most important issues that legislators are called on to decide. Research on roll-call voting behavior in state legislatures generally confirms this assumption. The political party is the most important cue-giving mechanism for determining how legislators will vote. The degree of partisanship may vary from issue to issue, but, if the political party does not organize the legislature, as in some one-party states, there is no voting cue or structure for voting behavior. Lance T. LeLoup examined voting behavior in Missouri and Ohio on five major issues—social welfare, natural resources, law and justice, state administration, and economic policy—and discovered that the legislators followed party voting lines for all issue areas.[40] Thus it appears that, in all but a handful of legislatures, a political party provides the main basis for voting behavior.

Two points are worth making at this time: First, not all issues are party oriented. In some legislatures, as few as 30 and as many as 90 percent of all roll-call votes are party votes.[41] State constitutions often require a roll call on final passage of every bill. The usual consequence is that a large proportion are either unanimous or nearly unanimous. These issues are not controversial and, therefore, not a measure of party, constituency, or pressure-group strength. The second point is that some unanimous roll calls are the end result of an agonizing process of conflict, negotiation, and compromise. The major issues have been settled in committee or among the party leadership before the bills reach the floor. The vote may then be unanimous because the legislators follow the cues set by their leaders beforehand. By excluding unanimous votes from examination, we are excluding a few of these controversial votes as well. In the last analysis, however, most contested roll-call votes are those that measure the effects we want to measure: the strength of a political party versus the other major contenders for the legislator's vote.

The package of bills a governor presents to the legislature as his policy program is the most important and, hence, the most controversial legislation considered. Those who study which issues are most likely to divide the legislators along party lines usually agree that three categories are most likely to cause conflict: (1) those in the administration's program; (2) social and economic issues that can divide the two parties along liberal-conservative lines and on which major interest groups have taken a stand; and (3) issues involving either the special interest of a state, such as reorganization and administration of state government, or the special interests of legislative parties such as the election of a speaker or adoption of legislative rules.[42] Studies of the bills composing a governor's program have only recently become a subject of research interest. Obviously, a governor's program covers the three categories listed above—elements of them all are included. In the last chapter, we listed the bills in the governor's program for 20 states in 1971. They ranged from environmental and health, education, and welfare legislation to reform of the election laws, civil service, and the judiciary. Certainly, a governor's program contains all the controversial categories. And surely, it is of utmost importance to the governor that his party elect a speaker of the house and president of the senate who are sympathetic to his policies. A majority of the major bills passed in an average session of a state legislature now emanate from the governor's office. As a result, he must devote most of his time and attention to the development and coordination of a legislative program and the strategy needed to secure its support. A governor will be judged by the people of a state not so much by what he proposes but by what he is able to accomplish.

Party Control of the Legislature[43]

The constitutional separation of powers between the executive and legislative branches of government is expected to be softened by the synthesizing effects of a political party. The minimum condition essential for parties to perform their supposed function of meshing the independent organs of government is their ability to capture both executive and legislative branches. Because of the reapportionment revolution in the '60's, this possibility now exists. By 1968, every state had reapportioned one or both houses of its legislature.

Practically speaking, the Republicans have a long way to go before they can hope to gain legislative majorities in the seven solid Democratic states. To do so would be about as noteworthy as if the Democrats gained control in both houses of Vermont, New Hampshire, Kansas, Wyoming, and North Dakota—all Republican legislatures. In ten competitive states, Republican governors can count on one or both houses being controlled by the Democrats. In at least three competitive states, Democratic governors can count on facing Republican majorities. Figure 6–3 indicates how many elections over 12 years resulted in dividing party control between the two branches of government. In 1974 for the first time during this period there was party meshing (under the Democrats) in more states than

FIGURE 6–3

---

*Party Control of State Legislatures and
Governorships, 1966–78[a]*

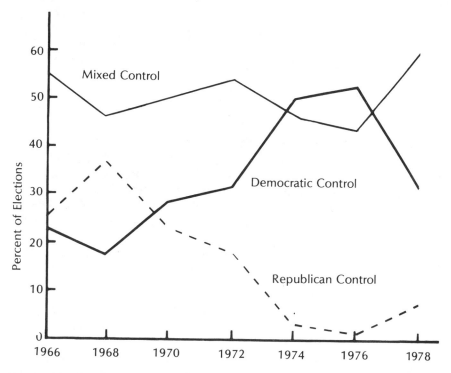

[a]Percent of the elections in 42 states resulting in the governorship and both houses of the legislature in partisan control or mixed control between the governorship and one or both houses.
The seven solid Democratic states mentioned in Table 4–2 were not included nor was Nebraska which has a nonpartisan legislature. Minnesota was not included prior to 1972 because its legislature was nonpartisan.
Source: Data used with permission of the Council of State Governments, *The Book of the States* (Lexington, Ky.: Council of State Governments), appropriate years.

those divided politically between the parties. If the governor's party controls the legislature, success in obtaining the passage of his program legislation will be increased.

Many advantages accrue to a governor who is backed by a majority. The speaker, majority leaders, chairmen, and majorities of committees are all from his party. The speaker of the house and the president pro tem and party leaders of the senate control the membership of committees and the assignment of bills. This gives the governor a control over legislation that he does not have with a minority. It was found that holding a legislative majority and hence the ability to organize procedures is a major contributor to the governor's success in getting his program passed.[44] Veto votes were used to measure gubernatorial influence in 58 house sessions in non-Southern states during the period 1946 to 1960. While a legislative majority can improve the prediction for a governor's success in achieving legislative support, it was also discovered that the percentage of seats a governor's party holds in the legislature can predict the support he will receive. Governors calculate closely and do not dispense more rewards or punishments than necessary to gain support for their projects. Minority-party governors can expect high support from their party members. However, they must also bargain with the opposition for some votes. The governor can handle a modest majority in the legislature. But, when his party has an overwhelming majority, coalitions form against him that he cannot manipulate with his traditional stock of rewards and punishments. The optimum legislative contingent, then, would appear to be a comfortable majority—say about 55 percent—in both houses of the legislature. Figure 6–3 reveals that over half the time governors face legislatures in which they do not have majorities. Prior to 1972, these divided situations were split evenly between Republican and Democratic governors. Until the election of 1974, when the Democratic tide produced 30 governors outside the South, only nine of which faced divided legislatures, the liability of divided control did not fall any heavier on the Republicans than on the Democrats. The strategy of dealing with the opposition to win enough votes to pass legislation is a common phenomenon these days. A governor who is in a strong position within his party can convince both his own party members and, when necessary, some of the majority to support his program.

Party Voting

Table 6–1 provides a summary of the discussion so far based on an examination of the roll-call votes pertaining to the governors' program bills in 20 state legislatures in 1971. The states are categorized according to their

TABLE 6–1

Party Voting in Twenty State Legislative Houses
In 1971: Indices of Support, Opposition, and
Likeness

STATE[a]	INDEX OF SUPPORT[b]	INDEX OF OPPOSITION[c]	INDEX OF LIKENESS[d]
One-Party Democratic			
Arkansas–D	58.8		
Mississippi–D	58.9		
*Tennessee–R	80.7	58.7	60.1
Average	66.1		
Modified One-Party			
New Hampshire–R	58.7	67.9	73.3
North Carolina–D	61.2	70.8	64.4
Wyoming–R	79.2	32.8	81.6
*Nevada–D	82.4	52.4	61.9
*Ohio–D	83.5	62.3	47.3
Average	73.0	57.2	65.7
Two-Party			
*Massachusetts–R	69.1	57.2	69.4
Rhode Island–D	74.9	86.5	30.3
Washington–R	75.2	29.2	73.5
Kentucky–D	77.3	55.2	68.6
Illinois–R	80.0	41.0	62.1
Wisconsin–D	80.4	62.5	47.7
*Montana–D	81.1	36.0	77.1
New York–R	84.0	50.7	55.5
Pennsylvania–D	87.7	65.7	43.9
*West Virginia–R	87.8	48.2	64.0
*California–R	88.7	65.7	34.0
Colorado–R	91.3	78.8	24.6
Average	81.5	56.4	54.2

[a] These are the states discussed in chapter 5 and listed in Table 5–6. The party affiliation of the governor is given. An asterisk indicates that the house contains a majority of the opposite party.

[b] Index of support = $\dfrac{\text{Governor's party votes cast for governor}}{\text{Total party votes}}$

[c] Index of opposition = $\dfrac{\text{Opposition party votes cast against governor}}{\text{Total party votes}}$

[d] Index of likeness: See footnote 45.

degree of two-party competition for governor over a 14-year period: The three indices are calculated to tell us about the support and opposition the governors faced from both parties under different conditions of competition. The index of support indicates how loyal a governor's party was when voting for his program bills. The second index tells us how loyally the opposition party closed ranks against the governor's program. The index of likeness measures the degree to which both parties supported the governor's program.[45] The index varies from zero to 100, with zero representing complete dissimilarity and 100 representing complete similarity in party voting responses. If there is strong party voting—both parties being cohesive—with one supporting and the other opposing the governor's program, the index of likeness is low. If both parties strongly support or oppose the governor's program, the index of likeness is high. The results in Table 6–1 indicate general trends but they do not reveal spectacular consistencies. We can see that the average party support for a governor is more pronounced in competitive states than in one-party or modified states. The average index of support in one-party states is 66; in modified one-party states, be they Democratic or Republican, the average support for the governor is 73; and, in competitive states, is 81.5.

The index of support is low in states that are completely dominated by the Democratic party, indicating that the governor has a difficult time obtaining votes from the members of his legislative contingent. Tennessee provides a variation on this theme because a Republican minority governor was able to obtain significant loyalty from his substantially outnumbered legislative contingent. The Republican loyalty in this session illustrates how a minority party must stick together and bargain with the majority to gain the necessary votes for passing a governor's program. The Democratic party, used to being in the majority, did not show the typical signs of cohesion one might expect of a party that had lost the governorship. Its average cohesion of 58.7 was similar to the other Democratic one-party states of Arkansas and Mississippi. In these three states, where the Democratic party is the overwhelming majority, party is not a source of voting cues. The governor has no dependable, cohesive faction to support his program; nor does he face a cohesive opposition. In his effort to win support for his program, he depends on the resources of his office and his skill in using them. The average index of support shows backing for some of his measures and failure to pass others. He may also anticipate coalitions that oppose his program and propose weak or minimal legislation. Samuel Patterson's study of the Oklahoma house in 1959 provides a good example of the fluidity of voting patterns in a one-party state where party did not provide voting cues. Only the governor's program revealed signs of party loyalty. All other voting patterns showed that the legislators responded to different voting cues as the issue areas differed. Patterson concluded that, in the absence of party as a reference group, a given legislator is likely to be independent in his voting.[46]

Governors in the competitive states must get every party vote they can garner to hold the line against the common enemy. In these states, the governor's party is likely to have a narrow majority. He therefore needs a loyal voting group. Another observation we can pull from the table is the much lower average voting cohesion among members of the governor's opposition party. While the mean index of support for the 20 legislatures is 78, the mean opposition score is 58. This indicates that there is opportunity for the governor's party to bargain for votes, perhaps with various promises of rewards and favors for constituents in the opposing legislator's district. There is also a higher index of likeness in modified one-party states where the governor has trouble obtaining voting support from his own party. This shows that the governor's party leaders have worked to obtain votes from the opposition, thus bringing the two parties into closer agreement. One further observation can be made: The seven states in which the governor's party is a minority in the house illustrate a higher-than-average level of support for the governor. This, again, indicates that the governor must extract every vote he can from his own party before he bargains with the opposition for its votes. American state legislatures have developed an alternative to the parliamentary system in which the executive always has a majority of the legislature. This alternative pattern features high support from the party of the executive whether it be a majority or a minority of the legislature, coupled with low opposition from the other party, rendering it vulnerable to defection.

Table 6–1 may raise more questions than it answers. We have noted general trends, but much more needs to be explained. In general, the competition-cohesion school of thought, which states that parties are more cohesive in two-party states, is confirmed. But the statistical correlation between state-wide competition and party support is only .50. Researchers have mentioned other forces that may affect the ability of the party to garner support. It is possible that competition itself masks other factors that are more plausible explanations for support.

Urban versus Rural States

Malcolm Jewell compared the degree of party loyalty in several competitive states. He discovered, as Table 6–1 indicates, that state-wide competition did not explain all party voting loyalty. He also found no correlation between the party division of legislative seats and voting loyalty. However, the legislatures he studied had a reasonably close party balance which may not have provided enough variation to test. Jewell turned to intraparty cohesion for an explanation. He advanced the proposition that there is more cohesion within parties from urban states because that's where he discovered a higher degree of party loyalty.[47] He concluded that in states with high party voting—the urban industrial states—each of the parties is likely to be relatively homogeneous in its composition. The Democrats draw their electoral strength from the metropolitan centers and particularly from labor groups, racial and ethnic minorities, Catholic voters, and persons with below-average incomes. The Republican vote is in the higher-income sections of the metropolis, the towns and cities, and some of the farm areas. The result of this polarization is that each legislative party is quite homogeneous in constituencies represented by its members. In states with lower levels of urbanization and industrialization and, therefore, few metropolitan centers, both parties are likely to draw a substantial proportion of their support from rural areas. Both parties usually have more diverse constituencies, making legislative party cohesion more difficult to achieve.[48]

Thomas Flinn tested this theory of party unity based on similarity of district in the Ohio Assembly of 1949 and 1959. He concluded, on the other hand, that differing constituencies do *not* give rise to intraparty voting disagreements and that policy differences between the parties are *not* due to differences in the constituency composition. This finding has since been confirmed by several studies.[49] Similarities in degree of constituency urbanization apparently do not form the basis for unity among legislators. Nor is there evidence that such similarities reflect the political recruitment of legislators with similar policy predispositions.[50]

While it is now generally agreed that urban-rural differences among legislators do not form the basis upon which political parties rely for cohesive support, there is undoubtedly some truth to the assertion that partisan differences may reflect broad ideological deviations, which are ultimately grounded in the different recruitment bases of opposing party organizations. These ideological divergencies can be seen as the two parties oppose each other on a wide range of issues. Duane Lockard attributes the cohesion in Connecticut's legislative parties to ideological similarities within each organization—the Democrats are generally liberal and the Republicans are generally conservative.[51] New York, Michigan, and Rhode Island are examples of issue-oriented parties where the Democrats are heavily committed to labor and welfare policies.

When all is said and done, the organizational strength of a state party and its governor as well as the efforts of the legislative party leadership can account for the voting loyalty of the legislators. The state party emerges as a major determinant of policy output. Its organization, then, is of vital importance to the policy-making process.

The Demands of the Legislator's District

There is another side to the story of legislative support. Parties are, after all, made up of legislators who are influenced by the interests of their constituencies as well as the demands for party conformity imposed by state leaders. As we have seen, the initial assumption of researchers who have studied the relationship of a legislator to his district was that the representative voted according to the socioeconomic interests of his constituency and that legislation represented the dominant interests of a majority of districts. This assumption was soon modified when it was seen that legislators from similar constituencies did not vot together as a bloc but were more likely to follow the leadership of their party. Thus it appears that the linkage between the economic interests of a constituency and its legislator's voting behavior is not direct but is modified by the intervening variable of party demands on the legislator.[52]

The degree of competition in a constituency, measured singly or in combination with economic characteristics, has been offered as an additional variable affecting the extremes in legislative voting loyalty. It is assumed that members with comfortable margins are a more-loyal group than those from competitive districts because they are freed from constituency pressures and can vote the party line without fear of voter retribution. On the other hand, legislators running in close races will reflect the interests of their constituencies, regardless of the party line. Thus, the most deviant legislators would be found from competitive, atypical districts.[53] This theory has been disproved, however, by studies made in Pennsylvania and Michigan. One study—of Michigan's legislature—concluded that the degree of interparty competition reflected in district general elections did not seem to affect the liberal-conservative voting behavior of representatives. It also found that the competitiveness or noncompetitiveness in district primary elections had no effect. Another observer, studying Pennsylvania's legislature, found little correlation between district competitiveness in the legislative race and party loyalty.[54]

My study, which examined the conditions under which a legislator would support his governor when pressured to do so, indicated very little correlation between a legislator's district primary or election competition and his support for the governor's legislative requests. Apparently, his response to a governor's demand for obedience is not based on his primary or election concerns. With respect to socioeconomic legislation, the control a governor exerts over his legislators is subject to the following generalizations: The pattern of support for a successful governor does not depend on socioeconomic or electoral variables within the legislators' districts. If the governor cannot control his legislators, the demographic character of the districts provides the major bases for factions to develop. This finding agrees with the studies of pressure-group success in state legislatures. Party is the major cue for a legislator's stand on issues, and lobbyists are independently successful only where the influence of party is weak. Lobbying activity is generally directed at legislators who sympathize with the policy positions of the group or groups involved. If this is consistent with the party's position, the groups achieve their ends. If a party cannot gain the loyalty of its legislators, the lobbyists can reinforce the dormant tendencies of those legislators.

In the Democratic party, a governor receives high support from the legislators in those areas where he has strong party support as measured by his primary vote. Loyal Democratic legislators come from areas of high party strength. In the Republican party, a governor's support cannot be geographically located in this way. Both Republican and Democratic governors are subject to the same generalization: control over their party's nominating organization brings legislative discipline.[55]

The primary vote, a measure of a governor's political leadership, indicates 1) the strength of the coalition the governor has been able to build for himself, or 2) the strength of the coalition that represents the continuing efforts of a party's state leadership. Actual and potential factions exist within the parties, and the governor must compete for the nomination. To do so, he will build a coalition within his party large enough to assure him of an uncontested primary nomination, or at least guarantee victory in the primary election. It would seem logical, therefore, that this faction include members of the legislature who come from areas where the governor has organization support. The legislative party, therefore, is not separated from the electoral party, but is a partner in the policy-making process. If the governor has party backing, he can introduce and get legislation passed that produces a wider distribution of benefits to the needy.

THE GOVERNOR AND THE
LEGISLATURE: PARTNERS OR RIVALS?

In this section we will make another test boring into the relationship between governor and legislature. The last chapter revealed that a governor's political and formal powers gave him command over his legislative party members. This was shown by the support they gave him on his program. This investigation is in the area of redistributive policy—policy that takes benefits from one group and gives them to another. The question is: What political and structural variables affect redistributive policy in the states? Redistribution entails the question of who gets what and who

pays how much for the public goods and services generated by governments. Redistributive policies involve intense conflict over the legitimacy
of the action. The reader is no doubt aware of what the major theme of
this book is: Cohesive parties will redistribute the burdens and benefits of
society to the advantage of the poorer members. Both parties will do this
because their respective leadership must establish a good record for the
next election. A fear of retribution hangs at the polls if they don't benefit
the lower-income classes. They may also fear riots and demonstrations
which would affect their ability to get reelected. We would expect that the
more cohesive a party, the more its governor and legislative leaders can
propose redistributive policies, and the more its legislators will provide
loyal support.

Redistributive policies are at the core of the governing process. The
degree to which the wealthy should be taxed to pay for state services is
a continuing controversy within both parties. A governor who proposes an
income tax fears for his next election. And yet he is pressured by demands
for education, welfare, and health care, which must be paid for by those
who have. Redistributive policies are also at the budgetary process base.
A budget must be passed by the state legislature. Submitted by the governor, it is his statement of the value of his program. The money will allow
him to initiate or continue major activities for the state. Where the money
comes from and to whom it goes is detailed in the budget. At the beginning of this chapter, we saw that oversight of the executive was one of the
main legislative functions. Review of the state budget is the major instrument for accomplishing this goal. Most of the improvements in staffing
committees have been geared toward permitting the legislature to evaluate and make changes in the governor's budget. The final step in increased
budgetary control is the development of legislative-based professional
staffs to generate independent sources of information. Hence, the budget
is becoming a much-amended document as legislatures increase their
ability to evaluate and analyze. Kenneth Boulding catches the essence of
the budget process in the following statement:

> A budget seems to me the prime expression of political decision. It may be
> arrived at, of course, by all sorts of bargaining and horse trading among
> people and organizations who are affected, but the essence of the political
> process in any organization, it seems to me, is to reach a decision on a budget,
> and to make this decision effective. The budget, therefore, is the typical
> institution of politics as the market is of economics, and indeed the politiciza-
> tion of a society can be measured by the extent to which the allocation of its
> resources is determined through budgets rather than through markets.[56]

We are interested in measuring redistributive policies so we can make
a comparison across the 20 states. If we find that states that tax wealth and

income and give generously to the poor have political, structural, or economic characteristics in common, we can assume that these economic and political characteristics give rise to redistribution. This is the purpose of this investigation. Recently, Fry and Winters made a systematic attempt to measure the level of redistribution in state government programs and policies.[57] Their measure has been widely employed and is given as "the ratio of expenditure benefits to revenue burdens for the three lowest income classes in the state." In other words, they found out how much the three lowest income groups paid in taxes and how that compared with what they gained in welfare benefits, schooling, and other services.

The measure of government redistribution used in this investigation is simpler to compute, although not as thoroughgoing and elegant, as the Fry-Winters Ratio. It captures simultaneously the idea of taking from the rich and giving to the poor. This index of redistribution, designed by Richard DeLeon, reflects the ratio between (1) the percentage of tax revenues derived from corporate and personal income taxes and inheritance and gift taxes and (2) the percentage of state welfare spending as a proportion of total expenditures.[58] This gives a crude but plausible index of how much is being taken from the wealthy. The percentage of a state's expenditures going for welfare spending provides an index of how much is being given to the poor. The reasoning behind this index is simple: State governments that *neither* take from the rich *nor* give to the poor are the least redistributive; governments taking from the rich *or* giving to the poor are somewhat redistributive; and governments that give *and* take are most redistributive in their taxation and spending policies.

This investigation proceeds in the same fashion as the first. Redistributive policies of the 20 states with which we have been working are the dependent outcome variables. According to our model of the policy-making process (Figure 1–4), we will consider all of the economic, social, and electoral indicators of the needs and demands of the people in these 20 states as well as the party organization and structural variables we have considered to date. We have discussed measures for gubernatorial party leadership and party support. We have also measured the formal powers of the governor, legislative party strength (in terms of percentage of seats), and the professionalism of the legislature. The needs and demands of the people are filtered through these political and structural processes before they emerge as policy outcomes. Appendix 3 lists these variables and how they are measured. We are interested in the variables that are most helpful in explaining the extent of redistributive policy in each state, and will use multiple-regression analysis to determine them. An explanation of this form of analysis may be found in the chapter 5 test of the governor's ability to command his legislative party support. The results of a multiple-regression analysis give us the effect of each variable on redistributive policy while taking all the others into consideration.

Figure 6–4 shows the following variables to be most highly associated with redistributive policies in these states: gubernatorial party leadership, legislative professionalism, and the strength of a governor's party in the senate. In this case, governor's party leadership represents an average leadership coalition of 15 years duration. It is not the strength of the incumbent governor we are measuring here, but the strength of the governor's ongoing coalition. This traditional leadership coalition within the political party can account for the level of redistribution in a state. Redistributive policies are the product of forces that are continuing in state politics. A test for the association between Republicans or Democrats

FIGURE 6–4

---

*Relationships among the Economy, The
Governor's Party Leadership, Legislative
Professionalism, Party Strength, and
Redistributive Policies*

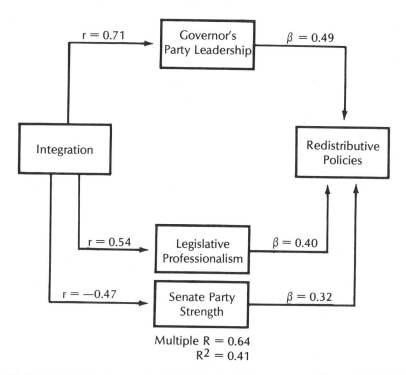

Multiple R = 0.64
R^2 = 0.41

Note: The beta weights (β) shown in the figure indicate the relative contribution of each independent variable to variation in the dependent variable (redistributive policies). The figure shows the governor's party leadership to be the most important explanatory variable in the 20 state legislatures. See Appendix 3 for measures of these variables.

and redistribution policies showed no apparent correlation. Evidently, both parties take similar stands on redistribution of wealth, but the success either party has depends on the continuing strength of a leadership coalition in the party. This is what we have been saying all along—it takes leadership on a continuing basis to provide programs for the poor.

The degree of professionalism in a legislature is also positively associated with the redistributive policies in the states. Apparently, a "reformed" legislature is able to be more receptive to the needs and demands of the people. This does not make it a rival of the governor but does make it better able to be a partner in the policy-making process. The governor and legislators, collectively, represent the same needs. With more staff assistance, better pay, and longer sessions in which to accomplish their programs, legislators can better serve the people of their state. The goal of reformers is to make the legislature independent of the executive. The major outcome of the reformed legislature is to make it better able to serve the constituents. Both strong party leadership and legislative professionalism are associated with states that have integrated cultures. States with wealth, education, urban areas, and professional talent are likely to have cohesive parties and professional legislatures.

It takes a degree of head scratching to account for the influence average senate party strength has on redistribution. This measure of the average percent of senate seats held by the governor's party indicates that the percent of seats a governor can control in his or her legislature will affect the degree of legislative support he can muster. Indeed, the percent of senate seats does correlate highly with the success a governor has in obtaining enough votes from his party members to pass legislation. Redistributive policies, then, are associated with states that have continuing leadership coalitions and professional legislatures. The influence of wealth and education is not direct but is filtered through the political process. A leadership coalition and a professional legislature make it possible for the leaders to propose, and see passed, measures that will serve the needs of the have-nots in a state.

CONCLUSIONS

This chapter has considered the legislative process from two perspectives. It examined the influence of the constituency on the legislator and his or her perception of himself or herself as a trustee or a delegate. The main conclusions were that the more a legislator sees his party as a means for advancement, the more likely it is the person will be a trustee, or one who tends to view state needs as more important than those of the district. We did not discover any correlation between competition in a district and the loyalty with which a legislator supports his or her party's program. Nor was there any reason to think that legislative voting loyalty is based on the degree to which a district conforms to the party mainstream. Perhaps a few deviant legislators can be found among those whose districts are most unrepresentative of the party's programs. Differing social and economic conditions and the conflicting demands of pressure groups can pull legislators away from their party's policy stands. The political leadership may allow some deviation when a legislator pleads hardship and begs to vote the interests of his or her district, perhaps in trade for a later loyal vote.

By all odds, the most important voting cue for a legislator is his or her political party. The leaders propose programs and expect voting compliance. Even in one-party states, there is more cohesion on the governor's program than on other issues. Every state governor proposes a program and budget that are subject to the legislative process. The success of a governor's program depends on the degree to which legislative leaders can garner support for the governor's policies. Where the governor has a strong coalition in the electoral party, he or she is better able to convince the legislators to support him or her. The governor can extract loyalty by promises of rewards or deprivation. The pressure groups deal with the party's leadership. If a governor's coalition has control over his or her party, the legislator knows that the governor can make good on promises. A governor's coalition may be part of an ongoing coalition in the electoral party. I found that the strength of a governor's coalition measured over a 15 year period was a major explanation for redistributive policies in the states.

In reformed legislatures where the legislators are better paid and better staffed, output of the policy-making process appears to be more responsive to the lower-income classes. We do not know whether this is because legislators have more assurance that their efforts are appreciated, that they represent a more qualified group because of more attractive rewards, or simply that they have the proper tools that give them competency to examine and respond to the proposals of an executive. Political party is the solvent for separation of powers between the legislative and executive branches of government. The closer legislators and governor are, as part of the same governing coalition, the better able a political party will be to propose and pass programs that represent a majority of the people.

NOTES

1. The Citizens Conference on State Legislatures, *State Legislatures: An Evaluation of Their Effectiveness* (New York: Praeger, 1971).

2. *Pennsylvania Legislative Journal-House,* 31 March 1971, p. 358.
3. Harold A. Katz, "The Illinois Experience in Legislative Modernization," in Donald Herzberg, *Strengthening the States: Essays on Legislative Reform* (Garden City, N.J.: Doubleday, 1971), p. 224.
4. Samuel C. Patterson, John C. Wahlke, and G. Robert Boynton, "Dimensions of Support in Legislative Systems," chapter 12 in Allen Kornberg and Lloyd A. Musolf, eds., *Legislatures in Comparative Perspective* (New York: McKay, 1973), pp. 282–313; Samuel C. Patterson and George R. Boynton, *Citizens, Leaders and Legislators: Perspectives on Support for the American Legislature* (Beverly Hills, Calif.: Sage Publications, 1974); George R. Boynton, Samuel C. Patterson, and Ronald D. Hedlund, "The Missing Links in Legislative Politics: Attentive Constituents," *The Journal of Politics* 31 (August 1969): 700–21.
5. Robert G. Dixon, Jr., *Democratic Representation: Reapportionment in Law and Politics* (New York: Oxford University Press, 1968), pp. 589–628.
6. Robert S. Erikson, "The Partisan Impact of State Legislative Reapportionment," *Midwest Journal of Political Science* 15 (February 1971): 70.
7. H. George Frederickson and Yong Hyo Cho, "Legislative Apportionment and Fiscal Policy in the American States," *Western Political Quarterly* 27 (March 1974): 5–37.
8. Richard Lehne, *Reapportionment of the New York Legislature: Impact and Issues* (New York: National Municipal League, 1972), pp. 49–52.
9. Lester G. Seligman et al., *Patterns of Recruitment* (Chicago, Ill.: Rand McNally, 1974), p. 6.
10. V. O. Key, Jr., *American State Politics,* pp. 169–96.
11. Frank J. Sorauf, *Party and Representation* (New York: Atherton Press, Prentice-Hall, 1963), pp. 107–20.
12. Richard J. Tobin, "Influence of Nominating Systems on the Political Experiences of State Legislators, *Western Political Quarterly* 28 (September 1975): 553–66.
13. Sarah McCally (Morehouse), *The Effects of Competition Upon The Structure and Function of State Political Parties* (Ph.D. dissertation, Department of Political Science, Yale University, 1964).
14. Malcolm E. Jewell, *Legislative Representation in the Contemporary South* (Durham, N.C.: Duke University Press, 1967), pp. 12–18.
15. Key, *American State Politics,* pp. 175–78.
16. Richard J. Tobin and Edward Keynes, "Institutional Differences in the Recruitment Process: A Four-State Study," *American Journal of Political Science* 19 (November 1975): 678–79.
17. Jewell, *Legislative Representation,* chapter 4.
18. David Ray, "Voluntary Retirement and Electoral Defeat in Eight State Legislatures," *Journal of Politics* 38 (May 1976): 426–33.
19. Alan Rosenthal, "Turnover in State Legislatures," *American Journal of Political Science* 18 (August 1974): 609–16.
20. John C. Wahlke, Heinz Eulau, William Buchanan, and Leroy C. Ferguson, *The Legislative System* (New York: Wiley, 1962), chapters 12 and 13.
21. Ibid., p. 281.
22. Malcolm E. Jewell and Samuel C. Patterson, *The Legislative Process in the United States,* 2d ed. (New York: Random House, 1973), p. 421.

23. Sorauf, *Party and Representation.*
24. Ronald D. Hedlund and H. Paul Friesma, "Representatives' Perceptions of Constituency Opinion," *Journal of Politics* (August 1972): 730–52.
25. Robert S. Erikson, Norman R. Luttbeg, and William U. Holloway, "Knowing One's District: How Legislators Predict Referendum Voting," *American Journal of Political Science* 19 (May 1975): 231–46.
26. John W. Soule, "Future Political Ambitions and the Behavior of Incumbent State Legislators," *Midwest Journal of Political Science* 13 (August 1969): 450.
27. Ohio Legislative Service Commission, *A Guidebook for Ohio Legislators* (Columbus, Ohio: 1970), p. iii.
28. Eugene W. Jones et al., *Practicing Texas Politics,* 3d ed. (Boston: Houghton Mifflin, 1977), pp. 274–77.
29. Richard Reeves, "The Other Half of State Government," *New York Times Magazine,* 2 April 1967, p. 86, quoted in Alan G. Hevesi, *Legislative Politics in New York State* (New York: Praeger, 1975), p. 10.
30. Alex B. Lacy, Jr., ed., *Power in American State Legislatures,* Tulane Studies in Political Science, Vol. XI (New Orleans, 1967), pp. 43–44.
31. Charles W. Wiggins, *The Legislative Process in Iowa* (Ames: Iowa State University Press, 1972), pp. 5–6.
32. Malcolm E. Jewell, *The State Legislature: Politics and Practice,* 2d ed. (New York: Random House, 1969), pp. 46-47.
33. *Ohio House Journal,* Vol. 134, Part I (1971–1972), pp. 72–75; and *Ohio Senate Journal,* Vol. 134 (1971–1972), pp. 96–97.
34. David B. Ogle, *Strengthening the Mississippi Legislature: An Eagleton Study and Report* (New Brunswick, N.J.: Rutgers University Press, 1971), p. 41.
35. Several items in this summary are drawn from Jesse Unruh and Donald G. Herzberg, "Legislative Reform: An Overview," chapter 10 in Herzberg and Unruh, *Essays on the State Legislative Process* (New York: Holt, Rinehart and Winston, 1970), pp. 105–106.
36. Alan Rosenthal, *Legislative Performance in the States* (New York: Free Press, 1974), p. 109.
37. Albert B. Roberts, "American State Legislatures: The Staff Environment," *Public Administration Review* 35 (September/October 1975): pp. 501–504.
38. John G. Grumm, "The Effects of Legislative Structure on Legislative Performance," in Richard Hofferbert and Ira Sharkansky, eds., *State and Urban Politics* (Boston: Little, Brown, 1971), pp. 298–322. See Appendix 4 for the variables considered in my updated version of Grumm's index and Appendix 8 for the state scores.
39. Edward G. Carmines, "The Mediating Influence of State Legislatures on the Linkage Between Interparty Competition and Welfare Policies," *American Political Science Review* 68 (September 1974): 1118–24.
40. Lance T. LeLoup, "Policy, Party, and Voting in U.S. State Legislatures: A Test of the Content-Process Linkage," *Legislative Studies Quarterly* 1 (May 1976): 213–30.
41. Malcolm E. Jewell and Samuel Patterson, *The Legislative Process in the United States,* 2d ed. (New York: Random House, 1973), pp. 445–46.
42. There are three studies from which this discussion was drawn: Malcolm E. Jewell, "Party Voting in American State Legislatures," *American Political*

Science Review, 49 (September, 1955): 773–791; Wayne L. Francis, *Legislative Issues in the Fifty States: A Comparative Analysis,* American Politics Research Series (Chicago, Ill.: Rand McNally, 1967); and Hugh L. LeBlanc, "Voting in State Senates: Party and Constituency Influences," *Midwest Journal of Political Science* 13 (February 1969): 33–57.

43. Portions of this chapter appeared in slightly different form in "The Governor as Political Leader" by Sarah Morehouse in Herbert Jacob and Kenneth N. Vines, eds., *Politics in The American States: A Comparative Analysis,* Third Edition, copyright © 1976, by Little Brown and Company Inc. and are reprinted by permission.

44. Sarah McCally (Morehouse), "The Governor and His Legislative Party," *American Political Science Review* 60 (December 1966): pp. 933–41; Francis, *Legislative Issues in the Fifty States,* p. 35.

45. Lee F. Anderson; Meredith W. Watts; Jr.; and Allen R. Wilcox, *Legislative Roll-Call Analysis* (Evanston, Ill.: Northwestern University Press, 1966), p. 44. The Index of Likeness is obtained by calculating the percentage of members of each party that voted in favor of the administration bill, subtracting the smaller percentage from the larger, and subtracting the resulting remainder from 100.

46. Samuel C. Patterson, "Dimensions of Voting Behavior in a One-Party State Legislature," *Public Opinion Quarterly* 26 (Spring 1962): 185–200.

47. Malcolm E. Jewell, "Party Voting in American State Legislatures." Jewell chose eight competitive states and limited his research to sessions in which the party balance in the legislature was reasonably close, for he assumed that there would be less party voting even in strong two-party states during the years of one-sided legislative control. He discovered, however, that the three states with the highest levels of party loyalty had long records of Republican legislative control, with only a few Democratic years, while the Democrats frequently held large legislative minorities and (except in Pennsylvania) won control of the governorship. In the states with a closer balance between the parties in the legislature, a lower level of party unity was found. He used all the roll call votes in a session and paid no attention to their sponsorship.

48. Duncan MacRae, "The Relationship Between Roll Call Votes and Constituencies in Massachusetts," *American Political Science Review* 46 (December 1952): 1046–55. MacRae maintained that those legislators who come from districts that are most typical of their parties tend to show highest party loyalty on roll calls. Those who come from districts atypical of their party tend to cross party lines more often. We do not know whether the roll calls selected by MacRae were administration-supported measures or whether deviations were sizable enough to prevent passage. Thomas R. Dye, "A Comparison of Constituency Influences in the Upper and Lower Chambers of a State Legislature," *Western Political Quarterly* 14 (June 1961): 473–81. Dye used all party opposition votes whether or not the issues were economic. He measured voting deviation. Bruce W. Robeck, "Legislative Partisanship, Constituency and Malapportionment: The Case of California," *American Political Science Review* 66 (December 1972): 1246–55. This study of the California Senate from 1957 to 1969 showed that the correlation between party loyalty and constituency characteristics increased sharply after reapportionment, which drastically increased urban representation. Robeck believes this was because the constit-

uencies within each party became more alike, and hence the difference between the parties increased.

49. Thomas A. Flinn, "Party Responsibility in the States: Some Causal Factors," *American Political Science Review* 58 (March 1964): 60–71; David R. Derge, "Metropolitan and Outstate Alignments in Illinois and Missouri Legislative Delegations," *American Political Science Review* 52 (December 1958): 1051–65.

50. Glen T. Broach, "A Comparative Dimensional Analysis of Partisan and Urban-Rural Voting in State Legislatures," *Journal of Politics* 34 (August 1972): 905–21.

51. Duane Lockard, *New England State Politics* (Princeton: Princeton University, Press, 1959), pp. 291–92. In the then essentially non-competitive states of New Hampshire, Maine, and Vermont, policy making was primarily a function of the dominant party in the legislature. The factions within this party, both inside and outside the legislature, determined the fate of legislation. In the competitive states of Massachusetts, Connecticut, and Rhode Island, Lockard discovered considerable discipline in both legislative parties. He used votes on which there was disagreement between the parties.

52. Hugh L. LeBlanc, "Voting in States Senates: Party and Constituency Influences," LeBlanc accepted for analysis all roll call votes of the session in which at least 10 percent of those voting dissented from the majority position. A second more rigorous test extracted only those roll calls in which party majorities stood in opposition to one another. Sorauf, *Party and Representation*, 141–44. Most writers used all party opposition votes, whether or not the issues were economic.

53. MacRae, "The Relationship Between Roll Call Votes," pp. 1046–55; Dye, "A Comparison of Constituency Influences," p. 477; Flinn, "Party Responsibility in the States," p. 67; Samuel C. Patterson, "The Role of the Deviant in the State Legislative System: The Wisconsin Assembly," *The Western Political Quarterly* 14 (June 1961): 460–72.

54. Robert W. Becker, Frieda L. Foote, Mathias Lubega, and Stephen V. Mosma, "Correlates of Legislative Voting: Michigan House of Representatives, 1954–1961," *Midwest Journal of Political Science* 6 (November 1962): 384–96. The number of members from districts classified as close was so small as to make the finding doubtful. With respect to primary competition, the hypothesis that a member would support the state party position if he won in a close primary is open to question. He would probably support the ideological position of the wing of the party from which he received help. This might not be the governor's position. Sorauf, *Party and Representation*, p. 141. Sorauf discovered a correlation between the results of the gubernatorial race in a legislative district and party loyalty. This may indicate a degree of state party organization and support in the district that does influence the behavior of a legislator.

55. Sarah McCally Morehouse, "The State Political Party and the Policy-Making Process," *The American Political Science Review* 67 (March 1973): 55–72.

56. Kenneth Boulding, *The Parameters of Politics* (Urbana, Ill.: University of Illinois Press, 1966), p. 10.

57. Brian R. Fry and Richard F. Winters, "The Politics of Redistribution," *Ameri-*

can *Political Science Review* 62 (June 1970): 508–22. For a comment on the
selection of variables, see John L. Sullivan, "A Note on Redistributive Politics,"
American Political Science Review 66 (December 1972): 1031–35.

58. This is a revision of his redistribution measure used in his article: Richard E.
DeLeon, "Politics, Economic Surplus and Redistribution in the American
States: A Test of a Theory," *American Journal of Political Science* (November
1973): 781–96. Assuming approximately equal means and variances for tax
revenues and welfare expenditures, the Redistribution Index is defined as RI=
$\sqrt{T^2 + S^2}$ where T = % Taxes and S = % Welfare expenditures.

CHAPTER SEVEN

THE "LEAST DANGEROUS" BRANCH

W. BRADLEY MOREHOUSE

The Preamble to the federal Constitution lists five fundamental purposes designed to be advanced by that great document. Among them is "to establish justice." Although justice is a concern of every branch of every American government, it is the peculiar preoccupation of the courts. In part because our perception of the courts is influenced by *national* media, and in part because the issues dealt with by the federal courts (and particularly the Supreme Court of the United States) in the last generation have often been of transcendent political, social, and economic importance (such as civil liberties, amelioration of the bitter fruits of slavery, women's rights, and Watergate), policial science has often regarded state courts as judicial stepchildren. But in the number and variety of the cases they decide and the immediate impact of those decisions on the parties involved, the state courts play a far more important role in the administration of justice than one would infer from their relative obscurity in terms of both popular interest and scholarly research. Few of the readers of this chapter will ever find themselves in a federal court (although all, of course, will be touched by federal decisions), whereas many (and probably most) will at some time or other find themselves in a state court, if only to answer a traffic summons or probate a will.

The Nature of Law

The word "law" is an embracing concept, at once something more and something less than ethics. It has been defined as "The whole body or system of rules of conduct, including both decisions of courts and legislative acts."[1] Justice Oliver Wendell Holmes observed in a celebrated article, "The prophecies of what the courts will do in fact, and nothing more pretentious, are what I mean by the law."[2] As society becomes more complex, as the role of government enlarges, and as population density increases, there is greater reliance upon law to impose rules of conduct that either were unnecessary or seemed unnecessary in simpler societies.

Constitutional Law

Our legal system comprises various types of law. Constitutional law stands at the pinnacle of the American judicial system. By its terms, the federal Constitution is supreme in the limited areas it covers, and all statutes, federal and state, that are repugnant to the Constitution must necessarily fall. Each state also has a constitution, in most cases a more detailed document than the federal Constitution. In general, constitutions, and particularly the United States Constitution, paint with a broad brush, dealing in noble concepts like "due process" or elastic phrases like "interstate commerce." It is for the legislatures and the courts to fill the gaps between the broad constitutional principles and to pronounce the law in the large areas on which constitutions are silent.

Common Law

One great division in our law is that between common law and statute law. In general, common law can be said to be judge-made law—law as it has evolved from actual cases—whereas statute law is legislative law. Historically, the first has been of greater significance in Anglo-American law, although the field of statute law is gradually broadening and any inconsistency between common law and statute law is resolved in favor of the latter.

Common law developed in England over the three to four centuries following the Norman Conquest in 1066. Chancellor Kent, an eminent American legal scholar, describes common law as: "Those principles, usages, and rules of action applicable to the government and security of persons and of property, which do not rest for their authority upon any express and positive declaration of the will of the legislature."[3] Our forefathers brought the common law to America as their judicial heritage, and it still flourishes throughout the United States, although the law of Louisiana is heavily influenced by Roman law through the Code Napoleon. Despite a common origin, changing conditions and divergent practices have created differences in the common law among the various states. The Seventh Amendment to the United State Constitution refers to the "rules of the common law." This reference is not to the common law of any individual state but to the common law of England (as it existed when we became an independent nation), a common law that comprehended (in addition to court decisions) such fundamental instruments as Magna Carta, the Petition of Right and the 1689 Bill of Rights, and such basic principles as the adversary system of criminal justice and trial by jury. In general, however, there is no federal common law. The early Supreme Court case of *Swift v. Tyson*, 16 Peters 1 (1842), empowered federal courts to determine common law independent of the states in which they sat. But this result was overturned in *Erie Railroad v. Tompkins,* 304 U.S. 64 (1937), and federal courts now apply the common law of the states in which they sit. In a celebrated book, Justice Holmes observed:

> The life of the law has not been logic; it has been experience. The felt necessities of the time, the prevalent moral and political theories, intuitions of public policy, avowed or unconscious, even the prejudices which judges share with their fellow-men, have had a good deal more to do than the syllogism in determining the rules by which men should be governed.[4]

Equity

In ordinary English usage, the word *equity* means natural justice or fairness. In legal history, equity is a system of justice ancillary to the common law, one developed because of certain weaknesses in the common law. For centuries it was administered by different courts (sometimes called chancery courts), but the courts of most American states now administer both law and equity, depending on the nature of the matter before them. The only states still having separate courts of equity are Arkansas, Delaware, Mississippi, and Tennessee.

The expression "there ought to be a law," is common. In many such cases, equity fills the breach, relying on "natural law" or essential fairness rather than precedent or statute. Perhaps the most familiar application of equity is injunctions. At common law, one who had wronged another could be made to respond in money damages, but he could not be forbidden or required to act (other than to pay the damages assessed). There are many wrongs for which money is not adequate compensation. My neighbor, for instance, may threaten to put an electrified fence between our properties. At common law, I could be compensated in money for the damages resulting from the fence, but I may not want the fence under *any* circumstances. If the fence is up, I can seek a mandatory injunction to compel its removal. If the building of the fence is merely threatened, I can seek a prohibitory injunction to prevent its erection. Both actions are those in equity although increasingly in modern law I would seek them from a single court administering both law and equity.

Statutes

Statutes are of course *legislative* enactments or acts. Within their scope, they supersede the common law. Even at their most comprehensive, however, they still cannot foresee and hence cover all varieties of conduct, and they often, indeed usually, include terms or phrases that are drawn from the common law. As a result, statutes have to be fleshed out, interpreted, and applied by common law precedents and principles.

It is true that codes and statutes do not render the judge superfluous, nor his work perfunctory and mechanical. There are gaps to be filled. There are doubts and ambiguities to be cleared. . . . We reach the land of mystery where constitution and statute are silent, and the judge must look to the common law for the rule that fits the case.[5]

Civil and Criminal Law

Another fundamental cleavage is between civil and criminal law. (The term "civil law" has another meaning, the law derived or developed from Roman law. Civil law in this sense can be said to be the law of Continental Europe and countries that trace their legal heritage to the Continent.) In Anglo-American jurisprudence, the phrase is used to cover the great body of rules of conduct, whether made by the courts or the legislature, relating to activities that are not covered by criminal law. Among the most significant areas of civil law would be contract law (dealing with agreements between persons or corporations), tort law (dealing with civil wrongs such as injuries resulting from an automobile collision), domestic law (dealing with relations between husband and wife and parent and child although the phrase is also used to distinguish international law from the laws applicable within a nation), and laws regarding wills, trusts, and the administration of estates.

All states have codified criminal law so that common law crimes no longer have a place in modern jurisprudence. Criminal law consists of legislative declarations (codes or acts) that prohibit specified conduct and can lead to fines, imprisonment, or even death for transgressors.

Civil law generally covers disputes between individuals (or businesses), whereas criminal law is invariably prosecuted by the government. The same action, however, can constitute both a crime and a tort. For instance, if I am mugged, the state can prosecute my assailant for assault at the time that I can bring an action against him for damages based on my expenses, pain and suffering and any permanent disability. (Unfortunately, the practical benefit of my right is limited by the ability of the defendant to pay a judgment.)

Distinctions Between State and Federal Law

The great bulk of law is administered by the state courts. This is especially true of criminal law, although there are certain interstate transactions defined by Congress as crimes. Federal courts play a significant role in the field of bankruptcy, and the Constitution gives federal courts concurrent jurisdiction with state courts over controversies concerning citizens of different states (where the amount involved is substantial). This jurisdiction is under increasing attack since it is no longer likely, for instance, that a Virginian would experience discrimination in a Massachusetts court, and vice versa. The federal and state courts exist side by side. There is no general right of cross appeal although state supreme court decisions can be appealed to the United States Supreme Court if a substantial federal question or a claimed violation of the federal Constitution is involved. Only a few such cases are heard annually, the Supreme Court rejecting most applications for review (called certiorari).

THE ORGANIZATION OF STATE COURTS

Although the judicial systems of no two of the fifty states are identical, all have at least one tier of trial courts of record* with general jurisdiction, an appellate court, usually called the supreme court, and various courts of specialized jurisdiction, such as probate matters, family relations, traffic infractions, and small claims. Almost half the states have both intermediate court of appeals and a supreme court. Many states also have two branches of general trial courts, one for comparatively minor matters and another for cases of larger consequence (often with the amount in controversy determining the courts jurisdiction). Figure 7–1 shows the relationships among various state courts.

Until recent years, most state court systems showed a tendency to become more complicated as new conditions, values, and interests spawned specialized courts. An example is traffic courts, developed because of the pervasiveness of the automobile and the fact that a high percentage of quasicriminal cases involve automobile offenses. Another example would be youth courts, a result of broadened public acceptance of the proposition that youthful offenders should be guided rather than punished and should be insulated from the main stream of the criminal law and the adult prison system. As with other organs of government, each court developed its own constituency with the result that there were entrenched obstacles to change. Recent years have seen a trend to simplification in a quest for efficiency. It is now thought that the consolidation of minor courts will permit the more effective use of judges, other court personnel, and courtrooms and reduce the backlog of cases which, in urban areas particularly, results in long delays (sometimes of three or four years) in the trial of an ordinary civil law suit. (The constitutional requirement of a speedy criminal trial militates against any comparable delays in the criminal law field, but the rising incidence of crime and the prece-

*A court of record is one in which a transcript of the proceedings is kept. Customarily, minor courts (such as traffic courts, small claims courts, and justice of the peace courts) are *not* courts of record.

FIGURE 7–1

State Court Organization

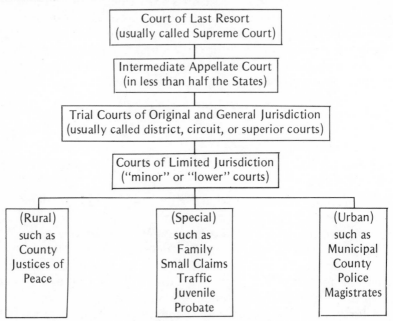

Source: Advisory Commission on Intergovernmental Relations, *State-Local Relations in the Criminal Justice System* (Washington, G.P.O.: August, 1971) p. 88.

dence given to criminal trials further delays the civil trial docket.) Although law is becoming increasingly specialized and requires judges of comparable sophistication, court reformers feel that one can have specialized judges within the same court system and that this is preferable to creating independent courts of limited jurisdiction.

SELECTION OF JUDGES

The early colonization of America coincided with the struggle in the Mother Country between Parliament and the Stuart kings, James I and Charles I. Bound up with this struggle was the attempt by the king to control the courts, an attempt that failed when the judiciary under Sir Edward Coke successfully asserted its independence. By the time of the Revolution, the independence of the judiciary from the executive or legislative branches of government was firmly entrenched in Anglo-American law and practice. In Colonial America, both governors and judges were generally appointed by the Crown. Accordingly, the revolutionary and postrevolutionary years saw a growth of legislative power at the expense of executive and judicial power. Despite this, none of the constitutions of the 13 original states provided for the popular election of judges. Consistent with the fact that the local assemblies had been the champions of the colonial cause prior to the Revolution (and the consequent beneficiaries of revolutionary success), eight of the original state constitutions provided that judges be elected by the legislature. In the remaining five constitutions, judges were appointed by the governors, but several provided that the *governor* be appointed by the legislature, so that the latter's influence was paramount.

Vermont, admitted to the Union in 1791 but under a 1777 constitution, was the first state to provide for the popular election of at least some judges, and Vermont's example was followed by Ohio, Georgia, Indiana, Mississippi, and Michigan. By the time of the Civil War, a majority of states provided that most or all judges be popularly elected for specific terms (in contrast with appointment for an indefinite period on good behavior). Following the Civil War and well into this century, the partisan election of judges—which had been viewed as a democratic reform—fell into disfavor, and the bulk of the states that joined the Union in the post-Civil War period did so under constitutions that provided for nonpartisan election.

At present, there are five principal means by which judges are chosen.

Under the partisan election form, judges run under party labels, and formal participation by political parties plays a significant role. Even in states using the partisan election method, however, interim appointments play a significant role. It is common for a judge to retire or resign before his term of office is up, permitting (often by prearrangement) the governor to fill the vacancy for the unexpired term. The incumbent then enters the partisan race already wearing the judicial robe, and judicial incumbents have a high success rate in elections, both because many judicial races are not contested and because the layman is handicapped in campaigning against a judge. Furthermore, a judge, unlike a governor, is seldom called on to make decisions that alienate large groups of voters.

Even in nonpartisan elections, party influence is often present. In general, judges are chosen (no matter what the formal method of election or selection) from among lawyers who have been actively engaged in politics and who enter the judiciary with a recognized, partisan political background.

The third method is through election by the legislature. In the fourth, judges are appointed by the governor (sometimes, as in the federal system, with the "advice and consent" of the legislature). The fifth plan is sometimes called the Missouri plan, having been adopted by that state in 1940. Under the Missouri plan, the governor selects the judge from among a panel nominated by a blue-ribbon commission. The plan requires electoral confirmation via popular referendum after one-year's service, with the judge running unopposed on his record. In practice, because of the image of a judge as a figure of authority and respect and because you "can't beat somebody with nobody," there is seldom any significant opposition, so that in practice the initial appointment confers tenure.

Although a number of studies have attempted to determine whether different systems lead to judges with different characteristics, the evidence is not compelling. The systems appear to exhibit some differences in the persons chosen but the differences are not pronounced.[6] Some studies of our appellate courts suggest that Republican judges differ from Democratic judges, the former displaying a somewhat greater sympathy for business and a greater distrust of government regulation. This comes as no surprise since many judges run under party labels and presumably share to some degree their party's philosophy, despite the fact that both major American parties embrace a wide spectrum of political views.[7] At least some differences that might appear to be due to differing selection processes are probably due to geography. For instance, most southern states have partisan elections so that generalizations about the sort of judge thrown up by partisan elections are likely to be misleading.[8]

Although frequent reform movements develop that are designed "to take the courts out of politics," usually by moving from a partisan election to a nonpartisan election or from an election to the Missouri plan, we know of no study that clearly shows the superiority of any one system so far as the ultimate product, the judge, is concerned. At most one can probably say that the Missouri plan permits a broader range of choice by including nominees who, by temperament, background, or the character of their law practice, would not choose to expose themselves to the give-and-take of a normal election. And yet that give-and-take helps create (or perhaps suggests) a sensitivity or empathy which is a valuable judicial quality, particularly at the trial-court level. See Appendix 5 for a breakdown by state of the selection process.

HOW COURTS OPERATE

One attribute that distinguishes courts from the executive and legislative branches of government is that they cannot initiate but must instead react. That is, they cannot decide a case until it is brought to them by a party with "standing," or the right to raise the point. They do not decide abstractions but only real contests, although some states permit the governor to call on its supreme court judges for an opinion on pending matters.

Typically, a civil case is started by the preparation of a complaint by the plaintiff's lawyer. The complaint is served on the defendant by a sheriff and returned to court, at which time the case is docketed. The defendant must then plead (respond in writing to the complaint). He may do so by admitting the facts in the complaint, but denying their legal sufficiency to state a cause of action. He may attack the court's jurisdiction over either the subject matter or himself as a party. He may attack the plaintiff's right to bring the action. He may move that the plaintiff amend his complaint by clarifying its allegations or claims for relief, or he may move to strike some of those allegations or claims as being improper. Ultimately, unless the case is disposed of on a jurisdictional basis—a successful attack on the court's jurisdiction, that is—is settled, or dies a natural death—because not pressed for one reason or another—the defendant must answer the complaint (or risk being defaulted) by admitting or denying its allegations and, at this point, the pleadings are "closed" and the case can be claimed for trial, either to the judge or a jury.

In an effort to lessen surprise, eliminate inconsequential or admitted matters from contest, and generally narrow and clarify the issues, parties under modern rules can smoke out their opponents' position by a variety of devices, among them interrogatories (questions the other party must answer under oath), discovery (requiring the other party to produce certain papers for review by the moving party), and deposition (under which the testimony of a party or witness is taken before a court stenographer, partly for trial preparation purposes and partly to nail the witness down).

Many courts require a pretrial conference among the parties' counsel and a judge, partly again to simplify the issues but also for settlement purposes. Litigation, particularly with long delays and numerous motions, is very expensive so a tolerable settlement is often preferable to an ultimate victory (and of course a settlement eliminates the element of doubt present in virtually every case). Most cases are settled, whether through preliminary negotiations between the parties, in the course of or as a result of the pretrial conference, or at some stage during or immediately preceding the trial.

At common law, the petty trial jury consisted of twelve persons with a unanimous decision required. In an effort to streamline procedure and reduce expenses, some states now permit juries as small as six and permit verdicts without unanimity—but never by a bare majority.[9]

Choosing a jury is often a time-consuming matter, particularly before judges who permit detailed and protracted questioning of each prospective juryman (the so-called voir dire). Ideally, each side wishes to have a jury preconditioned to its views. At the least, parties wish to preclude jury persons who, through background or interest, might be thought to sympathize with the adversary. Each side may have a prospective juror excused "for cause" (usually some connection with one of the parties or a response that suggests bias). In addition, each side is given a number of peremptory challenges under which it may have a prospective juror excused *without* showing any reason, the real reason being the gut reaction of an experienced advocate. The number of peremptory challenges in criminal cases is usually related to the gravity of the charge.

In a jury trial, the jury is the judge of the facts, although the judge instructs them on the law, and reaches the verdict, which the judge will accept unless it is so manifestly unjust or incorrect as to permit him to disregard it, in which event a new trial must be held unless the case is settled. In a court trial (before a judge), the judge both finds the facts and renders the judgment.

In civil actions, the plaintiff must prevail by a fair preponderance of evidence. In criminal cases, on the other hand, the state, that is the prosecution, must meet a stricter burden of proof because the accused can be convicted only if his guilt is determined "beyond a reasonable doubt." Moreover, the accused cannot be required to testify nor can his failure to testify be commented on adversely by the prosecutor or the court.

Just as most civil cases are settled short of trial, so most criminal cases are also disposed of without trial, via a process known as "plea bargaining." This is necessary because the courts lack the means physically to try more than a small fraction of the criminal cases brought before them every year. In practice it means that the prosecuting attorney negotiates with defense counsel to obtain a guilty plea, usually to a reduced charge and with the expectation, although without an actual commitment, of lenity in sentencing. As a result of this process, some persons plead guilty to crimes they did not commit, fearing the vagaries of justice and recognizing that their punishment is likely to be more severe if they insist on a trial and the result is adverse. To a much greater extent, persons accused (and guilty) of serious crimes are permitted to plead guilty to less-serious offenses and in many cases escape a punishment commensurate with their desserts. Although plea bargaining is a necessary evil and probably will continue to be widely used, it is disturbing in that the innocent are sometimes persuaded to plead guilty and that the guilty often return to society to continue their criminal careers.

Appellate Courts

Except for minor criminal infractions or civil actions involving small sums, the loser in a civil action or the convicted in a criminal action has a right of appeal. As noted earlier, about half the states have intermediate appellate courts. In these states, generally no right for appeal exists from the intermediate appellate court to the highest court, merely a right to petition the latter for review. This permits the supreme court to screen the cases it will entertain, reserving those of general interest or where it appears that serious error has been committed. No juries are called at the appellate level and no witnesses or new evidence. Instead, the matter comes before the appellate court on the record, that is the pleadings and relevant portions of the evidence as transcribed by court stenographers, of the trial. The record is supplemented by briefs—legal memoranda—

prepared by the parties and, generally, by a hearing at which counsel present oral arguments and undergo questioning from the appellate judges.

Quasijudicial Agencies

Many administrative boards, agencies, and commissions, whether elected or appointed, exercise judicial functions. In enacting zoning regulations, for instance, a zoning commission acts in a legislative capacity; but in applying those regulations to specific factual situations, the commission often acts in a judicial capacity, as does a zoning board of appeals in determining whether the regulations should be waived or varied for a particular property owner. The rate-making authority of public utilities or insurance commissions and the licensing authority of agencies such as liquor control commissions and professional standards boards all involve judicial powers to some extent. In many cases, there is a right of appeal to the courts, but in most such cases, just as in appeals generally, the case is heard on the record, and a presumption of validity attaches to the board's action.

Such regulatory agencies are likely to play an increasing role, supplementing and in some cases even supplanting the jurisdiction of established courts.

THE JUDICIARY'S SPECIAL ROLE IN AMERICAN LAW

One of the most quoted observations of Alexis de Toqueville is that "scarcely any political question arises in the United States that is not resolved, sooner or later, into a judicial question." In a famous 1906 address on the state of the law in the United States, Dean Roscoe Pound said much the same thing: "The subjects which our constitutional system commits to the courts are largely matters of economics, politics, and sociology, upon which a democracy is peculiarly sensitive. Not only are these matters made into legal questions, but they are tried as incidents of private litigation." And James Bryce observed, "No feature in the government of the United States has awakened so much curiosity in the European mind, caused so much discussion, received so much admiration, and been more frequently misunderstood, than ... the functions which it [the Supreme Court] discharges in guarding the arc of the Constitution."[10]*

The British Constitution is found in certain fundamental laws enacted

---

*It is possible that our reliance on the law impairs our ability to deal with social problems, by externalizing decisions that very well in fact involve active choice.

by Parliament, laws that Parliament has every constitutional right to re-peal and modify when it chooses. American constitutions, on the other hand, are organic laws superior to legislation. But the supremacy of consti-tutions is not self-executing, and the executive and legislative branches are not likely to defer to that supremacy, at least in matters in which they feel particularly self-righteous or assume the existence of an overwhelming public mandate, without a referee to see that they play by the rules. Just as the United States Supreme Court interprets and applies the federal Constitution, so the state supreme courts interpret and apply state consti-tutions. The power to declare executive or legislative action unconstitu-tional is an extraordinary power and one that makes the judiciary supreme on those infrequent occasions when the power must be exercised.

In Number 78 of the Federalist Papers, Alexander Hamilton wrote, "Whoever attentively considers the different departments of power must perceive, that, in a government in which they are separated from each other, the judiciary, from the nature of its functions, will always be the least dangerous to the political rights of the Constitution. . . ."

Despite the extraordinary power of judicial review, Hamilton's obser-vation that the judiciary is the "least dangerous" branch is certainly true, for courts cannot enforce their decisions against a determined governor or legislature. For instance, Thomas Jefferson is said to have observed, following the decision in *Marbury v. Madison,* 1 Cranch 137 (1803) in which the power of the United States Supreme Court to declare an act invalid was first enunciated, "John Marshall has made his decision. Now let him enforce it."

The concept of judicial review has been attacked as elitist and basi-cally undemocratic. Furthermore, it sometimes invites legislators to act irresponsibly, sacrificing a principle under popular pressure, secure in the belief that the courts will bail them out. In general, though, the power has been exercised sparingly and has been accepted, however grudgingly in specific cases, by the American people. Because the power is generally exercised in favor of unpopular causes or minorities, the willingness of the other branches of government—and of the populace generally—to accept dictation from the "least dangerous" branch is a tribute to their political maturity, their general sense of fairness, and the special veneration in which constitutions are held.

THE COURTS AND POLITICS

In the exercise of judicial review, supreme courts may be said at once to transcend politics and to influence politics directly and substantially. The courts transcend politics by invoking an authority (the constitution) which is supreme. They influence politics because their participation warps the political process, often decisively. An example of this on the national level is the legislative reapportionment decisions in the 1960s, by which the Supreme Court compelled legislative redistricting, thus ending the over-representation of rural areas and central cities to the benefit of the burgeoning suburbs.

The courts' involvement in politics and the political process goes far beyond the incidental and infrequent invocation of judicial reveiw. As we have seen, judges are often elected, many times running under partisan banners. Even appointed judges are only one step removed from politics, since they are appointed by politicians.[11] Furthermore, although courts do not exist to serve political parties, they are a substantial source of political patronage and probably are a more important *comparative* source than a generation ago because of the extension of civil service to many other areas of government. Courts are staffed not only by judges but by public prosecutors—called by various names such as district attorney, state's attorney, or prosecuting attorney; public defenders—representing the indigent accused; clerks; sheriffs; bailiffs; court stenographers; and various other functionaries. In many cases, each position is held by a party faithful.

The larger states have, quite literally, hundreds of judgeships, and each is regarded as a valuable political plum. Few cases arise where judicial salaries compare favorably with those of highly successful lawyers in private practice, but such lawyers do not generally aspire to judicial office, and judicial salaries *are* attractive to many members of the bar. In addition, judges are regarded as persons of substance and respect in the community. Furthermore, a judgeship can be granted not only as a mark of individual merit but as "recognition" to an ethnic or religious minority, particularly an ethnic or religious minority important to the party conferring the appointment or nomination. In general, elected judges have much longer terms than legislators. (The terms of state supreme court justices, for instance, run from 6 to 15 years.) Also, judicial elections are much less likely to be contested and the incumbent generally wins even where there *is* a contest so that a judicial appointment is not likely to be interrupted frequently by the necessity to expend time and money in seeking renomination or reelection. Judicial contests are also likely to be conducted with considerably more decorum and gentility than executive or legislative elections.* Finally, not only is a judge a man of respect, but he is a man of power, with the ability to make decisions which almost always are significant to the individual litigants before him and are sometimes significant for broader groups in the community.

---

*Judges in Illinois attended a "charm school" in 1979, to enhance their reelection chances. Among the recommendations: group advertising by incumbents (to avoid appearances of running against one another), a group "war chest" (with contributions just under the threshold of the Campaign Disclosure Act) and a regard for personal appearance (i.e., no cigars or loud shirts in public). "Illinois Judges Given Campaigning Tips," *American Bar Association Journal*, 65 (October 1979): 1461.

The difference in function between the trial and appellate courts probably results in somewhat different personnel being attracted to the two benches. Appellate courts act collegially. Appellate judges have time for reflection and research, removed from the hurly-burly of the court room. The trial judge, on the other hand, is forced to make numerous on-the-spot rulings and generally lacks the time or the facilities for extensive research. But he is likely to have been a trial lawyer himself and to relish the forensic combat in the courtroom. A trial judge is more likely than an appellate judge to "let his hair down," at least when closeted with counsel in his chambers.

Appellate court decisions are binding on lower courts within the same state but only where the facts in the later case are similar to those in the earlier decision or precedent. Trial-court decisions (which are not usually "reported," that is, printed as part of the state's permanent record of decisions) are not binding, although they may be persuasive because of their logic or the influence of the individual judge. Similarly, the appellate decisions of courts of sister states or other common law jurisdictions may be persuasive, but they are not binding outside the jurisdiction.

How the Public Perceives the Courts

The primary social controls over institutions are the ballot box and the market place. Although the ballot box has some influence over the courts, it is far from decisive even in jurisdictions where judges are elected in genuine contests under party banners. The market exercises little or no control over the administration of the courts. The tremendous increase in litigation, both criminal and civil, over the past 20 years does *not* mean that the courts are giving better service. In criminal law, it means weakened social constraints and a loss of shared values. In civil law, it means that we have become a highly claims-conscious people, particularly in urban areas. Until recent years, people accepted much loss or injury as merely bad luck. Increasingly, citizens feel a "psychology of entitlement," an interest in spreading individual misfortune over a wide group, as by insurance, and a willingness to sue neighbors, professionals (witness the explosion of malpractice claims against physicians, lawyers, and architects), and merchants whom, in a more homogeneous and simpler society, they would regard as friends or acquaintances rather than as potential defendants in a lawsuit.

In a period of public "accountability," courts are concerned with their image. The National Center for State Courts recently engaged the public survey firm of Yankelovich, Skelly & White, Inc., to determine public attitudes towards the justice system. The results were disquieting. Both the general public and community leaders are dissatisfied with the performance of courts and rank them lower than many other major American institutions. Perhaps the most disturbing, only 17 percent of those with the *greatest* knowledge of the courts voiced confidence in their operations, in contrast to 29 percent of those with limited knowledge. Specific questions revealed the fact that public knowledge of the courts and of certain fundamental elements of our law, such as the limited power of the United States Supreme Court over state courts and the state's obligation to prove the guilt of a criminal accused beyond a reasonable doubt, is woefully deficient. The greatest criticism of the courts, shared by 43 percent of the general public, was the courts' inability to reduce crime. In contrast, only 13 percent of judges and lawyers believed this to be a major problem.[12]

Unhappily, the public is likely to be dissatisfied with the courts so long as it blames them for continued high crime rates, rates that are due far more to "the revolution of rising expectations," structural poverty (relative to "rising expectations," even if not serious by traditional standards), the decline in opportunities for unskilled labor, and an alienation of large numbers of young people from the "establishment" than to any imperfections of the courts, although the legislative unwillingness to fund the court and corrective systems in proportion to increased needs is unquestionably an important factor. (As an example both of the litigious society and the niggardly financing of court systems, consider that the courts of Connecticut, a comparatively small state, handled more than a half million civil and criminal cases in 1978 on a budget of little more than $30,000,000 and with offsetting fees and fines of some $13,000,000.)

JUDICIAL REFORM

Reform, of course, is merely what its proponents call change. For instance, the trend from an appointed to a popularly elected judiciary in the pre-Civil War years was perceived as a reform, just as the trend *away* from partisan elections in more recent years is perceived as a reform. We should perhaps speak of modernization rather than use a value-laden and imprecise term like "reform."

Modernization is largely a response to the clogged docket and consequent long delays that are increasingly symptomatic of our courts. Magna Carta declared "To none will we sell, to none will we deny, to none will we *delay*, right or justice." (Emphasis added.) In criminal cases, an accused without means or roots in the community, and thus unable to raise bail, may be jailed for weeks or months awaiting a trial or hearing that may vindicate him. As indicated above, delays in civil cases are likely to be far longer, and witnesses die, move away, or forget what was once fresh in memory. In a message in December 1901, President Taft (later, as Chief

Justice of the United States, a vigorous and effective advocate for court reform), after referring to "the deplorable delays in the administration of civil and criminal law," went on to say, "A change in judicial procedure, with a view to reducing its expense to private litigants in civil cases and facilitating the dispatch of business and final decision in both civil and criminal cases, constitutes the greatest need in our American institutions."[13]

One growing response to the problem of clogged dockets is arbitration. Arbitration is usual in labor-management disputes and is used frequently in contract disputes, particularly complicated ones. Arbitration is generally held under the auspices and rules of the American Arbitration Association. Hearings are relatively informal and are often held before a panel of three, at least two of whom are specialists in the subject of the dispute. Arbitration is usually quicker and cheaper than court proceedings and has the added advantage of confidentiality. All states have laws that permit arbitration awards to be enforced through the courts. In 1979, New York began an experiment in requiring small litigants to accept official or court-administered arbitration, but with the proviso that a disappointed party could thereafter "have his day in court."

The rationalization of the court system by the elimination of specialized courts that have outlived their usefulness and the combination of courts of overlapping jurisdiction permits a more efficient use of courtrooms and judges.

At its August 1968 meeting, the house of delegates of the American Bar Association approved a model judicial article recommending a state court system consisting of a supreme court, an intermediate court of appeals, and a circuit court of general jurisdiction with rule-making power vested in the supreme court, or a committee to consist of judges, lawyers, legal scholars, and legislators, and with provision for the merit selection of judges. Although this action is not binding on state and local bar associations and still less, of course, on state governments, it is likely to have a persuasive impact over the years and reflects the current view of interested and informed professionals.

Perhaps the most pronounced and accelerating change in court modernization is the trend to professional management, centralization, and the exercise of rule-making powers to streamline litigation. Collectively, these trends virtually amount to a silent judicial revolution, particularly when one considers that the courts have been the most tradition bound of our political institutions.

In 1968, Congress created the Law Enforcement Assistance Administration, which has provided funds to the states for the courts, particularly for criminal administration. Until recent years it was common for courts of limited or special jurisdiction to be funded not by the state but through the fees and fines collected (one reason for the speed trap and the hasty arraignment of out-of-state motorists before the local justice of the peace). Increasingly, states are moving towards fully state-funded court systems under a budget which, in many cases, is prepared by the highest court.

The judiciary's rule-making authority, usually exercised through its highest court, is being used (as indicated above) to streamline the trial process, to expedite appeals, to enact codes of professional responsibility of bench and bar, to require continuing legal education for lawyers practicing in the courts, and to impose conflict-of-interest restrictions on judges.

A decade ago, only 25 states maintained an office of court administrator. The number has now swelled to 48, all but Mississippi and New Hampshire. This office tends to weaken the influence of local or political leaders on the number and assignment of judges and the erection or improvement of court facilities and, generally, permits judicial planning on a professional basis.

Unlike most European countries, where judges are trained as judges under a system independent of lawyers' training, the Anglo-American legal tradition contemplates that judges will be chosen from the bar, and it is usual for lawyers to ascend the bench with no specialized judicial training.[14] However, some 15 states now have broad judicial education programs. Perhaps the most ambitious, and the one that is likely to set the trend, is the California Center for Judicial Education and Research. Created in 1973, the center coordinates judicial education, disseminates educational material throughout the courts, provides a continuing education program, and gives special assistance to new judges.

Judicial councils exist in approximately three-fourths of the states, usually created by statute and usually comprised of judges, lawyers, legislators, and members of the general public. Judicial councils lack authority, their primary function being to investigate and recommend. They are a convenient liaison between legislatures and courts and are probably helpful in obtaining funding, which is especially important since the courts have no broad-based pressure groups hectoring the legislatures for constantly increased appropriations.

Despite modernization, centralization, and professionalization, it is fair to say that the courts are still intensely traditional and permeated with a resistance to change. The forms and ceremony that invest their operations are an outward and visible sign of this reliance on authority, precedent, and tradition. (Perhaps the only other American institution aside from the church in which forms and ceremonies play a comparable role is the university, where academic processions eclipse even the most awesome judicial pomp.) Moreover, the existing system is supported by powerful political forces that benefit from the status quo. Parties fearful of losing patronage, judges afraid of losing independence, and lawyers leary of having to play by new rules are barriers to change. The courts operate in relative obscurity—in contrast to the other two branches of the government—so they fail to generate public demand for reform. Despite these obstacles to modernization, it is probably fair to say that the courts have moved faster in the last 15 years than in the previous 50, and that the trend is accelerating.[15]

THE BAR

There are now more than 450,000 lawyers in the United States, about double the total only two decades ago. The number drawn from minorities, including women, has increased even more dramatically, so that the bar today is far more representative than in earlier generations. De Toqueville wrote of the bar, "In America there are no nobles or literary men, and the people are apt to mistrust the wealthy; lawyers consequently form the highest political class and the most cultivated portion of society." It is a long time since this has been the case. The historic view of a lawyer was as an officer of the court, an integral part of the scheme of justice. Increasingly, the lawyer is currently perceived merely as a paid servant of his client, justified in using any technical device to advance his client's interests. The change in the lawyer's role and the public's perception of that change have led to a loss of public esteem, a loss that must have been aggravated by the high percentage of lawyers involved in the Watergate fiasco. A generation ago, the average lawyer earned as much as the average doctor. His earnings are now far behind those of the average physician and somewhat behind the income of the average dentist. In part this is a result of the comparative ease of training lawyers, which can be done without the one-on-one training necessary in medicine and dentistry. Particularly with respect to physicians, it is probably due to the fact that most patients are covered by some form of medical insurance; and the success of Medicare has lead to pressure for "Judicare."

Some two-thirds of lawyers are in private practice (increasingly in partnerships, of which there are at least ten of more than 200 lawyers each). However, many thousands work for various levels of government, both within the court system and in government agencies; more thousands are employed by corporations; many teach; and many have moved elsewhere, using their legal training to advantage in business, accountancy, and other fields.

Over half the lawyers (251,000) belong to the American Bar Association, which is at once a trade group (advancing its members' economic interests) and a public-interest group (seeking to improve the administration of justice). In 1963, fewer than 11,000 new lawyers were admitted to practice. In 1977, more than 33,000 were admitted. Although substantial incomes are not uncommon in the bar, tens of thousands of lawyers barely make ends meet, and the situation is likely to worsen. In a recent speech to the annual meeting of the American Bar Association, S. Shepherd Tate, the incoming president, emphasized the financial problems of the bar and warned of unemployment facing many young lawyers. He cited a poll of Bar Association members (who are generally more successful than non-members) that showed median income dropping from $32,000 in 1975 to $30,000 in 1976.[16]

Although traditional areas of private practice have been eroded by such innovations as no-fault recovery in automobile cases and no-fault divorce, new challenges are emerging in such growing fields as environmental law, consumer law, and practice before federal, state, and local regulatory agencies. The image of the lawyer as spending most of his time in the courtroom has never been accurate for the bar in general and will become less so in the future. Increasingly, lawyers practice "preventive" law, aimed at keeping clients out of trouble rather than in getting them out of trouble. The effective practice of preventive law, however, depends on widespread awareness of a lawyer's function and the ready availability of lawyers on a basis the general public can afford.

In a May 1978 speech, President Carter said "We are over-lawyered and under-represented. Excessive litigation and legal featherbedding are encouraged." To the bar, the president's remarks must have seemed populist hyperbole, but the public received the speech with apparent agreement.

It can fairly be said that the American government is staffed by lawyers. This is true not only of the courts, but of the executive and legislative branches as well. The lawyer's image consequently suffers when, as now, there is a broad-based distrust of government.

The quality of justice depends not only on sound laws and fair judges. It depends equally on a bar that is well educated, honorable, and accessible. Today's lawyer is far better educated than yesterday's, and it is probably fair to say that the bar is quicker to clean house of undesirable members than are other professions. The availability, however, of lawyers to the average American is limited, limited both by the latter's ignorance and by high costs. Business, government, and the rich are adequately represented. Increasingly, the poor—particularly the urban poor—have access to lawyers through public-interest law firms (federally funded),[17] legal aid societies, and lawyers in private practice who sense an obligation to do some work on a pro bono publico basis. But the average middle-class American is often unaware of his need for a lawyer, ignorant as to how he can choose one both knowledgeable and trustworthy, and fearful (often with cause) of the resulting fees. Perhaps the greatest challenge facing the bar in the years ahead is the delivery of legal services to the average American at a price he can afford. Prepaid legal services, the use of paralegals, legal clinics, specialization, advertising (until recently forbidden by canons of legal ethics), and increased use of labor-saving machinery and equipment like automatic typewriters and computers are intriguing avenues for better service at reasonable cost.

For a recent, comprehensive report of the public's legal needs and how those legal needs are being met, see *The Legal Needs of the Public: Final Report of a National Survey,* American Bar Foundation, Chicago, Illinois (1978). A survey by the National Opinion Research Center found that the public consults lawyers most frequently in matters of estate planning followed by real estate and domestic matters. Although consumer problems, tort claims, and involvement with government agencies are legal problems that arise with frequency, the public is much less likely to consult a lawyer when faced with these problems, instead relying on self-help or other resource persons. Clients appear well satisfied with the service they receive, but the degree of satisfaction is highest where the lawyer can control the results (as in a will or a real estate closing), and lowest in adversary matters (such as suits or controversies) where optimum results are unlikely and at least one party is likely to be gravely disappointed.

CONCLUSIONS

State courts are an integral part of a state's political process. Perhaps the most conspicuous example of their political role is their ability not only to strike down executive and legislative actions when, in the court's judgment, those actions violate the state (or federal) constitution, but also to require fundamental changes in established practices the court deems unconstitutional.* Their participation in the political process is far more pervasive than their occasional and infrequent decisions as keepers of the constitutional ark. The great majority of judges come to the bench from a political life. For many, political involvement continues. Their perception of their role, their oath of office, and a desire to maintain the respect of bench and bar combine to keep most judges from frankly partisan decisions, let alone outright corruption. But judges cannot decide cases in a vacuum and each is influenced by his training, experience, background, and the social climate in which he functions. Particularly at the appellate court level, judges make policy—even those judges who honestly believe that their role is more passive and involves only the interpretation of

---

*One recent and conspicuous example of the latter power is the overthrow by a number of state supreme courts of the traditional local property tax base for funding public schools on the ground that it discriminates against poor districts and violates the constitutional mandate for a comprehensive public school system under state auspices.

law.[18] Although in most cases judges are divorced from the electorate and from the pressure groups* or lobbyists who seek to influence their coordinant branches, they cannot fail to be affected by the "felt necessities . . . the prevalent moral and political theories . . ." of their times, in Justice Holmes' words.

The courts are engulfed in a wave of increased criminal and civil litigation with little control over the causes for these burdens. It remains to be seen whether the recent genuine progress in raising the efficiency of the courts and making justice available to all Americans will continue. Increasingly, the public demands accountability and efficiency in all organs of government. The courts, most tradition bound of our government bodies, must adjust to new demands. An increased willingness to innovate and a subordination of tradition to efficiency are hopeful portents, but the final verdict has yet to be rendered.

NOTES

1. *Ballentine's Law Dictionary* (Rochester, N.Y.: Lawyers Co-Operative Publishing Company, 1948), p. 728.
2. "The Path of the Law," 10 *Harvard Law Review* (1897): 457 at 461.
3. James Kent, Vol. 1 of *Commentaries in American Law* (New York, 1826–30), p. 492.
4. Oliver Wendell Holmes, *The Common Law* (Boston, Little, Brown, 1922), p. 1.
5. Benjamin Nathan Cardozo, *The Nature of the Judicial Process* (New Haven, Conn.: Yale University Press, 1921), pp. 14, 18–19.
6. See in this regard Herbert Jacob, "The Effect of Institutional Differences in the Recruitment Process: The Case of State Judges," *Journal of Public Law* 33 (1964): 104–19.
7. Stuart Nagel, "Political Party Affiliation and Judges' Decisions," *American Political Science Review* LD (1961): 843–51.
8. Bradley C. Canon, "The Impact of Formal Selection Processes on the Characteristics of Judges—Reconsidered," *Law and Society Review* (May 1972): 579–92.
9. In *Ballew* v. *Georgia*, 435 U.S. 223, decided 21 March 1978, the U.S. Supreme Court decided that conviction by a *five*-man jury in a Georgia court deprived the accused of his rights under the Sixth and Fourteenth Amendments.
10. James Bryce, Vol. 1 of *The American Commonwealth* (New York: Macmillan, 1911), p. 242.
11. John E. Crow, "Subterranean Politics: A Judge is Chosen," *Journal of Public Law* 12 (1965): 275–87.
12. The survey is described in *New York Times,* 19 March 1978, p. 20.

*Pressure groups, although not characterizing themselves as such, sometimes influence decisions of major significance by the filing of amicus curiæ briefs with the court.

13. Bryce, *American Commonwealth*, Vol. 2, p. 683.
14. *New York Times*, 13 July 1978, featured an article about Joan Carey, a new trial judge, and pointed out that she took the bench with but one day's judicial training.
15. In 1978, Chief Justice Burger dedicated the new headquarters of the National Center for State Courts, a nonprofit research and development arm of state judiciaries. Under the Center's auspices, 375 judges and lawyers assembled in Williamsburg, Virginia, in March 1978 to draw a blueprint for state courts for the next generation. Drawing and implementing are two different things.
16. *New York Times*, 6 August 1978, p. 30.
17. The Legal Services Corporation has presented a budget request of $304 million to Congress for fiscal 1979 to complete a three-year plan to provide minimum access to civil legal assistance to *all* poor people in the United States (using the Office of Management and Budget's poverty threshold).
18. For perceptive comments on the judiciary's participation in the political process, see Henry Robert Glick and Kenneth N. Vines, *State Court Systems* (Englewood Cliffs, N.J.: Prentice-Hall, 1973), p. 59ff.; and Dr. Glick's *Supreme Courts in State Politics* (New York: Basic Books, 1971), p. 38ff.

CHAPTER EIGHT

THE POLITICS OF REDISTRIBUTION: WELFARE POLICY

On May 20, 1971, Governor Richard B. Ogilvie of Illinois delivered a special message on welfare reform to the 77th General Assembly. The governor said:

> The failures of this nation's welfare system are failures of historic magnitude. The example of Imperial Rome may prove to be prophetic for us. Welfare is warping our nation. The President did not overstate the crisis when he called the system "a monstrous, consuming outrage." It is a human outrage and a fiscal monster. It robs the poor of their dignity, and the taxpayers of their hard-earned dollars. The welfare system embodies all the worst of our failures —moral, fiscal, administrative, and legal. Where in the system do we find charity, service, work, dignity, respect, and responsiveness? Think of the children whose lives are being distorted by this hopeless environment, and what that means for the future.[1]

The concern of this chapter will be in the area of welfare policy. We will examine the way the different parts of our policy-making process work to produce welfare policy for the people of the various states. So far we have examined the way in which the citizens make their needs and demands known by voting, joining various groups to present claims, and working through their political parties to get their candidates elected to public office. We next examined the policy-making apparatus in the form of the decision makers: the governor, the legislature, and the courts. As we stated in chapter 1, the proof of the pudding is in the eating. We are concerned with party government and public policy. Policy is the result of the input of needs and demands of the people converted by the efforts of politicians into output which, we hope, will bear some relationship to those needs and demands. We assume that it is the quality of the efforts of those men and women who have been elected to public office that will be crucial in this transformation of needs into policy. The party as both an electoral vehicle and a governing vehicle provides the link between the people and their government. The quality of the party as an electoral and governing vehicle varies from state to state. It has been the hypothesis of this book that the states that have cohesive parties, which are united in the electoral stage and are able to present programs and policies to loyal legislators, will better serve the people than states in which parties are ridden with factions in the electoral and governing stages. Multifactionalism within a political party facilitates control over government policy by the "haves" in the society as opposed to the "have-nots." A unified party system provides a semblance of joint responsibility between the governor and the legislature. The independence of candidates in multifactional politics makes it possible to elect a governor who represents a minority of the people faced with a legislature, a majority of whose members are committed to inaction. It is time to test this contention of the late V. O. Key that governing parties with sufficient cohesiveness to pass programs to which they commit themselves will bring about a wider distribution of state expenditures across income classes.

WELFARE POLICY CONTRASTED WITH OTHER TYPES OF POLICY

Before continuing with the discussion of welfare policy, I want to discuss why I have given it the label "redistributive" policy. This will require a brief discussion of the difference between that concept and the "distributive" and "regulatory" policies discussed in the following two chapters.[2] Each of these policies involves different expectations on the part of the people, groups, and decision makers about who should be rewarded and who should be deprived, because every decision governments make entails rewarding some groups or classes and depriving others. Rewards may be given in terms of money or services or goods or rules that benefit one sector of the people over another. Those who lose may be the taxpayer, the group that does not receive the benefits, or the regulated group. Each of these types of policies brings forth its own arena of power. The groups or classes contending for power are different in the arena of welfare policy from those who contend in the arena of education policy and, again, from those who contend in arena of land-use regulation. The expectations on the part of the decision makers and the people being governed are different in all three areas. A brief discussion of each of these types of policies follows.

   1. *Redistributive policies* are concerned with relations among social classes. They are directed to the haves and have-nots. The aim of such policies is the redistribution of money from those who have to those who have none, based on the assumption that everyone is guaranteed a certain basic minimum existence even if he did not earn all of it or even any of

it. Redistributive policies take from those who earn income and give to those who cannot earn any or all of the money needed to support themselves because they are old, blind, or disabled or are children who are not yet able to work. These groups are the poor and represent about 11 percent of our total population. Almost half of all federal, state, and local social welfare expenditures go to aid those in the 11 percent of our population who are poor, or about nine million families. The state governments have a powerful say over who will receive this money within their borders. Some states give generously to the poor. Others do not. In our study of welfare policy, we will consider what it is about the characteristics of the people and the decision makers of the various states that can account for the wide disparity in providing for the poor.

2. *Distributive policies* involve giving benefits to a group of people without regard to the source of the resources paying for these benefits. Eyebrows will be raised when I categorize educational policy as distributive. It is the common belief that everyone is entitled to an equal education provided at public expense. The prevailing myth is that everyone receives free public education, no matter what their ability to pay may be. This education is to be provided equally to all through twelfth grade and to those who qualify at the university level. That is why education is usually categorized as redistributive. The distribution of education funds has not been equal. Money for education goes to the wealthy suburban community as a direct consequence of state-sponsored disparities in school funding. The states control funding and policies with respect to education. All federal funding amounts to only 10 percent of the total. As with welfare, some states have made a larger effort to distribute funds on a more equal basis. As a result of recent state-court decisions, some states are being forced to equalize their funding for education. It is in these states that educational policy is becoming more redistributive—more money for education is going to areas of need and less to the least needy areas. More on this in the next chapter.

3. *Regulatory policies* are specific in their impact on certain groups. Although the laws are stated in general terms ("This land must not be used for building houses"; "This farm land must never be developed"), the impact of regulatory decisions benefits some groups over others. Regulatory policy may represent the purest example of the group conflict described in chapter 3. According to the group theorists, policy is the result of the interplay of group conflict. Individual regulatory decisions are based on direct confrontation of indulged and deprived. In the case of land use, the developer and the environmentalist, the dredge operator and the sportsman confront each other and try to gain as favorable decisions as possible. What emerges is the result of this interplay of groups. While the environmentalists may win in establishing a land-use policy in the state, the developers may win in insisting on local autonomy in enforcement,

shifting enforcement into an arena in which they hope to prevail. Regulatory policies rest on the direct confrontation of groups in the political arena. Governmental decisions are the result of the pulling and hauling of such groups. The states are making regulatory decisions in transportation, air pollution, land use, and energy, to name a few. We will consider, in chapter 10, the land-use policies in the states and the reasons some states have developed more regulation than others and how this came about.

To summarize, we are going to consider three types of policy in the next three chapters. The three types are related to different types of decision making, public expectations, and group conflict. In the first, welfare, the type of policy is redistributive. It concerns the poor and the nonpoor, the haves and the have-nots. Money is taken from the nonpoor and given to the poor. The second policy, education, is distributive, although some may challenge this categorization. Funding of education has been so ordered by the states that the wealthy suburbs receive generous public money and the poorer towns and cities do not. Partly because the state decision makers stress local funding of education and partly because educational policy making is in the hands of those who represent the suburbs, the policy has never been redistributive and is only now changing in some states. Regulatory policy does not commit large amounts of the taxpayers' money to public policy but regulates the individual pressures that vie for favorable decisions. Here, the policy is the result of the interplay of interests that directly confront each other in the public arena. This policy has few of the attributes of distribution or redistribution. The public interest is represented by environmental groups, reform groups, and the like. The state becomes an arbiter rather than a giver or a taker, although, for each individual decision, there will be a winner or a loser. We proceed to a discussion of redistributive policy, a policy that deals with two major contenders, the poor and the nonpoor.

THE STRUCTURE AND SCOPE OF STATE WELFARE POLICY

Development of Welfare Policy

Governor Ogilvie, as the opening quote suggests, was not pleased with the welfare policies that existed in his state or in the nation. He blamed the federal government for not taking a more active role in providing fiscal relief to the states, as the number of people eligible for welfare grew by leaps and bounds. He blamed national economic policies that created unemployment and hence brought more people onto welfare rolls and made it difficult for those on welfare to get off. While state expenditures typically rise from 10 to 15 percent a year, the governor said, the welfare budget increased by approximately 30 percent in each of the two years previous to his address. In 1971, the amount was double that of three years before. The governor proposed a work requirement backed up by new public-sector jobs to help Illinois solve its welfare responsibilities. As we review the governor's remarks, it is obvious that welfare policy represents the "marble cake" notion of federal-state relationships described in chapter 1. Welfare policies set at the national level affect welfare policies at the state level. In general, the federal government provides grants to help defray state costs for providing financial assistance to the needy. In the particular program of aid to families with dependent children about which Governor Ogilvie was speaking, the federal government pays 55 percent of the total and states and cities pay the remainder. How did this "marble cake" arrangement come about in the area of welfare policy? After all, welfare was not regarded as the proper responsibility of the federal government at all until the 1930s.

"Decent provision for the poor," Samuel Johnson observed, "is the true test of civilization." It is doubtful whether we can measure up to this test at the present time. American programs in aid of the poor are based on English law dating as far back as the fourteenth century. Central was the distinction between the employable and the unemployable. The former were considered unworthy of assistance; the latter were considered deserving and various schemes were devised to help them, but aid was kept lower than potential earnings. It is not difficult to find this philosophy today in Congress and state legislatures. Central to much of the current discussion is that the employable poor are to blame for their condition.

Programs to provide money for the nonworking poor, or income maintenance programs as they are called, began to take their present shape during the two decades preceding World War I, a period marked by social reform. It was in the individual states that these programs began. State provisions for widows and orphans were consistent with the recognition that care of children is best carried on in their own homes. Widows and orphans were recognized to be "unemployable." Income was provided through the payment of "mother's allowances." Not all states provided such payments, and, in most instances, the amounts disbursed were modest indeed. By 1926, all but six states had mothers' aid programs; by 1933, old-age assistance was compulsory in 25 states, and 24 states aided the blind. Although state efforts were gaining momentum, the expanding aid offered by private, local, and state programs was completely snowed under by the Great Depression. Because the states could no longer provide for their poor, the federal government stepped in. New Deal Legislation designed two distinct income-maintenance systems that have survived to the present time. Enacted under the Social Security Act of

1935, these programs were the federal government's first involvement in general income maintenance for the needy. These two programs are based on the distinction between those who work and those who have little expectation of self-support. First, two contributory social insurance programs—unemployment insurance and old-age insurance—distribute income payments on the basis of prior earnings and tax contributions. With coverage extended to survivors and the disabled, and with health insurance also added, the original program of Old Age Insurance became Old Age, Survivors, Disability, and Health Insurance (OASDHI)—commonly called social security. Because benefits under the social insurance programs depend on prior earnings and labor-force attachment, only those with income in the past qualify for future payments. People covered under this program are entirely "respectable." They are workers who, for entirely understandable reasons such as retirement, death, disability, and temporary unemployment, are no longer working. The federal government supervises these programs and collects the taxes to fund them. We will not consider them as part of our study of welfare in this chapter. It should be noted, however, that one poor family in four receives these benefits, and these income supports have prevented many households from falling into poverty. Eligibility and benefit levels, however, are determined not on the basis of need but on the basis of past contributions. Millionaires over sixty-five routinely draw monthly stipends from Social Security because they have contributed to the system and believe they are entitled to its benefits.

The second set of programs provides assistance on the basis of need alone. This is the welfare system, as it has come to be called, because those who receive the benefits receive them on the basis of need and have rarely contributed anything toward their funding. The expectation in 1935 was that public assistance or welfare would wither away. This expectation, however, has not been realized. The states play a major role in the funding and operation of the welfare program. Welfare is second only to education in spending at the state level. All these programs provide benefits only to persons whose incomes are below a certain eligibility level. In addition, to receive cash assistance, the individual must be aged, blind, or permanently and totally disabled; or, in the case of a family with children, have lost support of a parent through death, incapacity, or absence from the home (AFDC); or, in some states, because of unemployment of the father (AFDC-UF). Welfare policy is the major instrument for states in coping with the problem of poverty. Indeed, before the federal government entered the picture, the states had developed welfare programs for needy children, the blind, and the elderly. Welfare is still regarded as a state responsibility, although the superior taxing powers of the federal government are used to assist states in meeting their welfare payments. It is assumed that state governments are better judges of recipient needs and what taxpayers can afford and are responsive to the political and socioeconomic characteristics of the states. Welfare, thus, competes with transportation, education, and environmental protection as a priority on the states' agenda. Some states provide generously for their poor. Others give niggardly benefits. We will examine why this is so, asking such questions as: What are the characteristics of the generous states as compared with those who treat their poor with less respect? Can the party system explain a portion of this question? Does the participation of the poor themselves affect the generosity of payments? Is the responsiveness of legislators a key to the answer?

This section on the development of welfare policy pointed out the basic distinction between the national social insurance programs and the public welfare programs. The recipients of the former include the great majority of all citizens, and benefits are uniform throughout the states. The insurance programs are managed almost entirely by the federal government. Welfare operates as a decentralized system: a marble cake with the primary responsibility for management left to the states who share almost equally in the expense. While the recipients of the social insurance program are given benefits by right, the recipients of welfare are considered charity cases and must demonstrate their need by proving that they are poor. We turn now to a description of contemporary welfare policy.

The Structure of Welfare Policy

The Aid to Families with Dependent Children Program (AFDC) is the largest, most costly, and most controversial component of public assistance. This cash assistance program operates to provide income for more than 10 million needy recipients in 3.5 million families, including over 7 million children. In May 1979, program payments totaled about $890 million. The federal share of the costs has been just over half the total amount. In general, AFDC provides for federal and state money to help defray costs of providing financial assistance to needy children who are under age 18 (or under 21 and attending school); living in the home of a parent or specified relative; and deprived of parental support or care because of the death, continued absence from home, or physical or mental incapacity of a parent—or, if a state so elects, the unemployment of a father. The state has the primary responsibility for initiating and developing its AFDC program. The decision to provide AFDC rests with the state, which thereby commits itself to administer it within the context of federal requirements. To receive federal funds, a state must submit and have approved by the Secretary of Health and Human Services a "state plan" describing the proposed system. To be approved for federal financial participation, a state plan for AFDC must provide, among other things, for the operation of the program in the entire state, and the program must be administered by a single state agency whose employees operate under civil service provisions. Eligibility may be determined by the state, but federal law provides that the recipient of aid must be in "need"; that the state must consider a person's available income and resources in determining the amount of assistance, and that the state must register for manpower services, training, and employment (the work incentive (WIN) program) all employable persons in the family. The state must also provide for a fair hearing for any person whose application for aid is denied. The state plan may not be approved if it includes a residence requirement that excludes an otherwise eligible person who is a resident of the state. This requirement is a result of a 1969 Supreme Court decision which ruled out residence requirements on the grounds that such requirements violated the equal protection of the law provided by the Fourteenth Amendment and interfered with the citizen's right to move. A resident is defined as anyone who is living in the state voluntarily with the intention of making it his home—not for a temporary purpose.[3]

Since 1965, the Social Security Act (Title XIX) provides basic medical services (including hospitalization and primary physical care) to all persons receiving cash assistance grants under AFDC and the Old Age, Blind, and Disabled Program and, at state option, nonwelfare-related persons whose resources are inadequate to meet necessary medical costs (considered "medically indigent"). Although states have considerable discretion in determining the scope of services available, the law requires all states to guarantee payments for eight basic categories of medical care under Medicaid. All states now provide Medicaid services as state policy for meeting the medical needs of the poor. The federal government pays, on an average, 55 percent of these funds. In 1968, Congress restricted Medicaid to families with an income of no more than a third above the state AFDC cut-off point, a step taken because several states had set significantly higher ceilings. Ceilings ranged in 1974 from $1,400 to $2,700 for individuals and from $2,700 to $5,600 for a family of four.[4] Twenty-nine states extend eligibility to persons who do not qualify for public assistance but whose income is sufficiently low to qualify them as "medically needy." The medical costs as well as the costs for administration are paid for on a cost-sharing basis according to a formula based on the per capita income of the state. In 1977, federal cost sharing was as high as 78 percent in Mississippi and, in 15 states, it was 50 percent—the statutory minimum. There is no doubt that this program has opened the doors of health care to many of the poor and near-poor who were either previously shut out or who were forced to rely on "free" care—when available.

The basis for determining the federal grants to the states for AFDC is one of two formulas specified in the federal act. The Medicaid formula (which may be applied toward AFDC money payment costs by states) provides a federal grant that funds from 50 to 78 percent of a state's total expenditures for AFDC and medical assistance. Most states have adopted this formula. The other formula is more complicated. Since there are only seven states still using this older formula, we will not elaborate upon it except to note that the states which continue to use it are the seven lowest-payment states (Alabama, Arizona, Georgia, Mississippi, South Carolina, Tennessee, and Texas). Apparently the provisions benefit their strategy. This formula provides reimbursement of $15 of the first $18 *per case* spent by a state plus a fraction of the remainder (from 50 to 65 percent, in inverse ratio to state percapita income) *up to a maximum of $32.* In general, the lower the grant and the higher the caseload, the greater the benefits that accrue to the states. This is apparently the reason the seven states with low payments keep the older formula.

Until January 1974, each state also set the eligibility criteria and the benefit levels for Old Age Assistance, Aid to the Blind, and Aid to the Permanently and Totally Disabled. For nearly four decades, assistance programs for these three groups of needy operated much as did AFDC. The federal government contributed a share of the cost, and the states decided who was eligible and what the payments would be. Payments were more generous than under AFDC because these people were the "respectable poor"—those who could not get work because they had understandable handicaps. On the other hand, parents who did not work were considered less respectable—and, presumably, their children were less respectable too, because the average payment for dependent children was far lower than the average payment to the other three groups.

Social Security amendments passed in 1972 thoroughly revamped this system for payments to the elderly, blind, and disabled. These amendments shifted to the federal government much of the responsibility for determining eligibility criteria and benefits levels. Effective January 1, 1974, the federal government provided national minimum standards of assistance and eligibility criteria for persons formerly covered under Old Age Assistance, Aid to the Blind, and Aid to the Permanently and Totally Disabled. The total number of 4.2 million persons were included in the SSI program in December 1978.[5] Less than 2 percent of the total number are blind. Those remaining are divided between the aged and disabled with the aged accounting for slightly under 50 percent of the recipients and the disabled slightly over 50 percent. In July 1975, the federal government guaranteed the aged, blind, and disabled a monthly income of $158 for an individual and $237 for a couple. This represented an increase in benefits paid by nearly half the states. Even so, the guarantee equaled only about 70 percent of the poverty level for individuals and 82 percent for couples.

States that had been paying more generously than the federal government are required to supplement national minimums to guarantee that no recipient will receive *less* aid as a result of the new programs. States may also supplement the federal assistance standard at their own expense, that is, without federal matching funds. The net effect of this innovation is a reversal of the traditional flow of revenue sharing with some states reimbursing the federal government for supplementation of cash assistance to the aged, blind, and disabled. As a result of these mandatory supplements and those the states add at their own expense, the average combined federal and state payments exceed those disbursed under the former programs. The states' share is now 25 percent of the total amount. The fact that some states want to provide more generously for the blind, disabled, and poor than the payments set by the federal government is a new concept in the whole notion of federalism. States that want the federal government to do better than its commitment give it the funds to do so for the poor within their borders. The interesting question to students of state government is what makes some states provide better than others for their aged, blind, and disabled poor?

There is one more program for the poor that falls entirely within the jurisdiction of the states. When all else fails, when someone is poor and *not* blind, old, disabled, or a child, the states pick up the tab. Operated outside the context of any federal standards, these programs vary widely from state to state in eligibility requirements, in amount and duration of payments, and in administrative procedures. In some states, the state public assistance agency administers the general assistance program. In others, local authorities administer the program with the supervision of the state. In still others, it is administered by the local governments without any kind of state supervision. The number of persons aided by general assistance varies according to general economic conditions. When economic conditions are bad and many are unemployed, the number of persons aided by general assistance tends to rise. In Pennsylvania and New York in June 1975, there was one general assistance beneficiary for every five recipients of AFDC; in Alabama there was one for every 2,560. The payments ranged from $134 per month in Massachusetts to $4.99 per month in Arkansas. General assistance payments are concentrated in large cities, and there is rapid turnover. Some states make only cash payments; others provide only medical care, hospitalization, or burial.

We have now outlined the structure and scope of state welfare programs. They are the second largest item in state budgets and are growing. The traditional programs for aid to the blind, aged, and disabled, which allowed state discretion with regard to eligibility and payment levels, now operate on a federal minimum and are administered largely by the federal government. The states, however, supply the government with supplemental payments over the federal minimum to provide more comfortably for their poor. These three programs are more "respectable" than the programs for poor children and their parents. A stigma attaches to the able poor, which may account for the reluctance of the federal government to take over basic funding and administration of that program. Assistance for

Table 8–1

Average Payments per Welfare Receipient, December 1978	
Aid to the blind	168.64
Aid to disabled	157.37
Old-age assistance	104.08
Aid to families with dependent children	87.65

Source: Table M–35, "Aid To Families With Dependent Children...," *Social Security Bulletin* (June 1979): 58; and Table M–25, Table M–27, and Table M–30, "Supplemental Security Income for the aged, blind and disabled...," *Social Security Bulletin* (April 1979): 65–67.

the blind has always been accorded a special status at state and federal levels, which accounts for the fact that payments are higher than those in other categories. Intensive lobbying on behalf of the blind has been rewarded by special legislation allowing larger exemptions of income in computing welfare grants than for other categories of assistance. This is still reflected in the payment levels for 1978, although the federal eligibility requirements are the same for all three groups under SSI. The aid-to-the-blind payments reflect preferential treatment for that group under state law and, hence, higher supplemental payments. The figures on average payments to recipients in Table 8–1 are representative of the lawmakers' estimation of "deservedness" of the groups served under the welfare assistance programs.

The Scope of State Welfare Policy

We have presented the structure of the welfare program as it is shared by the states and the federal government. It is indeed a marble cake with responsibility and money flowing both ways. While the federal level has now taken over the setting of eligibility and minimum payment levels for the aged, blind, and disabled under SSI, the states still exercise the option of providing more generously for their poor over the federal level of payment. Figure 8–1 lists the states in order of the percent of cases receiving the state supplementary payments. This is an indication of the concern of each state toward its poor in the aged, blind, and disabled categories.

The states make the determining decisions with respect to the Aid to Families with Dependent Children (AFDC). Here the federal government does not set the minimum standards, nor does it determine eligibility. No matter what the payment level, the federal government pays a proportionate share of state expenditures determined by the formula in the Social Security Act (50 to 78 percent). The wide variation in the standards set for eligibility, or needs standards as they are called, repre-

FIGURE 8–1

Percent of Total SSI Caseload Receiving
State Supplementary Payments, by State,
December 1975.

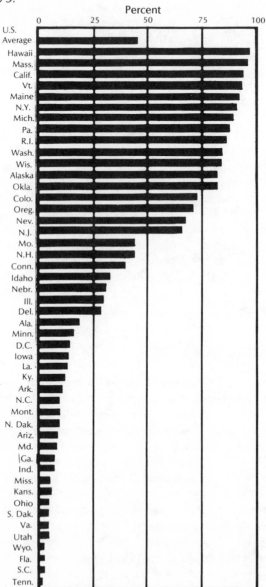

Source: Sue Hawkins, "State Supplementation Under SSI," *Social Security Bulletin* (February 1977): 16.

sents the concern a state has for its poor. The need standard normally reflects the cost of rent, utilities, food, clothing, and other basic expenses. In many states, however, there is little correlation between actual living costs and the established need standards. The monthly cost of basic needs calculated by the states for a family of four on AFDC in 1978 ranged from $187 (Texas) to $560 (Vermont).[6] But many states fail to pay even these low amounts. Only 25 states pay up to the full amount. In the others, the amount appropriated by the state legislature is not sufficient to pay the full amount according to their standard of need. Several states also have a statutory limit on the amount that may be paid to a family of a given size, regardless of the cost of the standard of need for a family of that size. In eight states, the largest amount paid is less than two-thirds of the minimum standards. In 1978, no state paid high enough benefits to keep an AFDC family out of poverty if the family had no other income or in-kind assistance. The map (Figure 8–2) shows the range of benefit levels by the largest amount paid for basic needs in April 1978 by state. This figure is the maximum payment or the largest monthly amount that can be paid under state law or agency regulations to a poor family of four living in the state.

We have noted the differences between the states in their payments for public welfare. We have not speculated why this is so, although it has been one of the hypotheses of this book that the strength of the political party system in a state system affects the redistribution of the money from the rich to the poor. The testing of this proposition will be undertaken later in this chapter. First we will comment on the tremendous growth of public welfare in the last 25 years. Following that we will describe the poor and the public attitudes concerning them. This will set the stage for our consideration of the reasons some states are more generous than others in caring for those who live in poverty.

The Growth of State Welfare Assistance

Figure 8–3 shows how state and local welfare expenditures for aid to the blind, old, and disabled and families with dependent children have sky-rocketed since 1950. As we have said, welfare is second only to education in priority for spending at the state level. By far the largest share of welfare spending can be accounted for by vastly increased costs of medical assistance. Since 1965 when the Social Security Act set up a joint state-federal program of medical assistance to people on welfare, state spending for medical assistance has risen from 30 percent to 44 percent of the welfare budget. Figure 8–3 indicates this increase; the middle line represents medical payments.

FIGURE 8–2

Largest Amount Paid for Basic Needs for a Family of Four, April 1, 1978
(In Dollars)

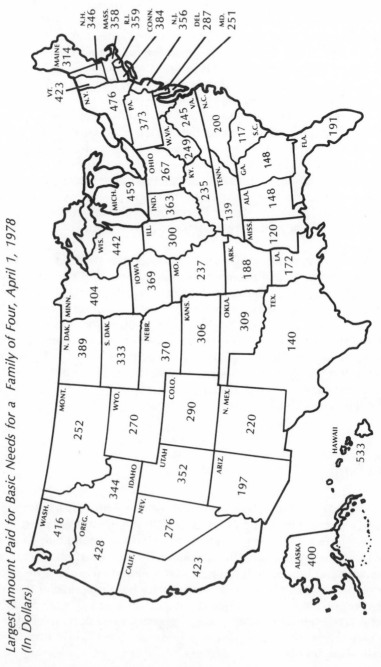

FIGURE 8–3

State and Local Public Aid Expenditures,
Selected Fiscal Years, 1950–76

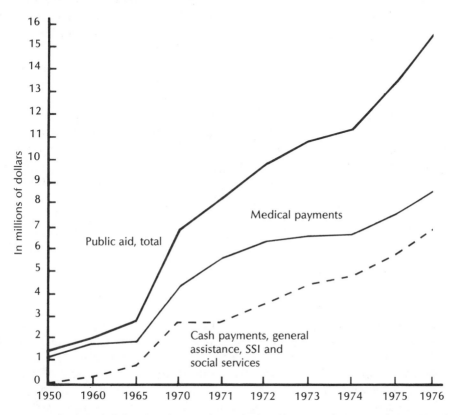

Source: Alfred M. Skolnik and Sophie R. Dales, "Social Welfare Expenditures, Fiscal Year 1976," *Social Security Bulletin* (January 1977): 7.

Aid to families with dependent children has grown tremendously since 1960, when it was about 29 percent of the total welfare budget, to 1976 when it surpassed medicare, claiming 46 percent of the total welfare spending in the states. This means that nearly half of all money spent on welfare goes to needy families with dependent children. This does not count the money spent on medical expenses for these same families. Because this program consumes such a large proportion of the welfare budget, we will concern ourselves with some of the reasons for its rapid growth as well as giving a description of the families who are served under it. The reasons for the expansion of AFDC are many and complex. Not only did more people become eligible, the benefits were also increased, and the stigma attached to welfare was moderated. Public assistance was projected as a right that people in need should be mobilized to exercise. We can barely touch on some of these reasons in the following paragraphs.

One of the most controversial reasons advanced for the increase in public welfare since 1960 is contained in the book by Pivan and Cloward entitled *Regulating the Poor.* Writing in 1971, the authors try to account for the rapid rise in welfare costs during the 1960s.[7] According to the authors, the government seeks to regulate the political and economic behavior of the poor by expanding or contracting the welfare payments. Their hypothesis is based on history. According to Pivan and Cloward, historical evidence suggests that relief arrangements are initiated or expanded during the occasional outbreaks of civil disorder produced by mass unemployment and are then abolished or contracted when political stability is restored. They argue that expansive relief policies are intended to mute civil disorder and restrictive ones to reinforce work norms. The authors review the events of the Depression as well as developments during the post-World War II period, including the civil disorder that broke out and spread during the 1960s and resulted in a great upsurge in relief rolls, especially after 1964. Hence, Pivan and Cloward's main thesis is that the welfare system is run by the government to define and enforce the terms on which different classes of people are made to do different kinds of work and has a great deal to do with maintaining social and economic inequities. Space does not allow a full discussion of this brilliant, though controversial thesis. The trend line in Figure 8–3 does not show fluctuations—just steady increases. The 1970s have been relatively quiet in terms of riots and militant welfare-rights groups, and the caseloads and benefits have risen steadily overall, facts that tend to refute the Pivan-Cloward hypothesis. In 1975, public-aid expenditures increased by 29.2 percent, and, in 1976, they increased by 20.2 percent, these years representing the two largest percentage increases since 1950. It would seem, therefore, that the explanation that welfare increases as a direct result of civil disorders is in error. This is not to say, however, that public participation and expectation have no influence on the level of welfare caseloads and payments. We will observe the relationship between public interest and welfare generosity at a later time. A governmental response to a favorable welfare climate of opinion is not the same as governmental response to riots and disorders.

Another point at variance with the Pivan-Cloward hypothesis is that welfare policy is not made by the federal government alone. It is made also by 50 states, each responding to varying conditions. The welfare map (Figure 8–2) reveals how different are the benefits the different states give their poor. We would expect that the states that experienced the most social disorder in the 1960s would show an accelerated increase in welfare caseloads and payments. While this was true in New York and California, it was not true in Pennsylvania, Illinois, or Michigan—all states with large cities experiencing civil disturbances. Public welfare payments are responsive to other inputs, apparently, than riots and disorders.

Several other reasons have been advanced for the increase in caseloads and money spent on welfare. One is the "expanded pool" reason. Rapid population growth has occurred since 1950. But, perhaps more important, were changes in family structure resulting in an increased number of households headed by women who are potential AFDC recipients. Not only did the rate of divorce increase by half during the 1960s, but the number of children involved per divorce decree also increased. In addition, the number of children born out of wedlock increased from one in 20 to one in 10. AFDC may, then, be viewed as a response to the single-parent family. But the program itself may induce families to modify their behavior to qualify for benefits. AFDC may encourage the very phenomenon to which it is a response, by inducing an unemployed man either to desert his family to make his dependents eligible for assistance or to fail to marry the mother. Charges that mothers on welfare have additional children for the purpose of qualifying for higher payments remain unproved, and many AFDC mothers practice birth control when it is made available.

There has also been an expansion of the "pool" through extension of coverage to groups not previously eligible. In 1961, Congress allowed states to grant assistance to families that were dependent because of the unemployment of an employable parent. This "unemployed father" component, now available in 26 states (1979) is restricted by federal regulations to those working fewer than 100 hours per month, no matter how meager their earnings. In 1967, a provision allowing the social welfare agency to disregard $30 per month plus work expenses and one third of additional earnings when determining if a family was poor added many families to the welfare rolls. In 1968 the Supreme Court struck down the "man in the house" rule, which held a man living in an AFDC home responsible for the child's support even if he was not legally liable. Later, other states were permitted to grant aid to children after age 18 who were attending school. This provision now holds in 40 states. The states themselves have also initiated more generous income disregards—whereby they ignore certain earnings in computing eligibility and payments—which have permitted many families to remain on the rolls after they begin to earn some money.

AFDC is now considered a way of life. Combined with food stamps and medical care, it provides a bare subsistence for many families, more than the meager earnings a mother might provide if she worked as a cleaning woman in a private household and had to place her children in a nursery. Although working may still provide more income than welfare alone to many families, combining these two sources may be preferable to either. It is therefore becoming the practice for work and welfare to go together. For a time, a family lives on both; then, as earnings rise, families move off the welfare rolls. Sixty percent of those on welfare leave within three years.[8]

For all these reasons—increased interest in the poor in some states, more demands by the poor, a greatly expanded pool of eligible families, and a general acceptance of the fact that work and welfare go together —welfare spending increased rapidly until 1976, although it has slowed in recent years. Even with all these reasons for the expansion of welfare, only 40 percent of all poor families (defined below) were on welfare in 1974. We turn our attention to those who are poor in our country in hopes that we may better understand the problem.

WHO ARE THE POOR?

The Circle of Poverty

The poor are caught in a vicious circle of poverty from which it is hard to escape. They manifest a number of characteristics which are a result of their poverty and which help to perpetuate it.[9] Because they are poor, their nutrition and health are poor; they cannot hold down good jobs; because they cannot keep jobs, they are poor. Because they are poor, they must go to work at an early age, and, because they cannot get educated, they earn less and remain poor.

The poor immigrants of the early 1900s have been replaced by large numbers of native-born Americans who find themselves outside the main-stream of economic life. They are the urban ghetto dweller, the rural farm worker, the immigrant to the city from the farm, the welfare recipient, the AFDC mother, the technologically displaced consisting of both young and old workers who do not know how to run the machines of modern industry, the minority-group members who are discriminated against in employment, education, and housing. Poverty is not now viewed by these people as a temporary condition. For the immigrant, work and education for his children could lift them above the poverty conditions into which they were born. For today's poor, poverty is viewed as a human condition of life. For many there is no escape.

We have in the United States social conditions that are characterized by extreme disparities between affluence and poverty. In spite of all the income support and welfare programs in the past 30 years, we have not altered the structure of this nation's income distribution. Table 8–2 shows that the wealthiest fifth of the nation's families received over 40 percent of all income, while the poorest 20 percent of American families receive

TABLE 8–2

*Distribution of Money Income by Share of
Aggregate Received by Each Fifth and Top
5 Percent of Families, Selected Years, 1947–70*

| | Percentage Distribution of Aggregate Income | | | | | |
YEAR	LOWEST FIFTH	SECOND FIFTH	MIDDLE FIFTH	FOURTH FIFTH	HIGHEST FIFTH	TOP 5 PERCENT
1947	5.1	11.8	16.7	23.2	43.3	17.5
1957	5.0	12.6	18.1	23.7	40.5	15.8
1962	5.1	12.0	17.3	23.8	41.7	16.3
1966	5.4	12.2	17.7	23.7	41.0	15.3
1970	5.5	12.0	17.4	23.5	41.6	14.4

Source: Ida C. Merriam, "Welfare and its Measurement," in Eleanor B. Sheldon and Wilbert E. Moore, eds., *Indicators of Social Change* (New York: Russell Sage Foundation, 1968), p. 735; U.S. Department of Commerce, Bureau of the Census, *Current Population Reports*, Series P–60, no. 80, "Income in 1970 of Families and Persons in the United States," (Washington, D.C.: U.S. Government Printing Office, 1971): p 28.

barely over 5 percent of the nation's income. This has not changed in 25 years. No wonder the poor believe they are trapped in a circle of poverty. Some escape, of course, to be replaced by others.

By another standard, the plight of the poor is growing worse. The gap between the living standards of the poor and the more affluent is increasing. Those families who are poor today must live on a smaller proportion of the medium income than poor families of 15 years ago. As the general American standard of living improves, the poor will become progressively worse off by comparison. The poor will be struggling for social survival even after the problems of physical survival have been solved. Those who remain relatively poor will inhabit an increasingly different world than the affluent. While the poor are not starving, they live considerably below general standards. This should be a source of worry to a nation that believes in equal opportunity.

Description of the Poor

The poor lack goods and services needed for an adequate standard of living. While it is difficult to measure poverty, we have come to use a standard developed by the Social Security Administration in 1964. This index is based on the cost of a minimum diet, estimated by the Department of Agriculture for a four-member family with two school-age children. The total cost of living of the low-income family is estimated to be three times its own food expenditures; thus a larger family will have a proportionately higher poverty threshold. Farm families are presumed to need only 85 percent of the cash income required by nonfarm families. A summary of the federal government's definition of poverty income based on 1976 prices is presented in Table 8–3.

Since 1970, the percentage of our people who live below the poverty level has hovered between 11 and 12. It had decreased rapidly during the 1960s. Most of this progress occurred during the second half of the decade when jobs were plentiful. In the last ten years however, the number of poor has remained at twenty-four to twenty-five million.

Who are these poor; what are they like? Table 8–4 shows that poverty is related to age, color, sex of family head, and place of residence. It is also related to work status and education achievement. Blacks are over three times as likely to be poor as whites. Families headed by women are six times as likely to be poor as families headed by males. Not shown in the table, but discovered by those who study poverty, is that families whose heads have eight years of schooling or less are six times more likely to be poor than families headed by persons with some college education. Overall changes in the number of poor people mask the considerable movement of persons into and out of poverty. That the total number of poor in 1976, for example was slightly lower than the total in 1975 was the net effect of the movement out of poverty by some fortunate enough to obtain

TABLE 8–3

Poverty Cutoffs in 1976 by Size of Family and by Farm-Nonfarm Residence

NUMBER OF FAMILY MEMBERS	NONFARM	FARM
1	$2,884	$2,438
2	3,711	3,128
3	4,540	3,858
4	5,815	4,950
5	6,876	5,870
6	7,760	6,585

Source: U.S. Department of Commerce, Bureau of the Census, *Current Population Reports,* Series P-60, no. 197 (September 1977) "Characteristics of the Low-Income Population" (Washington, D.C.: U.S. Government Printing Office, 1977), p. 20.

jobs or benefit by welfare payments and the movement into poverty by those who lost jobs or whose jobs did not pay them enough to stay out of poverty. In 1973, 50 percent of all AFDC families had been in the program less than two years.[10]

It is customary to describe the poor in terms of four major categories: the elderly, working-age adults who are employed, those of working age

TABLE 8–4

Characteristics of the Poor, 1976

CHARACTERISTIC	NUMBER (IN THOUSANDS)	POOR AS PERCENT OF TOTAL IN CATEGORY
Total	24,975	11.8
Race and Spanish origin		
White	16,713	9.1
Black	7,595	31.1
Other	667	17.8
Spanish origin	2,783	24.7
Age		
Under 18	10,273	16.0
65 and over	3,313	15.0
Type of residence		
Central city	9,482	15.8
Outside central city	5,747	6.9
Nonmetropolitan areas	9,746	14.0
Family status		
All families	5,311	9.4
Male head	2,768	5.6
Female head	2,543	33.0
White families	3,560	7.1
Male head	2,182	4.9
Female head	1,379	25.2
Black families	1,617	27.9
Male head	495	13.5
Female head	1,122	52.2
Unrelated individuals		
Total	5,344	24.9
Male	1,787	19.7
Female	3,557	28.7

Source: Same as for Table 8–3.

who are not employed, and children in poor families. Each group has its particular characteristics and needs.

Aged citizens have nearly as high an incidence of poverty as children. The major cause of poverty among the elderly is that few hold jobs. While some of the elderly poor are willing and able to work regularly, the vast majority cannot do so. An increasing number of our elderly persons live alone. They cannot indulge in much entertainment or recreation and are isolated and lonely because they cannot afford to visit others. Our society separates the elderly from its more active members. As a result many of the elderly live barren lives, away from the mainstream of society, and often burdened by feelings of unproductivity and helplessness.

Poor children, our poorest age group, are at the other end of the spectrum. Many children live in poverty because they are its cause. Low-income families are often driven into poverty by the addition of children. One study of poverty in 1966 discovered that 62.7 percent of all poor children are in the largest families (families with four or more children).[11] As we can see by consulting Table 8–4, children are far less likely to be poor if their household is headed by a male. Poverty experienced by children has several major effects. These are significant for the future of any attempt to reduce poverty. Severe poverty causes lack of adequate food and properly balanced diets. Recent research shows that such deprivation during the early years of life can affect the development of the brain. Poor families suffer from feelings of insecurity and lack of belonging. They may have poor verbal skills and do not engage in developed conversation. They do not see that reading is an escape from brutal reality. Children from such families are confronted by an alien atmosphere at school. They fall farther and farther behind. Many poor families need the earnings that children can bring in at an early age. Poverty compels some children to drop out of school by age 16 to go to work. Poverty certainly prevents children who might go to college from ever entertaining the possibility. For these reasons, poor children are one of the nation's greatest problems—one that is explosive as the gap between poverty and nonpoverty increases.

It is not commonly known that the working poor make up over half of our poor families. It is usually believed that lack of employment brings poverty, but employment itself does not bring an adequate income. Poverty is often the result of low-paying jobs as well as intermittent unemployment. The poor are the victims of forced idleness more frequently than the nonpoor. Low-paying jobs such as domestic service in private households or other service work, unskilled labor, or farming tend to lead to frequent unemployment. For the working poor, the problems are frequent joblessness, low wages, and inadequate skills. In families where one or both parents work and poverty still exists, there is engendered a lack of respect for the justice of the economic system or the value of legitimate employment. If the family cannot get welfare payments because their income is just above the poverty level before taxes, they most likely cannot benefit by Medicaid either. They are worse off than the nonworking poor. This condition may breed cynicism about the middle-class work ethic.

The nonworking poor are, contrary to popular belief, not a bunch of lazy and worthless people. Female-headed families make up a large proportion of these families, as is visible by inspection of Table 8–4. Poor males who do not work are likely (three-fifths of them) to be ill or disabled. In 70 percent of the female-headed families, the mothers need to stay home and take care of the children. Hence, children not only increase the chances of being poor, they make it impossible for a mother to get a job to provide for their support. Why are there so many poor families headed by females? This may result from the inability of poor males to obtain steady, well-paying jobs to support a household. For those who cannot, desertion and divorce appear to be common. This brings about illegitimacy. Another cause of poverty among female-headed households is the low level of assistance provided by many states to support such households. In many states, the amounts furnished by the authorities are far below the poverty thresholds for the various family sizes concerned. In states that do not allow payments to families with an employable male present, there is a real incentive for the father to leave so that the family may get welfare. This fosters the breakdown of the home as an economic unit, lack of respect for a father who cannot provide, destructive tensions that build up within the family, and the possibility of illegal activities such as prostitution, dope peddling, and gambling to bring in funds that do not have to be reported.

Attitude toward the Poor

Strong social mores reinforce a negative attitude toward the program of aid to families with dependent children. The program was originally designed to support orphaned children cared for by a widowed mother. Cash assistance is now provided to a parent or relative caring for poor children, and, in some states, to both parents where one parent is unemployed. We have social mores against illegitimacy that influence the negative attitude toward welfare mothers. Until court decisions came in the late 1960s, sanctions against sexual activity by mothers of dependent children receiving aid were rigidly enforced by many states. Spying on AFDC households to detect visits of unrelated males—a violation of "man-in-the-house rules" —cost more than benign neglect of the regulations.

Racial prejudice plays a role in negative attitudes toward the AFDC program. While whites still constitute a majority of recipients, the proportion of blacks on welfare has increased and with it negative racial attitudes. Again, this is a result of court-ordered constraints on states, especially

Deep South states, which formerly limited welfare to white recipients. Much of the recent increase in the number of nonwhite recipients of AFDC has been the result of admitting eligible persons who had been excluded by arbitrary state welfare administrations. This trend has exacerbated society's negative attitude toward welfare recipients.

Any substantial change in the conditions that maintain poverty in the United States will require a reorientation of social and political attitudes toward the poor. Americans generally tend to believe that the poor are responsible for their own poverty. This assumption of personal fault fits with our market economy and market-oriented values. We see personal income and industrial profit as positive societal values. On the other hand, expenditures for public assistance, social services, public housing, and medicaid are looked upon as costs. It is the redistribution of money from those who have to those who have not that is viewed as a bad investment rather than a positive one that may strengthen the fabric of our democratic system.[12] We will see that the states that provide the most generously for their poor are marked by integrated societies in which income is distributed more equally and in which there is public support for economic and social equality.

WHY DO THE STATES PROVIDE SO DIFFERENTLY?

This chapter began with the declaration that welfare policy was redistributive—it takes from the nonpoor and gives to the poor. Also mentioned was the ever-present speculation that it is the quality of the party system in a given state that is a major determinant of the way the state provides for its poor. If a political party is able to nominate, elect, and govern with a sufficient degree of cohesion, it listens to the needs of the poor and incorporates solutions in its policy program. Perhaps the party does not heed the needs of the poor out of brotherly love, but out of necessity to represent them to be reelected. Both Republican as well as Democratic governors need the votes in the cities, and both spend time building urban constituencies by campaigning on platforms promising aid and effort in meeting city needs. If the poor are able to present their demands; that is, if they are represented by welfare rights organizations, we would expect that they would fare better than those in states where they are not vocal. Political leadership cannot afford to ignore persistent demands. One might also expect that a more hospitable social environment might account for a more generous welfare policy. In states where the belief system supports the extension of benefits to the poor, we would expect to find more generous policies. Politicians respond to the desires of the people. In states where there is a party system organized enough to listen to the needs of the poor as expressed by organizations working in their behalf, or by a generally supportive belief system, they would be better served.

Welfare Policy and the Impact of Poverty

One might suspect that welfare policies of the states reflect the numbers of the poor. Those who believe that need itself determines expenditure would say that the more poor, the more people on welfare. Table 8–5 provides food for thought. For each state the following three items were measured: percent of families living in poverty as defined by the federal government; second, the ratio of families receiving welfare to those below the poverty level in each state; and third, a measure of the adequacy of the grants as the ratio of AFDC grants to average per capita income in the state. Here in one table we have a measure of need based on the percentage of the families below the poverty level and two measures of response to that need. The first response is indicated by the percentage of poor families to which the state gives aid. The larger the percentage, the more the state is concerned for its poor. The second response indicates how generous the state is toward its poor by giving the ratio of average grant size to average per capita income. What is termed welfare effort is a combination of the effort to cover as many of the needy as possible and the generosity of those payments. Inspection of Table 8-5 reveals that there is a negative correlation between need and welfare generosity in the states. In the states with the greatest need, as measured by numbers of families below the poverty line, the response both in terms of numbers on welfare and generosity of payments is lowest. In states where the need is lowest, the states are most generous on both counts. If the reader recalls chapter 2, the concepts of integration and the Gini index of income distribution will be familiar. These two indices reveal the degree to which a state has an economic and social culture based on education, professionalism, high media circulation, and equality of income distribution. The states with the lowest number of people below the poverty line are also high on integration and income equality. Those where large numbers are below the poverty line are the least integrated and most unequal with respect to income distribution. It is disheartening to face up to the grim picture indicated—that, in states where the need is greatest, the welfare effort is least generous. Even though it costs less to live in Mississippi or Alabama and therefore we might expect payments to be lower than in New York or Connecticut, the adequacy of the grants measured as a ratio of average per capita income is low. In the states with the greatest need, the grants are less than 10 percent of average income. Even in New York

TABLE 8-5

States Arranged According to Need and Welfare Effort, 1975

		Effort			
Need[a]	HIGH PERCENT SERVED[b] 80.0–129.0 ADEQUACY[c] 16.0–24.0	HIGH-MEDIUM[d] HIGH ON ONE MEDIUM ON OTHER	MEDIUM PERCENT SERVED 46.0–78.9 ADEQUACY 12.0–15.9	MEDIUM-LOW[e] LOW ON ONE MEDIUM ON OTHER	LOW PERCENT SERVED 28.0–45.9 ADEQUACY 7.0–11.9
PERCENT BELOW POVERTY LEVEL					
High 11.0–20.5 (14)			Kentucky	Oklahoma (1) West Virginia (1) Louisiana (2) North Carolina (1) South Carolina (2) Georgia (2) Tennessee (2)	Mississippi Arkansas Alabama Texas Florida New Mexico
Medium 7.1–10.9 (17)	New York Michigan Pennsylvania	Ohio (1) New Hampshire (2) Vermont (2) California (1) Illinois (1)	Virginia Maine *High Adequacy Low % Served*	Missouri (2) Nebraska (1) Montana (1)	Arizona

Low
5.0–7.0
(19)

		North Dakota	
		South Dakota	
		Idaho	
Rhode Island	New Jersey (2)	*High % Served*	Nevada (2)
Oregon	Connecticut (1)	*Low Adequacy*	Indiana (2)
Hawaii	Colorado (1)	Delaware	Wyoming (1)
Massachusetts	Alaska (1)	Maryland	
Washington	Iowa (2)		
Wisconsin	Utah (2)	Kansas	
	Minnesota (2)		

a Percent of families below the poverty level, 1975.
b *Effort 1* Ratio of AFDC families to families below poverty level, 1975.
c *Effort 2* Ratio of AFDC grants to average per capita income, 1975.
d Effort that is high is indicated in ( ).
e Effort that is low is indicated in ( ).

Source: *U.S. Statistical Abstract, 1979*, Table 730, p. 445; Table 764, p. 465. *U.S. Statistical Abstract, 1976*, Table 500, p. 319. *The World Almanac and Book of Facts, 1977* (New York: Newspaper Enterprise Association, Inc. 1977), p. 239. For adequacy of welfare grants, see Robert Albritton, "Welfare Policy," chapter 9 in Jacob and Vines, eds., *Politics in the American States: A Comparative Analysis*, Third Edition, pp. 369–73.

with most-generous welfare grants, the average payment is only a sixth of the average income in the state. Before we become overcynical to the point of thinking that need and concern for welfare have no connection, we should dig a little deeper into the reasons one political system might provide more generously than another for the needs of the poor. We have stated that welfare policy is redistributive policy. It takes from the haves and gives to the have-nots. We would not expect that, in a political system in which the haves had control both economically and politically, the have-nots would receive according to their needs. Political parties reflect the economic and social needs and feelings of the people. With a certain degree of organization and cohesion, political leaders can convert these needs and feelings into policy. The proper climate and the organization are both necessary.

A recent study sheds light on this relationship between the poor and the nonpoor and the belief system that is either supportive or hostile to welfare. According to Gronbjerg, two explanations account for the generosity (or lack of generosity) of welfare payments.[13] One lies in what she calls the "social stratification" approach. This explanation would anticipate the welfare system to be marked by notions of the proper place of the poor in the social and economic system. The other explanation is based on a different interpretation of the burden of responsibility in a society. To the extent that there is a system of beliefs that is widely shared and calls for equality of economic citizenship, the needs of the poor are regarded as the responsibility of the government. In these states, the poor also have an idea that they should receive economic citizenship. They believe they should press for benefits as well as apply for them in large numbers.

In states where society is more stratified, where the poor are accepted as a phenomenon, there is no belief that they should be brought into a fuller economic citizenship. Some of the poor in such a system are considered more deserving than others. In the southern states, those who are considered the "deserving poor" are the white, native-born, out-of-work poor. Here, the criterion for providing assistance may be the poor's place in the stratification system—not economic need alone. If there are large numbers of minorities who are considered less deserving, the welfare system will be restrictive and aid will be limited. In the southern states until recently, this was the case. Great pressure was exerted on the public assistance rolls, but also a stratification approach developed to granting such aid—restrictive policies to limit aid to those of appropriate status and to conserve scarce fiscal resources. Here, welfare is considered stigmatizing, and politicians share in the low public regard for welfare recipients. Welfare officials are reluctant to approve applications for welfare.

In states characterized by high incomes, high industrialization, high voter participation, large occupational elites, and high urbanization, the situation is the reverse. Here the need for assistance is less desperate, however, because of high industrialization and urbanization; notions of public or collective responsibility tend to be further advanced, and these outlooks are shared by politicans. Because their right to economic assistance is not questioned, the poor bring their needs to the attention of party leaders. Neither party can ignore these demands for fear of losing precious votes. To the extent that the parties are cohesive, these demands are met in the governing process.

Determinants of Welfare Policy

The previous section hypothesized that a link exists between the type of economic climate prevailing and the generosity with which a political system provides for its poor. We did not draw the inference that it was the socioeconomic structure that could explain all of welfare policy, but that it was important because it affected the beliefs of the people as well as the politicians working in their behalf. The theory of the policy-making process with which we are working and which was described in detail in chapter 1 (Figure 1–4) considers policy as the result of the needs and demands of the people converted by the efforts of politicians acting within certain institutional restraints. While this theory of the policy-making process is acceptable to most investigators, no general agreement has been reached as to the relative influence of the socioeconomic, political, and structural variables that contribute to policy output. The relationship between state party leadership and policy has not been studied. To my knowledge, the only measure of the contribution of state party leadership to policy was my "test boring" at the end of chapter 6, when I found a gratifying relationship between gubernatorial party leadership and redistributive policy. The major relationships that *have* been discovered link policy with the economy of the states. Thomas Dye, previously discussed in chapter 1, concludes that political system characteristics have relatively little impact on policy outcomes in the states. Economic development shapes both political systems and policy outcomes.[14] His study, however, leaves much unexplained interstate variation in policy output. Only one-half of the variation in policy could be explained by the combined force of all Dye's economic measures (and this occurred in only 35% of the cases). While there is no doubt that socioeconomic development affects the activities as well as the demands of the people in a state, the efforts of the political leadership must convert such demands into policy. The quality of the party leadership and the ability of the leaders to make promises and then to build legislative coalitions to put these promises into effect are crucial to the well-being of the citizens of the state—and especially to the least fortunate of those citizens, the poor.

As the student has progressed through the pages of this book, many independent variables that may explain the given type of policy output of a state's political system have been identified and described. We have identified party leadership as the ability to put together a coalition large enough to capture a nomination, campaign for office, and implement policy after the election. We have described and measured the formal power of a governor that allows him to exert leadership. We have described the means by which legislatures have become more professional and how this professionalism affects their ability to promote policies that redistribute the wealth of the state to the needy. The measures of all these variables are contained in Appendix 3.

The Measurement of Welfare Policy

Readers who have followed this discussion must be concerned about the number of variables that have been advanced as influencing policy. Policy itself has not yet been explained except in the simplest terms. What we need is a measure of welfare policy output with which to compare the states in the quality of services their poor citizens enjoy. Although welfare is the second largest category of spending in the states, there has been disagreement among researchers as to the measurement of welfare output. Some researchers use level of expenditures for various programs, but there is a risk in relying exclusively on total per capita expenditures as indicators of public welfare policy. The current expenditures may not be reliable indicators of the service provided to those on welfare. The level of spending does not tell us who is receiving the benefits nor the quality of the benefits received. Some outcomes are not intended by policy makers. For example, they may decide to spend more on welfare children to help them emerge from poverty and helplessness; but, if the money does not reach those most in need, the outcome is contrary to their intentions. Outcomes require measures different from outputs. Whereas state-government expenditures for welfare is an output, the proportion of the poor who are raised above the poverty level is an outcome. Whereas expenditures for Medicaid is an output, the increased health of the poor is an outcome. Outcomes are what concern people most. Citizens formulate demands, pay taxes, and seek to influence the decision makers—all to achieve desired outcomes. No consideration of policy is complete without a consideration of outcomes, although they have been the least-studied political concept and are often the most difficult to measure—in part because there are relatively few official indicators of outcomes whereas data about outputs are numerous.

The measure of welfare policy used in this test boring is composed of both output and outcome variables. The measure involves payments to families with dependent children and payments to the other three needy groups: the old, the crippled, and the blind.[15] The statistical technique used to cluster the variables around this dimension of welfare policy is factor analysis, which was described in chapter 2 (footnote 20).

Why Welfare Policies Differ[16]

Proceeding as we have in other test borings, we can discover what is related to generous or meager welfare policies in all 50 states. The computer was instructed to find the independent effects of a long list of possible determinants and then list them in order of impact.[17] We selected the top five variables and fitted them into the policy-making diagram. Figure 8-4 shows the results. Five variables are used in the explanation of welfare policy that have sufficient contributory power to be included: the input variables of integration and participation; and the process variables of governor's party leadership, formal power, and legislative professionalism.

Taken together, the governor's party leadership and his formal powers, which make it easier for him to exert his leadership, plus the professionalism of the legislature explain a significant portion of welfare policy. If we could measure it better, the governor's leadership might emerge as a stronger explanatory variable. Leadership is measured here as the average strength of the gubernatorial leadership coalition over a 15-year period. It indicates the ability of the party leaders and the gubernatorial candidates to build a coalition that can control nominating and hence electing and policy making.

The participation of the citizens of a state has a strong influence over policy in the welfare area. The more active the citizens, the more the decision makers respond to their demands. Insistent demands cannot be swept under the rug for fear that the next election will bring opponents into power. The hypothesis of those who study voter turnout has been that, the higher the participation rate overall, the higher the participation of low-income groups. The fact that participation is so strongly associated with welfare policy lends credibility to that hypothesis. The analysis provides an extremely appealing and sensible confirmation of this hypothesis of the policy-making process, which counts citizen effort as a major contributory cause.

What of the power of the economic variables in the paths that lead to welfare policy? Integration is the influential variable, as the value of its coefficient shows. Integration is also important in explaining the leadership of the governor and the formal powers given him as well as the services provided the legislators. The wealth, education, and communications ties existing in a state give rise to demands for political leadership, formal powers, and services to make it effective. It is important to note that this economic condition has more effect on the formal powers and services given a governor and legislature than on policy itself. Apparently the economy spurs demands on governors and legislators to restructure the decision-making process within the government. This fact tends to confirm Schlesinger's hypothesis that states that are affluent and economically complex need more formal centralized leadership. In addition, another characteristic of these states is a large urban population which

FIGURE 8–4

Relationships Among the Economy, Voter
Participation, Political Leadership, and
Welfare Policy

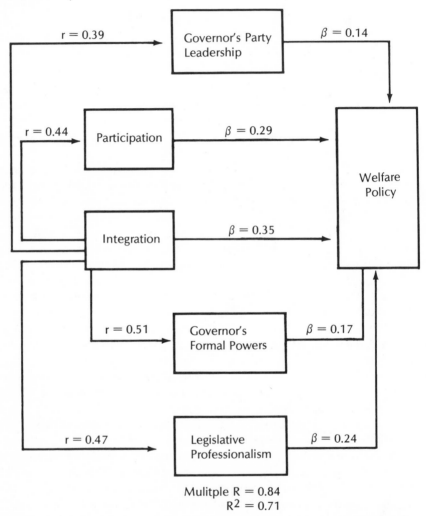

Mulitple R = 0.84
$R^2 = 0.71$

Note: The beta weights (β) shown in the figure indicate the relative contribution of each independent
variable to accounting for variation in the dependent variable (welfare policy). Taken together, the
political variables (participation, governor's leadership and formal powers, and legislative professionalism) contribute more to the variance (R^2) than the economic variable (integration).

generates poor and needy people. In summary, the effect of the economic
variable of integration is significant, but the demands that arise from the
economy are filtered through the political process. Integration explains
less of welfare policy (.54) than the political variables (.64).

Welfare policy appears to be determined by a combination of socio-economic, participation, and leadership variables. These influences taken together indicate that states with a high degree of professionalism, education, and personal wealth—as well as urban centers that spawn problems—tend to contain the elements of redistributive politics. It is there that the participation of low-income groups and the strength of the leadership bring about the provision of generous welfare payments to those in need. Apparently, both leadership and internal cohesion are required to mold policies like welfare programs, which bring about a wider distribution of the benefits of state expenditures across income classes.

FUTURE CHOICES

The common assumption by those who are concerned with the unequal treatment of the poor from state to state is that the national government must take the initiative to redistribute income to the poor in those states where the poor suffer most. It is not possible, however, to prove what constitutes the most desirable amount of redistribution. Any redistribution tends to improve the standard of living of the recipients at the expense of the taxpayers. This does not necessarily mean that the taxpayers are worse off. Recently, economists have emphasized that transfering income to low-income families may actually benefit those who give up resources that finance the redistribution. Higher incomes for the poor may benefit other people in a number of ways. Making the poor better off may help reduce crime, juvenile delinquency, or social unrest. Also present are the advantages that come from a share in the responsibility for a society that tries to guarantee that all of its citizens will share certain social and economic benefits. We have seen that the states that are higher on the integration scale also have a great desire to bring all their citizens up to a basic standard. Browning expects that many people are willing to pay $1,000 in taxes as their share of a $20 billion redistribution to the poor, which was the estimated cost of the presidential proposal considered by Congress in 1978. Those who are well off may care about the living standard of others.[18] For these reasons, a strong case can be made for having the government engage in redistribution.

Guaranteed Income

A variety of plans to reform the current welfare system have been proposed in recent years. The United States relies on a sizable array of policies to benefit the poor. These policies are not all equally effective, and proposals to change the welfare system differ over whether to scrap the existing and start fresh, or to use an incremental approach. Table 8–6 outlines two major policies for redistribution of income. There are others, of course, such as special tax advantages and minimum-wage laws and price ceilings with which we will not concern ourselves here. Table 8–6 covers most of the policies actually used in the United States and one category for which there is no U.S. program, namely, broad-based cash transfers. Many economists think that we should have a negative income tax or a program administered by the Internal Revenue Service which actually pays taxes to all who fall below a certain level of income. Hence, from the point of view of the internal revenue system, this is a negative income tax because the IRS must pay it—it is positive for those who receive it. Most proposals under the concept of a negative income tax or guaranteed income embody the following characteristics: (1) assistance is to be made available on the basis of need alone; (2) need and entitlement to public assistance would be objectively and uniformly measured throughout the nation in terms of the size and composition of the family unit, its income, and other resources; (3) assistance would be paid in cash, not kind, and should be given for free disposition by the recipient, not earmarked for certain purposes; (4) any tax imposed on income earned in addition to that provided by the supplement should be less than 100%. In other words, a family that earns money should not immediately have its guaranteed income reduced by the same amount. A tax rate of about 50% is the current thinking. Families that earn can keep their benefits up to a certain maximum—until their annual earned income reaches $8,400 (1978).

This was the substance of the program proposed by President Carter in August 1977 and resembled that of President Nixon, unveiled just eight years before. Both presidents said that this was a total reform. Carter's program would scrap the existing Aid to Families with Dependent Children (AFDC), Supplemental Security Income (SSI), and

TABLE 8–6

Policies for the Redistribution of Income

MAJOR CATEGORIES	EXAMPLES
I. Cash transfers	
(a) Broad-based	Negative income tax, wage subsidy
(b) Categorical	AFDC, Supplemental Security Income
II. In-kind transfers	
(a) Consumption	Food stamps, Medicaid, Medicare, public housing
(b) Human capital	Various training programs

Source: This table was adapted from one by Edgar K. Browning, *Redistribution and the Welfare System*, p. 31. (See note 18.)

food-stamp programs in favor of a standard, consolidated cash payment. In addition, about 1.1 million jobs would be created for needy families.

Incremental Reform

There are critics of this "total reform" approach. Two critics, Richard Nathan, senior fellow of the Brookings Institution, and Sar Levitan of the Center for Social Policy Studies argue that single cash payments would fail to meet the multiple needs of the poor. Both argue that existing program overlap is necessary to address the needs of a diverse population.

In a statement before the House Welfare Reform Subcommittee on October 12, 1977, Richard Nathan questioned whether we need a total reform as proposed by President Carter. Nathan claimed that the amount of growth in welfare programs has been tremendous in the years since President Nixon proposed his Family Assistance Plan. The food-stamp program now provides aid to the working poor at a rate higher than the Family Assistance Program would have. The new federal program of Supplemental Security Income for the aged, blind, and disabled provides relief to the states so that they can divert their attention to the poor families. There are now strong work requirements for receiving welfare assistance. Job programs currently are very large.

Nathan, a veteran in the welfare reform area, suggests that the incremental approach would be the best. It would leave intact the efforts of those states that now provide generously. It would call for full state administration of the welfare program instead of the mixture we have under the programs for the aged, blind, and disabled. To ensure that some states will not continue to treat their poor in a niggardly fashion, Nathan suggests a national minimum benefit level, uniformity in eligibility standards, and the addition of more working families.[19] Congress appeared to favor this approach as the 1980s began.

The incremental approach has much to recommend it. Many states have indicated that they are moving toward a society that cares for its poor. For example, 27 states now have welfare for male-headed families —a great increase. To scrap all existing programs and institute a nationally administered program would remove responsibility from many states, responsibility they have handled well. With a national minimum payment guarantee, the poor in niggardly states would be brought up to a minimum income. It is my view that states should be encouraged to provide for their poor. Their capability has increased in recent years. They now have four-year governors, reformed legislatures, and reorganized administrations. They are closer to the needs of their poor.

CONCLUSIONS

The marble-cake merging of responsibility for welfare produces a system of aid to families of dependent children where some poor states like Mississippi cannot pay recipients even minimally adequate benefits; some not-so-poor states like Delaware choose not to; and other states like New Jersey do pay poverty-level benefits, but do so at the expense of other valuable programs. In the test boring, we discovered that the economic and social structure of a state was important in determining the way it provided for its poor, but that this capability was not as important as the leadership and political arrangements. The degree to which the poor participate in their own system is important because the leadership cannot ignore the demands of the voters. The degree to which states have given their governors power to plan and execute the programs they deem necessary plays an important part in the redistribution of society's benefits to the poor. Reformed legislatures are better able to listen to both governors and constituents. And, finally, we noted the importance of that elusive character of political leadership itself—the ability of a party and the men and women within it to sustain a leadership group that continues to provide men and women who are experienced and capable to staff the government. Because the political arrangement a society makes to govern itself is so desperately important to the redistribution of the benefits, the obvious solution to the problem would be to encourage reform of the executive and legislature to bring about a more sensitive and equipped leadership. While party reform is more elusive, any arrangements that make it easier for party leaders to recruit, groom, and promote ambition for public office would also relate to the ability of the political system to benefit its people. But these reforms are not easily achieved and are almost entirely up to the discretion of the state political systems. Meanwhile, poor people are cold and hungry and neglected and hence without hope. Some solution must be worked out that will not penalize those poor who are fortunate enough to live in states whose political and economic arrangements have provided for them. Reform will be brought about, presumably, by the congressional leadership of those states that already provide generously. Thus, the national government must take the initiative to provide for the poor in states that fail to provide for them adequately.

Today we are on the threshold of deciding whether the support of minority rights should include social and economic rights as well. Many states have already decided this—by including large numbers of their poor and providing for them generously. In some states, the majority nonpoor are not willing to sacrifice some of their own economic and social rights. Incremental welfare reforms that establish a national minimum benefit for poor families appear to be the best solution. This preserves the programs in states that provide generously and forces the reluctant states to care for their poor.

NOTES

1. Richard B. Ogilvie, "Special Message on Welfare Reform," Illinois, *Journal of the House of Representatives* (20 May 1971), p. 1986.
2. It was Theodore J. Lowi who formulated these three types of policies. The discussion that follows is partially based on his description and partially based on my interpretation of his description. The adaptation of his typology to state policies is my own attempt. See Theodore J. Lowi, "American Business, Public Policy, Case Studies, and Political Theory," *World Politics* 16 (July 1964): 690–715.
3. Leon D. Platky, "Aid to Families With Dependent Children: An Overview, October 1977," *Social Security Bulletin* (October 1977): 17–18.
4. Sar A. Levitan, *Programs in Aid of the Poor,* 3d ed. (Baltimore: Johns Hopkins Press, 1976), p. 63.
5. Table M-25, "Supplemental security income for the aged, blind, and disabled: Number of persons receiving federally administered payments, by reason for eligibility and State, December 1978," *Social Security Bulletin* (April 1979): 65.
6. Elizabeth Chief, "Need Determination in AFDC Program," *Social Security Bulletin* 42 (September 1979): 20.
7. Frances Fox Pivan and Richard H. Cloward, *Regulating the Poor* (New York: Vintage Books, 1971).
8. This discussion draws from Levitan, *Programs in Aid of the Poor,* p. 34.
9. Dale Tussing, *Poverty in a Dual Economy* (New York: St. Martin's, 1975), p. 27.
10. U. S. Bureau of the Census, *Statistical Abstract of the U.S.* 1976 (Washington, D.C., 1976): p. 320.
11. Anthony Downs, *Who Are the Urban Poor?* CED Supplementary Paper, Number 26 (New York: Committee for Economic Development, 1968), p. 23.
12. Marian Lief Palley and Howard A. Palley, "National Income and Services Policy in the United States," chapter 18 in Dorothy Buckton James, ed., *Analyzing Poverty Policy* (Lexington, Mass.: Heath, 1975), p. 243.
13. Kirsten A. Gronbjerg, *Mass Society and the Extension of Welfare 1960–1970* (Chicago: University of Chicago Press, 1977). Others have found similar results. See Ernest H. Wohlenberg, "A Regional Approach to Public Attitudes and Public Assistance," *Social Service Review* 50 (September 1976): 491–505. Also see Gerald C. Wright, Jr., "Racism and Welfare Policy in America," *Social Science Quarterly* 57 (March 1977): 718–30.
14. Thomas R. Dye, *Politics, Economics and the Public: Policy Outcomes in the American States* (Chicago, Ill.: Rand McNally, 1966). Also see the discussion in chapter 1, and footnote 19 in this text.

15. See Appendix 6 for the variables used. The statistical technique used to cluster the variables around two major dimensions of welfare and highway-natural resources is known as factor analysis. This is described in chapter 2, footnote 20. From an original list of 26 variables, the analysis extracted these two dimensions or factors. The variables in the welfare factor are very different from those in the highway-natural resources factor

    The highway-natural resources factor involves traffic needs and sports— hardly life-and-death issues. I discovered that the independent variables that explain highways-natural resources policies are economic. The process whereby money is allocated to this type of policy is devoid of political leadership. There appear to be few issues in this field that array taxpayers and economic haves against recipients of services and the have-nots. Hence there may be no need for cohesive leadership.

16. Portions of this chapter appeared in slightly different from in "The Governor as Political Leader" by Sarah Morehouse in Herbert Jacob and Kenneth N. Vines eds., *Politics in The American States: A Comparative Analysis,* Third Edition, copyright © 1976 by Little Brown and Company Inc. and are reprinted by permission.

17. Multiple-regression analysis is explained in chapter 5.

18. Edgar K. Browning, *Redistribution and The Welfare System* (Washington, D.C.: American Enterprise Institute for Public Policy Research, 1975), p. 95.

19. Testimony sent by Richard P. Nathan, Brookings Institution.

CHAPTER NINE

THE POLITICS OF DISTRIBUTION: EDUCATION POLICY

On August 30, 1971, the California Supreme Court accepted the argument that education represents a "fundamental interest" in a landmark case that became the model for many other suits filed after its decision. The court held that the state school finance system was unconstitutional under the state's equal protection clause because it made the quality of education a function of local school districts' taxable wealth. The court concluded:

> For the reasons we have explained ... the system conditions the full entitlement to such interest on wealth, classifies its recipients on the basis of their collective affluence, and makes the quality of a child's education depend upon the resources of his school district and ultimately upon the pocketbook of his parents. We find that such financing system as presently constituted is not necessary to its attainment of any compelling state interest. Since it does not withstand the requisite "strict scrutiny," it denies to the plaintiffs and other similarly situated the equal protection of the laws.[1]

That landmark case of *Serrano v. Priest* confirmed the fact that education has been distributive policy. Court cases have arisen in 40 other states since 1973 based on the same issue—that education in those states was based on wealth and hence the states were not providing their poor children with an education equal to that of the wealthy. This was not the first time a declaration on educational equality had been made. The Supreme Court of the United States had so stated in 1954, nearly 20 years earlier, when it pronounced in ringing terms that, in public education, the doctrine of separate but equal was no longer valid. *Brown v. The Board of Education of Topeka, Kansas* called for massive desegregation throughout the country and particularly in the southern states. The substance of that decision was that education had not been equally provided—that white children had benefited by the distribution of the privileges of education.

Distributive policy, then, is policy that benefits certain groups at public expense. The money that pays for educational policy is collected from those who earn, and the benefits and services that education has to offer are distributed to certain other groups (defined by the California supreme court as "wealthy"). The difference between welfare policy and education policy as it has been carried out is this: Welfare policy takes from those who have and gives to those who have not, although the generosity of payments differs from state to state; education policy takes from those who have and gives major benefits to an even smaller group of those who have, a group distinguished by race and wealth. Education policy is usually called redistributive policy because the constitutions of all states provide for free public education for all children. The redistributive benefits of education, however, have not come up to the provisions of state constitutions. While the purpose is redistributive, the practice has not been. Figure 9–1 illustrates the point I am making.

We will see that the states are making an effort to bring education policy up to the provisions of their state constitutions as a result of state court decisions that impel them to do so. We would predict that states striving to make their education more redistributive will be those in which the needs and demands of the people can find expression through the organization of the political party. Perhaps state supreme courts—in the forefront of the recent effort—also respond to the needs and feelings of their states' people. It is too early to measure accurately the results of the current effort to equalize education in the states, but we will discuss in a later section the attempts that are being made. First, we will consider the purpose of education in a state political system. Following that, we will devote attention to the groups that make demands on the system in an effort to gain the benefits of education policy. How the decision makers respond to these groups will follow. By that time, we may have an idea why educational policy has been distributive and why it is changing to redistributive. We will discuss attempts by state policy makers to make educational policy redistributive in three policy areas: desegregation, equalization of financing, and higher education.

EDUCATION IN THE STATES: PURPOSE AND PERFORMANCE

In chapter 1, we developed a diagram of the policy-making process modeled after the political system of David Easton. Under the concept of inputs into the policy-making process, we described citizen support, which may be expressed as positive action such as voting or paying taxes and making requests, or as negative action such as withdrawal, refusal to

FIGURE 9–1

The Politics of Redistribution and
Distribution

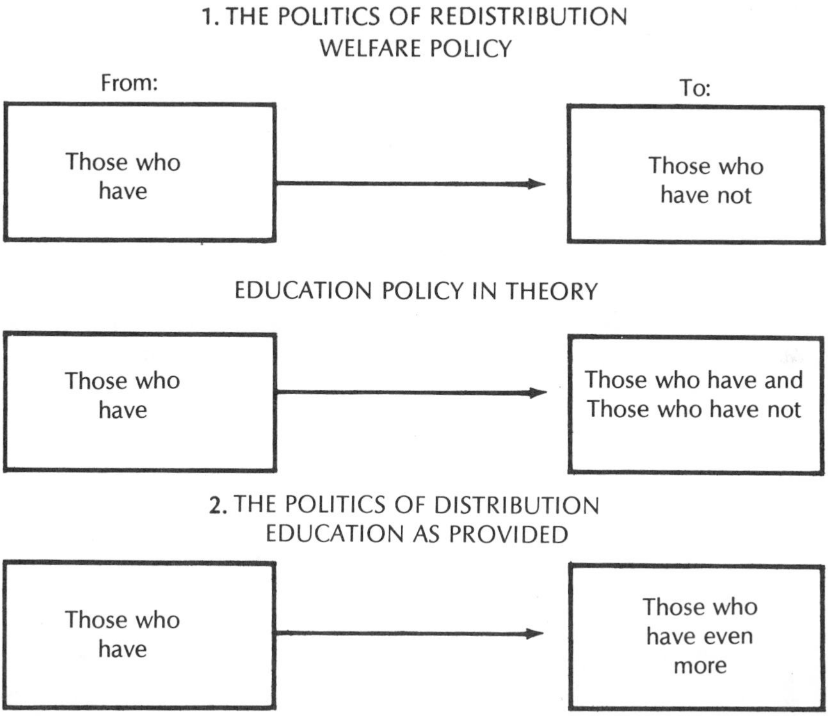

1. THE POLITICS OF REDISTRIBUTION
WELFARE POLICY

From:

To:

Those who have	⟶	Those who have not

EDUCATION POLICY IN THEORY

Those who have	⟶	Those who have and Those who have not

2. THE POLITICS OF DISTRIBUTION
EDUCATION AS PROVIDED

Those who have	⟶	Those who have even more

pay taxes, demonstrations, and sit-ins. We have continuously referred to this diagram throughout the book as we proceeded step-by-step to discuss its components. We discussed voters and elections. We discussed the demands placed on the policy makers by pressure groups and political parties. We considered the governor, the legislature, and the courts as policy-making agencies that receive the demands and supports. Now we are considering the outputs of this policy-making process. Education policy has responded to the needs and demands of groups, and, as we have seen, the groups that have benefited the most have been those who had the most resources to bring to bear on the policy makers. Policies are made in response to demands and support, and some balance must be struck between the inputs and the outputs or the policy-making system will not continue to be viable. There are times when the decision makers appear blind to needs that may be unexpressed. An unexpressed need poses a special problem. The poor and uneducated may not know how to bring their needs to the decision makers. If their needs are neglected long enough, they may erupt in violence—the only way they know how to express demands. The relationship of education to the state is dramatically illustrated in the 1968 Report of the National Advisory Commission on Civil Disorders. The Report considered the role of education as crucial in the maintenance of American social and political systems.

> But the most dramatic evidence of the relationship between educational practices and civil disorder lies in the high incidence of riot participation by ghetto youth who had not completed high school. Our survey of riot cities found that the typical participant was a high school dropout. As Superintendent Briggs of Cleveland testified before the Commission:
>
> "Many of those whose recent acts threaten the domestic safety and tear at the roots of the American democracy are the products of yesterday's inadequate and neglected inner-city schools. The greatest unused and underdeveloped human resources in America are to be found in the deteriorating cores of America's urban centers."[2]

Education, then, is related to the way people feel about their government. If they believe they are a part, that they know how to participate if they have a demand, they will generally be supportive. If they think they are not equipped to make demands, that their government does not care, they will be alienated, will withdraw until such time as their demands may erupt in violence. Education shares with voting the quality of being anterior to all other values in a democratic society. In fact, as between the two, education deserves precedence as the indispensable basis of political life.

Education, then, performs a vital function for a political system. The way the system receives support is a function of the educational institutions that induct the youth into the prevailing political culture. While the exact impact of education on political socialization has not yet been established, education taking place in schools contributes to the development of the basic political orientations of children. Education has an influence on how the child and the future citizen will see himself as a potential participant in the political process. Education also plays a selection and recruitment function; that is, it screens and trains those who will join the elite ranks. As Professor John Coons said: "At the pinnacle of our economic temple still flies the standard of universal access to the levers of opulence and nobility. Beyond argument, the prime mover in the modern labor market is education. In a free-enterprise system, its differential provision by the public school ... means that certain participants in the economic race are hobbled at the gate—and hobbled by the public handicapper."[3] Thus education, by default or design, may close or widen the elite-mass gap depending upon the particular school system.

Support for the Political System: Unequally Acquired

The political system needs a reservoir of diffuse support to maintain itself. This is acquired as the schools and other agents of socialization build a reservoir of approval and favorable predisposition toward the system. Diffuse support for the system enables it to survive periods of unrest. Loyalty to and acceptance of the symbols and laws of government are important factors in the maintenance of the system. What is equally important, however, is for citizens to feel a sense of involvement in the system—a belief that they have a right to participate and to be heard. Apparently, this sense of involvement is not conveyed equally to children of all socioeconomic groups.

Edgar Litt studied three schools near Boston and discovered that, while children of all social strata received formal training in the elements of democratic government, the formal instructional programs and the textbooks used in working-class schools emphasized the duties and responsibilities of citizens rather than their rights and freedoms.[4] Working-class students, as opposed to students from affluent communities, were oriented toward an idealistic view of the political process, and they had a passive view of themselves. Only in the upper-middle-class school was there much attempt to communicate a "real" image of government, that is, an image of people engaged in power struggles, or groups in conflict, and of ordinary citizens taking an active part. Litt concluded that those students from the wealthy schools were being trained to fill the activist roles into which their socioeconomic status would lead them as they take over positions of prominence in the world of work. Children of a less-privileged social class faced a handicap for future political involvement in the socialization they received. They absorbed the consensus values of American political life, but were not taught the skills they needed to be anything but passive participants in politics. What is sinister about all this is the relationship between the curriculum content and the wealth of the school districts. We need to know, of course, if the curriculum content does indeed affect the attitudes of the school children. Perhaps they are not as receptive to curriculum content as we might expect. I am not impressed with the relationship that has been discovered between curriculum content and attitudes. Perhaps the sinister division of curriculum into anticipated high- and low-class participation is not as effective as it is sinister. The main point is that there does appear to be a difference in the attempted socialization of children depending on their expected future role in society. This does not square with the constitutional guarantee of equal education offered by all states to their citizens.

Selection and Recruitment of Leadership: Unequally Bestowed

The other function of education for a political system is selection and recruitment; education screens and trains those who will join the elite ranks. An elite is defined for our purposes as a group of persons who exercise political power in a society whether they occupy a formal political position or not. Theoretically, the opportunity to join the ranks of leadership should be open to anybody with ability. "Strive and you will succeed" is part of our mythology. In addition to providing the opportunity for some to join the elite, the educational system should function to provide everyone with the intellectual skills that will allow them to cope with the complex choices and situations of conflicting value which they will encounter in our postindustrial society. They should be able to do this as free self-confident people rather than as dependents lacking the elementary intellectual ability required for the carrying on of day to day affairs. Equality of opportunity implies strongly that an individual of any racial or social group has the same probability of succeeding as does an individual of any other race or social group. Given equality of opportunity, there should be a random relationship between the racial and social position of parents and the lifetime attainments of their offspring. While recruitment for the ranks of the elite will always be won by the most able, the proper functioning of the schools would result in the eligibility of able individuals from all social groups. Education in our society should function so that able children of each socioeconomic group would begin their adult lives with equal chances of success in matters such as pursuing further education, obtaining a job, and participating in the political system.

Education is a form of human capital development. Economists have used the human-capital approach to understand the process of increasing social and private well-being through investing in the health, education, and training of people. They have found that financial investments in raising the health and education of human beings yield substantial social and economic dividends to society. Economists believe that returns on human-capital investment exceed those from physical capital.

Both people and society suffer from individual educational handicaps. For those persons who lack adequate schooling, economic self-sufficiency becomes meaningless. They suffer frustration and defeat. At worst, they live a life of crime and decadence. From the point of view of society, this is a double burden. Not only do the undereducated fail to contribute their share, but everyone else is deprived of the benefits of those individuals who, if properly schooled, could have made a significant contribution. Society cannot tolerate vast numbers of unskilled and underdeveloped individuals. In the past, the schools of our country fostered economic opportunity. Today, because of the unequal distribution of resources, schools are no longer able to offer equality of opportunity.

The fact that equality of opportunity does not exist has been amply documented. While the adoption over a century ago of Horace Mann's idea of free public education for all has led to universal schooling of Americans, the quality of education provided to an individual and his subsequent educational achievement and post-school performance are determined to a substantial degree by his social and economic circumstances. At one extreme, children from wealthy families tend to have waiting for them the highest quality of available educational services. This provides them with an opportunity to maximize their intellectual potential and thereafter to apply their learning in a fashion that will lead to high income, high social status, and, consequently, elite rank. At the other extreme, a child from a socially less-advantaged and economically depressed home typically has waiting for him low-quality school services that inhibit development of his intellectual capacities and that subsequently curtail his ability to earn a living and achieve fulfillment. Reasons given for these circumstances vary. Those who think that they are caused by racial and geographical segregation see hope that the conditions can change. This point will be discussed in a later section.

Samuel Bowles and Herbert Gintis take a more conspiratorial view of the inequalities of schooling in our society.

> More fundamentally, the contradictory nature of liberal educational reform objectives may be directly traced to the dual role imposed on education in the interests of profitability and stability; namely, enhancing workers' productive capacities and perpetuating the social, political, and economic conditions for the transformation of the fruits of labor into capitalist profits. It is these overriding objectives of the capitalist class—not the ideals of liberal reformers —which have shaped the actuality of U.S. education and left little room for the school to facilitate the pursuit of equality or full human development. When education is viewed as an aspect of the reproduction of the capitalist division of labor, the history of school reforms in the United States appears less as a story of an enlightened but sadly unsuccessful corrective and more as an integral part of the process of capitalist growth itself.[5]

According to Bowles and Gintis, there is no way for education to serve as the proper method of increasing economic opportunity for deprived groups so long as the responsibility for education remains in the hands of the upper economic elite. Local school boards made up of the upper classes have a vested interest in preferential education. In spite of educational rhetoric to the contrary, it is the children of the well-to-do, not the children of the poor who have benefited most from public education at public expense. The community pays for providing a minority of the children with an economic advantage over the rest. At the same time, education operates as a social sorting device enabling the well-to-do children to retain or improve their advantage while doing very little for the rest.

Because we are so wedded to our capitalist system, they say, we are also wedded to finding nonsocialist approaches to social reform. Massive income redistribution, as we saw in the last chapter, has been unacceptable. So has broad-scale intervention in the economy. We therefore attach ourselves to the notion that education can provide the skills and attitudes that will cause unemployment and poverty to disappear. The economic elite promote this notion because they fear tampering with basic social, structural, or economic characteristics. In this way, educational reform has actually hindered economic reform. Obviously there is no way to reform the schools according to Bowles and Gintis so long as our capitalist economy exists. The capitalist economy is dominated by the imperatives of profit and domination rather than by human need. Unless we have greater economic equality, we can never have educational equality, according to the writers. It is interesting to note that the facts of our educational inequalities, admitted by most thoughtful people, have been interpreted by Bowles and Gintis to be a result of our capitalist system. While they admit that desegregation and a more equitable school financing system are steps in the right direction, they are advocates of an overhaul of the whole economic system. We cannot take the space to do more than note their interpretations of our current inequities. School policy has been largely a local–state function and while it has not been dictated by some grand capitalistic design, it has been largely controlled by local school boards composed of upper-class members. The fact remains that the commonly acknowledged functions of education, which are to promote (1) equality of political participation and (2) equality of opportunity to join the ranks of the elite, have not been met by our state governments.

FEDERAL, STATE, AND LOCAL
RESPONSIBILITY: THE MARBLE CAKE

Education is a state function administered locally. It is the most expensive state function, consuming about 40 percent of total expenditures. Each state through its constitutional arrangements, judicial decisions, and legislative and executive actions, as well as its local administrative agencies, provides the legal context in which school districts operate. The local school district is legally a creature of the state. In 1977, public schools received 48.3 percent of their funds from local sources, 43.3 percent of their support from the states, and 8.3 percent from federal money. Since 1970, the state share has gone up, the local share has gone down, and the federal share has remained about the same. The reader may want to contrast this division of responsibility for the funding and policy making in education with the marble-cake arrangement for welfare. The federal government funds over half of the program of Aid to Families with Dependent Children. The streak in our hypothetical marble cake would be of nearly equal width in the federal and state layers and dwindle to nothing in the local layer. The cake has a very different marbling effect for the division of responsibility in education between the layers of government. In the education cake, the streak begins with a scanty dimension in the federal layer and is divided about equally between the state and local layers (with a slightly wider lump in the local portion). I hope this visualization technique is meaningful. It is intended to illustrate the fact that different policies are shared in different ways between the federal, state, and local layers of government.

Education Is a State and Local Responsibility.

Unlike most other nations of the world, our country treats education as a state and local function. In the early days of the Republic, the Northwest Ordinance and land-grant provisions of statehood acts encouraged educational use of the proceeds from public land sales; but the educational function, by the ordinary interpretation of the Constitution, remained a power of the states under the Tenth Amendment. It was not until the middle of the nineteenth century that the notion of public responsibility for universal, free, and common education came into being, largely because of the efforts of Horace Mann and his fellow reformers. (Recall that Bowles and Gintis would not agree with this interpretation). As public schools developed, schooling as a state and local responsibility was reinforced. Mann's distinctive innovation of local, lay control of education was adopted everywhere, and the nation was composed of thousands of school districts, often not geographically or administratively related to other local jurisdictions, and with separate taxing power. When, after the Civil War, the states began to exercise their constitutional prerogatives in the area of education, they found that local citizens everywhere remained intensely interested in retaining and exercising this control over schools. The states usually accepted this tradition of local control and confined their activities to setting minimum standards and providing basic levels of financial support for local school districts. They let the districts decide whom to hire and how much to spend. Except for broad grants of economic support to public education through the sale of public lands (extended to the area of higher education through the Morrill Act), the federal government's only educational policy activity during the nineteenth century was the establishment in 1867 of an Office of Education to collect and disseminate information about education in the United States.

The Federal Role

The Elementary and Secondary Education Act of 1965 was the breakthrough in the involvement of the federal government in the financial support of schools. Before ESEA, a few modest federal grant programs had been initiated:

1. Title III of the National Defense Education Act of 1958 (NDEA), financial assistance for strengthening instruction in science, mathematics, modern foreign languages, and other critical subjects;
2. Title V-A of NDEA, guidance, counseling, and testing;
3. Vocational Education (aid for vocational education from all federal programs);
4. School Lunch and Milk Program; and
5. School assistance in Federally Affected Areas (general aid to offset increased school costs related to federal employees and school construction money for similar purposes);

but none of these implied across-the-board support to public schooling, and, altogether, federal grants for elementary and secondary education contributed little in the way of financial support to most school districts.

Unlike all its predecessors and companions, Title I of ESEA with its allotment system based on poverty criteria promised to deliver significant financial resources (50 percent or more of local pupil expenditures for each eligible student) to most school districts in the nation.[6] This act was widely heralded as a major political feat. It served the purposes, however, of many state and local officials who were reluctant to distribute state funds to the most needy areas in the state. Localities, confined largely to one tax source (property) that did not expand apace with needs, were increasingly concerned about tax competition with other jurisdictions for population and business, especially since they were unsuccessful in persuading states to shoulder any additional share of the expense. They eyed the progressive and elastic federal revenue system with envy and were eager to tap its largesse.

Under the landmark Education of All Handicapped Act of 1975 (PL 94–142), states have had to provide a free and appropriate education to all school-aged handicapped children. By 1980, they had to do the same for all those aged 3 to 21. Passage of PL 94–142 marked a major change in national policy toward education of the handicapped. The law was preceded by a series of court rulings in the early 1970s to the effect that handicapped children had a constitutional right to a free and appropriate public education. In addition, the Education of All Handicapped Law required that handicapped children be educated in regular classrooms along with other children to the extent consistent with their special needs. It also required that schools plan for each handicapped child individually and gave parents rights to contest school decisions affecting their children. Congress set an ambitious schedule of increasing assistance to states and local schools to help finance education for the handicapped, but the federal government is dropping farther and farther behind on its commitment, and school districts are complaining that they can't afford to meet the federal mandate unassisted.

In enacting ESEA and the Education of All Handicapped Act, the federal government was responding to widespread distress in the American educational system. In doing so, however, it was also establishing clear, continuing limitations on the federal role. The programs were clearly not general aid, and deliberately so. Each was of a categorical nature, designed to target federal funds at particular shortcomings in existing educational programs—such as neglect in the education of poor or handicapped children or the absence of a spirit of innovation. The ESEA programs were also intended to provide some general financial assistance to particularly poverty-stricken school districts, but the giant step to a "general aid" program, that is, help with the basic operating costs of local schools, was not taken. In addition, the federal government intended to honor "local control of schools" in deference to the existing political and constitutional arrangements governing public education. Lastly, federal support was subject to the annual congressional appropriations process with appropriation levels to be determined each year. This is unlike Aid to Families with Dependent Children or Medicare, for instance, where the federal government guarantees a certain percentage of state yearly expenses.

Likelihood of Dimiminished Federal Role in School Aid

For three major reasons there is little likelihood that the federal government will expand its role in school aid to the states beyond its present effort. (Its share of funding has gone down slightly since 1975.) The first is that local and state officials have not been too pleased with the operation of the programs. Annual federal appropriations were chronically tardy, and the auditing practices were demanding and clumsy. Many local district board members and administrators have been extremely vocal in proclaiming an erosion of their authority to operate the schools, saying that the federal government has more influence over the schools than the amount of federal dollars appropriated would warrant. While the dollars have not increased dramatically, the reporting requirements and the attendant paperwork have. Different federal bureaus have different reporting requirements, some calling for semiannual reports, some quarterly, and some monthly. Whether the new Department of Education will be able to exert some control over the excessive amount of paperwork required in the programs remains to be seen. Established in 1979, the department will combine the Office of Education of the Department of Health, Education, and Welfare with a variety of educational programs scattered throughout dozens of agencies.

State and local officials also object to other requirements of the new laws. With respect to the requirements of the Education of All Handicapped Act, states have objected that the federal law preempts much of the activity that has taken years of effort to provide. State laws differ widely and quite often do not contain the same provisions as PL 94-142. To qualify for funds, states have had to amend their own laws to bring their special education programs into compliance with the federal legislation. Finally, federal funding never reached expected levels, thus leaving the states holding the bag. They must provide for programs mandated by federal law without the funds to pay for them.

Secondly, Congress was disgruntled by the way the funds were spent as well as by the results. The states differed in the degree to which they carried out the intention of the Elementary and Secondary Education Act. A study of the use of federal aid to six states reported:[7]

1.   Federal aid to education in the aggregate has only a slight equalizing tendency at best, and within a number of metropolitan areas, it displays distinctly disequalizing characteristics;
2.   The degree of equalization, where it does exist, is usually too small to offset pre-existing disparities among school districts;
3.   Although Title I of ESEA does flow in greater proportion to poorer and higher-need school districts, a number of other federal programs operate to help the rich districts get richer.

Finally, the major pressures for additional educational financing by the federal government were abating in the seventies. The public school enrollment increases ended. As pupil increases ended, so did much of the demand for teachers. In some areas, enrollment has declined drastically enough to close whole schools. In 1973, a study by the Advisory Commission on Intergovernmental Relations, entitled *Financing Schools and Property Tax Relief: A State Responsibility*, concluded that the states possess resources to cope with school finance on their own.[8] In addition to this, the Supreme Court declared in March 1973 in the *Rodriguez v. San Antonio Independent School District* case that the equal protection clause of the Fourteenth Amendment to the federal Constitution does not require that states equalize disparities among school districts. There is little doubt but that the federal government is standing firm in its position that education is a responsibility of the state governments and will provide little additional money in the future. It is, then, up to the states to finance and manage their own systems of education. Many are achieving major reforms in school financing as well as integration. Many are not. It behooves us to examine the conditions under which the decision makers of the states make the fateful decisions in the largest area of state policy.

GROUPS AND INTERESTS AND BASES OF POWER

The Myth of Neutrality

The myth that education should not be involved in politics or that politics should not be in education virtually ruled the minds of many professors of education. Education was a priesthood, and the practice of its expertise, supported by the public's emotional response to sacred values, insulated it from the political arena. Because of the myth, the education profession rejected the two-party system and the mainstream of political life as too corrupt to let education thrive in it. A corollary of the myth suggested that regularly elected representatives in American government could not be trusted by educators and that the welfare of children would require instead separate elections and agencies on the local level. In line with this, nonpartisan elections also would ensure the sacred quality of the school board. At the state level, the education agency would respond to the wishes of the school educators of the state as organized into educational associations of nonpartisan boards of education. Education would be insulated from politics because politics was too "dirty" a process to trust with the education of innocent children.

This myth could survive so long as the public believed it and believed that it was serving the interests of their children. Probably many educators also believed it sincerely and rested comfortably with the idea that the children were better educated by policies set by "neutral" administrators —far from the political scuffles of partisan elections. This has always been a myth. Even in the palmy days of "insulated" education, policies never were effectively insulated from the political process. State legislators always voted the budget for the state portion of school expenses. The school administrators always made their demands known to the state education agencies. In actuality, therefore, education has always been involved in the political process.

What has been devious, however, has been the effect of the myth. If the people as well as the politicians allowed educational policy to be made by the "priesthood," it was made by a small group of privileged educators who were not responsible for their actions to elected leaders or the voters. Avoiding the two-party system in school districts has often carried with it the penalty created by the lack of a loyal opposition—the destruction of the system's capacity for self-criticism. The nature of the politics of education is characteristic of a closed society. In Iannaccone's words:

> The dominant pattern of pedagogical politics at the state level also displays the tendencies toward: (1) the elimination of even a loyal opposition, (2) a reward pattern for maintaining the status quo, (3) the absence of adequate self-criticism, and (4) the establishment of an internal educational power elite.[9]

We started this chapter by stating that educational policy has until very recently been distributive. That is, the greatest benefits of education have gone to certain groups even though the stated purpose of education is redistributive. The reason for this lies in the practice of the myth of the educational priesthood. Because education was insulated from politics, the needs and demands of the people were not brought to the regular decision sites of government. Educational policy was the province of the educators, and they could notice or ignore the needs and demands of the population. The recent round of state supreme court decisions, which state that education has not been provided on an equal basis to all the state's children, illustrates how insulated from the political process educational policy making had become. Because the regular agencies of policy making had not responded, resort was made to the courts. There is evidence that the old order of insulation is changing. Education, the largest single enterprise of state government, is becoming a part of the political process and hence is headed toward redistributive policy.

The reader recalls that, when we discussed pressure groups, we used a four-part formula for describing their power: the base, the means, the scope, and the amount. A pressure group with resources such as votes, internal cohesion, and money, for instance—and skill in converting these into policy—will have a greater amount of power than a pressure group that does not have these attributes. We would assume that a group such as the state educational association would have more power in some states than in others. The combination of the prevailing myth of neutrality plus a cohesive internal structure of power would yield major power over policy. On the other hand, if the political party system did not subscribe, or was beginning to change its previous sentiments toward neutrality, and, if the parties were also cohesive, the educational groups might have to operate within the political arena of two-party politics. I would predict that as the myth of neutrality broke down—as it has in nearly every state in the last few years—the states that had a tradition of strong parties would encourage fragmented educational groups, and states where the parties were weak would encourage strong educational associations. To offer some proof of this theory, let's take a look at some of the major pressure groups at the state level.

The Professional Interest Groups: The Teachers and Administrators

For many years, the most numerous interest group—the teachers—had only potential political power. Traditionally, school teachers have been reluctant to employ collective action because they were told by the administrators that a unified front at the state level would be more beneficial to their interests. This traditional doctrine emphasized the "authority" of the superintendent and favored teacher participation only for its effect on morale building and resultant improved performance. For years the National Education Association and the state affiliates maintained the norms of a unified profession that should not split into opposing interest groups competing for scarce resources and should not engage in public conflict. The NEA, as the leading national organization, concentrated its efforts at the national and state level. The group has impressive resources. It has over a million members, about 52 percent of our public school teachers.[10]

The grand coalition of teachers and administrators within the NEA, however, has fallen apart. The issues that had joined them before 1900 in establishing the public school system and defending it after that broke as governors, legislators, and courts began to question the equity of the allocation patterns of school finance that had been decided by the "priesthood" for so long. Newly militant teachers were also increasingly reluctant to accept allocation decisions by local superintendents and school boards. By 1975, the teachers had formed a national coalition and were the most powerful lobby at the state level. These divisions over priorities for money and value within the profession have spawned professional competitors in the form of teachers and administrators who argue their cases before school boards, legislatures, and governors.

A notable division also exists within the teaching profession itself. The American Federation of Teachers restricts its membership to teachers or to administrators with no direct authority over teachers. The AFT has state affiliates, a membership concentrated in large cities or suburbs, and a budget much smaller than the NEA. AFT executives contend that professional unity is a myth because value conflicts are inevitable between teachers and their managers, the school administrators. The AFT's willingness to resort to a strike has proven attractive to big-city teachers and has shattered the "noblesse oblige" ethic of the NEA. The AFT observes that administrator groups such as the American Association of School Administrators have usually been a majority on the NEA governing boards and has branded the NEA a "company union." The fact remains that the teachers associations, the affiliates of the NEA, enroll by far the largest membership, from roughly twice to hundreds of times as large as the other organizations. The AFT membership ranks second in a number of states, but the federation is virtually nonexistent in many states lacking large urban centers. The administrator groups represent the fewest individuals, ranging from 67 in Florida to 3,229 in California.[11]

A fourth group, usually mentioned briefly in the lineup of professional educational interest groups, is the National School Boards Association and its state affiliates. The school board associations are usually smallest in size if only institutional memberships are counted, but they rank ahead of the administrator groups in number of persons represented. School board associations are comprised of five or so people from each town or city elected to the local school board. They represent the citizens and hence are not strictly "professional" educators. We have observed that school boards have also been under the influence of the school administrators. As long as the school administrators could hold together the coalition of teachers and school boards as spokespersons for education interests at the state level, the monolithic as well as "neutral" educational lobby could function as a single, major power center. After the teachers and administrators split up, the school boards, who, after all, must deal with both at the local level, were out in the cold so far as an alliance was concerned. They now join the coalition of teachers and administrators only when they can agree among themselves. In general, the state school boards associations are not able to exert an influence comparable to the teachers' associations.

Allies of the Professional Interest Groups

The National Congress of Parents and Teachers is not only the largest of the professionals' allies, but the largest volunteer organization in the nation. The PTA is a loose confederation of 43,000 local units (with over 9 million members).[12] The major influence of the PTA is at the local level, and there it is generally observed to be dependent on school administrators. Even with a large membership, the influence of the PTA is minimal over school policy. Most parents are apathetic or ignorant of educational matters. James Koerner expresses my sentiments about the PTA: ". . . that the American PTA is rarely anything more than a coffee-and-cookies organization based on vague good will and gullibility. It is chiefly useful to the administrators for raising money for special projects and persuading parents who are interested enough to attend meetings that the local schools are in the front ranks of American education."[13] While the potential power in the PTA is great—about half the parents of public school children belong—it has weak leadership or leadership that goes along with the professionals when they agree among themselves and stands aside when they don't. There are state PTAs in all the states but they rarely have any legislative or statewide influence. There is an elaborate organizational structure of local, community, district, regional, and state PTAs. This cumbersome apparatus precludes any real policy making. The major purpose of the PTA has become the maintenance of the existing order. It also provides the administrators with a major resource: numbers.

Professionally oriented interest groups can also be found among numerous organizations that embrace education as a secondary concern. The League of Women Voters and the American Association of University Women are examples. These organizations exist for general social improvements, some of which touch on school programs and process. State branches of federations of women's clubs, library associations, and leagues for mental health have all been found involved with education on occasion. The first two of these groups are concerned with school finance in many states at present and may or may not come out as allies of the professional educators. These groups are generally high-status groups, that is, this is their major resource, and they enjoy considerable political influence on matters about which they are concerned. A study of educational coalitions in 12 states indicates that the major member groups consist of the educational organizations (teachers—both association and federation; administrators and school boards) and perhaps one or two closely related school groups like PTAs and, less frequently, the AAUW chapter. In only two states in the study does the coalition include a broad range of noneducational organizations. In Tennessee, the coalition includes such diverse groups as the American Legion, the AAUW, the Junior Chamber of Commerce (Jaycees), the Citizens Committee for Better Schools, and the Federation of Business and Professional Women. In Colorado, coalition membership is perhaps even more diverse, reaching to the Colorado Association of Commerce and Industry, cattlemen, mining interests, sheepmen, and other farm representatives.[14] Of particular interest is the finding that Chambers of Commerce are in the coalition in some states. One would suppose that they would oppose school tax increases and bond proposals. On the other hand, these organizations may be pushing for broad-based taxes levied impartially on all sectors of the state. By definition, such taxes are state taxes—most commonly on sales. Sales taxes, in particular, come to be preferred by business groups as they seek to shift burdens to the nonbusiness sector of the community. A heavy property tax on a manufacturing concern will raise costs for the firm: a sales tax does not appear to have such adverse effects.

Coalitions and Political Party Strength

The coalitions that the professional educators build within their respective states to further their interests have been the subject of several additional studies. In 1967, Iannaccone found four major types of coalitions in the eleven states he examined. The typology is based on the type of influence each coalition has over the state legislature. The first type is characterized by localism. Both legislators and school people represent their school district first of all. Included in this type is an attitude of provincialism, jealousy, and fierce defense of one's home district against outsiders, especially the state.

The second type of organizational structure linking the profession to the legislature is characterized by a statewide pattern of interaction. The professionals speak to the legislature on behalf of education. They are composed of the groups mentioned earlier: teachers, administrators, school boards, and the PTA. This is called the statewide monolithic structure. The professionals speak with a united voice.

The third type is a fragmented relationship among the educational interests. We have already hinted at this when we indicated that teacher unionism is breaking up the old coalition of state educational groups formerly composed of a united alliance of teachers and administrators. Here statewide associations of school board members, teachers of the AFT and NEA state affiliates, school administrators, and parent groups come to the legislature disunited, often in conflict rather than consensus.

The fourth type is statewide syndical. The link between the school people and the legislature is provided by a formal governmental unit. The Illinois School Problems Commission provides the only instance of this type of pattern. The commission includes most of the major interests that had a direct stake in the outcome of public school decisions. It is structured to provide those interests with a direct and official voice. What is provocative about Iannaccone's hypothesis is his theory that states move from one typology to the next. Each type represents a phase in the changing pattern of state educational politics. A change in the legislature brought about by reapportionment may change the balance of power in the educational structure. On the other hand, as the educational coalition breaks down, the legislatures and governors step in to exercise more control.[15] We would expect that states with cohesive political parties would be the first to break down the grand coalition of educators as the myth of the sacredness of education faded away and educational problems entered the political process. States in which urban districts make demands for additional funds or increased integration would progress from a monolithic to a fragmented type of educational interest structure. Rural, suburban, and city interests divide the coalition. Table 9-1 illustrates the preceding points. Unfortunately we have only 18 states represented by the table, but

TABLE 9–1

Progression in the Pressure-Group Politics of
Education

PARTY STRENGTH[a]	PHASE I DISPARATE (LOCALLY BASED)	PHASE II MONOLITHIC (STATEWIDE)	PHASE III FRAGMENTED (STATEWIDE)	PHASE IV SYNDICAL (STATEWIDE)
Strong	Vt. (1967)		Mich. (1974)	
		Mass. (1967) →	Mass. (1974)	
		N.Y. (1967) →	N.Y. (1974)	
		R.I. (1967)		
			Wis. (1974)	
			Minn. (1974)	
		Colo. (1974) →	Colo. (1974)	
		Va. (1972)		
Moderate	N.H. (1967)	N.J. (1967)	Neb. (1974)	Ill. (1967)
		Mo. (1964)	Cal. (1974)	
Weak	Texas (1972)			
	Ga. (1974) →	Ga. (1974)		
	Fla. (1974) ————————————→		Fla. (1974)	

[a] Party strength is measured as in Table 4–1.
Source: The dates following the states indicate the following: 1967, Lawrence Iannacone, *Politics in Education*; 1974, JAlan Aufderheide, "Educational Interest Groups ... "; 1964, Nicholas A. Masters et al., *State Politics and the Public Schools* (New York: Knopf, 1964); 1972, Joel S. Berke and Michael W. Kirst, *Federal Aid to Education* ... , chapters 6 and 7.

we can get an idea of the progression. Since Iannaccone wrote in 1967, three states have moved from the monolithic phase of educational pressure-group structure into the fragmented phase. They are all states with strong party systems. (We have no results on Rhode Island to tell us whether that state has also progressed into the fragmented phase.) The Aufderheide study made in 1974 indicates also that some states are moving out of the locally based phase into Phase II or Phase III. The major impact of the table is that two-thirds of the states in Phase III are strong party states, which confirms the hypothesis that strong parties are associated with fragmented pressure groups. Apparently a close relationship exists between the strength of political parties and the ability of pressure groups to make demands. For a considerable period, parties were content to let the educators "run the show." So long as the people subscribed to the sacredness of education—that is, so long as the people were content to let the chief priests of the educational establishment make policy, the politicians stayed out of the way. Politicians do not ask for trouble. Generally, they try to go along with what the public wants. However, as the cities began to make demands (fortified by increased representation in state legislatures) that the politicians could not ignore, or as the state courts placed a mandate upon the legislatures to redistribute educational funds, the political parties began to represent these demands. No longer could they let the educators run the show. The educators themselves began to disagree and the old coalition fell apart.

THE PROCESS OF MAKING SCHOOL DECISIONS

This section discusses the location and process of making school decisions. We begin with decision making that is closest to the parents and children —the local school district.

The 16,000 School Districts

The states have delegated authority to the local school district for the administration of free public education. Once the township school was prevalent in America, but now there are districts incorporating just elementary or high schools or both, which may also include vocational and other special-education schools. The school district is set up to reflect and administer the local citizens' schooling needs. It incorporates the voters of a designated geographical area whose needs in education are administered by a school board (nearly always elected but sometimes appointed) which appoints a superintendent (in a few places, elected) to whom is given the tasks of administering the schools in the district.

The balance of power in most local systems is strongly in favor of the superintendent of schools, in large part because of the failure of the school boards to exercise a greater voice in policy. This accusation would probably be denied by the administrators themselves who would claim that the board makes policy and the administrators carry it out. This view is also proclaimed by their national organization, The American Association of School Administrators. A recent study of the governance of American schools concluded that school boards are not instruments of democracy in the sense that they represent the people. In three areas, the traditional school board has fallen down according to the authors:

1. In the area of selection of members, the writers found that competition for the places on the school board are limited, and sponsorship and preemptive appointments are common. Challenges to the status quo are infrequent; incumbents are but rarely challenged and more rarely still defeated.
2. In the area of interaction with constituents, the writers found that

communication was sparse. The board felt threatened when any but harmless group activity flourished because it might mean that not all was well in the district, that the natives were restless.

3. In the area of the ability of the board to control the superintendent, the writers found that the majority of boards found no conflict between their responsibilities to the public and their obligations to the school administration. Members of the board displayed deference to the superintendent. Higher-status boards were even more likely than lower-status boards to stay clear of the day-to-day administration. The writers found that boards that were more political—in other words, those whose members were recruited through the political process and who ran in partisan elections—were more likely to challenge the superintendent. Unfortunately, the majority of boards did not appear to be political.[16]

This study reinforces the main argument of the present book—that political parties have an important role to play in our states, namely, the function of recruiting, electing, and governing. Zeigler and Jennings found that where this is lacking, as it is in most jurisdictions because of the strong myth of nonpartisanship in education, the people were not properly represented.

An area in which the people participate directly in school decisions at the local level is financing. There is no public policy in state government in which the exercise of popular sovereignty takes place more frequently than school financing—and schools have for decades required the largest state and local expenditures. The importance of school fiscal referenda—bond, tax levy, and budget "elections"—has become evident recently in the newspaper reporting of crises in schools across the nation because of voter defeats of school budgets, bond proposals, and tax levies. Recall that we have said repeatedly that the primary source of revenue for local governments is the property tax and that the primary expenditure of local government is schools. The two are linked in the voters' minds. The voters' tolerance of school tax rate increases and bond issues has declined markedly since the 1950s when school proposals rarely lost. Numerous referenda have generated intense community conflict and have produced fiscal crises for many school systems. One estimate is that there are about 7,000 tax levy and budget elections annually across the country with eight states accounting for over 5,000. There are amazing differences in the frequency of levy elections. Oklahomans vote in more than 1,800 such elections each year; New York has 800 budget elections; and there are 600 tax levy referenda in Ohio and Michigan; while the other states have less than a dozen.[17]

By 1968, the rate of budget and tax levy defeats was alarming to school officials in several states, and efforts were made to modify or abolish the referendum system. There is no question but that the referendum system can cause uncertainty and instability in school financing and operation. As Hamilton and Cohen point out, it is not mere coincidence that most of the school crises and all of the school closings have occurred in referenda states.[18] Some states impose more restrictions on the referendum system, and more stability of finance is assured. Another study tested for the changing attitudes of voters on the subject of school finance over the years since 1969. By 1972, in a national sample 56 percent of the parents of children in the public schools as well as 56 percent nonparents would oppose a school financial issue that required additional tax support.[19] In June 1978, the voters of California in a statewide referendum approved by 64 percent an amendment to the constitution limiting property taxes. Clearly, where the option exists to register disapproval of the local property tax, many voters are doing so. The result of all this will undoubtedly be some form of local tax relief. The states with their superior taxing power will be forced to aid local communities in meeting their school budgets. We return to this problem later on.

Education Agencies at the State Level

The hierarchy of school agencies at the state level is patterned after the local level. The hierarchy is frequently referred to as the state education agency (SEA), but it is tripartite. A state board of education (SBE) and chief state school officer (CSSO) emerged with responsibility for oversight and policy making in at least half the states by 1900 and exist in all states today. (Wisconsin has no SBE.) The state department of education (SDE) is charged with daily administration. These agencies have varying amounts of input in the policy-making process depending on economic and political factors.

The method of selection and the powers given to the state boards of education do have some impact on their influence, but regardless of whether they are elected or appointed, the state boards have little capability as actors in the educational policy systems of the states. There have been some notable exceptions: the involvement of Texas' state board of education in the school finance issue and Minnesota's in the school desegregation issue. Most boards have the authority to set policy regarding curriculum standards as well as authority over teacher certification. A study of twelve states, however, shows no strong evidence that boards initiate many proposals or mobilize support in these or other areas.

The major finding of the study is that state boards primarily gave legitimation to the proposals made by chief state school officers.[20] Members of the state boards of education perceived that the CSSOs were highly influential. Where differences of opinion exist among education interests in a state, the studies show that the chief's position will more likely reflect the interests of management (administrators and school boards) than those of teachers. Perhaps this is because most chiefs and their top staff members have had experience as administrators and reflect this perspective. If there is a fracturing of education groups, the teacher groups, because of superior numbers, generally gain access to the legislature, while the CSSOs serve as a point of access for the administrators.

According to the study, CSSO influence with the legislators is related to their method of selection and to several other political variables. Apparently, independently elected CSSOs develop programs and policies of their own, which, because of their electoral backing, bear weight with the legislators. If the CSSO is appointed by governor, he or she undoubtedly reflects the governor's program and has less impact on the legislators. The 12-state study also found moderate relationships between interparty competition (which is a surrogate for party cohesion) and voting turnout and legislative influence of the CSSO, and the relationships were negative.[21] Apparently, the CSSO does not have as much power in the legislatures of states in which the voters express an interest and in which party cohesion exists. This accords, although somewhat modestly, with the major hypothesis of the present book, that is, that the strength of the political party and interest of the electorate can account for the type of policy in a state. In states where the parties are weak and the voters apathetic, policy making responds to other pressures—it does not represent the needs and demands of the people as well as in states where a responsible party system does exist.

The state department of education is usually described as the executive or implementing arm of the policy-making state board. Since we have already stressed that most boards of education lack real policy-making powers, and that they are primarily legitimating agencies for the CSSOs who head the state departments of education, we are led to the conclusion that the CSSOs and their departments traditionally have been the arena where educational policy has been made. The SDE has had close ties with the professional statewide associations of teachers, administrators, and curriculum specialists who provide demands and supports for SDE's decisions and recommendations to the board. For many years the SDEs responded to their constituency of professional interest groups and of malapportioned state legislatures, both favoring rural areas. The increasing impact of state and federal aid is bringing more attention to the cities and hence to an expanding SDE role throughout the state. The legislature and governor will try to exert more influence over the SDEs of the future. Because the allocation of education funds is a major issue in the states and because the state share is increasing, governors must ensure that the SDEs are responsive to their wishes rather than to the traditional educational establishment.

In most states, the control structure for public higher education is independent of that for elementary and secondary education. SEAs rarely have permanent, well-established relations with colleges and universities, even though such links would be highly desirable. Colleges and universities are usually governed by boards of trustees or regents, and it is customary for the governor to nominate members, often subject to confirmation by the upper house of the legislature. The picture has been one in which higher education is fragmented with each institution's governing board and academic administrators desiring to deal directly with the governor. In the typical state, community colleges, state colleges, and state universities are all separately organized under their own boards. Today, there is a strong movement toward reformed organization for higher education through some coordinative device that will reduce institutional autonomy and independence and ensure common overall planning. State after state has established coordinating boards. While some effort has been devoted to voluntary coordination, the wave of the future is clearly to take many broad educational policy decisions out of the hands of individual institutions and place them under single boards with substantial coercive powers.[22]

The Governor

As education became a political issue, as it was drawn inevitably into the forefront of politics by disagreements over desegregation, finance, unionization of teachers, and so on, the governors and their parties had to take notice, propose policy, and attempt to see this policy through the legislatures. We would predict that governors who can get their parties to back their proposals will have a better chance to see their proposals become law. Most of the 12 governors interviewed in the study by Campbell and Mazzoni thought that education was a campaign issue in 1970. Governors in Minnesota, Michigan, Wisconsin, and Florida were actively involved in defining educational issues so as to stress the need for reform in school finance and taxation. In Georgia, Tennessee, and Texas, governors focused on educational programs. In Georgia, a major issue was early childhood education; in Tennessee, it was kindergarten education; in Texas, the issues were vocational and technical education.[23] Once a proposal has emerged from the governor's office, his staff members research the issue and make recommendations for legislation. In this process, they may seek the advice of state education agencies and CSSOs but they are not bound by these agencies and often seek advice elsewhere. In addition, where educational interest groups are fragmented, we would not expect any one group to be ascendant. When governors possess power, they can control

SEA budget requests, influence state legislatures and state boards of education to do their bidding, and employ state personnel boards and finance agencies to keep SEAs under control.

As we would expect from our analysis of the political leadership role of the governor, his success in legislative enactment of his educational policies depends on the strength of his legislative contingent or his skill in obtaining enough votes from the opposition to pass his program, if his party is in the minority. In New York, the governor calls in his legislative leaders and maintains close contact with them throughout the session. They do much of his legislative work for him. In the 1970–71 legislative sessions in Tennessee, California, and Massachusetts, the governors were faced with majorities in opposition. They had to enter into coalitions with the party leadership on the other side. In Massachusetts, the Republican governor appealed to a strong liberal Democratic faction as well as compromising with the legislative leadership. On the other hand, in Florida, Georgia, and Texas, where the governor had legislative majorities, these were so large that factions developed that he could not control. In Florida, the executive cabinet included six other elected officials, among them the CSSO who could lobby directly in the legislature if more funds were desired.[24]

In the states where governors have become involved in the educational policy-making process, the educational output reflects this involvement. Hines discovered that states where the governor is assertive in educational policy making have made a greater effort to tax their citizens to redistribute the benefits of education. These states also spend more on education.[25] Thus, it appears that, as the governors take on education as a policy issue, it enters the political arena. Legislatures view it as a plank in the governor's program and react to it accordingly. More effort is made to tax the citizens of the state to provide the benefits of education.

The Legislature

While the governor and the legislature necessarily interact in the policy-making process, many factors determine how the legislators will react to the governor's proposals. As the governors become more involved in the educational policy-making process, legislatures have also begun to reform their operations to better enable them to cope with these increasing demands for policy enactment. In fact, a high degree of gubernatorial involvement goes along with a reformed legislature. Legislatures are developing countervailing capacities in building up their own independent resources in the form of increased professional staffing and research capabilities. These resources permit the legislature to perform an independent examination of proposals coming from the governor's office as well as from various education groups and agencies.

Another reform of the state legislative process, which makes it more likely that the legislature will become the focus of educational policy, is greater representation of urban and suburban areas in state legislatures as a result of the Supreme Court's one-man, one-vote reapportionment decision in *Baker v. Carr.* Before this decision allowed for a fuller representation of urban and suburban legislators, a rural localism pervaded the state legislatures in many states. Bailey describes these proponents of localism in the Northeast:

> These stalwarts are emphatically not against good schools. Their main concern, however, is to oppose, and, if possible, to thwart, the pernicious growth of the power of state government. . . . Their legislative frame of reference begins—and all too often ends—with consideration of their own community's advantage. They grapple with law-making by applying the only standards they feel sure of—hometown benefit.[26]

Governors must grapple with vestiges of this attitude over 16 years later. In Minnesota, Governor Anderson's education proposals were never assigned to the education committee because it appeared likely that the conservative chairman would bottle up the proposals. Instead they were sent to the fiscal committees as part of the budget. As a result, the house education committee, which had traditionally made revisions in the school finance formula in conjunction with the state department of education and educational interest groups (especially the Minnesota School Boards Association), was effectively bypassed. The short-circuiting of this committee reduced the power of the conservative education chairman as well as lessened the impact of the education lobby, which had enjoyed direct access to the education committee.[27]

Increasing fragmentation of interest groups, a condition predicted by Iannaccone more than ten years ago, has the result of increasing the role of the legislature in educational policy. Some school-aid proposals force a realignment of the traditional educational coalitions. Proposals that would help poor districts at the expense of rich ones may immobilize the statewide education groups whose constituencies include all types of groups. In the past, groups could get together periodically with key legislators on the education and appropriation committees to increase the existing state-aid formula. Now the old alliances are breaking apart and the hold these groups have on key committees is diminishing. In summary, the three reasons the legislature is better able to cope with educational policy are: professionalism, reapportionment, and the diminished power of the educational lobby because of fragmentation of interests within it.

The Courts

It has become evident that parents, students, educators, and political leaders accept the involvement of the courts in the educational process. We will mention briefly the role the courts play in the educational decision-making process at the state level. There is a marble-cake relationship between the federal and state courts in the division of responsibility for education. Table 9–2 indicates the division of the state and federal court cases that affected the schools from 1946 to 1971.

John C. Hogan identifies five stages in the evolution of the roles of both state and federal courts in education in three principal areas: race, wealth, and individual rights.[28]

1. The stage of strict judicial laissez faire. From 1789 to about 1850, the federal and state courts ignored education. The state courts left it to the educators. School policies were generally reviewed only for reasonableness, and, unless they were shown to be arbitrary or capricious, the courts would not question the wisdom of school rules.
2. The stage of state control of education. During the period from about 1850 to 1950, state courts asserted that education was exclusively a state and local matter. There developed during this period a broad body of statutory and decisional law at the state level that permitted and encouraged school policies and practices which did not meet minimum constitutional standards.
3. The reformation stage. Federal court involvement in education after 1950 came about primarily because of state statutes and educational policies that required separation of the races in the schools. In *Brown v. Board of Education of Topeka,* decided in 1954, the U.S. Supreme

TABLE 9–2

State and Federal Court Cases That Have Affected the Organization, Administration, and Programs of the Schools (1946–71)

PERIODS	TOTAL	STATE COURT	FEDERAL COURT
1946–56	7,203	7,091	112
1956–66	4,420	3,691	729
1967–71	3,510	2,237	1,273
Totals	15,133	13,019	2,114

Source: The three periods in this table were taken from a more complete table of the same name. Reprinted by permission of the publisher from John C. Hogan, *The Schools, the Courts, and the Public Interest* (Lexington, Mass.: Lexington Books, Heath, 1974), p. 7.

Court declared that such statutes and policies violated the equal protection clause of the Fourteenth Amendment and were therefore
unconstitutional.

4. The stage of "education under supervision of the courts." Concurrent
   with the reformation stage, a discernible tendency has developed for
   both state and federal courts to expand the scope of their powers over
   the schools (for example, intervention in matters affecting the administration, organization, and programs of the schools; retaining jurisdiction over cases until their mandates, orders, and decrees have been
   carried out). This is clearly a new judicial function.

5. Hogan calls this last stage the stage of "strict construction" at the
   federal level. I call it "the stage of education as a fundamental interest" at the state level. This stage was first associated with school financing systems in August 1971 when the Supreme Court of California
   announced in *Serrano v. Priest* (quoted in the introduction to this
   chapter), that education is a "fundamental interest," and that principle was quickly cited with approval and followed in courts across the
   country, e.g., Texas, Minnesota, New Jersey, and Connecticut. However, the Supreme Court of the United States two years later in *San
   Antonio Independent School District v. Rodriguez,* refused to accept
   the "right-to-education" argument, saying that education is not one of
   the rights specified in the *federal* Constitution. (This is why Hogan
   gives this section the title of "strict construction.") The door was left
   open, however, for state court review of such systems on state constitutional grounds. Many challenges have arisen to school finance structures that are now before the state courts. Apparently, the Supreme
   Court is now about to back away from its earlier "reformation" stage
   and leave education to state control. This means that education will
   be distributed to the children of the various states as a consequence
   of state political and social structures for decision making.

Shortly we will consider both race and wealth as factors affecting the
distribution of education benefits to the children in this country. Federal
and state courts are involved in both areas. A third area of court involvement is the expanding area of student and teacher rights. Courts have
been asked to review the constitutionality of school rules and practices
pertaining to freedom of expression (pure speech and symbolic expression), hair styles and grooming, behavior and campus discipline, preg-
nancy, corporal punishment, admission and graduation requirements,
suspension, expulsion, and so on. Use of test scores for pupil placement and
teacher employment and promotion purposes has been successfully challenged in the courts. Because of the long period of judicial laissez faire, a
body of decisional law has developed at the state level that permitted
school authorities to make rules and regulations governing student and

teacher conduct, but that failed to meet the requirements of the First Amendment freedoms. Much of the recent federal court activity in this area has been to correct this situation.

We are interested in education as redistributive policy—in other words, as a service that should be offered to all children. In this chapter, we concern ourselves with equality of education as it is offered in our states. We will not further consider student and teacher rights as guaranteed by the First Amendment, although it is a major area in which the courts have spoken in recent years.

EDUCATION AS DISTRIBUTIVE POLICY HEADED TOWARD REDISTRIBUTIVE POLICY

In the introduction to this chapter, I stated that education as it has been offered in the states of this country has been distributive rather than redistributive, as it is promised in each state constitution. The taxpayers of each state pay for education, the primary benefits of which go to well-to-do children. The neediest children get the least benefits of education in our states. Policy that benefits specific groups at taxpayers' expense is distributive policy. Hence, education policy has been distributive. Due to recent court decisions and efforts on the part of those pleading the cause of the disadvantaged, however, education is heading away from distributive toward redistributive policy in many states. In these states, political leaders and educators are attempting to redistribute the advantages of education in order that those who have may receive equally with those who do not have—taking primarily from children in the white suburbs and giving to the children in poor and black inner cities. In the following three sections, we will discuss educational policy as distributive headed toward redistributive in three areas: desegregation, finance, and higher education.

School Desegregation

Many people are not aware of what it was like to be a black citizen in the South in 1954. All the public schools were segregated; public accommodations were segregated; only a minute percentage of registered voters were black; and black public officeholders were virtually nonexistent. Black families earned less than half the medium income of white families, and illiteracy rates were overwhelmingly high. Then, on May 17, 1954, the United States Supreme Court decided *Brown v. Board of Education (Brown I)*, holding unanimously that segregation of white and black children in state public schools, solely on the basis of race and pursuant to statutes permitting or requiring such segregation, denied to black children the equal protection of the laws guaranteed by the Fourteenth Amendment. State-imposed segregation of the races in public schools "generates a feeling of inferiority as to their status in the community that may affect their hearts and minds in a way unlikely ever to be undone."[29]

When the courts, state or federal, act on such a momentous policy issue, it is because the political process has been unresponsive. This is still the case in school desegregation, although the problem has moved north. In 1954, however, the focus of school desegregation was in the South. On May 31, 1955 *Brown II,* the implementation decision, was handed down, again by a unanimous Court ordering segregated public school systems to "effectuate a transition to a racially nondiscriminatory school system ... with all deliberate speed." The Court gave local school authorities the primary responsibility for the implementation supervised by the federal district court.

Little was accomplished in the way of desegregation in the South in the years immediately after 1955. While significant desegregation did occur voluntarily or with a minimum of resistance in some border states, in the 11 states of the Confederacy, school desegregation cases became mired in delaying tactics and obstructionism at the federal district level. In Virginia, the resisters halted all steps to racial integration for almost five years. In 1958, pursuant to the governor's recommendation, the General Assembly of Virginia enacted an appropriation bill rider cutting off state funds to localities that integrated their schools. Governor Almond also supervised the passage of the "Little Rock" bill which provided for the automatic closing of any public school patrolled by United States military forces.[30]

By the early 1960s, the federal government recognized that "all deliberate speed" had not taken place. Opinion polls in the North reported the sympathy of the North to faster desegregation in the South. At that time, the desegregation of only two percent of black students in the Deep South could not be reconciled with the *Brown* decision. Congress then passed the 1964 Civil Rights Act, Title VI of which was a straightforward declaration that nondiscrimination in public schools receiving federal financial support represented the will of the national legislature. Funds would be withheld from districts that failed to comply. This marked the end of massive resistance in the South. Table 9–3 reveals the state of desegregation in the South in 1963–64, a situation that prompted congressional action. With both the judicial and executive branches of the U.S. government joined in concentrated effort, substantial progress began to be made in the South. By 1966, 14 percent of southern black school children attended predominantly white schools. This figure rose to 18 percent by 1968, and then jumped dramatically to 40 percent by 1970. By 1972, the

TABLE 9–3

Status of Southern School Desegregation,
1963–64

COMPLIANCE AND STATES	DISTRICTS DESEGREGATED[a] (PERCENT)	BLACKS IN DESEGREGATED SCHOOLS (PERCENT)
Token compliance	26.5	2.26
Arkansas	5.7	.33
Florida	23.9	1.53
North Carolina	23.4	.54
Tennessee	31.5	2.72
Texas	29.3	5.52
Virginia	43.0	1.63
Minimal compliance	1.77	0.13
Alabama	3.51	.007
Georgia	2.21	.052
Louisiana	3.00	.602
Mississippi	0.00	.000
South Carolina	.92	.003

[a]Only for districts containing both races.
Source: Adapted from a table by the same name in Frederick M. Wirt and Michael W. Kirst, *The Political Web of American Schools* (Boston: Little, Brown, 1972), p. 185.

South led the nation in school desegregation with more than 46 percent of its black school children attending predominantly white schools.[31] Overall, the southern experience with desegregation should be judged a qualified success. In spite of the fact that the number of private schools burgeoned from 1965 to 1970 as a haven for white escapists, their attendance represents only 5 percent of all southern white school children.[32] Much of the South is nonmetropolitan, and many blacks live outside the central cities. A majority of southern school districts consist of medium- to small-sized cities and towns and rural areas where the accomplishment of desegregation is relatively easy and where the whites cannot flee to the suburbs nor afford the high costs of private schools for their children.

Outside the South, the vast majority of blacks live in large cities. It is in these major metropolitan areas that desegregation is most difficult because the whites can move to the suburbs and can afford to send their children to private schools, if necessary. Whites have migrated to the suburbs in a steady stream, with the result that central cities and their suburbs are now stratified by race. School districts are mostly contiguous with municipal boundaries, which makes school desegregation nearly impossible if left up to the local school district. In other words, where residential living patterns separate the races, statutes requiring such segregation may not exist; segregation simply occurs by fact. This is the distinction between de jure segregation promoted by law and de facto segregation brought about by living patterns. The Supreme Court has noted this difference and made a shift in interpretation from process (laws) to outcomes (results of laws and decisions). In 1973, in *Keyes v. School District No. 1*, the Denver decision, the Court said that states and school districts must be responsible for the results of their decisions, even though the decisions are not racist in themselves. If, for example, a district (city) built a new school in an entirely black neighborhood, it would be presumed that the school was constructed in order that a segregated policy might be enforced.

Many proponents of desegregation carry this argument one step further and state that metropolitan residential segregation is a denial of equal educational opportunity. Many have concluded that the only effective remedy is consolidated desegregation planning over entire metropolitan regions affecting central cities and suburbs alike. Residential preferences thus would not exclusively determine school assignments, and the racial stratification between central cities and suburbs would be broken. Suits for consolidated desegregation already have been brought and approved by federal district judges in two prominent cases involving the Richmond and Detroit metropolitan areas. In both cases, the United States Supreme Court refused to sanction consolidation. In *Milliken v. Bradley*, the Detroit case, a justice indicated that an interdistrict remedy would be appropriate where it could be shown that state authorities had acted to deny equal opportunities.

There is no doubt, however, that the Supreme Court is backing away from desegregation decisions. In effect, the Court seems to be saying that the state political process must solve the tough desegregation decisions of the North. Nothing says that a state may not adopt a metropolitan remedy to its segregated schools. The fact that the Supreme Court says that a state is not forced to do so unless it can be shown that it is deliberately segregating the races does not prevent the state from positive action. The Court cannot substitute itself for the political process. Returning to the Detroit case for a moment: After the district court had tried to desegregate the city within its limits—a difficult task in a school district more than 75 percent black—and the NAACP appealed the case, the appellate court recognized the validity of both sides. The court said that only a politically generated solution, in which the suburbs are induced to share Detroit's predicament would have any prospect of success. This solution is better performed by the legislative and executive branches of the government.

The yellow school bus is the symbol of the attempt to integrate the schools. Although it has been the traditional daily mode of transporting children, busing for the purpose of racial balance has provoked violence in the streets. It is no wonder the courts have backed away, leaving the solution to "the political process." The political process can be rough. In a school district near San Francisco, a leader of the anti-busing movement said:

> I would do everything in my power to resist it. . . . Under no circumstances will my kids ever ride a bus for even one minute for the purpose of integration.[33]

In Boston, white parents protested en masse, spat on popular Senator Edward Kennedy, and kept children home from school in defiance of federal judge Garrity's integration orders.[34]

Why does busing evoke such violence between whites? A thoughtful study of a school district near San Francisco identified the two white groups in conflict: the working class and lower-middle-class conservatives who were overtly racist and the upper-middle-class liberals who controlled the school board and who favored integration.[35] The liberals, however, could not accomplish their goals of integrating the schools. Their failure to do so lay in their inability to cope with racial conflict. Their plans were incoherent, inept, and politically unfair and were bound to arouse large numbers of formerly inactive men and women who were most immediately threatened by the integration of the schools. For these people, race is not an abstract problem far from home, as it is for many upper-middle-class liberals. Their jobs, their neighborhoods, their schools are threatened by upward mobility among blacks. With little to show for a lifetime of hard work and striving, the working-class conservatives in the district near San Francisco were not about to make way for newcomers.

For too long, educational policy had been made by a small upper-class elite—a policy that left the working class and lower-middle-class out. When the upper-class liberals sought to integrate the schools under the threat of court action, the working classes moved into the political arena in large numbers. Every dimension of racism was exposed—stereotyping, hostility, unreasoning fear, special fantasies, prejudice, in an attempt to thwart integration and oust the liberal coalition from power. In the end, they succeeded. They defeated the integrationist school board by a 2.5 to 1 victory and dashed the dream of desegregating the ghetto schools. This story illustrates the difficulty encountered as community after community attempted integration in the years following the Brown decision. The courts have backed down now, leaving integration to the political process, and the political process has not coped with the racial tensions in our society. Given these tensions, integration of the schools has slowed; delays are granted by the courts and cases are not reopened. Black children continue to go to segregated ghetto schools.

Table 9–4 discloses the degree of desegregation that exists in the 40 states that have appreciable minority populations. There appear to be

TABLE 9–4

Desegregation in Public Schools, 1976

MINORITIES AS PERCENT OF ALL SCHOOL-AGE CHILDREN*	PERCENT OF MINORITY CHILDREN ATTENDING DESEGREGATED SCHOOLS (UNDER 50% MINORITY GROUP)		
	20–40%	41–60%	61–100%
6–14%	Connecticut Ohio	Massachusetts Indiana Wisconsin	Utah Nebraska Kansas Oregon Rhode Island Washington Wyoming Kentucky South Dakota
15–29%	Tennessee Illinois Michigan Missouri New Jersey Pennsylvania	Virginia Alaska Arkansas Delaware Florida	Nevada Oklahoma Colorado
30–53%	Mississippi New York Louisiana New Mexico South Carolina Texas	Alabama Georgia Maryland North Carolina Arizona California	

* The term minorities refers to Blacks, American Indians, Alaskan natives, and Hispanics.
Source: Data used with permission of The Council of State Governments, Table 2, "Fall Enrollment in Public Elementary and Secondary Day Schools, 1975–1976 and 1976–1977," *The Book of the States, 1978–1979*, Vol. 22, (Lexington, Ky.), p. 337 and Table 246, "Minority Enrollment in Public Elementary and Secondary Schools by Minority Group School Enrollment—States, 1976" *U.S. Statistical Abstract, 1979*, p. 152.

three distinct groups of states: (1) the first (in the upper right corner of the table) is a group of states with small numbers of minority school children and in which it is not so difficult to integrate; (2) the second group (in the middle row of the table) represents many large industrial states with significant numbers of minority school children in ghettos in large cities that have not integrated their schools to any great extent because of the existing de facto segregation; (3) the third group of states, states in the deep South as well as New York and California, have made extraordinary progress in integrating their schools so that they are between 30 to 60 percent integrated. Comparison of the present status of the southern states with their status ten years ago reveals tremendous progress in desegregation (see Table 9–3).

Education is a state function. The fact that it has been performed by local school districts does not mean that it is not a state responsibility. For example, in Cleveland in the fall of 1976, the local and state boards of education placed a full-page advertisement in the daily papers calling for cooperation with court-ordered desegregation. In Columbus, a Metropolitan Columbus Schools Committee composed of community groups, business and industry leaders, foundations, and local citizens helped the city initiate system-wide busing to achieve desegregation. A community-awareness program featured billboards, TV spots, a school child's jingle, neighborhood programs, and a telephone factline.

Solutions to desegregation will call for imaginative policy making at the state and local level. In a district where the students are more than 75 percent black, one type of solution is called for. In another, such as Hartford, Connecticut, community interest and geographical feasibility have made modest metropolitan desegregation work. In certain places, busing may work, and, in others, busing will be resented. Magnet schools whose special curriculums draw students from a large area have afforded an exciting educational opportunity to students from an entire city, as in Dayton, Boston, and Houston. Many solutions can be wrought, given the willingness and imagination of educators, community leaders, and political leaders.

School Finance Reform

The American educational system is characterized by widespread inequality. In the previous section, we described the inequality of educational opportunity received by black children. This section will consider the inequality of opportunity in education received by *poor* children. There is an overlap here, of course, because so many of the black children are poor. The bias against the poor may be found both in the quality of education offered them and in the average number of years they complete. The result is a substantial difference between the amount of resources our society invests in the typical poor youth and its expenditure on children whose parents are average or above average in economic status.

Professor Coons tells the story of two schoolboys who lived in California in 1970.[36] They could be any color, but they were, in fact, white from a white neighborhood. One lived on 36th Street in Oakland, California; his friend lived across the street in Emeryville. Every weekday morning at 8:00 they separated, each to attend his assigned public school—one in the Oakland system, one in the Emeryville district. The state of California, like most states, has provided a system guaranteeing to one child a superior education, while to the other it offers one that is mediocre or inferior. Oakland spent $600 to $700 on the first child; the Emeryville student went first-class at nearly three times that expense. Coons pointed out that this situation was not extreme nor extraordinary. The spectrum of school districts in California included expenditures both higher and considerably lower than these. This was the picture in other states in 1970 and does not differ radically from conditions today in most states. In Illinois, expenditures ranged from $390 for students in the lowest ranks to $1,129 for those in the highest, and, in Connecticut, Massachusetts, New Jersey, and New York, the situation was not much better.[37] Coons contended that there is something incongruous about a differential of *any* magnitude, the sole justification for which is an imaginary school line between two children.

Our state governments, by leaving the financing and administration of education to the local level, embrace the philosophy that, as a rule, the quality of education should be in direct proportion to the wealth of the school district; in general, this also means that quality will be in inverse proportion to the needs of children. The primary dependence of public education on the real property tax and the localization of that tax's administration and expenditure have combined to make the public school into an educator for the educated rich and a keeper for the uneducated poor. Education policy has been clearly distributive. It has systematically given benefits to wealthy districts and has discriminated against poor districts.

How has this come about in states that proclaim equality of education in their constitutions, as every state does? Political forces support the status quo. For generations, the topic of raising and distributing revenues for public schools was the domain of a small group of specialists. The people who dealt with the subject were finance officials in state education departments, a few legislators who had made the area their speciality, a professor or two from a state teachers college, representatives from the state school boards association, and the American Association of School Administrators. The topic of school financing was clouded in jargon indigenous to this exclusive group. The subject received little attention from the public and, hence, was not a political issue. During our discussion of pressure groups, we noted that a locally based or a monolithic structure of education groups could accomplish its ends away from public scrutiny. It was only when the structure crumbled into fragments that the political process began to receive the demands and, in response, assign priorities to them.

Any change in the existing distribution of resources to schools will be resisted by powerful forces. Districts favored by a superior tax base are likely to be opposed to change on all grounds; districts of average affluence are apathetic but can also be opposed to change because they fear loss of control. Poor districts, alone, have a clear interest in change, but they do not have sufficient strength in the legislatures to bargain alone for redistribution. They must ally themselves with the poorer suburbs or with the poorer rural districts.

Three major forces brought about the impetus for change from the usual distributive politics of education to that of redistribution. The first consisted of a group of economists, political scientists, and public administrators who began to examine the way the schools were financed. Going beyond the intricacies of the complicated aid formulas (which we will mention later), the new specialists turned their attention to the results of these formulas. They found that the existing school finance systems did not go very far toward equalizing tax burdens and educational spending among different school districts. Spending per pupil varied widely, as Coons illustrates. Local tax rates also varied markedly. But what was particularly disturbing was the demonstration that communities with high tax rates frequently achieved only average or even lower-than-average spending levels. By contrast, the higher-spending districts were able to support their budgets with only moderate or low local tax effort. This is because the amount of money available for education depends on the amount of property wealth that happens to exist within the district. The total value, composition, and amount of property (the tax base), the accuracy of assessment procedures used to measure that value, and the tax effort (rate) applied all affect the amount of money raised for education. Citizens in property-poor districts may produce less revenue per child at a higher tax rate than their property-rich neighbors. As a result, their children may receive less in the way of educational services.

There were other defects in the system. For example, there was a concentration of disadvantaged and handicapped pupils in the largest cities where the general financial situation was undergoing marked deterioration and where the cost of living was highest in the state. Despite this situation, state-aid systems were geared to the 1920s when cities were rich and needed little aid, while their environs were poor. On the average, 40 percent more central city than suburban residents earned poverty-level wages. Home and rental values, the basis of property taxation, increased only half as fast in central cities during the 1960s. The crime rate was twice as high. While central cities spent two-thirds or more of their budgets for nonschool expenditures, suburbs spent less than half. City residents were paying 30 percent higher per capita taxes for inferior services. Table 9-5 gives this disparity in spending related to the wealth of the district in 1970. There are two sets of states in which the disparity between wealthiest and poorest districts is the greatest. Some of these ratios are indicated in parentheses. In these states, which are in the Good-Effort box, the political process has managed to equalize spending so that the amount spent per pupil between the poorest district and the wealthiest districts (90th percentile) is less than 2 to 1. The states boxed in the lower right are singled out for lack of effort. In these states there is the least disparity between the districts in taxable wealth, and yet per pupil spending ranges from 2 to 1 to nearly 3 to 1. Table 9–5 also shows that a group of states (located

TABLE 9–5

Relationship Between Property Wealth and
Spending per Pupil, by State, 1970

RATIO OF PROPERTY VALUE PER PUPIL: WEALTHIEST-TO- POOREST DISTRICT	RATIO OF HIGHEST TO LOWEST DISTRICT SPENDING PER PUPIL		
	EQUAL 1.0 TO 1– 1.9 TO 1	MEDIUM 2.0 TO 1– 2.2 TO 1	UNEQUAL 2.3 TO 1– 4.3 TO 1
	Good Effort		
High 19.0 to 1–182.8 to 1	Kansas (182.8 to 1) New Mexico New York (84.2 to 1)	Michigan Oklahoma Wisconsin (77.9 to 1)	Arizona California Illinois Missouri Nebraska (45.1 to 1) Texas
Medium 8.6 to 1–17.4 to 1	Arkansas Colorado Florida Kentucky Louisiana South Carolina Utah	Indiana Massachusetts New Jersey Ohio Pennsylvania Tennessee	Maine South Dakota Washington
			Delinquent
Low 1.7 to 1–6.8 to 1	Alabama Delaware Georgia Idaho Iowa Maryland Mississippi Nevada North Carolina Virginia West Virginia Wyoming	Connecticut Minnesota Oregon Rhode Island	Alaska Montana New Hampshire North Dakota Vermont

Source: Adapted from Table 31, "Ratio of Assessed Valuation per Pupil in District With Largest Valuation per Pupil to that in District with Smallest Valuation per Pupil for Each State, 1968–1969"; and Table 33, "Ratio of Expenditure per Pupil at The 90th Pupil Percentile to Lowest per Pupil Expenditure in Each State, 1969–1970," (Advisory Commission on Intergovernmental Relations, *Financing Schools and Property Tax Relief* ..., 1973), pp. 98, 100–101.

in the lower left of the table) have small disparities in per pupil spending mainly because little difference in taxable wealth exists between their wealthiest and poorest districts. The states in the upper right area of the table are those in which the political process could not equalize spending between the districts. Well-known constitutional challenges have been made to the inequities of spending in two of these states (California and Texas).

While these findings were emerging, the second force in the form of a "taxpayers' revolt" was taking place across the country. The rise in total educational spending had outrun most other sectors of the economy, and taxes were going up at an alarming rate. State after state set record levels for defeating school budgets and bond issues. A recent state to do so is California whose voters approved of Proposition 13 in June 1978, which limited property taxes by constitutional amendment. The proposition in a single stroke slashed the total income of local governments in the fiscal year beginning July 1 by more than 22 percent, on the average. For some communities and school districts that depend heavily on the property tax, the proposition reduced income by as much as 70 percent.

A final force undermining the stability of the existing school finance systems was a series of constitutional challenges. In a 1970 landmark decision, the California Supreme Court ruled that school finance laws should not invidiously discriminate against the poor by making the quality of a child's education a function of the wealth of his parents and neighbors. Serrano (the case) triggered a chain reaction. Between 1971 and 1977, similar challenges were waged in 40 states to strike down state systems of school finance. These decisions affect every state in the union except Hawaii, which has a statewide revenue-raising system.

In the Texas case, *San Antonio v. Rodriguez* (1973), the state appealed to the United States Supreme Court. It was argued that economic discrimination rather than racial discrimination was being practiced by the state of Texas and that the U.S. Constitution forbade such action by the states. The Court in March 1973 handed down a sharply divided 5 to 4 decision reversing the district court's decision. The Court rejected the argument that the constitutional provision for "equal protection of the laws" forbade the operation of public education under the system of enormous disparities found in most states and metropolitan areas. The Court held that education is not among the rights afforded explicit protection under our federal Constitution. This ended the series of cases that relied upon the Fourteenth Amendment to invalidate school finance laws.

As a result of new research, the taxpayers revolt, and the legal challenges, changes are taking place in the way revenues are raised and distributed for public education. Several state courts have overturned school finance laws on the basis of state constitutions. Decisions in California,

New Jersey, Connecticut, and New York will require substantial reforms in educational financing. The reform must take place in the legislature and must have the approval of the governor and political party leaders.

Table 9–6 illustrates three hypothetical communities and the disparities in property wealth per pupil and the tax effort as well as the types of municipal services offered the residents and the quality of the educational services given the pupils. The disparities in property wealth between the three communities are moderate compared to the possible ratios illustrated in Table 9–5. Note that Bigtown's tax rate is much higher than the rural community of Apple Valley or the Cadillac suburb. Bigtown can raise less than one-half as much money per pupil as Cadillac, even though Cadillac has a much lower tax rate. In addition, Bigtown must tax its residents heavily for nonschool services such as welfare and health, which are not necessary expenditures in Cadillac or Apple Valley. Note also how much more Cadillac spends per pupil and per teacher than either Apple Valley or Bigtown. Given inequalities such as this, which are typical, how can a state overcome disparities in expenditures caused by variations in local wealth? Of course, state aid to education can help equalize the money spent on education in the communities.

This distribution of money for "equalization" usually takes place through a formula where state dollars are distributed in inverse proportion to local wealth. In other words, the lower the district wealth, the more state aid it receives. As a result the combination of state aid and local revenues enables a poor district to spend more nearly at the same per pupil level as a rich one. To move toward more equal spending per district, state governments must redistribute funds from rich districts to poor ones. But this effort raises serious political opposition from representatives of wealthy districts. State legislatures have typically avoided direct confrontation on this issue and have settled for a modest step toward equalization in the form of foundation plans, which tend to help the poorest school districts without seriously penalizing wealthy ones. Under a foundation program, state aid makes up the difference between what local districts can raise with a state-mandated minimum property tax rate and an established minimum per pupil expenditure. However, the minimum expenditures were set so low that little equalization actually occurred. Until recently, little support existed for more thorough-going measures of equalization at the state government level.

State legislatures are now rising to the challenge. The period from 1970 to 1975 produced fundamental school finance reform in 20 states. During that time, the most popular way to reform a state's aid system was to implement a guaranteed tax base program under which the state guaranteed a certain dollar yield per pupil for each level of local tax effort. Colorado, Connecticut, Illinois, Kansas, Michigan, New Jersey, Ohio, and Wisconsin are examples of states whose new finance structures include a

TABLE 9–6

Variations in Cost and Quality of Services in
Three Hypothetical Communities, 1978

	APPLE VALLEY	BIGTOWN	CADILLAC
Characteristics	Residential farming community. Little industry	Urban; industry, offices, apartments, university, hospitals, inner-city run-down areas	Suburban residential, some industry, corporate headquarters
Tax statistics	School tax: 20 mills[a] Non-school: 10 mills Total: 30 mills $25,000 property wealth per pupil	School tax: 30 mills Non-school: 30 mills Total: 60 mills $30,000 property wealth per pupil	School tax: 14 mills Non-school: 11 mills Total: 25 mills $150,000 property wealth per pupil
Municipal services	State trooper, volunteer fire dept., private library, road maintenance and repair, dog pound	Police, fire dept., library, sewers, garbage collection, recreation program, parks, swimming pools, senior center, health clinic, welfare, museum	Police, fire dept., library, sewers, garbage collection, recreation program, parks, swimming pools, senior center, skating rink, golf course
Educational system			
Per pupil expenditure	$950	$1,325	$2,450
Median teacher salary	$11,800	$14,750	$19,000
Pupils per professional staff	23	16	14.5
Percent of grads in post-high school education	50	58	70
Libraries	High school only	High school, some larger elementaries	Each school building

[a] A mill is a tenth of a cent and is commonly used in referring to tax assessments in order to avoid (or minimize) the use of decimals. For example, in this table a 20 mill tax rate would result in an actual tax of $20 on each $1,000 of assessed value (which may vary markedly from market value).
Source: Barbara Sacks, "School Finance in Connecticut" *State Board Report* (Hamden, Conn; League of Women Voters of Connecticut, September 1978), p. 5.

type of guaranteed yield equalization formula. States establish a minimum tax base per pupil and allow districts to set their own tax rates. State aid makes up the difference between what a district can raise with its actual tax base and what it could raise if it had the guaranteed tax base. Sometimes states combine the foundation and guaranteed tax base programs. Returning to our three hypothetical communities shown in Figure 9-2, we see that, under a guaranteed tax base program, Bigtown with its high tax effort would receive enough equalization aid to make its spending per pupil exceed that of Cadillac. Because so many of Bigtown's children need special education, this program allows the city to meet their needs. Cadillac receives no equalization funds. Apple Valley receives funds commensurate with its tax rate.

Other states—for example, Minnesota, Montana, Utah and New Mexico—adopted high foundation-level programs. The new aid programs greatly increased the state role in supporting public education from an average of thirty-nine per cent to an estimated average of fifty-one per cent. Local property tax relief occurred in nearly all of the reform states with property tax reductions on average exceeding ten per cent in Colorado, Florida and Wisconsin.[38]

Political success in educational reform demands the development of a new coalition of educational consumers. In the recent New York case (Summer 1978) in which the Supreme Court said that the use of the property tax to finance public education was unconstitutional, the plaintiffs were 27 suburban and rural school districts as well as New York City, Buffalo, Syracuse, and Rochester. Apparently, the suburbs contain poor districts as well as wealthy ones, since Levittown, hardly a large city or a rural district, initiated the suit. We can expect that existing groups that stand to gain from the status quo will quickly organize in response to new plans that would change the accepted order of things. Groups such as school administrators, teachers, and taxpayers may try to block reform. In the end, the situation boils down to the determination of priorities by the political process. The redistribution of education funds is no longer a closed decision-making process. Equality of education will depend on political parties, governors, and legislators in response to the demands of those who are disadvantaged by the present system.

Higher Education

While higher education is primarily a publicly supported institution, it has not equally benefited all sectors of the public. College resources have been preferentially distributed to the sons and daughters of the American upper class. The politics of distribution whereby private groups appropriate

FIGURE 9–2

Equalizing Resources
Guaranteed Tax Base Program:
Guaranteed Tax Base of $75,000 per Pupil

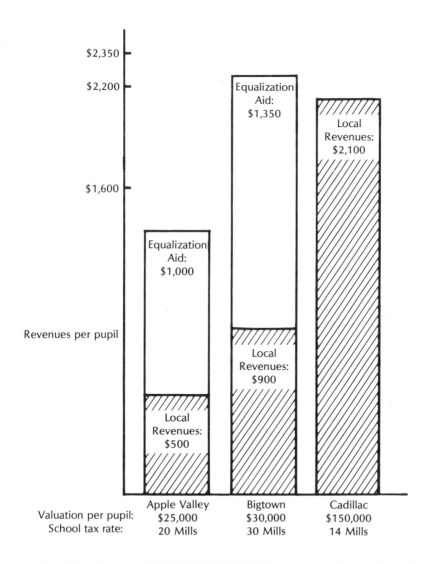

Source: Adapted from Figure 3 EQUALIZING RESOURCES, by Margaret E. Goertz, "Designing a School Finance System for Connecticut" in *What Are Connecticut's Choices Under Horton v. Meskill?* papers presented at Connecticut School Finance Seminar, North Haven, Connecticut, March, 1978, sponsored by the Connecticut Bar Foundation, Inc., the Connecticut Public Expenditure Council Inc., and the League of Women Voters of Connecticut Education Fund, p. 41.

a public resource is a feature of many government programs in the United States, but it is of particular interest here since attendance at college can help to perpetuate or undermine a society's class hierarchy. In the view of two sociologists, evidence shows that higher education plays an active role in closing opportunities to most young people except those from upper-class families. "Rather than equalizing opportunities, the state appears to be actively involved in perpetuating upper-class privilege from generation to generation."[39]

Since World War II, state governments have invested huge resources to meet the expanding demand in the field of higher education. In the 1930s, the bulk of higher education was provided by private colleges and universities. Now the greatest portion comes from public institutions supported by the taxpayers' money. Seventy percent of America's seven million college students are enrolled in public colleges that are state supported. Ira Sharkansky believes that state activity in public higher education reveals the states "at their best." This contention, of course, is a relative one and one that must stand the test of redistributive policy— policy that provides equal opportunity at public expense. Sharkansky states, "Higher education is different from other services in that it promises vast future payoffs for individuals and communities. By assuming responsibility for higher education, the states are doing more than just training students."[40]

There are considerable variations from state to state in programs of higher education. State universities in California, Wisconsin, and Michigan have long been ranked with the most prestigious of the private universities, and they now provide models for other states to follow. California's model has three components:[41]

1. A major university that provides a wide range of graduate instruction, subsidizes faculty research, and admits the best of high school graduates.
2. Several four-year institutions to concentrate on baccalaureate-level education and limited master's programs in education and business.
3. Many two-year institutions for commuters to provide programs in vocational training and the equivalent of freshman and sophomore liberal arts programs.

As we have seen, the impact of state policy activity has decidedly negative consequences for lower-income and black persons in the area of elementary and secondary education. Its impact in the area of higher education may be even more unfortunate. Here the offspring of the lower-income classes partake of educational opportunity at a much lower rate than the offspring of the financially better off. One study of those finishing secondary schooling in 1960, for instance, shows that 49 percent of the young men enter college the following year. When this overall average is broken down, it is found that only 24 percent of the men from the poorest fifth of the nation's families started college. By contrast, 81 percent of those from the richest fifth of families began their higher education.[42] In availing themselves of higher education, the poorer students wind up with middling curricula at two-year colleges. Students from upper-income families tend to go to more costly public colleges (universities rather than four- or two-year colleges), and attend them longer than do students from lower-income families.[43] The result of these conditions is commented upon by Douglas Windham after an extensive examination of who pays and who benefits from public higher education in Florida: "Not only is public higher education ... not a factor which provides extra opportunities for the poor ... but ... the system is taking more from lower groups than it returns to them."[44] While this comment has been contested, there is the unmistakable conclusion that, no matter how taxes are raised, state funds for higher education apparently benefit institutions frequented by the middle class and the rich more heavily than those attended by the poor. The taxpayer is spending more funds for the well-to-do student than for the less-affluent student.

It is not easy to define equality of opportunity for higher education, but it is not hard to show that, by any reasonable definition, we do not have it now. In the conclusion to their analysis of the higher education system in California, which confirms the findings above, Hansen and Weisbrod make several policy proposals. One is to provide substantial grants to low-income students to help offset the cost to them and their parents of giving up much of their immediate (albeit low) earning capacity. Because the writers found that those who benefit most from the public higher education system are, in general, those who are least in need of help in paying for what they receive, the writers suggest a change in the state and local tax structure to make it more progressive or a change in the tuition policies in higher education—to charge on the basis of ability to pay, and, where necessary, to provide generous supplements to low-income students.[45]

Why Some States Are Changing

Education policy, until recently distributive, is becoming redistributive. It is the type of policy that takes the strength of a united party, the leadership of a strong governor, and the efforts of a reformed legislature to put into effect. Before, it was the work of a small group outside the political process, like most distributive policy. Now it is made by political leaders responding to needs and demands. Figure 9–3, which represents the 50 state systems, illustrates this point. The output, or policy variable, is the

FIGURE 9–3

Relationships Among the Economy,
Political Leadership, and Change in
Welfare-Education Policy, 1968–72

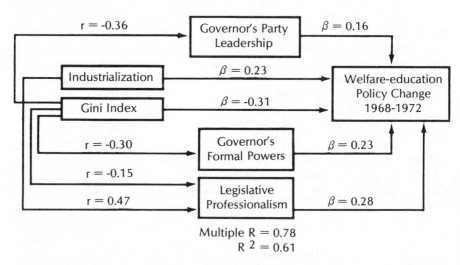

Multiple R = 0.78
$R^2 = 0.61$

Note: The beta weights (β) shown in the figure indicate the relative contribution of each independent variable to variation in the dependent variable (welfare-education policy change, 1968–72). Taken together, the political variables (governor's leadership and formal powers and legislative professionalism) contribute more to the variance (R^2) than the economic variables (industrialization and Gini index).

change in education and welfare policies from 1968 when the ferment in education erupted in 1972. During that period, the desegregation of northern cities as well as the distribution of education funds became part of the political process. The mix of welfare and education variables that measure the changes are noted in Appendix 7. The two education variables in the welfare education mix are per capita education expenditures, indicating the degree of dedication to education by the state, and the percent of high school students who graduate, indicating the attractiveness of education for all groups.[46]

Again we see that the governor's party leadership and his formal powers that make it possible for him to exert his leadership plus the professionalization of the legislature explain a significant portion of welfare-education policy change from 1968 to 1972. In states that have strong parties, that can control nominations and promote policies that can be put into effect by governors and legislatures, the change in welfare and education is greatest. Before the mid-sixties, we would not expect education to respond to political factors, but it is apparent that, after that time, the greatest change in education policy was made in states where the governor and the politicians make education a priority.

While the economic variables do not explain as much of the change as the political variables (the efforts of men and women in the system), the gini index of income distribution as well as the industrialization of the state explain a portion of the change in welfare-education policy. The increases in provision for education and welfare appear to be in states where there is not such a great difference in the distribution of income (the larger the gini index, the more unequal the distribution of income; hence the negative correlation with the policy variable). An industrial tax base as well as a more equal distribution of income indicates a society that is, economically speaking, capable of being taxed for education and welfare services. The fact that the political variables account for more of the change reveals that it is the efforts of the men and women in the political process that can represent the needs and demands in education and welfare and convince the people that the expenditures are necessary.

CONCLUSIONS

The fact that education has not been provided equally to all students has been amply documented. Even though each state constitution guarantees free public education at state expense, and hence education should be redistributive policy, it has been appropriated by the upper class and has been distributive policy. At one extreme, children from upper-income families have waiting for them the highest quality of available educational services. They are well prepared to go to college at public expense. At the other extreme, a child from a socially less-advantaged and economically depressed home has waiting for him low-quality school services that inhibit development of his intellectual capacities and curtail his ability to earn a living and achieve fulfillment.

There are several reasons education until recently was distributive policy. The myth that education should not be involved in politics was perpetuated by the school people who probably believed it to a certain extent, but it served their interests well. Education was insulated from the political system by nonpartisan boards of education and by special education budgets funded by special taxes and spent by neutral educators. At the state level, a grand coalition of teachers, administrators, and school boards worked through the state education agency to distribute state funds in a way that would benefit the upper-class communities. The cities lacked enough political clout to contest this distribution. This myth could persist so long as the people believed it and did not pressure the politicians. The legislators, overwhelmingly from rural and suburban communities, supported the distribution of funds by formulas that benefited their constituencies. Reapportionment, followed by a break in the monolithic union of school administrators and teachers, resulted in the politics of education "going public." When education entered the public arena, when the educators were challenged by integrationists and disgruntled parents in the North, the distributive aspects of education were revealed. The integrationists and the poor turned to the courts when the legislatures and education agencies did not respond quickly enough. The courts have spoken and, it appears, are leaving the problem of equality of education to the political process. In state after state, the courts place a mandate on the legislatures to work out plans for the redistribution of funds for education. It is now up to the political parties, the governors, and the legislatures to make education redistributive.

NOTES

1. *Serrano v. Priest*, 5 Cal. 3d 584, 96 Cal. Rptr. 601, 487 P.2d 1241 (1971), subsequent opinion, 45 U.S.L.W. 2340 (Dec. 30, 1976).
2. *Report of the National Advisory Commission on Civil Disorders* (New York: Bantam, 1968), pp. 424–25.
3. John E. Coons; William H. Clune, III; and Stephen D. Sugarman, *Private Wealth and Public Education* (Cambridge, Mass.: Harvard University Press, 1970), p. xxi.
4. Edgar Litt, "Civic Education, Community Norms and Political Indoctrination," *American Sociological Review* 28, no. 1 (February 1963): 69–75.
5. Samuel Bowles and Herbert Gintis, *Schooling in Capitalist America* (New York: Basic Books, 1976), p. 49.
6. The following discussion draws upon the article by P. Michael Timpane, "Reform Through Congress, Federal Aid to Schools: Its Limited Future," *Law and Contemporary Problems* 38 (Winter–Spring 1974): 492–512.
7. Joel S. Berke and Michael W. Kirst, *Federal Aid to Education: Who Benefits? Who Governs?* (Lexington, Mass.: Heath, 1972), 22.
8. Advisory Commission on Intergovernmental Relations, *Financing Schools and Property Tax Relief—A State Responsibility* (Washington, D.C.: January 1973).
9. Lawrence Innaccone, *Politics in Education* (New York: Center for Applied Research in Education, Inc., 1967), p. 11.
10. Frederick M. Wirt and Michael W. Kirst, *The Political Web of American Schools* (Boston: Little, Brown, 1972), p. 51.
11. JAlan Aufderheide, "Educational Interest Groups and the State Legislature," chapter 5 in Roald F. Campbell and Tim L. Mazzoni, Jr., *State Policy Making for the Public Schools* (Berkeley, Calif.: McCutchan Publishing Corp., 1976), p. 179. This is based on a study of twelve states.
12. Wirt and Kirst, *The Political Web*, p. 53.

13. James D. Koerner, *Who Controls American Education* (Boston: Beacon Press, 1968), p. 148.
14. JAlan Aufderheide, "Educational Interest Groups," pp. 198–99.
15. See Iannaccone, *Politics in Education.*
16. L. Harmon Zeigler, M. Kent Jennings, and G. Wayne Peak, *Governing American Schools* (North Scituate, Mass.: Duxbury Press, 1974).
17. Howard D. Hamilton and Sylvan H. Cohen, *Policy Making by Plebiscite: School Referenda* (Lexington, Mass.: Health, 1974), pp. 1–16.
18. Ibid., p. 267.
19. Philip K. Piele and John S. Hall, *Budgets, Bonds and Ballots: Voting Behavior in School Financial Elections* (Lexington, Mass.: Heath, 1974), pp. 54–55.
20. Campbell and Mazzoni, *State Policy Making,* chapters 1, 2, 3.
21. Ibid., p. 121.
22. John W. Lederle, "Governors and Higher Education," in Thad Beyle and J. Oliver Williams, *The American Governor in Behavioral Perspective* (New York: Harper & Row, 1972), pp. 232–35.
23. Edward R. Hines, "Governors and Educational Policy Making"; chapter 4 in Campbell and Mazzoni, *State Policy Making,* pp. 139–41.
24. Ibid., 160–62.
25. Ibid., 167–68.
26. Stephen K. Bailey, *Schoolmen and Politics: A Study of State Aid to Education in the Northeast* (Syracuse, N.Y.: Syracuse University Press, 1962), p. 47.
27. Peggy M. Siegel, "The Politics of School Finance Reform," chapter 6 in Campbell and Mazzoni, *State Policy Making,* pp. 238–39.
28. John C. Hogan, *The Schools, The Courts and The Public Interest* (Lexington, Mass.: Heath, 1974). This discussion draws heavily on chapters 1 and 6 of his book.
29. 347 U.S. at 494.
30. James W. Ely, Jr., *The Crisis on Conservative Virginia: The Byrd Organization and The Politics of Massive Resistance* (Knoxville, University of Tennessee Press, 1976), p. 71.
31. Everett F. Cataldo, Michael Giles, and Douglas S. Gatlin, "Metropolitan School Desegregation: Practical Remedy or Impractical Ideal?" *The Annals of the American Academy of Political and Social Science* (November 1975): 98.
32. Ibid., pp. 98–99.
33. Lillian B. Rubin, *Busing and Backlash* (Berkeley: University of California Press, 1972), p. 7.
34. Robert C. Lineberry and Ira Sharkansky, *Urban Politics and Public Policy,* 3d ed., (New York: Harper & Row, 1978), p. 309.
35. Lillian Rubin, *Busing and Backlash,* 90.
36. Coons et al., *Private Wealth and Public Education,* pp. xviii–xix.
37. Advisory Commission on Intergovernmental Relations, *Financing Schools and Property Tax Relief,* Table 33, "Ratio of Expenditure Per Pupil at the 90th Pupil Percentile to Lowest Per-Pupil Expenditure in Each State, 1969–1970," pp. 100–101.
38. Education Finance Center, Education Commission of the States, *School Finance Reform in the States,* 1976–1977 (Denver, Colo.: Education Commission of the States, 1976), p. 3.

39. Michael Unseem and S. M. Miller, "The Upper Class in Education," *Social Policy* 7 (January/February 1977): 28.

40. Ira Sharkansky, *The Maligned States* (New York: McGraw-Hill, 1972), p. 82.

41. Ibid., p. 84.

42. Unseem and Miller, "The Upper Class in Education," p. 28.

43. Jerome Karabel, "Community Colleges and Social Stratification," *Harvard Educational Review* 42, no. 4 (November 1972).

44. Douglas Windham, *Education, Equality and Income Redistribution* (Lexington, Mass.: Heath, 1970), p. xiiv.

45. W. Lee Hansen and Burton A. Weisbrod, *Benefits, Costs and Finance of Public Higher Education* (Chicago: Markham, 1969), chapter 6.

46. See Appendix 6 for a list of the policy variables subject to analysis and for the sources for the 1972 variables. The sources for the 1968 variables are earlier volumes of the same documents, and I would be happy to provide the exact citations. For measurement of time changes in policy output for the two factors, the factor analyses could not be performed separately for the data in each of the two years, since the loadings of the factors are not the same, and there is no equivalency. For comparing the policy changes from 1968 to 1972, each state was treated as two different states: the state in 1968 and the state in 1972. Thus the number was effectively doubled, and a factor analysis was run on the 100 units of analysis. In this way, the two scores were created for each state (one for 1968 and one for 1972), and the scores are comparable as is evident from the method of creation. Hence, it makes sense to analyze time changes for each of the states.

CHAPTER TEN

THE POLITICS OF REGULATION: LAND USE

The regulation of privately owned land for the public interest is fraught by intense conflict among competing groups, each of which claims a legitimate right to its use. Consider the remarks of the following decision-makers as they try to solve the land use puzzle. At the conference of governors in 1974, Governor Link of North Dakota stated:

> I must urge all governors, then, to consider the situation of North Dakota at present. The nation is facing an energy crisis and it is looking for a method of attaining self-sufficiency by, among other things, utilizing the coal resources of North Dakota....The developing world food shortage could shortly prove that the use of productive agricultural land for lignite production may be ill-considered. A national choice must soon be made: should North Dakota be utilized for food production or energy production—both may not be possible.[1]

Land regulation came to Vermont sooner than in most states, Governor Thomas P. Salmon said, because "We were always aware that we had something special, worth preserving."[2] Insulated for many years by both choice and physical barriers, Vermonters have recently had to defend their land from affluent outsiders seeking a rural stake in life. Lacking the policy tools, technical assistance and resources to cope with the multi-million-dollar developers, the towns were helpless to prevent their mountains from being carved into quarter-acre lots. The recreation dollars were welcomed, but the ravage of the tranquil countryside was not. Compact villages and scattered farms were hidden beneath tract housing, trailers, ski trails, and strip development. Streams became polluted as towns dumped their raw sewage, which was joined by overflow from poorly planned septic systems and ran down the mountainside.

For the urban poor living in an environment of poverty, rats, lead poisoning, carbon monoxide, and noise, the sensible thing would be to pack up and leave. There is a land of promise less than twenty miles away, but to the impoverished family it is no more accessible than Shangri-la.

The suburbs zone their land for single-family use, thus making the price of a house prohibitive. A county in California requires a 500-square-foot "green area" for each new housing unit planned. This increases the cost of multiple-unit housing and makes low to moderate cost construction impossible. No wonder environmentalism is seen by the poor as an upper-middle-income suburban thing. Inner-city State Senator Richard H. Newhouse of Chicago said: "Don't you admit that it's kind of silly to talk about conservation of resources, because for the poor there aren't any resources. All life's energies are taken up with just plain existence." Newhouse claims that green areas have no reality for the poor. "Talking about open space is not likely to draw a great deal of attention in the pool room," he said.[3]

The examples just given illustrate pressures on the use of land that is owned by people, corporations, and business, in other words privately held. The American ethic is that private land belongs to the owner to be used as he pleases. In North Dakota, Vermont, Illinois, and California, the land which was just discussed by the governors and senator was in private hands. Yet in each case there was a public interest involved which the speaker proclaimed. In each case, a perfectly valid claim could be made for alternate use of the land; in North Dakota the conflict lay between present energy and future food production; in Vermont between recreation and preservation, and in Illinois and California between the right of the poor to enjoy housing and provision for green space.

REGULATORY POLICY

The idea that land cannot be exploited by its owner, but is a resource which has common properties like air and water and hence is subject to governmental regulation, is new. In the last ten years, states have come to recognize that some land in private hands must be regulated for the public good. This has been called the "quiet revolution," as state after state sought to regulate the use of land among competing pressures to arrive at a balance between private desires and public needs. Society is drawing away from the idea that land's only function is to enable its owner to make money. It is realizing that important social and environmental goals require more specific controls on the use that is made of scarce land resources. Faced with scarcity, we must regulate what remains by centralized political decision making. We must come to terms with what Kenneth Boulding calls a "spaceman economy."[4] In a spaceman economy, human welfare does not depend on rapid consumption or more and more consumers because these are potentially fatal, but on the extent to which we can wring maximum comfort and fulfillment for a reasonable population from minimum resources. This will be hard to accomplish because the

American ethic is so firmly ingrained. The basic political policy which will attempt to solve the problem of scarcity is called regulatory policy.

In the beginning of chapter 8 we considered three types of policy: redistributive, distributive, and regulatory. Each of these types of policy involves different expectations on the part of the people, groups, and decision-makers with respect to who should be rewarded and who should be deprived, because every decision which emerges from the political process involves depriving some groups or classes and rewarding others. In the case of welfare, or redistributive policy, the haves are taxed to support the have-nots, who because of age, sickness, or adversity cannot support themselves. In education policy, which is distributive policy, public funds are distributed unequally to a specific group of schools and not to all who have supposedly equal claim. This is done outside the public arena in the offices of the state education departments where the educators and administrators devise the distribution of funds.

Regulatory policy is intended to regulate the activities of known groups according to a general rule of law. Each decision involves rewarding or depriving the groups which contend face-to-face on a case-by-case basis. Most of these groups are private, although some public agencies are involved in the competition for use of the land (Department of Public Works, mass transit authority, sewer district, Housing Authority, for example). In each area of regulatory policy, the groups which contend are highly salient. For example, landowners and developers and environmentalists are main contenders in land use policy. Although the laws or regulations are stated in general terms such as: "Tourist-attracting development should be encouraged without disturbing the attractions of the natural landscape," it can be predicted that each decision made under this somewhat general policy would benefit either the environmentalist or the developer, those who want open space or those who need homes. Regulatory policy may be the purest example of the group conflict described in chapter 3. Because land use regulations take place in thousands of local jurisdictions, some decision-makers are "captured" by the developers and some by the environmentalists. Individual regulatory decisions involve direct confrontation of the indulged and the deprived. Regulatory policy is the result of this continuous interplay of the groups, both in its initiation and in its practice.

The general pattern of regulation is for the legislature to pass broad policy goals and then establish a regulatory commission or other agency to develop and administer the detailed technicalities of implementing the goals. Needless to say, the groups which are subject to regulation are much interested in the whole process, from the creation of regulatory power which has not previously existed to the implementation of the regulations on a continuing basis. Political relationships within the regulatory policy area are visible and competitive. Typically, the governmental regulatory agency makes a decision that confers some benefit—a permit to develop, or a subdivision, to a developer to the exclusion of the environmentalists or sportsmen. At a later time the agency may block construction in a woodland, a decision that supports the environmentalists. There is high degree of competition for favorable decisions. In general, developers and construction unions would prefer to avoid government regulation altogether, but where regulation is unavoidable, they pursue several options. One is to press for regulation that is either favorable or not too bothersome to their interests. For instance, in the area of coastal regulation, the distinction between coastal *management* and *conservation* is much more than semantic. Management means a tradeoff between environment and development, while conservation makes explicit the primacy of the environmentalists. Both coalitions try to write the initial legislation to favor their interests. The placement of the regulatory agency is also of prime concern. If it is lodged within an environmental protection agency, the bias in favor of conservation is stronger than if it is given independent status. Hence developers or those in favor of weak regulation prefer independent regulatory commissions.

The conclusion to be drawn from all this is that regulatory policy concerns many different groups which are highly visible and competitive. Its proper aim is to balance the many claims to keep any one from dominating the resource that is being regulated. This is done in the public interest. However, the public interest is often vague and regulation is very specific, so a relationship between the regulated and the regulators often develops on the operating level where the decisions are made on a case-by-case basis. Matthew Holden has observed that specialized regulatory agencies distribute advantages and disadvantages but that "the distributions which occur are seldom consistent with the distributions which one would have expected if one took the policy norms involved in the creation of the agencies as clues to the agencies' most likely behavior."[5]

Where does the political party come into the regulatory arena? We have made the claim throughout the pages of this book that the type of political party system which exists in a state determines the quality and distribution of policy. If this is so, we would expect that it would take strong political parties to balance the insistent demands of groups in the regulatory process. Each regulatory decision involves rewarding some groups and depriving others. The stronger a political party's leadership, the more it can balance the demands of groups which compose its coalition. We would expect that a cohesive party will be able to enact and implement policies which do not benefit environmentalists over developers, suburbanites over the homeless, big farmers over little farmers. The political party influences the type of regulatory policy that is passed and the location and powers of the agency that will oversee the task of regulation. If the party can impose order on the regulation of land in the public interest, it will not let any one group become too powerful. It will authorize a regulatory agency to oversee the thousands of decisions made at the local level to see if they conform to land use law. It will give the agency authority to intervene if the proper balancing between environmental and social interests is not achieved. The quality of the political party as an electoral and governing vehicle varies from state to state. We hypothesize that the states which have strong and cohesive party systems will consider the needs of the lower-income groups as well as the environmentalists and grant the regulatory agency the authority to balance those needs.

This chapter continues with a description of our land and previous attempts to regulate its use on the local level. As the land becomes despoiled, as housing becomes scarce, more regulation is necessary, and state governments are taking the responsibility when local governments falter and federal help is not forthcoming. A discussion of the groups involved in the land use struggle is followed by a description of the decision-making arenas in which they operate. The chapter concludes with a description of regulation as a symbolic process, seldom subject to the public will but rather more to the desires of those it attempts to regulate. It is only through the efforts of a strong party system, which listens to demands of the low- to middle-income groups and which can regulate in their behalf, that land use policy will arrive at a balance between competing demands of environmentalists and housing groups.

LAND USE: STATE RESPONSIBILITY, PRIMARILY LOCAL CONTROL

A Word about Our Land

Our land is vastly more productive than that of the world as a whole. The "big three" of land use in terms of acres are grazing, forestry, and cropland, occupying 34, 32, and 23 percent respectively of the total area of the 48 contiguous states. Two other important uses of land—urban development and recreation—together account for 4 percent of the total area, but these uses affect far more people than the others and generate the intense need for land use control. These five uses comprise 93 percent of the total land area; the other 7 percent is used for water management and storage, transportation, mining, and defense, or is idle land.

Land use is affected by social, economic, and technical trends. By 1970, 73 percent of the U. S. population was urban, living on about 2 percent of the land area. The value of this 2 percent was approximately 50 percent greater than the value of all the other 98 percent. In recent decades the U. S. population has become more urbanized, more suburban-

ized, more metropolitanized, and more "coastalized."[6] People are moving
to towns and cities from rural areas. Within urbanized areas, people have
been moving to suburbs. They have also been moving to locations near the
coasts. By 1970, half the population lived no more than 50 miles from a
coast (including the Great Lakes coasts).

Most of our land is and will remain privately owned. (About one-third
of our total land area is publicly owned, largely by the federal government.) The privately owned land has been subject to the policy of unfettered economic growth. It was treated as indestructible. It was also treated
as a commodity, ignoring its biological role as a crucial link in the web of
life. Its use and abuse was a matter to be determined exclusively by the
owner.

The Origins of Regulation

As the nation began to shift from rural to urban, owners learned that the
economics of city life could bring about a decline in property value. Measures to protect residential and "high class" business areas from encroach-
ment by industry and tenements were taken by zoning blocks or
residential areas for single purpose uses. From 1909 to 1926 the legality
of zoning was debated in the courts. Some courts ruled in favor of this
procedure and some against. Since land was viewed as an economic commodity and was considered personal property, there was the question as
to whether zoning or restricting the use of a man's property could be
construed as the taking of property without "due process" as secured by
the Constitution. In 1926 the landmark *Euclid v. Ambler Realty Co.* case
was heard by the U.S. Supreme Court. In essence the court ruled that:

> States are the legal repository of police power. (An) enabling act for zoning
> is the grant of this power to a municipality for regulating the height, area and
> use of buldings, and the use of land. In the exercise of this grant the regula-
> tions must be reasonable and not arbitrary or discriminatory. They must have
> a substantial relation to the health, safety, morals, comfort, convenience, and
> welfare of the community.[7]

Thus it was established that municipalities did have the right to enact
zoning laws if authorized by their state governments. It is important to
realize that all zoning power legally emanates from the state, and in order
for a municipality to use this power it must be granted directly from the
state or through a state enabling act. Implicit in this is the power of the
state itself to exercise police power through zoning. In the early years, the
states preferred to delegate this power. They followed a federal model

"Standard State Zoning Enabling Act." It was not until 1961 that the Hawaii legislature enacted a state zoning program to be administered by the state itself. But this is ahead of the story for now.

From the beginning the state governments saw land use control as an urban problem and delegated it to the cities. The number and kinds of zoning increased; greater flexibility was introduced through open space ratios, floor plan ratios, and performance standards. Planned unit development—the uniting of compatible uses and the relaxation of standard restrictions according to a development plan—was added to the kit of zoning devices. This complexity cannot hide the fact that local zoning remains as it was from the beginning—local control of land use by local agencies controlled by local interests. It has become apparent that the local zoning ordinance, virtually the sole means of controlling land use for 50 years, has proved woefully inadequate to combat many problems of state-wide significance such as environmental pollution, social problems, salvaging of farm land, and saving of the coasts. Traditionally states provided little or no technical help or advice and almost no state supervision over the exercise of delegated powers. State legislatures, state executive offices, and even to a considerable extent state courts washed their hands of involvement in land use control.

Other Powers Over the Use of Private Land

Beside the police power which is legally lodged in the state and may be granted to the cities and counties to allow them to enact zoning ordinances, there are three other potential powers over the use of private land. The second, the power to tax land, has traditionally been used by local governments, although it may be invoked by the states. The third power, the power of eminent domain, has been used by all three levels of government. The fourth power, that of the public purse, had been a tool in the hands of the state and national governments, primarily the national. A brief discussion of each power follows and is basic to the understanding of the marble-cake relationship between the three levels of government and the possibility of change in this relationship.[8]

A basic governmental power over land is taxation. As we noted in the last chapter during the discussion of sources of funding for education, taxes on land are the mainstay of local government. Every property owner pays taxes directly; every tenant helps to pay his landlord's taxes. Taxes are also one of the largest costs of land ownership; they not infrequently take a fourth to half of the income from the land. In suburban and urban areas, desired governmental services such as schools, libraries, and recreation can only be obtained by taxes on real estate. The landowner is caught between his desire for services and his dislike of paying more taxes. A farmer may be forced off his land if the taxes go up because he can no longer farm it for profit. This power plus the one previously discussed, zoning, are exercised almost exclusively by local governments. The states could, however, exercise the option of using both powers.

The third basic power which has an impact on land use is that of eminent domain, to take private land needed for public purposes. Prime examples are slum clearance, as exercised by local governments, highways, a state and national exercise, and park additions, which is typical of all three levels of government. The government's power is practically unlimited, subject to the requirement that the land is needed for a public purpose. The courts have placed different interpretations on "public purpose" over time, and some land uses—slum clearance for example—are today acceptable whereas once they would not have been. The private land so taken must be paid for, under the provisions of the fifth amendment, and the private landowner can always insist upon a court-determined price for his land, which is usually generous. The power of eminent domain is important not so much for the area of land taken, which is rather small, but for the strategic nature of the lands. Much legal controversy today is concerned with the power of zoning and the power of eminent domain. When land is zoned to preclude certain uses, the owners and developers may insist that it constitutes a "taking"—in other words it has been rendered as useless to the owner as if the government had indeed taken it by eminent domain, and the owner therefore should be compensated.

An exceedingly important governmental power over land is the power of the purse. Both land use and landowners are materially affected by the way in which government at all levels, but especially the federal government, spends funds for various public purposes. The variety of the programs is so great and the scope is so large that the programs have considerable indirect impact on land use. Flood protection and irrigation activities enable private landowners to make maximum use of their land. The federal government has heavily subsidized highway construction, airport construction, and in an earlier day, railroad construction. It has also subsidized electric power production and transmission, especially into rural areas. It has provided financial help for forest fire control and other forest programs. And it has provided direct payments to millions of farmers to carry out soil conservation measures, to reduce crop acreage, or to carry out other programs. Millions of acres of cropland have been taken out of active use and are idle. All of these programs affect land use. Although they do not *require* owners to engage in certain land use activities, they offer a considerable monetary incentive for them to do so. The power of the purse will be the major way in which the federal government may exert control over land use in the future. It may provide sticks and carrots in the form of withdrawing or providing money to states that engage in desired programs.

A New Role for States

To date we have discussed four methods of control over land use that can be employed by government. Zoning and taxation are used by local governments. Eminent domain is practiced by all layers of government, and the power of the purse is the main technique of the state and federal governments. In terms of all land use power, however, the local governments have traditionally exercised almost exclusive control. In the last 15 years this division of responsibility has begun to change. In a number of states, the state government has begun to exercise direct control over the use of some kinds of land. The impetus for this involvement has come from the states themselves in response to local and statewide needs. In 1961, the legislature of the new state of Hawaii took the first step in what Bosselman and Callies have termed "the quiet revolution in land use control"[9] by adopting a statewide Land Use Law. Under this law, a state Land Use Commission was directed to classify all of Hawaii's 6,424 square miles into urban, rural, agricultural, or conservation districts. The law gave the Hawaiian state government an unprecedented degree of control over the state's land resources. During the next 15 years support for an increased state role in land use regulation began to spread. Each year after 1970, additional states began to regulate developments whose large scale, growth-inducing potential or environmentally sensitive location made them of more than local concern. Often they did so because of some particular crisis within their borders—a second home boom in Vermont, a water shortage in Florida, or the possibility of new coastal refineries in Delaware. In some states, the mandate is limited to "critical areas," such as the seacoasts in California and Delaware. In others the state reviews all construction projects beyond a certain size and all subdivisions with more than a specified number of lots, no matter where the project is located. Other states mandate the planning criteria to be followed by local and regional governments. All fifty states have some form of statewide land controls.

The following approaches to land use management have been initiated by the states in the past several years.[10] Several states have initiated statewide programs of land resource management which involve the development of a comprehensive plan. When the state does the zoning (using its police powers to enforce the plan), it can exercise broad control over the land for social, economic, and political purposes. Usually there is a joint agreement between the state and local governments for the administration of the state plan. The most noted example of this approach is the 1961 Hawaii State Land Use Law mentioned earlier.

In other states the regulation of certain types of development is performed on the state level. Table 10–1 presents the programs in existence in 1975. Large-scale development, the siting of power plants, commercial, and industrial locations can threaten the environmentally fragile, agricultural, and scenic lands within a state. Often there is no regulatory authority to control the location of these developments, or municipalities may be incapable or unwilling to try to control developments because of their size. Rather than trying to manage all the land within their borders, several states have designed plans that will regulate only specific types of development. In this functional approach, the aim is to control the location of industrial or commercial sites, to achieve an improved environmental quality, or to provide more low-income housing on scattered sites. The State of Washington uses this approach. In 1970, Washington created a Thermal Power Plant Evaluation Council. The Council has the power to adopt guidelines for plant location, conduct hearings, and make recommendations to the governor concerning site applications. The Governor is the final authority for the state to approve or reject site applications. Massachusetts has an Anti-Snob Zoning Law which provides for the siting of subsidized housing for low- and moderate-income families. This provides for state authority to override the decisions of local zoning and other boards. In these cases the state has taken over the power to regulate certain types of land use in line with plans made at the state level. While this is not a comprehensive plan of statewide regulation, it is a more assertive program than merely granting the towns the authority to zone, which was the prevailing practice until recently.

Another way in which states can regulate land without regulating *all* the land within their borders is by managing only certain geographic or critical areas. These areas can be located specifically—in wetlands, coasts, and marshes where nature must be protected to save the lives of small water creatures, plants, and possibly all life itself. This type of management has proven to be the most popular form of state land use control activity. It is like the functional approach described above except that the areas can be located geographically. California is the most prominent example. In November 1972, California voters empowered the state to regulate in this manner all development along the California coastline— in most instances 1,000 yards inland from mean high tide. The 1973 Florida legislature passed an act that designated the Big Cypress Swamp as an area of critical state concern. The legislature found that "the Big Cypress Area is an area containing and having a significant impact upon environmental and natural resources of regional and statewide importance."[11] North Carolina defines areas along its outer banks as critical; Vermont labels all land above a 2,500 foot elevation critical, and New York's Adirondack Park is termed a critical area.[12]

In some states the principal reason for state involvement is the failure

TABLE 10–1

State Land Use Programs 1975

	POWER PLANT SITING[a]	COASTAL ZONE MANAGEMENT[b]	WETLANDS MANAGEMENT[c]	DESIGNATION OF CRITICAL AREAS[d]	DIFFERENTIAL ASSESSMENT LAWS[e]	FLOOD PLAIN MANAGEMENT[f]	SURFACE MINING[g]
Alabama	—	*	—	—	—	*	2
Alaska	—	*	—	—	2	—	—
Arizona	*	—	—	—	1	*	—
Arkansas	*	—	—	—	1	*	2,3
California	*	*	—	*	3	*	1
Colorado	—	—	—	—	1	*	1
Connecticut	*	*	*	—	2	*	—
Delaware	—	*	*	*	1	—	—
Florida	*	*	*	*	1,3	—	2
Georgia	—	*	*	—	—	—	2,3
Hawaii	—	*	—	*	2	*	1
Idaho	—	—	—	—	1	—	1
Illinois	—	*	—	—	2	*	2,3
Indiana	—	*	—	—	1	*	2,3
Iowa	—	—	—	—	1	*	2,3
Kansas	—	—	—	—	—	—	2,3
Kentucky	*	—	—	—	2	—	2,3
Louisiana	—	*	*	*	—	—	—
Maine	—	*	*	*	2	*	2
Maryland	*	*	*	*	2	*	2,3
Massachusetts	*	*	*	*	2	*	—
Michigan	—	*	—	—	3	*	1
Minnesota	*	*	*	*	2	*	1
Mississippi	—	*	*	—	—	*	1

TABLE 10-1

Continued

	POWER PLANT SITING[a]	COASTAL ZONE MANAGEMENT[b]	WETLANDS MANAGEMENT[c]	DESIGNATION OF CRITICAL AREAS[d]	DIFFERENTIAL ASSESSMENT LAWS[e]	FLOOD PLAIN MANAGEMENT[f]	SURFACE MINING[g]
Missouri	—	—	*	—	1	*	1
Montana	*	—	—	*	2	*	2,3
Nebraska	—	—	—	—	2	*	—
Nevada	*	—	—	*	2	—	—
New Hampshire	*	*	*	—	2,3	*	—
New Jersey	—	*	*	—	2	—	2
New Mexico	*	—	—	—	1	*	1
New York	*	*	*	*	2	*	1
North Carolina	—	*	*	—	2	—	2
North Dakota	*	—	—	—	1	—	2
Ohio	*	*	—	—	2	*	1
Oklahoma	—	—	—	*	1	—	2
Oregon	*	*	*	*	2	—	2
Pennsylvania	—	*	*	—	2	—	—
Rhode Island	—	*	—	—	2	—	—
South Carolina	*	*	—	*	2	—	2
South Dakota	—	—	—	—	1	—	2
Tennessee	—	—	*	—	—	—	2,3
Texas	—	*	—	—	2	—	1
Utah	—	—	*	—	2	—	2
Vermont	*	—	*	—	3	*	1
Virginia	—	*	*	—	2	—	2,3
Washington	*	*	*	—	2	*	2

West Virginia	—	*	*	—	—	2,3
Wisconsin	*	*	*	*	*	1
Wyoming	*	—	—	—	1	2

Note: * indicates that a State has a program in one of the above categories but does not constitute an evaluation of the effectiveness of the program, nor does it indicate that the program is based on specific enabling legislation.

a State has established criteria or planning for the identification of suitability of power plant and transmission lines and has authorized a state regulatory agency.

b State is participating in coastal zone management program authorized by the Coastal Zone Management Act of 1972.

c State has authority to plan or review local plans or the ability to control land use in the wetlands.

d State has established rules, or is in the process of establishing rules, regulations, and guidelines for the identification and designation of areas of critical state concern (e.g., environmentally fragile areas, areas of historical significance).

e State has adopted tax measure which is designed to give property tax relief to owners of agricultural or open space lands.

1. Preferential Assessment Program—Assessment of eligible land is based upon a selected formula, which is usually use-value.

2. Deferred Taxation—Assessment of eligible land is based upon a selected formula, which is usually use-value and provides for a sanction, usually the payment of back taxes, if the land is converted to a noneligible use.

3. Restrictive Agreements—Eligible land is assessed at its use-value, with a requirement that the owner sign a contract and a sanction, usually the payment of back taxes if the owner violates the terms of the agreement.

f State has legislation allowing regulation of floodplains.

g State regulations of surface mining.

1. State has structural authority.

2. Preferential Assessment Program—Assessment of eligible land is based upon a selected formula, which is usually use-value.

3. Deferred Taxation—Assessments of eligible land is based upon a selected formula, which is usually use-value and provides for a sanction, usually the payment of back taxes, if the land is converted to a noneligible use.

Source: Data used with permission of The Council of State Governments, *The Book of the States, 1976–1977*, Vol. 21 (Sexington, Ky.: Council of State Governments, 1976), p. 478 and grateful acknowledgement to the Urban Institute for these excerpts from Nelson Rosenbaum, *Land Use And The Legislatures* (Washington, D.C.: The Urban Institute, 1976), pp. 44–45.

of local areas to take any responsibility for planning or zoning. Under this approach, a state usually administers land use controls in all or a portion of unregulated county and municipal lands until the county or municipality enacts regulatory legislation of its own. This type of regulation is only a temporary solution at best. Unless it is related to a more comprehensive program, it provides no more effective land management than when each municipality acts as an autonomous unit—which is the traditional way of doing things. In Oregon's comprehensive land use law, there is a provision which requires all local governments to adopt a comprehensive plan and methods for implementing it (zoning, subdivision regulations, and so on). The state, through the planning agency, the Land Conservation and Development Commission (LCDC), is authorized to develop a comprehensive land use plan and implementation methods for any land not protected by local authorities.

The preceding discussion illustrates the different types of land use programs that have originated in the states in the last ten to fifteen years. Recognizing that misuse and pollution of existing land brought predictions of worse to come, the states began to take over from the localities the traditional function of regulating land use. We must not lose sight of what this means in terms of the groups that contend for the right to develop the land. It means that the state takes over the arena in which the contest is fought. Instead of local developers confronting local environmentalists and citizen's groups, the stage is set on the state level. The groups that have the determination and the funds confront each other in this arena. The transfer of the regulation to the state level may mean that some groups have an advantage which they did not enjoy at the local level. If the regulation is done through an environmental agency, the assumption would be that the decisions may favor the conservationists—as long as they keep up their interest. Regulatory policy, wherever it takes place, involves the confrontation of groups on a case-by-case basis with the government providing the forum and the rules for the contest.

What about the Federal Government?

THE FAILURE OF FEDERAL LAND USE LEGISLATION.   So far in this discussion we have discussed the local and state involvement in land use without mention of the role of the federal government. How does our marble cake look in the case of land use? In the division of responsibility for land use between the layers of government in our marble cake, a mere trickle in the federal layer widens in the state layer and broadens out to the thickest portion in the local level (resembling an Erlenmeyer flask). What explanation is there for the lack of federal government initiative in land use programs? For the last forty years we have become used to federal involvement in new kinds of social and economic programs, even if it only follows the actions of the more advanced states. The recent revolution in land use is an exception. It has to a great extent been initiated by the states themselves in response to problems within their borders. National legislation to encourage controlled land use was introduced in Congress from 1970 through 1975 but has yet to become law. Perhaps a brief study of the coalitions favoring and opposing the national legislation may be some indication of the groups which operate on the state level to favor or oppose land use planning.[13]

The general intent of federal land use policy would be to aid the states in their efforts to prevent urban sprawl, protect environmentally critical areas, encourage economic development, and plan for orderly use of land. This would be done through the power of the purse. In the first place, there was considerable disagreement among a number of executive branch agencies. The strongest spokesmen for a bill of the type supported by Representative Morris Udall and Senator Henry Jackson between 1970 and 1975 came from the Department of the Interior and the Environmental Protection Agency. The forces within the administration opposed to such a bill included the Federal Energy Administration (which feared slowdowns on energy facility siting decisions) and the Department of Housing and Urban Development (which wanted jurisdiction over land use itself through the comprehensive planning section of an existing statute). In the Executive Office, The Domestic Council and the Office of Management and Budget (headed by a former HUD secretary, a vigorous opponent of land use control) also opposed the Land Use Legislation. Groups from the outside formed two large coalitions: (1) to favor a reasonably strong bill or (2) to favor a weak bill or no bill at all. The major supporting groups included all of the environmentalist groups, the AFL-CIO, the United Auto Workers, the general purpose state and local government units (The National League of Cities, U.S. Conference of Mayors, The Council of State Governments, The National Governor's Conference, and the National Association of Counties), and the National Association of Realtors. In opposition were the home construction industry (both the builders and the construction unions), rural groups (Farm Bureau Federation and the National Cattlemen's Association), the U.S. Chamber of Commerce, and ideologically conservative groups fearing increasing "socialism" (The American Conservative Union and the Liberty Lobby). A high degree of emotional lobbying surrounded the consideration of the bill in the House of Representatives. It was too hot an issue for the House to wish to decide. The result is that decisions on land use remain decentralized to the state level. In some states the relative power of the coalitions varies and different types of land use legislation are passed. Regulatory policy inevitably involves conflict. With that conflict as intense as it was in the House of Representatives, the legislators shied from creating a regulatory power within the Department of the Interior which would contain such potential warfare.

The rejected federal legislation expressed the need for greater state involvement in land use management and provided federal financial assistance without sanctions to induce the states to achieve greater control over the use of the land. While direct state planning and regulation of land use would be allowed, the language and the Senate hearing testimony made it clear that substantial delegation of power to local government was preferred. The underlying assumption of the proposals was the inability of local government to make planning and regulation land use decisions consonent with the best interests of the state. The proposed legislation provided a framework for decision making to ensure that decisions regarding areas of statewide concern were decided (ultimately) at the state level. For reasons expressed above it does not appear likely that this legislation will be passed in the near future, and the states are proceeding by themselves to cope with their land use problems.

Coastal Zone Management Act

There is only one federal program to date (1979) which directly stimulates and facilitates state action on reform of land use governance. The Coastal Zone Management Act of 1972 became operational in 1974 and was designed to encourage states to manage their coastal resources comprehensively. Thirty states, including those on the Great Lakes, are eligible for grant money under the program. This program is administered by the Department of Commerce's National Oceanic and Atmospheric Administration, Office of Coastal Environment. Direct exercise of the police power by state governments, based upon a plan of development, was at the heart of the proposal. The Act encouraged states to engage in a study and planning process before undertaking legislative action, and therefore state legislatures began receiving proposals in 1976 for reallocation of authority over the shorelands. After this planning period, funds are available only for administration and management of the program adopted by the state (contingent upon federal approval).

The states are given considerable latitude under the Act to design a comprehensive management program that suits their own needs. The policy of the Act is to balance development on the nation's coasts with ecological, cultural, and historic values. The state is ultimately responsible for the development and preservation of the coastal zone. One of the most interesting aspects of the Act is the requirement that the management program must provide "for adequate consideration of the national interest involved in the siting of facilities necessary to meet requirements which are other than local in nature." The question arises whether this could mean an express federal preemption of state powers. Some states have been particularly concerned about the location of deep water ports, power plants, offshore wells, and coastal refineries. If these are deemed to be in the national interest, the environmentalists may not agree to the legislation, envisioning nuclear power plants standing along the coast with federal blessing. The program is to be administered by a single state agency designated by the governor. The agency is required to involve local governments in the management program and to coordinate all plans and activities in the coastal zone. Each of the thirty states involved in the planning process for implementation of this legislation are currently enmeshed in the bargaining that inevitably surrounds the initiation of new regulatory authority. It can be anticipated that intergovernmental rivalries, environmental groups, developers, and landowners will all converge on the state capitols.

Other Federal Programs

A Task Force sponsored by the Council of State Governments identifies 137 federal programs that have a direct impact on land use through construction of buildings or public facilities or through conservation or protective measures.[14] These programs illustrate the power of the purse over land use. They do not involve comprehensive planning and could complicate state efforts to plan for land. Two federal laws establish regulatory programs which are of particular interest in managing the use of land. These are the Federal Water Pollution Control Act and the Clean Air Act, both administered by the Environmental Protection Agency. The agency that decides where sewers will locate or be extended is also deciding indirectly where industry will locate. The agency which can determine where major sources of pollution can locate (highways and airports, for example) is also involved in land use. No mechanism is provided to insure that decisions made through these procedures will be consistent with each other or with overall state land use policy. Hence federal-mission-oriented agencies may hinder rather than help state efforts in land use planning.

We conclude this discussion of the local, state, and federal role in land use management with the observation that most land use is controlled by the local governments through the use of zoning power—a power which has been granted them by the states. Because there are now many areas of statewide concern which the local governments cannot control effectively, the states are beginning to assume more power. The federal government has tried and failed to pass general land use legislation to encourage, through the power of the purse, state efforts to plan. We saw that the groups that supported or opposed this legislation were too strong to allow the regulatory policy to be passed. Only one land use law in coastal zone management has managed to make it through the national legislative process. Other legislation of an environmental nature affects land use, but creates mission-oriented agencies which may exert a negative influence on state land use planning efforts. The interests that favor and oppose land use legislation are concentrating their efforts at the state level, where the major battles over planning for critical areas is taking place. We turn now to a discussion of the groups and interests which are locked in this struggle for land use regulation.

GROUPS AND INTERESTS AND BASES OF POWER

Politics makes strange bedfellows. This old adage is nowhere more true than in a study of land use planning and management. Governor Nelson Rockefeller said that he did not use labels like "liberal" and "conservative" because they are confusing and misleading.[15] This is also relevant, and we must remember both bits of political wisdom as we proceed with a discussion of the groups that contend in the arena of land use regulation. Assuming that groups try always to maximize their own self-interest through the governing process, it follows that they will support any set of rules that will bring them rewards. They will try to co-opt any group of decision-makers that deals out rewards and deprivations in the political process. While Conservatives generally support less government and Liberals more government, there are times when Conservatives need the government to protect their property and Liberals need less restrictive government to advance their interests. The following Table 10–2 contains some surprises, therefore. It places the Minority Rights and Open Housing Groups on the "No Regulation" column along with the traditional conservative groups like the Developers, Real Estate Brokers, and Farmers. It places the traditional conservative landed gentry citizens' groups in the column with the liberal environmentalists, both of whom believe that government must regulate the land to preserve it for the future. However, even as we place the groups such as farmers and developers in the "no regulation" column, we must recognize that in some states where pressure groups are strong and united, it is in the interest of a determined coalition to control the regulatory process against weaker rivals or anticipated enemies. Bureaucrats are found in both columns because regulation represents a loss of power to some and increase of power to others. Recall that on the national level, the proposed land use bill was supported by the Environmental Protection Agency and the Department of the Interior, both of whom stood to gain in power, and was opposed by the Federal Energy Administration, the Department of Housing and Urban Development, and the

Office of Management and Budget, which feared that they would lose control over the planning process. Local-level bureaucrats are generally fearful that if the state assumes more power, it will be taken from them; state-level bureaucrats are generally in favor of state regulation, particularly if they are in the environmental protection agency that will do the administering.

TABLE 10–2

Interest Groups in Land Use Regulation on
State and Local Level

THOSE DESIRING NO REGULATION	THOSE DESIRING REGULATION
Open Housing Minority Rights Groups (no regulation on the local level: possible regulation on state level if Anti-Snob Legislation)	Citizens' Groups (regulation on the local level: enabling legislation on state level)
Developers	Environmentalists
Real Estate Boards	
Construction Unions	Labor Unions
Chambers of Commerce	
Farmers	
Conservatives	Liberals
Bureaucrats	Bureaucrats

Minority Rights Groups versus Local Citizens' Groups

For the Minority Rights Groups, the exclusionary zoning in suburbia is regulation to be abolished in the effort to open up the suburbs to moderate- and lower-income people. Exclusionary zoning is the practice of zoning residential districts heavily or entirely for expensive, large-lot development. It has come to be recognized as that form of zoning which municipalities employ to exclude lower-income groups by erecting a barrier of prohibitively high priced, large-lot, single-family zoning. The price of housing on large lots is too high for the lower- to middle-class family. This type of zoning is supported by local citizens groups who want to protect their property against outsiders. They fear low-income people because they think they bring crime, children, and higher taxes to the community. The environmentalists on the local level also support the exclusionary zoning under a program of preserving open space. They want land to remain undeveloped so that they can enjoy scenery, hiking, and camping. They also want land to remain undeveloped so that wildlife can be preserved and fragile creatures that spawn in the wetlands can be allowed to preserve a chain of life. At the same time the National Association for the Advancement of Colored People urges Blacks to do battle in the townships and villages to lower zoning barriers and create new opportunities for housing closer to jobs at affordable prices. Since these exclusionary decisions are made at the local level under a broad grant of authority from the state, the proponents of opening up land for the use of lower-income and Black people must fight each community on a case-by-case basis, or try to seek redress in the courts or in state legislatures. The suburbs have little desire to protect interests other than their own. They depend on local property taxes, and the more valuable the property the better services they can provide for those already in residence. Hence, most suburbs successfully resist pressures at the local level for major changes in their zoning policies, particularly when the aim is the expansion of housing opportunities for lower-income and minority groups. They can, simultaneously, seek shopping centers and corporate headquarters.

A variety of urban interest groups have joined the NAACP to try to open up the suburbs. National civil rights and religious groups, labor unions, foundations, and public-interest organizations have been drawn to the issue. In general these groups have tried to change policy on the state level in an attempt to get favorable judicial decisions or legislative action to increase the access of lower-income and minority groups to land and housing in many local jurisdictions. These groups also have local affiliates which try to organize on a town-by-town basis to challenge local zoning. These groups have not been successful, mainly because they cannot mobilize sufficient support in the suburbs where they are trying to open up zoning. Linowes and Allensworth explain why this is so:

> The upper-middle-class suburbs have a great deal of influence with state legislatures, state executives, the federal government, and the courts at both levels. As long as the upper-middle-class controls the land-use system, it is not clear how other classes can gain.[16]

The writers go on to say that those who are in a position to do something about housing for the poor and Blacks are invariably progovernment. Their view is that liberals will not accept the position that the elimination of government from the "whole field" of land use would be preferable to the existing system, insofar as the interests of Blacks and other racial or economic minorities are concerned. According to Linowes and Allensworth, liberals equate government with help for the disadvantaged, and cannot see that government is the cause of the problem, not the means of solving it. The writers see the strategy of the developers as the main hope of the disadvantaged groups. The developer's strategy is to make land controls more flexible and to give developer interests more of a say in their exercise. The result will be more development, and even regulated development, the writers say, will end up serving wider segments of the population than more rigid controls. In concluding their argument, the writers state that: "Developers may be motivated principally by profit, but they are much more likely to serve useful policy ends than their opposite number.[17] Michael Danielson, however, does not share this optimism. He notices a difference between the National Association of Home Builders, who can and do oppose exclusionary zoning, and the local builders, who defend the status quo because their attachments to local governments are strong and their personal economic stakes in the existing housing and land use system are substantial.[18] Few local developers or realtors are likely to bite the hand that feeds them. They cannot be counted on to join forces with the poor who wish to have access to suburban living. Whether or not we agree with the writers that the developers represent the best ally of the disadvantaged, we turn now to a discussion of the roles of the developers and the environmentalists in the land use battle.

Property Owners and Developers versus Environmentalists

It is the view of the environmentalists that ecologically uninformed planning and development is creating significant and avoidable adverse impacts on the environment, particularly lands near or under major bodies or courses of water which possess significant natural and scenic values. They complain that land use decisions are made without adequate opportunity for members of the public to be informed about the impact of or the alternatives for such decisions or to become involved in them. Groups such as the Sierra Club and the Audubon Society have been involved in conservation for decades, but the heightened interest in the movement around 1970 spawned new groups that have grown in influence as a result of public recognition that America's natural and recreational resources are dwindling. The environmentalists are not always united, however. There are preservationists who would like to stop all development in wetland or coastal areas—to pursue a "forever wild" policy. The conservationist is presumably more amenable to some development, if carefully planned. The diversity among the environmental groups was dramatized by the battle over the San Onofre, California, nuclear generating station. The issue of nuclear power generation, coupled with the proposed destruction of an attractive length of coastline, brought forth a broad cross-section of environmentalists to make clear their opposition before the commission. But one group, the Sierra Club, was divided on the issue. One faction was willing to face the risks of nuclear hazards and some coastal trade-off in exchange for the cleaner environment promised by the availability of nuclear generated energy.[19]

There is also a growing awareness that ecology is elitist. It is often a matter of the rich man's politics of choice versus the poor man's politics of necessity. Environmentalists are not the steelworkers, or assemblyline workers, or small farmers, or hotel clerks. They are lawyers, junior faculty, editors, writers, corporate vice-presidents, and leisure-class women. The citizens' groups which try to save their neighborhood character on the local level are also environmentalists on the state and national level.

This is not to imply that virtue lies on the side of the developers or their allies, the landowners and construction unions. In the recent past, the developers' claims to private property rights and resulting profits were quite acceptable to land use decision makers and, when not, were quite consistently upheld in the courts. As long as the developers could control decisions in local jurisdictions, they were content to maintain a low profile. As long as the state governments allowed the local jurisdictions to make the key land use decisions, developers did not push for any land use legislation—indeed it was in their interests to defeat it. In California, a group called "Committee Opposed to Ecology Issues" had been meeting for several years prior to 1972 and had as its main goal the blockage of coastal legislation. The Committee consisted of 34 industry lobbyists, including representatives of Southern California Edison Company, Standard Oil, the California Real Estate Association, and various other organizations who benefited by local decision making.[20] These names appear in the Ralph Nadar study of the organizations that control land use in California. The Nadar study revealed that remarkably few corporations own much of the state. Twenty-five landowners hold over 16 percent of the state's privately held land. These few who hold much of California's land control their own political and economic destinies.[21]

The combined force of all these companies, plus the public relations firm of Whitaker and Baxter, could not stop the environmentalists in 1974 from initiating and getting enacted the measure on coastal zone conservation known as Proposition 20. The Coastal Alliance, consisting of a coalition of over sixty groups which worked for the initiative, was joined by the Sierra Club, The League of Women Voters, The California Medical Association, the Federation of Western Outdoor Clubs, the United Auto Workers Union, the American Institute of Architects, Common Cause, The American Association of University Women, and many others.[22] In the official ballot summary of the issues behind Proposition 20, the Coastal Alliance stated that the coast had been plundered by haphazard development and land speculation. Beaches and campgrounds formerly open were closed. Wildlife habitats were buried under streets and vacation homes for the wealthy. Land speculators banked their profits, posted their "no trespassing signs," and left the small property owner with the burden of increased taxes to pay for streets, sewers, police, and fire protection. The coast continued to shrink.[23]

On the other hand, the land developers and oil and utility companies stated that the proponents of Proposition 20 devised a scheme for appropriating private property without paying for it. In contrast to the arguments of the Coastal Alliance, the opponents stated that Proposition 20 would make beach lands a haven for the rich, who already have developed "exclusive playgrounds." They stated that the foremost motivation of the Initiative's elitist proponents was to preclude the enjoyment of coastal areas by retired and working people. Those who gave forth this rhetoric were on record by law, for their contributions to the Citizens against the Coastal Initiative. They included:[24]

Land Developers	Deane and Deane, Inc.	$ 50,000
	The Irvine Company	50,000
Oil Companies	Standard Oil—Calif.	30,000
	Union Oil	10,000
	Gulf Oil	10,000
	Standard Oil—N.J.	25,000
	Getty Oil	5,000
Contracting Firm	Bechtel Corp.	25,000
Farm Equipment	Allis Chalmers	10,000
Conglomerate	Dart Industries	13,000
Electric Companies	General Electric	25,000
	Pacific Gas and Electric	251,000
	Southern Cal. Edison	25,000
Railroad	Southern Pacific	20,000

In addition, some land owners, banks, industrialists, and oil companies from outside the state gave money to defeat the proposition. It is interesting that both sides claimed the "little guy"—the worker and the retired who needed sun and rest. In the end the proponents of the measure won by 55 percent of the vote. While they did not have the money, they did have other resources that mattered. They had *time* in the form of numerous volunteer workers; they had *skill* provided by legal advice and campaign firms. Numbers and time are resources which can be used skillfully to overcome groups with greater monetary advantage. Groups which lack one resource can achieve their ends by using other resources to advantage. However, the whole issue over the Coastal Zone Conservation indicated that the fight would be carried into the regulatory arena after the regional commissions were organized. All observations confirm the fact that this is true.

Farmers Divided

In general, farmers both large and small, do not want regulation. In the case of the small farmer, it means that his land may be zoned for farming and he will not be able to sell it or dispose of it as he wishes. Small farmers traditionally have been hostile to public land controls throughout the United States. It was representatives of this group that appeared in Washington in massive numbers to defeat the national land use bill in 1974. Typical of the groups that came were:[25]

Mississippi Forestry Association
Louisiana Forestry Association
Texas Forestry Association
North Carolina Forestry Association
Nebraska Farm Bureau
Iowa Farm Bureau Federation
Illinois Agricultural Association
Missouri Farm Bureau Federation
New Mexico Cattle Growers' Association
South Dakota Stock Growers' Association
Texas Sheep and Goat Association
Oklahoma Cattlemen's Association

The small farmer may be justifiably fearful of the corporate farmer. The corporate landholder's concern is with maximizing profit by changing land use, be it plantations, ranching, timber, mining, or development. According to Robert Fellmeth, author of the Nadar study of land use in California, Southern Pacific still holds almost two million acres of land. In addition to leasing its land for oil and mineral exploration, for agricultural use, for grazing purposes, and for timber, Southern Pacific is opening up vast tracts for development—"bulldozing lots for sale to speculators."[26] The small farmer is no match for the huge corporate conglomerate. He is unable to accumulate the resources of land and credit that would give him advantages equal to those of the corporate farmer. Why then does the small farmer oppose regulation? It may be that he fears that any land regulation would naturally be subject to the manipulation of the corporate landowners, and hence damaging to him. It also may be that he is traditionally against *any* form of regulation of his most precious resource—his land.

It is surprising, therefore, that the first state-wide land use law was enacted in 1961 primarily to protect Hawaii's farmers. However, the farmers in Hawaii are large-scale growers. Only a handful of families and groups in the state own about 90 percent of the private land (about half of the total land area), with one organization alone controlling about a tenth of it. The private holdings include nearly all the tillable agricultural land.[27] Much of the property in large holdings is used for pineapple and sugarcane, although some of it was being converted to development near urban areas. Much of the land in plantations is leased by growers, who may, in fact, be divisions of a giant landholding corporation. The corporate landholder's concern is with maximizing profits by changing land use, be it for plantations, development, or other uses. The growers, of course, wanted to protect the plantations. In the 1950s the possibility that the large landowners might withdraw their leases and sell to developers loomed as a specter for plantation agriculture. The growers, hardly small farmers, but smaller at least than the landowners, wanted to protect their interests and the first total state-wide land use law was passed. Hawaii drew on a strong tradition of central control of land and of concentrated land ownership. This provided the impetus for the state land use law. Absent was the influence of any sizable bloc of small farmers. Also less potent at the time was the power of the development interests representing housing needs and the tourist industry. The large growers as a group separate from the landowners, held the power. This power will inevitably give way to a balance of interests in the future. Agriculture has slipped to third place in the economic life of Hawaii, and growth and urbanization pressures are strong. In 1975, there was widespread criticism of the Land Use Commission. The monopoly held by the growers has been broken and new adjustments must be made to accommodate the newer pressures in the regulatory process.[28]

It is surprising that the first all-encompassing state land use law in the continental United States should also be in a farming state. The Vermont *Land Use and Government Control Act* of 1970 was supported by the farmers. Apparently the rapid conversion of agricultural land to nonfarm uses and the resulting disruption caused by the invasion of developers, who came to provide the recreational, residential, and commercial ski and resort facilities the newcomers demanded, caused farmers to favor some form of regulation. The taxes of farmland rose near these developments, making it too difficult for the family farmer to continue. There was a resentment of outsiders and the feeling that the legislation would "punish" them. Apparently there was little pressure group activity at the time the bill was passed. The popular and ambitious governor spoke for the "insiders" or native Vermonters who feared new developments in the southern part of Vermont, and especially one proposed by the International Paper Company. Since most native Vermonters were small farmers, the legislation was not opposed—the farmers believed the governor and state legislature spoke for them. Here we have a case where the farmers were strong enough—indeed, spoke for the state—so that they did not oppose planning which they could control. A great deal of land use regulation depends on the power of the competing groups. If one group is strong enough to be in the driver's seat, there is no reason to oppose the legislation.

Bureaucrats Divided

The general rule that informs all group pressure is that of advantage. To what extent will the regulation advantage or disadvantage the group? All activity is concentrated around that end.

The first division among bureaucrats is that of local versus state regulation. Local officials may fear that statewide land use regulation will stifle their economic growth and their chances to capitalize on industrial or tourist-oriented development. A planning board member from a county in North Carolina's outer banks argues, "We don't want our destiny controlled by the governor. We want to control it ourselves."[29] Similar fears are expressed in the impoverished communities of northeastern Vermont, the Adirondacks, and rural Colorado. On the other hand, a shift of local control to the state means a shift in the power of individuals. Regulation of land use at the local level can be used to reward political friends and penalize enemies. One state legislator, a supporter of a state land use bill, said of the local officials who opposed it, "These guys want to keep this their own ball game. There are a lot of political contributions from people in the development business. The local officials don't want it all going to (the governor)."[30]

The second division among bureaucrats exists on a horizontal dimension. Just as the proposed national land use bill was opposed by some agencies in the administration and executive branch, we can anticipate that such bureaucratic rivalries exist on the state level. Scores of state agencies are now pursuing narrow land-use-related goals. State agencies that control pollution, such as the Environmental Protection Agency, approve sewage treatment plants that open up new lands to urbanization. State land planners, with a more comprehensive view, will oppose these same projects because they encourage development in critical areas. Since energy has become a constant worry and a high priority, rivalries between agencies responsible for power plant siting and other land use exist on the state as well as national level. Delaware has state zoning in the sense that it has prohibited new heavy industry from locating in a strip 1 to 5 miles wide along its coastline. Although the law is quite simple in its prohibition of heavy industry, there is an argument as to which industries are "light" and therefore acceptable. In 1973 a state board which issues permits overruled the recommendation of the state planner and agreed to consider a permit for a "light" chemical plant that would include four or five 25,000 gallon tanks and three 50-foot high distillation columns.[31]

What about Political Parties?

What is the role of the political party in land use regulation? It is, frankly, very early to tell. What we will look for is the role of the party in containing pressure group activity so that regulation can proceed without constant bias in favor of any one group. As stated before, political parties that are cohesive enough to make electoral promises which they can put into effect are most likely to control pressure group activity. Pressure groups can work within such parties, but not dominate them. In order to contain pressures within the regulatory area, a program proposed and enacted by a cohesive party would place regulatory activity within the purview of the governor, and not in an independent agency. In this way a strong governor and an active legislature could oversee the politics of regulation with an eye to a balancing of interests.

One study that is directly addressed to the role of the political party in environmental policy predicted that, in view of the Republican Party's pro-business orientation, aversion to government controls, and conservative stance toward governmental action on social problems, Republican legislators would be less likely to support pro-environmental proposals than Democrats. The test took place in Oregon in 1971, and all environmental issues (pollution, natural resources, wildlife, natural beauty, and population control) were considered. The hypothesis received considerable support. The writers conclude that the parties differ substantially in a policy area heretofore regarded as nonpartisan. They muse about the practical implications of their results and arrive at a final recommendation that it would still be more efficacious for environmentalists to single out those regarded as exceptionally good or poor candidates and support or oppose them regardless of party.[32] Charles E. Little's study of land use legislation in Oregon confirms the wisdom of this advice. Oregon's Senate Bill 100, passed in 1973, was an ambitious and comprehensive state land use measure which established mandatory land use planning by all local units of government. In addition, the law established a state land use commission, the Land Conservation and Development Commission (LCDC), empowered to review local plans for their consistency with state goals and guidelines. Little found that while it appeared that Democrats favored the land use legislation, the geographical location of the legislator had more explanatory power than party. Here are his tabulations 'for legislators from both houses on SB 100, the land use legislation:[33]

SB 100		YES	NO
Democrats	(52)	37	13
Republicans	(38)	21	17
Willamette	(60)	49	9
Other	(30)	9	21

Mushkatel and Medler provide a further refinement of Little's thesis that land use planning has geographical support in Oregon and conclude that the issue is a class-based one. The better-off counties and cities favor land use planning while the less well off reject it. In Oregon, high levels of unemployment tend to be located in the more rural counties—counties which rejected land use planning on a subsequent referendum in 1976. In addition, timber-dependent counties were also hostile to land use planning. These counties lie outside the Willamette Valley, where 70 percent of the people reside. The less well off want to catch up to the rest of Oregon and believe that state-imposed guidelines for land use are a threat to future development.[34]

In conclusion, studies of the role of parties in Oregon land use decisions are not definitive in helping us understand their importance for land use policy. We know that parties are weak in Oregon and pressure groups are strong. Contrary to the strong party states, parties in Oregon do not provide a vehicle for containing and mediating class conflict. Apparently the poorer counties do not find a champion in the Democratic party which would be expected to represent them. Oregon may represent the classic case of regulatory policy dominated by class conflict. In an effort to understand how groups can influence the decision-makers, we proceed with a discussion of the arenas in which decisions are made.

THE PROCESS OF MAKING LAND USE DECISIONS

Poliscide: The Killing of Weston, Illinois[35]

The following story provides an introduction to the fragmented decision-making process through which regulatory policy is made. Responsibility for decisions is divided between several governments, hence groups with more resources and incentives are likely to prevail over groups that do not have the money or the knowledge to make the process serve them. This story, called "Poliscide," shows how a struggling blue-collar community was killed by groups in the county which did not want it to live. The enemy groups used political fragmentation to serve their interests. It was not so much that the state or the national government wanted to kill Weston, Illinois; it was simply that they preferred to remain ignorant about the location of the atom smasher which eventually killed the town —not by an explosion, but by deliberate political annihilation.

Two years before the accident at the nuclear power plant at Three Mile Island in Pennsylvania in March, 1979, the American public had the almost eighteenth-century faith that science and technology had all the answers. Nuclear power was supported by 70 percent of Americans and even the location of a plant in the home community was approved by over half.[36] Before the nuclear accident, the location of power plants was the responsibility of local governments in most states. Radiation danger was not one of the criteria which guided the choice of the location of the power plant. Business and economic development wishes dominated the site selection process as local governments vied for the privilege of locating the plant within their borders. While state and national safety requirements must now be considered when a new power plant is given a site, the following story illustrates how groups can still use political fragmentation of the regulatory process to serve their interests. It describes how groups which can dominate the decision-making process can get what they want at the expense of groups that are not as powerful.

Weston, Illinois, was a working class suburb thirty miles west of Chicago. It consisted of 71 farms and 100 "tract" houses. Among its citizens were farmers, tenant farmers, gentlemen farmers, ordinary white-collar commuters, blue-collar workers who could buy a cheap house, and land speculators waiting to subdivide. The wealthy county of DuPage, where this struggling community tried to exist, had one of the highest median family incomes in the United States and was determined to prevent the "urbanization and proletarianization" of Weston. It had tried to prevent the new homes from being built, the incorporation of the village itself, and finally the expansion. The county had succeeded in persuading the Federal Housing Administration and the Veteran's Administration to refuse to provide insured mortgages for Weston—much as they have done in urban slums.

Weston did not fit into the future of the suburban county as envisioned by county and regional planners. It was in the middle of open country slated for clean industry and possibly a college. The county did not want low-cost development of housing units to fit the lower-middle-class notion of the suburban dream. The county planners wanted to control the growth of the country along their notion of suburbs as elegant, white, and wealthy. Clean industry is better than lower-middle-class people, they thought.

How did Weston get started in the first place, given the open hostility to its existence on the part of the county planners? It all began when a land speculator bought a 420-acre farm whose owner could not afford to pay the higher taxes on his increasingly valuable land. The speculator sold the land to a land development corporation which planned to build enough low rental blue-collar homes to incorporate as a village, and then to subdivide two lot parcels into three and proceed to build more expensive homes for middle-class residents. The original homes were modest and the residents were convinced to incorporate as a village, a procedure which was initiated by the signatures of only 35 electors. The county fought the developers every step of the way and, as a result of the delay, the developers went bankrupt and turned to a crime syndicate for financing. Even the crime syndicate could not thwart the opposition of DuPage County when the upper classes declared war on the lower. Transiency, rentals, intense land use, and a working class population guaranteed the opposition of the upper classes. But the Weston residents, living in rented homes, still dreamed of a middle-class city of their own as promised by the developers.

It was into this milieu that the idea of an atom smasher was dropped. The state wanted the 200-billion electron volt accelerator located near Chicago to stop the scientific brain drain and to help keep the Chicago metropolitan area alive. Governor Kerner was willing to leave the acquisition of the site to the county and to remain ignorant of the county plans. The county seized on this opportunity to rid itself of the town of Weston. It first sold the residents on the idea that the accelerator could bring about their dream—a thriving city. They received this news enthusiastically, and the Village Board invited the accelerator to locate in their community. Eventually the local planners found out that their hopes for a new city were based on false assumptions, but by the time they did, the villagers and farmers did not have enough time to organize opposition to the site selection or to prevent the taking of their property for the purpose of building the smasher. (They were compensated, but the transactions were made under duress and were probably not fair market value.) Twenty months later, no legal trace of the village or farms remained. National Accelerator Laboratory personnel occupied the village and farmhouses while supervising construction of the underground ring, two miles in diameter, in which atoms would be accelerated, shot at, and smashed. The final result is that no low-cost project penetrated DuPage County, and with the absorption of the last large tracts of undeveloped land by the accelerator and by upper-class developments, there is not likely to be such a penetration.

This study shows how a wealthy suburban county managed to make pawns of the national government as well as the state government in its strategy of county planning and development. It was able to do this because the choice of the site of the atom smasher was made locally. Had the Village officials been able to see what lay ahead, they could have resisted the selection of their community for the accelerator, or they might have been able to negotiate its location away from their homes. But they were not sophisticated enough to have that much clout. Who could have come to their aid? It is the thesis of this book that a cohesive political party with strong leadership and an open housing platform might have come to the rescue of Weston, Illinois. The politicians at the state level were the only ones who could have saved the town from extinction. They were the only ones who could have balanced the demands of the wealthy suburbs against the needs of the working classes for homes outside the center city at prices they could afford. The state could do this only if it had assumed the power to regulate the location of power plants—a power which Illinois had not given its state government. We proceed to a discussion of the levels of government which participate in the making of land use policy.

The 14,000 Local Governments

It is in the nature of the regulatory process that it rewards some groups at the expense of others. Because most land use decisions are made at the local level, groups which win in some areas lose in others. Local land regulation agencies have been accused of serving developer interests as well as "citizens' groups." It was the traditional assumption that the local government bias favored economic growth and development over other interests and values. Linowes and Allensworth counter with the claim that developers' claims to private property rights and the resulting profits are no longer considered legitimate in many quarters. According to them, power has shifted away from developers to citizens' groups.[37] They claim that the more you try to use government to solve a problem the worse the problem gets, because government is no more than the classes or interests controlling it. If upper-middle-class interests control the government, the decisions will be made in the interests of the upper middle class, as they were in DuPage County, Illinois. Linowes and Allensworth contend that land use controls should be more flexible in order to serve wider segments of the population.

Theoretically, local government asserts the public interest in regulating changes in the use of private land. The fact that both developers and citizens' groups are disappointed reveals that local decision-makers respond to the strongest local pressures. Local control of land use means local zoning and subdivision regulations have succeeded only in preserving existing neighborhoods from invasions of nonresidential uses or "nonconforming residential uses," such as multi-family housing or small-lot developments. On the urban fringe of the cities, market forces have ordained new shopping centers or high rises which bring valuable revenue to tax-needy governments.

Perhaps it would be well at this point to review the status of local governments with respect to planning and zoning. Up until recently the contribution of the states to land use has been limited to approving enabling legislation permitting local governments to plan and zone. Enabling legislation does not mandate or require local action, as is the case with most state legislation, but permits it under certain conditions. These conditions may specify which local governments are authorized to do planning and zoning—for example cities with populations over 5,000. Within the states the political system is unitary, meaning that all powers reside in the state governments and the local governments are subservient or merely "creatures" of the state. Local governments in this sense include cities, counties, townships, towns, villages, boroughs, special districts, and others. The idea that local governments are creatures of the state has been sustained by the Supreme Court. Since localities are creatures of the state, they can do only what the state permits or directs them to do.

Until recent years, it was zoning and not planning that had taken the lead. The states enacted zoning-enabling legislation years before they did anything about planning. It should be noted that planning is only advisory, and although it theoretically should precede actual land regulation (zoning), states and communities have typically opted for zoning first. Zoning is law and it must be "obeyed." It details the use of this or that piece of property—whether a hotel or a high rise or a house with two acres of land or a park can be built on it—while planning merely suggests possible uses for the land. Planning is a guide for future use, while zoning stipulates that use here and now. Today all states authorize their localities to plan, either through enabling legislation or in other ways, such as city charters or direct legislation. The standard legislation calls for the establishment of independent planning commissions. The reasoning was that planning should be removed from the political process. More recent arguments hold that there is no way to divorce planning from politics, and that planning should be put under officials who are politically responsible and accountable, that planning has to be implemented to be effective, and that it cannot be implemented if it is not integrated into the mainstream of local government.

We are faced with a record of local government failure to deal with land use conflicts. These failures stem from the fact that individual local governments cannot take into account the interests of the wider public significantly affected by the outcome of a given land use policy. It has been estimated that there are 14,000 local governments in the United States which exercise some form of land use control. More than 10,000 have planning boards, and a slightly smaller number have a zoning ordinance or subdivision regulations with the planning board as the administrator.[38] The effects of land use changes can spill over these jurisdictional boundaries in obvious ways. Robert G. Healy describes the following situation:

Take, for example, the location of an oil refinery on the New England coast, a possibility that has been the source of several land use controversies and a major impetus to Maine's Site Location of Development Law (1970). If built in the small town of Machiasport, Maine, a $150 to $300 million refinery would be assessed at $113 to $225 million—75 to 150 times the town's present assessed valuation. Under present state law, the property taxes generated would not be shared with surrounding towns, even though these latter would have to house substantial numbers of new workers and would have to provide them with schools, roads, utilities, and other public services.[39]

Growth itself is one of the greatest jurisdictional spillovers. During the rapid change of California's Santa Clara Valley from cropland to suburbia, no single local government could have chosen not to change. Although each municipality had zoning power, no one government could have resisted the growth and remained farmland. Economics and the political pressures it generates makes holding out against development impossible.

The environmentalists see the destruction of the wilderness as a breach of faith with nature. But the local official on the zoning board is hard pressed not to give in to his friend or customer. If the petitioner explains that his livelihood depends on the approval of the request, the board member has made an enemy for life. New York's Adirondack Park provides an example of this controversy. Visitors to this wild forest area feared that a second-home boom would destroy the habitat of wildlife and the wilderness visitors enjoyed. Residents of the towns within the borders of the proposed park felt that the proposed land regulations would preserve them in picturesque poverty for the benefit of wealthy environmentalists. Thus there are many conflicts of interest in the regulation of land. It is of note that both the environmentalists and the landowners and developers are turning to the state governments as the solution to the land use puzzle. Each group has its own definition of better planning, depending on the group's self-interest or its conception of the public interest. While developers would prefer no planning at all, they realize that planning can support and encourage development. Thus both groups have suffered defeat at the local level and reason that they have something to gain from state government planning of land use.

The Governor, The Bureaucracy, and the Legislature

Recently, Governor Byrne of New Jersey called a halt to all development in the Pine Barrens, awaiting a study of their environmental significance. The governor stated that they were the habitat of many forms of wildlife and an exceedingly important aquifer.

The governors of Vermont, Florida, and Oregon initiated land use plans and guided them through the legislatures. Governor Tom McCall put the problem to the 57th Legislative Assembly of Oregon. "There is a shameless threat to our environment," McCall charged, "and to the whole quality of life—the unfettered despoiling of the land." The Governor continued in the following vein. "We are in dire need of a state land use policy, new subdivision laws, and new standards for planning and zoning by cities and counties. The interests of Oregon for today and in the future must be protection from the wastrels of the land."[40] Governor McCall was successful in getting what he wanted, but not without help from his friends, the environmentalists, and more than a few compromises with his enemies, business, industry, and the developers.

The governor's interest and support is undoubtedly crucial for the passage and continuing success of a land use program. The location of the agency to plan and administer the land use program is a key factor in its effectiveness. As each state moves into the arena of land use legislation, it will have to decide the nature of the state's lead agency for implementation of that legislation. The predominant location for the lead agency is in the state planning office. Most states place the program under the governor's direction. In all cases where the state planning office is the lead agency, it has the responsibility for the formulation of broader goals and policies. Figure 10–1 indicates the location of a land use planning agency under the Environmental Planning Director, headed by a state planning agency. That the bureaucracy has an independent influence in and of itself has been amply documented by many analysts. The governor is just one person and his staff is small. His powers over the bureaucracy will depend, as much as anything, on his willingness to go to the public to defend his programs and bring pressure on the agencies. One of the key features of state executives is the extent to which they are dominated by boards and commissions. This, in turn, leads to administrative decentralization and makes it even harder for the governor to control. Important policy-making powers are concentrated in the Boards (see the Environmental Quality Council in Figure 10–1),which in turn can exercise important policy and administrative authority over agency staff .

It is the state legislatures that must establish the land use program and its implementation. In addition, the land use policies set forth in the legislation and the program for carrying them out are subject to the continuing responsibility of legislative oversight. In two states, Colorado and Oregon, the legislatures have set up joint committees on land use. One or two other states use a select committee made up of the chairmen or other representatives of committees whose jurisdiction is related to land use. In most other states the committees dealing with natural resources, environmental affairs, or state government have jurisdiction.

Subgovernments

We have set up the formalities of the structure of land use planning and implementation, but this does not tell us much about how the system really works. We know that the interest groups have a vital interest in the subject. How do they bring their influence to bear on the state agencies? While it is too early to portray the manner in which the regulation of land use works in the states, it is clearly relevant to consider how regulatory agencies have operated in other areas and predict that this may come

FIGURE 10–1

Location of Land Use Planning Agency

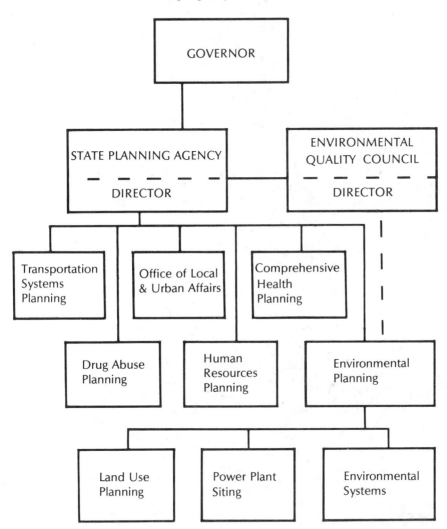

Source: This figure is used with permission of the Council of State Governments and is adapted from the Minnesota State Planning Agency in *Land Use: Policy and Program Analysis,* No. 3, *Organization, Management and Financing of State Land Use Programs* (Lexington, Ky: Council of State Governments, 1974), p. 60.

about in the area of land use policy. In general a close relationship develops between the regulators and the regulated. Occasionally this linkage has been called a "complex" or "subgovernment." Figure 10–2 illustrates this subgovernment between the bureaucracy, the legislative oversight

FIGURE 10–2

A Subgovernment

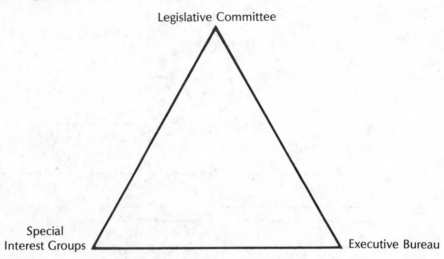

committee, and the special interest groups—in this case the most likely groups would be the builders, the developers, and the environmentalists. A subgovernment is likely to develop when there is widespread apathy on the subject on the part of the general public. It is also typified by relatively autonomous bureaucratic agencies able to cultivate ties of their own outside the executive branch. The reason these agencies develop relationships outside the government among those they are supposed to regulate is that these relationships help reduce friction for the policy-makers and help build up predictability. Hence regulatory policy brings about the natural tendencies of the regulators to develop relationships of mutual trust and interdependency with the regulated. The interest groups most capable of cultivating such intimate relationships with legislative committees and their bureau counterparts are those possessing several of these attributes:[41]

1. a clearly defined stake in the land use regulatory area
2. legitimacy in the eyes of legislative committee members
3. money enough to afford lobbyists at the state level and staffs able to conduct research of use to the committee's work
4. additional funds to help support individual committee members' electoral campaigns
5. organizational bases (real estate groups, business firms, etc.) at the local level to which the committee members themselves belong.

While the developers have more of these resources than the environmentalists, they will not have as much power when the land use program is first set up, and the environmentalists have tremendous incentive. The bureaucracy will line up with the environmentalists, even though both social and environmental concerns supposedly are encompassed by state land use policies. Danielson is pessimistic about the ability of state government to serve the housing needs of the poor as well as protecting the environment:

> In all but a few states, environmental protection has been the paramount concern in the design of state land-use controls . . . Far from seeking to expand housing opportunities, almost all the new laws aim to limit development. In so doing, state land use and environment control which affect housing inevitably restrict housing opportunities.[42]

There are several counteractive forces at work in the land use area. In the first place, the interest of the governor can be a deterrent to the capture of the agency and the legislative committee by an interest group. The governor may be able to create strong supervision over the ageny.[43] He may engage public interest in the plan. He may be able to counteract the effects of interest group subgovernments with the effects of a determined party program. Table 10–3 indicates that there is a tendency for states that have strong pressure groups to have weak planning agencies, and for states that have weak pressure groups to have significant planning systems. This "report card" on the status of the states' planning efforts represents a period ending in 1972. At that time each state was given grades of Significant, Moderate, or Limited for each of its several activities in development, public involvement, and generation of official interest. Table 10–3 reveals general tendencies only, however. Forty percent of the weak pressure group states had significant plans, and 40 percent of the strong pressure group states had limited plans. This indicates that states in which pressures are strong may not be able to pass significant regulatory legislation. Remember that business and real estate and developer groups prefer no regulation at all as a first choice. However, the observer will note that there is a cluster of states in the upper right cell of the table that is composed of states in which pressure group strength is strong and regulation is significant. A casual review of these states reveals that several of them instituted regulation that favored the strongest groups in the state. Needless to say, a strong pressure group which can dominate the politics of a state will prefer to regulate in its own favor. This happened in Hawaii, where the plantation growers of pineapple and sugarcane got control over the first state-wide land use program. In Oregon, where businesses and developers are strong, the passage of land use regulatory legislation depended on their support. It had rough going, as told by Charles E. Little.

TABLE 10–3

State Planning Effectiveness by Pressure-Group
Strength, 1972

PLANNING EFFECTIVENESS[a]	PRESSURE-GROUP STRENGTH[b]		
	WEAK	MODERATE	STRONG
Significant	New York	Delaware	Hawaii
	Wisconsin	Vermont	Washington
	Massachusetts	Virginia	New Hampshire
	New Jersey	Maine	Oregon
		California	Georgia
		Maryland	Texas
		Pennsylvania	
Moderate	Connecticut	Arizona	Iowa
	Minnesota	Kansas	South Carolina
	Rhode Island	Illinois	New Mexico
			North Carolina
			Florida
			Oklahoma
			Louisiana
Limited	North Dakota	South Dakota	Montana
	Colorado	Missouri	Nebraska
	Michigan	Nevada	Arkansas
		Utah	Alaska
		Idaho	Kentucky
		Wyoming	Alabama
		Indiana	Mississippi
		Ohio	Tennessee
			West Virginia

[a]The planning effectiveness for each state was determined by assigning values to the grades given by Catanese for each of nine planning activities. The values were summed. The total possible score was 27; the minimum was 9 (Sig = 3; Mod = 2; and Lim = 1)
[b]Pressure group strength is measured as in Table 3–3
Source: Data used with permission of The Council of State Governments from Anthony James Catanese, "Reflections on State Planning Evaluation," The Council of State Planning Agencies and the Council of State Governments, eds., State Planning Issues, 1973 (Lexington, Ky.: Council of State Governments, 1973), p. 27.

After it was over, Governor McCall received a plaque from the Associated Oregon Industries lauding his "consistent cooperation with business and industry" to win his goal of a beautiful Oregon "preserved from pollution and prepared for progress."[44]

State Courts

Most of the case law in zoning and land use control can be traced to the state courts, and most of it deals with local zoning decisions. The United

States Supreme Court has considered very few zoning cases since its famous *Euclid* decision, and it has ruled on the subject only four times since.[45] Most of the litigation in land use regulation has been left within the province of the state courts, and it has become an important part of their workload. Cases are generally brought in the trial court and may be appealed all the way up through the intermediate court to the highest court in the state, and after this, if a federal question is involved, they may be taken to the United States courts.

The reason for the heavy involvement of the courts in the land use question is based on the Fifth Amendment to the Constitution of the United States which states: "... nor shall private property be taken for public use, without just compensation, ..." a provision generally echoed and often strengthened or extended by state constitutions. This brief phrase involves troublesome ambiguities when it is applied to regulation of the use of private land in the interests of the general public. Questions such as:

1. When is property "taken" by regulation—when the owner's exercise of full and complete ownership is restricted in any way, or limited severely, or when the land is completely removed from his control?
2. What is "public use"—enjoyment, absence of nuisance, or physical occupation?
3. What is "just compensation"—does the securing of advantages to society as a whole provide compensation which is just for some limitations on the use of land, or does any loss in value resulting from such limitations require monetary compensation?

The taking issue involves a balancing of individual and social rights and obligations. It is a serious problem whenever there is substantial pressure for urban growth, particularly where the environment is sensitive. Efforts to achieve balance through legislation and litigation furnish solutions to this problem. Resolution of the uncertainty is crucial in determining how the development and use of land can be successfully regulated.

It appears that the state courts have been more tolerant of state land use regulation than they are of local controls. They have typically been sympathetic to a wide construction of state powers in this area and have tended to side with public over private rights in such matters as state zoning of shorelines and coastal areas, state regulation of wetlands, direct state control of floodplains, regional planning set up by the state, airport zoning under state powers, and general state zoning (although there are very few such cases).[46] In one recent Wisconsin case, *Just v. Marinette County* (1972), a state court upheld the Wisconsin Shoreland Zoning Law of 1970 which regulates land 1,000 feet back from all lakes and 300 feet from river basins. The court ruled that the measure does not represent an unreasonable exercise of police power and that the state is perfectly justified in limiting the use of private property so that it remains in its largely natural state to prevent harm to public rights.[47]

It is in the area of local zoning that the most frequent and bitter cases are fought. As groups attempt to break down local zoning for development, it is not clear what regulation is in the public interest. Here the public is involved on both sides, with the regulatory agency taking one or the other side. The courts must decide whether a combination of large landowners, developers, speculators, working-class Whites, farmers, Blacks, and open-housing and civil rights groups should prevail over middle- and upper-class citizens' groups, wealthy estate owners, and environmental organizations. No wonder zoning cases account for much of the workload of the courts.

THE FUTURE OF LAND USE REGULATION

Since the major thesis of this book has been that political parties play a determining role in the quality-of-life decisions of state governments, some speculation about their role in the area of land use planning is in order. There are very few studies of the effects of parties on land use decisions. The three case studies, all drawn from Oregon, concluded that parties played a minimal role in balancing the interests of the poor who need housing and jobs and the well-to-do who want to protect their neighborhoods from development. Oregon is a state in which parties are not able to act cohesively in nominating, electing, and governing. Political parties that are able to make electoral promises which they can put into effect are more likely to control pressure group activity. Each political party contains elements of the poor who need housing, workers who need jobs, environmentalists, and middle-income homeowners who fear that a large development nearby will drive down their property values. It is the job of the political parties to mediate among the needs of the diverse groups which make up their respective coalitions and attempt to provide a balance between them so that the regulatory decisions that emerge will not be biased in favor of one group only.

To illustrate how crucial it is for the political party to represent the public interest, we turn to a concept of the regulatory process which claims that there is no such thing as "the public interest." All the disorganized public receives from regulatory policies are "symbolic goods."

The Symbolic Aspects of Regulation

Murray Edelman claims that when we examine the divergence between the political and legal promises of regulatory policy on the one hand and the actual distribution of rewards and deprivations on the other, we see that the regulatory process is largely symbolic. The unorganized are assured that the government is actively regulating in the public interest, while in effect it is distributing rewards to the powerful.[48] Here is how it works:

1. Resources—permits, land, power—are given to organized groups in proportion to their relative bargaining strength. They are frequently not given to unorganized group interests as promised in regulatory statutes.

2. Symbolic goods such as legislative wrath against forces threatening "the little man" reassure the unorganized that their appeals are noted and that something is being done; this tends to pacify them and keep them content. For instance, some states have passed legislation which purports to locate low-to-moderate income housing in certain areas. When this does not happen, the deprived groups show little tendency to protest or display their awareness of the deprivation. They remain quiescent.

3. Conflict is ritualized and regularized in regulatory agencies to reduce anxiety and uncertainty for those who are regulated and to legitimate authority. When there is conflict among the regulated, the regulatory agencies are generally composed of representatives from each of the major interests. At one time the Oregon Land Conservation and Development Commission was composed of a realtor, an attorney active in environmental organizations, a farmer, a marine biologist, a local government official, a former director of the state's Department of Environmental Quality, and a past president of the League of Women Voters. Through such a membership, major contending interests are represented.[49] However, this alliance does not necessarily defend the "public interest." It will continue to serve the interests of the strongest group, and the other rival groupings are silenced because they are participants.

4. Organized groups use regulatory agencies to make good their claims on tangible resources. Regulatory agencies are captured by the regulated. This does not mean that the same groups capture every land use regulatory agency. Environmental groups can capture some regulatory agencies and developers can capture others. However, the recent logic of state planning favors the environmental and antidevelopment position, although both social and environmental concerns supposedly are encompassed by state land use planning policies. Bernard Frieden points out that environmental opposition to homebuilding has almost no connection to mainstream conservation issues, such as protecting wildlife and eliminating environmental health hazards.[50] Housing proposals seldom conflict with these goals. The consistent environmental theme against homebuilding is simply the need to save open

space. The open space that local growth opponents want is usually for private use, not public parks. Environmentalists form effective alliances with other resident groups and use the rhetoric of public purpose to fight new housing, but the goals they pursue are private ones. They want open space primarily to protect their own social and tax advantages. This illustrates how environmental and citizens' groups use the public regulatory agencies to protect their private interests.

Figure 10–3 illustrates the symbolic politics of regulation. Here the public receives symbolic assurances that the regulatory agency is protecting its interests. Even when this does not happen, the public remains apathetic. It is not effectively organized. Environmental degradation and lack of decent housing may result from the regulatory process while the

FIGURE 10–3

The Symbolic Politics of Regulation

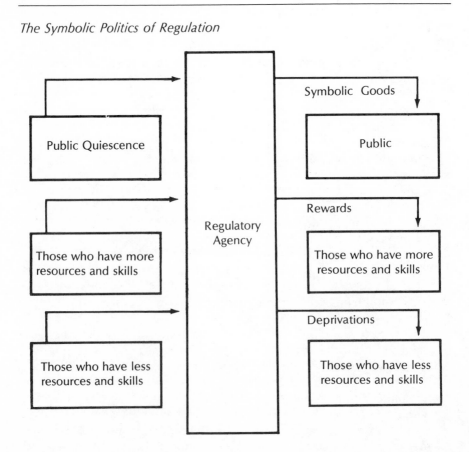

public remains quiescent. Those groups which have more resources and skills receive rewards, and those who have less receive deprivations. A law without identifiable public support is virtually unenforceable in a democratic system. As an example, the Connecticut Coastal Area Management legislation is limited by the fact that it precedes any public recognition of need to protect coastal resources. In California, Washington, and North Carolina there were citizen perceptions of threatened natural resources. These state programs represent the Cadillacs and Mercedes of coastal area management. The people of Connecticut are not yet sure whether they want even a Honda Civic.[51] It will be difficult for the Department of Environmental Protection to administer a regulatory program along the Connecticut coast in the absence of public interest in balancing social and environmental concerns.

The Role of the Political Party in the Future of Land Use Regulation

The political party is the vehicle through which groups make known their needs and demands. If a group is silent, it is not represented in the political process. We discovered that welfare programs were most generous to the poor in those states where the lower-income groups participated in the political process and where the governor and the political parties were strong enough to act on their needs. Education became more redistributive when legislators were challenged by integrationists and disgruntled parents. The more active the citizens, the more the decision-makers respond to their demands. Insistent demands cannot be ignored for fear that the next election will bring opponents into power. The stronger the leadership within the political party, the more likely it is that the party can act on behalf of the groups which put demands upon it. It takes a cohesive party to fashion a program that will not benefit one group to the exclusion of others. A combination of strong groups and weak parties results in the benefits going only to the groups that have money and power.

We would expect the same to be true in the regulatory process. In the area of regulation, the public interest is formally taken by the regulatory agency. It carries out the mandate it was given by the legislature. In a state where the political parties are strong, we would expect that the land use regulatory agency would have power to bring local regulatory agencies into conformity with a state land use plan. The methods used would insure that the interests of all groups were balanced in the regulatory process. Figure 10–4 contains some information which is useful to evaluate our hypothesis. The states are coded according to the degree of state authority over the land use programs. The first designation involves a significant degree of state regulation. The 11 states in this category require permits for certain types of development, can initiate review of local plans,

FIGURE 10–4

State Authority Over Land-Use Programs

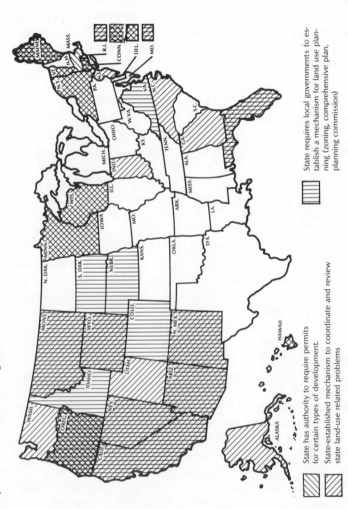

State has authority to require permits for certain types of development.

State-established mechanism to coordinate and review state land-use related problems

State requires local governments to establish a mechanism for land use planning (zoning, comprehensive plan, planning commission)

Sources: Data used with permission of The Council of State Governments, *The Book of the States, 1976–1977*, Vol. 21, (Lexington, Ky.; Council of State Governments, 1976), p. 478 and grateful acknowledgement to the Urban Institute for these excerpts from Nelson Rosenbaum, *Land Use and The Legislatures* (Washington, D. C.: The Urban Institute, 1976), pp. 9–30; data from Alvin Mushkatel and Linda Mushkatel, "The Emergence of State Planning and its Potential Impact on Urban Areas," *State and Local Goverment Review*, 11 no. 2 (May 1979): 56–57.

and modify local plans and regulations where necessary. An example of this is the Vermont permit review for certain size developments. The second category involves a measure of state coordination and control which involves a periodic review of local regulations and controls of state concern. Some of the states in this category use a double-veto system because both state and local approval is required. The double-veto system preserves considerable power at the local level. A state may block development, or impose conditions on development that has been approved locally, but the state does not have the authority to overrule a local government's decision and approve a development vetoed by the local authority. The state cannot override the resistance of local governments to low- and moderate-price housing. The third category involves state action in requiring local governments to establish planning agencies and providing them with guidelines. Under this system, state intervention occurs but once. Once a plan is drawn up or the guidelines are approved, the local authorities carry out the land use regulation. In this last category, state authority over land use is minimal.[52]

Our hypothesis that strong party states will develop more control over the land use planning and implementation process is confirmed by the information contained on the map. Out of the 11 states which exert considerable authority over land use planning, seven are strong party states (Vermont, Connecticut, Massachusetts, New York, Delaware, Minnesota, and Wisconsin). This provides us with a foundation, at least, to speculate about the role of the political party in the politics of regulation. The most cohesive parties are organized to govern in the interests of those they represent. Within each party are urbanites who need housing and suburbanites who favor protecting the environment. The public interest involves a balancing of housing and environmental protection which can only be provided by a mechanism such as a political party. No single interest group can have such a wide range of interests. Thus, as with the politics of distribution in the case of education, it takes the determined efforts of the political party to make the regulations protect the *public* interest rather than the interests of the strongest groups with a stake in land use policy.

CONCLUSIONS

Involvement of the public is vital to any land use program. Furthermore, citizen participation in land use planning should not be limited to administrative hearings on the scope and content of state land use programs. An administrative or judicial appeals process should be provided to give standing to all those whose social and environmental interests have been substantially harmed by land use decisions.

Although it is tempting to tout the advantages of a state "take-over" in the area of land use control, state regulation should be used sparingly and only in certain areas which have scenic, historic, or environmental value of more than local concern. Also necessary areas for state regulation would be developments of regional impact or benefit such as power plants, landfills, and low-income housing that are rejected by localities but which produce significant benefits for larger areas.

With the exception of these areas, the state should allow local governments to plan and implement the vast majority of local land use decisions. Local government is the most accessible to the citizens. It is far easier for them to go to the town hall than to the state capital. Developers and large environmental groups can hire lobbyists. Citizens cannot. While it is true that the most enlightened development decisions do not always flow from citizen participation, it is the type of decision that will work because it has been forged by compromise between the contending factions in full view of the public. If apathy governs, then the apathetic will receive no more than symbolic goods, and the rewards and deprivations will flow to the stronger interests.

The regulation of land use is a new area. The role of the political party is just beginning to emerge in importance. This can be seen in the states which have given their land use planning agencies authority over certain areas of critical concern to the public interest. In weak party states, the land use planning process is manipulated to give the strongest pressures the most favorable decisions. As land becomes more precious, political party leaders will become vital to the effective regulation of land use in the public interest.

NOTES

1. Arthur A. Link, "A Basic Issue: Energy or Food?" in National Governors' Conference, *Innovations in State Government* (Washington, D.C.: National Governors' Conference, 1974), pp. 151–52.
2. Speech to Council of State Governments Symposium, Rosslyn, Virginia, 11 April 1973, quoted in Phyllis Myers, *So Goes Vermont* (Washington, D.C.: The Conservation Foundation, 1974), p. vii.
3. State Senator Richard H. Newhouse, Chicago, Remarks at a Conservation Foundation Conference, "Environmental Quality and Social Justice," Woodstock, Ill., 15 November 1972, quoted in Conservation Foundation Letter, *The Environment of the Poor: Who Gives a Damn?* (Washington, D.C.: Conservation Foundation, 1973), p. 7.

4. Kenneth E. Boulding, "Is Scarcity Dead?" *Public Interest* 5 (Fall 1966): 42–43.

5. Matthew Holden, Jr., *Pollution Control as a Bargaining Process: An Essay on Regulatory Decision Making* (Ithaca, N.Y.: Cornell University Press, Publication No. 9, October 1966).

6. This term as well as this discussion is borrowed from the following article by Carl H. Madden, "Land as a National Resource," in The American Assembly, Columbia University, *The Good Earth of America: Planning Our Land Use* (Englewood Cliffs, N.J.: Prentice-Hall, 1974), pp. 6–30.

7. Council of State Governments, *The Land Use Puzzle* (Lexington, Ky.: Council of State Governments, 1974), p. 4.

8. This discussion draws upon the following source: Marion Clawson, "Land In Our Daily Lives," in Virginia Curtis, ed., *Land Use and the Environment, An Anthology of Readings* (Chicago: American Society of Planning Officials, 1973), pp. 51–52.

9. Fred Bosselman and David Callies, *The Quiet Revolution in Land Use Control* (Washington, D.C.: Council on Environmental Quality, 1971).

10. This discussion draws heavily on: Council of State Governments, *The Land Use Puzzle,* pp. 15–19.

11. The Big Cypress Conservation Act of 1973, Sec. 380.055(1) (1973).

12. Alvin Mushkatel and Linda Mushkatel, "The Emergence of State Planning and Its Potential Impact on Urban Areas," in *State and Local Government Review* 11 (May 1979): 53–59.

13. This discussion is based on the section on land use in chapter 5 of Randall B. Ripley and Grace A. Franklin, *Congress, the Bureaucracy, and Public Policy* (Homewood, Ill.: Dorsey Press, 1976), pp. 106–108.

14. Council of State Governments, *Land: State Alternatives for Planning and Management* (Lexington, Ky.: Council of State Governments, 1975), p. 19.

15. This sentence was written on the day Governor Nelson Rockefeller died (26 January 1979). He is to be remembered for his dedication to political activity, which he dignified by his interest and illuminated by his enthusiasm.

16. R. Robert Linowes and Don T. Allensworth, *The Politics of Land-Use Law: Developers vs. Citizens in the Courts* (New York: Praeger, 1976), p. 14.

17. Linowes and Allensworth, *The Politics of Land-Use Law,* p. 15.

18. Michael N. Danielson, *The Politics of Exclusion* (New York: Columbia University Press, 1976), p. 139.

19. Melvin B. Mogulof, *Saving The Coast* (Lexington, Mass.: Heath, 1975), p. 31.

20. John Brigham and Michael Semler, "Interest Groups and the Governmental Process: Public Policy for the California Coast," chapter 6 in John Brigham, ed., *Making Public Policy* (Lexington, Mass.: Heath, 1977), p. 354.

21. Robert C. Fellmeth, *Politics of Land: Ralph Nader's Study Group Report on Land Use in California* (New York: Grossman, 1973).

22. Brigham and Semler, "Interest Groups and the Governmental Process," p. 373.

23. Ibid., p. 379.

24. Ibid., pp. 373–74.

25. R. Robert Linowes and Don T. Allensworth, *The States and Land-Use Control* (New York: Praeger, 1975), p. 62.

26. Fellmeth, *Politics of Land,* p. 19.
27. Linowes and Allensworth, *The States and Land-Use Control,* p. 61.
28. This discussion draws on Phyllis Myers, *Zoning Hawaii* (Washington, D.C.: Conservation Foundation, 1975).
29. Quoted in Robert G. Healy, *Land Use and The States* (Baltimore: Johns Hopkins Press, 1976), p. 162.
30. Ibid., p. 163.
31. Ibid., p. 152.
32. Riley E. Dunlap and Richard P. Gale, "Party Membership and Environmental Politics: A Legislative Roll-Call Analysis," *Social Science Quarterly* 55 (December 1974): 670–90.
33. Charles E. Little, *The New Oregon Trail* (Washington, D.C.: The Conservation Foundation, 1974), p. 30.
34. Alvin Mushkatel and Jerry Medler, "Urban-Rural Class Conflict in Oregon Land-Use Planning," *Western Political Quarterly* (September 1979): 338–49.
35. The following discussion draws on the book by Theodore J. Lowi and Benjamin Ginsberg, eds., *Poliscide* (New York: Macmillan, 1976).
36. Adam Clymer, "Poll Shows Sharp Rise Since '77 in Opposition to Nuclear Plants," *New York Times,* 10 April 1979, p. 1.
37. Linowes and Allensworth, *The Politics of Land-Use Law,* pp. 1–16.
38. Linowes and Allensworth, *The States and Land-Use Control,* p. 46.
39. Healy, *Land Use and The States,* p. 7.
40. Little, *The New Oregon Trail,* p. 7.
41. This discussion is based on that by Cynthia H. Enloe, *The Politics of Pollution In A Comparative Perspective: Ecology and Power in Four Nations* (New York: Longmans, 1975), pp. 168–71.
42. Danielson, *The Politics of Exclusion,* p. 287.
43. David L. Rosebaugh, "State Planning as a Policy-Coordinative Process," *American Institute of Planners Journal* 42 (January 1976), pp. 57–58.
44. Little, *The New Oregon Trail,* p. 35.
45. Linowes and Allensworth, *The States and Land-Use Control,* p. 179.
46. Ibid., pp. 180–81.
47. Ibid., p. 180.
48. Murray Edelman, *The Symbolic Uses of Politics* (Urbana: University of Illinois Press, 1964), chapters 2 and 3.
49. David E. Ervin et al., *Land Use Control* (Cambridge, Mass.: Ballinger Publishing Company, 1977), p. 50.
50. Bernard J. Frieden, *The Environmental Protection Hustle* (Cambridge, Mass.: MIT Press, 1979), pp. 9–10.
51. Sarah McCally Morehouse, "The Future of Long Island Sound: The Beginning of Public Debate," in *Long Island Sound: The People and the Environment,* Proceedings of a two-day symposium sponsored by The Oceanic Society and The Connecticut Humanities Council (Stamford, Conn.: The Oceanic Society, 1978), pp. 176–77.
52. Alvin Mushkatel and Linda Mushkatel, "The Emergence of State Planning," p. 57.

CHAPTER ELEVEN

PARTY GOVERNMENT IN THE AMERICAN STATES: A SUMMARY

Although an emphasis on party government is not currently popular, it has been a major theme of this book. Party government involves the ability of the men and women who operate under a party label to recruit and elect candidates for public office who are broadly representative of the party's voters and, when elected, to present, enact, and implement programs that reflect the needs, aspirations, and demands of the same voters. I have stated boldly that the ability of a state political party to perform the functions described above affects the quality of life of the citizens of the state. No single-issue group can do this vital job of aggregating and mediating the preferences of a mass electorate by nominating candidates for public office and converting these preferences into specific electoral and policy decisions. The Anti-abortionists, the Conservationists, the Feminists, even the Liberal activists within the Democratic Party and the right-wing activists within the Republican, are not concerned with aggregating and mediating the preferences of the many and converting them into election decisions and policy. In the tunnel vision of these groups, the parties are impediments to the channeling of their single-issue programs. Compromise, which is the result of aggregating and converting the needs of many into specific policy decisions, is a dirty word to single-issue crusaders. And yet it is commonly agreed that parties that are split into factions do not represent the needs of the people as well as those in which a more cohesive system of nominating, electing, and governing prevails.

Another currently fashionable opinion is that the parties are not so much to be maligned as to be buried. In the eyes of a sizable and respectable group of writers, political parties have become obsolete. Since 1972 political analysts have bemoaned the fact that our party system has suffered severe setbacks in its ability to nominate and elect candidates. "Politics without Parties" and "Reform is wrecking the U.S. Party System" are counsels of despair. In fact, the smoke-filled room where the bosses compromised on the candidate most acceptable to all has historical acceptability among those who comment on the latest ineptness of the party to fulfill its functions. The basis for the requiem played over the political party is the reform of the presidential nominating process initiated in 1972 and further entrenched in 1976. The reform movement has shifted the responsibility for the nomination of the President of the United States from a coalition of state party leaders to the electorate which registers its choice in presidential primaries in most of our states. We will consider the impact of these reforms later in these conclusions, but it is necessary to be clear-headed about just which parties the analysts are talking about. It is obvious that they are concerned with the national parties and their weakened condition. However, the national parties never were more than a coalition of state parties which managed to agree on a suitable presidential candidate every four years. It is true that the state party leaders are now prevented from brokering the convention choice of a presidential nominee by virtue of the recent "reforms" in the national nominating process. But because their national nominating function has been removed, does that automatically mean that the state parties are themselves weakened in their job of recruiting, nominating, and electing at the state level? The analysts have not answered that one, but I believe that this book helps answer the question. In many of our states, the political parties *are* organizations capable of party government, as illustrated by their ability to nominate, elect, and govern.

A third group that denigrates the party government idea is the economic-determinism school, which has maintained for some time that the efforts of politicians have a very minor role to play in the outputs of state governments. In their view, economic development shapes both political systems and policy outcomes. States where the people are wealthy and well-educated spend more for welfare and education; states where the people are poor and uneducated do not. This cannot be denied. But in politics, as in all human effort, it is not the extremes which need to be explained, but the marginal differences. Why do two states with the same economic conditions provide differently for their children, their poor, and their aged? Why does one state by a series of decisions arrive at such an extraordinarily different policy outcome from a state in the same economic and social circumstances? The economic determinism school leaves much unexplained variation in policy output. Although socioeconomic development certainly affects the activities as well as the demands of the people in a state, the efforts of political leaders must convert these demands into policy. The quality of the political leadership, the ability of the leaders to make promises and then to build legislative coalitions to put these promises into effect, are crucial to the well-being of the citizens of the state. Governments in many states either surpass or fail to reach the policy norms that are associated with their levels of economic development.

There are, therefore, three current arguments or viewpoints against the concept that party government exists and can be used as a yardstick to measure the output of state political systems. They can be summarized thus:

1. The parties are undemocratic because nominating decisions are made by a small group of party regulars and are not open to popular control. They should be reformed further to facilitate widespread participation in the nomination process. The reforms should discourage the efforts of regulars to form coalitions within the party. The eradication of parties as organizations should pave the way for government more responsive to mass sentiment.
2. The parties have been so weakened by the reformers that they are incapable of fulfilling their proper function of nominating, electing, and governing. Hence party government is dead.
3. It does not matter whether parties are reformed or unreformed because the efforts of politicians do not matter to the most important result—the policies produced by the decisional system.

With these three strikes, it appears foolhardy to continue to affirm that the efforts of politicians and the political parties which they operate are important to the public welfare. And yet the research reported in this book indicates that there exists a wide variation in the political party systems in the states and that these variations do contribute to differences in the quality of life of the people.

If we believe that the political parties have a central role to play in state politics, we need to confront several broad problems. The first involves the importance of the states as actors in the federal system. If they have a declining role in the evolving federal system, then the importance of party government diminishes. If our federal system has become so centralized that the states are simply administrative conduits for national policy, then the efforts of state politicians do not make much difference. Related to the responsibilities which the parties confront is the type of state government structure to which they elect and through which they govern. Are they handicapped by lack of formal power to perform their job of electing and governing?

If we believe that political parties have a central role to play in state political systems, what internal problems do they exhibit which prevent them from governing effectively? Assuming that we need stability, firmness, and competence, how can these exist in political systems that exhibit erratic and atomized politics? What contributes to the deterioration of the political party? What can explain its success in some states and its ineffectiveness in others?

This chapter will consider three major issues:

1. The place of the states in the federal system, the responsibilities they
    are called upon to perform, and the role of the party in this evolving
    federalism;
2. The ability of state political parties to perform their functions of nomi-
    nating, electing, and governing; and
3. The emerging trends and the ranges of choice open to maintain party
    government in the American states. In other words, can we con-
    sciously affect the performance of the parties?

THE STATES IN THE FEDERAL SYSTEM

This book began with the story of the New York City fiscal crisis of 1975.
As the book has been written, the solution to the crisis (although not to the
conditions that created the crisis) has evolved, and the evolution has born
witness to the new federalism of today. The old theory of federalism was
based on separate levels of government separately financed. In 1854,
President Franklin Pierce vetoed a bill that would have provided federal
land grants to the states to support facilities for the insane. In doing so, he
declared:

> [Should Congress] make provision for such objects, the fountain of charity will
> be dried up at home, and the several states, instead of bestowing their own
> means on the social wants of their people, may themselves, through the strong
> temptation, which appeals to states as to individuals, become humble suppli-
> cants for the bounty of the Federal Government, reversing their true relation
> to this union.[1]

This pronouncement was suitable to reflect the first reaction of President
Ford and a majority of Congress to the New York City fiscal crisis. Yet the
subsequent reversal of Ford's position and the provision of direct federal
loan guarantees to the City marked the evolution from layer-cake-federal-
ism to the marble-cake federalism which we have today. The concept of
marble-cake federalism involves shared fiscal responsibility for a common
problem along all three layers of government. However, the fact that we
now have a marble-cake federalism does not mean that we have worked
out the solutions to shared management of joint problems. In fact, the
federal government treats New York City aid as a regrettable but temporary condition resulting from the failure of a single city to "live within its
means." The fact that no older inner city has met this standard for three
decades (if the standard implies providing local services only to the extent
that they can be supported from the local tax base) was not faced squarely.

Subsequent events in Detroit, Cincinnati, and other cities suggested that this attitude would only postpone the day of reckoning and indicated that future municipal crises would be dealt with in the traditional crisis atmosphere. As Congress granted federal long-term guarantees (up to 15 years) for New York City bonds in 1978, both supporters and critics were quick to assert that this would be the last time the federal government would come to the aid of New York City. In addition they said the program caused an unfortunate federal involvement in local affairs which should not serve as a precedent for other cities. Thus marble-cake federalism as a concept is an operating principle, as illustrated by the granting of federal aid to states and localities, but control or management of the relationship among the three layers of government still has to be worked out. It would appear to be up to the states to provide long-term solutions to the plight of the cities within their borders.

The enactment of revenue sharing in 1972 was an historic occurrence that reflected the plight of the states in the wake of the first recession since most of them had become heavily dependent upon the income tax. During the period from 1954 on, the states had expanded their share of financial support toward localities by more than half. By the time of the recession, such states as New York were allocating more than 80 percent of state revenues to aid localities. It was no wonder that the recession hit the larger states and their cities since they had become financially interwoven. The results of revenue sharing are as problematic as the outcome of the New York City crisis. Revenue sharing has given money with no strings attached to all state and local governments. States must also stand by while smaller towns build firehouses and parks with their entitlements and must use state money to go to the aid of the large cities because the revenue-sharing funds are not sufficient to meet their needs. Again, the principle of the marble-cake was not questioned, but administration of the federal funds posed new problems for state governments.

The marble-cake concept of federalism, then, does not solve the question of the political relationship among the three layers of government. The New York City crisis was solved on a temporary basis—and the federal government made it clear that it would not repeat the performance for other ailing cities. Revenue-sharing funds were distributed according to a formula to all state and local governments. The states received only one-third of the funds and hence could not control the flow of the major share of the money crossing their borders.

Just to add to the complications surrounding the federal relationship, all three layers of government are reeling in the face of taxpayer reaction to 15 years of state and local tax increases to meet the needs of the core cities. As Governor Carey said in 1974, "the days of wine and roses" are over for New York. In June 1978 the California voters approved Proposition 13, the constitutional amendment that cut $7 billion from local property taxes. In the November 1978 elections a record number of ballot initiatives and referenda to curb taxing or spending were held. Most were passed. Tax cuts and retrenchment of services became the overriding theme in the 1978 primaries and general elections. State after state cut taxes and spending. Some state actions were drastic. Wisconsin refunded nearly $1 billion to taxpayers from a surplus, declared a two-month moratorium on payment of income taxes, and lowered tax brackets. Minnesota enacted a tax law that cost the state $712 million a year. Cuts in services were held to a minimum because most states had built up surpluses under the general prosperity of the preceding period. (They had learned from the recession of 1971. It would not be until 1981 that the surpluses would run down to critical balances.) In the meantime, the federal government drastically cut the urban program. According to Robert Nathan, senior fellow at the Brookings Institution, the net result was to cut total authority for the overall urban program to $2.5 billion, 18 percent of what was originally posed and loudly trumpeted when it was proposed.[2]

What can we conclude about the evolving nature of federalism based on the foregoing recital of events? It appears that states have more responsibility whether the federal funds in the marble cake increase or decrease. The federal government responded to the Proposition 13 philosophy by drastically curtailing services. The states must also respond, but for them it is a matter of hard decisions. They can cut taxes and spending, but there are still the poor to be helped, the children to be educated, and the environment to be cleaned. The hard choices come with the decisions on priorities of expenditures. The cities do not have the revenue to maintain a sufficient level of services. The federal government cut expenditures in response to the spirit behind Proposition 13. The states are left holding the bag. It is they who must be responsive to their citizens, who must aggregate their preferences and act in accordance with their demands. It is they who must mobilize support for the hard choices between alternatives. The federal government is too remote from the people to deal with the human issues that confront them. A political leader can have meaningful contact with only a certain number of people. A legislative body can be only so big if it is to remain able to deliberate and make decisions. The states are in a key position to deliver the governmental services demanded of them even while they remain small enough to maintain a high level of political communication between governors and governed. They are the only American polities able to meet both conditions.

There have been other times when the states *should* have been ready to provide both communication between the citizens and their government and the services which the citizens demanded, but they have not always been equipped to do so. In 1956, V. O. Key observed that the combination of party system and the structure of representation in most states incapacitated the states politically and diverted demands for political action to Washington. He concluded that most states were not utilized to the limit of their potentiality in the total task of government.[3] Since then the states have reformed many aspects of their governmental structure to make them more representative and better able to provide needed services. Many of these organizational rigidities were incorporated in the state constitutions, which had to be amended. Not all states have eliminated the crippling constitutional limitations. But most state governments are now distinctly more modern than they were in the 1950s or 1960s. The states now have legislative bodies equitably representing their populations. With both houses in their bicameral systems subject to the one-person-one-vote rule, the states can claim greater equality of popular representation than the national Congress, whose Senate grossly over-represents the people of small states. In addition to their reapportioning, state legislatures have modernized in other significant respects. For example, 42 states had formal or informal arrangements for annual legislative sessions by the mid-seventies, compared to only 20 in 1962-1963. Legislatures now deal with more bills and have longer sessions, higher salaries, streamlined procedures, and larger and better paid staffs. Membership in the state legislatures is more attractive than it has been in the past, and there has been a marked increase in the number of state legislators seeking reelection rather than voluntarily retiring after short-term service.

The governorship has been strengthened to permit its occupant to deal with the new demands imposed upon the state governments. Forty-six governors now have four-year terms compared to only 32 in 1960, and 43 states now allow a governor at least a second term as compared to 31 in 1960. Another means for enhancing gubernatorial leadership is executive control of budget making. In all but 19 states the governor has the sole responsibility for preparing the budget, and in 37 states he has the item veto—a potentially potent instrument for influencing final policy outcomes in the appropriation process.

In addition to the structural changes in state institutions, there are changes in taxation that have allowed the states to manage increased expenditures. Individual and corporate income taxes have been added to the various sales and gross receipts taxes in an effort to make the tax structures more progressive and to provide property tax relief for local governments. Thus changes in state taxation are part of a modernization at the state level that has accompanied reform of governmental structures.

V. O. Key bemoaned the fact that party competition did not exist in most of the states and that in many power was completely monopolized by one party. Twenty-five years later, he would have cause to rejoice at the degree to which two-party competition has spread to all but eight states in the Union. In all but these eight, either party can attain the governorship. V. O. Key believed that only in the alternation in office between two parties can popular will be translated into governmental action. Key assumed that where the conditions of party competition existed, parties were cohesive and would translate election promises into policy, not so much from conscience as from fear of retribution at the polls. At present all but eight states are competitive, which raises the question: are the people in consequence better governed? At least the conditions for party government exist.

We have completed the review of the increasing responsibilities of the state governments as they face the 1980s. We have noted that they have reformed their procedures and their structures. They have caused their legislatures to become more representative and their governors better equipped. They are now competitive between the parties. The stage is set for party government. Yet almost no state has thought of measures that can strengthen the capability of the parties to recruit, elect, and govern. Curious that so much reform has been expended on governmental structures and procedures and that so little has been given to the political organizations of men and women who provide the link between the people and their government. How capable are the parties to carry out their functions of recruitment, electing, and governing? We turn our attention to this in the next section.

THE RECORD: DOES PARTY GOVERNMENT MAKE A DIFFERENCE?

Nominating

Party government involves the ability of the men and women who operate under a common party label to recruit and nominate candidates for public office and to win in the party's name in order to govern in the interests of the voters who put them there. The conditions for a proper nominating process require that there be a stable group of party leaders who are interested in maintaining the party as an organization. These leaders should be able to spot capable men and women in the state and interest them in working for the party. Party work may involve making speeches, running party meetings, and other ways of proving oneself to the leadership. If the recruits indicate that they are capable of running for public office and governing in coalition with others who are also elected, the leaders back them for nomination. The state chairmen are especially interested in recruiting state legislators who can be both successful and loyal.

All states now require state-level candidates to be nominated by primary. This is a major hurdle, and the leaders must firmly implant the party label on their favored candidate for governor and work to ensure his or her nomination in the primary election. The coalitions necessary to win the primary election carry over into the general election, and provide the nucleus for a statewide effort to place the candidate before the general electorate. At least this is how the nominating process *should* work. In some states, it actually does work this way. In others, state political parties are a shambles of scrapping candidacies, competing coalitions, and disorganization. A formal corps of leaders may exist, but it is powerless to compete with self-recruited candidacies and their supportive coalitions. What signs exist that state political parties are becoming better equipped to handle the job of recruiting and nominating?

For one thing, most state parties now have permanent headquarters. State party chairmen place considerable importance upon maintaining full-time headquarters, most of which have been opened since the early 1960s.[4] Four reasons have been suggested for this development. The first is the spread of two-party competition in most of the states. Once a party wins the governorship, it looks to a repeat of that performance and establishes headquarters to aid the attempt. This is true of the Republican party in the South. The second reason is the growth of political technology. This aids in the centralization process of the political party. Because few single candidates can afford to foot the bill for statewide public opinion polling, computerized information retrieval systems, and media services, the state parties have created their own professional staffs to operate the new technologies. The third reason is reaction to national party demands. Although the total effect of these demands may insulate the state parties from the national nominating process, meeting some of the nationally imposed requirements has created the need for a central bureaucracy at the state level to closely define and monitor their own procedures. The reform of campaign finance has also required the state parties to keep careful control over their fund raising and spending. The fourth reason for the development of full-time headquarters is the emergence of communication among state chairmen. There is now a state chairmen's organization which operates within each party and is a means for discussing common problems and joint strategy.[5]

Political parties appear better equipped than ever to form coalitions in the nomination process which will carry over into the election and governing process. However, the major hurdle is the statewide primary form of nomination mandated by state law. The best party candidates can lose in this process, which throws the decision open to those who turn out to vote on primary day. Primary voters are a very different lot from the general electorate. Furthermore, they may not be representative of their own party's voters and may be able to nominate a candidate in the primary who will ruin the party's chances of winning. On the other hand, this primary process may bring unrepresentative nominees to both parties, and the voters of the state will be cheated out of a leader who is broadly representative of their interests. Within the framework of the primary, the media picks up the job of the party leaders. Private interests work to build up candidates. Invisible power structures dupe the electorate. V. O. Key puts the problem succinctly:

> The question boils down ultimately to whether Joe Doakes, Republican political leader and elective official, will on the average act in one way if he is continuously aware that he acts as a member of a Republican group with both a past and a future and another way if he looks upon himself as a self-made tribune of the people who got where he is under his own power and has but one short life to live.[6]

The question before us is: to what extent have the leaders of the political parties managed to nominate their choice for governor working within the framework of the primary? At the last count (1979) there were sixteen states in which the party leaders make endorsements for governor. State laws mandate nominating conventions in a few states, and in others the party organization is authorized to make some type of formal endorsement of candidates, usually in a convention, before the primary election. As noted in chapter 4, Iowa and South Dakota hold post-primary conventions if no candidate receives over 35 percent of the primary vote. It is in these states that the party leaders and workers can groom candidates and count on nominating them for statewide office if they prove themselves. The party conventions are out to pick winners, and they scrutinize the potential candidates with the idea of nominating the candidate most representative of the state's electorate. In the states with pre-primary endorsements, the party choice is noted on the ballot. The party voters can see immediately which candidate is endorsed. What is of major importance is the fact that the pre-primary endorsements occur in the strong party states. Eleven of the 15 strongest political party systems use some form of pre-primary endorsement. These states are able to build voting coalitions behind their candidates to ensure that the primary winner will take the primary by 80 to 100 percent. In these states there is the realization that the business of developing and pushing candidates for governor cannot be settled by the process of self-selection by aspiring office-seekers At least in these states, candidates who receive the nod of the party leaders have an organization with which to begin the process of winning the election and governing.

Electing

What is the role of the political party in electing candidates to the governorship and the legislature? Many state chairmen are active in election campaigns for the whole party ticket. The candidates campaign together and urge votes for the whole party list. The party is well staffed in the counties and precincts and party workers campaign for the whole ticket. This type of party has been able to resolve its differences well before the nomination, and its agreed-upon slate is usually nominated in the primary. The result is that, in the general election, the party faces the electorate as a single and united election participant. This is the ideal. Unfortunately, this happens in a bare majority of cases. Elections are won many times over by gubernatorial candidates who have not taken their party by storm. For all winners in both parties, barely 50 percent of the elections put into office a governor who has a working majority of his party behind him (80 to 100 percent of the primary vote). The open primary form of nomination presents to the electorate candidates who have not formed broad coalitions for the process of electing and governing. Well over a majority of the time, both parties send first-term governors into the state house with less than 70 percent of their party's backing. The new governor faces a legislature in which sit bitter remnants of the factions that opposed him in the primary contest. With this start he must put together a coalition to back his policies. If he does manage to unite his party during his term as governor, he has a better chance in the next election. Incumbents win with a party united behind them over 95 percent of the time. The incumbent governor can face the legislature knowing that out there in that sea of faces there are friends whom he has made and perhaps enemies he has tamed over the last four years.

While incumbent governors are generally able to win in primaries with their parties united behind them, the mechanics of the primary form of nomination prevents most state parties from engineering coalitions on behalf of new gubernatorial candidates. In the fifteen states we mentioned, the parties make the attempt to control the nominations of all gubernatorial candidates in order to make a united front in the election. It has been a hypothesis of this book that the factions which contend during the process of nominating the governor also contend in the governing process. To the extent that a governor has worked within the machinery of the party and has its support, he can count on its help in governing. His faction, if it is large enough, can be counted on to produce the votes he needs when he proposes measures to the legislature for passage. A governor hamstrung by factions cannot hope to govern effectively. Governing parties need internal cohesion to pass programs to which they commit themselves.

Governing

Is it true, as V. O. Key has stated so often, that political organization affects the quality and distribution of services? My research confirms that it does.

Party government is based on the link between the electoral party and the governing party. The governor is leader of both and as such he begins to make policy as he campaigns for the office in the form of the party platform. If he wins the election, he develops this policy into an administrative program and presents it to the legislature. This type of party dictates the conditions under which the governor operates to fashion his policy. In states with weak political parties, those in which the party organization is no more than a holding company for rival factions and shifting coalitions, the party has no platform except those of the individual members of the party who are running for office. In the primary contest, the platforms of the candidates for the governorship represent the views of the candidates and need not, and usually do not, contain uniform provisions. As a result, when the primary is over, the platforms of the winning gubernatorial candidate, the other elected candidates, and those of the legislative members are not necessarily related. The governor runs on his own program. There is no party organization, no party support for his efforts. In states with cohesive parties, the potential governor heads the state ticket and the others who run on it, such as the state legislators, and other candidates campaign on the same platform. This platform has been adopted by the state convention, and provides the party leaders and candidates with a convenient source for political positions on the issues.

Each year the governor presents a State of the State address to a joint gathering of both legislative houses. In this he outlines the substance of the program he wants passed for the session. This is translated into administration bills which are introduced in most states by the governor's party leaders in the house or by legislators whom the governor may specify. Party politics, especially state political leadership, affects the conversion of need into policy. The legislature is a potential partner in the policy-making process. The degree to which it is a partner is deeply involved with the type of political party that operates in the state both inside and outside the legislature.

While the political party as a governing instrument is central to the policy-making process, the efforts of the men and women who operate under its banner can be aided or hamstrung by the laws, procedures, and powers given to the various actors in the process. The states have come far in reforming their executive and legislative branches by constitutional and legislative means. As mentioned earlier, governors have been given longer terms. Their formal powers of appointment, budget initiation, and item veto enhance their ability to see their programs through the legislature. The legislatures, on the other hand, have professionalized their operations and become more representative. With the heavy weight of responsibility they carry, the legislators are due the necessary tools. A state which gives its legislators the staff and help they need may also give them an awareness of their importance in the governing process. Adequate sources of information, adequate secretarial services, adequate space, and so on make legislatures more responsive to the needs and concerns of the citizens. Because the legislature is the principal political arena for converting party programs into public policy, and because the conversion process should be effective to the degree that the legislature is organizationally capable, it is reasonable that the linkage between party and program promises would be stronger among states with strong effective legislative systems than among those with weak legislatures.

Test borings into the ability of the governor to obtain the loyalty of his party for his programs have confirmed the fact that the governor's political leadership over his electoral party, combined with his formal gubernatorial powers, are the major explanations. If the governor was successful in building a coalition to support him in the primary and election, he is also successful in building a coalition within the legislature to pass his legislation. The high correlation between outside party cohesion and legislative loyalty supports the theory that the governor's electoral party generates discipline within the legislative party. In states where legislative party loyalty is low, the political party outside the legislature is not strong. This is, to my knowledge, the first attempt to test the strength of the outside party on the support for the program of the governor. The test was methodologically rigorous and confirms the theory that party government exists in a significant number of our states.

While we have tested the ability of a governor to get support for his program bills, skeptics may suggest that this is not a full measure of how the people of a state are being served. How can we tell whether the poor are provided for or whether the children are fairly educated? Perhaps the governor's program does not provide for them. Just because we have a measure of party cohesion outside the legislature linked with legislative loyalty within, how can we know that unified parties provide for the people of their states better than parties that are fractured? Party government is not a favored concept, as I stated in the beginning of this chapter. There are those who deprecate the role of parties and try to handicap their work. There are those who believe parties are too weak to perform their proper functions of nominating, electing, and governing. There are those who believe that social and economic conditions determine welfare and education services.

In spite of all those skeptics, there are state political systems which are responding to the needs of their people, and a major actor in this response is the political party. Another test boring, as rigorous as the first, investigated the relationship between the strength of the political party, the political system, and welfare and education policy. The political party was measured as a continuing organization able to nominate its candidates throughout a 15-year period. Measured this way, the party is an organization with a memory and a future. The leadership needs to be concerned with perpetuating the organization and backing candidates who will support its image. The results of the test showed that the political party, the powers of the governor, and the professionalism of the legislature were able to explain why some states provide for their poor and their children more generously than others. And these three variables could also explain why some states were able to innovate and increase services for their citizens over a four year period from 1968–1972. Both education and welfare are redistributive policies—policies which redistribute the benefits of society to provide for more equality across income groups. Because party government is a continuing force in state politics, redistributive policies are produced by a political party with continuous leadership. The conditions under which the politicians operate also influence the ability of the system to produce welfare and education policies that equalize the services of the state. Apparently a reformed legislature is able to be more receptive to the needs and demands of the people. This does not make it a rival of the governor but a partner in the policy-making process. The governor and the legislature represent the same needs.

If a political party is able to nominate, elect, and govern with a sufficient degree of cohesion, it listens to the needs of the poor and disadvantaged and incorporates solutions in its policy program. Perhaps it does not heed their demands out of brotherly love, but out of the necessity to represent them in order to be reelected. Both Republican and Democratic governors need the vote in the cities and both spend time building urban constituencies by campaigning on platforms and promising aid and effort to meet city needs. If the poor are able to present their demands, they fare better than if they are not vocal. Political leadership cannot afford to ignore persistent demands. In states where the belief system supports the extension of benefits to the poor, as discussed in chapter 8, we would expect to find more generous policies. In states where there is a party system that is organized enough to listen to the needs of the poor, we find that they are better served.

The critics of party government who claim that social and economic conditions create the party system as well as the outputs of the state political process may still remain unconvinced by the test borings. It is true that the degree of industrialization in a state influences the needs and demands of its citizens. If the state has reached an advanced post-industrial condition, the quality of education may be higher and the smaller numbers of poor may be better cared for. The analyses in this book have taken these factors into consideration by testing all variables in relationship to each other. It is true that the wealth, education, and communication systems that exist in a state give rise to demands for political leadership and the formal powers and services to make it effective. In all cases, however, the economic conditions of a state have had less effect on the redistributive services than the combination of the political party and the political structures within which the party operates.

We have tested the ability of the state political party to nominate, elect, and govern. We discovered that there are political parties in about one-third of our states where a leadership corps can schedule ambition and build electoral coalitions around the candidate of its choice. We have seen that the strength of the political party plays a part in the ability of its most important political figure, the governor, to attract support for his program in the legislature. We have also noted that the institutional reforms which many states have made in the last few years aid the parties in their efforts to represent and govern. The obvious conclusion is that we should have more reform of the executive and legislature to provide the party leaders with the proper tools. But what of the party as an organization itself? What type of change can help it become more representative and better able to govern? We turn our attention to this problem in the last section of this book.

EMERGING TRENDS AND RANGES OF CHOICE

The 1970s have not been kind to political parties. The national political parties may be likened to two trees with dead limbs and branches. To the eye they are dead. What is not seen by those who despair of their death is that the roots are still alive and well. The roots are tapping the well-springs of renewal in the state political systems.

The Effects of National Party Reforms

In 1978 one of our foremost political party theorists, Everett Carll Ladd, lamented:

> The institutional parties are crumbling. That is the decisive electoral fact of our day. Lacking the coalescing bonds that parties once provided, the various units of government will find it harder than ever to pull together toward coherent policy.[7]

Why are party theorists lamenting the death of the national political parties? Austin Ranney does not believe the Republic would collapse, at least, not right away.

> The party labels would persist for a while and serve as cues for the dwindling number of voters for whom they were still meaningful. The candidate organizations, the women's caucuses, the black caucuses, the right to life leagues, and the like would become the only real players in the game. The mass communications media would become the sole agencies for sorting out the

finalists from the original entrants and for defining the voters' choices. And the societal functions of interest-aggregation, consensus-building, and civil war-prevention would presumably be left to the schools, the churches, and perhaps Common Cause and Nader's Raiders.[8]

Both of the above writers lament the demise of the national political parties. The basis for their assertion that reform has wrecked the national party system lies primarily with the reforms which both national parties have been implementing in the 1970s to make themselves superficially more democratic. They originated largely within the Democratic party, but have engulfed the Republicans as well. The tumultuous 1968 Democratic convention created a commission, headed first by Senator George McGovern and later by Representative Donald Fraser of Minnesota, to reform the party's system of delegate selection. The changes required almost all delegates to be chosen through primary elections, or through caucuses or conventions open to all party adherents and committed to proportional representation for minority candidates. Also proscribed was the practice whereby "certain public or party office holders are delegates to county, state and national conventions by virtue of their official positions." The Republicans, meanwhile, were also adopting new procedures for delegate selection that were as anti-party as those of the Democrats. Many of the Democrats' changes, particularly the increased use of primaries, have been written into state law and so apply to both parties. The most important effect of these reforms has been to destroy the mechanisms through which state party leaders controlled presidential nominations. The presidential selection process has been reduced to a system of chaotic individualism. Potential candidates gather about themselves organizations of their own choosing. They need only capture the voters in a sufficient number of state conventions or primaries to receive the nomination. And these candidates may not represent the preferences of the party's rank and file. Who can say that Carter was representative of the Democratic party's voters or that Reagan was the choice of the "middle of the road" Republicans? Yet both were successful in capturing their party's nomination. Thus the national parties are becoming extinct as organizations that can fulfill one of the major functions of party—that of recruiting and nominating candidates who are broadly reflective of their parties.

More party-weakening measures have also been passed at the national level. Federal funding of presidential campaigns, voted into law as a means of "cleaning up" national politics, has reduced the dependency of candidates on party and on the interest groups that have served as prime building blocks of party organization. More party-weakening measures are in the works. President Carter has proposed a constitutional amendment to eliminate the electoral college and substitute direct election of the chief executive. This would further reduce the role of state parties by making state boundaries irrelevant to election outcomes. Candidates would be freer to campaign without regard to state party systems and their vote-getting functions.

The fact that the new delegate-selection process would weaken the party was largely unforeseen by most McGovern-Fraser commission members. In 1978 the Democratic National Committee voted to make all Democratic governors, U.S. Senators, and Congressmen voting delegates to the national conventions by dint of their office, thus acknowledging and honoring the ability of party leaders to assume leadership in the presidential selection process. However, the 1978 Democratic midterm conference further weakened the delegate-selection process for the 1980 presidential convention by banning the last remaining vestige of the winner-take-all primary, the one which uses single member delegate districts. This further restricts the states from trying to engineer a block of delegate districts. The conference was not attended by many of the party leaders and members of the House and Senate who felt it would serve no useful purpose. This is the state of our national parties. The problem that faces the state political parties is the question of survival until the national climate becomes more favorable. State parties must insulate themselves from the national parties in the first move to weather the storm.

In the first place, the state political leaders found the new rules for caucuses and conventions complex and unpalatable. They were likely to be "taken over" by presidential coalition strategists who roamed about the country like Chinese war lords manipulating the established routines and thwarting the leaders' control over the nominating process. Seeking to insulate themselves from such maneuvering, the state leaders set up presidential primaries in which the war lords could do battle against each other without spoiling the state party's own game of nomination. Hence there was an explosion in the number of primaries—from 17 in 1968 to 23 in 1972, to 30 in 1976, and at least five more for the 1980 convention. Whereas less than half of all delegates to the 1968 convention were chosen by primaries, nearly three-fourths of the 1976 delegates were chosen that way. While it is hard to predict the end result of the continuing insulation of the state parties from the national, this is the rational course for them to take. In fact, they may be waiting for the time when a convention is deadlocked between three or more candidates, a likely event, considering the absence of any control over the national nominating process. Then the possibility of brokering a candidate who is more satisfying to mass preferences will again emerge. There appeared to be among President Carter and his strategists a move toward party regulars for the renomination in 1980. An incumbent president is, after all, a "regular" and wants to have as much help from the established state organizations as possible. The national party is, as always, a coalition of state parties who collect for the single purpose of nominating and electing a president. The state parties can function without this national event. In an open presidential contest, it appears that potential candidates can bypass the organizing and electoral efforts of the state parties. But we shall see how long the estrangement lasts. In the meantime, many state political parties are becoming stronger vehicles for performing their functions of nominating, electing, and governing.

Party Renewal

The tap root of the political party is alive and well. The voters continue to divide their loyalties between the two parties in fairly even proportions, and this competition has spread to almost all the states. In spite of assertions of the voting analysts that the voters are less attached to party than they used to be, they are not ready to abandon the party labels which have become household words and to which they cling like old furniture. Thus political parties are meaningful in the hearts and minds of the voters. This sentiment ensures that political parties as labels, as standards under which candidates run for office, are very much alive and well. Since the major prize of the presidential nominating contest is the capture of the party label, this attests to the party's significance as the major electoral device. Many think this is all that need be expected of the party in today's world. But the party as a label is not enough. The party owes more to the voters than that. It should provide them with a candidate who fairly reflects their needs. It should also provide them with a group of candidates who are linked to the extent that they share common ideas and loyalties to a program. The party should be able to capture the governorship and a goodly portion of legislative seats—enough to put its program into effect.

Because approximately one-third of our state political parties are effective mechanisms for recruiting and nominating, and because we have discovered that the cohesion which accompanied this ability of the party leaders to exert control over the electoral party carries over into the governing process, uniting the legislators to respond to their governor's program, it behooves us to set up the conditions under which this type of party government can take place. In this way the people of the states can be better served. The political party is a primary institution of society. It is as important as the legislature, the executive, and the court system. Measures have been initiated to make these latter institutions better able to serve the people's needs, at the same time that the political party has been enervated by misguided reforms. What can be done to strengthen the state political parties at this time?

Consideration should be given to assuring that a continuing leadership group can exist in the state headquarters of the party. The average state chairman is in office a little over two years. Some state parties have a two-year limit on the tenure of chairmen; this practice should be abolished. Thought should be given to making the job more attractive. It should be salaried to keep those who find they must leave for financial reasons. While chairmen must continue to serve at the pleasure of the state committee and the governor, a state chairman who seeks to assure the survival of the party as an organization is likely to enjoy a long tenure. My research assures me that the party which has a continuing leadership, which can engineer coalitions for its nominee, is the best vehicle for responsible government.

Along with continuing leadership, state parties should enter the business of polling and mass media. They should attempt to provide technical assistance to candidates in the general election with regard to engaging the services of professional firms and evaluating their product. Some state parties hold workshops for their candidates and their staffs to help them prepare for their election campaigns. Campaign management firms are rivals to political party organization. Displacement occurs as the firm provides to candidates all the campaign services which the party could provide. Because they are expensive, only wealthy candidates can afford them. Because they require no more than money for their efforts, the elected official owes them no loyalty. They do not demand allegiance to policy or program as does the political party.

While the direct primary form of nomination has seriously weakened our state political parties, primaries are here to stay. But it is possible to guarantee by law that the party leadership will have a more direct role to play in recruiting candidates and scheduling their ambitions. Pre-primary conventions are the principal vehicle for assuring that the state leadership has the ability to plan for nominations which are in accord with the party's voters. Several states require that persons who challenge the endorsed candidate must win a certain percentage of a pre-primary convention in order to have a primary at all. This is a challenge primary form and would strengthen the hands of the party leaders, while at the same time assuring that their choice could be challenged if a certain percentage of party delegates were dissatisfied.

A Black leader in Connecticut emphasizes the point that the open primary is not as democratic as it sounds:

> There is a move on in Connecticut to abolish the convention system of endorsing political candidates in favor of direct or open primaries. . . . As one who has had much exposure to the political process, and as a black person, I believe open primaries will prove to be the most devastating deterrent to the political progress of black people since the poll tax and restrictions on voter registration used mostly in the South. . . .Under the convention system, delegates are selected on the local level, where negotiations with leaders of the party

achieve a balanced ticket of candidates reflecting ethnic, geographic, age, and sex considerations. Political leaders don't do this out or love or affection; they do it to win elections.[9]

It is certainly not too much to ask that those who help select the party nominee in a primary should be party members with more than a passing attachment to the party. The purpose of a primary is to nominate the candidate most likely to win in the general election. If the primary is open to any voter, the nominee may represent an unrepresentative but determined segment of the electorate who "raided" the primary with that exact purpose. State laws should restrict voting in primaries to those who have registered with a party several months in advance of the primary. Some loyalty to the future of a political party as an organization should be required to allow a voter to participate in its most important function— that of nominating the standard bearer.

Enthusiasm for public financing has been dampened by the recent tax revolt and the feeling that governments should be doing less rather than more. There are 17 or so states which publicly finance elections. Some of these states raise funds through an income tax checkoff system similar to the national one. Much rhetoric surrounds the use of public funds for campaigns, but not so much is expended on the implications of the various plans for the party system. Public financing is not a panacea, as the reformers assert. It will bring fundamental changes in the political structure and electoral processes. Public funding of political campaigns, made doubly attractive by limits on private contributions, may accelerate the trend toward candidate independence and diminish the role of the parties. The results may be the growth of personalized politics and a diminished ability to produce legislative coalitions which agree on a party program. The parties need continuing, not diminishing, relationships with legislators carrying the party label. Accordingly, in states where the idea of public funding has come, there should be means for channeling the candidate funding, at least in the general election, through the parties. The way to get more accountability and responsibility through political finance would be through adequately funded political parties, not through increased candidate independence.

Representative government is unthinkable without political parties. That is why so much attention has been given to parties as institutions in our states. In about one-third of them, political parties are able to go about the process of nominating, electing, and governing in a cohesive and organized way that far outshines our national political parties. In fact, most of our state political party systems are now more cohesive than the national party system. This has profound implications for the future of federalism. Presidents swept into office by personal electoral organizations have very little in common with the state party systems which send their delegates to Congress. There is an increasing estrangement between the presidential and congressional parties, the latter better representing the grass roots of party strength in America. This will affect the sharing of federal powers, with the probable swing back to the states in the future. Federal funds will continue to be made available to the states with few strings attached. It is therefore imperative that the institutions in the states that are best able to represent the needs and desires of the people be strengthened to do the job. As the party system lies at the heart of the governing process, so, too, do parties provide an ongoing political vehicle for the mass of people who lack wealth or power.

NOTES

1. President Franklin Pierce, quoted in Edward K. Hamilton, "On Nonconstitutional Management of a Constitutional Problem," *Daedalus* 107 (Winter 1978): 113.
2. John Herbers, "A Year after Proposition 13, Governmental Bodies Vie To Trim Taxes and Costs," *New York Times*, 4 June 1979, B15.
3. V. O. Key, *American State Politics* (New York: Alfred A. Knopf, 1956), p. 267.
4. Malcolm E. Jewell and David M. Olson, *American State Political Parties and Elections* (Homewood, Ill.: Dorsey Press, 1978), pp. 69–70.
5. Huckshorn, *Party Leadership in the States* (Amherst: University of Massachusetts Press, 1976), p. 255.
6. Key, *American State Politics*, p. 272.
7. Everett Carll Ladd, Jr., *Where Have All the Voters Gone? The Fracturing of America's Political Parties* (New York: W. W. Norton, 1978), p. 76.
8. Austin Ranney, "The Political Parties: Reform and Decline," chapter 6 in Anthony King, ed., *The New American Political System* (Washington, D.C.: American Enterprise Institute for Public Policy Research, 1978), p. 247.
9. Otha M. Brown, "Political Black Out," *Connecticut Magazine* (April 1979): 10.

FACTOR ANALYSIS OF SOCIOECONOMIC VARIABLES IN THE AMERICAN STATES[a]

Integration 1970	
VARIABLE	**LOADING**
Income/capita	.87
% population over 25, college graduates	.79
% employed persons in finance and insurance	.79
% population urban	.78
% employed persons professionals	.77
% population foreign white stock	.77
Retail trade sales/capita, 1967	.71
% farms with sales greater than $40,000, 1969	.65
Population density	.46
Newspaper circulation (copies/1,000)	.43
Average acreage/farm, 1969	.26
Value added/capita, manufacturing	.12
% employed persons in manufacturing	−.16
% employed persons in agriculture	−.32
% population black	−.48
PTV = 38	

Industrialization 1970	
% employed persons in manufacturing	.91
Value added/capita, manufacturing	.89
Population density	.64
% population black	.41
% population urban	.30
Income/capita	.24
% employed persons in finance and insurance	.23
Newspaper circulation (copies/1,000)	.21

APPENDIX 1 (CONTINUED)

Industrialization 1970 (Continued)

VARIABLE	LOADING
% population foreign white stock	.15
Retail trade sales/capita, 1967	−.09
% employed persons professionals	−.19
% population over 25, college graduates	−.22
% farms with sales greater than $40,000, 1969	−.23
% employed persons in agriculture	−.60
Average acreage/farm, 1969	−.71
PTV = 23	

[a] David R. Cameron and Richard I. Hofferbert, "Sociopolitical Dynamics and Policy Innovation: The Case of State Education Finance," mimeograph. For a complete list of loadings, variables, and their sources, contact David R. Cameron and Richard I. Hofferbert. The data are available in machine-readable form from the Historical Data Archive, Interuniversity Consortium for Political Research, P.O. Box 1248, Ann Arbor, Michigan 48106.

RANKING OF THE STATES ON THE INDEX OF THE FORMAL POWERS OF THE GOVERNOR, 1971

	TENURE POTENTIAL[a]	APPOINTIVE POWERS[b]	BUDGET POWERS[c]	VETO POWERS[d]	TOTAL INDEX
New York	5	5	5	5	20
Illinois	5	5	5	5	20
Hawaii	5	5	5	5	20
Wyoming	5	4	5	5	19
Michigan	5	4	5	5	19
Minnesota	5	4	5	5	19
New Jersey	4	5	5	5	19
Pennsylvania	4	5	5	5	19
California	5	3	5	5	18
Utah	5	3	5	5	18
Connecticut	5	4	4	5	18
Delaware	4	4	5	5	18
Colorado	5	3	5	5	18
Ohio	4	3	5	5	17
Massachusetts	5	5	4	3	17
Missouri	4	3	5	5	17
Tennessee	3	5	5	4	17
North Dakota	5	2	5	5	17
Nebraska	4	4	4	5	17
Maryland	4	2	5	5	16
Virginia	3	5	5	3	16
Alabama	4	3	5	4	16
Arizona	5	1	5	5	16
Washington	5	2	5	3	15
Alaska	4	2	4	5	15
Idaho	5	2	5	3	15
Kentucky	5	4	4	4	15

APPENDIX TWO (CONTINUED)

	TENURE POTENTIAL[a]	APPOINTIVE POWERS[b]	BUDGET POWERS[c]	VETO POWERS[d]	TOTAL INDEX
Montana	5	3	4	3	15
Wisconsin	5	2	5	3	15
Louisiana	4	2	4	5	15
Oregon	4	3	5	3	15
Iowa	2	3	5	5	15
West Virginia	4	3	4	4	15
Oklahoma	4	1	5	4	14
Georgia	3	1	5	5	14
Florida	4	2	5	3	14
Nevada	4	2	5	2	13
Vermont	2	4	5	2	13
Arkansas	2	2	5	4	13
Maine	4	2	4	2	12
Kansas	2	1	4	5	12
Rhode Island	2	4	4	2	12
New Mexico	3	1	5	3	12
South Dakota	1	2	5	3	11
New Hampshire	2	2	5	2	11
North Carolina	3	3	4	1	11
Indiana	3	5	1	2	11
Mississippi	3	1	1	5	10
Texas	2	1	3	3	9
South Carolina	3	1	1	3	8

The states are assigned points according to the pointing system used by Joseph Schlesinger, "The Politics of the Executive," *Jacob and Vines*, 2d ed., pp. 222–34.

[a] Four-year term, no restraint on re-election (5 points)
  Four-year term, one re-election permitted (4 points)
  Four-year term, no consecutive re-election permitted (3 points)
  Two-year term, no restraint on re-election (2 points)
  Two-year term, one re-election permitted (1 point)

[b] The points are based on the state scores on the Appointive Powers Index.
  Strong (5 points)
  Strong-moderate (4 points)
  Moderate (3 points)
  Moderate-Weak (2 points)
  Weak (1 point)

The scores themselves are based on the appointive powers of the governor over the sixteen major functions and offices listed by Schlesinger. For each function, the appointive power is scaled according to the governor's powers of appointment according to the following formula:

$$\text{Appointive Power} = \frac{\text{Values of } P_1 + P_2 + P_3 + \ldots P_n}{\text{Maximum values of } P_1 + P_2 + P_3 + \ldots P_n}$$

where P 5 if governor appoints;
        4 if governor appoints and one house of legislature approves;
        3 if governor appoints and both houses of legislature approve;
        2 if appointed by director with governor's approval or by governor and council;

---

1 if appointed by department director, board, by legislature, by civil service;

0 if elected by popular vote;

and where the subscript indicates the chief administrator for each of the sixteen major functions and services.

c 5 if the governor has the responsibility for preparing the budget and shares it only with persons appointed directly by him;

4 if the governor has the responsibility for preparing the budget but shares it either with a civil service appointee or an appointee of someone other than himself;

3 if the governor shares responsibility with the legislature;

2 if the governor shares responsibility with another major elected official (no contemporary examples)

1 if the governor prepares the budget only as a member of a group, usually consisting of other elected state officials or members of the legislature.

d 5 Very strong (Item veto plus at least 3/5 of legislature to override)

4 Strong (Item veto plus majority of legislature to override)

3 Medium (Item veto plus more than majority of members of legislature present to override)

2 Weak (No item veto, but special legislative majority to override)

1 Weakest (No item veto and simple legislative majority required to override, or no veto at all)

Source: Data used with permission of The Council of State Governments, *The Book of the States, 1972–1973,* Vol. 19, (Lexington, Ky.: Council of State Governments), pp. 72–73, 151, 154–155, 166–170.

APPENDIX THREE

VARIABLES USED IN THE MULTIPLE REGRESSION ANALYSES TO MEASURE THE RELATIONSHIPS BETWEEN INPUT, PROCESS, AND POLICY

VARIABLES	INDEX	INDEX MEASURES
I. Input		
A. Economic development	Industrialization[a] 1970	Manufacturing Variables
	Integration[b] 1970	Wealth, Professionalism, Education, Media Variables
	Gini Coefficient[c] 1970	Income Distribution
B. Electoral competition	Proportion	Average percentage of popular vote won by governor's party 1956–70
	Duration	Percentage of all terms for governor held by governor's party 1956–70

| | Margin of victory | Average difference between percent of vote for governor for each party, 1956–70 |
| C. Popular participation | Voting interest[d] | Average percent of voter turnout in gubernatorial elections 1956–70 |

II. Process

A. Party organization

1. Governor's leadership — Nominating control
   1. Gubernatorial nominee's percent of primary vote in 1970 (pre-session) and 1972 (post-session)
   2. Average primary vote for successful nominee of governor's party 1956–70

2. Legislative party cohesion

Index of support $= \dfrac{\text{governor's party votes cast for governor}}{\text{Total party votes cast}}$

Index of success $= \dfrac{\%\text{ of party votes cast for governor}}{\%\text{ party votes needed for passage}}$

Index of opposition $= \dfrac{\text{Opposition party votes cast against governor}}{\text{Total party votes}}$

Index of likeness

See Chapter 6, footnote 45

Roll call votes on governor's program bills in 1971 (twenty state legislative sessions: House and Senate)

VARIABLES	INDEX	INDEX MEASURES
Party program	Governor's party	D or R (D = 2; R = 1)
B. Structural variables	Formal Powers of the governor[e] 1971	Tenure potential
		Appointive powers
		Budget powers
		Veto powers
	Legislative party size	Percentage of seats held by the governor's party in House and Senate: average 1956–1970; 1971 session only
	Majority of House or Senate	Yes—2
		No—1
	Legislative professionalism[f] 1970–1971	Compensation
		Length of session
		Legislative services expenditures
		Legislative services provided
		Av. population/house seat
III. Output: public policy	Index of redistribution[g] 1971	Ratio between tax sources and welfare spending
	Welfare factor[h] 1972	Average welfare payments to dependent children, blind, disabled and old age recipients
	Welfare-education change, 1968–1972	Change in spending for welfare and education from 1968–1972
	Highways-natural resources factor[i] 1972	Highways and outdoor recreation expenditures
	Highways-natural resources change 1968–1972	Change in spending for highways and natural resources 1968–1972

Sources:

a, b David R. Cameron and Richard I. Hofferbert, "Sociopolitical Dynamics and Policy Innovation, The Case of State Education Finance, 1960–1970," (mimeograph) The University of Michigan. See Appendix I.

c David R. Morgan, *Handbook of State Policy Indicators* (Norman, Okla.: Bureau of Government Research, University of Oklahoma, 1974), Table 7, p. 26.

d Vote as a percentage of the civilian population of voting age. Sources: U.S. Department of Commerce, Bureau of the Census, *Statistical Abstract of the United States*, 1959 and 1969; Current Population Reports, Series P–25, No. 342 (June, 1966) and No. 479 (March 1972). Note: The Census Bureau does not give civilian resident population after 1968, so I used an estimation procedure to obtain it for 1970 based on the ratio of civilian resident to total resident population for 1968.

e Joseph A. Schlesinger, "The Politics of the Executive," in Herbert Jacob and Kenneth Vines (eds.) *Politics in the American States*, second edition, 222–34. See Appendix 2.

f John G. Grumm, "The Effects of Legislative Structure on Legislative Performance," in Richard Hofferbert and Ira Sharkansky (eds.) *State and Urban Politics*, 315–17. See Appendix 4.

g Richard E. DeLeon, "Politics, Economic Surplus and Redistribution in the American States: A Test of a Theory," *American Journal of Political Science* (November 1973): 781–796. See Chapter 6, footnote 58. Source: U.S. Bureau of the Census, State Government Finances in 1972.

h, i Ira Sharkansky and Richard Hofferbert, "Dimensions of State Politics, Economics and Public Policy," *American Political Science Review*, 63 (September 1969): 872–879. See my paper "The Impact of the Governor's Party on Public Policy" presented to the Midwest Political Science Association Annual Meeting, May 1–3, 1975, Chicago, Illinois (University Microfilms, Ann Arbor, Michigan), pp. 20–21, Appendix 4 and 5. The same policy variables used by Sharkansky and Hofferbert to perform their policy factor analysis in 1962 were collected for 1968 and 1972. The variables took a long time to collect and I will be happy to produce more information about sources. The same procedures used by those writers to eliminate variables which loaded high on two factors or no factors were used in this analysis. The procedures used to arrive at the difference in Welfare-Education and Highways-Natural Resources Policy between 1968 and 1972 is explained in footnote 46, Chapter 9. See Appendices 6 and 7.

VARIABLES CONSIDERED AND USED IN THE PROFESSIONALISM INDEX[a]

VARIABLES SUBJECT TO ANALYSIS

1. Biennial compensation of legislators, 1970–71
2. Expenditures for legislative staff and services, 1971
3. Length of regular plus extra sessions in calendar days, 1970–71
4. Legislative Services Score, 1970
5. Average population per house seat, 1970
6. Average population per senate seat, 1970
7. Number of bills introduced in the 1970–71 sessions
8. Number of enactments in the 1970–71 regular and extra sessions
9. First term membership in the senate, by percent, 1971
10. First term membership in the house, by percent, 1971
11. Number of standing committees in house, 1971
12. Number of standing committees in senate, 1971

LOADINGS FOR FIRST FIVE VARIABLES ON THE LEGISLATIVE PROFESSIONALISM INDEX

1. Biennial compensation of legislators, 1970–71	.915
2. Expenditures for legislative staff and services, 1971	.913
3. Length of regular plus extra sessions in calendar days 1970–71	.724
4. Legislative Services Score 1970	.589
5. Average population per house seat 1970	.882

[a] John G. Grumm, "The Effects of Legislative Structure on Legislative Performance," 315–317. The Index of Legislative Professionalism as developed by John Grumm from data from the 1960's was reformulated from data for 1970–1971. Grumm chose the first four variables for inclusion in the index and then examined the eight others for their correlations with the original four. He selected the number of bills introduced as a fifth variable based on its high average correlation with the original four. The relationships among the variables apparently changed over the ten-year period, because the average population per house seat emerges as the fifth variable based on its high correlations with the original four. The five variables were subjected to the same analysis Grumm used, and the unrotated first factor loadings were used to compute factor scores for each of the states.

APPENDIX FOUR (CONTINUED)

Sources: The following sources were used for the variables on the list:

1. The Citizens Conference on State Legislatures, *Report on Salaries, Expenses in 50 State Legislatures As 1973 Sessions Begin, Research Memorandum* 16 (Kansas City, Mo.: The Citizens Conference on State Legislatures, December, 1972) :6–7.

2. U.S. Department of Commerce: Social and Economic Statistics Administration: Bureau of the Census, *State Government Finances in 1971*, Series G-71, No. 3 (Washington: U.S. Government Printing Office, 1972) 34.

3. Data used with permission of The Council of State Governments, *The Book of the States, 1972–1973*, Vol. 19, (Lexington, Ky.: Council of State Governments), 60–61.

4. This variable was based on the 1969–1970 Legislative Evaluation Study by the Citizens Conference on State Legislatures. The score was constructed by means of a point system based on answers to questions asked on the Functional and Informational Schedules. The questions were concerned with staff support, facilities, service agencies, office space, research and legal staffing, and fiscal review capabilities. I assigned points to each state for each question according to the preferred answers. I merely added the points for each state (total possible, 170). I did not attempt to weight the answers. See the complete report by the Citizens Conference on State Legislatures, *State Legislatures: An Evaluation of Their Effectiveness* (New York: Praeger, 1971) Appendices A–C. Contact me for any questions about my scoring procedures.

5. Data used with permission of The Council of State Governments, *The Book of the States, 1972–1973*, Vol. 19, (Lexington, Ky.: Council of State Governments), 65.

6. *Ibid.*, 64.

7. *Ibid.*, 74–75.

8. *Ibid.*

9. Council of State Governments, *State Elective Officials and the Legislatures*, Supplement I to the *Book of the States*: 1969 and 1971.

10. *Ibid.*

11. Data used with permission of The Council of State Governments, *The Book of the States, 1972–1973*, Vol. 19, (Lexington, Ky.: Council of State Governments), 67.

12. *Ibid.*

FINAL SELECTION OF JUDGES

Alabama	Appellate, circuit, district, and probate judges elected on partisan ballots. Judges of municipal courts are appointed by the governing body of the municipality.
Alaska	Supreme court justices, superior, and district court judges appointed by governor from nominations by Judicial Council. Approved or rejected at first general election held more than 3 years after appointment. Reconfirmed every 10, 6, and 4 years, respectively. Magistrates appointed by and serve at pleasure of the presiding judges of each judicial district.
Arizona	Supreme court justices and court of appeals judges appointed by governor from a list of not less than 3 for each vacancy submitted by a 9-member Commission on Appellate Court Appointments. Maricopa and Pima County superior court judges appointed by governor from a list of not less than 3 for each vacancy submitted by a 9-member commission on trial court appointments for each county. Superior court judges of other 12 counties elected on nonpartisan ballot (partisan primary); justices of the peace elected on partisan ballot; city and town magistrates selected as provided by charter or ordinance, usually appointed by mayor and council.
Arkansas	All elected on partisan ballot.
California	Supreme court and courts of appeal judges appointed by governor with approval of Commission on Judicial Appointments. Run for reelection on record. All judges elected on nonpartisan ballot.
Colorado	Judges of all courts, except Denver County and municipal, appointed initially by governor from lists submitted by nonpartisan nominating commissions; run on record for retention. Municipal judges appointed by city councils or town boards. Denver County judges appointed by mayor from list submitted by nominating commission; judges run on record for retention.
Connecticut	All appointed by legislature from nominations submitted by governor, except that probate judges are elected on partisan ballot.
Delaware	All appointed by governor with consent of senate.
Florida	All trial judges are elected on a nonpartisan ballot. All appellate judges are appointed by the governor with recommendations by a Judicial Nominating Commission. The latter are retained by running on their records.

Georgia	All elected on partisan ballot except that county and some city court judges are appointed by the governor with consent of the senate.
Hawaii	Supreme court justices and circuit court judges appointed by the governor with consent of the senate. District judges appointed by chief justice of the state.
Idaho	Supreme court and district court judges initially are nominated by Idaho Judicial Council and appointed by governor; thereafter, they are elected on nonpartisan ballot. Magistrates appointed by District Magistrate's Commission for initial 2-year term; thereafter, run on record for retention for 4-year term on nonpartisan ballot.
Illinois	All elected on partisan ballot and run on record for retention. Associate judges are appointed by circuit judges and serve 4-year terms.
Indiana	Judges of appellate courts appointed by governor from a list of 3 for each vacancy submitted by a 7-member Judicial Nomination Commission. Governor appoints members of municipal courts and several counties have judicial nominating commissions which submit a list of nominees to the governor for appointment. All other judges are elected.
Iowa	Judges of supreme, appeals, and district courts appointed initially by governor from lists submitted by nonpartisan nominating commissions. Appointee serves initial 1-year term and then runs on record for retention. District associate judges run on record for retention, if not retained or office becomes vacant, replaced by a full-time judicial magistrate. Full-time judicial magistrates appointed by district judges in the judicial election district from nominees submitted by county judicial magistrate appointing commission. Part-time judicial magistrates appointed by county judicial magistrate appointing commissions.
Kansas	Judges of appellate courts appointed by governor from list submitted by nominating commission. Run on record for retention. Nonpartisan selection method adopted for judges of courts of general jurisdiction in 23 of 29 districts.
Kentucky	All judges elected on nonpartisan ballot.
Louisiana	All elected on open (bipartisan) ballot.
Maine	All appointed by governor with confirmation of the senate, except that probate judges are elected on partisan ballot.
Maryland	Judges of court of appeals, court of special appeals, circuit courts, and Supreme Bench of Baltimore City appointed by governor, elected on nonpartisan ballot after at least one year's service. District court judges appointed by governor subject to confirmation by senate.
Massachusetts	All appointed by governor with consent of Executive Council. Judicial Nominating Commission, established by executive order, advises governor on appointment of judges.

APPENDIX FIVE (CONTINUED)

Michigan	All elected on nonpartisan ballot, except municipal judges in accordance with local charters by local city councils.
Minnesota	All elected on nonpartisan ballot. Vacancy filled by gubernatorial appointment.
Mississippi	All elected on partisan ballot, except that city police court justices are appointed by governing authority of each municipality.
Missouri	Judges of supreme court, court of appeals, circuit and probate courts in St. Louis City and County, Jackson County, Platte County, Clay County, and St. Louis Court of Criminal Correction appointed initially by governor from nominations submitted by special commissions. Run on record for reelection. All other judges elected on partisan ballot.
Montana	All elected on nonpartisan ballot. Vacancies on supreme or district courts and Worker's Compensation Court filled by governor according to established appointment procedure (from 3 nominees submitted by Judicial Nominations Commission). Vacancies at end of term may be filled by election, except Worker's Compensation Court. Gubernatorial appointments face senate confirmation.
Nebraska	Judges of all courts appointed initially by governor from lists submitted by bipartisan nominating commissions. Run on record for retention in office in general election following initial term of 3 years; subsequent terms are 6 years.
Nevada	All elected on nonpartisan ballot.
New Hampshire	All appointed by governor with confirmation of Executive Council.
New Jersey	All appointed by governor with consent of senate except that judges of municipal courts serving one municipality only are appointed by governing bodies.
New Mexico	All elected on partisan ballot.
New York	All elected on partisan ballot except that governor appoints chief judge and associate judges of court of appeals, with advice and consent of senate, from a list of persons found to be well qualified and recommended by the bipartisan Judicial Nominating Commission, and also appoints judges of court of claims and designates members of appellate division of supreme court. Mayor of New York City appoints judges of the criminal and family courts in the city.
North Carolina	All elected on partisan ballot. By executive order, governor has established 1-year trial system for merit selection of superior court judges.
North Dakota	All elected on nonpartisan ballot.
Ohio	All elected on nonpartisan ballot except court of claims judges who may be appointed by chief justice of supreme court from ranks of supreme court, court of appeals, court of common pleas, or retired judges.

Oklahoma	Supreme court justices and court of criminal appeals judges appointed by governor from lists of 3 submitted by Judicial Nominating Commission. If governor fails to make appointment within 60 days after occurrence of vacancy, appointment is made by chief justice from the same list. Run for election on their records at first general election following completion of 12 months' service for unexpired term. Judges of court of appeals, and district and associate district judges elected on nonpartisan ballot in adversary popular election. Special judges appointed by district judges. Municipal judges appointed by governing body of municipality.
Oregon	All judges except municipal judges are elected on nonpartisan ballot for 6-year terms. Municipal judges are mostly appointed by city councils except 1 Oregon city elects its judge.
Pennsylvania	All originally elected on partisan ballot; thereafter, on nonpartisan retention ballot, except police magistrates, city of Pittsburgh—appointed by mayor of Pittsburgh.
Rhode Island	Supreme court justices elected by legislature. Superior, family, and district court justices and justices of the peace appointed by governor, with consent of senate (except for justices of the peace); probate and municipal court judges appointed by city or town councils.
South Carolina	Supreme court and circuit court judges elected by legislature. City judges, magistrates, and some county judges and family court judges appointed by governor—the latter on recommendation of the legislative delegation in the area served by the court. Probate judges and some county judges elected on partisan ballot.
South Dakota	All elected on nonpartisan ballot, except magistrates (law trained and others), who are appointed by the presiding judge of the judicial circuit.
Tennessee	Judges of intermediate appellate courts appointed initially by governor from nominations submitted by special commission. Run on record for reelection. The supreme court judges and all other judges elected on partisan ballot, except from some municipal judges who are appointed by the governing body of the city.
Texas	All elected on partisan ballot except municipal judges, most of whom are appointed by municipal governing body.
Utah	Supreme court, district court, and circuit court judges appointed by governor from lists of 3 nominees submitted by nominating commissions. If governor fails to make appointment within 30 days, chief justice appoints. Judges run for retention in office at next succeeding election; they may be opposed by others on nonpartisan judicial ballots. Juvenile court judges are initially appointed by the governor from a list of not less than 2 nominated by the Juvenile Court Commission, and retained in office

APPENDIX FIVE (CONTINUED)

Utah (continued)	by gubernatorial appointment. Town justices of the peace are appointed for 4-year terms by town trustees. County justices of the peace are elected for 4 years on nonpartisan ballot.
Vermont	Supreme court justices, superior court judges (presiding judges of county courts), and district court judges appointed by governor with consent of senate from list of persons designated as qualified by the Judicial Selection Board. Supreme, superior, and district court judges retained in office by vote of legislature. Assistant judges of county courts and probate judges elected on partisan ballot in the territorial area of their jurisdiction.
Virginia	Supreme court justices and all judges of circuit courts, general district, and juvenile and domestic relations district courts elected by legislature. Committee on district courts, in the case of part-time judges, certifies that a vacancy exists. Thereupon, all part-time judges of general district courts and juvenile and domestic relations courts are appointed by circuit court judges.
Washington	All elected on nonpartisan ballot except that municipal judges in second-, third- and fourth-class cities are appointed by mayor.
West Virginia	Judges of all courts of record and magistrate courts elected on partisan ballot.
Wisconsin	All elected on.nonpartisan ballot.
Wyoming	Supreme court justices and district court judges appointed by governor from a list of 3 submitted by nominating committee and stand for retention at next election after 1 year in office. Justices of the peace elected on nonpartisan ballot. Municipal judges appointed by mayor.
Dist. of Col.	Nominated by the president of the United States from a list of persons recommended by the District of Columbia Judicial Nomination Commission; appointed upon the advice and consent of the U.S. Senate.
American Samoa	Chief justice and associate justice(s) appointed by the U.S. Secretary of Interior pursuant to presidential delegation of authority. Associate judges appointed by governor of American Samoa on recommendation of the chief justice, and subsequently confirmed by the senate of American Somoa.
Guam[†]	All appointed by governor with consent of legislature from list of 3 nominees submitted by Judicial Council for term of 5 years; thereafter run on record for retention every 5 years.
Puerto Rico	All appointed by governor with consent of senate.

[†] Reflects 1976 survey.

Source: Data used with permission of The Council of State Governments, *The Book of the States*, Vol. 22, (Lexington, Ky.: Council of State Governments, 1978–1979), pp. 90–91.

POLICY VARIABLES SUBJECT TO ANALYSIS[a]

EDUCATION
1. Percent of ninth grade students (1968) graduating four years later
2. Percent of candidates passing selective service mental examination
3. State and local government expenditures for education per capita

HIGHWAYS
4. Total road mileage per capita[b]
5. Rural road mileage per rural resident[b]
6. Municipal road mileage per urban resident
7. Percent of designated Interstate mileage completed[b]
8. Population per highway fatality[b]
9. State and local government expenditures for highways per capita[b]

WELFARE
10. Average payment per recipient, Aid to Families of Dependent Children[b]
11. Average payment, Old Age Assistance[b]
12. Average payment, Aid to the Blind[b]
13. Average payment, Aid to the Permanently and Totally Disabled[b]
14. Incidence of AFDC recipients among dependent children below the poverty level[b]
15. Incidence of OAA recipients among persons over 65 years of age below the poverty level
16. Incidence of AB recipients among persons below the poverty level
17. Incidence of APTD recipients among persons below the poverty level[b]
18. State and local government expenditures for public welfare per capita[b]

HEALTH
19. Proportion of white infants surviving their first year of life
20. Proportion of non-white infants surviving their first year of life
21. State and local government expenditures for health, hospitals, and sanitation per capita

NATURAL RESOURCES
22. Visits per 10,000 population to state parks
23. Fishing license holders per 10,000 population[b]
24. Hunting license holders per 10,000 population[b]
25. State and local government expenditures for parks and recreation per capita[b]

GENERAL
26. Total state and local government general expenditures per capita[b]

APPENDIX SIX (CONTINUED)

[a]The data all pertain to 1972 except as otherwise noted.

[b]Variables surviving test for high loading on a single factor.

Sources: The same policy variables used by Sharkansky and Hofferbert to perform their policy factor analysis in 1962 were collected for 1972. Ira Sharkansky and Richard I. Hofferbert. "Dimensions of State Policy" in Herbert Jacob and Kenneth N. Vines, eds., *Politics in the American States: A Comparative Analysis*, Second Edition, Little Brown and Company Inc., footnote 22, 587–588. Reprinted by permission. The variables took a long time to collect and I will be happy to produce more information about sources. State and local government expenditures for various items can be found in the Bureau of the Census publication: *Governmental Finances in 1971–1972*, Table 22. The sources for the following variables are listed:

1. N.E.A. Research National Education Association, *Rankings of the States 1973*, Table D-6.

2. Department of the Army, Office of the Surgeon General, *Health of the Army, Supplement, 1973*, Table 38.

4, 5, 6. U.S. Department of Transportation, Federal Highway Administration, Bureau of Public Roads, *Highway Statistics*, 1972, Table M-1. Because the Census Bureau does not prepare intercensal estimates on the urban/rural population, I estimated the 1972 rural and urban population for the states assuming linear population change from 1960–70. I obtained these population figures from the 1970 Census Report PC (1)-A1, Table 18. Percentages for 5 and 6 were based on these estimated figures.

7. U.S. Department of Transportation, Federal Highway Administration, Bureau of Public Roads, *Public Roads*, 1973, Table I, "The National System of Interstate and Defense Highways."

8. Bureau of Public Roads, *Highway Statistics*, 1972, Table HA-1.

10–13. U.S. Department of Health, Education and Welfare, Social and Rehabilitation Service, *Public Assistance Statistics, June 1972*, No. (SRS) 73-0311, (10/3/72), Tables 7, 4, 5, 6.

14–17. I obtained the number of recipients from Bureau of the Census, *Statistical Abstract, 1973*, Table 500. Because data on income by state is only available from the decennial census, I based the percentages on poverty level statistics from the 1970 Census found in *Census of Population*, 1970, Vol. i, *Characteristics of the Population*, Part 1, *U.S. Summary*, Section 1, Chapter C, Table 182.

19, 20. Department of Health, Education and Welfare, Public Health Service, National Center for Health Statistics, photocopied Table 2–6 giving infant death rates by color for 1970, the last year for which data by race are available. I estimated the proportions for 1972 on the rate of change 1968–1970.

22. National Conference on State Parks, National Recreation and Park Association, *State Park Statistics 1970*. (August 1971): pp. 18–20. These were the latest attendance figures.

23, 24. U.S. Department of the Interior, Fish and Wildlife Service, News Release, April 29, 1973: "Number of Paid Hunting License Holders ... Fiscal Year 1972," and "Number of Paid Fishing License Holders ... Fiscal Year 1972." The Department issues an annual report, *Federal Aid in Fish and Wildlife Restoration*, which includes these statistics.

LOADINGS OF POLICY VARIABLES ON TWO PRINCIPAL FACTORS

VARIABLES[a]	WELFARE-EDUCATION	HIGHWAYS-NATURAL RESOURCES
AFDC Payments (10)	.863	.021
AB Payments (12)	.808	−.160
Total Expenditures per capita (26)	.779	.249
AFDC Recipients below poverty level (14)	.759	−.419
APTD Payments (13)	.751	−.219
Expenditures for Welfare per capita (18)	.722	−.347
OAA Payments (11)	.660	−.049
Population per highway fatality (8)	.614	−.598
APTD Recipients below poverty level (17)	.488	−.232
Expenditures for parks and recreation per capita (25)	.463	−.042
Hunting Licenses (24)	−.154	.866
Fishing Licenses (23)	−.175	.841
Total Road mileage (4)	−.140	.828
Rural Road mileage (5)	−.098	.827
Expenditures for highways per capita (9)	.039	.796
Interstate mileage completed (7)	−.412	.361
Percent of Total Variance	32.4	27.7

[a]The parenthesized numbers correspond to the variable numbers in preceding table. The same procedures used by Sharkansky and Hofferbert to eliminate 1962 variables which loaded high on two factors or no factors were used in this analysis. See Ira Sharkansky and Richard I. Hofferbert "Dimensions of State Policy" in Herbert Jacob and Kenneth Vines eds., *Politics in the American States: A Comparative Analysis*, 2nd edition (Boston: Little Brown and Company Inc. 1971), Footnote 22, pp. 587–88. Reprinted by permission. A separate factor analysis of the variables that remained is presented in this table. The values derived from this final analysis constitute the bases for constructing indices for each state's standing on the two policy factors. The Welfare-Education factor for 1972 has become primarily a welfare factor. It retains four of the original welfare expenditures for 1962 and adds three more. Total expenditures per capita is a highly loaded variable indicating the expenditures on welfare are highly related to total expenditures. Expenditures for parks and recreation emerge as a Welfare-Education factor. There are

APPENDIX SIX A (CONTINUED)

less highway fatalities in the Welfare-syndrome (a welcome by-product of more welfare spending?). The Education variable did not emerge in this 1972 factor. The Highways-Natural Resources Factor retains four of the 1962 variables and adds two more Highway variables. Two variables which loaded high on this factor in 1962 are no longer associated with it: old age recipients below the poverty level and expenditures for parks and recreation which is now a Welfare variable.

LOADINGS OF POLICY VARIABLES ON TWO PRINCIPAL FACTORS: POLICY CHANGES 1968–1972[a]

VARIABLES	POLICY CHANGE WELFARE-EDUCATION	POLICY CHANGE HIGHWAY-NATURAL RESOURCES
1. Total government expenditures	.885	.211
2. AFDC recipients below poverty	.841	.355
3. AFDC payments	.822	.037
4. Total expenditures for welfare	.807	−.233
5. AB payments	.797	−.089
6. Total expenditures for education[b]	.775	.345
7. APTD payments	.722	−.170
8. OAA payments	.677	.008
9. Total expenditures for health	.672	−.201
10. Total expenditures for parks	.629	−.088
11. APTD recipients below poverty	.587	−.255
12. High school graduates[b]	.483	.306
13. Total road mileage	−.070	.825
14. Rural road mileage	−.010	.819

APPENDIX SEVEN (CONTINUED)

VARIABLES	POLICY CHANGE WELFARE-EDUCATION	POLICY CHANGE HIGHWAY-NATURAL RESOURCES
15. Hunting licenses	−.200	.814
16. Fishing licenses	−.121	.783
17. Total expenditures for highways	.224	.740
18. Municipal road mileage	−.162	.595
Percent of total variance	36.6	22.9

KEY:

1. Total state and local government general expenditures per capita
2. Incidence of AFDC recipients among dependent children below the poverty level
3. Average payment per recipient, Aid to Families of Dependent Children
4. State and local government expenditures for public welfare per capita
5. Average payment, Aid to the Blind
6. State and local government expenditures for education per capita
7. Average payment, Aid to the Permanently and Totally Disabled
8. Average payment, Old Age Assistance
9. State and local government expenditures for health, hospitals and sanitation per capita
10. State and local government expenditures for parks and recreation per capita
11. Incidence of APTD recipients among persons below the poverty level
12. Percent of ninth grade students graduating four years later
13. Total road mileage per capita
14. Rural road mileage per rural resident
15. Hunting license holders per 10,000 population
16. Fishing license holders per 10,000 population
17. State and local government expenditures for highways per capita
18. Municipal road mileage per urban resident

[a]See chapter 9, footnote 46, for an explanation of this factor analysis.
[b]Education variable which emerged in this factor analysis of policy change.

FACTOR SCORES FOR THE STATES ON SOCIOECONOMIC, LEGISLATIVE PROFESSIONALISM AND POLICY FACTORS

STATE	INDUSTRIAL-IZATION	INTE-GRATION	PROFES-SIONALISM	WELFARE	WELFARE-EDUCATION CHANGE 1968–1972
Alabama	0.60	−1.57	−0.43	−0.99	1.09
Alaska	−1.81	.53	a	a	a
Arizona	−1.59	1.18	−0.03	−0.38	1.36
Arkansas	0.16	−1.81	−0.79	−1.38	.73
California	0.11	1.56	4.00	2.13	1.64
Colorado	−0.71	1.11	−0.11	.02	1.15
Connecticut	1.45	1.77	−0.39	1.04	1.77
Delaware	0.52	0.90	−0.20	0.79	1.77
Florida	−0.11	0.45	0.74	−1.03	1.02
Georgia	0.48	−0.94	−0.54	−1.08	1.12
Hawaii	−0.55	1.12	0.44	2.16	2.13
Idaho	−1.02	−0.37	−0.72	−0.07	1.02
Illinois	1.07	0.78	1.55	0.74	1.78
Indiana	1.15	−0.41	−0.08	−1.01	1.20
Iowa	−0.41	0.03	−0.25	0.55	.94
Kansas	−0.43	0.00	−0.62	−0.54	.38
Kentucky	0.29	−1.48	−0.55	−1.05	.73
Louisiana	0.08	−0.96	−0.29	−0.94	.64

APPENDIX EIGHT CONTINUED

STATE	INDUSTRIAL-IZATION	INTE-GRATION	PROFES-SIONALISM	WELFARE	WELFARE-EDUCATION CHANGE 1968–1972
Maine	0.06	−0.59	−0.75	−0.00	1.25
Maryland	0.18	0.81	0.13	0.19	1.25
Massachusetts	1.21	1.66	1.04	2.08	2.19
Michigan	1.31	−0.01	1.74	0.91	2.00
Minnesota	−0.13	0.29	0.29	0.76	1.62
Mississippi	0.17	−2.10	−0.68	−1.39	1.14
Missouri	0.43	−0.20	0.11	−0.51	1.07
Montana	−1.57	0.00	−0.75	−0.31	.90
Nebraska	−0.77	0.17	−0.70	−0.51	.99
Nevada	−1.56	1.16	−0.65	0.04	1.19
New Hampshire	0.79	0.00	−0.62	1.17	1.79
New Jersey	1.67	1.50	1.21	0.80	1.66
New Mexico	−1.84	0.25	−0.73	−0.72	.77
New York	1.08	1.71	2.49	2.12	1.90
North Carolina	0.85	−1.54	−0.08	−1.17	.84
North Dakota	−1.77	−0.70	−0.87	0.37	.87
Ohio	1.35	−0.14	1.15	−0.62	1.03
Oklahoma	−0.35	−0.37	0.16	−0.18	.63
Oregon	−0.18	0.38	−0.18	−0.01	.91
Pennsylvania	1.17	−0.06	1.47	0.76	1.74
Rhode Island	1.53	0.77	−0.56	0.30	.92
South Carolina	0.86	−1.75	−0.47	−1.94	.84
South Dakota	−1.75	−0.77	−0.89	−0.30	.78
Tennessee	0.76	−1.20	−0.33	−1.24	.85
Texas	0.05	0.06	0.49	−1.28	.83
Utah	−0.62	0.27	−0.95	0.18	1.24
Vermont	−0.54	−0.23	−1.21	0.77	1.13
Virginia	0.12	−0.42	−0.16	−0.70	1.20
Washington	−0.01	0.95	0.07	0.85	1.62
West Virginia	0.22	−1.61	−0.52	−0.31	1.25
Wisconsin	0.52	−0.32	0.42	0.93	1.80
Wyoming	−2.04	0.13	−1.43	0.01	.65

[a] Alaska was omitted from the regression analysis when I discovered that her score on the Welfare variable was two and a half times greater than that of the next highest state. Her policy makers do not operate within the usual socioeconomic restraints. She has a disproportion of resources to population. The state budget has quadrupled to about $400 million annually in the last decade under the influence of social programs voted by a legislature secure in the knowledge that the oil lease money was at hand and that perhaps more was to come.

INDEX